GENESIS

This commentary is an innovative interpretation of one of the most profound texts of world literature: the book of Genesis. The first book of the Bible has been studied, debated, and expounded as much as any text in history, yet because it addresses the weightiest questions of life and faith, it continues to demand our attention. The author of this new commentary combines older critical approaches with the latest rhetorical methodologies to yield fresh interpretations accessible to scholars, clergy, teachers, seminarians, and interested laypeople. It explains important concepts and terms as expressed in the Hebrew original so that both people who know Hebrew and those who do not will be able to follow the discussion. "Closer Look" sections examine Genesis in the context of cultures of the Ancient Near East. "Bridging the Horizons" sections enable the reader to see the enduring relevance of the book in the twenty-first century.

Bill T. Arnold is Director of Hebrew Studies and the Paul S. Amos Professor of Old Testament Interpretation at Asbury Theological Seminary. He has authored, co-authored, or co-edited eight books, including most recently the *Dictionary of the Old Testament: Historical Books* (with H. G. M. Williamson, 2005); *Who Were the Babylonians?* (2004); *A Guide to Biblical Hebrew Syntax* (with John H. Choi, Cambridge University Press, 2003); and *1 and 2 Samuel: The NIV Application Commentary* (2003).

Advance Praise for Genesis

"Arnold's commentary is a welcome addition to the current proliferation of Genesis commentaries. Because of the care, depth, scope, and interpretive sensibility of the author, it is sure to become a major and definitive work for subsequent interpretation. Arnold moves easily between synchronic and diachronic questions and makes his way knowingly from Ancient Near Eastern materials to contemporary theological concerns. The several topical studies amid the commentary are judicious and illuminating. The commentary is well researched with ready appeal to the vast literature on the texts. This book is of particular interest because it exhibits for us the working processes of an interpreter who brings his readers along in the venture."

– Walter Brueggemann, Columbia Theological Seminary

"Arnold succeeds brilliantly in drawing together in an accessible manner the best of previous scholarship on Genesis in order to inform his fresh, positive, and theologically insightful commentary. This work will quickly become a first port of call for busy readers who require a sure guide to the range of responsible interpretations of this seminal biblical book."

– H. G. M. Williamson, Regius Professor of Hebrew, University of Oxford

NEW CAMBRIDGE BIBLE COMMENTARY

GENERAL EDITOR: Ben Witherington III

HEBREW BIBLE/OLD TESTAMENT EDITOR: Bill T. Arnold

EDITORIAL BOARD
Bill T. Arnold, *Asbury Theological Seminary*
James D. G. Dunn, *University of Durham*
Michael V. Fox, *University of Wisconsin-Madison*
Robert P. Gordon, *University of Cambridge*
Judith Gundry-Volf, *Yale University*
Ben Witherington III, *Asbury Theological Seminary*

The *New Cambridge Bible Commentary* (NCBC) aims to elucidate the Hebrew and Christian Scriptures for a wide range of intellectually curious individuals. While building on the work and reputation of the *Cambridge Bible Commentary* popular in the 1960s and 1970s, the NCBC takes advantage of many of the rewards provided by scholarly research over the last four decades. Volumes utilize recent gains in rhetorical criticism, social scientific study of the Scriptures, narrative criticism, and other developing disciplines to exploit the growing advances in biblical studies. Accessible, jargon-free commentary, an annotated "Suggested Reading" list, and the entire New Revised Standard Version (NRSV) text under discussion are the hallmarks of all volumes in the series.

PUBLISHED VOLUMES IN THE SERIES
Genesis, Bill T. Arnold
Exodus, Carol Meyers
Judges and Ruth, Victor H. Matthews
1–2 Corinthians, Craig S. Keener
The Gospel of John, Jerome H. Neyrey
James and Jude, William F. Brosend II
Revelation, Ben Witherington III

FORTHCOMING VOLUMES
Deuteronomy, Brent Strawn
Joshua, Douglas A. Knight
1–2 Chronicles, William M. Schniedewind
Psalms 1–72, Walter Brueggemann and William H. Bellinger, Jr.
Psalms 73–150, Walter Brueggemann and William H. Bellinger, Jr.
Isaiah 1–39, David Baer
Jeremiah, Baruch Halpern
Hosea, Joel, and Amos, J. J. M. Roberts
The Gospel of Matthew, Craig A. Evans
The Gospel of Luke, Amy-Jill Levine and Ben Witherington III
The Letters of John, Duane F. Watson

Genesis

Bill T. Arnold

Asbury Theological Seminary

CAMBRIDGE
UNIVERSITY PRESS

CAMBRIDGE UNIVERSITY PRESS
Cambridge, New York, Melbourne, Madrid, Cape Town, Singapore, São Paulo, Delhi

Cambridge University Press
32 Avenue of the Americas, New York, NY 10013-2473, USA

www.cambridge.org
Information on this title: www.cambridge.org/9780521000673

First published 2009

Printed in the United States of America

A catalog record for this publication is available from the British Library.

Library of Congress Cataloging in Publication Data

Arnold, Bill T.
Genesis / Bill T. Arnold.
   p.   cm. – (The new Cambridge Bible commentary)
Includes bibliographical references and indexes.
ISBN 978-0-521-80607-7 (hardcover : alk. paper) – ISBN 978-0-521-00067-3 (pbk. : alk. paper)
1. Bible. O.T. Genesis – Commentaries.   I. Title.
BS1235.53.A76   2008
222′.11077 – dc22   2008027146

ISBN   978-0-521-80607-7 hardback
ISBN   978-0-521-00067-3 paperback

For

David Wesley

Jeremy Clark

Alexander Joseph

Psalm 127:3—5

Contents

Supplementary Sections

Preface

Writing a biblical commentary is a precarious enterprise. If the commentary one writes is technical and scholarly ("critical" in the parlance of scholarship), it will most certainly be judged too advanced for a general readership, in addition to the close scrutiny one expects from scholars and serious students of the Bible. If, on the other hand, the commentary is written for pastors or students, it will certainly seem inadequate to scholars because it cannot address all the issues, even all the *important* issues. Moreover, writing a relatively small commentary on a monumental classic such as Genesis is all the more challenging. The history of interpretation of the book of Genesis is an academic discipline in its own right. The amount of secondary literature on the book is unprecedented. I have been reminded at every step that a commentary of this size simply cannot comment on everything I would have liked, and the more advanced reader will want to keep close to hand the more advanced commentaries (especially Westermann).

My appreciation goes out to Ben Witherington, who conceived this series and serves as its General Editor. I owe much to Andy Beck of Cambridge University Press, for reasons too numerous to list here. Brent A. Strawn, who served as a "hired hand" to edit an early draft of the manuscript, was insightful, as usual. I also express my appreciation to Andrew Gilmore, Jeremiah Clements, and Jason Jackson, who served as research assistants during the time I worked on this project, and to Shaylin Clark for compiling the indexes. Finally, I offer this volume to my three sons, who enrich their parents' lives immeasurably. David, Jeremy, and AJ confirm the psalmist's wisdom: "the sons of one's youth" are a great blessing.

Bill T. Arnold

A Word about Citations

All volumes in the *New Cambridge Bible Commentary* (NCBC) include footnotes, with full bibliographical citations included in the note when a source is first mentioned. Subsequent citations include the author's initial or initials, full last name, abbreviated title for the work, and date of publication. Most readers prefer this citation system to endnotes that require searching through pages at the back of the book.

The Suggested Reading lists, also included in all NCBC volumes after the Introduction, are not a part of this citation apparatus. Annotated and organized by publication type, the self-contained Suggested Reading list is intended to introduce and briefly review some of the most well-known and helpful literature on the biblical text under discussion.

Abbreviations

AA	*American Anthropologist*
AASOR	Annual of the American Schools of Oriental Research
AB	Anchor Bible
ABD	*Anchor Bible Dictionary.* Edited by D. N. Freedman. 6 vols. New York, 1992.
ABRL	Anchor Bible Reference Library
AHw	*Akkadisches Handwörterbuch.* W. von Soden. 3 vols. Wiesbaden, 1965–1981.
ANET	*Ancient Near Eastern Texts Relating to the Old Testament.* Edited by James B. Pritchard. Third edition. Princeton: Princeton University Press, 1969.
AOAT	Alter Orient und Altes Testament
AOS	American Oriental Series
ASOR	American Schools of Oriental Research
AsTJ	*Asbury Theological Journal*
BASOR	*Bulletin of the American Schools of Oriental Research*
BDB	Brown, F., S. R. Driver, and C. A. Briggs, *A Hebrew and English Lexicon of the Old Testament.* Oxford, 1907.
BEATAJ	Beiträge zur Erforschung des Alten Testaments und des antiken Judentum
BETL	Bibliotheca ephemeridum theologicarum lovaniensium
BHS	*Biblia Hebraica Stuttgartensia.* Edited by K. Elliger and W. Rudolph. Stuttgart: Deutsche Bibelgesellschaft, 1983.
Bib	*Biblica*
BJS	Brown Judaic Studies
BN	*Biblische Notizen*
BRev	*Bible Review*
BWANT	Beiträge zur Wissenschaft vom Alten und Neuen Testament
BZ	*Biblische Zeitschrift*
BZAW	Beihefte zur Zeitschrift für die alttestamentliche Wissenschaft

CAD	*The Assyrian Dictionary of the Oriental Institute of the University of Chicago*. Edited by A. Leo Oppenheim et al. Chicago: University of Chicago Press, 1956–2007.
CAH	*The Cambridge Ancient History*. Edited by I. E. S. Edwards and John Boardman. 14 vols. Cambridge: Cambridge University Press, 1970–.
CANE	*Civilizations of the Ancient Near East*. Edited by Jack Sasson. 4 vols. New York, 1995.
CBQ	*Catholic Biblical Quarterly*
CBQMS	Catholic Biblical Quarterly Monograph Series
CDA	*A Concise Dictionary of Akkadian*. Jeremy A. Black, Andrew R. George, and J. N. Postgate. Santag 5. Wiesbaden: Harrassowitz, 2000.
ConBOT	Coniectanea biblica: Old Testament Series
COS	*The Context of Scripture*. Edited by William W. Hallo and K. Lawson Younger, Jr. 3 vols. Leiden: Brill, 1997–2002.
CTU	*The Cuneiform Alphabetic Texts from Ugarit, Ras Ibn Hani, and Other Places*. Edited by M. Dietrich, O. Loretz, and J. Sanmartin. Münster: Ugarit–Verlag, 1995.
CurBS	*Currents in Research: Biblical Studies*
DCH	*Dictionary of Classical Hebrew*. Edited by D. J. A. Clines. Sheffield: Sheffield Academic Press, 1993–.
DDD²	*Dictionary of Deities and Demons in the Bible*. Edited by K. van der Toorn, B. Becking, and P. W. van der Horst. Second edition. Leiden: Brill, 1999.
DOTHB	*Dictionary of the Old Testament: Historical Books*. Edited by Bill T. Arnold and H. G. M. Williamson. Downers Grove, Ill.: InterVarsity, 2005.
DOTP	*Dictionary of the Old Testament: Pentateuch*. Edited by T. Desmond Alexander and David W. Baker. Downers Grove, Ill.: InterVarsity, 2003.
ErIsr	*Eretz-Israel*
FCB	Feminist Companion to the Bible
FOTL	Forms of Old Testament Literature
FRLANT	Forschungen zur Religion und Literatur des Alten und Neuen Testaments
GKC	*Gesenius's Hebrew Grammar*. Edited by E. Kautzsch. Translated by A. E. Cowley. Second edition. Oxford: Clarendon Press, 1910.
HALOT	Koehler, L., W. Baumgartner, and J. J. Stamm. *The Hebrew and Aramaic Lexicon of the Old Testament*. Translated and edited under the supervision of M. E. J. Richardson. 4 vols. Leiden: Brill, 1994–1999.
HAR	*Hebrew Annual Review*

HSM	Harvard Semitic Monographs
HSS	Harvard Semitic Studies
HTR	*Harvard Theological Review*
HUCA	*Hebrew Union College Annual*
IBC	Interpretation: A Bible Commentary for Teaching and Preaching
ICC	International Critical Commentary
IDB	*The Interpreter's Dictionary of the Bible.* Edited by G. A. Buttrick. 4 vols. Nashville: Abingdon, 1962.
IDBSup	*Interpreter's Dictionary of the Bible: Supplementary Volume.* Edited by K. Crim. Nashville: Abingdon, 1976.
IEJ	*Israel Exploration Journal*
Int	*Interpretation*
ITC	International Theological Commentary
JAAR	*Journal of the American Academy of Religion*
JANESCU	*Journal of the Ancient Near Eastern Society of Columbia University*
JAOS	*Journal of the American Oriental Society*
JBL	*Journal of Biblical Literature*
JCS	*Journal of Cuneiform Studies*
JEA	*Journal of Egyptian Archaeology*
JJS	*Journal of Jewish Studies*
JLSP	Janua Linguarum: Series Practica
JNES	*Journal of Near Eastern Studies*
JSOT	*Journal for the Study of the Old Testament*
JSOTSup	Journal for the Study of the Old Testament: Supplement Series
JTS	*Journal of Theological Studies*
MARI	*Mari: Annales de recherches interdisciplinaires*
NAC	New American Commentary
NCBC	New Cambridge Bible Commentary
NIB	*The New Interpreter's Bible*
NIBCOT	New International Biblical Commentary on the Old Testament
NICOT	New International Commentary on the Old Testament
NIDB	*The New Interpreter's Dictionary of the Bible.* Edited by Katharine Doob Sakenfeld. 5 vols. Nashville: Abingdon, 2006–.
NIDOTTE	*New International Dictionary of Old Testament Theology and Exegesis.* Edited by Willem A. Van Gemeren. 5 vols. Grand Rapids, Mich.: Zondervan, 1997.
OBO	Orbis biblicus et orientalis
OBT	Overtures to Biblical Theology
OEANE	*The Oxford Encyclopedia of Archaeology in the Near East.* Edited by Eric M. Meyers. 5 vols. New York: Oxford University Press, 1997
OIP	Oriental Institute Publications

OrAnt	*Oriens antiquus*
OTG	Old Testament Guides
OTL	Old Testament Library
OtSt	Oudtestamentische Studiën
PIAS	Publications of the Institute for Advanced Studies, the Hebrew University of Jerusalem
PEQ	*Palestine Exploration Quarterly*
PTMS	Pittsburgh Theological Monograph Series
RA	*Revue d'assyriologie et d'archéologie orientale*
RANE	*Readings from the Ancient Near East: Primary Sources for Old Testament Study.* Bill T. Arnold and Bryan E. Beyer. Grand Rapids, Mich.: Baker Academic, 2002.
RB	*Revue biblique*
RlA	*Reallexikon der Assyriologie.* Edited by Erich Ebeling, et al. Berlin: Walter de Gruyter, 1932–.
SAOC	Studies in Ancient Oriental Civilizations
SBLABS	Society of Biblical Literature Archaeology and Biblical Studies
SBLDS	Society of Biblical Literature Dissertation Series
SBLMS	Society of Biblical Literature Monograph Series
SBLRBS	Society of Biblical Literature Resources for Biblical Study
SBLSymS	Society of Biblical Literature Symposium Series
SBLWAW	Society of Biblical Literature Writings from the Ancient World
SBTS	Sources for Biblical and Theological Study
SemeiaSt	Semeia Studies
SHCANE	Studies in the History and Culture of the Ancient Near East
SJOT	*Scandinavian Journal of the Old Testament*
SSN	Studia Semitica Neerlandica
SubBi	Subsidia biblica
TDOT	*Theological Dictionary of the Old Testament.* Edited by G. Johannes Botterweck and Helmer Ringgren. Translated by J. T. Willis, G. W. Bromiley, and D. E. Green. 15 vols. Grand Rapids, Mich.: Eerdmans, 1974–.
TOTC	Tyndale Old Testament Commentaries
TUAT	*Texte aus der Umwelt des Alten Testaments.* Edited by Otto Kaiser and Riekele Borger. Gütersloh: G. Mohn, 1983–1997.
TynBul	*Tyndale Bulletin*
TZ	*Theologische Zeitschrift*
UF	*Ugarit-Forschungen*
VT	*Vetus Testamentum*
VTSup	Vetus Testamentum Supplements
WMANT	Wissenschaftliche Monographien zum Alten und Neuen Testament

WBC	Word Biblical Commentary
WTJ	*Westminster Theological Journal*
YNER	Yale Near Eastern Researches
ZA	*Zeitschrift für Assyriologie*
ZAW	*Zeitschrift für die alttestamentliche Wissenschaft*

I. Introduction

〜❧〜

The book of Genesis addresses the most profound questions of life. Who are we? Why are we here? And, more to the focus of Genesis, who is God, how does God relate to the universe, and what are the origins of God's chosen people, Israel? Many cultures, ancient and modern, have produced similar philosophical speculations about the nature of God, humanity, and cosmic origins, but none has left the impact on world history and thought as enduring as that of Genesis.

The book is comprised of two large blocks of material, the Primeval History (Gen 1–11) and the ancestral narratives (Gen 12–50).[1] These have been linked together in order to express a certain theological perspective, intended to establish the background necessary for reading the rest of the Pentateuch and beyond. Essential to that perspective in Genesis is the careful identification of the national God of ancient Israel, Yahweh, with the Sovereign God of creation as well as the self-revealing, promise-giving, and covenant-making God of Israel's ancestors. The God encountered in Genesis is therefore also the God of the plagues, the exodus from Egypt, the covenant, the law, the monarchy, the prophets, and the exile and restoration. Genesis is preparatory to a larger story.

This commentary will hold two commitments in focus related to methodology. (Unless the reader is especially interested in questions of method or composition, it may be advisable to skip the rest of this introduction and move directly to the commentary itself.) The first commitment has to do with the literary genre of the book of Genesis in light of scholarship on ancient Near Eastern literature generally. Gains

---

[1] Although originally, the flood may have constituted the end of the primeval age; Theodore Hiebert, *The Yahwist's Landscape: Nature and Religion in Early Israel* (New York: Oxford University Press, 1996), 80–82. Others contend that Gen 1–9 is an individual unit, or that the ancestral period must include the genealogy of Shem (11:10–26). See respectively, W. Malcolm Clark, "The Flood and the Structure of the Pre-Patriarchal History," *ZAW* 83 (1971): 184–211, and Naomi A. Steinberg, "The Genealogical Framework of the Family Stories in Genesis," *Semeia* 46 (1989): 41–50. Because of the symmetrical arrangement of the *tôlĕdôt* structuring clauses (see below), I have used the traditional division between Gen 1–11 and 12–50 here.

in our understanding of comparative materials from the ancient world have shed light on Genesis, affecting the way we read both the Primeval History and the ancestral narratives. The literary position of the Primeval History is unique in biblical literature because it has no local *co-text*, or immediately preceding materials to aid the reader in understanding. Thus the ancient Near Eastern comparative materials are all the more important for understanding the socio-historical realities of Genesis. Without belaboring the details of these comparative methods, this commentary will summarize key conclusions concerning the Primeval History's arrangement of themes common to other ancient cultures along a time continuum using cause and effect.[2] Such an approach demonstrates how these materials have been transformed in the biblical account, altering their original meaning and import. The implications of such an approach will broaden the reader's appreciation for the importance of these chapters in ordering the theological world of ancient Israel.

The identification of the ancestral narratives as Israel's proto-historical, national epic will likewise yield important results for our interpretation of the book.[3] The book of Genesis has been categorized largely as a composite of myth and legend since the days of Hermann Gunkel. Such an identification has tended to preclude subsequent scholarship from regarding the Yahwist, and the book of Genesis as a whole, as a work of history. More recently, John Van Seters has demonstrated that the Yahwist was first and foremost a historian, and by investigating the roles of myth, legend, and etiology in ancient history writing, he has also demonstrated that Genesis is "a type of antiquarian historiography concerned with origins and a national tradition of people and places."[4] So although the ancestral narratives are not the same type of history writing we know in the Deuteronomistic History, such as in the Court History (2 Sam 9–10; 1 Kgs 1–2), they are nonetheless far from myth and legend. They may rightly be identified, therefore, as Israel's proto-historical writings, or a national epic account of origins.

---

[2] Thorkild Jacobsen, "The Eridu Genesis," *JBL* 100 (1981): 513–29, esp. 528; and Patrick D. Miller, Jr., "Eridu, Dunnu, and Babel: A Study in Comparative Mythology," *HAR* 9 (1985): 227–51, esp. 231. Both reprinted in Richard S. Hess and David T. Tsumura, eds., "*I Studied Inscriptions from Before the Flood*": *Ancient Near Eastern, Literary, and Linguistic Approaches to Genesis 1–11* (SBTS 4; Winona Lake, Ind.: Eisenbrauns, 1994), 129–42 and 143–68 respectively.

[3] Frank M. Cross, *Canaanite Myth and Hebrew Epic: Essays in the History of the Religion of Israel* (Cambridge, Mass.: Harvard University Press, 1973); David Damrosch, *The Narrative Covenant: Transformations of Genre in the Growth of Biblical Literature* (San Francisco: Harper & Row, 1987); Abraham Malamat, "The Proto-History of Israel: A Study in Method," in *The Word of the Lord Shall Go Forth: Essays in Honor of David Noel Freedman in Celebration of His Sixtieth Birthday*, eds. Carol L. Meyers and Michael P. O'Connor (ASOR Special Volume Series 1; Winona Lake, Ind.: Eisenbrauns, 1983), 303–13.

[4] John Van Seters, *Prologue to History: The Yahwist as Historian in Genesis* (Louisville, Ky.: Westminster/John Knox Press, 1992), 22. However, I find his comparisons with Greek and Mesopotamian historiography of the first millennium BCE inadequate foundation for his late date of the Yahwist as a prologue for the Deuteronomistic History. See Bill T. Arnold, "History and Historiography, OT," *NIDB* 2: 833–37.

The second methodological commitment of this commentary is the importance of combining traditional historical-critical scholarship (source, form, and redaction criticism) with more recently developed synchronic approaches (narrative criticism and discourse analysis) as a means of closing the gap between today's reader and an ancient book like Genesis. A predilection to any single method (which characterizes many biblical commentaries) occasionally results in mechanical readings that may strip a text of its voice. It is my belief that a balance between older diachronic approaches and the newer synchronic readings will be most effective, especially for drawing out the significance of a text for contemporary clergy or students. Thus, I have attempted to strike a balance in the use of the various methodologies, old and new alike.[5]

The complexities of combining synchronic and diachronic approaches for biblical books are numerous. Many positions are possible along a continuum between those who, on the one hand, use redactional and diachronic historical studies of a text as a means of defining the structure, and on the other hand, those who investigate structure and synchronic relationships with little regard for the compositional history of the text. As a means of revealing my approach in this commentary, and therefore avoiding a complete philosophical defense for this approach (which requires a monograph instead of a brief commentary), I simply assert here that I favor an approach that reads the text twice, once for its compositional history as a means of informing the second reading, which emphasizes the synchronic structure of the whole.

In this manner, and in the interest of saving space, I will not rehearse the complex issues related to the original sources of Genesis, but will discuss them only briefly below (see "composition" pp. 12–18). My primary task in this volume, therefore, will be to comment on the text as we have received it. I will occasionally refer to the "narrative" of Genesis, by which I mean the macro-structure of extended portions of the book. By "text" I mean a particular pericope or selection of text under consideration, often a given chapter or group of chapters. Upon occasion, the fruits of traditional historical–critical research have an important bearing on the interpretation of the canonical or final shape of the text. So for example, the relationship between the two creation accounts in Genesis 1 and 2 is sometimes misunderstood because the phrase "these are the generations of . . . " (so important

---

[5] I am not the first to make this case, of course; cf. David L. Petersen, "The Formation of the Pentateuch," in *Old Testament Interpretation: Past, Present, and Future. Essays in Honor of Gene M. Tucker*, eds. James L. Mays, David L. Petersen, and Kent H. Richards (Nashville: Abingdon Press, 1995), 31–45; Hoftijzer prefers the terms "structure" and "compositional/redactional history" to "synchronic" and "diachronic" respectively because of ambiguous ways in which these terms are used; Jacob Hoftijzer, "Holistic or Compositional Approach? Linguistic Remarks to the Problem," in *Synchronic or Diachronic? A Debate on Method in Old Testament Exegesis*, ed. Johannes Cornelis de Moor (OtSt 34; Leiden, New York: E.J. Brill, 1995), 98–114.

in the canonical shape of the book) is taken as a *sub*scription of chapter 1. In this case, the unit breaks are 1:1–2:4a and 2:4b–25. However, if we take the expression as the priestly *super*scription of the second creation account (traditionally identified as Yahwistic) and assume rather the units to be 1:1–2:3 and 2:4–25, we have a new understanding of how the chapters are complementing each other.[6] The priestly editor has intentionally produced a coherent structure that stresses the continuity between the two accounts. Thus for example, the divine mandate of the first account ("fill the earth and subdue it" 1:28) is unpacked in the purpose clause of the second ("to till it and keep it," 2:15). The two have been tied together by the redactional process so that we must read them together in light of each other, producing a kind of binocular perception of the creation. And so, both a redactional, diachronic reading, and a canonical, synchronic reading are useful for understanding Genesis.

My procedure throughout has been to read each text in the Hebrew original with these methodological commitments in view, checking the Greek of the Septuagint and other versions as appropriate for textual clarity. At this initial stage, I drew up my preliminary comments before turning to the text of the NRSV itself, as well as a series of other commentaries on Genesis, several leading monographs and other secondary literature in order to provide the reader with an up-to-date interaction with the scholarship as much as possible. I have attempted to honor the original insights of others where appropriate without burdening the reader with unnecessary footnote references.

STRUCTURE AND CONTENT

Genesis is one of the most intentionally structured books of the Bible. Here I will survey the uses of a specific structuring device used to create its literary unity, as well as overview several of the book's main features.

The unique tôlĕdôt structuring device. The final editor of the book has used a clearly discernible structuring clause, to arrange the book into eleven panels of texts, placed side-by-side in a continuous whole (the first panel, 1:1–2:3, does not use the device). This structuring device is comprised of the term *tôlĕdôt*, "offspring, descendants; (family/clan) history," in the clause "these are the descendants of [personal name]" to introduce each new portion of the text.[7] The origins of the expression are most

---

[6] F. M. Cross, *Canaanite Myth and Hebrew Epic* (1973), 302; Brevard S. Childs, *Introduction to the Old Testament as Scripture* (Philadelphia: Fortress Press, 1979), 145.

[7] Specifically, this clause is found in 2:4; 5:1; 6:9; 10:1; 11:10; 11:27; 25:12; 25:19; 36:1; 36:9; 37:2. The first example is exceptional because "heavens and earth" occurs instead of a personal name. Another alternate has "sons of [personal name]" instead of the personal name itself, and the occurrence in 5:1 is exceptional because the phraseology is slightly different, "This is the list of the descendants of Adam." The clause is repeated in the text devoted to Esau's descendants (36:1,9), yielding a total of eleven occurrences of the expression in Genesis.

likely to be found in the use of genealogies (see pp. 9–10), but we have good reason to assume it was expanded intentionally by the editor of the book of Genesis in order to bring order to the whole (see commentary at 2:4 pp. 54–55).

Although the issues are quite complex, it seems reasonable to assume the *tôlĕdôt* clause was originally used to designate the descendants of a single individual in genealogical fashion.[8] As a noun pattern of the verbal root *yālad*, "to father, give birth to," the plural noun *tôlĕdôt* refers to that which is generated or produced by the individual in question. Uses in which it refers to the "generations" of heaven and earth in more metaphorical fashion (2:4) are therefore most likely derived from the genealogical uses. The particular occurrence in 5:1 is different from others in the addition of the word "list" ("document, scroll" *sēper*), which may reflect the most ancient title for such genealogies and suggests that the other *tôlĕdôt* clauses in Genesis are derived from this one. The distinctive genealogical style introduced at 5:1 is continued in Shem's genealogy (11:10–26) and implies that together they were once part of a very ancient genealogical "document" (*sēper*), which was used by priestly authors to periodize primeval times, first from creation and the Eden narratives to the flood, and then from the flood to Abram.

This more natural genealogical use of the *tôlĕdôt* clause has been adapted to a narrative format by the editor at 6:9 in order to return to a thread related to Noah: "Noah was a righteous man." This narrative thread was dropped at 5:32 in order to include notations on intermarriage between the sons of God and human daughters, along with additional reasons for the great flood (6:1–8). Similarly, the *tôlĕdôt* clause of 10:1 is likely an editorial link, since v. 1b appears to be original to the source behind this text.[9] In this way, it seems likely that the *tôlĕdôt* clauses themselves, with the sole exception of 5:1, were an invention of our priestly redactor (see pp. 16–18).

While the *tôlĕdôt* clauses probably originated as introductions to genealogical lists, they are at times used in Genesis to introduce narrative portions as well. Thus Genesis is comprised of two types of materials, narrative accounts and lists of various sorts, especially genealogies; these might conveniently be termed *narrative* and *numerative* texts.[10] The *tôlĕdôt* clause is twice followed by temporal clauses, both to narrate creation (2:4 and 5:1), and three times followed by descriptive nominal clauses (6:9; 11:10; 37:2). Others are followed by simple narrative verbal clauses, at

---

[8] A demonstrative introduces the identification nominal clause, "these *are the generations of*," and the progenitor's name follows *tôlĕdôt* in a construct state, "of Terah," for example. In several cases, the ancestor's name is doubled immediately after the clause, as in "... these are the descendants of Terah ... Terah was the father of Abram ... " (11:27, cf. 6:9; 11:10; 11:27; and similarly 36:1–2).

[9] And perhaps following naturally from 6:10 before it.

[10] Claus Westermann, *Genesis 1–11: A Commentary* (Minneapolis: Augsburg Pub. House, 1984), 3. His original, *Erzählung* and *Aufzählung*, makes for more catchy alliteration than in translation; Claus Westermann, *Biblischer Kommentar, Altes Testament: Genesis*, eds. Siegfried Herrmann and Hans Walter Wolff (Volume I/1; Neukirchen-Vluyn: Neukirchener Verlag des Erziehungsverein, 1974), 4.

times as part of the genealogical birth announcements (e.g., "Terah was the father of Abram . . . ," 11:27). The result of the combined narrative and numerative uses of the *tôlĕdôt* clause is an organization of the book into ten panels of material, eleven counting the creation overture in 1:1–2:3, arranged as follows:

2:4a	*tôlĕdôt* of heaven and earth	2:4b–4:26
5:1a	*tôlĕdôt* of Adam	5:1–6:8
6:9a	*tôlĕdôt* of Noah	6:9–9:29
10:1a	*tôlĕdôt* of Noah's sons	10:1–11:9
11:10a	*tôlĕdôt* of Shem	11:10–26
11:27a	*tôlĕdôt* of Terah	11:27–25:11
25:12a	*tôlĕdôt* of Ishmael	25:12–18
25:19a	*tôlĕdôt* of Isaac	25:19–35:29
36:1a	*tôlĕdôt* of Esau (again at 36:9a)	36:1–37:1
37:2a	*tôlĕdôt* of Jacob	37:2–50:26

These ten portions are devoted equally to (1) the origins of the universe and the early history of humanity, and (2) the prehistory of the Israelite nation preserved in the account of the ancestral family. Thus five *tôlĕdôt* clauses are used to provide genealogical structure for the Primeval History (1:1–11:26), while five are devoted to the ancestral narratives (11:27–50:26). The materials of Genesis are disproportionately focused on the ancestral narratives, while at the same time, the equal distribution of the *tôlĕdôt* clauses provides a certain symmetry to the whole. Indeed, it is possible that the fivefold symmetry in the two portions of Genesis is related to palistrophic or chiastic structure known to be present elsewhere in Genesis, or to be compared to the fivefold division of the Pentateuch itself.[11]

The alternation between *tôlĕdôt* for numerative purposes and *tôlĕdôt* for narrative purposes, or between genealogy and narrative in Genesis, may be compared to watching a movie on DVD in the privacy of one's home.[12] The genealogies are times when we "fast-forward" through the story, getting only the barest of minimum details in quick summation, except on occasions when the editor slows down enough to highlight certain particular features, such as Enoch's exemplary walk with God, or Nimrod's impressive urban accomplishments (5:22–24 and 10:8b–12, respectively). In fast-forward mode, we get only name, length of years, list of children, and perhaps death. The narratives, by contrast, move along at a deliberate pace – at times even in "slow motion" – because the details of the narrative are so important. The effect is an overarching narrative trajectory, intentionally established by the editor using the *tôlĕdôt* clauses in order to give the impression of a slow and gradual narrowing

[11] Joseph Blenkinsopp, *The Pentateuch: An Introduction to the First Five Books of the Bible* (ABRL; New York: Doubleday, 1992), 59, and on the *tôlĕdôt* clauses generally, 58–59 and 99–100.

[12] I owe this metaphor to J. G. Janzen, *Abraham and All the Families of the Earth: A Commentary on the Book of Genesis 12–50* (ITC; Grand Rapids, Mich.: Eerdmans, 1993), 4.

focus, with fewer and fewer participants, accenting the particularizing effects of the blessings of God.[13]

Origins – primeval and ancestral. The book of Genesis is about beginnings. It begins with God because God himself has no beginning. But the origin of everything else apart from God is explained here. That is to say, this book explains the origins for everything the Israelites believed important for understanding their salvation history, and therefore Genesis provides what is needed for reading the rest of the Bible. In general, this includes cosmic origins and Israelite origins. The Primeval History describes the origins of the universe and God's plan to relate to it, and especially to humans, while the ancestral narratives present the origins of the nation Israel.

These two portions of Genesis – the cosmic origins of the Primeval History and the Israelite origins of the ancestral narratives – work in introductory, concentric circles, drawing the reader ever closer to an understanding of God's relationship first with the cosmos generally, and then with God's chosen people, Israel. The ancestral narratives in particular, the accounts of Abraham, Isaac, and Jacob, including the story of Joseph embedded near the conclusion, provide an essential ideological foundation for what follows in Exodus, Leviticus, Numbers, and Deuteronomy (e.g., Exod 2:24; Deut 1:8; 34:4). The saving acts of Yahweh on Israel's behalf (the plagues of Egypt, the miraculous crossing of the Sea of Reeds), and the covenant at Mount Sinai were based on the ancestral covenant and its intentions for the nation Israel. While there is little mention of the events of the Primeval History in the Pentateuch, Gen 1–11 form an important introductory role as well, not just for the Mosaic religion of ancient Israel but for the rest of the Bible.

We should not be surprised by a lack of connection between the people, places, and events of the Primeval History on the one hand, and what we might call verifiable history in contemporary research on the other. The very nature of the material as Israel's mytho-historical literature, devoted as it is to the origins of the universe, make it impossible to find such historical traces. The literary genre "mytho-historical" in no way identifies these chapters as myths or mythical, but rather draws attention to the way in which themes previously regarded simply as mythological are arranged along an historical time line using cause and effect.[14]

Attempts to find historical traces in the ancestral narratives have been no more fruitful. Against the trend of much scholarship of the past three decades, it has been argued recently that Genesis preserves traces of Israelite heritage extending back to the Bronze Age (3200–1200 BCE).[15] Such historical traces, it is alleged, locate Israel's

---

[13] Josef Schreiner, "*tôlĕdôt,*" *TDOT* 15:582–88, esp. 586.

[14] T. Jacobsen, "The Eridu Genesis," esp. 528.

[15] Daniel E. Fleming, "Genesis in History and Tradition: The Syrian Background of Israel's Ancestors, Reprise," in *The Future of Biblical Archaeology: Reassessing Methodologies and Assumptions,* eds. James K. Hoffmeier and A. R. Millard (Grand Rapids, Mich.: Eerdmans, 2004), 193–232.

identity in social categories that are not uniquely Israelite, but rather are pre-Israelite in origin and attested in the ancestral traditions of Genesis. Specifically the tradition of ancestral roots in northern Syria is currently inexplicable from the perspective of an Israelite living in the first millennium BCE. Rather, the identity of an ancestral homeland in Syrian Haran in the north presents a tantalizing connection with the tribal confederacies known from the Mari texts, especially the southwestern division of a confederacy known as Binu Yamina, which spanned all of modern Syria.[16]

Yet the first attested extra-biblical reference to "Israel" dates from the very end of the Bronze Age.[17] This fact, together with the absence of archaeological or epigraphical evidence for Israel's existence before the thirteenth century BCE, and the apparent origins of these ancestral traditions in the Iron Age (especially Iron I, 1200–1000 BCE), have led historians to conclude that Israel's history begins in, and only in, the Iron Age. Understood in this way, the ancestral traditions narrated in Genesis reflect only the Israel of the Iron Age, and not that of the Bronze Age, which it purports to narrate. Thus the period of the ancestors disappears altogether.[18] However, when the biblical sources are subjected to standards demanded of other ancient Near Eastern texts – assuming proper critical precautions when reading distinctly literary reformulations of oral traditions such as the ancestral narratives, but at the same time not requiring of the biblical materials standards demanded nowhere else – the Israelite traditions about origins in the Bronze Age must be taken seriously. So, for example, when first-millennium Assyrian and Babylonian historians speak of a religious and cultural (and indeed, ethnic) continuity with their origins in the Bronze Age, today's historians typically give credence to such textual claims.[19] In the same way, traces of Israel's earliest history are likely contained

---

[16] For details of this potential background for Israel's ancestors, and further exploration of the possible connection between biblical "Benjaminites" with Mari's Yaminites and the city of Haran, see Daniel E. Fleming, "Mari and the Possibilities of Biblical Memory," *RA* 92 (1998): 41–78, esp. 59–73; and again, Daniel E. Fleming, "Genesis in History and Tradition."

[17] James K. Hoffmeier, "The (Israel) Stela of Merneptah," *COS* 2.6:40–41.

[18] M. P. Maidman, "Historiographic Reflections on Israel's Origins: The Rise and Fall of the Patriarchal Age," in *Hayim and Miriam Tadmor Volume*, eds. Israel Eph'al, Amnon Ben-Tor, and Peter Machinist (ErIsr 27; Jerusalem: Israel Exploration Society, 2003), 120–128. And so some today date the Pentateuch quite late, perhaps as late as the third century BCE; e.g., Russell E. Gmirkin, *Berossus and Genesis, Manetho and Exodus: Hellenistic Histories and the Date of the Pentateuch* (Library of Hebrew Bible/Old Testament Studies 433.15; New York: T&T Clark, 2006).

[19] William W. Hallo, *Origins: The Ancient Near Eastern Background of Some Modern Western Institutions* (SHCANE 6; Leiden: E.J. Brill, 1996), 314–15. Although several socio-cultural features of the early second millennium BCE have been overstated as parallels with the ancestral narratives, others continue to warrant our attention as potential recollections of memories preserved through oral traditions, as argued recently by Amihai Mazar in Israel Finkelstein and Amihai Mazar, *The Quest for the Historical Israel: Debating Archaeology and the History of Early Israel* (SBLABS 17; Leiden/Atlanta: Brill/Society of Biblical Literature, 2007), esp. 57–59.

in the Genesis traditions of Mesopotamian roots and sojourns in Syria–Palestine and Egypt. Although historical details of these Bronze Age origins are currently beyond our grasp and will no doubt continue to be debated, we have good reason to look to the Bronze Age for Israel's beginnings. But given what we know about these historical periods currently, the most we can hope for is to establish a plausible setting for the events of the ancestral narratives in light of the broad contours of ancient Near Eastern social and political history.[20]

Genealogies. Such a book of origins, organized as it is with the *tôlĕdôt* structuring device, has a great interest in genealogies. Genesis contains two types of genealogies: the "linear" or vertical genealogy, which traces a single line of descent, and "segmented" or horizontal genealogy, which traces various descendants. The form of the genealogy depends upon its function in the text. So, for example, "the descendants of Adam" are listed in a linear genealogy through ten generations from Adam to Noah, in which a single son is named for each descendant and only passing reference is made to "other sons and daughters" (5:1–32). The genealogy then segments at the tenth generation in order to introduce all three sons of Noah, who became the father of Shem, Ham, and Japheth (5:32). By contrast, "the descendants of Noah's sons" are presented in a segmented genealogy, listing the sons according to their families, languages, lands, and nations, in order to describe the human race in the post-flood era (10:1–32).[21] It is possible to trace through this system of genealogies in Genesis a line of descent for all of humanity through twenty-five generations from Adam to the children of Jacob, the ancestor of the Israelite clans and families, thus creating a literary framework or skeleton for the entire book.[22]

Anthropologists have contributed to our understanding of the role of genealogies in the Bible by identifying processes of "divergence," "invergence," and "segmentation."[23] As this relates to the book of Genesis, each patriarch is the father of other children who are not part of the Israelite ancestry and who become the ancestors of other people groups in the known world. Through this process of differentiation, or *divergence*, the book gives explanation to other populations in a kind of ethnic

---

[20] J. Blenkinsopp, *The Pentateuch* (1992), 126–29.

[21] Among many resources on biblical genealogies, see especially the following: Yigal Levin, "Understanding Biblical Genealogies," *CurBS* 9 (2001): 11–46; Sven Tengström, *Die Toledotformel und die literarische Struktur der priesterlichen Erweiterungsschicht im Pentateuch* (ConBOT 17; Lund: Gleerup, 1982); Robert R. Wilson, *Genealogy and History in the Biblical World* (YNER 7; New Haven: Yale University Press, 1977); Ronald S. Hendel, *Remembering Abraham: Culture, Memory, and History in the Hebrew Bible* (New York: Oxford University Press, 2005), 9–13; and Richard S. Hess, "The Genealogies of Genesis 1–11 and Comparative Literature," *Bib* 70 (1989): 241–54; repr. in R. S. Hess and D. T. Tsumura, *I Studied Inscriptions from Before the Flood* (1994), 58–72.

[22] Frank Crüsemann, "Human Solidarity and Ethnic Identity: Israel's Self-Definition in the Genealogical System of Genesis," in *Ethnicity and the Bible*, ed. Mark G. Brett (Biblical Interpretation Series 19; Leiden: E.J. Brill, 1996), 57–76 esp. 58–60.

[23] See especially the important work of Karin R. Andriolo, "A Structural Analysis of Genealogy and World View in the Old Testament," *AA* 75 (1973): 1657–69, esp. 1657–63.

map of the world, and explains further the way Israel related to those populations. In distinction to this use of genealogies to describe the world's populations in a process of branching, Israel's lineage itself is traced through a straight line, from Adam to Jacob through *invergence*. In each generation, only one son continues the Israelite ancestry. This process is used in Genesis to present and discuss each of the "other" descendants of Israel's ancestors first before picking up the descent line of interest. Once the promised seed begins multiplying, this lineal process of alternating divergence and invergence ends with the segmented genealogy of Jacob, whose twelve sons become the twelve tribes of Israel. The lineal descent gives way to twelve sub-units in a single generation, and from that point forward, *segmentation* becomes primary in Genesis (cf. 29:31–30:24). Once the children of Jacob are born, the genealogical focus of the book is on the branches of the ancestral family, all considered *within* the covenant blessing of Israel's ancestry, rather than certain branches that are excluded (e.g., Ishmael, Esau). Through this process of segmentation, all the tribes are equally part of the Israelite nation, which illustrates that the covenant blessings are becoming a reality.

The Bible's genealogies are thus a means of providing social identification for a person or people group, making important assertions about identity, territory, and relating them to others in the narrative.[24] In a sense, such genealogies are more natural to the ancestral narratives, and so it has been suggested that the use of the genealogies in the Primeval History of Gen 1–11 was continued from their use in Gen 12–50 as a means of overlaying formal literary structure upon otherwise disparate and in some cases, unrelated materials.[25] Whether or not this is indeed the case, the genealogies of the Primeval History may be said to replace the role of theogonies, or the birth of the gods, in ancient Near Eastern accounts of creation. In other words, divine birthing, parenting, and the succession of births (sky-god and earth-god, fresh-water god and salt-water god, etc.) all play an important role in ancient cosmogonies throughout western Asia. But in Gen 1–11, these are replaced by genealogies of humankind's earliest ancestors.[26]

Etiologies. Etiology may be defined as "a narrative designed in its basic structure to support some kind of explanation for a situation or name that exists at the time of the storyteller."[27] The term "etiology" may thus be applied to any narrative giving the past, historical reason for a present reality (the present of the author), and is a

---

[24] Gary N. Knoppers, "Intermarriage, Social Complexity, and Ethnic Diversity in the Genealogy of Judah," *JBL* 120 (2001): 15–30, esp. 18.

[25] C. Westermann, *Genesis 1–11* (1984): 8–9.

[26] On the nature of theogonies in ancient Near Eastern creation myths, see Frank M. Cross, *From Epic to Canon: History and Literature in Ancient Israel* (Baltimore: Johns Hopkins University Press, 1998), 73–83 and pp. 45–47 below.

[27] George W. Coats, *Genesis, with an Introduction to Narrative Literature* (FOTL 1; Grand Rapids, Mich.: Eerdmans, 1983), 10; Burke O. Long, *The Problem of Etiological Narrative in the Old Testament* (BZAW 108; Berlin: Töpelmann, 1968).

purely descriptive term.[28] As a literary feature, it is most characteristic of traditional, perhaps originally oral materials. Often in Genesis, an episode is concluded with an etiological connection that helps the reader understand why something *is as it is*, and secondarily prepares the reader for the next unit of the book. So, for example, the Primeval History uses etiologies to explain sabbath law (2:1–3), marriage (2:24), serpentine locomotion (3:14), human hatred of snakes (3:15), pain in childbirth (3:16), and many others, while the ancestral narratives explain the name Beer-lahai-roi (16:14), the name Zoar (19:22), and many others (the commentary below will note these as they occur). So in its two portions – Primeval History and ancestral narratives – the book of Genesis is both retrospective and anticipatory, looking back at events of the past that effected some important sociological or cultural change and anticipating the continued effects of that change for the nation Israel. Etiologies are the preferred way of marking those changes, and tying the events of the past with the author's present.

Yet one large block of material in Genesis is an exception to this observation and requires further comment. Hermann Gunkel argued convincingly that Gen 37–50 needs to be distinguished from the "legend cycles" of the other ancestral narratives in 12–36 by its coherent composition.[29] Unlike a row of pearls on a somewhat inconspicuous thread, as we encounter in the Abraham and Jacob narratives in Gen 12–36, most of the Joseph narrative is a well-organized whole. Contained in these chapters is the "Joseph Novel" comprised of Gen 37, 39–45, and parts of 46–50, which explains the coherent composition (see "Overview of the Joseph Narrative" below at pp. 313–17). The Novel itself, as distinct from the Joseph narrative overall, uses repetition in speeches liberally, and characterizes the main protagonist, Joseph, with complex detail as opposed to the one-dimensional characterization most common in Gen 12–36. Also, the Joseph Novel diminishes the prominence of places, such as Hebron, Penuel, Bethel, etc., and instead Jacob dwells generally "in the land of Canaan." Furthermore, the Joseph Novel contains no theophanies, such as those so central to the Abraham and Jacob narratives, but instead "belief in providence has taken the place of belief in theophanies."[30] In addition to these several distinctive features of the Joseph Novel, we note a complete absence of etiologies in Gen 37 and 39–45. The Joseph narrative at large contains only four examples of etiology in

---

[28] Alan R. Millard, "Story, History, and Theology," in *Faith, Tradition, and History: Old Testament Historiography in its Near Eastern Context*, eds. A. R. Millard, James K. Hoffmeier, and David W. Baker (Winona Lake, Ind.: Eisenbrauns, 1994), 37–64 esp. 40–41.

[29] For part of what follows here, see Hermann Gunkel, *Genesis: Translated and Interpreted*, trans. Mark E. Biddle (Macon, Ga.: Mercer University Press, 1997), 381–83; Hermann Gunkel, *The Legends of Genesis: The Biblical Saga and History*, trans. William H. Carruth (New York: Schocken Books, 1964), 77–117.

[30] H. Gunkel, *Genesis: Translated and Interpreted* (1997), 382. Even in the Novel's use of dreams, the least sensory form of revelation, God no longer appears to speak. Gunkel also noted the differences in the way foreigners are portrayed in the Joseph Novel compared to the other ancestral narratives of Genesis.

contrast to the high concentration of etiologies in Gen 1–36, and these occur in the narrative seams around the Novel.[31] The original Joseph Novel shows no interest in etiological origins of social or political institutions because it is motivated by different theological interests, which will be detailed in the commentary below (see especially 45:5–8 and 50:20).

Geography. Finally, with regard to structure and content, the reader should note the interesting geographical arrangement in the book of Genesis. The Primeval History displays a remarkable western orientation by its frequent references to things in the "east." Yahweh God planted Eden there (2:8), the Tigris flows from Eden east of Assyria (2:14), Adam and Eve were driven east of Eden (3:24), Cain lived in Nod, east of Eden (4:16), the descendants of Shem lived in the eastern hill country (10:30), and early humanity migrated to Shinar from the east (11:2). The ancestral narratives, on the other hand, highlight several specific localities in Syria–Palestine, especially Shechem, Hebron, Bethlehem, and Bethel, while also tracing ancestral journeys to northern Mesopotamia and Egypt. Indeed, it has been observed that Gen 1–11 is set against a Mesopotamian background, while Gen 12–36 has Syria–Palestine primarily in view and Gen 37–50 is largely focused on Egypt.[32]

COMPOSITION

Theories on the composition of the book of Genesis have a long and complicated history. I offer here a brief overview of that history, and summarize the assumptions at work in this commentary. From the Enlightenment in the eighteenth century, various scholars across Europe began speculation about sources used in the composition of the book of Genesis, and this source-critical approach crystallized in the works of Karl H. Graf and Julius Wellhausen in the so-called Graf–Wellhausen synthesis of the Documentary Hypothesis.[33] This hypothesis inaugurated an era of general consensus on the documents behind the Pentateuch and their transmission history, in which it was taken for granted that earlier Yahwistic (J for Jehovistic) and Elohistic (E) sources were combined as a product of the early divided monarchy of ancient Israel. This so-called JE source was combined much later with a D source, which was essentially the core of the book of Deuteronomy composed in the seventh century BCE, and finally with a priestly source (P) produced as part of the postexilic

---

[31] The birth of Perez and Zerah (38:29–30), Joseph's statute in Egypt (47:26), the elevation of Ephraim over the firstborn Manasseh (48:20), and the naming of Abel-mizraim (50:10–11).

[32] William W. Hallo, "Biblical History in Its Near Eastern Setting: The Contextual Approach," in *Scripture in Context: Essays on the Comparative Method*, eds. Carl D. Evans, William W. Hallo, and John B. White (PTMS 34; Pittsburg: Pickwick Press, 1980), 1–26 esp. 15.

[33] For bibliography and more on what follows here, see Bill T. Arnold, "Pentateuchal Criticism, History of," *DOTP*, 622–31, esp. 622–26.

restoration. Wellhausen so persuasively made the case for this four-source theory (the now familiar "JEDP"), the hypothesis essentially convinced most of the scholarly world by the turn of the twentieth century. Scholars continued working on the pre-history and compilation of these sources themselves, as well as their tradition history, analyzing larger complexes of tradition.[34] But by and large, the four-source hypothesis was fundamental to these investigations.

The first period in this overview may therefore be called the *regnant source analysis* of Pentateuchal studies, dating from Wellhausen (1844–1918) until approximately 1970. Essentially, the conclusions of the four-source Graf–Wellhausen hypothesis were unchallenged, although there were many developments and nuanced interpretations along the lines of form-critical and tradition-critical investigation. The second development in critical studies of Genesis may be called *nascent literary criticism*, in which rhetorical or aesthetic criticism attempted to overcome the atomizing excesses of source- and form-criticism.[35] The closing decades of the twentieth century witnessed a burgeoning secondary literature exploring the rhetorical sophistication of these narratives, often assuming a dichotomy between "final form" readings and source criticism, or to put it another way, between diachronic approaches (most coming before approximately 1970) and synchronic approaches. Many of these newer approaches were also less likely to accept the classical expression of the four-source theory, and although there was certainly no uniformity in this, the Graf–Wellhausen formulation no longer dominated the field of research.

The third stage of Pentateuchal research may be called the *maturation of literary criticism*. While some proponents of rhetorical criticism continue to jettison the source-critical approach altogether, more are regretting the retrenchment of scholars into synchronic and diachronic camps, rejecting this as a false dichotomy, and attempting to hold together a source approach with a sensitivity to the rhetorical sophistication of the text. In particular, I have been most impressed by recent appeals for a balance between the diachronic and synchronic approaches, especially in the way we should think of the *intra*textuality of ancient compositions, which is especially true of a book like Genesis. We may speak of *inter*textuality as the way a text is interwoven with references, allusions, even quotations, with other texts and indeed, with an entire cultural system (although the definition of "intertextuality" is contested). On the other hand, *intra*textuality refers to the way a later text "builds

---

[34] Form-critical investigation, pioneered by Hermann Gunkel and Hugo Gressmann, and tradition–historical research led first and foremost by Gerhard von Rad and Martin Noth dominated much of the early twentieth century.

[35] This development is often traced to James Muilenburg's 1968 presidential address to the Society of Biblical Literature, published as "Form Criticism and Beyond," *JBL* 88 (1969): 1–18. The assumption is simplistic since his paper did not launch a new movement, but it has become symbolic nonetheless. Also, although not precisely correct, we may include the rise of so-called canonical criticism in this category, often associated with Brevard S. Childs and James A. Sanders, although the former resisted such a categorization.

itself around an earlier text, claiming to reproduce it."[36] So the resultant composite text claims the authority of the earlier text it has incorporated, even as it has absorbed and transformed it. Thus the process of exegesis is not unlike the following analogy.[37] Traditional historical–critical scholarship may be compared to "strip mining," in which layers of traditions and sources are opened up like a seam in the earth's surface. Newer literary and canonical approaches are more like a "wilderness preserve," in which the boundaries and integrity of a text are protected and admired. Ultimately, however, we must combine the investigation of the final form of the text with a "geological" approach, in which the contours of the text's landscape are scrutinized and hypotheses are developed to explain how the landscape was created. Such an approach contributes depth perception to our exegesis, and avoids the extremes of either the strip-mining or preserve approaches.

In this commentary, my own approach assumes the essential validity of the source analysis, although I will not draw frequent attention to this because of the limited size of the volume. I offer here a brief explanation of my assumptions, which the reader may consult at various times in the commentary for clarification.[38] The book of Genesis as we now have it was composed of the following sources. The *first* in the series is the old epic narrative of Israel's history written at a point in time impossible for us to determine. This great epic account is distinguished in a number of ways, such as theology and literary style,[39] but especially in the ways it uses the sacred name for God, YHWH/Yahweh, or "the Lord" in most translations, and

---

[36] David M. Carr, *Reading the Fractures of Genesis: Historical and Literary Approaches* (Louisville, Ky.: Westminster John Knox Press, 1996), 12–13; and cf. Kirsten Nielsen, "Intertextuality and the Hebrew Bible," in *Congress Volume, Oslo 1998*, eds. André Lemaire and Magne Sæbø (VTSup 80; Leiden: Brill, 2000), 17–31. And on the rapprochement between diachronic and synchronic studies more generally, see in addition to David Carr, John Barton, "Intertextuality and the 'Final Form' of the Text," in *Congress Volume, Oslo 1998*, eds. André Lemaire and Magne Sæbø (VTSup 80; Leiden: Brill, 2000), 33–37; and Daniel B. Mathewson, "A Critical Binarism: Source Criticism and Deconstructive Criticism," *JSOT* 26 (2002): 3–28.

[37] Noted by a number of scholars for over a century, and conveniently summarized by Carr, to whom I am indebted for this discussion (*Reading the Fractures* [1996]: 15).

[38] The present Hebrew text of Genesis contains many late features, but these likely have little to do with the actual time of composition. For discussion of the origins of Biblical Hebrew, how it evolved over time, and the promises and pitfalls of using these data for dating biblical texts, see Jens B. Kofoed, *Text and History: Historiography and the Study of the Biblical Text* (Winona Lake, Ind.: Eisenbrauns, 2005), 113–63. For a thorough refutation of the Graf–Wellhausen hypothesis, opting instead for a composition of the Pentateuch in the first half of the first millennium BCE, and still allowing for "various types" of literature, see Richard S. Hess, *Israelite Religions: An Archaeological and Biblical Survey* (Grand Rapids, Mich.: Baker Academic, 2007), 46–59, esp. 58–59.

[39] By "literary style," I mean much more than mere lexical or syntactical preferences, but a register of set phrases in a rhythmic–verbal style characteristic of the classical strata of Biblical Hebrew narrative and shared with ancient Semitic epic poetry. This style is most prevalent in the Abraham and Jacob narratives. See Frank H. Polak, "Linguistic and Stylistic Aspects of Epic Formulae in Ancient Semitic Poetry and Biblical Narrative," in *Biblical Hebrew in Its Northwest Semitic Setting: Typological and Historical Perspectives*, eds. Steven

therefore the author is often referred to as the Yahwist (or J). Although some believe the Yahwist lived and worked in the exilic or post-exilic periods of Israel's history, I assume the more traditional position that the Yahwist was a historian of the southern kingdom, writing during the eighth or ninth centuries BCE, or before.[40] Indeed, a strong case can be made for a tenth century origin for Israel's national epic, and some even assume it may be precisely fixed to the reign of David.[41] The extent of the work has been much debated. One proposal assumes a single Yahwistic author, living in the ninth century BCE, writing a continuous story from the creation of the world (Gen 2:4) through the Davidic kingdom to David's successor, Solomon (1 Kings 2:5–46).[42]

In the classic understanding of the documentary approach to Pentateuchal origins, the Yahwistic source was itself a composite of earlier sources, especially including those of the older traditions from the northern kingdom, often associated with an Elohistic author (or E). It is doubtful whether E ever existed as an independent and complete work, and a growing number of scholars have come to think of it as a supplement to J.[43] Thus the siglum used to designate the Yahwist in the secondary literature on Genesis is often JE, although R[JE], for redactor of the JE materials, is strictly more *apropos*. The composite nature of JE is most apparent in Genesis but

E. Fassberg and Avi Hurvitz (PIAS 1; Winona Lake, Ind./Jerusalem: Eisenbrauns/Hebrew University Magnes Press, 2006), 285–304, and the bibliography there.

[40] For arguments in favor of an exilic date based on Mesopotamian and Greek parallels, see J. Van Seters, *Prologue to History* (1992). For opposite conclusions based on some of the same parallels, see Moshe Weinfeld, *The Promise of the Land: The Inheritance of the Land of Canaan by the Israelites* (Taubman Lectures in Jewish Studies 3; Berkeley: University of California Press, 1993), 1–21. The view that the matrix for Israelite history writing, including J, was the literary tradition found in the Northwest Semitic inscriptions of the ninth–seventh centuries BCE has much to commend it; see John A. Emerton, "The Date of the Yahwist," in *In Search of Pre-Exilic Israel: Proceedings of the Oxford Old Testament Seminar*, ed. John Day (JSOTSup 406; London: T & T Clark International, 2004), 107–29, and John A. Emerton, "The Kingdoms of Judah and Israel and Ancient Hebrew History Writing," in *Biblical Hebrew in Its Northwest Semitic Setting*, eds. S. E. Fassberg and A. Hurvitz (2006), 33–49.

[41] Robert B. Coote and David R. Ord, *The Bible's First History: From Eden to the Court of David with the Yahwist* (Philadelphia: Fortress Press, 1989). Coote and Ord assume that J is an exemplar of what anthropologists term the "great tradition," literature developed in and for an urban context at the courts and chapels of ancient monarchs. The nomadic pastoralists that appear in Genesis were, in this scenario, the powerful Bedouin sheikhs of David's day, who banded with him in his rise to power. See also George Mendenhall, "The Nature and Purpose of the Abraham Narratives," in *Ancient Israelite Religion: Essays in Honor of Frank Moore Cross*, eds. Patrick D. Miller, Jr., Paul D. Hanson, and S. D. McBride (Philadelphia: Fortress Press, 1987), 337–57, who argues that David's monarchy was legitimized by replacing the common eponymous ancestor Jacob with Abraham in an attempt to bring together the urban Canaanite population and the village Yahwists.

[42] Richard E. Friedman, *The Hidden Book in the Bible* (San Francisco: HarperSanFrancisco, 1998), esp. 3–56.

[43] Sean McEvenue, "The Elohist at Work," *ZAW* 96 (1984): 315–32; Jean L. Ska, "Gn 22, 1–19: Essai sur les niveaus de lecture," *Bib* 69 (1988): 324–37.

impossible to disentangle thereafter in Exodus–Numbers. All of this merely illustrates the fact that the earliest stages of tradition transmission for the materials in Genesis are beyond our ability to reconstruct.[44]

The *second* source discernible in Genesis and elsewhere in the Pentateuch is attributable to priestly tradents, and therefore typically known by the standard siglum P. Like JE, this source is distinguished by theology and style, and by its habitual use of Elohim, "God," rather than Yahweh. An impressive consensus has emerged on the identification of the priestly material in Genesis, and the current debate is devoted more to the nature of the material than to its scope.[45] On the other hand, a few interpreters argue that the priestly material is redactional only, an expansionistic stratum rather than an independent source or document.[46] Yet this approach has been convincingly countered.[47] I have also been convinced by the impressive linguistic data garnered in recent decades to argue in favor of a pre-exilic date for the priestly material, over against the more traditional source-critical assumption that P is post-exilic.[48]

Third, I also assume the Pentateuch contains materials originating from a Holiness school distinct from other priestly materials (often labeled as H), which was comprised primarily of Leviticus 17–27. Recent work on these portions has shown convincingly, in my opinion, that both the priestly materials and the Holiness texts have pre-exilic origins, and that H assumes earlier P traditions (reversing the

---

[44] D. M. Carr, *Reading the Fractures of Genesis* (1996), 36–37.

[45] Marc Vervenne, "Genesis 1,1–2,4: The Compositional Texture of the Priestly Overture to the Pentateuch," in *Studies in the Book of Genesis: Literature, Redaction and History*, ed. André Wénin (BETL 155; Leuven/Sterling, Va.: Leuven University Press/Uitgeverij Peeters, 2001), 35–79, esp. 37–38.

[46] F. M. Cross, *Canaanite Myth and Hebrew Epic* (1973), 293–325.

[47] See the objections of J. A. Emerton, "The Priestly Writer in Genesis," *JTS* 39 (1988): 381–400; Klaus Koch, "P – kein Redaktor! Erinnerung an zwei Eckdaten der Quellenscheidung," *VT* 37 (1987): 446–61; B. Renaud, "Les généalogies et la structure de l'histoire sacerdotale dans le Livre de la Genèse," *RB* 97 (1990): 5–30.

[48] See the many works of Avi Hurvitz on this topic, e.g., Avi Hurvitz, "Once Again: The Linguistic Profile of the Priestly Material in the Pentateuch and its Historical Age: A Response to J. Blenkinsopp," *ZAW* 112 (2000): 180–191, and for a convenient recent survey of other relevant literature, see R. S. Hendel, *Remembering Abraham* (2005), 109–17. For decades, many Jewish scholars have argued that P antedates the book of Deuteronomy and is therefore pre-exilic, although Christian scholarship has typically followed the Wellhausenian approach that P is post-exilic; for discussion and bibliography, see Moshe Weinfeld, *The Place of the Law in the Religion of Ancient Israel* (VTSup 100; Leiden: E. J. Brill, 2004). Weinfeld especially argues that the distinctive themes of P are due to its origins in the sanctuary and priesthood, not to its late origins in the postexilic period (80–81), and further that D originated either among the common people (79), or among the royal court (81). Zevit proposes a date in the late tenth century BCE; Ziony Zevit, "Philology, Archaeology, and a Terminus a Quo for P's ḥaṭṭāʾt Legislation," in *Pomegranates and Golden Bells: Studies in Biblical, Jewish, and Near Eastern Ritual, Law, and Literature in Honor of Jacob Milgrom*, eds. David P. Wright, David N. Freedman, and Avi Hurvitz (Winona Lake, Ind.: Eisenbrauns, 1995), 29–38.

assumed sequence of earlier source critics).[49] Perhaps less conventionally, I am not convinced the Holiness texts comprised a pre-existing document, which was later edited into our final form of Genesis. Rather, I propose that the Holiness editor has composed portions of Genesis as new material and edited the whole. So, for example, Gen 1:1–2:3 and the *tôlĕdôt* structuring clauses may be explained as the Holiness redactor's way of introducing and tying together the authoritative and long-revered Yahwistic traditions with the equally authoritative but more recent priestly materials. The result is a unified whole.

The final source, the Joseph narrative in Gen 37–50, or more particularly the Joseph Novel (37, 39–45, and portions of 46–47; see commentary at Gen 37), had a different editorial history. While earlier source critics sought J and P origins behind the current Joseph Novel, that search has rightly been abandoned. The Novel is now seen as having an independent history, its sources now largely unreconstructable.[50] It has been adapted for use in Genesis, and its final portions were interspersed with the editor's additions using traditional materials from the J and P sources in Gen 46–50. Thus Genesis is a carefully structured composite text of ancient Yahwistic and priestly materials, edited and joined together by a redactor of the Holiness tradition, who also incorporated a Joseph Novel near the conclusion.[51] We may continue to use the sigla J (or JE) and P to maintain continuity with the history of scholarship, although the definitions and criteria for these sources can no longer be retained as used in the classical Graf–Wellhausen model.

The process of composition of the book of Genesis, using these various sources and traditions of ancient Israel, may be compared to the composition of the gospels of the New Testament.[52] As the gospel authors collected the narratives and teachings of Jesus, combining both written and oral sources, producing "an orderly account" (Luke 1:1–4), so a final redactor has done so for ancient Israel's traditions devoted

---

[49] On the priority of P to H, see Jacob Milgrom, *Leviticus 17–22: A New Translation with Introduction and Commentary* (AB 3A; New York: Doubleday, 2000), 1319–67; and Israel Knohl, *The Sanctuary of Silence: The Priestly Torah and the Holiness School* (Minneapolis: Fortress Press, 1994).

[50] D. M. Carr, *Reading the Fractures of Genesis* (1996), 283–89.

[51] As I have stated, these are my "assumptions," being only the departure point for the commentary offered here. At this moment in the discipline, another view is gaining favor, which takes P as the first overarching history of early Israel, assuming a postexilic Priestly author used a collection of "non-P" materials (those formerly attributed to J) to create the master narrative of the Pentateuch; see the editors' introduction in Thomas B. Dozeman and Konrad Schmid, eds., *A Farewell to the Yahwist? The Composition of the Pentateuch in Recent European Interpretation* (SBLSymS 34; Boston: Brill, 2006), 1–7, and the other essays there. These scholars are establishing a new series of questions for investigation, but so far their solutions lack explanatory power. Others have argued for an exilic Yahwistic editor of the whole Pentateuch, a theory that raises more difficulties than it settles; Christoph Levin, "The Yahwist: The Earliest Editor in the Pentateuch," *JBL* 126/2 (2007): 209–30.

[52] For this comparison, see John E. Hartley, *Genesis* (NIBCOT 1; Peabody, Mass.: Hendrickson Publishers, 2000), 16–17.

to origins – primeval and ancestral.[53] I propose that the final edition of Genesis is the result of a similar process by an editor of the Holiness school of pre-exilic Israel, who combined and organized these various materials into a continuous and meaningful whole.

THEOLOGY

Genesis is above all a theological book. Its theological propositions and convictions are foundational for the rest of the Bible. Much could be said about the book's views of God, humanity, sin, the need for reconciliation, and the nature of salvation. Numerous treatments are easily found elsewhere, and limited space precludes discussions of these here.[54] In addition, I have noted these important contributions of the book in the commentary throughout. Suffice here to highlight two especially central theological themes of the book of Genesis, which contribute to the confluence of ideas flowing into what eventually became Judaism and Christianity, and to comment especially on the relation of these two to an additional theme at the core of Old Testament theology.

The additional theme at the core is that of Israel's soteriological understanding of Yahweh/God as the One identified and defined in God's salvation of Israel.[55] In the Hebrew Scriptures generally, the doctrine of salvation is primary to that of creation.[56] Israel first knew Yahweh as a saving God, determining and defining himself as the One who released Israel from bondage in Egypt, delivered Israel from the desert and into the Promised Land. These foundational experiences, including the covenant between God and Israel made in the Sinai Desert, comprised Israel's foundational experiences of God. These saving acts of Yahweh constituted Israel's primal experience, and became the foundation for other theological speculation about God. Thus Israel first knew Yahweh in his soteriological role, the savior of

---

[53] Of course, my approach spurns entirely the recent attempt to deny anything like editions of literary works in antiquity, including the role of editors and redactors; John Van Seters, *The Edited Bible: The Curious History of the "Editor" in Biblical Criticism* (Winona Lake, Ind.: Eisenbrauns, 2006).

[54] C. Westermann, *Genesis 1–11* (1984), 64–69; Claus Westermann, *Genesis 12–36: A Commentary* (Minneapolis: Augsburg Pub. House, 1985), 105–13; Victor P. Hamilton, *The Book of Genesis. Chapters 1–17* (NICOT; Grand Rapids, Mich.: Eerdmans, 1990), 38–59; Gordon J. Wenham, *Genesis 1–15* (WBC 1; Waco, Tex.: Word Books, 1987), xlv–liii.

[55] By stating that this theme is "at the core of Old Testament theology," I do not mean to endorse it as the theological center or organizing tenet (German *Mitte*) for the Old Testament, such as is often said of covenant, promise, etc. I mean instead to call attention to the primacy of salvation in the Hebrew Scriptures, and to Israel's understanding of salvation as in some way the origin for the two other ideas discussed here.

[56] Assumed to be true by many scholars since a famous paper by Gerhard von Rad first published in 1936; Gerhard von Rad, "The Theological Problem of the Old Testament Doctrine of Creation," in *The Problem of the Hexateuch and Other Essays* (New York: McGraw-Hill, 1966), 131–43.

ancient Israel. The two additional themes so central to Genesis were developed through theological reflection and contemplation on Yahweh as savior.

First, Israel's overarching convictions about God as Creator and the nature of the universe are set out here in particularly careful terms. Other passages of Scripture, of course, often assume what we learn here, or assert additional specifics about creation. But only here does the Bible intentionally establish a paradigm for God's creative activities, drawing out especially the singular sovereignty of the Creator, the goodness of the creation, and the relationships inherent in the created order, including the various interpersonal relationships of humans. The Israelites reflected on the significance of creation in light of their historical experiences of Yahweh acting in national life and history in the plagues and exodus, resulting in the most profound exploration of the themes of creation in human history: the opening chapters of the Bible.[57] The Primeval History in Gen 1–11 is, in fact, the result of deep, contemplative exploration of God's relationship with the entire universe *in light of* God's intervention in the life and history of national Israel.

Second, I propose that the ancestral narratives of Gen 12–36, and to a lesser extent the Joseph narrative in Gen 37–50, also resulted from Israel's contemplative reflection on its own origins in light of that salvation known in the plagues and the exodus event. The central theme of this portion of the Bible is, simply said, revelation. The sovereign God, Lord Yahweh of creation and salvation, appears here time and again to Israel's ancestors as the revealing God, the One intent on making himself known to Israel's patriarchs and matriarchs. The nature of God as the self-introducing Yahweh will be observed at numerous points throughout the commentary (see Closer Look at pp. 135–36). Thus Genesis delineates God as the creating and revealing God in a way that prepares for his soteriological roles in the rest of the Bible.

---

[57] Explored again recently in Neil B. MacDonald, *Metaphysics and the God of Israel: Systematic Theology of the Old and New Testaments* (Milton Keynes, Bucks/Grand Rapids, Mich.: Paternoster/Baker Academic, 2006), 3–113.

II. Suggested Readings on Genesis

*T*he following suggestions are neither exhaustive nor exhaustively annotated. The amount of secondary literature on the book of Genesis is enormous, so the list offered here is merely a guide to further reading and research, as is done in other volumes in this series. The intent is to serve as a point of entry for students of the book of Genesis, providing an up-to-date reading list for *some* of the most helpful literature available. For more complete bibliography, see the critical commentaries mentioned in the first section below.

COMMENTARIES

A magisterial work that has commanded the attention of all interpreters of Genesis since its publication is Claus Westermann's three-volume work published in English translation in 1984–86 (trans. John J. Scullion; Minneapolis: Augsburg Publishing House; German edition in 3 vols.; Neukirchen-Vluyn: Neukirchener Verlag des Erziehungsverein, 1974–82). Westermann's bibliographies are exhaustive to the date of his German edition, and even though he was writing just as the newer literary approaches were burgeoning, he at times interacts with those early efforts as well. Gordon J. Wenham's volumes are rich in literary and theological connections (2 vols.; WBC 1 and 2; Dallas, Tex.: Word Books, 1987 and 1994) and Victor P. Hamilton is most helpful for his frequent philological observations, and specifically Christian applications in the sections devoted to "New Testament Appropriation" (2 vols.; NICOT; Grand Rapids, Mich.: Eerdmans, 1990 and 1994). The commentary of Nahum M. Sarna also contains consistently pertinent insight on the text of Genesis, as well as critical engagement with the ancient Near Eastern and later Rabbinical materials (JPS Torah Commentary; Philadelphia: Jewish Publication Society, 1989). A few of the older commentaries may still be read with much profit, especially Hermann Gunkel, now available in English (trans. Mark E. Biddle; Macon, Ga.: Mercer University Press, 1997) and John Skinner (ICC 1; New York: Scribner, 1910). Two commentaries that are especially thought-provoking theologically are

Gerhard von Rad, of course (OTL; Philadelphia: Westminster Press, 1961) and Walter Brueggemann (IBC; Atlanta: John Knox Press, 1982).

The following additional commentaries have their own strengths and weaknesses, but all make contributions to the reading of Genesis in their own ways.

Alter, Robert. *Genesis: Translation and Commentary*. New York: W.W. Norton, 1996.

Baldwin, Joyce G. *The Message of Genesis 12–50: From Abraham to Joseph*. Bible Speaks Today. Downers Grove, Ill.: InterVarsity Press, 1986.

Brodie, Thomas L. *Genesis as Dialogue: A Literary, Historical, and Theological Commentary*. New York: Oxford University Press, 2001.

Cassuto, Umberto. *A Commentary on the Book of Genesis*. 1st English ed.; Jerusalem: Magnes Press, Hebrew University, 1972.

Cotter, David W. *Genesis*. Berit Olam. Collegeville, Minn.: Liturgical Press, 2003.

Driver, S. R. *The Book of Genesis, with Introduction and Notes*. 14th ed.; Westminster Commentaries 1. London: Methuen, 1943 [1904].

Fretheim, Terence E. "The Book of Genesis." *NIB* 1: 319–674.

Gibson, John C. L. *Genesis*. Daily Study Bible Series. 2 vols. Philadelphia: Westminster Press, 1981–1982.

Gowan, Donald E. *From Eden to Babel: A Commentary on the Book of Genesis 1–11*. ITC. Grand Rapids, Mich.: Eerdmans, 1988.

Hartley, John E. *Genesis*. NIBCOT 1. Peabody, Mass.: Hendrickson Publishers, 2000.

Janzen, J. G. *Abraham and All the Families of the Earth: A Commentary on the Book of Genesis 12–50*. ITC. Grand Rapids, Mich.: Eerdmans, 1993.

Kidner, Derek. *Genesis: An Introduction and Commentary*. TOTC. Downers Grove, Ill.: InterVarsity, 1967.

Mathews, Kenneth A. *Genesis 1–11:26*. NAC 1A. Nashville: Broadman & Holman Publishers, 1996.

Mathews, Kenneth A. *Genesis 11:27–50:26*. NAC 1B. Nashville: Broadman & Holman Publishers, 2005.

Roop, Eugene F. *Genesis*. Believers Church Bible Commentary. Scottdale, Pa.: Herald Press, 1987.

Ross, Allen P. *Creation and Blessing: A Guide to the Study and Exposition of the Book of Genesis*. Grand Rapids, Mich.: Baker Book House, 1988.

Sailhamer, John H. "Genesis." Pages 2:1–284 in *The Expositor's Bible Commentary*. Edited by Frank E. Gaebelein. Grand Rapids, Mich.: Zondervan, 1976.

Speiser, E. A. *Genesis: Introduction, Translation, and Notes*. AB 1. Garden City, N.Y.: Doubleday, 1964.

Towner, W. S. *Genesis*. Westminster Bible Companion. Louisville, Ky.: Westminster John Knox Press, 2001.

Vawter, Bruce. *On Genesis: A New Reading*. Garden City, N.Y.: Doubleday, 1977.

Waltke, Bruce K., and Cathi J. Fredricks. *Genesis: A Commentary.* Grand Rapids, Mich.: Zondervan, 2001.
Walton, John H. *Genesis.* NIV Application Commentary. Grand Rapids, Mich.: Zondervan, 2001.

LITERARY STUDIES

I include selections for both synchronic and diachronic studies here, as per the discussion in the introduction. Source analysis of the Pentateuch since the days of H. B. Witter (1683–1715) and Jean Astruc (1684–1766) has focused first on the book of Genesis. Today scholars continue to devote much attention to the book as a vital part of investigations on the composition of the Pentateuch in general, as well as for the rhetorical artistry of Genesis in particular. Consequently, I mention here only a few suggested readings as an introduction to this topic.

A definitive work on the current state of source-critical investigation of Genesis is that of David M. Carr, which I have cited several times in the commentary (*Reading the Fractures of Genesis: Historical and Literary Approaches* [Louisville, Ky.: Westminster John Knox Press, 1996]). Also quite helpful, and somewhat less technical, as introductions to the complex issues on this topic are the works of Joseph Blenkinsopp (*The Pentateuch: An Introduction to the First Five Books of the Bible* [ABRL; New York: Doubleday, 1992]) and Jean L. Ska (*Introduction to Reading the Pentateuch* [Winona Lake, Ind.: Eisenbrauns, 2006]). See also Gary N. Knoppers and Bernard M. Levinson, *The Pentateuch as Torah: New Models for Understanding its Promulgation and Acceptance* (Winona Lake, Ind.: Eisenbrauns, 2007).

The work most helpful to me in writing this commentary from the perspective of the newer rhetorical approach is that of my teacher, Rabbi Herbert Chanan Brichto (*The Names of God: Poetic Readings in Biblical Beginnings* [New York: Oxford University Press, 1998]). His book is not a commentary *per se*, but as the subtitle indicates, it is a study of Genesis (especially Gen 1–22) in light of Brichto's highly refined poetic sensitivities, the blueprint for which he presented systematically elsewhere (*Toward a Grammar of Biblical Poetics: Tales of the Prophets* [New York: Oxford University Press, 1992]). His insights are often helpful, even profound, although many of his historical-critical conclusions are idiosyncratic. Other works, devoted to literary artistry or discourse linguistics, are listed here that often have Genesis as the object of discussion (e.g., Alter, Sternberg, and Heller).

Alter, Robert. *The Art of Biblical Narrative.* New York: Basic Books, 1981.
Clines, David J. A. *The Theme of the Pentateuch.* JSOTSup 10. Sheffield: University of Sheffield, 1978.
Coote, Robert B., and David R. Ord. *The Bible's First History: From Eden to the Court of David with the Yahwist.* Philadelphia: Fortress Press, 1989.
Fokkelman, J. P. *Narrative Art in Genesis: Specimens of Stylistic and Structural Analysis.* SSN 17. Assen: Van Gorcum, 1975.

Heller, Roy L. *Narrative Structure and Discourse Constellations: An Analysis of Clause Function in Biblical Hebrew Prose*. HSS 55. Winona Lake, Ind.: Eisenbrauns, 2004.

Humphreys, W. L. *The Character of God in the Book of Genesis: A Narrative Appraisal*. Louisville, Ky.: Westminster John Knox Press, 2001.

Longacre, Robert E. *Joseph, a Story of Divine Providence: A Text Theoretical and Textlinguistic Analysis of Genesis 37 and 39–48*. Second edition; Winona Lake, Ind.: Eisenbrauns, 2003[First edition, 1989].

Rendsburg, Gary A. *The Redaction of Genesis*. Winona Lake, Ind.: Eisenbrauns, 1986.

Sternberg, Meir. *The Poetics of Biblical Narrative: Ideological Literature and the Drama of Reading*. Indiana Studies in Biblical Literature. Bloomington: Indiana University Press, 1985.

Turner, Laurence A. *Announcements of Plot in Genesis*. JSOTSup 96. Sheffield: JSOT Press, 1990.

FEMINIST STUDIES

For nearly four decades now, biblical scholars have made unprecedented progress on the role of women in the Bible, and various exegetical studies have investigated the status and role of women in ancient Israel. A vast amount of secondary literature is appearing on this topic. I have found most convenient as an introduction to the topic, the dictionary edited by Carol L. Meyers, Toni Craven, and Ross S. Kraemer, which is cited frequently in the commentary (*Women in Scripture: A Dictionary of Named and Unnamed Women in the Hebrew Bible, the Apocryphal/Deuterocanonical Books, and the New Testament* [Boston: Houghton Mifflin, 2000]). In addition to entries on nearly every topic related to this subject, complete bibliography up to 2000 can also be found there. I simply highlight several other important works here.

Bird, Phyllis. "'Male and Female He Created Them': Gen 1:27b in the Context of the Priestly Account of Creation." *HTR* 74 (1981): 129–59.

Clines, David J. A. "What Does Eve Do to Help? and Other Irredeemably Androcentric Orientations in Genesis 1–3." Pages 25–48 in *What Does Eve Do to Help? And Other Readerly Questions to the Old Testament*. Edited by David J. A. Clines. JSOTSup 94. Sheffield: JSOT, 1990.

Davies, Philip R., and David J. A. Clines. *The World of Genesis: Persons, Places, Perspectives*. JSOTSup 257. Sheffield: Sheffield Academic Press, 1998.

Meyers, Carol L. *Discovering Eve: Ancient Israelite Women in Context*. New York: Oxford University Press, 1988.

Meyers, Carol L. "From Household to House of Yahweh: Women's Religious Culture in Ancient Israel." Pages 277–303 in *Congress Volume: Basel, 2001*. Edited by André Lemaire. VTSup 92. Leiden: Brill, 2002.

Meyers, Carol L. "Everyday Life in Biblical Israel: Women's Social Networks." Pages 185–204 in *Life and Culture in the Ancient Near East*. Edited by Richard E. Averbeck, Mark W. Chavalas, and David B. Weisberg. Bethesda, Md.: CDL Press, 2003.

Meyers, Carol L. "Hierarchy or Heterarchy? Archaeology and the Theorizing of Israelite Society." Pages 245–54 in *Confronting the Past: Archaeological and Historical Essays on Ancient Israel in Honor of William G. Dever*. Edited by Seymour Gitin, J. E. Wright, and J. P. Dessel. Winona Lake, Ind.: Eisenbrauns, 2006.

Trible, Phyllis. *God and the Rhetoric of Sexuality*. OBT 2. Philadelphia: Fortress Press, 1978.

Trible, Phyllis. *Texts of Terror: Literary-Feminist Readings of Biblical Narratives*. OBT 13. Philadelphia: Fortress Press, 1984.

Trible, Phyllis, and Letty M. Russell. *Hagar, Sarah, and Their Children: Jewish, Christian, and Muslim Perspectives*. Louisville, Ky.: Westminster John Knox Press, 2006.

SOCIOLOGICAL AND ANTHROPOLOGICAL STUDIES

Several of the most important contributions in this category overlap with those in the feminist or literary categories, and others will appear lastly in the monograph section. So, for example, I have included the early monograph by Ronald S. Hendel in the more general category of "additional monographs" but his work was one of the early attempts to take anthropology seriously as it relates to the oral traditions of Genesis (*The Epic of the Patriarch: The Jacob Cycle and the Narrative Traditions of Canaan and Israel*; HSM 42; [Atlanta: Scholars Press, 1987]). For general introduction, one should see Charles E. Carter ("Opening Windows onto Biblical Worlds: Applying the Social Sciences to Hebrew Scripture," in *The Face of Old Testament Studies: A Survey of Contemporary Approaches*; eds. David W. Baker and Bill T. Arnold [Grand Rapids, Mich.: Baker Books, 1999], 421–33), in addition to the works listed here, most of which contain portions specifically dedicated to Genesis.

Carter, Charles E., and Carol L. Meyers, eds. *Community, Identity, and Ideology: Social Science Approaches to the Hebrew Bible*. SBTS 6. Winona Lake, Ind: Eisenbrauns, 1996.

Esler, Philip F. *Ancient Israel: The Old Testament in Its Social Context*. Minneapolis: Fortress Press, 2006.

Lawrence, Louise J., and Mario I. Aguilar. *Anthropology and Biblical Studies: Avenues of Approach*. Leiden: Deo, 2004.

Niditch, Susan. *Chaos to Cosmos: Studies in Biblical Patterns of Creation*. Studies in the Humanities 6. Chico, Calif.: Scholars Press, 1985.

Niditch, Susan. *Oral World and Written Word: Ancient Israelite Literature*. Library of Ancient Israel. Louisville, Ky.: Westminster John Knox Press, 1996.

Steinberg, Naomi A. "The Genealogical Framework of the Family Stories in Genesis." *Semeia* 46 (1989): 41–50.

Steinberg, Naomi A. *Kinship and Marriage in Genesis: A Household Economics Perspective.* Minneapolis: Fortress Press, 1993.

ADDITIONAL MONOGRAPHS AND ARTICLES OF INTEREST

Of the enormous amount of other secondary literature, I simply list here monographs and articles I have found especially helpful in writing this commentary.

Andriolo, Karin R. "A Structural Analysis of Genealogy and World View in the Old Testament." *AA* 75 (1973): 1657–69.

Brett, Mark G. *Genesis: Procreation and the Politics of Identity.* Old Testament Readings; London: Routledge, 2000.

Clifford, Richard J., and John J. Collins. *Creation in the Biblical Traditions.* CBQMS 24. Washington, D.C.: Catholic Biblical Association of America, 1992.

Clines, David J. A. "Theme in Genesis 1–11." *CBQ* 38 (1976): 483–507.

Clines, David J. A. "Beyond Synchronic/Diachronic." Pages 52–71 in *Synchronic or Diachronic? A Debate on Method in Old Testament Exegesis.* Edited by Johannes Cornelis de Moor. OtSt 34. Leiden, New York: E.J. Brill, 1995.

Coats, George W. *From Canaan to Egypt: Structural and Theological Context for the Joseph Story.* CBQMS 4. Washington, D.C.: Catholic Biblical Association of America, 1976.

Coats, George W. *Genesis, with an Introduction to Narrative Literature.* FOTL 1. Grand Rapids, Mich.: Eerdmans, 1983.

Dozeman, Thomas B., and Konrad Schmid. *A Farewell to the Yahwist? The Composition of the Pentateuch in Recent European Interpretation.* SBLSymS 34. Atlanta/Boston: Society of Biblical Literature/Brill, 2006.

Emerton, John A. "The Origin of the Promises to the Patriarchs in the Older Sources of the Book of Genesis." *VT* 32 (1982): 14–32.

Emerton, John A. "The Priestly Writer in Genesis." *JTS* 39 (1988): 381–400.

Emerton, John A. "The Date of the Yahwist." Pages 107–29 in *In Search of Pre-Exilic Israel: Proceedings of the Oxford Old Testament Seminar.* Edited by John Day. JSOTSup 406. London: T & T Clark International, 2004.

Hendel, Ronald S. *The Epic of the Patriarch: The Jacob Cycle and the Narrative Traditions of Canaan and Israel.* HSM 42. Atlanta: Scholars Press, 1987.

Hendel, Ronald S. *The Text of Genesis 1–11: Textual Studies and Critical Edition.* New York: Oxford University Press, 1998.

Hendel, Ronald S. *Remembering Abraham: Culture, Memory, and History in the Hebrew Bible.* New York: Oxford University Press, 2005.

Hess, Richard S., P. E. Satterthwaite, and Gordon J. Wenham. *He Swore an Oath: Biblical Themes from Genesis 12–50.* 2nd ed. Carlisle, U.K./Grand Rapids, Mich.: Paternoster Press/Baker Book House, 1994.

Hess, Richard S., and David T. Tsumura. *I Studied Inscriptions from Before the Flood: Ancient Near Eastern, Literary, and Linguistic Approaches to Genesis 1–11.* SBTS 4. Winona Lake, Ind.: Eisenbrauns, 1994.

Hiebert, Theodore. *The Yahwist's Landscape: Nature and Religion in Early Israel.* New York: Oxford University Press, 1996.

Humphreys, W. L. *Joseph and His Family: A Literary Study.* Columbia: University of South Carolina, 1988.

Kass, Leon. *The Beginning of Wisdom: Reading Genesis.* New York: Free Press, 2003.

Kselman, John S. "The Book of Genesis: A Decade of Scholarly Research." *Int* 45/4 (1991): 380–392.

Levenson, Jon D. *Creation and the Persistence of Evil: The Jewish Drama of Divine Omnipotence.* San Francisco: Harper & Row, 1988.

Lundbom, Jack R. "Abraham and David in the Theology of the Yahwist." Pages 203–9 in *The Word of the Lord Shall Go Forth: Essays in Honor of David Noel Freedman in Celebration of His Sixtieth Birthday.* Edited by Carol L. Meyers and Michael P. O'Connor. ASOR Special Volume Series 1. Winona Lake, Ind.: Eisenbrauns, 1983.

Millard, A. R., and D. J. Wiseman. *Essays on the Patriarchal Narratives.* Leicester, England: InterVarsity Press, 1980.

Miller, Patrick D., Jr. *Genesis 1–11: Studies in Structure and Theme.* JSOTSup 8. Sheffield: University of Sheffield, 1978.

Mitchell, Christopher W. *The Meaning of brk "to bless" in the Old Testament.* SBLDS 95. Atlanta: Scholars Press, 1987.

Moberly, R. W. L. *The Old Testament of the Old Testament: Patriarchal Narratives and Mosaic Yahwism.* OBT. Minneapolis: Fortress Press, 1992.

Moberly, R. W. L. *Genesis 12–50.* OTG. Sheffield: JSOT Press, 1992.

Nicholson, Ernest W. *The Pentateuch in the Twentieth Century: The Legacy of Julius Wellhausen.* Oxford: Clarendon, 1998.

Rogerson, J. W. *Genesis 1–11.* OTG. Sheffield: Sheffield Academic, 1991.

Van Seters, John. *Prologue to History: The Yahwist as Historian in Genesis.* Louisville, Ky.: Westminster John Knox Press, 1992.

van Wolde, Ellen J. *Words Become Worlds: Semantic Studies of Genesis 1–11.* Biblical Interpretation Series 6. Leiden: E.J. Brill, 1994.

Wallace, Howard N. "The Toledot of Adam." Pages 17–33 in *Studies in the Pentateuch.* Edited by John A. Emerton. VTSup 41. Leiden: E.J. Brill, 1990.

White, Hugh C. *Narration and Discourse in the Book of Genesis.* Cambridge: Cambridge University Press, 1991.

Williamson, Paul R. *Abraham, Israel and the Nations: The Patriarchal Promise and its Covenantal Development in Genesis.* JSOTSup 315. Sheffield: Sheffield Academic Press, 2000.

Wynn-Williams, Damian J. *The State of the Pentateuch: A Comparison of the Approaches of M. Noth and E. Blum.* BZAW 249. New York: Walter de Gruyter, 1997.

Wénin, André. *Studies in the Book of Genesis: Literature, Redaction and History.* BETL 155. Leuven/Sterling, Va.: Leuven University Press/Uitgeverij Peeters, 2001.

III. Commentary Part One:
The Primeval History – Genesis 1–11

GENESIS 1:1–2:3 CREATION OVERTURE

(1:1) In the beginning when God created[a] the heavens and the earth,

(1:2) the earth was a formless void and darkness covered the face of the deep, while a wind from God[b] swept over the face of the waters.

(1:3) Then God said, "Let there be light"; and there was light.

(1:4) And God saw that the light was good; and God separated the light from the darkness.

(1:5) God called the light Day, and the darkness he called Night. And there was evening and there was morning, the first day.

(1:6) And God said, "Let there be a dome in the midst of the waters, and let it separate the waters from the waters."

(1:7) So God made the dome and separated the waters that were under the dome from the waters that were above the dome. And it was so.

(1:8) God called the dome Sky. And there was evening and there was morning, the second day.

(1:9) And God said, "Let the waters under the sky be gathered together into one place, and let the dry land appear." And it was so.

(1:10) God called the dry land Earth, and the waters that were gathered together he called Seas. And God saw that it was good.

(1:11) Then God said, "Let the earth put forth vegetation: plants yielding seed, and fruit trees of every kind on earth that bear fruit with the seed in it." And it was so.

(1:12) The earth brought forth vegetation: plants yielding seed of every kind, and trees of every kind bearing fruit with the seed in it. And God saw that it was good.

(1:13) And there was evening and there was morning, the third day.

---

[a] Or "when God began to create" or "In the beginning God created".

[b] Or "while the spirit of God" or "while a mighty wind".

(1:14) And God said, "Let there be lights in the dome of the sky to separate the day from the night; and let them be for signs and for seasons and for days and years,

(1:15) and let them be lights in the dome of the sky to give light upon the earth." And it was so.

(1:16) God made the two great lights – the greater light to rule the day and the lesser light to rule the night – and the stars.

(1:17) God set them in the dome of the sky to give light upon the earth,

(1:18) to rule over the day and over the night, and to separate the light from the darkness. And God saw that it was good.

(1:19) And there was evening and there was morning, the fourth day.

(1:20) And God said, "Let the waters bring forth swarms of living creatures, and let birds fly above the earth across the dome of the sky."

(1:21) So God created the great sea monsters and every living creature that moves, of every kind, with which the waters swarm, and every winged bird of every kind. And God saw that it was good.

(1:22) God blessed them, saying, "Be fruitful and multiply and fill the waters in the seas, and let birds multiply on the earth."

(1:23) And there was evening and there was morning, the fifth day.

(1:24) And God said, "Let the earth bring forth living creatures of every kind: cattle and creeping things and wild animals of the earth of every kind." And it was so.

(1:25) God made the wild animals of the earth of every kind, and the cattle of every kind, and everything that creeps upon the ground of every kind. And God saw that it was good.

(1:26) Then God said, "Let us make humankind in our image, according to our likeness; and let them have dominion over the fish of the sea, and over the birds of the air, and over the cattle, and over all the wild animals of the earth, and over every creeping thing that creeps upon the earth."

(1:27) So God created humankind in his image, in the image of God he created them; male and female he created them.

(1:28) God blessed them, and God said to them, "Be fruitful and multiply, and fill the earth and subdue it; and have dominion over the fish of the sea and over the birds of the air and over every living thing that moves upon the earth."

(1:29) God said, "See, I have given you every plant yielding seed that is upon the face of all the earth, and every tree with seed in its fruit; you shall have them for food.

(1:30) And to every beast of the earth, and to every bird of the air, and to everything that creeps on the earth, everything that has the breath of life, I have given every green plant for food." And it was so.

(1:31) God saw everything that he had made, and indeed, it was very good. And there was evening and there was morning, the sixth day.

(2:1) Thus the heavens and the earth were finished, and all their multitude.

(2:2) And on the seventh day God finished the work that he had done, and he rested on the seventh day from all the work that he had done.

(2:3) So God blessed the seventh day and hallowed it, because on it God rested from all the work that he had done in creation.

*G*enesis 1 has been studied, debated, and expounded as much as any text in world history.[1] Scholars and amateurs alike have poured over this text for twenty-five hundred years, and it continues to demand our attention because of its arresting content and architectonic style. Its position at the beginning of Genesis, like a keystone supporting the book's structure, gives this introductory chapter a unique importance as revered Scripture in diverse faith communities and denominations.

The Bible's first chapter has an elegant prose more akin to poetry and may, in fact, have been based on a poem originally.[2] With a lilting and graceful rhythm, this chapter describes the beginning of the universe, the beginning of time and space, or put simply, the beginning of everything except God, who has no beginning. However, the uniqueness of Gen 1 lies not in its literary style or content but in this simple fact: it has no preceding literary context. Contemporary studies in literary theory have taught us that a passage's context is the most important determining feature of interpretation, and especially the immediately preceding unit of the text; that which comes immediately prior to a text assists most in our interpretation. Gen 1 is the only passage of the biblical canon without such an immediately preceding context. Its position at the head of the Bible means it charts the course for the reader. The ancient Near Eastern background for Gen 1 is even more important than usual in the process of interpretation. In a way, the ancient cosmogonies of Egypt and Mesopotamia become the interpretive context for Gen 1, and the commentary below will make frequent reference to them.[3]

The author of Gen 1 was a member of Israel's priestly caste, who lived and wrote during pre-exilic times and not, as was once routinely asserted, during the

---

[1] The chapter break at 1:31 rather than 2:4 is from the medieval Vulgate translation (thirteenth century CE), and is especially unfortunate in this case. For the sake of convenience, I will refer to 1:1–2:3 simply as Gen 1, and to 2:4–25 as Gen 2.

[2] For an attempt to advocate a poetic reading of Gen 1, see Frank H. Polak, "Poetic Style and Parallelism in the Creation Account (Gen. 1:1–2:3)," in *Creation in Jewish and Christian Tradition*, eds. Henning Reventlow and Yair Hoffman (JSOTSup 319; Sheffield: Sheffield Academic Press, 2002), 2–31.

[3] Such background was, of course, instinctive for ancient readers but needs to be kept constantly before us as twenty-first-century interpreters. For many today, the lack of immediately preceding literary context is taken as permission to read contemporary sensibilities into Gen 1, and since our context is so technological and scientific, this has produced a regrettable and unnecessary dichotomy between science and religion. Keeping the ancient Near Eastern backdrop for Gen 1 in mind helps avoid this pitfall.

post-exilic period.[4] The chapter was composed intentionally as a prologue to what
follows in Genesis, and perhaps beyond in Exodus, Leviticus, and Numbers. The
author may have relied on older sources, such as a brief description of creation
in terms of divine actions or commands (see comment at p. 39 on "divine *fiat*"),
but this is far from certain. He was familiar with Egyptian and Mesopotamian
cosmogonies and intended to present an alternative worldview, although I believe
the polemical nature of Gen 1 has been overstated and is not the primary *raison d'être*
for the chapter. Rather, this author, in addition to refuting the regnant mythological
conceptions of creation known throughout the ancient world, wanted primarily
to give explanation for the unique and exalted position of humanity in God's
resplendent creation, which is "good" in every respect (see at vv. 26–31). The author
was also interested in explaining the nature of the animal kingdom as a prelude
to Israel's dietary laws (see at vv. 24–25), and the nature of Sabbath as central to
Israel's religion (see at 2:1–3). These theological concerns may indicate the author
was a member of Israel's priestly Holiness School, so that Gen 1 was intended to
supply what was missing from the narratives in 2:4–4:26, and to prepare the reader
for Exodus–Numbers (see Introduction).[5]

The most prominent literary feature in Gen 1 is its recurring formulaic structure
and symmetry. This recurring formula presents in rhythmic detail the creation of the
heavens and the earth with all of their components, and does so using the Sabbath
theme so important in Israelite thought. The repetition of the formula for the seven
days creates a pulsating effect that invites the reader to consider the grandeur of
the topic. The symmetry of the text derives also from its correspondence of created
objects in the first six days of creation; day one corresponds to day four, day two to
five, and day three to six.[6] Such literary symmetry mirrors the balance and order
of the created cosmos itself. Rhetoric imitates reality, as nothing is left to chance.
Creation by God's word marches forward inexorably, encountering no resistance
whatsoever, as plants, animals, and finally humans are created according to the will
and design of that divine word.

Recurring literary formulas in the Bible are a means to an end – never an end in
themselves. So here, the formula has regular and predictable features as it presents
in parade-like fashion the components of the cosmos at creation. But those features
are also fluid. Gen 1 is not bound or limited in any way by the individual features
of the formula as it highlights the most important aspects of the presentation. The
features of the formula are as follows.

---

[4] See the introduction for details, and Moshe Weinfeld, *The Place of the Law in the Religion
   of Ancient Israel* (VTSup 100; Leiden: E. J. Brill, 2004), 95–109.

[5] Edwin Firmage, "Genesis 1 and the Priestly Agenda," *JSOT* 82 (1999): 97–114.

[6] For reservations about this thematic structure, see William P. Brown, *Structure, Role,
   and Ideology in the Hebrew and Greek Texts of Genesis 1:1–2:3* (SBLDS 132; Atlanta, Ga.:
   Scholars Press, 1993), 92–95. Brown, however, requires too much precision of the text by
   comparing it to the clearer symmetry of the Septuagint.

1. Introduction: "And God said . . . "
2. Volitive command: "Let there be . . . "
3. Indicative result or commentary: "and it was so" or "and God made"
4. Divine evaluation: "God saw that it was good"
5. Naming of created object: "God called . . . "
6. Concluding merism: "there was evening and there was morning"
7. Enumerative summary: "the [X] day"

The flexibility of the formula is illustrated by the absence of items three, four, and five in certain of the days of creation, nor is this precise sequence always required.[7] The third component, the creative result or commentary, may appear as a simple statement of accomplishment, as in day one, "and there was light" or day two, "and it was so." It may also be an expansion upon the creative activity in the form of commentary explaining what has just been stated, as for example in day one: "and God separated the light from the darkness." Twice the creative period is compound or complex, in that it narrates more than one creative act. So days three and six repeat the introduction and volitive command (components 1 and 2). Day three thus narrates creation of both earth (vv. 9–10) and vegetation (vv. 11–12), and day six living creatures (vv. 24–25) and humankind (vv. 26–30).

The simple but profound elegance of "in the beginning when God created . . . " is difficult for us to appreciate fully (1:1). In the context of the ancient Near East, such an assertion was astounding! Commentaries since the early 1900s, as a result of the influential works of Hermann Gunkel, have routinely explored the possible connections of Gen 1 with the Babylonian Creation Epic (or *Enuma Elish*, see Closer Look, pp. 33–34).[8] Typically, it has been assumed that the Hebrew account relied on the Babylonian one, and most have argued that the biblical account served as a polemic against ancient Near Eastern speculation about the origins of the cosmos. However, it must be admitted that many of the similarities are common to most ancient cosmogonies, and Gen 1 is not genetically related to the *Enuma Elish*, nor is it necessarily a direct polemic against it.[9] There may be points of

---

[7] The evaluation clause is missing in day 2 and the naming clause in days 4, 5, and 6. Additionally, the complex nature of the third component of the formula, the indicative result or commentary, takes a variety of forms in days two through five.

[8] Hermann Gunkel, *Creation and Chaos in the Primeval Era and the Eschaton: A Religio-Historical Study of Genesis 1 and Revelation 12*, trans. K. W. Whitney, Jr. (Grand Rapids, Mich.: Eerdmans, 2006); trans. of *Schöpfung und Chaos in Urzeit und Endzeit: Eine religionsgeschichtliche Untersuchung über Gen 1 und Ap Joh 12* (Göttingen: Vandenhoeck und Ruprecht, 1921[1895]); Hermann Gunkel, *Genesis: Translated and Interpreted*, trans. Mark E. Biddle (Macon, Ga.: Mercer University Press, 1997); trans. of *Genesis* (Göttingen: Vandenhoeck und Ruprecht, 1910[1901]).

[9] Wilfred G. Lambert, "A New Look at the Babylonian Background of Genesis," *JTS* 16 (1965): 287–300; repr. in Richard S. Hess and David T. Tsumura, eds., *I Studied Inscriptions from Before the Flood: Ancient Near Eastern, Literary, and Linguistic Approaches to Genesis 1–11* (SBTS 4; Winona Lake, Ind.: Eisenbrauns, 1994), 96–113.

contact as we shall see, and it is likely the author of Gen 1 was aware of the Babylonian account as well as several other competing explanations of the world's origins. So in a most general way, it seems likely that references here to the "deep" (v. 2), the splitting of primeval waters (v. 6), the "image of God" (vv. 26–27), and divine "rest" at the conclusion of creation (2:3), may all be subtle allusions to those competing philosophies. But Gen 1 has so profoundly transcended the other cosmogonies that the author hardly seems concerned to point out the specific points of departure. Rather, in constructing an entirely new and different edifice, "stones in the new temple have been taken from the old shrine of Baal."[10] Polemic refutation is hardly the *raison d'être* for Gen 1, although in a general way, it is the byproduct of the author's purpose. As an entirely new worldview, Gen 1 includes polemic but transcends competing theologies by presenting a new paradigm altogether.

We fail to appreciate the profundity of vv. 1–3 for two primary reasons, among several others. First, it is exceedingly familiar to those of us in the West, who still benefit from the long years of Judeo–Christian education and influence. Second, we have overemphasized the similarities between Gen 1 and the other ancient cosmogonies without fully appreciating the differences. This text soars above them in such a way as to deny *implicitly* any possibility of the theologies expressed in the Egyptian or Mesopotamian accounts. If we consider it an ideological polemic, we must admit it is not specifically so and only indirectly. It contains no theomachy, or cosmic conflict among the gods, or victory enthronement motif. Both are excluded by "in the beginning when God created . . ."! Israel's God has no rivals. There can be no struggle with forces opposed to his actions or corresponding to his power. There can be no victory enthronement motif because God's victory was never in doubt; rather, God has never *not* been enthroned. There can be no enthronement portrait here because God has not *become* sovereign; he has simply never been *less than* sovereign.

In this way, Gen 1 refutes not only the competing cosmogonies of the ancient Near East; it disallows any competing ideologies *within* ancient Israel itself. Reading this text only as a polemic against Egyptian and Mesopotamian accounts is too negative an assessment, because in fact the author has a positive agenda. He is not only interested in showing the *Enuma Elish* (or others) to be false, but in creating for Israel a new way of thinking about God. This text aims to establish a beachhead in the religious and cultural war occurring in Israel's monarchy. The author stakes a claim to territory belonging to those who belittled the role of Sabbath, of the dietary laws, and of the image of God in humans.

---

[10] Flemming F. Hvidberg, "The Canaanite Background of Gen I-III," *VT* 10 (1960): 285–94, esp. 293.

A CLOSER LOOK — CREATION ACCOUNTS IN THE ANCIENT NEAR EAST

The great riverine cultures of Mesopotamia and Egypt produced mythological traditions concerning creation and early human history. In addition, we have evidence from the Syrian port-city of Ugarit and traces elsewhere of cosmogonic speculation in Syria–Palestine.[11]

First, the Egyptian material offers several interesting parallels with Genesis 1, including the belief in a creator god who made the universe by verbal fiat.[12] The so-called *Memphite Theology* is preserved on a monumental inscription placed in the temple of the god Ptah at Memphis, probably composed during the thirteenth century BCE.[13] In this text, Ptah creates by divine word and was "satisfied" (or "rested") after his work. Even more striking is the *Instruction of Merikare*, which avers that the deity subdued chaos (or "the water monster"), created heaven and earth for the sake of humanity, breathed life into their nostrils, created them according to his likeness ("images" from his body), and finally, that he created for them plants and animals, fish and fowl for food.[14]

Second, the Mesopotamian materials are helpful for understanding the broader worldview, although they have fewer direct parallels than the Egyptian.[15] The *Epic of Atra-ḫasis* can be dated to around 1700 BCE, although its actual composition may have been centuries earlier.[16] The reason this text is of such great interest is the way it presents in sequence the creation of humankind and its near extinction in the flood. The Babylonian *Epic of Creation* (better known by the Akkadian title

---

[11] Plato's work, *Timaeus of Locri*, also offers interesting parallels; William P. Brown, "Divine Act and the Art of Persuasion in Genesis 1," in *History and Interpretation: Essays in Honour of John H. Hayes*, eds. Matt P. Graham, William P. Brown, and Jeffrey K. Kuan (JSOTSup 173; Sheffield: JSOT Press, 1993), 19–32.

[12] John D. Currid, "An Examination of the Egyptian Background of the Genesis Cosmogony," *BZ* 35 (1991): 18–40, esp. 20–21; James P. Allen, *Genesis in Egypt: The Philosophy of Ancient Egyptian Creation Accounts* (Yale Egyptological Studies 2; New Haven: Yale Egyptological Seminar, 1988).

[13] James P. Allen, "From the 'Memphite Theology,'" *COS* 1.15:21–23.

[14] Miriam Lichtheim, "Merikare," *COS* 1.35:61–66, esp. 65.

[15] For comparison with creation and flood stories from Mesopotamia, see Jeffrey H. Tigay, "On Evaluating Claims of Literary Borrowing," in *The Tablet and the Scroll: Near Eastern Studies in Honor of William W. Hallo*, eds. Mark E. Cohen, Daniel C. Snell, and David B. Weisberg (Bethesda, Md.: CDL Press, 1993), 250–255. And the older discussion of G. R. Driver is still useful; "Appendix: Problems in the Book of Genesis in the Light of Recent Babylonian, Assyrian and Egyptian Research," in S. R. Driver, *The Book of Genesis, with Introduction and Notes* (Westminster Commentaries 1; London: Methuen, 1943), 417–54.

[16] W. G. Lambert, A. R. Millard, and Miguel Civil, *Atra-ḫasīs: The Babylonian Story of The Flood* (Winona Lake, Ind.: Eisenbrauns, 1999); Stephanie Dalley, *Myths from Mesopotamia: Creation, the Flood, Gilgamesh, and Others* (Oxford: Oxford University Press, 2000), 1–38; Benjamin R. Foster, "Atra-ḫasis," *COS* 1.130:450–453; Wolfram von Soden, "Der altbabylonische Atramchasis-Mythos," *TUAT* 3/4:612–45.

Enuma Elish) was probably composed around the eleventh century BCE, although there may have been precursors.[17] It relates the cosmic battle between Tiamat, the monstrous matrix goddess personifying the primeval ocean, and the young god Marduk, patron deity of Babylon. The victorious Marduk kills Tiamat and creates the universe from her carcass. Thus the *Enuma Elish* typifies cosmogonies of the ancient world, but is in reality more about Marduk's rise to supremacy than about the creation of the universe. For our purposes, it is more instructive as a general introduction to Babylonian religion and worldview than as specific background for Genesis 1. Fragments of the Sumerian *Eridu Genesis* have been preserved in various versions from approximately 1600 BCE.[18] It puts in sequence the creation of humanity, the institution of kingship, the first cities, and a great flood in a way reminiscent of Genesis.

Third, the West Semitic background for Genesis 1 may be reflected in the Ugaritic *Baal Cycle*, in which the storm-god Baal defeats Yam, the sea-god, and Mot, the underworld-god in order to secure kingship.[19] Dated to the fourteenth century BCE, it tells of Baal's struggle for supremacy in the West Semitic pantheon and of his right to succeed the chief older deity, El. It has been proposed that Genesis 1 should be read as a demythologized Canaanite *Chaoskampf,* assuming the wind of 1:2 is related to the wind Baal used against the sea monster in the *Baal Cycle,* and that *těhôm* ("deep") has Canaanite mythological origins (but see the commentary).[20]

The Bible's first paragraph – simple enough in English translation – is actually quite problematic in the Hebrew syntax. The first sentence of the Bible, indeed the first word, presents interpreters with some of the most complex and difficult questions of the Bible.[21] Without getting into details here, the basic question is the syntactical

---

[17] Benjamin R. Foster, "Epic of Creation," *COS* 1.111:390–402; Wilfred G. Lambert, "Enuma Elisch," *TUAT* 3/4:565–602.

[18] Thorkild Jacobsen, "The Eridu Genesis," *COS* 1.158:513–15; Miguel Civil, "The Sumerian Flood Story," in W. G. Lambert, A. R. Millard, and M. Civil, *Atra-ḫasīs: The Babylonian Story of The Flood* (1999), 138–45; Thorkild Jacobsen, "The Eridu Genesis," *JBL* 100 (1981): 513–29.

[19] Dennis Pardee, "The Baʿlu Myth," *COS* 1.86:241–74; and for the first two tablets, see Mark S. Smith, *The Ugaritic Baal Cycle* (VTSup 55-; Leiden: E.J. Brill, 1994). For perhaps the earliest example of this mythological theme, see Jean-Marie Durand, "Le mythologème du combat entre le dieu de l'orage et la mer en Mésopotamie," *MARI* 7 (1993): 41–61.

[20] John Day, *God's Conflict with The Dragon and The Sea: Echoes of a Canaanite Myth in The Old Testament* (University of Cambridge Oriental Publications 35; Cambridge: Cambridge University Press, 1985), 50–53. See also F. F. Hvidberg, "The Canaanite Background of Gen I–III"; Nicolas Wyatt, "Interpreting the Creation and Fall Story in Genesis 2–3," *ZAW* 93 (1981): 10–21; and Mark S. Smith, *The Origins of Biblical Monotheism: Israel's Polytheistic Background and the Ugaritic Texts* (New York: Oxford University Press, 2001), 167–71.

[21] On the difficult syntactical features of vv. 1–3, which cannot be treated at length in a commentary of this size, see Michaela Bauks, *Die Welt am Anfang: Zum Verhältnis von Vorwelt und Weltentstehung in Gen 1 und in der altorientalischen Literatur* (WMANT 74;

relationship of v. 1 to v. 2, and the relationship of both of these together to v. 3. To complicate matters further, debates about these verses are rarely conducted in a detached non-emotional manner based solely on the particulars of Hebrew syntax. Longstanding theological convictions about the subject matter often impinge upon the way interpreters read this text.

The traditional interpretation takes v. 1 as in independent sentence, and this translation is still preserved in the footnotes of the NRSV: "In the beginning God created the heavens and the earth." In this case, v. 1 may be taken as a superscription or title for the whole chapter. Verse 1, then, stands outside of the six-day creative pattern, and 1:2–2:3 is thus a commentary on "God created" in v. 1. God's creative activity becomes a process of organizing, partitioning, and developing the chaos of v. 2. This interpretation requires taking "earth" (*hāʾāreṣ*) in v. 2 in a very different way than in v. 1, which led Hermann Gunkel years ago to argue that it means "chaos" in v. 2.[22]

A second interpretation of this traditional reading is to take an independent sentence in v. 1, not as a superscription or title, but as a summary statement describing the "first" creation, namely of heaven and earth. In this reading, v. 2 becomes a description of the kind of earth God created at first, and prepares for a "second" creation in vv. 3–10, in which heaven is created on day two (vv. 6–8) and earth on day three (vv. 9–10). In this interpretation, v. 1 is thus an initial step in the creation of the world, but a separate step from the formal creation described in vv. 3–31.[23]

The approach adopted in the NRSV, upon which this commentary is based, differs from both of these traditional interpretations. This reading gives primacy to comparisons of vv. 1–3 with other ancient creation accounts, which begin with subordinate, temporal clauses (such as Gen 2:4b; 5:1; and the *Enuma Elish*). Thus v. 1 is a dependent, temporal clause, followed by the main clause in v. 2: "In the beginning when God created . . . , the earth was a formless void . . . " (NRSV). Even this temporal reading of v. 1 has an alternate interpretation. Instead of dependent upon v. 2, perhaps v. 1 is dependent upon v. 3, in which case v. 2 is a parenthetical comment: "When God began to create heaven and earth (the earth being unformed and void, . . .), God said, . . . " (cf. NJPS). This last approach answers more questions than it raises, and is for the meantime the best reading of vv. 1–3. To the question whether God used preexistent material to create the universe or rather he created it "out of nothing" (the early Jewish–Christian doctrine of *creatio ex nihilo*, first explicitly occurring in 2 Macc 7:28; and see Rom 4:17; Heb 11:3), it must be admitted

---

Neukirchen-Vluyn: Neukirchener Verlag, 1997), 65–92; and W. P. Brown, *Structure, Role, and Ideology in the Hebrew and Greek Texts of Genesis 1:1–2:3* (1993), 62–73.

[22] H. Gunkel, *Genesis* (1997), 104.

[23] This is the approach taken in the Septuagint translation; W. P. Brown, *Structure, Role, and Ideology in the Hebrew and Greek Texts of Genesis 1:1–2:3* (1993), 31–35.

that Gen 1 neither precludes nor defends the possibility, and we must look elsewhere for data to decide the issue.[24] However, such a concept is not false to the intent of Gen 1. Indeed, had we an opportunity to pose the question to the author of this text, we may assume with Westermann and others that he would "certainly have decided in favor of *creatio ex nihilo.*"[25]

With no introduction and little fanfare, the text announces with utmost simplicity that it was God – and God *alone* – who created the cosmos. The Semitic merism "the heavens and the earth" (v. 1) emphasizes that God is responsible for all observable cosmic phenomena, the universe, for which there is no separate word in Biblical Hebrew.[26] The use of "heaven" and "earth" in the rest of the account will have a much more restricted meaning, heaven being the domed sky created in vv. 6–7 and earth being the land inhabited by the humans and animals, and created in vv. 9–10.

The creative action that God takes in v. 1 is the verb *bārā'*, which is regularly overloaded with theological content by commentators of this text. Routinely, exegetes aver that Israel's God is the only subject of this verb in the Hebrew Bible and that its accusative is always of product and never of material.[27] Various theological conclusions are often drawn from these observations, including *creatio ex nihilo*, and God's sovereignty and power in creating effortlessly.[28] These concepts are present in Gen 1, or in the case of creation without the use of preexistent matter, are at least compatible with the passage and asserted elsewhere in Scripture (Pss 33:6, 9; 148:5). However, this is entirely too much for our little verb to bear. The assertion that Israel's God is always and only the subject of this verb is slightly misleading, since an identical root (*bārā'* III) means to "separate (as by cutting)," and is perhaps not a separate root at all, but only a distinct use for another derived stem.[29] Furthermore,

[24] Michael A. Fishbane, *Biblical Text and Texture: A Literary Reading of Selected Texts* (Oxford: Oneworld, 1998), 3–16.

[25] Claus Westermann, *Genesis 1–11: A Commentary* (Minneapolis: Augsburg Pub. House, 1984), 108–9; Johannes P. Floss, "Schöpfung als Geschehen? Von der Syntax zur Semantik in der priesterschriftlichen Schöpfungsdarstellung Gen 1,1–2,4a," in *Nachdenken über Israel, Bibel und Theologie: Festschrift für Klaus-Dietrich Schunck zu seinem 65. Geburtstag,* eds. Hermann M. Niemann, Matthias Augustin, and Werner H. Schmidt (BEATAJ 37; Frankfurt am Main: P. Lang, 1994), 311–18.

[26] Nahum M. Sarna, *Genesis: The Traditional Hebrew Text with the New JPS Translation* (JPS Torah Commentary; Philadelphia: Jewish Publication Society, 1989), 5; Jože Krašovec, "Merism – Polar Expression in Biblical Hebrew," *Bib* 64 (1983): 231–39; Herbert C. Brichto, *Toward a Grammar of Biblical Poetics: Tales of the Prophets* (New York: Oxford University Press, 1992), 42. See the latter especially on what he calls extended complex merism. The use of the "solitary" definite article marks "heavens and earth" as unique, they are without parallel or equal; see Bill T. Arnold and John H. Choi, *A Guide to Biblical Hebrew Syntax* (Cambridge: Cambridge University Press, 2003), 31.

[27] See, e.g., John Skinner, *A Critical and Exegetical Commentary on Genesis* (ICC 1; New York: Scribner, 1910), 14–15.

[28] Werner H. Schmidt, *Die Schöpfungsgeschichte der Priesterschrift zur Überlieferungsgeschichte von Genesis 1, 1–2, 4a und 2, 4b-3, 24* (WMANT 17; Neukirchen-Vluyn: Neukirchener Verlag, 1973), 166–67, and many others.

[29] That is, the verb's use as "create" occurs only in the Qal and Niphal, while the supposed separate root appears only in the Piel for "cut." Jan Bergman, Karl-Heinz Bernhardt,

although it is true that creating (*bārā'*) never mentions the material out of which something is created, it is frequently used together with other verbs that do, such as "do, make" (*ʿāśâ*, vv. 26–27). Thus it seems likely that the verb *bārā'* has developed from "separate by cutting" (the supposed *bārā'* III),[30] and that it has here an intentional, and no less theologically significant connotation of creating by cutting, shaping, or fashioning (not unlike the use of *yāṣar* in 2:7, see below). Indeed, it seems likely our author has intentionally begun the story with a theologically loaded word play in the first two words of the Bible, using the consonants *br'* in an alliterative sequence: *běrēʾšît běrōʾ*, "In the beginning when [God] created . . . "[31] The word play anticipates the specific manner in which God brings order and shape to his creation, by dividing and separating, as in light from darkness and waters from waters (Hiphil of *bdl*, vv. 4, 7, 14, and 18 below). God masterfully divides the cosmos by a series of "cuts" and differentiates its components into "kinds."[32] Without reading too much into this particular verb, it is no doubt still true that this creative activity in 1:1–2:3 is clearly reserved for the domain of the sovereign God of Israel. Creating in this way is something only God can do.

The parenthetical v. 2 details three circumstances of the cosmos at its beginning. Components of the universe at this time were "the earth," "the deep," and "the waters," presumably portraying a disk of land with water over and below it. The state of things before the first divine command of v. 3 was undeveloped and uninhabitable. The land itself was an unproductive emptiness, winds blowing across its seas and darkness covering its subterranean waters. The three clauses of v. 2 describe this "earth," which was not then as we know it today (or as it was known by the first readers of Genesis). First, the earth was "unformed and void" (*tōhû wābōhû*), a nominal hendiadys in which two nouns are bound together to refer to a single referent (one noun typically modifies the other in translation, as in NRSV's "a formless void"). This undeveloped (or pre-developed!) place is not a land of ominous "chaos" as often assumed, which might otherwise imply an independent threat to the cosmos or to God's creative decrees. Rather, "formless void" implies an unproductive "emptiness" strangely different from the world later to teem and

G. Johannes Botterweck, and Helmer Ringgren, "*bārā'*," *TDOT* 2:242–249, esp. 246; Raymond C. Van Leeuwen, "*br'*, create," *NIDOTTE* 1:728–35, esp. 731–32. Thus it is still true that its use in the Qal and Niphal always has God as subject, and it appears to be used intentionally in Gen 1 with distinctive theological import, albeit more subtle than commonly assumed. Wilfred G. Lambert, "Technical Terminology for Creation in the Ancient Near East," in Jiří Prosecký, ed., *Intellectual Life of the Ancient Near East: Papers Presented at the 43rd Rencontre assyriologique international, Prague, July 1–5, 1996* (Prague: Oriental Institute, 1998), 189–93.

30 C. Westermann, *Genesis 1–11* (1984), 98–100.
31 Thus an epanastrophic word play; Jack M. Sasson, "Wordplay in the OT," *IDBSup* 968–70, esp. 968. My vocalization represents a reconstruction of the temporal clause with infinitive construct. The traditional interpretation of the Masoretic Text also preserves the word play, *běrēʾšît bārā'*.
32 David J. A. Clines, *The Theme of the Pentateuch* (JSOTSup 10; Sheffield: University of Sheffield, 1978), 73–77.

swarm with plants, animals, and humans.[33] This is no threatening, chaotic state but a neutral "emptiness" needing only God's powerful word to transform it and fill it.

Second, darkness was over the face of "the deep" (*těhôm*). This term was once assumed to be evidence of direct dependence of the Israelite creation account on Babylonian mythology, especially in light of its etymological affinities with Tiāmat, the matrix goddess personifying primeval ocean in *Enuma Elish*. While it is apparent that Hebrew *těhôm* and Akkadian *tiāmtu/tâmtu* are derived from a common Semitic root, direct borrowing is unlikely.[34] So it may be said that *těhôm* "seems to be etymologically akin to (but not derived from) the word *tiamat*."[35] To be sure, the use of *těhôm* in v. 2 without the definite article may reflect a vague conception of mythological origins, in which case our text is refuting it subtly. But Gen 1 has nothing like the titanic struggle between the creator-god and personified ocean known from ancient cosmogonies (see Closer Look, pp. 45–47), and it certainly does not have *Enuma Elish*'s Tiāmat in view. This is no direct polemical statement, intending to demythologize an offensive mythical idea, as once assumed.[36] Instead, the "deep" in v. 2 reflects other ancient creation accounts in which a primeval flood is present at the beginning,[37] or it simply refers to an enormous mass of subterranean water, which was taken to be the source of all earthly bodies of water, as Gen 7:11 implies (where "deep" is again *těhôm*).[38]

Third, a "wind from God" swept over the waters. A superlative use of "God" (Heb *'ělōhîm*) might mean this phrase should be "a mighty wind" or "an awesome gale" (see NRSV footnote), but such an interpretation would be unique for this particular phrase and unlikely in Gen 1.[39] The use of *rûaḥ* is fascinating because it could be either "wind" or "spirit," or in certain metaphorical contexts, both. Wind often serves an innervating and rejuvenating function in the Bible, especially when serving as an agent of God. Similar terms are used when God blows a wind over the earth to tame the flood waters (Gen 8:1) and to part the waters of the Re(e)d Sea

---

[33] David T. Tsumura, *Creation and Destruction: A Reappraisal of the Chaoskampf Theory in the Old Testament* (Winona Lake, Ind.: Eisenbrauns, 2005), 9–35, and on less linguistic grounds, see Terence E. Fretheim, "The Book of Genesis," *NIB* 1:319–674, esp. 356.

[34] The Hebrew term cannot be a loan word from Akkadian since it would have retained the feminine morpheme and would not have inserted an "h" where we would expect a long vowel. Instead, Hebrew *těhôm* is more likely related to Ugaritic *thm*, which more naturally denotes "ocean." D. T. Tsumura, *Creation and Destruction* (2005), 36–53; Alexander Heidel, *The Babylonian Genesis: The Story of the Creation* (Chicago: University of Chicago Press, 1951), 98–101.

[35] Derek Kidner, *Genesis: An Introduction and Commentary* (TOTC; Downers Grove, Ill.: InterVarsity, 1967), 45.

[36] Tsumura has persuasively argued on linguistic grounds against parallels between Gen 1 and ancient Near Eastern combat myths; D. T. Tsumura, *Creation and Destruction* (2005); see also W. G. Lambert, "A New Look at the Babylonian Background of Genesis," 293–96.

[37] C. Westermann, *Genesis 1–11* (1984), 106.

[38] J. Day, *God's Conflict with The Dragon and The Sea* (1985), 50.

[39] E. A. Speiser, *Genesis: Introduction, Translation, and Notes* (AB 1; Garden City, N.Y.: Doubleday, 1964), 5.

(Exod 14:21). In a tantalizing way, this announcement that the "wind/spirit of God" was hovering over the waters announces God's presence on the scene, anticipating God's dramatic decree in v. 3.

God speaks and changes everything, with remarkably simple and concise language (vv. 3–5). These verses on the creation of "light" (*'ôr*) are not a deeply philosophical treatise on the nature of physics, on which some interpreters rave about light as the first-fruits of creation, the sublimest element, and the finest of all elementary powers.[40] Instead, this author intends to describe creation in a six-day pattern, moving inexorably to an all-important seventh. For this reason, the creation of light is first and fundamental to the rest, because it makes possible the first separations and divisions of creation; that is, light from darkness, day from night, and therefore the alternating sequence of days. What God has created in vv. 3–5 is *time*, which is more important than space for this chapter.[41] Only through this orderly progression through the six days will God now bring order to the cosmos, and this prepares for the importance of the seventh day (2:1–3), which is paramount for this author.

God's method of creation – divine *fiat*, or spoken word[42] – is known elsewhere in the ancient world. The Babylonian lord of creation, Marduk, proves his worth as divine king by means of a star, which is created at his command and disappears at his command.[43] Similarly in the Memphite theology of Egypt, the god Ptah creates by means of his heart and tongue, which is to say, by the word of his mouth.[44] Like a king issuing a decree, the creative orders are given and fulfilled.[45] In this case, however, there is no one else there to receive the command and carry out the order. This is truly a creative command unlike others, because the very speech of God brings something into existence that did not have independent, previous existence.[46] It is also interesting that this is the only time in Gen 1 that creation occurs by *fiat* alone. Elsewhere in the chapter God speaks and then takes action to "make" or otherwise bring about the feature of creation.[47]

This is the first occurrence of the word "good" (*tôb*) in the Bible (v. 4). It recurs frequently in the rest of the chapter as the fourth component of the daily creative

---

[40] Gerhard von Rad, *Genesis: A Commentary* (OTL; Philadelphia: Westminster Press, 1961), 51.

[41] Walter Vogels, "The Cultic and Civil Calendars of the Fourth Day of Creation (Gen 1,14b)," *SJOT* 11/2 (1997): 163–80: esp. 178–79; C. Westermann, *Genesis 1–11* (1984), 112.

[42] From the Latin Vulgate translation of v. 3, *fiat lux*, "let there be light."

[43] *Enuma Elish* IV:19–28; B. R. Foster, "Epic of Creation," 397.

[44] J. P. Allen, "From the 'Memphite Theology,'" 22.

[45] The "word" and "action" intersections in Gen 1:1–2:3 have yielded theories about an original source describing creation in terms of divine actions (*Tatberichte*), which were subsequently expanded by divine commands (*Wortberichte*). For summary and critique, see Gordon J. Wenham, *Genesis 1–15* (WBC 1; Waco, Tex.: Word Books, 1987), 7–8; and M. Weinfeld, *The Place of the Law in the Religion of Ancient Israel* (2004), 98–99.

[46] C. Westermann, *Genesis 1–11* (1984), 111.

[47] Victor P. Hamilton, *The Book of Genesis, Chapters 1–17* (NICOT; Grand Rapids, Mich.: W.B. Eerdmans, 1990), 119.

formula ("divine evaluation"). Its recurring use in the formula weaves "the notion of cosmic goodness into the very fabric of creation."[48] This is no moral or ethical goodness, since no evil or bad thing is yet a potentiality in God's perfect work. That will come later (2:9). Rather this evaluation of light as "good" implies that it, and the rest of creation, are precisely what God had in mind. It is just what God ordered, no more and no less than perfection, and completely satisfying to God in every respect. The often repeated comparison of God to an artisan is appropriate. After completing his work, God inspects it and finds it pleasing. The cosmos fulfills its purpose for creation, and all its features function just as God intended. The world and everything in it pleases God.

Another component of the recurring formula, which makes its appearance here for the first time, is the concept of naming: "God called the light Day, and the darkness he called Night" (v. 5). This, the fifth element of the formula, is important because of the nature and role of name-giving in ancient Hebrew traditions, and in the ancient Near East generally. The function of names themselves is more significant in ancient cultures than today because the giving of names was more than a mere identification tag. Names were sometimes seen as a hypostasis, or the very essence of a thing. The opening lines of the Babylonian creation epic, *Enuma Elish*, equate naming with existence, showing that naming is often determinative of existence.

> When on high no name was given to heaven,
> Nor below was the netherworld called by name, . . . [49]

A few lines later, the epic describes the primordial period when only Absu and Tiamat existed.

> When no gods at all had been brought forth,
> None called by names, no destinies ordained,
> Then were the gods formed within these two.
> Lahmu and Lahamu [the first gods born] were brought forth,
> Were called by name.

Many other examples illustrate that throughout the ancient world, naming and existence were often equated.[50] In Gen 1:5, name-giving is part of God's creative activity.

---

[48] Susan Niditch, *Oral World and Written Word: Ancient Israelite Literature* (Library of Ancient Israel; Louisville, Ky.: Westminster John Knox Press, 1996), 14.

[49] For this translation and the next, see B. R. Foster, "Epic of Creation," 391.

[50] In the Ugaritic Baal Cycle, the wise, craftsman double-deity, Kothar-wa-Khasis created and named two clubs for Baal to use in his battle against Yamm. In a name-giving formula, Kothar pronounced their names, Yagrušu and ʾAyyamurru (both meaning "Driver"), and charged them with "driving out" Yamm from the throne of his royal dominion; *CTU* 1.2.IV.11–15a, and 18b-23a, see M. S. Smith, *The Ugaritic Baal Cycle* (1994), 322–323; D. Pardee, "The Baʾlu Myth," 248–49. In this case, the name-giving identifies function, or perhaps represents magical incantations to empower the weapons (so-called "nomen omen").

He completes the creative work by naming light "Day" and darkness "Night," perhaps also determining their functions.

God will continue naming the objects of his handiwork on days two and three. The dome or firmament created on day two is named "Sky" (or simply, "heaven," v. 8), the dry ground of day three is named "Earth" (or "land"), while the collected waters beneath the dome he called "Seas" (v. 10).[51] Elsewhere in the chapter, the name-giving gives way to other creative activities. God simply calls forth a new component of the universe from one of these primary features, such as vegetation from earth (v. 11), or living creatures from earth and seas (vv. 20 and 24). At other times, God "makes" (from the verbal root, *ʿśh*) new components as a feature of one of these previously named objects, such as sun and moon in the sky (vv. 16–17), wild animals in the earth (v. 25), and humankind as ruler of all other creatures in sky and earth (v. 26). This amounts to a materialization or physicalizing of the rest of creation subsequent to his naming the primary components in vv. 3–10. The naming of Day, Night, Sky, Earth, and Seas establishes the essential components of the universe, from which others are derived or to which others are added.

The formulaic pattern for creating is now established for the rest of the days of creation. On day two (vv. 6–8), God spoke into existence a dome or firmament (*rāqîaʿ*). Just as God separated light from darkness, so now he cuts apart the celestial waters above from terrestrial waters below using the new dome to partition them (v. 6). The cosmology presented by this image is quite unlike our contemporary scientific understanding. This ancient cosmology, which the Israelites shared with their neighbors, included a flat disk-shaped earth with mountains at its ends supporting a multi-layered sky, or domed firmament.[52] The sun, moon, and stars crossed this dome in regular and predictable patterns. Moreover, the dome had chambers through which the water above it came down as rain, and there was also water under the earth, and water around the whole making up the cosmic seas (details to be recalled in the flood narrative, 7:11).

Although I have argued that Gen 1:1–2:3 is not a direct polemic against the Babylonian creation epic, *Enuma Elish*, and is certainly not directly borrowed from it, a parallel must be admitted between it or its precursors and vv. 6–7. Just as God divides the cosmic waters into two parts, so Marduk used the winds to conquer Tiamat, the divine creatrix-ocean, and then after inspecting her carcass, he split her

---

51 Similarly in Gen 2:19, the man's naming of all animals and birds created by Yahweh God grants a creative function to the human.

52 J. E. Wright, "Biblical Versus Israelite Images of the Heavenly Realm," *JSOT* 93 (2001): 59–75; Douglas A. Knight, "Cosmogony and Order in the Hebrew Tradition," in *Cosmogony and Ethical Order: New Studies in Comparative Ethics*, eds. Robin W. Lovin and Frank Reynolds (Chicago: University of Chicago Press, 1985), 133–57, esp. 138; Othmar Keel, *The Symbolism of the Biblical World: Ancient Near Eastern Iconography and the Book of Psalms* (New York: Seabury Press, 1978), 16–60.

in two, creating a heavenly dome with half and the earth with half.[53] Since these are the only examples of the splitting of a body of water as part of the creation image, it seems likely that a parallel exists here between Genesis and the Babylonian account.[54] This text is at least aware of other explanations for world origins, even as it thoroughly objectifies and de-personalizes the waters.

The third day has two acts of creation. The first uses the familiar formula to narrate the creation of "Earth" and "Seas," their naming, and their evaluation as "good" (vv. 9–10). The second tells of earth's involvement in the production of vegetation (vv. 11–13). Verse 11 contains a word play that simply cannot be captured in translation. The verb ("put forth") and the object ("vegetation") are derived from the same root, and imply that the vegetation had no existence prior to the spoken command.[55] This rhetorical feature and others like it in the context (vv. 15 and 20) highlight God's artistry in creation: His rhetoric is a creative force and is *itself* also rhetorically artistic.[56] The ensuing result statement ("the earth brought forth vegetation," v. 12) changes the verb and therefore also drops the word play, thereby intensifying the rhetorical artistry of God's speech. The word play is also the first example of God handing over his creative power, encouraging the "land" just created to produce on its own. In this regard, the rhetorical force of God's creative word prepares for the task he has in store for humanity (v. 28).

The literary formula – minus the name-giving – is used in vv. 14–19 to narrate events of the fourth day. The reasons God made the sun and moon are clear: they are to serve as lamps in the dome of the sky to separate light from darkness perpetually (a process God began on day one, v. 4), and to rule over day and night, giving light upon the earth. Thus a function belonging to God (i.e., separation of light from darkness) is being granted to components of the cosmos to be continued as an essential feature of the creation. The great lamps are also to become signs and seasons throughout the years, which implies more than simply establishing the pattern of the four seasons. It seems likely this also refers to the special functions of the sun and moon in the sacred seasons of the worship of Yahweh, especially as defined in Leviticus 23 (where the word translated in v. 14 as "seasons," *mô'ǎdîm*, is translated "appointed festivals," and see Ps 104:19).

The objectification of sun, moon, and stars also merits comment. In religious thought of the ancient world, the sun and moon were leading deities, often the most important gods of the pantheons of the ancient Near East. The use of "greater

---

[53] B. R. Foster, "Epic of Creation," 398–400.

[54] W. G. Lambert, "A New Look at the Babylonian Background of Genesis," 293–95; David B. Weisberg, "Loyalty and Death: Some Ancient Near Eastern Metaphors," *Maarav* 7 (1991): 253–67, esp. 263–65. For essential differences between the two, see Jon D. Levenson, *Creation and the Persistence of Evil: The Jewish Drama of Divine Omnipotence* (San Francisco: Harper & Row, 1988), 121–22.

[55] Hebrew *tadšē'... deše'*, and thus, an "effected" object accusative; B. T. Arnold and J. H. Choi, *A Guide to Biblical Hebrew Syntax* (2003), 15.

[56] W. P. Brown, "Divine Act and the Art of Persuasion in Genesis 1," in *History and Interpretation: Essays in Honour of John H. Hayes* (1993), 24–27.

light" and "lesser light" avoids the Hebrew words for sun and moon (*šemeš* and *yārēaḥ*, respectively), which could have been taken for the ordinary names for the deities, Shemesh and Yarikh.[57] These great subjects, worshiped in the ancient world, have instead become physical objects of God's creative work. Ancient religion was almost always chained to the natural rhythms of time, irrevocably associated with the personification of Sun, Moon, and Stars. But these personified powers have been "demoted in Genesis to mere artifacts, lamps rising and setting on command of the One Creator."[58]

The fifth day (vv. 20–23) begins with another word play, using again the "language of production" as we saw in v. 11: "let the waters bring forth swarms of living creatures" (literally, "let the waters swarm with swarmers").[59] God's words are themselves artistic, as he hands over the creative activity to the waters (v. 20). While God has again delegated creative responsibility to one of the primary components of the cosmos, it is still only God who creates (again, *br'* v. 21).[60]

The fifth day contains the first occurrence of divine "blessing" (v. 22). This will become an important theme elsewhere in Genesis, and it recurs even in this first creation account. God's blessing of all living creatures here anticipates his blessing of humankind in v. 28, and with similar effect. In both cases the divine blessing is articulated as a command to "be fruitful and multiply," and fill those reaches of the universe intended for them. Indeed, the blessing to procreate distinguishes "living creatures," animals and humans alike, from sun, moon, stars and other parts of the universe. The capacity to reproduce is the fundamental definition of what it means to be a "living creature."[61] The command "be fruitful and multiply" is a verbal play (*pĕrû ûrĕbû*), which may be intended to bring to mind the nominal hendiadys "formless void" of v. 2 (*tōhû wābōhû*). In this case, the living creatures of God's creation are hereby empowered to perpetuate God's life-giving creativity by bringing still more life into the world, by filling up and inhabiting that which was previously empty and uninhabitable.

As we have seen, the creative formula could be adapted to narrate more than one creative event for each day. So day three narrated creation of both earth (vv. 9–10) and vegetation (vv. 11–12). Now day six presents the creation of both living creatures (vv. 24–25) and humankind (vv. 26–30), a subset of living creatures. The first act of creation on day six is that of all land creatures; that is, cattle, creeping things, and wild animals of every kind (vv. 24–25). Genesis will typically divide the animal

---

[57] Edouard Lipiński, "Shemesh," *DDD²* 764–68; and B. B. Schmidt, "Moon," *DDD²* 585–93.

[58] Herbert C. Brichto, *The Names of God: Poetic Readings in Biblical Beginnings* (New York: Oxford University Press, 1998), 69.

[59] Hebrew *yišrĕṣû . . . šereṣ*; W. P. Brown, "Divine Act and the Art of Persuasion in Genesis 1," in *History and Interpretation: Essays in Honour of John H. Hayes* (1993), 24–27.

[60] It may be that "create" is used again here for the first time since v. 1 in order to emphasize that God himself is responsible even for the "great sea monsters" (*tannînim*), which are sometimes perceived by ancient Israelites as mythological antagonists to God; V. P. Hamilton, *The Book of Genesis, Chapters 1–17* (1990), 129–30.

[61] C. Westermann, *Genesis 1–11* (1984), 138–39.

kingdom into three parts, but not always the same three: here domesticated animals, creepers, and wild animals but elsewhere the three categories will be birds, creepers, and beasts (or simply "animals," v. 30, and compare 6:20 and 8:17).[62] While God "made" these creatures (ʿśh, v 25), the earth itself is once again given a role in the production (as in vv. 11–12).

The chapter reaches a climactic moment at vv. 26–27. The first appearance of humankind is distinguished by a different kind of divine speech.[63] In creative decrees thus far in Gen 1, God has simply spoken things into existence ("Let there be . . . "), ordered a redeployment of something ("Let the waters . . . be gathered . . . "), or called upon elemental components of the cosmos to bring forth secondary creations of their own accord ("Let the earth put forth vegetation . . . "). The lofty words of v. 26 make this event distinctive: "Let us make humankind in our image, according to our likeness." This is a moment that God and all of creation have awaited. Two features of this decree highlight its importance, which have however also exercised readers for centuries and made this one of the most widely debated texts of the Bible. The first is the use of the plural pronouns "us" and "our," which in the Hebrew is present even in the verb itself (the first common plural, *naʿăśeh*), and the second is the concept that God creates humankind "in his image" and according to his "likeness." On the first issue, early Christian interpreters often assumed trinitarian concepts were behind the plurals in vv. 26–27, while others have explored alternative explanations, including the presence of a heavenly audience of angelic hosts.[64] It is best to accept the plural cohortative as an especially emphatic exhortation of self-deliberation or determination, expressing the measured and intentional action God is about to take (compare Gen 11:7). In this case, the verse does not refer to plural persons or beings involved in the act of human creation, but is a pregnant way of saying that God deliberated with himself about the creation of humankind. God's speech makes clear the uniqueness of humanity in creation. Rather than create by simple *fiat* or through surrogates such as earth or water, God himself decisively steps in to make humankind.

The second important issue of vv. 26–27 is the interpretation of "image" or "likeness" of God. The term *imago Dei*, "image of God," so important in the history of theological ideas, is derived from the Latin Vulgate's translation of v. 27: ". . . in the image of God (*ad imaginem Dei*) he created them." The amount of scholarly literature on this expression is enormous.[65] Speculation has been wildly diverse

[62] For a different approach, see John H. Walton, *Genesis* (NIV Application Commentary; Grand Rapids, Mich.: Zondervan, 2001), 127 and 341–42.

[63] On the translation of *ʾādām* as "humankind" rather than the personal name, "Adam," see the commentary below at 2:7.

[64] C. Westermann, *Genesis 1–11* (1984), 144–45; G. J. Wenham, *Genesis 1–15* (1987), 27–28; and V. P. Hamilton, *The Book of Genesis, Chapters 1–17* (1990), 132–34.

[65] Gunnlaugur A. Jónsson, *The Image of God: Genesis 1:26–28 in a Century of Old Testament Research* (ConBOT 26; Stockholm, Sweden: Almqvist & Wiksell, 1988); J. R. Middleton, *The Liberating Image: The Imago Dei in Genesis 1* (Grand Rapids, Mich.: Brazos Press, 2005); C. Westermann, *Genesis 1–11* (1984), 147–155.

through the centuries, but found certain reasonable controls once ancient Near Eastern materials were deciphered and compared to Israelite literature. On the basis of numerous parallels from both Egypt and Mesopotamia, it has become clear that the phrase is related to royal language, in which a king or pharaoh is the "image of (a) god."[66] Thus humans are created to function as the divine image through the exercise of "dominion" and "rule," which of course is reinforced by the statement "and let them have dominion over . . . " (v. 26). This statement in v. 26 should be interpreted as a purpose clause, expressing the motivation behind God's creation of humans in his image: "in order that they may have dominion over . . . "[67] The image of God is about the exercise of rulership in the world. While it may be objected that an entire species of humans cannot stand in God's place as an individual king, it seems likely that the office of God's representative has been "democratized" in 1:26–27.[68]

Thus, God has created all types of animals – flyers, creepers, and swimmers – each with appropriate physical traits for its respective domain: sky, land, and water. With the creation of the human in vv. 26–27, however, physical characteristics are not determined necessarily by a creature's environment. This creature is unlike others, and is intended to rule and have dominion over the whole. It is therefore appropriate that God, the sovereign Creator of the universe, has in a sense replicated himself in creating this unique creature, the human.[69]

A CLOSER LOOK – ANCIENT NEAR EASTERN RELIGION AND THE BIBLE

Creation myths of the ancient Near East reflect two standard types or genres: theogony ("origin of the gods") and cosmogony ("origin of the universe").[70] On the one hand, the theogony recounts the birth and succession of the gods, especially the olden gods. Its language is embedded in time – in bygone days, in the beginning – although the mythological language of theogony points beyond itself to the structures of reality at all times, which encompass gods and humans alike. Theogony also uses language of sexual activity among the gods as the means of creation, typically

---

[66] Hans Wildberger, "Das Abbild Gottes, Gen 1.26–30," *TZ* 21 (1965): 245–59; 481–501; Boyo Ockinga, *Die Gottebenbildlichkeit im alten Ägypten und im Alten Testament* (Ägypten und Altes Testament 7; Wiesbaden: In Kommission bei O. Harrassowitz, 1984).

[67] That is, the imperfect of *rdh* with *waw* conjunctive to connote purpose; B. T. Arnold and J. H. Choi, *A Guide to Biblical Hebrew Syntax* (2003), 92.

[68] See the objections of C. Westermann, *Genesis 1–11* (1984), 152–154; and the answer of J. D. Levenson, *Creation and the Persistence of Evil* (1988), 111–116.

[69] Philip R. Davies, "Making it: Creation and Contradiction in Genesis," in *The Bible in Human Society: Essays in Honour of John Rogerson*, eds. M. D. Carroll R., David J. A. Clines, and Philip R. Davies (JSOTSup 200; Sheffield: Sheffield Academic Press, 1995), 249–56, esp. 251.

[70] Frank M. Cross, "The 'Olden Gods' in Ancient Near Eastern Creation Myths and in Israel," in *From Epic to Canon: History and Literature in Ancient Israel* (Baltimore: Johns Hopkins University Press, 1998), 73–83.

involving pairs of gods, often binary opposites (fresh-water and salt-water, sky and earth).

The cosmogony, on the other hand, recounts a conflict between the old and the young gods. The results of this colossal struggle are victory for the young gods, establishment of kingship among the gods, and an orderly government for the cosmos. Human kingship is thus patterned after the cosmic government, and is given religious justification through the rites of the cult. Language of time may again be used, but primarily such cosmogonic myths recount primordial events and institute the cyclical realities of the cosmos. Most of our available creation myths combined the two types, using the theogony as a prologue to the cosmogony.

What we have in Genesis 1 is closer to theogony than cosmogony. There is no cosmogonic struggle, no titanic conflict from which God emerges victorious to establish kingship over the universe. Rather we begin with the language of time, "in the beginning," and quickly encounter the binary pairs – heaven and earth, wind and watery bareness, darkness and light. Strikingly, those olden pairs are all transformed to natural objects. They have been objectified as part of God's creative activity; demythologized, de-deified, and materialized as part of creation. Also more akin to the theogonies of the ancient world, Genesis 1 functions as a prologue, not for another mythological genre, cosmogony, but for the great epical history of the Garden of Eden, the flood, and Israel's ancestors.

Such differences are so profound, they require further comment. Far from differences of mere literary form or style, the notable contrasts between Genesis 1 and the ancient Near Eastern creation accounts are essential and deeply important as an introduction to the rest of the Bible. In a word, ancient religion was polytheistic, mythological, and anthropomorphic, describing the gods in human forms and functions, while Genesis 1 is monotheistic, scornful of mythology, and engages in anthropomorphism only as figures of speech.[71] The religion expressed in the various ancient Near Eastern cosmogonies (see Closer Look, pp. 33–34) assumes that the locus of ultimate power is not with the gods, but is an impersonal force beyond them, to which even the gods are susceptible. Thus magic is central to ancient religion, as witnessed by the use of spells and incantations as a means for even the gods to exert power over each other and over nature.

Genesis 1, then, is revolutionary in that this inanimate and impersonal power in the ancient Near Eastern accounts here becomes the "infinite source of all existence."[72] Far from inanimate and impersonal, this Power has attributes that can only be called personal. Although this Power is non-sexual, it would be inadequate

---

[71] H. C. Brichto, *The Names of God* (1998), 57, and for more on what follows here, see his 57–62; and Yehezkel Kaufmann, *The Religion of Israel, from its Beginnings to the Babylonian Exile* (Chicago: University of Chicago Press, 1960), 21–26.

[72] H. C. Brichto, *The Names of God* (1998), 60.

to refer to "it," and so Power becomes "he." Gender is thus the necessary mandate of God's personhood. This Power commands, evaluates, and moves effortlessly through his work of creating. Other ancient religions were naturalistic and magical, while biblical religion is supernaturalistic and intensely personal, prohibiting magic as manipulative and foolish.[73] As a result, Israel's conception of the cosmos in Genesis 1 is structured and orderly, the express thoughts of the mind of God, and spoken effortlessly into existence by God's decree. Genesis knows no impersonal, ultimate power beyond God and therefore the cosmos is secure and whole. And humankind is the apex of that secure orderliness. Adam and Eve do not live in a world of competing deities churning with impersonal, amorphous power. Rather, humans inhabit a space and time expressly made for them, which is "good" in every respect, and which makes it possible for them to relate rightly to God, trusting without manipulating.

Like the divine "blessing" bestowed on the living creatures (v. 22), God's blessing of humankind is a command to "be fruitful and multiply," and thereby to fill up and inhabit that portion of the cosmos set apart especially for them (v. 28). Unlike that first blessing, however, we have here an additional command to "subdue" the earth and to "have dominion" over all living creatures of days five and six. The blessing of God thereby declares that God is favorably disposed toward humankind, details the natural order of things built into creation, and expresses God's will that humans represent him on earth by exercising dominion.[74]

The culminating events of day six are highlighted by a slight alteration in the fourth component of the creative formula – the divine evaluation. For the first time in Gen 1, that which God has made is "*very* good" (v. 31). Furthermore, this final evaluative statement relates to the entire created order instead of simply the creatures of day six. Heaven and earth together with their respective components reflect their Creator more completely than any of the separate components could do alone.[75]

The seven-part creative formula is suspended altogether for a terse but important conclusion in 2:1–3.[76] The completion statement in v. 1 is loaded with meaning:

---

[73] The differences between Israelite religion and that of its neighbors have been overstated at times. There were, in fact, many points of similarity between Israel and the polytheistic cultures of the ancient Near East; see J. J. M. Roberts, "Divine Freedom and Cultic Manipulation in Israel and Mesopotamia," in *Unity and Diversity: Essays in the History, Literature, and Religion of the Ancient Near East*, eds. Hans Goedicke and J. J. M. Roberts (Baltimore: Johns Hopkins University Press, 1975), 181–90; repr. in J. J. M. Roberts, *The Bible and the Ancient Near East: Collected Essays* (Winona Lake, Ind.: Eisenbrauns, 2002), 72–82.

[74] Christopher W. Mitchell, *The Meaning of* brk *"to bless" in the Old Testament* (SBLDS 95; Atlanta: Scholars Press, 1987), 62–63, and 165–66.

[75] G. J. Wenham, *Genesis 1–15* (1987), 34.

[76] See the commentary at 2:4 below for a note on whether this unit should end at 2:3 or 2:4a.

"Thus the heavens and the earth were finished." This clause and other features of 2:1–3 contain undeniable similarities with the instructions for building the wilderness tabernacle found in Exod 25–31 and 34–40, and especially the linguistic ties in Exod 39 and 40.[77] Through architectural similarities, the Bible asserts that in both cases – the construction of the world and of the tabernacle – a significant work has been completed. The comparison between this world-building project and the tabernacle-building project of Sinai becomes a metaphor used elsewhere in the Bible.[78] The entire cosmos may be viewed as a temple for God's sovereign rule. Conversely, Israel's sanctuaries, both the wilderness tabernacle and Solomon's temple, may be seen as microcosms of the universe, places of cosmic order in which God's reign is unquestioned and unending.

The concept of God's "rest" is somewhat misleading in English, since it may give the wrong impression that God was weary and needed a break from his labors (2:2). The concept is cessation of work, not resuscitation due to fatigue. Comparisons with creation accounts from the ancient Near East are again instructive. Both the *Enuma Elish* and the Ugaritic *Baal Cycle* close their creation accounts in cultic dramas, in the building of great temples, and in the case of *Enuma Elish*, specifically as a place of "rest."[79] Likewise in the Memphite theology of ancient Egypt, the god Ptah rested after creating everything.[80] At the conclusion of each of these, the cultic drama gives reason for the preeminence of a deity, of a temple, or of a specific cultic feature of life or worship. Similarly at the conclusion of Gen 1:1–2:3, we have an etiological account, explaining the origins of an important Israelite cultic concept – the Sabbath.

The institution of the Sabbath is again an occasion of divine blessing (see vv. 22 and 28). Here God does not bless animals or humans for purposes of procreation and dominion, but rather he consecrates the seventh day (2:3). The sequence of main verbs in v. 3, "blessed" and "hallowed," uses the second verb to expand or clarify the meaning of the first.[81] Both verbs are illocutionary speech acts, performative utterances that themselves accomplish the action, and there is no need to assume magic or some self-fulfilling power inherent in the words.[82] The "hallowing" (declarative

---

[77] Specifically 39:32, 43; 40:33–34; see Joseph Blenkinsopp, "The Structure of P," *CBQ* 38 (1976): 275–92, esp. 275–82.

[78] J. D. Levenson, *Creation and the Persistence of Evil* (1988), 78–90. Levenson also illustrates the use of this metaphor elsewhere in the ancient Near East. Interestingly, the prescriptive chapters of the tabernacle texts (Exod 25–31) contain seven subsections, each beginning with "The Lord spoke to Moses," with the last one (31:12) containing instructions for the Sabbath, paralleling closely this seven-stage creation of the cosmos; see Carol L. Meyers, *Exodus* (NCBC; Cambridge: Cambridge University Press, 2005), 224.

[79] *Enuma Elish* VI:51–54; B. R. Foster, "Epic of Creation," esp. 401.

[80] J. P. Allen, "From the 'Memphite Theology,'" esp. 23.

[81] The so-called "epexegetical" use of the *waw* consecutive; B. T. Arnold and J. H. Choi, *A Guide to Biblical Hebrew Syntax* (2003), 86–87.

[82] C. W. Mitchell, *The Meaning of* brk *"to bless" in the Old Testament* (1987), 64–65.

Piel of *qādaš*) specifies what type of pronouncement God is making and declares a change of status for the seventh day.

The significance of the Sabbath in ancient Israel can hardly be overstated. At the conclusion of the creation overture to the entire Bible, the six days of creation come to fruition in the institution of a day of rest. And it is not only an explanation of God's resting or a place for God's repose. Rather it institutes "blessing" and "holiness" for the created order. The Sabbath encompasses all of the best of God's intentions for the cosmos. Yet since the days of Julius Wellhausen, scholarship has routinely assumed that the concept of Sabbath changed radically in the post-exilic period, taking on a more legalistic form assumed to be reflected in Gen 2:1–3.[83] Such a position is hard to justify in light of the great antiquity of the concept of Sabbath in ancient Israel. Interestingly, the seven-day sequence was a common literary motif in fourteenth century Ugaritic inscriptions for "expressing extended processes," especially evident in the building of a palace for Baal, which took seven days.[84] It has also been suggested that the institution of a seven-day Sabbath in ancient Israel is an intentional apologetic or polemical argument against a Mesopotamian fifteen-day cycle that celebrated and honored the full moon.[85] In this case the old Israelite Sabbath ideology made such celebration impossible. Whether intentionally polemical or not, it is hard to say, but it is certainly true that the seven-day week is a somewhat artificial construct. Unlike the year, the month, or the day, all of which have basis in observable cosmic phenomena, the week is not based on recurring movement among the stars or planets. The seven-day week ending in a sanctified Sabbath is unique to Israel among ancient Near Eastern philosophies.[86] By definition, this institution of the Sabbath presents an alternative view of reality. Faithful Israelites would find it difficult to pay homage to deities and religious festivals connected to the stars and planets while also honoring the Lord of the Sabbath.

Narration of the seventh day is completely different from the previous six, obvious by the suspension of the creation formula used for the first six days. Beyond this literary observation, it should be clear that the seven-day pattern of Gen 1:1–2:3

[83] Wellhausen averred that post-exilic legalistic Judaism killed the vibrant religion of the earlier Israelites. Thus circumcision and the Sabbath were symbols that bound together the Jewish diaspora; Julius Wellhausen, *Prolegomena to the History of Israel* (Atlanta, Ga.: Scholars Press, 1994), 114–16, and 341; repr. of *Prolegomena to the History of Israel*, trans. J. Sutherland Black and Allan Enzies (Edinburgh: Adam & Charles Black, 1885).

[84] D. Pardee, "The Ba'lu Myth," esp. 261, n. 175.

[85] William W. Hallo, *Origins: The Ancient Near Eastern Background of Some Modern Western Institutions* (SHCANE 6; Leiden: E.J. Brill, 1996), 127. Hallo is of the opinion (with Cassuto before him) that the Hebrew notion of sabbath was instituted *in opposition* to the Mesopotamian system, making it impossible to celebrate a day of the full moon (Ibid., 127–28). For a different approach, see Michael A. Fishbane, *Biblical Interpretation in Ancient Israel* (Oxford: Clarendon Press, 1988), 149–50.

[86] Jack M. Sasson, "Of Time and Immortality: How Genesis Created Them," *BRev* 21/3 (2005): 32–41, 52–54, esp. 37.

transforms something as simple as the weekly calendar, with its regular twenty-four hour periods, into a constant reminder of God's creative sovereignty. *Every week* of human history becomes a mnemonic stroll through creation itself. Having been a staple of Western culture for so long, it may be difficult for today's readers to grasp the weight of this introduction of the concept of one day of rest in seven. Indeed, our easy acceptance of such an idea may lead us to read 2:1–3 as anticlimactic to what is an otherwise spectacular account of creation.[87] Our difficulty is in reading the institution of the Sabbath as merely a cultic dogma, almost as though it were an afterthought in the creation of the world. On the contrary, by placing it here, at the conclusion of the creation of the world, the author has created an elaborate theology of Sabbath that must not escape us. The seven-day structure together with the creation of sourceless light in 1:3 has lifted Israel's sights above the ancient religions and their infatuation with the natural rhythms of time itself. The deities so frequently worshipped in antiquity responsible for the seasons of nature – sun, moon, and stars – have been transformed into mere lamps illuminating the creation at the command of the one and sovereign Creator. Like the first word uttered in the creation process, "Let there be light," this last word – a blessing of the Sabbath – pertains to time itself, and therefore speaks to the role of Sabbath for the entire cosmos and not just for Israel.[88]

By arriving at the Sabbath in its conclusion, this narrative has arrived at its hymn of praise of the Creator. The *Enuma Elish* concludes in praise of Marduk and several hymns from ancient Egypt draw close to renouncing polytheism altogether in favor of ascribing powers and attributes to a single deity, almost as though monotheism is struggling to find articulation.[89] In Gen 1:1–2:3 we find eloquent expression of the one deity, all-powerful and sovereign in "the beginning," who is also personal and intimately related to his created order. But the creation narrative's doxology – the institution of the Sabbath – goes beyond a hymn of praise because it asserts that time itself is God's domain. It summons the reader to renounce dominion over time and all the uses we humans have for time. The reader is invited to acknowledge the lordship of the Creator over time itself, and therefore to renounce one's autonomy by embracing God's dominion over time and over oneself. Keeping the Sabbath is equated with acceptance of the sovereign lordship of God.[90]

---

[87] On this notion of the anticlimax of 2:1–3, and for more on what follows, see H. C. Brichto, *The Names of God* (1998), 66–70.

[88] Frank H. Polak, "Poetic Style and Parallelism in the Creation Account (Gen. 1:1–2:3)," in *Creation in Jewish and Christian Tradition*, eds. Henning Reventlow and Yair Hoffman (JSOTSup 319; Sheffield: Sheffield Academic Press, 2002), 26.

[89] H. C. Brichto, *The Names of God* (1998), 69.

[90] Matitiahu Tsevat, "The Basic Meaning of the Biblical Sabbath," in *The Meaning of the Book of Job and Other Biblical Studies: Essays on the Literature and Religion of the Hebrew Bible*, ed. M. Tsevat (New York: Ktav Publishing House, 1980), 39–52, esp. 48–49; repr. from *ZAW* 84 (1972): 447–59.

The author of Gen 1 produced a new creation story for Israel; whether he used sources and how extensive they might have been is impossible to determine. His purpose is clear in 2:1–3. This author has intentionally turned the creation story into an etiology for the Sabbath: "the priestly author's crystallization of Gen 1 was for the distinct purpose of providing a basis and a motivation for the Sabbath."[91] This author is also aware that he is not the first nor the last word on creation but one voice of a choir.[92] He is aware of how other Israelites have spoken of the origins of things (especially 2:4–25), and perhaps of how others in Mesopotamia and Egypt have done so as well. He does not insist that all of these are wrong and that he alone has it right. Rather, Gen 1 fills in the gaps and supplements what we find in 2:4–25, and together they provide a rich tapestry of creation theology.

BRIDGING THE HORIZONS — GENESIS 1 AND THE IDEOLOGIES OF THE AGES

Genesis 1 has held fast against the ideological storms of human speculation for more than two and a half millennia: from polytheism to atheism (including dualism, deism, and agnosticism), and concepts such as nihilism, materialism, astrology, and a host of others, and varieties of these. With raw simplicity, this text frames the biblical storyline with its assertions: God exists as a singular and personal entity; God alone created the world and did so effortlessly; the world is inherently good, including everything in it and especially the humans; the humans hold a unique role in the world as God's regents; and finally, the seventh day of the week is different from the others and is an especially appropriate time to reflect on these truths. Wherever and whenever human ideologies have gone astray, they have often involved a rejection or neglect of these truths.

The importance of such concepts for reading and understanding the rest of the Bible is obvious, and will become clear in this commentary as we continue through the book of Genesis. Beyond this foundational role of Gen 1 for reading the Bible, and obviously for religion and theology, it is also instructive to consider the contributions of this text more generally for contemporary explanations of life in our universe. In an age of rapidly expanding knowledge and exponential advances in scientific research, especially as it relates to the birth of the universe as much as twenty billion years ago and the evolution of the first humans five million years ago, this text continues to offer an intellectual benchmark for readers of faith. The supposed dichotomy between religion and science is one of the most unfortunate

---

[91] M. Weinfeld, *The Place of the Law in the Religion of Ancient Israel* (2004), 99. More broadly, it may be argued that Gen 1 establishes a priestly reality of (1) Sabbath, (2) other feast days, weeks, and years, and (3) kashrut, or dietary requirements; M. S. Smith, *The Origins of Biblical Monotheism* (2001), 169.

[92] C. Westermann, *Genesis 1–11* (1984), 173–74.

developments of contemporary thought. As science continues to make advances in our understanding of cosmic and human origins, Gen 1 continues to offer answers to the "Who" and "Why" questions that all of us ask instinctively. Instead of assuming that Genesis and science offer rival perspectives or mutually exclusive explanations, we should consider the potential for mutual instruction in future theories of origins, especially as this text speaks to issues of purpose and meaning in ways science is not equipped to address.

GENESIS 2:4–3:24 HUMAN ORIGINS, PART 1: THE GARDEN OF PARADISE

(2:4) These are the generations of the heavens and the earth when they were created. In the day that the LORD God made the earth and the heavens,

(2:5) when no plant of the field was yet in the earth and no herb of the field had yet sprung up – for the LORD God had not caused it to rain upon the earth, and there was no one to till the ground;

(2:6) but a stream would rise from the earth, and water the whole face of the ground –

(2:7) then the LORD God formed man from the dust of the ground, and breathed into his nostrils the breath of life; and the man became a living being.

(2:8) And the LORD God planted a garden in Eden, in the east; and there he put the man whom he had formed.

(2:9) Out of the ground the LORD God made to grow every tree that is pleasant to the sight and good for food, the tree of life also in the midst of the garden, and the tree of the knowledge of good and evil.

(2:10) A river flows out of Eden to water the garden, and from there it divides and becomes four branches.

(2:11) The name of the first is Pishon; it is the one that flows around the whole land of Havilah, where there is gold;

(2:12) and the gold of that land is good; bdellium and onyx stone are there.

(2:13) The name of the second river is Gihon; it is the one that flows around the whole land of Cush.

(2:14) The name of the third river is Tigris, which flows east of Assyria. And the fourth river is the Euphrates.

(2:15) The LORD God took the man and put him in the garden of Eden to till it and keep it.

(2:16) And the LORD God commanded the man, "You may freely eat of every tree of the garden;

(2:17) but of the tree of the knowledge of good and evil you shall not eat, for in the day that you eat of it you shall die."

(2:18) Then the LORD God said, "It is not good that the man should be alone; I will make him a helper as his partner."

(2:19) So out of the ground the LORD God formed every animal of the field and every bird of the air, and brought them to the man to see what he would call them; and whatever the man called every living creature, that was its name.

(2:20) The man gave names to all cattle, and to the birds of the air, and to every animal of the field; but for the man there was not found a helper as his partner.

(2:21) So the LORD God caused a deep sleep to fall upon the man, and he slept; then he took one of his ribs and closed up its place with flesh.

(2:22) And the rib that the LORD God had taken from the man he made into a woman and brought her to the man.

(2:23) Then the man said, "This at last is bone of my bones and flesh of my flesh; this one shall be called Woman,[c] for out of Man[d] this one was taken."

(2:24) Therefore a man leaves his father and his mother and clings to his wife, and they become one flesh.

(2:25) And the man and his wife were both naked, and were not ashamed.

(3:1) Now the serpent was more crafty than any other wild animal that the LORD God had made. He said to the woman, "Did God say, 'You shall not eat from any tree in the garden'?"

(3:2) The woman said to the serpent, "We may eat of the fruit of the trees in the garden;

(3:3) but God said, 'You shall not eat of the fruit of the tree that is in the middle of the garden, nor shall you touch it, or you shall die.'"

(3:4) But the serpent said to the woman, "You will not die;

(3:5) for God knows that when you eat of it your eyes will be opened, and you will be like God, knowing good and evil."

(3:6) So when the woman saw that the tree was good for food, and that it was a delight to the eyes, and that the tree was to be desired to make one wise, she took of its fruit and ate; and she also gave some to her husband, who was with her, and he ate.

(3:7) Then the eyes of both were opened, and they knew that they were naked; and they sewed fig leaves together and made loincloths for themselves.

(3:8) They heard the sound of the LORD God walking in the garden at the time of the evening breeze, and the man and his wife hid themselves from the presence of the LORD God among the trees of the garden.

(3:9) But the LORD God called to the man, and said to him, "Where are you?"

(3:10) He said, "I heard the sound of you in the garden, and I was afraid, because I was naked; and I hid myself."

(3:11) He said, "Who told you that you were naked? Have you eaten from the tree of which I commanded you not to eat?"

(3:12) The man said, "The woman whom you gave to be with me, she gave me fruit from the tree, and I ate."

(3:13) Then the LORD God said to the woman, "What is this that you have done?" The woman said, "The serpent tricked me, and I ate."

[c] Heb *ishshah*.
[d] Heb *ish*.

(3:14) The LORD God said to the serpent, "Because you have done this, cursed are you among all animals and among all wild creatures; upon your belly you shall go, and dust you shall eat all the days of your life.

(3:15) I will put enmity between you and the woman, and between your offspring and hers; he will strike your head, and you will strike his heel."

(3:16) To the woman he said, "I will greatly increase your pangs in childbearing; in pain you shall bring forth children, yet your desire shall be for your husband, and he shall rule over you."

(3:17) And to the man he said, "Because you have listened to the voice of your wife, and have eaten of the tree about which I commanded you, 'You shall not eat of it,' cursed is the ground because of you; in toil you shall eat of it all the days of your life;

(3:18) thorns and thistles it shall bring forth for you; and you shall eat the plants of the field.

(3:19) By the sweat of your face you shall eat bread until you return to the ground, for out of it you were taken; you are dust, and to dust you shall return."

(3:20) The man named his wife Eve, because she was the mother of all living.

(3:21) And the LORD God made garments of skins for the man and for his wife, and clothed them.

(3:22) Then the LORD God said, "See, the man has become like one of us, knowing good and evil; and now, he might reach out his hand and take also from the tree of life, and eat, and live forever" –

(3:23) therefore the LORD God sent him forth from the garden of Eden, to till the ground from which he was taken.

(3:24) He drove out the man; and at the east of the garden of Eden he placed the cherubim, and a sword flaming and turning to guard the way to the tree of life.

*T*his unit explains the nature of human existence, both in its beauty and in its brokenness. In a graphic and earthy style quite dissimilar from 1:1–2:3, these chapters address some of the most poignant questions of life. Why are we here? What is our role in the world? What is the nature of human sexuality? Why do men and women relate to each other as they do? Why is death inevitable?

These chapters preserve early traditions that once served as part of Israel's sweeping national epic, which included the Eden narratives, Cain and Abel, the flood story now combined with other materials in Gen 6–9, and ancestral accounts of Abraham, Isaac, and Jacob.[93] The expression in 2:4a, "these are the generations of

---

[93] Theodore Hiebert, *The Yahwist's Landscape: Nature and Religion in Early Israel* (New York: Oxford University Press, 1996); David Damrosch, *The Narrative Covenant: Transformations of Genre in The Growth of Biblical Literature* (San Francisco: Harper & Row, 1987). Some date the epic to a much later time in Israel's history; John Van Seters, *Prologue to History: The Yahwist as Historian in Genesis* (Louisville, Ky.: Westminster/John Knox Press, 1992). See the introduction for more on these sources of Genesis. For the term "mythos" rather than "epic," see H. C. Brichto, *The Names of God* (1998), 441–42, n. 11.

[*tôlĕdôt*] the heavens and the earth" is the first of the *tôlĕdôt* clauses of Genesis, and is the only one introducing the generations of an object, "heavens and earth," rather than a personal name (see the introduction). Thus v. 4a introduces the epic narrative of the Garden of Eden and binds it to the creation story of Gen 1, creating a layered and complex perception of creation. As summarized in the introduction, we have reason to believe the *tôlĕdôt* of 2:4 was created new by the author of 1:1–2:3, based on the older model of 5:1, which probably preserves the original use of "generations" (see commentary below, p. 85). The purpose for 2:4a was to tie the new priestly account of creation to the older account of 2:4b–3:24, which presumably by that time wielded impressive authority. Thus the older authoritative epic account of human origins has been absorbed and supplemented by the more comprehensive priestly account in Gen 1.

It has occasionally been assumed that the *tôlĕdôt* clause in 2:4a is a summary of the acts of creation in 1.1–2.3, and was an original part of a Priestly document (P). If so, the verse (and chapter) divisions are better fixed at 1.1–2.4a.[94] However, there is good reason to believe the *tôlĕdôt* clauses were independent of the Priestly document as I have explained in the introduction, and that 2:4 introduces the next block of material so that the unit division used here is to be preferred.[95] This approach is also instructive for our understanding of how these two creation accounts are functioning together. While some earlier source approaches tended to dissect and atomize these texts, an understanding of 2:4a as an intentional link between Gen 1 and Gen 2–3 teaches us how these accounts of creation were intended to sound together. The editor of the final text has produced a continuity between them, adapting and adopting the authority of the older account, and creating a new text that is greater than the sum of its parts.[96] They may have come from different authors originally, but Gen 1 and Gen 2–3 have been edited together in such an intentional way as to produce a binocular or synoptic view of creation. Gen 2–3 now takes a "second look."

Although Gen 2 is devoted to creation of "the earth and the heavens" (v. 4b), its scope is nothing like the universal perspective of Gen 1's "the heavens and the earth" (1:1). The interests here are much more narrowly focused: creation of the human (vv. 4b–7), the garden as his home (vv. 8–17), creation of the animals, and lastly, the woman as an appropriate partner for the man (vv. 18–25). One immediately striking

---

[94] C. Westermann, *Genesis 1–11* (1984), 81; and for an example from a distinctly non-documentarian approach, see H. C. Brichto, *The Names of God* (1998), 37. The literature on this verse is enormous due to the difficulties of identifying it either as subscription for 1:1–2:3 or as superscription for 2:5–25, for which see J. Skinner, *A Critical and Exegetical Commentary on Genesis* (1910), 40–41; and T Stordalen, "Genesis 2,4: Restudying a *locus classicus*," *ZAW* 104 (1992): 163–77.

[95] Sven Tengström, *Die Toledotformel und die literarische Struktur der priesterlichen Erweiterungsschicht im Pentateuch* (ConBOT 17; Lund: Gleerup, 1982), 54–58.

[96] On the role of the redactor in this process and the need for both diachronic and synchronic approaches for this particular text, see Rolf Rendtorff, "Canonical Readings of the Old Testament in the Context of Critical Scholarship," *AsTJ* 54/1 (1999): 5–11: esp. 8–9.

feature is the new designation for God in 2:4b, "the LORD God." While Gen 1 uses "God," *ĕlōhîm*, consistently throughout, in Gen 2–3 we encounter right away the compound designation *yhwh 'ĕlōhîm*, Yahweh/the LORD God, which occurs nowhere else in Genesis. The synoptic reading produced by the editor quite naturally invites us to identify the God of Gen 1 with Yahweh God of Gen 2–3. By reading them together, we are thrust at once into the heart of Israelite theology, which equates the God of the ancestors of Genesis 12–36 with the God of Moses and Sinai, whose name is Yahweh (Exod 3:15–16; 6:2–8). Israel's covenant God is also the sovereign Creator of the universe. The simple juxtaposition of Yahweh and Elohim as a compound name for God ensures that we read Gen 1 and Gen 2–3 *together*, in binocular fashion, and that we understand that the God of Israel's covenant is also the God of creation.[97]

Beyond the different name for God, the literary style of Gen 2–3 is obviously quite distinct from Gen 1, as is noticeable immediately by the use of intricate word plays and proverbs rather than the repetitive formula-frames we saw in Gen 1.[98] A distinction in theology is also noticeable. Gen 1 portrays the transcendent and sovereign Creator commanding order from chaos by a series of cuts and separations, structuring the world and its inhabitants according to types and categories. Now, 2:4–25 complements that portrait with one in which the immanent and intensely personal Yahweh Elohim, LORD God, shapes humanity from clay like a potter (2:7). Rather than dicing and splicing the cosmos into structured categories and distinguishing types, this account emphasizes the joints and connections that bind the whole together: humans are related to the dust (note the word play at v. 7, see below), men and women are forever joined (another word play at 2:23), as are humans and animals (2:19–20). The whole is intended to create a world in which Yahweh God relates naturally and peacefully to humans.

The syntax of 2:4b–7 is not unlike that of 1:1–3.[99] As I suggested in the commentary on Gen 1, the Bible opens with a dependent, temporal clause (1:1), followed by parenthetical circumstantial clauses (1:2) before the main clause (1:3): "When God began to create heaven and earth (the earth being unformed and void, . . .), God said, . . . " Similarly here, v. 4b is the introductory dependent, temporal clause, vv. 5–6 the parenthetical comment with circumstantial clauses, and v. 7 the main clause: "In the day that the LORD God made the earth and the heavens (there being no plant of the field, . . .), then the LORD God formed man . . . "[100] Unlike Gen 1, for which the

---

[97] The literary technique may be called synoptic/resumptive-expansion, and will be encountered again in Genesis. See H. C. Brichto, *Toward a Grammar of Biblical Poetics* (1992), 13–19, although I do not accept Rabbi Brichto's overall rejection of the source critical approaches.

[98] S. Niditch, *Oral World and Written Word* (1996), 28–33. On the literary problems of Gen 2:4b–3:24 itself, see J. Van Seters, *Prologue to History* (1992), 107–34.

[99] And perhaps also like that of the *Enuma Elish*; E. A. Speiser, *Genesis* (1964), 19.

[100] The NRSV's use of double-hyphens marks the parenthetical comments differently; compare NJPS.

appearance of humankind was reserved for the climactic day six, here humankind arrives early and dramatically in the first main sentence. The human being "is now the pivot of the story, as in chapter 1 he was the climax."[101]

The circumstances of the earth at the beginning made it uninhabitable: no plant life was possible because of lack of rainfall and lack of planter, while only subterranean waters were present.[102] The idea that rainfall is essential for the growth of vegetation is a central feature of this narrative, and surely reflects the rain-based, dryland farming characteristic of the highlands of Syria–Palestine, in which biblical Israel lived. Here we have an important distinction between this account and origin myths found elsewhere, especially the great river valley civilizations of Egypt and Mesopotamia, where agriculture was dependent primarily on irrigation of the rivers.[103] Yet this account also has points of contact with ancient Near Eastern texts. First is a rare uncontested loanword from Mesopotamia in v. 6, *'ēd*, "stream," which clearly indicates that the waters in question here are subsurface flows rather than run-off or rainwater.[104] The second relates to the remarkable statement that Yahweh God blew the breath of life into the nostrils of the human (v. 7), which bears similarity to the *Instruction of Merikare*, in which the Egyptian god Re "made breath for their [humankind's] noses to live."[105]

Despite such points of contact with the ancient Near East, the creation of the human in v. 7 is more powerfully and philosophically stated than any others. Using familiar terminology from the artistic craft of the potter, Yahweh God formed (*yāṣar*, "shaped") the man, breathed life into his nostrils, and he became "a living being."[106] Of course, this last phrase has been debated for centuries and has played an enormous role in theological and philosophical speculation. Regardless of one's convictions about the nature of human life, we must not require this verse to say more than it intends. The "living being" is not some disembodied component of the human being, distinct from his physical existence; a "soul" comprising one

---

[101] D. Kidner, *Genesis* (1967), 58.

[102] The *waw* + subject + predicate constructions of vv. 5–6 mark this material as background information; Alviero Niccacci, *The Syntax of the Verb in Classical Hebrew Prose* (JSOTSup 86; Sheffield: JSOT Press, 1990), 35–41.

[103] T. Hiebert, *The Yahwist's Landscape* (1996), 36.

[104] Attested in both Sumerian, a d e a, "ground-flow, irrigation" and Akkadian, *edû*, "flood, ground-flow"; Paul V. Mankowski, *Akkadian Loanwords in Biblical Hebrew* (HSS 47; Winona Lake, Ind.: Eisenbrauns, 2000), 25–27.

[105] A parallel closer than Mesopotamian exemplars; Miriam Lichtheim, *Ancient Egyptian Literature: A Book of Readings* (Berkeley: University of California Press, 1973–1980), vol. 1.106; Miriam Lichtheim, "Merikare," *COS* 1.35:61–66, esp. 65; James K. Hoffmeier, "Some Thoughts on Genesis 1 & 2 and Egyptian Cosmology," *JANESCU* 15 (1983): 39–49.

[106] The idea of God as Potter occurs also in Mesopotamia, where according to the most common tradition, humanity was made from clay; Wilfred G. Lambert, "Technical Terminology for Creation in the Ancient Near East," in Jiří Prosecký, ed., *Intellectual Life of the Ancient Near East: Papers Presented at the 43rd Rencontre assyriologique international, Prague, July 1–5, 1996* (Prague: Oriental Institute, 1998), 189–93.

portion of a person's whole being. Rather the "living being" denotes the totality of the human.[107] Beyond the specific terminology used in v. 7, the importance of the human is clarified by his role in the earth. Far from a divine afterthought, as he is in certain ancient Near Eastern cosmogonic myths, the human is part of the solution to earth's problems. The lack of someone to till the ground (v. 5) is supplied by the human who plays the central role in this passage (v. 15). Humankind is earth's keeper.

The word translated "man" in v. 7 (*'ādām*) will later become a personal name, Adam (4:25, where see comment). In this verse, however, it is a common noun comprised of the same consonants as the word "ground" (*'ădāmâ*) and therefore forming a word play: "... the Lord God formed man (*'ādām*) from the dust of the ground (*'ădāmâ*)." The terminology solidifies the human's connections to the earth: he was created from it, his job is to cultivate it (2:5,15), and at death he will return to it (3:19).[108]

As God was a potter in v. 7, he becomes a gardener in v. 8: "the Lord God planted a garden in Eden." The domicile for the human is described as a luscious garden in the region of "Delight" (or simply "Eden"), located vaguely "in the east." Once routinely believed to be related to a Sumero–Akkadian term for "steppe, plain" the name Eden is more naturally associated with a West Semitic root *'dn* ("pleasure, luxury"), now attested in a ninth-century BCE Old Aramaic inscription from Tell Fekheriye.[109]

This garden has impressive trees, which play an important role in the narrative (v. 9). Among the trees at the center of the garden was "the tree of life," the fruit from which resulted in an unnaturally long lifespan (perhaps even immortality, 3:22). Trees were a nearly universal symbol of life in the ancient Near East, and "trees-of-life" particularly represented the divine power responsible for fertility in plant life.[110] In Israel, the lampstand (*měnōrâ*) in the wilderness tabernacle (and later, in the Solomonic temple) had enormous iconic power as attested by its similarity to stylized trees in the art of the Late Bronze and Iron Ages.[111] The light it provided contributed to the sense of God's presence in the tabernacle (and temple), and to the

---

[107] For recent survey of the issues and careful treatment of *nepeš ḥayyâ*, "living being," see Lawson G. Stone, "The Soul: Possession, Part, or Person?" in *What about the Soul? Neuroscience and Christian Anthropology*, ed. Joel B. Green (Nashville: Abingdon Press, 2004), 47–61, esp. 53–57.

[108] G. J. Wenham, *Genesis 1–15* (1987), 59.

[109] Alan R. Millard, "The Etymology of Eden," *VT* 34 (1984): 103–6; and for the inscription, see Alan R. Millard, "Hadad-yithʿi," *COS* 2.34:153–54.

[110] Othmar Keel, *Goddesses and Trees, New Moon and Yahweh: Ancient Near Eastern Art and The Hebrew Bible* (JSOTSup 261; Sheffield: Sheffield Academic Press, 1998), 16–57.

[111] Carol L. Meyers, *The Tabernacle Menorah: A Synthetic Study of a Symbol from the Biblical Cult* (ASOR Dissertation Series 2; Missoula, Mont.: Published by Scholars Press for the American Schools of Oriental Research, 1976), 95–130; O. Keel, *Goddesses and Trees, New Moon and Yahweh* (1998), 56–57.

concept that Israel's sanctuaries may be seen as microcosms of the universe, places of cosmic order in which God's reign is unquestioned and unending, much like the Garden of Eden. Another tree, "the tree of the knowledge of good and evil" was also apparently at the center of the garden. Although its name is obscure, perhaps intentionally so, eating its fruit results in a sort of cognitive enlightenment, which is not good, however, since it also bears moral culpability. The river flowing from Eden watered the garden and then branched into four other fresh-water rivers to irrigate the surrounding region (vv. 10–14). Thus the problems of earth at its inception (lack of irrigable water and lack of planter, vv. 5–6) have been met with the creation of the human and the garden.

Next, Yahweh God placed the human in the garden "to till it and keep it" (v. 15). The human has been put in the garden for a distinct purpose.[112] He is not there solely for self-gratification or enjoyment, but as the representative of Yahweh God to cultivate the earth (*ʿbd*, or simply "serve" it) and as the one responsible for keeping or protecting it (*šmr*, "save, protect"). Gen 1 emphasized the intimate relationship between God and humanity in the "image of God" concept (1:26–27). Here the intimacy is expressed in very different terms. God has entrusted the garden to the human, as his sole representative on earth, to develop it and guard it as humanity's home; a place where humans will have all their needs satisfied, and will live in freedom with each other and with God. There is, however, one stipulation. Just as v. 9 is the first mention in the Bible of any potential "bad" thing ("knowledge of good and *evil*"), so now the human receives the first prohibition (v. 17): "you shall not eat." Indeed, vv. 16–17 contain the first commandment of God to humanity. The one requirement for maintaining the equilibrium of peace and tranquility in the garden of Paradise, indeed for maintaining life itself, was the willingness to hear God's command to stay away from a single tree.

For the first time in the Bible, we encounter something that is "not good" (v. 18). Yahweh God determines that the human should not be alone, and sets out to make for him "a helper as his partner" (*ʿēzer kĕnegdô*). This phrase and passage can be abused, and certainly has been at times in history, to suppress the role of women in society or to argue for the supremacy of men in their relationship with women. But the text itself will not support contemporary forms of sexism, because such sexism is itself "disavowed" by Gen 2–3 in general, despite the overall patriarchal orientation of its ancient Near Eastern background.[113] The text's use of *ʾādām* as a generic term for humanity, the placement of the creation of woman at the culmination of the narrative in chapter 2, and the woman's intelligence and sensitivity in chapter 3 all contribute to the overall egalitarian thrust of the text in light of its patriarchal setting (see Closer Look "The Role of Women in Genesis 2–3" at p. 73).

---

[112] Both "to till it" and "keep it" are infinitives construct of purpose; B. T. Arnold and J. H. Choi, *A Guide to Biblical Hebrew Syntax* (2003), 71.

[113] Phyllis Trible, "Depatriarchalizing in Biblical Interpretation," *JAAR* 41 (1973): 30–48.

The phrase itself, "a helper as his partner," occurs only here in the Bible. The compound preposition *kĕnegdô* implies complementarity (hence the NRSV's "as his partner"), so the need is for someone "corresponding to him" as his counterpart.[114] While in English, the term "helper" may imply subordination or inferior rank, this is not the case in Hebrew. Various uses of the verb *ʿzr*, "help, support" refer to God's help for humans or of military help, and the noun *ʿēzer*, "help(er)" can likewise be used of God.[115] In such cases there is no hint of inferiority or subservience.[116] Because of the preceding paragraph, we should read the "help" that Eve supplied in light of humankind's task in v. 15, which is to cultivate and tend the earth. The man's strength alone is insufficient for this task. But the immediate context also has marriage and procreation in view, as well as general human companionship. Indeed, this story of human origins may be related to the lives of ordinary women in the highland villages of early Israel, whose societal and household roles may be reconstructed on the basis of archaeological and anthropological parallels. Prior to the monarchy, the subsistence work of families required the interdependence of men and women to perform the tasks facing families, such as clearing the dry and rocky land for agriculture and producing children to help with the farming.[117] At this early stage of Israelite thought, egalitarian views of the roles of men and women were God-given and unquestioned. Sadly, this would not continue to be the case.

God formed all animals "out of the ground" (v. 19), as he had done in creating the human and the trees (vv. 7 and 9). By pronouncing the name of each as they were created, the human participated in the creative process with God. When no suitable "helper as his partner" was found among them, Yahweh God 'constructed' the woman. Whereas potter terminology was used again for creation of animals in v. 19 (*yṣr*, "shaped"), the clause in v. 22 for the creation of the woman uses building terminology ("the rib . . . he made into a woman," *bnh* + preposition *l*). Taking material from the man, Yahweh God built a woman as a living work of art.[118] When God presents her to the man, the latter's response is revealing (v. 23). His "at last" signals joy at meeting a suitable companion in distinction to the animals. The poetic assertion that she is his "flesh and bone" (likely the source of the common English idiom "flesh and blood") is the Hebrew expression of kinship relationships and

---

114 *HALOT* 2:666; *DCH* 5:604.

115 Edouard Lipiński and Heinz-Josef Fabry, "*ʿāzar*," *TDOT* 11:12–18.

116 Phyllis Trible, *God and the Rhetoric of Sexuality* (OBT 2; Philadelphia: Fortress Press, 1978), 90; see however the reservations of David J. A. Clines, "What Does Eve Do To Help? and Other Irredeemably Androcentric Orientations in Genesis 1–3," in *What does Eve Do To Help? And Other Readerly Questions to the Old Testament*, ed. David J. A. Clines (JSOTSup 94; Sheffield: JSOT, 1990), 25–48, esp. 27–37.

117 Carol L. Meyers, *Discovering Eve: Ancient Israelite Women in Context* (New York: Oxford University Press, 1988), 92–94.

118 Christoph Uehlinger, "Eva als 'lebendiges Kunstwerk': Traditionsgeschichte zu Gen 2,21–22(23.24) und 3,20" *BN* 43 (1988): 90–99.

identifies her essence.[119] The man and the woman are uniquely each other's in a way that defines what it means to be human, which also distinguishes them from the animals.

Typical of this passage is the role of word play to crystallize the importance of the event. As the NRSV footnotes indicate, the words "woman" and "man" are very similar in Hebrew although not related by etymology: *'îš* and *'iššâ*, "man" and "woman" respectively.[120] The woman is the only component of creation in Gen 2 not taken "from the ground" (vv. 7, 9, 19), rather "out of Man this one was taken." As the human was formed from the dust of the ground (*'ādām* from *'ădāmâ*), so woman is built from the man (*'iššâ* from *'îš*). This folk etymology emphasizes their similarities while acknowledging their distinct differences. They are appropriately and distinctively individual, so as to be able to procreate, but also alike enough to be singly human.

Also characteristic of Gen 2–3 and indeed of much of Genesis is the role of etiology. Just as Gen 1 culminated in an etiological explanation for the cultic institution of Sabbath, so now Gen 2 concludes with the social institution of marriage (v. 24). The verse's opening "therefore" (*'al-kēn*) introduces the narrator's voice and brings us to an important consequence of the male–female relationship, and some would say to the goal toward which the narrative has been driven from the beginning.[121] Thus marriage is not simply about romance or raising a family, but about reuniting two parts of a sexual whole. The mysterious power driving the sexes together is explained in the common fleshly bond they had with each other originally, at the beginning of time. The power of sexual love is located in the primordial communal unity of the first two humans, which becomes a paradigm for all marriages. "Every marriage is a union; not a union of two strangers, but rather a reunion, a reconstitution, so to speak, of the primordial unity."[122]

Genesis 2 ends in a brief notation about the innocence of the first human couple (v. 25). Although they were "naked" (*'ărûmmîm*), there was no shame in it. Such an assertion surely draws a contrast between that primordial Edenic condition and all subsequent human personality. Nakedness and shame were thought to be naturally linked in cause and effect bond (3:7). But it has not always been so, which raises a question. What has happened? The suspense is not sustained long, as the narrative next explains how the first human couple lost their innocence.

The narration of Gen 3 takes us in a different direction. The preceding paragraphs have explained why humans have an intimate relationship with the earth, the

---

[119] N. P. Bratsiotis, "*bāśār*," *TDOT* 2:317–332, esp. 327–38; Karl-Martin Beyse, "*'eṣem*," *TDOT* 11:304–9, esp. 306.

[120] The "man" in question here (*'îš*) typically denotes an individual male, while (*'ādām*) is the generic term for humanity.

[121] So G. von Rad, *Genesis* (1961), 84; but see the objections that v. 24 is an addition and not central to the story; C. Westermann, *Genesis 1–11* (1984), 233.

[122] H. C. Brichto, *The Names of God* (1998), 79.

animals, with each other as sexual partners, and especially with God. Gen 3:1–7 continues the etiological interests by narrating how all of these relationships changed dramatically from their original conditions. Although philosophical and theological treatments routinely refer to this passage as "the fall" of humankind, the Hebrew word for "fall" (*npl*) is not used here. Nor is this concept used anywhere in Israel's Scriptures to relate this passage to humanity's fall from a state of grace infecting all subsequent humans. It was only in the traditions of later Judaism that the concept was first expressed, which was subsequently developed by the Apostle Paul, and especially by St. Augustine.[123] For the meantime, we may think of Gen 3 simply as "the transgression," while acknowledging that most of our faith traditions embrace this text as the cornerstone for further theological reflection on the human condition.

The syntax of 3:1 marks a new subject and announces a new character. The identity of this serpent (*nāḥāš*, Hebrew's most common word for "snake") has posed a perplexing question for interpreters.[124] Christian readers routinely identify him as Satan because of allusions to this text in the New Testament (e.g., John 8:44; Rom 16:20; Rev 12:9; 20:2). However, there is nothing in Israel's Scriptures that would equate the serpent with Satan, especially since ancient Israelites did not embody all evil in a single personage. The association with Satan in this text cannot be accredited to an earlier Yahwistic source or the final form of Genesis. Explicit equation of the serpent with the satan ("adversary"), or Satan, the accusing adversary of God, appears first in later Jewish and early Christian apocalyptic works (e.g., Wis 2:23–24; Sir 21:2; 4 Macc 18:8; Rev 1:9; 14–15; 20:2).

Our answer must therefore come from elsewhere. The power of snake-imagery in the ancient world cannot be denied. Serpents were noted for their wisdom, protection, healing, and knowledge of death.[125] The serpent's ability to produce venom meant it was a threat to life, and paradoxically its ability to slough off its own skin seemed to give it the ability to renew life. Among the several ways in which snakes and snake-like creatures came to be worshipped in religions of the ancient Near East, one was as part of the Canaanite fertility cult that later Israelite prophets condemned.[126] One possibility is that the mythological figure behind the serpent is Canaanite Baal, appearing in the form most tempting to ancient Israel, that of

---

[123] For references and critique, see C. Westermann, *Genesis 1–11* (1984), 275–76, and James Barr, *The Garden of Eden and the Hope of Immortality* (Minneapolis: Fortress, 1993), ix.

[124] C. Westermann, *Genesis 1–11* (1984), 237–39.

[125] And several of these characteristics are found in the Hebrew Bible; for the literature and summary, see Ronald S. Hendel, "Serpent," *DDD²* 744–47.

[126] Jeremy A. Black and Anthony R. Green, *Gods, Demons, and Symbols of Ancient Mesopotamia: An Illustrated Dictionary* (Austin: University of Texas Press, 1992), 166–68; Howard N. Wallace, *The Eden Narrative* (HSM 32; Atlanta, Ga.: Scholars Press, 1985), 147–81.

a serpent.[127] In this theory, the Garden of Eden reflects an old Canaanite myth of a sacred grove, with a tree of life, living waters, guardians at the entrance, and especially a serpent. Thus it is possible an ancient story has been demythologized in order to expose the real nature of Canaanite Baalism, and not only to expose it, but to universalize the experience for all Israel so that obedience to Yahweh's voice and repudiation of Baalism becomes paramount for all. It may be objected that such a reading runs counter to the explicit assertion of v. 1 that the serpent was one of the creatures "that the Lord God had made."[128] How can the serpent represent the archenemy of true faith when it is explicitly introduced as created by God? But the objection misses the symbolic transformation of the Canaanite mythology. God has created everything, including even the insidious serpent, which some unenlightened Israelites are tempted to follow. The transformation is profound because the serpent has no special powers beyond his ability to lie, trick, and confuse. But even these powers are only available to him when standing (or slithering) before humans. Before God himself, his answer will be one of resolute silence (3:14–15).

The serpent is "crafty" (or "shrewd," *'ārûm*), indeed more so than any other animal (3:1). The term has been chosen as a deliberate word play on the description of the humans as "naked" in the previous verse (*'ărûmmîm* in 2:25).[129] The *nude* humans have been duped by the *shrewd* serpent; they want to be shrewd (v. 6), but in the end they are only nude (v. 7).[130] The concept of wisdom is related to all this because the serpent knew something they did not, and indeed the object under discussion is the fruit of the *knowledge*-tree. The serpent informs them that God knows eating the fruit will give the humans knowledge that will make them like God, "*knowing* good and evil" (3:5).

The serpent's motivation is not stated, but a clue may lie in the characterization of him as one of the wild animals that "the Lord God had made" (3:1a), perhaps a reference to God's creation of all the animals as possible partners for the man (2:18–20). Since the serpent was "more crafty" than all the rest, he must have been the most likely candidate as a helping partner (*'ēzer kĕnegdô*) for the man, which

[127] F. F. Hvidberg, "The Canaanite Background of Gen I-III." Hvidberg avers that, if he is right about the identification of the serpent as "Prince Baal" (Bel-Zebul), the adversary of Yahweh in the struggle for Israel's soul, then "the old Jewish-Christian belief that the serpent is the devil is far more historically true than late Judaism and early Christianity could conceive"; Ibid., 288; see also Walther Eichrodt, *Theology of the Old Testament* (OTL; Philadelphia: Westminster Press, 1961–1967), 2:405.

[128] C. Westermann, *Genesis 1–11* (1984), 238; G. J. Wenham, *Genesis 1–15* (1987), 72.

[129] The words are not related etymologically, although they are used here in a deliberate spelling to sound nearly identical; Herbert Niehr, "*'āram*," *TDOT* 11:361–66, and for the suggestion that the serpent in Gen 3 is a figure evolved from the Egyptian goddess Renenutet, in order to critique the assumption that the serpent deity could be reconciled with Yahweh, see esp. 362–63.

[130] The English "nude"/ "shrewd" word play attempts to mimic the original; as in G. J. Wenham, *Genesis 1–15* (1987), 72.

may further explain the serpent's ability to speak, reason, and engage the woman in dialogue (she did not seem surprised). As the animal most like the man and therefore the best candidate as his companion, the serpent may therefore be motivated by resentment of the woman. He has been rejected as companion to the man, while the woman is the perfect fulfillment of the man's and God's desires. This may also explain why the serpent approaches the woman instead of the man; he is attacking his competition.[131]

A CLOSER LOOK — THE PROBLEM OF EVIL

The presence of the serpent in the Garden of Eden naturally raises the philosophical question of the problem of evil in the world: If God is all powerful and all good, and his creation itself is good, why does evil exist in the world?

Genesis 1 and 2 have been unequivocal in the assertion that God's created order is "good" in every respect. On the other hand, the "chaos" or unproductive emptiness, of Gen 1:2 has not been destroyed, but merely transformed and controlled by partitioning.[132] God limits and controls the primordial chaos, but he does not banish it entirely. Similarly, God's first creation, light, does not banish darkness forever, but is distinguished from it and alternates with it to establish day and night. Darkness is not eliminated but controlled through its regular alternation with light. Chaos is still present, but safely controlled and contained by God. In Gen 2, possibility for the return to chaos is present in the first divine command to humans: " . . . you shall not eat" (2:17). The point of departure for Gen 1–3 is not how evil invaded God's created order, but the fact that the humans rebelled! The text seems more interested in the nature of human rebellion, its consequences, and how to reverse its effects. So Genesis raises the question of the problem of evil for us philosophically, but it is not prepared to supply an answer.

Elsewhere the Bible takes steps toward an answer. The exilic prophecies we now call Second Isaiah (Isa 40–55) contain this astonishing statement on the lips of Yahweh himself (Isa 45:7).

I form light and create darkness,
I make weal (*'ōśeh šālôm*) and create woe (*bôrē'rā'*);
I the LORD do all these things.

It is possible that this and other such assertions in Isaiah 40–48 especially are intentionally critiquing and correcting Gen 1. So, it may be argued, mythological notions such as the existence of primeval matter before creation, the image of God,

---

[131] For this interpretation, see L. G. Stone, "The Soul: Possession, Part, or Person?" in *What About the Soul? Neuroscience and Christian Anthropology* (2004), 58–59.

[132] For some of what follows, see J. D. Levenson, *Creation and the Persistence of Evil* (1988), 121–27.

the consultation with heavenly council, and God's work and rest are perhaps refuted by certain cosmogonic hymns of Isaiah 40–48.[133] In this vein, Isa 45:7 asserts that despite appearances in Genesis, even evil is within God's purview, indeed, God himself created it.

Elsewhere, the Bible defends the nature of God by asserting that evil is an exception to the rule that one generally gets what one deserves (Job; Eccl.). In principle, the bad things that occur are a consequence of one's behavior, so that we can expect to reap what we sow (Deut 28; Ps. 7:13–17 [Eng. 12–16]; Hos 8:7, etc.). But the righteous sufferer, Job, illustrates that the rule does not always hold up during the circumstances of life. Ultimately we must admit the Bible does not offer a definitive answer to this question.

The contribution of Gen 1–3 to this problem is that human rebellion is the real source of evil, not God. Evil was present in potentiality in the Garden of Eden because of the inherent libertarianism of creation, or free will of humanity. "The source of evil is not metaphysical but moral."[134] The statement in Isa 45:7 is not interested in secondary causes, and asserts that God and God alone is sovereign, even over the ill-conceived choices of humanity.

The serpent engages the woman in conversation with a subtle and seemingly innocent question (3:1b). As innocent as it may sound in translation, however, the question itself implies astonishment that God would make such an unreasonable demand and exaggerates the details of the command itself. Yahweh God had, in fact, granted permission to eat freely from "every tree of the garden" with a single exception (2:16–17). Yet the serpent's question turns it all around. His query opens the dialogue by asking indignantly whether God actually prohibited her from eating from *any* of the good trees of the garden – a conversation starter with a barb. The woman immediately corrects the serpent, and the word order of her answer is emphatic: "from the fruit of the trees of the garden we may eat" (3:2, literal translation). But the serpent's question of distortion had opened the possibility of an alternate interpretation of God's command, reflected in her slight addition "nor shall you touch it."[135] "It is as though she wanted to set a law for herself by means of this exaggeration."[136]

The serpent's conversation starter now turns to its insidious purpose by responding specifically to her point of exaggeration. "You will not die" is a direct challenge

[133] M. Weinfeld, *The Place of the Law in the Religion of Ancient Israel* (2004), 110–117.

[134] N. M. Sarna, *Genesis* (1989), 16.

[135] Among other more subtle changes in the tenor of the original command; see Kenneth A. Mathews, *Genesis 1–11:26* (NAC 1A; Nashville: Broadman & Holman Publishers, 1996), 235–36.

[136] G. von Rad, *Genesis* (1961), 88; Walter Brueggemann, *Genesis: A Bible Commentary for Teaching and Preaching* (IBC; Atlanta: John Knox Press, 1982), 48.

to God's authority and character (3:4, compare 2:17). This is followed by a less direct nuancing – a reinterpretation of God's command, where we learn just how shrewd the serpent really is (3:5). Here he uses half-truths to distort the whole truth; misinformation to cloud reality. In a certain twisted sense, human eyes will indeed be opened, and they will, in fact, gain knowledge (3:5, compare 3:7).[137] And the narrative goes quickly to its sorry conclusion. The misdeed was infectious and communal: "and she also gave . . . and he ate" (3:6). No sooner had they eaten than their eyes were opened, their innocence irreversibly lost (3:7).

The real point of the narrative returns in v. 7 when the humans learn they are "naked" (*ʿêrummîm* again[138]), reminding the reader of their shameless innocence in 2:25 and the serpent's shrewdness in 3:1. They have gained the serpent's shrewdness (*ʿārûm*, v. 1), and become shrewd themselves (*ʿêrummîm*, v. 7), which is to say they have become shamefully naked. The issue here is shameful nakedness rather than simple nudity, linking concepts of nakedness and knowledge, and implicitly sexuality (cf. vv. 10–11).[139] They sacrificed their blissful innocence at the altar of self-serving knowledge, especially in light of the limited pleasure afforded in the fruit (v. 6): "good for food . . . a delight to the eyes . . . to be desired to make one wise . . . " As Gen 1 is the answer to polytheism, atheism, and nihilism (see Bridging the Horizons at Gen 1, p. 51), so this text belies hedonism. It is impossible to hold that self-gratification and pleasure are the principal virtues of life and should be the aim of our actions if we grant the truth of this text: obedience to the Creator and relating rightly to God are the principal virtues of life. Indeed, Adam and Eve in Gen 2 had all that the hedonist could hope for. But the sole purpose for Eden was right relationship with Eden's Maker, as the humans learn in Gen 3.

After this transgression, the reader is prepared for swift and terrible annihilation of the human couple. Instead, they hear "the sound of the Lord God walking in the garden" and subsequently they hear his voice calling to them (3:8–9). The grace of God was evident in the creation of the world and of Eden, with appropriate blessings and gifts (Gen 1:1–2:24). But this is somehow different. There in Gen 1 and 2 we savor God's acts of power and grace, but this gracious forgiveness and divine mercy in the face of human recalcitrance is a new and somehow deeper insight into the character of God. Even so, v. 8 begins a new section of Gen 3 devoted to the consequences of transgression. So the chapter moves summarily from crime (vv. 1–7) to punishment (vv. 8–24). This is the first time we encounter this theme that extends into the rest of the Primeval History (Gen 1–11), and indeed throughout the Pentateuch as a whole: "Creation-Uncreation-Re-creation."[140] The sinful actions of humanity

---

[137] R. W. L. Moberly, "Did the Serpent Get it Right?" *JTS* 39 (1988): 1–27.

[138] Spelled in the expected form, since the alternate spelling of 2:25 was used to prepare for the word play of 3:1.

[139] H. C. Brichto, *The Names of God* (1998), 82–83.

[140] D. J. A. Clines, *The Theme of the Pentateuch* (1978), 61–79.

reverse the creative activity of God, presenting a suspenseful question whether God will be merciful or punish. The narrative relieves the suspense with punishment that never exceeds the crime, and with surprising glimpses of the forgiving heart of God.

In Gen 3:8–13, Yahweh God exposes the transgression. As the man and woman were ashamed in each other's presence (3:7), now they realize their guilt and shame in the presence of God. The sound of Yahweh walking about in the garden in the dusk's coolness may or may not have originated in the concept of a sacred tree in a cultic place.[141] But in this context, it clearly connotes the intimacy that God and humanity enjoyed in Eden prior to the transgression. And this is the tragedy, because the loss of that free intimacy is apparent to the humans instantaneously. They were ashamed to be in God's presence, and so they hid themselves "among the trees of the garden," thus attempting to turn God's good and gracious gifts (2:16) into barriers against his wrath.

The Bible has no portraits of divine pathos more tender than Yahweh's voice in Eden intoning (3:9): "Where are you?" Only a single word in Hebrew, this rhetorical question evokes the stern but loving voice of a father addressing a wayward child. It might be translated, "And what have you been up to just now?"[142] The question is not meant to elicit information about their whereabouts, as though God is confused by their absence. Rather God is encouraging introspection; why exactly are they just there, beyond those trees, hiding from the Lord who has provided all their needs and blessed them abundantly?

Having now been exposed, the man emerges from hiding and attempts a feeble explanation (3:10). Yahweh God assumes the position of a divine Prosecutor, asking two penetrating questions intended to explore the contours of the crime. The defense offered by the humans is laced with recrimination, self-preservation, and deflection of blame (3:12–13), all of which, of course, are endemic to the nature of humans, as we all recognize. The grammatical syntax of the man's response, and to a lesser extent the woman's, isolates the accused for emphasis: "The woman . . . *she* gave me fruit from the tree, and I ate." And so Adam blamed Eve (and God implicitly), and Eve blamed the serpent. Of course the reader understands how this works, because Cain blamed Abel (Gen 4:5), Joseph's brothers blamed him (Gen 37:4), the Israelites blamed Moses (Exod 16:2–3; Num 14:2–4), King Saul blamed his subjects (1 Sam 15:24), and on it goes. Finger-pointing is the response of choice wherever guilt is present.

The Prosecutor has heard enough, there being no need to hear from the serpent. His verdict announces punishment for all three protagonists in turn, first the serpent (3:14–15), next the woman (3:16), and last the man (3:17–19). The punishments are announced in poetry, which may reflect the cultural expectations for legal

---

[141] O. Keel, *Goddesses and Trees, New Moon and Yahweh* (1998), 41–42.

[142] E. A. Speiser, *Genesis* (1964), 25.

verdicts.[143] True to the etiological interests of this narrative, the punishments explain much about the resultant state of things for each personage. So we learn here why serpents crawl on the ground (3:14), why enmity persists between humans and serpents (3:15), why there is a close association between sexual pleasure and the pain of childbirth (3:16), why life and toil are inextricable and death is unavoidable (3:17–19).

The judgments meted out are often called "curses," although only the serpent and the soil are actually cursed by God. The rest are to be seen as logical and natural corollaries of the role played by each transgressor. Indeed, in the Hebrew Scriptures, divine punishment mirrors precisely the sin being punished. Judgment and punishment follow a sort of "poetic justice," meaning the penalty inflicted on the sinner matches repayment in kind for the harm done in the offense.[144] Such commensurate justice is a reflection of God's character as experienced by ancient Israel and expressed often in creedal form: Yahweh is "a God merciful and gracious, slow to anger, and abounding in steadfast love and faithfulness . . . forgiving iniquity and transgression and sin . . . yet by no means clearing the guilty . . . " (Exod 34:6–7; cf. texts dependent upon it: Exod 20:5–6; Num 14:18–19; Neh 9:17; Pss 86:15; 103:8; 145:8; Joel 2:13; Jonah 4:2).

The serpent's punishment (3:14–15) involves both a life function (i.e., a new style of locomotion) and a relationship, as will be the case also with the humans.[145] This curse does not mean the serpent once walked upright with legs anymore than it wants the reader to assume the serpent will now literally eat dust as opposed to its previous fare. Rather these are idioms for humiliation. The serpent, who had been characterized as the shrewdest of all the animals, will now become the most humble. The changed relationship is between the offspring of the woman and that of the serpent, which relationship will henceforth be marred by enmity (3:15). The concluding lines of poetry in the serpent's curse are fraught with translation difficulties: "he will strike your head, and you will strike his heel." The verb "strike" has been used twice by NRSV in order to retain a word play, which evidently involved two different but similar verbal roots originally: "crush" (*šwp*) and "snap at, hound" (*š'p* or *šwp*).[146] The original sense was something like, "he will crush (*yĕšûpĕkā*) your head, and you will snap at (*tĕšûpennû*) his heel." Whatever the philological specifics, this new cursed relationship is one in which humans and serpents habitually try

---

[143] C. Westermann, *Genesis 1–11* (1984), 257.

[144] Patrick D. Miller, Jr., *Sin and Judgment in the Prophets: A Stylistic and Theological Analysis* (SBLMS 27; Chico, Calif.: Scholars Press, 1982).

[145] Jerome T. Walsh, "Genesis 2:4b-3:24: A Synchronic Approach," *JBL* 96 (1977): 161–77, esp. 168; repr. in R. S. Hess and D. T. Tsumura, eds., *I Studied Inscriptions from Before the Flood* (1994), 362–82.

[146] Both verbs, however, are rare and used mostly in obscure poetic texts, which puts us on uncertain footing, and *š'p* "snap at," could be written also with internal *waw* (*šwp*), which complicates matters further; Cornelis Van Dam, "*šwp*," *NIDOTTE* 4:66–68.

to kill each other. Occurring as it does at the conclusion of God's curse against the serpent, the reader is to assume the human has a distinct advantage in this contest. In fact, it may be that the particular form and function of the verb in the second clause connotes attempt or endeavor rather than fact: "you will try to snap at his heel."[147] Thus the woman's seed will defeat the serpent, while the serpent will try in vain to bite the heel of his enemy.

In addition to the complexities of the poetry, 3:15b has a long and complicated interpretation history. Judaism found in these words a messianic hope for victory over Satan, as evidenced by the translations.[148] Subsequently, interpretations of the curse as a prophecy of Christ's victory over Satan became popular among a few early Christians (Justin and Irenaeus), and finally became widespread in the modern era.[149] Such interpretations assume "offspring" (*zera*) should be taken singularly, referring to Christ as the woman's seed, rather than collectively to denote humankind in general. As such, this verse was labeled the *protevangelium*, the "first good news," or first messianic prophecy, despite scant New Testament associations (Rom 16:20, and perhaps Heb 2:14 and 1 Cor 15:25). Yet as one recent interpreter has observed, "the verse is good news whether we understand *zera* [offspring] singularly or collectively."[150] Although it must be cautioned that messianic prophecy is not intended in 3:15, it remains an attractive appropriation of these words to find their fullest meaning (*sensus plenior*) in a future member of the human race destroying the serpent as part of God's redemptive plan, especially as it might relate to ancient Israel's royal ideology.[151]

The woman's punishment is equally difficult (3:16). Unlike the other two, her sentencing contains no causal clause, as begins Yahweh's speech to the serpent ("*because* you have done this,..." 3:14) and to the man ("*because* you have listened to the voice of your wife,..." 3:17). It is entirely possible the woman is somehow less culpable because she was deceived ("tricked" is her word, 3:13) by the serpent, in distinction to the willful rebellion of the serpent and the man.[152] Nevertheless, her punishment involves impairment of her roles in life, since she was created as the man's companion and as the mother of his children (2:20–24, although the role of childbearing is implicit only). As the serpent's punishment was both functional and relational (i.e., he became a crawler and has enmity with the woman's seed), so the woman will experience pain in childbirth and pain in relating to the

---

[147] Paul P. Saydon, "The Conative Imperfect in Hebrew," *VT* 12/1 (1962): 124–26, esp. 126.

[148] G. J. Wenham, *Genesis 1–15* (1987), 80–81.

[149] C. Westermann, *Genesis 1–11* (1984), 260–61.

[150] V. P. Hamilton, *The Book of Genesis, Chapters 1–17* (1990), 200.

[151] So G. J. Wenham, *Genesis 1–15* (1987), 81; and V. P. Hamilton, *The Book of Genesis, Chapters 1–17* (1990), 200, n. 20; both relying to some degree on William S. LaSor, "Prophecy, Inspiration, and *Sensus Plenior*," *TynBul* 29 (1978): 49–60, esp. 56–57.

[152] K. A. Mathews, *Genesis 1–11:26* (1996), 248, which may also be implied by the Apostle Paul in 2 Cor 11:3, and compare 1 Tim. 2:13–15.

man.[153] Discussion of these punishments often debates their *prescriptive* versus *descriptive* intent. Are the punishments announced here intended simply to *describe* life after the transgression, and resulting from it? This is unfortunately the way things are in life, no doubt about it. Or, are they to *prescribe* Yahweh God's decree or will for life after the transgression? This is the way life *should be* now that the humans have lost their innocence. Without doubt, 3:16b has been used at times to advocate suppression of women (see Closer Look at "The Role of Women in Genesis 2–3" at p. 73), which is an unfortunate reading of "he shall rule over you" as prescriptive, as though this is Yahweh God's decretive plan for the post-transgression world. But the pain of childbirth in the first half of the verse is without doubt descriptive. Whatever the nuanced meanings of the archaic poetry and terminology, now partly lost to us, the rulership of the man is no more prescriptive than pain in childbirth. If God had decreed strife as indispensable to marriage, then God would also have prescribed as much pain as possible in childbirth. Neither is intended by this text.

All such prescriptive approaches miss the point of human responsibility and the nature of punishment in the Hebrew Scriptures. The judgments of 3:15–19 are announcements of the consequences of their actions, and those consequences are perfectly commensurate with their crimes. The ancient Israelites were unconcerned about secondary causes, and therefore all of these consequences are related directly to Yahweh God: "I will put enmity between you and the woman . . ."; "I will greatly increase your pangs in childbearing. . . ." But in so announcing the judgments, God is describing the new circumstances of life on earth for the serpent, the woman, and the man, rather than decreeing his first and best will for them.

Along the lines of this *descriptive* approach, 3:16b contains fascinating and perhaps decisive parallels with Gen 4:7. The terms "desire" (noun, *těšûqâ*) and "rule" (verb *mšl*) occur together again there in a similar context, in what appears to be an idiomatic expression. Their recurrence so near each other in chapters 3 and 4 is illuminating in itself, but what is especially striking is the rarity of the noun "desire," which occurs only three times in the Bible (Gen 3:16; 4:7, and Song 7:11 [Eng. 7:10]). In Gen 4:7, sin's "desire" for Cain connotes an attempt to control and dominate Cain, and therefore the woman's "desire" for the man may likewise be an impulse to break the egalitarian relationship and initiate a struggle to dominate him.[154] Just as Cain must master ("rule," *mšl*) sin, so the man will rule the woman, and the marriage relationship will degenerate into a struggle for dominance: "to love and to cherish" will become "to desire and to dominate."[155] In this light, it is

---

[153] Carol Meyers translates the woman's punishment as requiring toil and the bearing of children, highlighting the need for both productivity and procreativity in early Israelite culture; C. L. Meyers, *Discovering Eve* (1988), 117–21. For more on all the issues discussed here, see the classic study of Phyllis Trible, *God and the Rhetoric of Sexuality* (OBT 2; Philadelphia: Fortress Press, 1978).

[154] Susan T. Foh, "What Is the Woman's Desire?" *WTJ* 37 (1975): 376–83.

[155] D. Kidner, *Genesis* (1967), 71.

also possible that the form and function of "rule" in the second clause connotes attempt or endeavor rather than fact: "he will attempt to rule over you."[156]

Yahweh God's judgment on the man (3:17–19) is also both functional and relational. This time the two punishments are interwoven, since the ground becomes intractable to his cultivation (relational) resulting in painful toil and burdening his eating (functional).[157] In essence, his crime results in another curse, this time against the ground so that he must labor for his subsistence. The poetry ties his crime and punishment together tightly through the five occurrences of the verb "eat" (*'kl*). Because Adam *ate* of the tree he was commanded not to *eat*, he will now be forced to *eat* of the cursed ground, *eating* plants of the field and *eating* bread by the sweat of his brow. He ate the wrong thing, so now he will eat food acquired through labor, reminding him of his human weaknesses and limitations. And his humanity comes to the fore again by means of the previous word play on "man" and "ground" (cf. 2:7). The punishment is announced to "the man" (*'ādām*), but it consists of a curse against "the ground" (*'ădāmâ*) on account of him, and to which he will return because he is, after all, from the dust of the ground.

In one sense, the man and woman share the same punishment – "pain" (*'iṣṣābôn*[158]), hers in childbirth and his in painful toil. Hers is more intimately associated with her purpose in life, while his is an *ad hoc* arrangement, creating a different role for him. Eden's "free lunch" has been turned into a "no work – no eat" plan. The need to work the ground for meager existence reflects realities of Syria–Palestine more than the rich alluvial soil of southern Mesopotamia, and this may reflect again the western orientation of the text even while the setting is in the east.[159] The memory of Israel's ancestry in ancient Mesopotamia provides the backdrop for the harsh realities of a life in the Levant, where husbands and wives had children and raised their families while working the rocky ground for meager subsistence.

The unit closes with narrative explanations for Eve's name, the ubiquitous use of clothing for humans, and why the loss of Eden is irreversible (3:20–24). Eve receives her name before Adam's is used in the narrative (cf. commentary at 4:25). Her name, like names often in the Bible, is a popular etymology associating the name with the root "to make alive" (**ḥwy*), and in this form, "Life-giver," it anticipates Gen 4:1.[160]

---

[156] Similar to the possible volitive imperfect in 3:15; V. P. Hamilton, *The Book of Genesis, Chapters 1–17* (1990), 202, n. 25; P. P. Saydon, "The Conative Imperfect in Hebrew," although Saydon considers only v. 15.

[157] J. T. Walsh, "Genesis 2:4b–3:24: A Synchronic Approach," 168.

[158] As in v. 16, but obscured by NRSV's "toil" in v. 17.

[159] T. Hiebert, *The Yahwist's Landscape* (1996), 51–62, without accepting, however, Hiebert's suggestion that the Garden of Eden should be equated with a primitive Jordan Valley prior to its catastrophic ruin in the conflagration of Sodom and Gomorrah.

[160] Scott C. Layton, "Remarks on the Canaanite Origin of Eve," *CBQ* 59/1 (1997): 22–32:31. Layton shows that "Eve" should be added to the list of symbolic names in the Hebrew Bible found in Werner Weinberg, "Language Consciousness in the Old Testament," *ZAW* 92 (1980): 185–204, esp. 197.

As an act of loving kindness, Yahweh God replaced their poor loincloths made of sewn fig leaves (3:7) with garments of pelt more suitable for their new lives outside Eden.

The loss of Eden itself is important because it also involves, of course, loss of its tree of life (vv. 22–24). In explaining why humans must die, the text serves the same function as certain ancient Near Eastern myths. So, for example, in one such story, the wiseman, Adapa, listens to the advice of a deity he has offended and rejects another deity's offer of the bread of life and the water of life, and he thereby loses immortality for himself and all humanity.[161] In ancient Mesopotamia, loss of immortal life is an almost comic tragedy and humans are ridiculed by the gods (in Adapa's case). But in Gen 3:22–24, Yahweh God banishes the humans from Eden as an act of grace and mercy, just as he lovingly clothes them in v. 21. To be sure, God resolutely throws them out and locks the door behind them. But in so doing, God is also protecting humans from overreaching their grasp, almost as though God is ensuring their continuing humanity as opposed to a lesser option – that of becoming trapped in immortality. To be human is thus to live in a balance between boundless potentiality and a "grounded" realism that life is short. This balance understands that being human holds potential for life with God in a world less than it was created to be, while humans *can* become (nearly) what they were created to be. On the other side, this balance also understands the limitations of human existence, and loathes the human impulse to reach for more than humans can achieve. It is this delicate balance, accomplished when Yahweh God sealed Eden off, ensuring that humans will remain free moral agents and thus essentially human, which is above all what Yahweh God desires in creation.

Genesis 1–3 constructs an anthropology that is foundational for the rest of the Bible. Humankind has a complex nature, created to have dominion in the likeness of God, created with an essentially good nature, but also created with a free will and independence to act as they choose.[162] Gen 3 serves as an indictment against the human misuse of that freedom to near ruinous effect. As central as its etiological interests are, Gen 3 is not merely an attempt to explain the origins of evil, or even to explain how sin and death came into the world; it is about more than "a snake

---

[161] Stephanie Dalley, *Myths from Mesopotamia: Creation, the Flood, Gilgamesh, and Others* (Oxford: Oxford University Press, 2000), 182–88; Benjamin R. Foster, "The Adapa Story," *COS* 1.129:449. "Adapa" is in fact a phonetic variant of *Adam(a); Richard S. Hess, *Studies in the Personal Names of Genesis 1–11* (AOAT 234; Kevelaer, Neukirchen-Vluyn: Verlag Butzon & Bercker, Neukirchener Verlag, 1993), 64–65. For the important ways in which the Gilgamesh Epic helps understand the explanation of death in Gen 3:22–24, see H. C. Brichto, *The Names of God* (1998), 86–96.

[162] Humankind is thus created "with a task, a liberation, and an indictment"; Douglas A. Knight, "Cosmogony and Order in the Hebrew Tradition," in *Cosmogony and Ethical Order: New Studies in Comparative Ethics*, eds. Robin W. Lovin and Frank Reynolds (Chicago: University of Chicago Press, 1985), 143.

talking, a woman balking, and a God stalking."[163] This text is primarily interested in why the individual human, *by nature of his or her humanity*, is forever afflicted by alienation, guilt, and the inevitability of death, and yet why humans still have this potential for life with God.

> The narrative of Gen 2–3 will always retain its meaning for humankind. Something basic is said about humanity that no religious or ideological, no scientific, technical or medical development or change can or will in any way alter. It is part of human existence that a person is fallible. One cannot be a human being other than a fallible human being.[164]

For this reason, the subsequent concept of "original sin" articulated by the New Testament and codified in church dogma is altogether reasonable and compatible with this text (e.g., Rom 5:12–21).[165] But that is not to say that "the fall" is explicitly taught here, nor any abstract concept of universal sin transmitted to successive generations infecting all humanity. Rather Gen 2–3 situates humankind's position vis-à-vis God as one of opposition and estrangement, and gives explanation only for the common experience of all humans in alienation, guilt, and death.

A CLOSER LOOK — THE ROLE OF WOMEN IN GENESIS 2–3

Many interpreters through the centuries have placed principal blame for the transgression in the Garden of Eden on the woman, or otherwise used this text to suppress women in a multitude of ways. In particular, the circumstances of Eve's creation to be "a helper as his partner" (2:18, 20), her role in conversing with the serpent and first taking the fruit (3:1–7), and the specifics of her share of the punishment (3:16) have led some to argue for a complementarian (as opposed to egalitarian) role for women in the family, in church or synagogue, or in society generally. While such approaches are reprehensible to today's sensibilities, it is not sufficient merely to deny that it was Eve's fault or to assert her equality. Fortunately since the 1970s several studies have reconsidered the subtleties of the text and improved our understanding of its contours.

A significant turning point was Phyllis Trible's article in 1973, in which she honestly addressed the "patriarchal" nature of Israelite religion and literature.[166] Trible argued that the "intentionality of biblical faith" is above all salvific, for both women and men, and that the "hermeneutical challenge" today is "to translate biblical faith without sexism." Specifically with regard to Gen 2–3, Trible demonstrated that by

---

[163] H. C. Brichto, *The Names of God* (1998), 81.

[164] C. Westermann, *Genesis 1–11* (1984), 277.

[165] H. C. Brichto, *The Names of God* (1998), 96; cf. also Mark E. Biddle, *Missing the Mark: Sin and its Consequences in Biblical Theology* (Nashville: Abingdon Press, 2005).

[166] P. Trible, "Depatriarchalizing in Biblical Interpretation"; all quotes in this paragraph are from her page 31.

comparison with the patriarchal orientation of the ancient Near East, the biblical portrait of humankind as "Adam" is an intentionally generic term and therefore disavows or precludes sexism. The androcentric and patriarchal point-of-reference in the text is not to be denied, but to be read in context of the ancient world in which it was produced.

Trible advanced our understanding of these texts in ways hard to overstate, although there are several points at which her arguments can and should be critiqued. In particular, Phyllis Bird has cautioned that the ancient writers were not feminists, and that they were often making no comment at all on the relationship between the sexes, either complementarian or egalitarian.[167] On the "helper" role of Eve, D. J. A. Clines has corrected the view that the term actually bears connotations of superiority, based allegedly on God's occasional appearance as "helper," and that in fact, it carries no implications regarding status.[168] Relying on archaeology and anthropology, Carol L. Meyers studied the subsistence work of families in the highland villages of premonarchic Israel, and reconstructed the societal and household roles of ordinary women during this early period.[169] In light of her research, the Eden narrative may be said to reflect culturally specific realities of a vital interdependence between men and women, an egalitarian local life, perhaps prior to its disruption by the early monarchy, which presumably eroded the status of women. More recently, Meyers has observed that several examples of female professionals can be found in ancient Israelite culture, which means that the designation "patriarchal" may not be strictly appropriate for all aspects of its society.[170] Jo Ann Hackett has observed that women's status in society ordinarily improves only in exceptional periods of social dysfunctionality, and it is possible the power Eve exerted in Eden reflects an egalitarian ideal for ancient Israel that was not the norm in much of its history.[171]

---

[167] Phyllis Bird, "'Male and Female He Created Them': Gen 1:27b in the Context of the Priestly Account of Creation," *HTR* 74 (1981): 129–59; repr. in R. S. Hess and D. T. Tsumura, eds., *I Studied Inscriptions from Before the Flood* (1994), 329–61, and compare P. Trible, *God and The Rhetoric of Sexuality* (1978), 12–23.

[168] D. J. A. Clines, "What Does Eve Do To Help? and Other Irredeemably Androcentric Orientations in Genesis 1–3," in *What Does Eve Do To Help? And Other Readerly Questions to the Old Testament* (1990), esp. 27–32.

[169] C. L. Meyers, *Discovering Eve* (1988), 117–19.

[170] She has recently made the case that, since ancient Israel was not truly egalitarian, we should think in terms of the anthropological model "heterarchy" rather than simple patriarchy or hierarchy. This approach would enable us to avoid simplistic binary interpretations of the diversity and complexity of Israelite society; Carol L. Meyers, "Hierarchy or Heterarchy? Archaeology and the Theorizing of Israelite Society," in *Confronting the Past: Archaeological and Historical Essays on Ancient Israel in Honor of William G. Dever*, eds. Seymour Gitin, J. E. Wright, and J. P. Dessel (Winona Lake, Ind.: Eisenbrauns, 2006), 245–54.

[171] Jo Ann Hackett, "Women's Studies and the Hebrew Bible," in *The Future of Biblical Studies: The Hebrew Scriptures*, eds. Richard E. Friedman and H. G. M. Williamson (SemeiaSt; Atlanta: Scholars Press, 1987), 141–64, esp. 150–54.

Such refinements of Trible's initial work will no doubt continue to improve our understanding of these important texts. They are not quite so androcentric and patriarchal as at first assumed, although Trible's central point on translating biblical faith without sexism is valid and remains a significant goal for all future research in this area.

GENESIS 4:1–26 HUMAN ORIGINS, PART 2: CAIN, ABEL, AND THE FIRST HUMAN INSTITUTIONS

(4:1) Now the man knew his wife Eve, and she conceived and bore Cain, saying, "I have produced a man with the help of the LORD."

(4:2) Next she bore his brother Abel. Now Abel was a keeper of sheep, and Cain a tiller of the ground.

(4:3) In the course of time Cain brought to the LORD an offering of the fruit of the ground,

(4:4) and Abel for his part brought of the firstlings of his flock, their fat portions. And the LORD had regard for Abel and his offering,

(4:5) but for Cain and his offering he had no regard. So Cain was very angry, and his countenance fell.

(4:6) The LORD said to Cain, "Why are you angry, and why has your countenance fallen?

(4:7) If you do well, will you not be accepted? And if you do not do well, sin is lurking at the door; its desire is for you, but you must master it."

(4:8) Cain said to his brother Abel, "Let us go out to the field." And when they were in the field, Cain rose up against his brother Abel, and killed him.

(4:9) Then the LORD said to Cain, "Where is your brother Abel?" He said, "I do not know; am I my brother's keeper?"

(4:10) And the LORD said, "What have you done? Listen; your brother's blood is crying out to me from the ground!

(4:11) And now you are cursed from the ground, which has opened its mouth to receive your brother's blood from your hand.

(4:12) When you till the ground, it will no longer yield to you its strength; you will be a fugitive and a wanderer on the earth."

(4:13) Cain said to the LORD, "My punishment is greater than I can bear!

(4:14) Today you have driven me away from the soil, and I shall be hidden from your face; I shall be a fugitive and a wanderer on the earth, and anyone who meets me may kill me."

(4:15) Then the LORD said to him, "Not so! Whoever kills Cain will suffer a sevenfold vengeance." And the LORD put a mark on Cain, so that no one who came upon him would kill him.

(4:16) Then Cain went away from the presence of the LORD, and settled in the land of Nod, east of Eden.

(4:17) Cain knew his wife, and she conceived and bore Enoch; and he built a city, and named it Enoch after his son Enoch.

(4:18) To Enoch was born Irad; and Irad was the father of Mehujael, and Mehujael the father of Methushael, and Methushael the father of Lamech.

(4:19) Lamech took two wives; the name of the one was Adah, and the name of the other Zillah.

(4:20) Adah bore Jabal; he was the ancestor of those who live in tents and have livestock.

(4:21) His brother's name was Jubal; he was the ancestor of all those who play the lyre and pipe.

(4:22) Zillah bore Tubal-cain, who made all kinds of bronze and iron tools. The sister of Tubal-cain was Naamah.

(4:23) Lamech said to his wives: "Adah and Zillah, hear my voice; you wives of Lamech, listen to what I say: I have killed a man for wounding me, a young man for striking me.

(4:24) If Cain is avenged sevenfold, truly Lamech seventy-sevenfold."

(4:25) Adam knew his wife again, and she bore a son and named him Seth, for she said, "God has appointed for me another child instead of Abel, because Cain killed him."

(4:26) To Seth also a son was born, and he named him Enosh. At that time people began to invoke the name of the LORD.

Genesis 4 is organized around birth announcements ("Now the man/ Cain/Adam knew his wife... and she [conceived and] bore..." vv. 1, 17, 25), which divide the materials into three components. First, Cain's birth announcement is immediately expanded into a narrative on his murder of Abel (vv. 1–16). Second, Enoch's birth announcement introduces etiological explanations of the first human cultural institutions, including urbanization, pastoral agriculture, music, and metallurgy (vv. 17–22), and is expanded further with poetic fragments about Lamech (vv. 23–24). Finally, Seth's birth announcement briefly calls attention to the importance of his line for its contributions to public worship (vv. 25–26).

This chapter illustrates a literary style that will become standard for much of the rest of Genesis. We have here a mixture of narrative and genealogical material, or "narrative" and "numerative."[172] The narrative portions constitute expansions or elaborations on the genealogical notices, which presumably were primary. Moreover, the announcement of Seth's birth (4:25–26) anticipates Gen 5:3, and illustrates another important literary technique of Genesis, and to some degree in the Bible generally – that of the eclipse of birth order or rank. In the ancient world, privilege is ascribed to the firstborn son, who ordinarily is granted precedence over his brothers,

---

[172] Westermann's "Erzählung" and "Aufzählung," see C. Westermann, *Genesis 1–11* (1984), 3–4, Claus Westermann, *Genesis 12–36: A Commentary* (Minneapolis: Augsburg Pub. House, 1985), 54–58; and my introduction, p. 5.

and receives a double share of inheritance (Gen 43:33; 49:3; Deut 21:15–17).[173] This "right of the firstborn" (*mišpaṭ habbĕkōrâ*), or principle of primogeniture, will be assumed in several of the genealogies of Genesis in such phrases as "Patriarch A became the father of patriarch B, . . . and had other sons and daughters." Patriarch B is presumed in such lists to be the firstborn, and is the one through whom the ancestral line is traced. However, the heroes of Genesis – those ancestors of Israel whose stories are told in the narrative sections – are generally not the firstborn. Seth, Isaac, and Jacob are all younger brothers, while the birth rank of Abraham is somewhat ambiguous, and Noah serves as an exception. Gen 4 thus explains how the firstborn, Cain, is disqualified, the second son is dead, and how the younger son, Seth, becomes the ancestor of Israel, among Adam's "other sons and daughters" (Gen 5:4).

In addition to the interlocking use of narrative and numerative materials, and the theme of the younger son supplanting the older, Gen 4 also illustrates the important role of genealogical materials in the message of Genesis (see Closer Look at p. 82). On the one hand, each patriarch is the father of other children who are not part of the Israelite ancestry and who become the ancestors of other people groups in the known world. Through this process of differentiation, the book gives explanation to other populations in a kind of ethnic map of the world, and explains further the way Israel related to those populations. On the other hand, while the world's populations are described through this process of branching, Israel's lineage is traced in distinction to these through a straight line, from Adam to Jacob.[174] In each generation, only one son continues the Israelite ancestry. This process is used routinely in Genesis to present and discuss to the full extent required by the narrative each of the "other" descendants of Israel's ancestors first before picking up the descent line of interest. So in Gen 4, Cain and his son, Enoch, are discussed and in a sense, placed aside before taking up the account of Seth. Another literary feature of this technique is the way each unit often concludes with a brief notation on the patriarch of interest, in this case Seth (4:25–26), before the next unit turns to his descent line in more detail, from Seth to Noah and his sons (5:1–32).[175]

Life outside the Garden of Eden is different. The Bible's first birth announcement signals the changes (v. 1): sexual relations, conception, birth, and the naming of children.[176] The man and woman find comfort in their relationship with each

---

[173] Bill T. Arnold, "*bkr*," *NIDOTTE* 1:658–59; and for more on this, see Frederick E. Greenspahn, *When Brothers Dwell Together: The Preeminence of Younger Siblings in the Hebrew Bible* (New York: Oxford University Press, 1994).

[174] Karin R. Andriolo, "A Structural Analysis of Genealogy and World View in the Old Testament," *AA* 75 (1973): 1657–69, esp. 1657–63. See the Introduction above for discussion of Andriolo's work identifying processes of "divergence," "invergence," and finally, "segmentation," which becomes primary with Jacob's twelve sons.

[175] So, e.g., Noah is introduced in 5:28–32 and 6:8, and becomes the central character in the next *tôlĕdôt* section, 6:9–9:29.

[176] Birth narratives of the Bible share features in Ugaritic literature, such as the tales of Kirta and Aqhat, as well as elsewhere in the ancient Near East; Ronald S. Hendel, *The Epic of*

other, and in the bearing and raising of children. Death is inescapable, but life continues through one's children.

The syntax of v. 1 indicates a new subject and a turn in the narrative.[177] Cain's name is explained by a popular etymology, which is standard in biblical birth narratives, while Abel's name ("breath, nothingness") is left unexplained somewhat like the ephemeral character himself. It has been assumed by many that the occupations of Cain and Abel, shepherd and tiller of soil, reflect strife between social groups in early human civilization and that this narrative explains why God favored one over the other. More likely the narrator intends us to understand that the harsh realities of life outside the Garden of Eden require a division of labor. Cain takes up the job of his father as "tiller of the ground," phraseology reminiscent of Gen 3:23, while Abel launches out as a stockbreeder.[178] Such a mixed economy of agriculturalists and pastoralists, which in fact mirrors early civilization closely, is not likely to reflect predetermined conflict as much as the necessity of codependence in the post-transgression world. The new realities after Eden require division of labor and cooperation.

The text does not explain why Yahweh favored Abel's offering above Cain's (vv. 3–5). Both primitive occupations resulted in sacrifice. Indeed, it was inconceivable for ancient Israelites that either form of worker – shepherd or farmer – could receive the produce without acknowledging and respecting the source at work in the yield.[179] This text does not institute sacrifice as a religious observance but assumes it as a logical corollary between work and thanksgiving. And it is too early to have specific prescriptions about the nature of sacrifice, so we are unable to discern whether Cain's was less appropriately offered. It is possible that the mention of the "fat portions" of Abel's "firstlings of his flock" is to be contrasted with Cain's "offering," making Cain's appear parsimonious. Abel willingly and voluntarily came with his best, while Cain seems to have brought what was at hand. But in Cain's response and Yahweh's warning (vv. 6–7) we learn "that the cause of Cain's dissatisfaction lies in himself."[180] This, in fact, is the trajectory assumed by authors of the New Testament, who assumed Abel's offering reflected an inner faithfulness missing in Cain's (Heb 11:4; 1 John 3:12).[181]

---

the Patriarch: The Jacob Cycle and the Narrative Traditions of Canaan and Israel (HSM 42; Atlanta: Scholars Press, 1987), 37–59.

[177] The same syntax may also, however, indicate anterior action, such as an English pluperfect, implying coitus took place inside Eden and birth took place outside Eden; H. C. Brichto, *The Names of God* (1998), 97.

[178] Verses 2–5 are structured chiastically relying predominantly on the personal names; Francis I. Andersen, *The Sentence in Biblical Hebrew* (JLSP 231; The Hague: Mouton, 1974), 122.

[179] C. Westermann, *Genesis 1–11* (1984), 295.

[180] J. Skinner, *A Critical and Exegetical Commentary on Genesis* (1910), 106.

[181] Another possibility is that Cain's offering is rejected because it was drawn from the ground cursed in Gen 3:17; Frank A. Spina, "The 'Ground' for Cain's Rejection (Gen 4): 'adamah in The Context of Gen 1–11," *ZAW* 104 (1992): 319–32; G. A. Herion, "Why God Rejected Cain's Offering: The Obvious Answer," in *Fortunate the Eyes that See: Essays in*

Verse 7 is one of the most important verses in Gen 4 and also one of the most difficult in the whole book. Many proposals for emendations and alternative interpretations are possible.[182] Regardless of the linguistic specifics, the idea is clearly a warning; Cain is free to resist or to give in to sin. For the first time in the Bible, the word "sin" occurs (*ḥaṭṭā't*), which sheds light on the role of Gen 3 in Israelite conceptions of sin, in light of the many parallels between Gen 3 and 4. Like Eve before him, Cain is clearly in danger of another serious breach. But unlike Eve's conversation with the serpent, Cain's problems are arising from within himself. God warns Cain that sin, the besetting impulse among humans for rebellion against God, is like a wild beast "lurking at the door" and Cain must master it. In all likelihood, NRSV's "sin is lurking at the door" should be take as "sin is a demon at the door" as a metaphor on the seriousness of Cain's situation.[183] He is teetering on the precipice of disaster, and it is entirely up to him which way he turns. Cain is a free moral agent and must master his own impulses or suffer the same consequences as his parents, or worse!

That which began in the Garden of Eden continues in a more disturbing way among humans East of Eden. The transgression has become a premeditated, violent act – fratricide. Humans, having been given freedom and warnings about the consequences of their actions, nevertheless commit violent acts, which alienate God and violate each other. The prevalent characteristic of humans has become the propensity to harm each other. Life in the Garden of Eden was one of plenty for Adam and Eve and there was no competition between them. Outside of Eden, humans reduced life to a zero-sum game. Whatever is gained by one individual is necessarily taken from someone else in this human reconfiguration of God's created order. Rather than producing new roles and relationships, humans replicate the given, assuming that anything gained by one must be lost by another. Instead of a plentiful Eden in which humans are encouraged to be creative in their own right, humans have created a world in which they gain by taking from others.[184]

The account of Cain's murder and its punishment is replete with parallels to Gen 3. The premeditated act is followed by a presumption of hiddenness ("in the

---

Honor of David Noel Freedman in Celebration of His Seventieth Birthday, ed. Astrid B. Beck (Grand Rapids, Mich.: Eerdmans, 1995), 52–65.

[182] On the textual, lexical, and grammatical difficulties, see C. Westermann, *Genesis 1–11* (1984), 299–300; G. J. Wenham, *Genesis 1–15* (1987), 104–6; V. P. Hamilton, *The Book of Genesis, Chapters 1–17* (1990), 225–28.

[183] Assuming instead a nominal clause, in which *rōbēṣ*, "lurker" is related to Akkadian *rābiṣu(m)*, "demon," or at times a malevolent doorstep demon lurking at the entrance of a building to threaten the occupants (*AHw* 935); E. A. Speiser, *Genesis* (1964), 33, and on the long history of this interpretation, C. Westermann, *Genesis 1–11* (1984), 299.

[184] See the anthropologist Karin Andriolo for some of this, although she draws a much heavier distinction along gender lines than I am doing here; Karin R. Andriolo, "Myth and History: A General Model and Its Application to the Bible," *AA* 83 (1981): 261–84: esp. 270–71.

field," v. 8, cf. 3:8). God's poignant question calls the sinner out of hiding ("Where is…?" v. 9a, cf. 3:9). The sinner's recrimination ("Am I my brother's keeper?" v. 9b, cf. 3:12–13) is followed by direct and undeniable evidence of wrongdoing (v. 10, cf. 3:11) and punishment involving a curse (vv. 11–12, cf. 3:14–19). The transgression of Gen 3 and Cain's murder of Abel in Gen 4 share emphasis on the personal moral responsibility of human actions. The man, woman, and their children are not automatons, androidic creations who simply do what they are told. Yahweh assumes Cain is responsible for his behavior, and he alone must bear the responsibility.

Cain's occupation, his crime, and his punishment are all related to the "ground" (ʾădāmâ, vv. 2, 3, 10, 11, 12, and 14, where NRSV has "soil"). That by which Cain sustained his life also bore witness against him. The ground that yielded its produce for Cain cried out because it also opened its mouth to receive innocent blood from Cain's hand. Yahweh does not curse the ground itself, which was the punishment of Cain's father (3:17) but rather Cain is cursed "from the ground" (v. 11). Because of his sin, the ground will no longer yield *at all*, and therefore he must leave to find other sustenance. His banishment is a necessity of the barren soil, which witnessed his unspeakable crime, and now he will be even further removed from beautiful Eden, humankind's first home.

Cain's objection (vv. 13–14) needs to be understood in light of ancient Israelite cultural conventions.[185] Because of Israel's corporate perception of reality, any crime against an individual was also a crime against that individual's kinship group. Punishment was exacted by a member of the offended group, an "avenger of bloodshed" (gōʾēl haddām), who was to kill the murderer of one's kin and thereby avenge the crime. If the criminal's kinship group refused to hand him over, the entire group became susceptible to vengeance, and a war was likely between the two groups. If the offender's group believed their member to be guilty, they could protect themselves simply by driving the criminal away. Such banishment meant the criminal had no protection from any avenger of bloodshed that caught him. Similarly, Cain objects, his banishment is as good as death (v. 14). Expulsion from the ground and from Yahweh means Cain has no protection against oppressive avengers.[186]

In this light, Yahweh's provision for Cain is especially gracious (vv. 15–16).[187] As God lovingly clothed Adam and Eve before banishing them (3:21), so here God pronounces "sevenfold vengeance" (cf. v. 24) and seals it with a mark on Cain before banishing him. Much speculation has gone into the nature of the mark (or "sign," ʾôt) protecting Cain.[188] But the point is that Yahweh has provided for Cain, even as

---

[185] For more on what follows, see H. C. Brichto, *The Names of God* (1998), 99–100.

[186] On the question of who these other peoples were, who might meet Cain and execute him (v. 14), see C. Westermann, *Genesis 1–11* (1984), 310–11.

[187] D. J. A. Clines, *The Theme of the Pentateuch* (1978), 65.

[188] Most assuming some physical mark on the forehead; e.g., N. M. Sarna, *Genesis* (1989), 35, although it is also possible the author did not know and did not care because the narrative is relating primeval history and portrays a world of time and place different and unfamiliar; C. Westermann, *Genesis 1–11* (1984), 313–14.

he was evicted from "the [protective] presence of the Lord" and was forced to settle in the land of Nod ("Wandering," "Homelessness"), still farther east of Eden.

The first portion of Gen 4 was introduced by Cain's birth announcement. The rest is also organized by births: Cain's genealogy is announced with the birth of Enoch (vv. 17–24) and Adam's genealogy is picked up again with the birth of Seth (vv. 25–26). The genealogy of Cain is a septet (vv. 17–22); a group of seven generations in linear fashion, which gives way at the seventh generation to a segmented genealogy (see introduction for definitions of these).[189] In the linear portion (vv. 17–19), we have only one expansion at v. 17 in the account of urbanization. The segmented portion, listing the four children of Lamech (vv. 20–22) has three expansions, giving account of other developments in human civilization: (a) pastoral nomadism ("those who live in tents and have livestock" as opposed to urban-dwellers), (b) musicians, and (c) metallurgy. Such etiological use of the genealogies gives account of the origins of human civilization.[190] Before placing Cain aside and taking up the more important line of Seth, the text explains that Cain's family made their own contributions to human civilization. As Cain and Abel had divided the labor between them (v. 2), so now his descendants develop specializations that will remain important throughout history (cf. v. 26).

The seventh line in Cain's genealogy, Lamech, is expanded further with poetic fragments about Lamech (vv. 23–24).[191] This family was responsible for developing a large portion of human civilization, yet the problem of Cain's violence, the "sin" principle introduced in v. 7, has only intensified. Lamech boasts to his wives of exacting vengeance out of proportion to the crime committed against him; execution in payment for a wound (v. 23). The escalation of violence in the world is captured in the limerick, "If Cain is avenged sevenfold, truly Lamech seventy-sevenfold" (v. 24). The linguistic links with v. 15 appear to emphasize that the principle of justice appropriate to the crime is forsaken by Lamech's generation. Yahweh could be expected to exact punishment against those who harm Cain, but Lamech's irrational self-defense is inhumane.[192]

At the conclusion of the *tôlĕdôt* unit (2:4–4:26), the main character for the next *tôlĕdôt* is introduced, Seth (vv. 25–26). The NRSV's "again" (*'ôd*) ties Seth's birth announcement together with vv. 1–2 and the birth of Seth's older brothers. For the first time, the common noun "man" (*'ādām*) is used as a personal name, Adam.[193]

---

[189] And on the role of the seventh position in genealogical lists, see Jack M. Sasson, "A Genealogical 'Convention' in Biblical Chronology?" *ZAW* 90 (1978): 171–85.

[190] On these arts of civilization in the ancient Near East generally, see John H. Walton, Victor H. Matthews, and Mark W. Chavalas, *The IVP Background Bible Commentary: Old Testament* (Downers Grove, Ill.: InterVarsity Press, 2000), 34–35.

[191] Stanley Gevirtz, *Patterns in the Early Poetry of Israel* (SAOC 32; Chicago: University of Chicago Press, 1973), 25–34.

[192] Jesus reversed precisely Lamech's boast, calling his followers to show mercy commensurate to Lamech's violence (Matt 18:21–22).

[193] Richard S. Hess, "Splitting the Adam: The Usage of *'ādām* in Genesis," in *Studies in the Pentateuch*, ed. John A. Emerton (VTSup 41; Leiden: E. J. Brill, 1990), 1–16. As a personal

In v. 1, its use as a common noun (*with* the definite article), "the man knew his wife," ties the births of Cain and Abel to the preceding Eden narrative, where it denotes the generic "the human." In v. 25, its use as a personal name (*without* the definite article) denotes the personal name, Adam, and thereby links Seth's birth narrative to the genealogy of Gen 5.

As before, we have the etiological naming – "Seth" sounds like "appointed" – with more interest in assonance and word play than accurate etymology. There are only two generations listed here, Seth and Enosh, but this line is to be picked up and developed significantly in the next chapter. The central feature of Seth's family is the brief note that during this period, "people began to invoke the name of the Lord" (v. 26). The expansion of genealogy is thus compared to those devoted to cultural developments in Cain's family (vv. 17–24). Cain's line established cultural and societal conventions for humanity, whereas Seth's line is noted for religious contributions. To invoke (literally "call upon") Yahweh's name is likely a reference to the institution of public worship among all nations and the development of religious practices in general compared to the other achievements of civilization.[194] Having made the contrast between the two branches of Adam's family, Cain and Seth, Cain's line will now be placed aside and the more important line of Seth is taken up in Gen 5.

A CLOSER LOOK – GENEALOGIES IN THE BIBLE

Genealogies do not make for exciting reading. Yet, two books of the Hebrew Bible have a concentration of genealogies, Genesis and 1 Chronicles, and other selected passages in the Bible have them embedded in narratives. For centuries, biblical researchers assumed the genealogies were little more than relics from Israel's ancient tribal ancestry, with little value in the interpretive process. The genealogies were, it was believed, a simple means of linking narrative accounts together to drive the storyline forward, like beads on a string.

In recent decades, cultural anthropologists working together with biblical scholars have changed all this. We now know that the Bible has two distinct types of genealogies, that such oral genealogies in tribal traditions were marked primarily by fluidity and flexibility, and that examples in the Bible represent a distinct literary genre with important contributions to the texts. The two types of genealogies (linear and segmented, see introduction, pp. 9–10) are distinct from each other in

name, Adam, is attested in west Semitic, with exact parallels in Amorite and Eblaite; R. S. Hess, *Studies in the Personal Names of Genesis 1–11* (1993), 59–62. Moreover, the hero of an Akkadian myth with parallels to the early chapters of Genesis and known from across the ancient Near East is named "Adapa," which may be a phonetic variant of **Adam(a)*; Ibid., 64–65. Copies of the story are attested from the city of Assur and as far away as El-Amarna in Egypt, which suggests the Syro–Palestinian scribes were acquainted with the myth. For translation and discussion, see S. Dalley, *Myths from Mesopotamia* (2000), 182–88.

[194] C. Westermann, *Genesis 1–11* (1984), 339–40; G. J. Wenham, *Genesis 1–15* (1987), 115–16.

form and function. This important aspect of everyday village life determined an individual's status in a personal lineage, so that a tribe's larger status in the people group was laid out by the specific pedigree among the other clans and tribes. In the Bible, genealogies become a literary genre, which can serve this individual function (Abram in 11:27–32), or can be transformed to explain Israel's national identity, and so to place Israel in proper perspective among the other nations (Gen 10). In the case of Genesis, genealogies also provide the literary backbone, the skeleton for the entire book (see introduction). Important individuals or people groups are highlighted for special comment, as though the author lifts a character for further commentary or explanation. I have often referred to this as "expansions" or "elaborations" on the part of the author. The literary result is that the genealogies are one of two types of material in Genesis, the other being narrative, which tells the story. Rather than seeing the genealogies as unfortunate necessities, we must read them as essential components of our story.

The New Testament makes similar use of genealogies. Both Matthew and Luke use elaborate genealogies to introduce the leading character of the gospel story, Jesus, and to legitimize his identity as the Messiah (Matt 1:1–17; Luke 3:23–38). Josephus also notes the importance of genealogical lineage in Jewish thought (*Life* §§3–6; *Ag. Ap.* 1.7, §§30–36.)

GENESIS 5:1–32 THE SCROLL OF ADAM'S DESCENDANTS

(5:1) This is the list of the descendants of Adam. When God created humankind, he made them in the likeness of God.

(5:2) Male and female he created them, and he blessed them and named them "Humankind" when they were created.

(5:3) When Adam had lived one hundred thirty years, he became the father of a son in his likeness, according to his image, and named him Seth.

(5:4) The days of Adam after he became the father of Seth were eight hundred years; and he had other sons and daughters.

(5:5) Thus all the days that Adam lived were nine hundred thirty years; and he died.

(5:6) When Seth had lived one hundred five years, he became the father of Enosh.

(5:7) Seth lived after the birth of Enosh eight hundred seven years, and had other sons and daughters.

(5:8) Thus all the days of Seth were nine hundred twelve years; and he died.

(5:9) When Enosh had lived ninety years, he became the father of Kenan.

(5:10) Enosh lived after the birth of Kenan eight hundred fifteen years, and had other sons and daughters.

(5:11) Thus all the days of Enosh were nine hundred five years; and he died.

(5:12) When Kenan had lived seventy years, he became the father of Mahalalel.

(5:13)   Kenan lived after the birth of Mahalalel eight hundred and forty years, and had other sons and daughters.

(5:14)   Thus all the days of Kenan were nine hundred and ten years; and he died.

(5:15)   When Mahalalel had lived sixty-five years, he became the father of Jared.

(5:16)   Mahalalel lived after the birth of Jared eight hundred thirty years, and had other sons and daughters.

(5:17)   Thus all the days of Mahalalel were eight hundred ninety-five years; and he died.

(5:18)   When Jared had lived one hundred sixty-two years he became the father of Enoch.

(5:19)   Jared lived after the birth of Enoch eight hundred years, and had other sons and daughters.

(5:20)   Thus all the days of Jared were nine hundred sixty-two years; and he died.

(5:21)   When Enoch had lived sixty-five years, he became the father of Methuselah.

(5:22)   Enoch walked with God after the birth of Methuselah three hundred years, and had other sons and daughters.

(5:23)   Thus all the days of Enoch were three hundred sixty-five years.

(5:24)   Enoch walked with God; then he was no more, because God took him.

(5:25)   When Methuselah had lived one hundred eighty-seven years, he became the father of Lamech.

(5:26)   Methuselah lived after the birth of Lamech seven hundred eighty-two years, and had other sons and daughters.

(5:27)   Thus all the days of Methuselah were nine hundred sixty-nine years; and he died.

(5:28)   When Lamech had lived one hundred eighty-two years, he became the father of a son;

(5:29)   he named him Noah, saying, "Out of the ground that the LORD has cursed this one shall bring us relief from our work and from the toil of our hands."

(5:30)   Lamech lived after the birth of Noah five hundred ninety-five years, and had other sons and daughters.

(5:31)   Thus all the days of Lamech were seven hundred seventy-seven years; and he died.

(5:32)   After Noah was five hundred years old, Noah became the father of Shem, Ham, and Japheth.

G enesis 5 contains remarkable similarities with Cain's genealogy (4:1, 17–22): both begin with Adam, both have ten names, both contain the names Enoch and Lamech, and both highlight Enoch for special notation.[195] The two lists also contain significant differences, which have long been explained in terms of source distinction, typically between the Yahwist (4:1, 17–22) and the Priestly source

---

[195]   H. C. Brichto, *The Names of God* (1998), 308–12; David M. Carr, *Reading the Fractures of Genesis: Historical and Literary Approaches* (Louisville, Ky.: Westminster John Knox Press, 1996), 68–73.

(Gen 5).[196] The *tôlĕdôt* clause of v. 1 is different from others in Genesis in the addition of the word "list" ("document, scroll" *sēper*), which may reflect the most ancient title for such genealogies and suggests that the other *tôlĕdôt* clauses in Genesis are derived from this one. The distinctive genealogical style introduced here (see below) is continued in Shem's genealogy (Gen 11:10–26) and implies that together they were once part of a very ancient genealogical "document" (*sēper*), which was used by priestly authors to periodize primeval times, first from creation and Eden narratives to the flood, and then from the flood to Abram.[197]

The "list of the descendants [*tôlĕdôt*] of Adam" (v. 1) introduces a linear genealogy of ten generations, branching into a segmented genealogy at the tenth generation, Noah (see introduction on genealogies). After the *tôlĕdôt* clause, vv. 1b–2 introduce the chapter using numerous lexical links with Gen 1: "created," "humankind" (*'ādām*), "made," "likeness," "male and female," "blessed." The temporal clause at the beginning of this introduction, "When God created . . . ," relates to my temporal interpretation of Gen 1:1 (see pp. 35–37 above). All of these features result in a first-order intertextuality in which particular signifiers embedded in the texts lead us to read Gen 1 and Gen 5:1–2 together.[198] The Eden narrative and Cain–Abel narrative have fleshed out details, and now the text draws us back to the main thread holding the entire Primeval History together.

The use of plural pronouns throughout v. 2 together with the pair "male and female" indicates that "humankind" (*'ādām*) is intentionally gender neutral and used in these texts as a generic term for humanity. The peculiar passive, "when they were created" emphasizes the passivity of the humans in the naming process, which completes the act of creation. The text is about to explain how Adam actively continued God's creative work through fathering a child. But this is not to suggest that humanity had anything to do with God's initial creative brilliance as narrated in Gen 1; humans were completely passive throughout. Only God can accomplish such a thing.

The birth of Seth is reported first (vv. 3–5). The distinctive style of this genealogy, and repeated only in Shem's genealogy (11:10–26), is as follows: "When A had lived *x*-years, he became the father of B; and A lived after the birth of B *y*-years, and had other sons and daughters." In Gen 5, this is followed by another sentence: "Thus all the days of A were *z*-years; and he died." The genealogical formula contains three uses of the verbal root *yld* in the causative form (Hiphil, "became the father of" or simply "had"), which is related to the noun form *tôlĕdôt*, "line of descendants," suggesting this important structuring device in Genesis was original to Gen 5.

196 J. Wellhausen, *Prolegomena to the History of Israel* (1994), 308–9.
197 Frank M. Cross, *Canaanite Myth and Hebrew Epic: Essays in the History of the Religion of Israel* (Cambridge, Mass.: Harvard University Press, 1973), 301–2.
198 Compare the three phases of intertextuality of Kirsten Nielsen, "Intertextuality and the Hebrew Bible," in *Congress Volume, Oslo 1998*, eds. André Lemaire and Magne Sæbø (VTSup 80; Leiden: Brill, 2000), 17–31.

Only Seth in this chapter is born in the "likeness" (*dĕmût*) and "image" (*ṣelem*) of his father (v. 3). The already unmistakable linkage of this statement with Gen 1:26–27 is strengthened by the recurrence of "likeness" in 5:1, which prepares for this statement: "When God created humankind, he made them in the *likeness* of God." As God created humans in his image in order to have dominion over the created order, so now Adam becomes the father of Seth in his (Adam's) image. The image of God is carried forward, so Seth will rule and have dominion over that which was his father's. Without this statement, we might haven taken Gen 1:26–27 as *sui generis*, leaving open the possibility that a primeval human being in God's image might have been unique to that ancient period and having little to do with later humans. But since Seth was made in Adam's image, and Adam was made in God's, the image of God becomes an actuality for all humans.[199] On the other hand, Seth is in *Adam's* image, which gives him an unfortunate bipolarity. Seth, and all in his line (and all later humans) are in the image of Adam as much as of God, and he is therefore a mixture of the regal image of God and the flawed image of Adam, resulting in "the ambivalence of humankind."[200] Seth and all humans after him represent the greatest potential for God's created order, and at the same time they present potential for the greatest evil.

The announcement of Adam's death (v. 5) raises an interesting question: How are we to understand the long lifespans of primitive humans? Israel appears to have shared the views of other ancient peoples that ancestors long ago before the great flood lived extraordinarily long lives. The Sumerian King List, for example, lists eight rulers reigning for a total of 241,000 years![201] There are significant differences here, however, in that Gen 5 details lifespans in the hundreds of years, reaching the limit in Methuselah's 969 years (v. 27), whereas ancient Sumerian rulers are said to have reigned an eye-popping tens-of-thousands of years; e.g., "Alulim became king and reigned for 28,000 years, . . . Alalgar reigned for 36,000 years," etc. Countless attempts have been offered to explain these numbers, although none has resulted in a satisfying solution, whether taken as symbolic, theological, or somehow historical (i.e., calculating the numbers as sexagesimal or some other system).[202] Whatever we make of the lifespans of the antediluvian patriarchs, the text emphasizes the irretrievable differences between that distant age and our own. Just as the Eden narrative portrayed a world in which talking snakes and trees of life needed no

---

[199] G. von Rad, *Genesis* (1961), 70–71.

[200] W. Brueggemann, *Genesis* (1982), 68.

[201] Walter Beyerlin, *Near Eastern Religious Texts relating to the Old Testament* (OTL; Philadelphia: Westminster Press, 1978), 88–89; *RANE* 150–51; and for comparisons with Gen 5, see John H. Walton, *Ancient Israelite Literature in Its Cultural Context: A Survey of Parallels between Biblical and Ancient Near Eastern Texts* (Grand Rapids, Mich.: Zondervan, 1989), 127–31.

[202] The quest is complicated further by intractable text critical problems between the Masoretic Text, the Septuagint, and the Samaritan Pentateuch; G. J. Wenham, *Genesis 1–15* (1987), 130–34.

particular explanation, so the antediluvian ancestors aged exceedingly slowly. It was a far away, shadowy past in which the image of God was carried forward in the line of Seth. Moreover, the steady decrease in lifespans from the antediluvian patriarchs of Gen 5 (908 years on average) to that of the lineage of Shem in Gen 11:10–26 (averaging 333 years) may be intended to chart the effects of sin on the vitality of human life (but see 6:3). Indeed, Abraham lived to be 175 (Gen 25:7), Jacob 147 (Gen 27:28), and the average Israelite may expect seventy years or eighty if strength prevails (Ps. 90:10).

Adam's days and children are summarized, and the text announces starkly in a single word in Hebrew, "and he died" (v. 5). The first obituary in human history is a moment anticipated since Gen 2:17 when Yahweh God warned of death. As a recurring feature of the genealogical formula in Gen 5, the simple statement, "and he died" is repeated for each antediluvian ancestor down to Noah, with the exception of Enoch (vv. 5, 8, 11, 14, 17, 20, 27, 31). Death has become a stark reality; indeed an expectation! The inescapable repetition in the chapter, "and he died," explains that now death can be expected as the common experience of all Adam's children.

The list of descendants moves in an uninterrupted line from Seth to Noah, using the genealogical formula to present in each case the firstborn son (vv. 6–32). The only exceptions to this formulaic presentation are Enoch and Noah, who are highlighted for special treatment. The formula is modified only slightly for Enoch (vv. 21–24). However, the list is segmented at Noah in order to introduce his three sons (v. 32), which prepares the reader for a brief aside before narrating the flood in great detail (6:1–9:27). After the long narrative insertion on the flood, the genealogical formula for Noah is taken up again at 9:28–29, immediately before the *tôlĕdôt* clause of 10:1 introducing the table of nations.

Israelite genealogies tend to highlight especially noteworthy ancestors by placing them in the seventh position in the list, and at times in the fifth position of a genealogical order.[203] Such a literary convention was not followed rigidly, but allowed ancient authors to focus didactic efforts on one or sometimes two positions in the genealogical tree. Thus Cain's genealogy was segmented at the seventh generation, Lamech, who was lifted for special treatment, and noted for exacting vengeance "seventy-sevenfold" (Lamech, 4:19–24). In Seth's genealogy, Lamech is moved to the ninth position, although interestingly his ages before and after the birth of Noah are multiples of seven (182 and 595), and he lived a total of 777 years (vv. 28–31). So unlike Cain's genealogy and its interest in the cultural innovations of Lamech's family, Gen 5 is more interested in lifting Enoch for special treatment in the seventh position, and culminates in the tenth position at Noah.

Immediately prior to this *tôlĕdôt* section (5:1), Seth's line was already identified as the one responsible for the religious cult and the institution of public worship

---

203 For some of what follows, see J. M. Sasson, "A Genealogical 'Convention' in Biblical Chronology?" esp. 173–76.

(4:25–26). Significantly, in the seventh position of this line, Enoch is especially identified as one who "walked with God" and broke the cycle of death (vv. 21–24). Modifications of the genealogical formula make the point. The clause "and A *lived* after the birth of B *x*-years" has become "and Enoch *walked with God* after the birth of Methuselah three hundred years" (v. 22). Similarly, the concluding clause of the formula "and he died" has been completely replaced (v. 24): "Enoch walked with God; then he was no more, because God took him." The same terminology, "walked with God" (iterative Hithpael of *hlk*) describes Noah as an especially righteous individual (6:9), and connotes a life of consistent fellowship with God. The faithful devotion of this simple 'walk with God' is precisely the piety fostered by the Old Testament, in contrast to the harsh legalism so often associated with it.[204] Enoch shows that there is more to life than living and dying; there is the possibility of consistent and steady relationship with God. In this way, Enoch's genealogical notation (vv. 21–24) hints at – and perhaps points forward to – the role of faith as the antidote to the vicious cycle of sin and death unleashed in the world by the actions of humankind. Interestingly, the Eden narrative also portrays Yahweh God "walking in the garden" (again iterative Hithpael of *hlk*) at a time when the humans had ceased walking with him because of their transgression (Gen 3:8). Enoch and Noah walked with God, while Adam and Eve hid from him.

Whatever the meaning of "God took him" (v. 24), Enoch's fate was not the stinging "and he died" we had come to think was unalterable. He has amended the lifecycle of the genealogical formula: live, father a son, live some more, have other children, then die. Death is not the last word after all. Enoch offers a solution to the transgression and violence that has marred God's creation; that is, a life with God that somehow transcends life and death itself. Genesis will have much more to add to this by elaborating on this life of righteousness, fleshing out the piety that is present here but indefinitely described.

GENESIS 6:1–8 DIVINE–HUMAN MARRIAGES, AND REASONS FOR THE FLOOD

(6:1) When people began to multiply on the face of the ground, and daughters were born to them,

(6:2) the sons of God saw that they were fair; and they took wives for themselves of all that they chose.

(6:3) Then the LORD said, "My spirit shall not abide in mortals forever, for they are flesh; their days shall be one hundred twenty years."

(6:4) The Nephilim were on the earth in those days – and also afterward – when the sons of God went in to the daughters of humans, who bore children to them. These were the heroes that were of old, warriors of renown.

---

[204] D. Kidner, *Genesis* (1967), 81.

(6:5) The LORD saw that the wickedness of humankind was great in the earth, and that every inclination of the thoughts of their hearts was only evil continually.

(6:6) And the LORD was sorry that he had made humankind on the earth, and it grieved him to his heart.

(6:7) So the LORD said, "I will blot out from the earth the human beings I have created – people together with animals and creeping things and birds of the air, for I am sorry that I have made them."

(6:8) But Noah found favor in the sight of the LORD.

*T*he *tôlĕdôt* of Adam, which began in 5:1, concludes with these two paragraphs: intermarriage of the sons of God and human daughters, resulting in a superrace (vv. 1–4) and Yahweh's resolve to destroy wicked humankind (vv. 5–8). These accounts continue the interests and themes of the Eden narrative (Gen 2–3) and the Cain and Abel account (Gen 4). So, for example, the theme of the human–earth bond (*'ādām/'ădāmâ*, cf. 2:7) returns when the human (NRSV's "people," v. 1, *'ādām*) begins to overpopulate the face of the ground (*'ădāmâ*), and Yahweh resolves to wipe away the human (*'ādām*) from the face of the ground (*'ădāmâ*, v. 7). Based on other thematic links, it is likely that these paragraphs were originally part of Israel's epical national history (Eden narrative, Cain and Abel, the flood, etc.), although vv. 1–4 may have origins in ancient mythology (see below). The specific explanation for the flood in vv. 5–8 may have been cut away from the flood narrative proper by the final editor of Genesis in order to introduce the flood account formally by the *tôlĕdôt* clause in v. 9, and therefore many interpreters take vv. 5–8 together with that unit as an introduction.[205] However, as it now stands, the paragraph concludes Adam's genealogy (5:1) and introduces the lead character for the next *tôlĕdôt* section, Noah (5:28–29; 6:8). In these two paragraphs the narrator's voice tells what the characters' actions in Gen 3–4 have shown to be true: humans are sinful and God is justified in sending a flood.

The first episode (vv. 1–4) is one of the most extraordinary in the Bible. The details themselves are narrated in vv. 1–2, followed by their consequences in the divine speech of v. 3 and the narrator's etiological note in v. 4. The reference to population increase is not surprising in light of the recurring "other sons and daughters" in Gen 5. The idea that numerous human daughters would populate the earth is only natural. What is entirely unnatural is the attraction these fair creatures held for the sons of God and the resultant marriages and births of superhuman warriors, the Nephilim. Interpreters have made every effort to explain this text in some way other than the plain and obvious meaning of the words before us. Such interpretive

---

[205] E.g., C. Westermann, *Genesis 1–11* (1984), 393–412; V. P. Hamilton, *The Book of Genesis, Chapters 1–17* (1990), 272–79; W. S. Towner, *Genesis* (Westminster Bible Companion; Louisville, Ky.: Westminster John Knox Press, 2001), 77–85.

efforts have included theories on human marriages between the faithful Sethites and wicked Cainites, or dynastic rulers and their polygamous marriages and ruthless off-spring, or otherwise demonic and/or angelic interpretations.[206] However, the clear sense of the text is simply that of preternatural beings (i.e., not entirely supernatural creatures but certainly not wholly natural either) fathering semi-human offspring of great exceptional military strength, and perhaps of great stature.[207] Such divine–human unions are attested in other cultures of the ancient world, including Baby-lonian, Egyptian, Ugaritic, Hittite, and Greek.[208] The Gilgamesh Epic attributes Gilgamesh's prodigious energy and powers to his parentage, and the fact that he is two-thirds divine.[209] Yahweh's announcement that humans will have no possibility of finding immortality (v. 3) is also reminiscent of the themes of the Gilgamesh Epic.

Clearly this little pericope has its origins in the traditional mythology of the ancient Near East. However, it has been adapted by the Israelite authors to explain more than simply where the Nephilim came from and why humans have a restricted lifespan of 120 years (v. 3). Yahweh is not counted among these "sons of God." In fact, Yahweh stands aside from them and condemns the unions they initiate with the humans. It has been somewhat demythologized by its placement in the primeval "history," tying the era of the Israelite authors to that distant past but also explaining the many drastic differences between the author's day and that ancient age. By placing vv. 1–4 immediately prior to the traditional Israelite explanation for the flood (vv. 5–6) the editor has transformed it and used it to show further why the flood was necessary.[210] Illicit relations between celestial beings and human daughters belong to a far distant era different from that of the author, in antediluvian days, and illustrates the lawlessness and disorder of that time.

The second episode (vv. 5–8) is the narrator's substantiation of Yahweh's speech and judgment (v. 3), and further justifies the decision to annihilate all creatures (v. 7). Verse 5 is perhaps the most emphatic articulation of the human condition in the Bible. Yahweh "saw" or perceived clearly the undeniable reality of the human condition: every imaginative and cognitive impulse of the human heart was per-sistently evil. The wickedness that the humans first introduced into the world has become pervasive, and now characterizes the human heart – evil is, in fact, the

---

[206] Willem VanGemeren, "The Sons of God in Genesis 6:1–4 (An Example of Evangelical Demythologization)," *WTJ* 43/2 (1981): 320–348.

[207] This is the "face value" of the text, as well as the oldest interpretation; cf. *1 En.* 6–11 and *Jub.* 5:1.

[208] Simon B. Parker, "Sons of (the) God(s)," *DDD²* 794–800, esp. 796; C. Westermann, *Genesis 1–11* (1984), 379–81.

[209] His father was Lugalbanda and his mother the goddess Ninsun, "Lady Wildcow"; Andrew George, *The Epic of Gilgamesh: The Babylonian Epic Poem and Other Texts in Akkadian and Sumerian* (London: Penguin, 2003), 2.

[210] Ronald S. Hendel, "Of Demigods and the Deluge: Toward an Interpretation of Genesis 6:1–4," *JBL* 106 (1987): 13–26, esp. 23–26.

profile of everything human. A progression of evil is discernible in the text, from the transgression in Eden, to its definition of "sin" in the Cain–Abel episode (4:7), to the widening and deepening pervasiveness of human wickedness (6:1–8). "The Lord saw" is a reversal of the positive evaluation of everything God created (1:31): "*God saw* everything that he had made, and indeed, it was very good." Reference to the human "heart" (*lēb, lēbāb*) denotes more than one's emotions, as is often asserted, since the heart is also the seat of one's intellect and will.[211]

Humanity's heart is evil, and Yahweh's heart is broken (v. 6). The narrator exposes Yahweh's inner life as painfully grief-stricken and deeply distressed. "Pain" has become the common experience of all humans in this world (*'iṣṣābôn* in 3:16,17 and 5:29) and is paralleled by the anguish of God (the verb *'ṣb*, "it grieved him," v. 6). The Bible's emotive language portrays no Aristotelian unmoved Mover, but a passionate and zealous Yahweh moved by his pathos into action. NRSV's "so the Lord said" might be better translated, "so the Lord *decided*" (v. 7), thus introducing his measured decree.[212] Specific terms and themes of v. 7 combine the creation account of Gen 1 with the "man"–"ground" emphases of the Eden narrative, in order to show that all has been undone.[213] The result is a divine decree that is both devastating and undeniably just. God's magnificent creation has been irrevocably ruined, and his passion and sorrow drive God into action.

Verse 8 is a strong disjunctive sentence (so NRSV's "but Noah . . . "). The reader has been prepared to meet Noah (5:28–29, 32), although his role could not have been anticipated. The text has built strong moral grounds for the flood based on the wickedness of humans and the pathos of a just God. But again, it is the "grace" (Heb *ḥēn*, NRSV's "favor") of Yahweh that intervenes. The reader has no reason for hope based on vv. 1–7. And yet here stands Noah as someone valued in Yahweh's sight. The expression "to find grace/favor in one's eyes" is to receive acceptance and approval, reflecting the nearly universal tendency to look into the eyes of another to discern whether they are favorably disposed or not.[214] Noah does not somehow limit God's plans but rather becomes the excuse God is seeking in order to avoid the disaster. Yahweh's approval of Noah turns the tide of evil and destruction. "The one who is grieved at heart before the inevitable obliteration is the one with whom the single human being finds favor."[215]

---

[211] The heart was the locus of a variety of emotions, as well as of thought (*HALOT* 2:513–516, esp. 514; *DCH* 4:497–509, esp. 498; BDB 523–525, esp. 524 number 9); Mark S. Smith, "The Heart and Innards in Israelite Emotional Expressions: Notes from Anthropology and Psychobiology," *JBL* 117/3 (1998): 427–36.

[212] Siegfried Wagner, "*'āmar*," *TDOT* 1:328–45, esp. 333.

[213] Howard N. Wallace, "The Toledot of Adam," in *Studies in the Pentateuch*, ed. John A. Emerton (VTSup 41; Leiden: E.J. Brill, 1990), 17–33, esp. 29–33.

[214] Terence E. Fretheim, "*ḥnn*," *NIDOTTE* 2:203–6; the term 'grace' (*ḥēn*) is also a play on Noah's name (*nōaḥ*).

[215] C. Westermann, *Genesis 1–11* (1984), 411.

GENESIS 6:9–9:29 THE GREAT FLOOD

(6:9) These are the descendants of Noah. Noah was a righteous man, blameless in his generation; Noah walked with God.

(6:10) And Noah had three sons, Shem, Ham, and Japheth.

(6:11) Now the earth was corrupt in God's sight, and the earth was filled with violence.

(6:12) And God saw that the earth was corrupt; for all flesh had corrupted its ways upon the earth.

(6:13) And God said to Noah, "I have determined to make an end of all flesh, for the earth is filled with violence because of them; now I am going to destroy them along with the earth.

(6:14) Make yourself an ark of cypress wood; make rooms in the ark, and cover it inside and out with pitch.

(6:15) This is how you are to make it: the length of the ark three hundred cubits, its width fifty cubits, and its height thirty cubits.

(6:16) Make a roof for the ark, and finish it to a cubit above; and put the door of the ark in its side; make it with lower, second, and third decks.

(6:17) For my part, I am going to bring a flood of waters on the earth, to destroy from under heaven all flesh in which is the breath of life; everything that is on the earth shall die.

(6:18) But I will establish my covenant with you; and you shall come into the ark, you, your sons, your wife, and your sons' wives with you.

(6:19) And of every living thing, of all flesh, you shall bring two of every kind into the ark, to keep them alive with you; they shall be male and female.

(6:20) Of the birds according to their kinds, and of the animals according to their kinds, of every creeping thing of the ground according to its kind, two of every kind shall come in to you, to keep them alive.

(6:21) Also take with you every kind of food that is eaten, and store it up; and it shall serve as food for you and for them."

(6:22) Noah did this; he did all that God commanded him.

(7:1) Then the LORD said to Noah, "Go into the ark, you and all your household, for I have seen that you alone are righteous before me in this generation.

(7:2) Take with you seven pairs of all clean animals, the male and its mate; and a pair of the animals that are not clean, the male and its mate;

(7:3) and seven pairs of the birds of the air also, male and female, to keep their kind alive on the face of all the earth.

(7:4) For in seven days I will send rain on the earth for forty days and forty nights; and every living thing that I have made I will blot out from the face of the ground."

(7:5) And Noah did all that the LORD had commanded him.

(7:6) Noah was six hundred years old when the flood of waters came on the earth.

(7:7) And Noah with his sons and his wife and his sons' wives went into the ark to escape the waters of the flood.

(7:8) Of clean animals, and of animals that are not clean, and of birds, and of everything that creeps on the ground,

(7:9) two and two, male and female, went into the ark with Noah, as God had commanded Noah.

(7:10) And after seven days the waters of the flood came on the earth.

(7:11) In the six hundredth year of Noah's life, in the second month, on the seventeenth day of the month, on that day all the fountains of the great deep burst forth, and the windows of the heavens were opened.

(7:12) The rain fell on the earth forty days and forty nights.

(7:13) On the very same day Noah with his sons, Shem and Ham and Japheth, and Noah's wife and the three wives of his sons entered the ark,

(7:14) they and every wild animal of every kind, and all domestic animals of every kind, and every creeping thing that creeps on the earth, and every bird of every kind – every bird, every winged creature.

(7:15) They went into the ark with Noah, two and two of all flesh in which there was the breath of life.

(7:16) And those that entered, male and female of all flesh, went in as God had commanded him; and the LORD shut him in.

(7:17) The flood continued forty days on the earth; and the waters increased, and bore up the ark, and it rose high above the earth.

(7:18) The waters swelled and increased greatly on the earth; and the ark floated on the face of the waters.

(7:19) The waters swelled so mightily on the earth that all the high mountains under the whole heaven were covered;

(7:20) the waters swelled above the mountains, covering them fifteen cubits deep.

(7:21) And all flesh died that moved on the earth, birds, domestic animals, wild animals, all swarming creatures that swarm on the earth, and all human beings;

(7:22) everything on dry land in whose nostrils was the breath of life died.

(7:23) He blotted out every living thing that was on the face of the ground, human beings and animals and creeping things and birds of the air; they were blotted out from the earth. Only Noah was left, and those that were with him in the ark.

(7:24) And the waters swelled on the earth for one hundred fifty days.

(8:1) But God remembered Noah and all the wild animals and all the domestic animals that were with him in the ark. And God made a wind blow over the earth, and the waters subsided;

(8:2) the fountains of the deep and the windows of the heavens were closed, the rain from the heavens was restrained,

(8:3) and the waters gradually receded from the earth. At the end of one hundred fifty days the waters had abated;

(8:4) and in the seventh month, on the seventeenth day of the month, the ark came to rest on the mountains of Ararat.

(8:5) The waters continued to abate until the tenth month; in the tenth month, on the first day of the month, the tops of the mountains appeared.

(8:6) At the end of forty days Noah opened the window of the ark that he had made

(8:7) and sent out the raven; and it went to and fro until the waters were dried up from the earth.

(8:8) Then he sent out the dove from him, to see if the waters had subsided from the face of the ground;

(8:9) but the dove found no place to set its foot, and it returned to him to the ark, for the waters were still on the face of the whole earth. So he put out his hand and took it and brought it into the ark with him.

(8:10) He waited another seven days, and again he sent out the dove from the ark;

(8:11) and the dove came back to him in the evening, and there in its beak was a freshly plucked olive leaf; so Noah knew that the waters had subsided from the earth.

(8:12) Then he waited another seven days, and sent out the dove; and it did not return to him any more.

(8:13) In the six hundred first year, in the first month, the first day of the month, the waters were dried up from the earth; and Noah removed the covering of the ark, and looked, and saw that the face of the ground was drying.

(8:14) In the second month, on the twenty-seventh day of the month, the earth was dry.

(8:15) Then God said to Noah,

(8:16) "Go out of the ark, you and your wife, and your sons and your sons' wives with you.

(8:17) Bring out with you every living thing that is with you of all flesh – birds and animals and every creeping thing that creeps on the earth – so that they may abound on the earth, and be fruitful and multiply on the earth."

(8:18) So Noah went out with his sons and his wife and his sons' wives.

(8:19) And every animal, every creeping thing, and every bird, everything that moves on the earth, went out of the ark by families.

(8:20) Then Noah built an altar to the LORD, and took of every clean animal and of every clean bird, and offered burnt offerings on the altar.

(8:21) And when the LORD smelled the pleasing odor, the LORD said in his heart, "I will never again curse the ground because of humankind, for the inclination of the human heart is evil from youth; nor will I ever again destroy every living creature as I have done.

(8:22) As long as the earth endures, seedtime and harvest, cold and heat, summer and winter, day and night, shall not cease."

(9:1) God blessed Noah and his sons, and said to them, "Be fruitful and multiply, and fill the earth.

(9:2) The fear and dread of you shall rest on every animal of the earth, and on every bird of the air, on everything that creeps on the ground, and on all the fish of the sea; into your hand they are delivered.

(9:3) Every moving thing that lives shall be food for you; and just as I gave you the green plants, I give you everything.

(9:4) Only, you shall not eat flesh with its life, that is, its blood.

(9:5) For your own lifeblood I will surely require a reckoning: from every animal I will require it and from human beings, each one for the blood of another, I will require a reckoning for human life.

(9:6) Whoever sheds the blood of a human, by a human shall that person's blood be shed; for in his own image God made humankind.

(9:7) And you, be fruitful and multiply, abound on the earth and multiply in it."

(9:8) Then God said to Noah and to his sons with him,

(9:9) "As for me, I am establishing my covenant with you and your descendants after you,

(9:10) and with every living creature that is with you, the birds, the domestic animals, and every animal of the earth with you, as many as came out of the ark.

(9:11) I establish my covenant with you, that never again shall all flesh be cut off by the waters of a flood, and never again shall there be a flood to destroy the earth."

(9:12) God said, "This is the sign of the covenant that I make between me and you and every living creature that is with you, for all future generations:

(9:13) I have set my bow in the clouds, and it shall be a sign of the covenant between me and the earth.

(9:14) When I bring clouds over the earth and the bow is seen in the clouds,

(9:15) I will remember my covenant that is between me and you and every living creature of all flesh; and the waters shall never again become a flood to destroy all flesh.

(9:16) When the bow is in the clouds, I will see it and remember the everlasting covenant between God and every living creature of all flesh that is on the earth."

(9:17) God said to Noah, "This is the sign of the covenant that I have established between me and all flesh that is on the earth."

(9:18) The sons of Noah who went out of the ark were Shem, Ham, and Japheth. Ham was the father of Canaan.

(9:19) These three were the sons of Noah; and from these the whole earth was peopled.

(9:20) Noah, a man of the soil, was the first to plant a vineyard.

(9:21) He drank some of the wine and became drunk, and he lay uncovered in his tent.

(9:22) And Ham, the father of Canaan, saw the nakedness of his father, and told his two brothers outside.

(9:23) Then Shem and Japheth took a garment, laid it on both their shoulders, and walked backward and covered the nakedness of their father; their faces were turned away, and they did not see their father's nakedness.

(9:24) When Noah awoke from his wine and knew what his youngest son had done
to him,

(9:25) he said, "Cursed be Canaan; lowest of slaves shall he be to his brothers."

(9:26) He also said, "Blessed by the LORD my God be Shem; and let Canaan be
his slave.

(9:27) May God make space for Japheth, and let him live in the tents of Shem; and
let Canaan be his slave."

(9:28) After the flood Noah lived three hundred fifty years.

(9:29) All the days of Noah were nine hundred fifty years; and he died.

*T*his is, without doubt, one of the best-known stories in world literature. The
unit covered here contains several smaller, independent paragraphs, all of
which will require comment below. I have treated them together as a single unit
because they are centered on the flood itself, with a clear introduction and conclusion.

For over two centuries, scholars have recognized this portion of Genesis as the
best example of the composite nature of the book. Despite the editorial unity of the
passage overall, it is composed of a least two independent and preexisting sources
or traditions. The history of these traditions and the way in which they have been
intertwined has been an irresistible topic of interest over the years, and in fact, the
flood story has been the *locus classicus* for understanding the characteristics of these
traditions. So scholars have routinely reconstructed a J source (Yahwistic) and a
P source (Priestly, see introduction on these sources) behind the existing text of
Gen 6:9–9:29, although today it is more common to speak simply of priestly and
non-priestly strands, allowing also for editorial extrapolations.[216]

For the purposes of this commentary, a summary of a few of the differences
between the underlying traditions may help the reader of the NRSV text understand
why the account as it now stands contains obviously contradictory statements. First,
a cursory reading of the account reveals perplexing commands to take "two of every
kind" of animal into the ark (6:19–20; 7:15–16a) and then to take "seven pairs" of all
clean animals and a single pair of unclean animals into the ark (7:2–3). Second, the
chronology of the flood is specifically given in two distinct methods. On the one
hand, the water rose for one hundred fifty days and receded another one hundred
fifty days (7:24; 8:3), and together with a drying period, the flood lasted just over
a year, measured according to Noah's age (7:11; 8:13–14). On the other hand, the
flood consisted of "forty days and forty nights" of rain after seven days of waiting
(7:4). Combined with a large number of other indicators of tradition transmission,
scholars have identified the "two-by-two" arrangement of the animals as priestly,
together with the year-long chronology of the flood. The "seven pairs" of clean

---

[216] For excellent summary of the issues, see D. M. Carr, *Reading the Fractures of Genesis*
(1996), 48–62.

animals and one pair of unclean is non-priestly (or simply J), along with the forty days and forty nights of rain chronology. There are of course many other indications of this analysis, but this simplification gives the reader an idea of the nature of the sources behind the present text. While it may seem odd to us at first that an editor retained such discrepancies, we may assume that the sources or traditions underlying the whole had already attained authoritative status, and the editor valued the traditions enough to retain the inconsistencies, which were not problematic in ancient literature.

Many explanations have been offered for the current unity of the flood story. A variety of models have attempted to identify which strand (priestly or non-priestly) was primary, and therefore which expanded the other.[217] Others have offered a palistrophic structure, or "chiasm," in which the first item matches the final item, the second item matches the penultimate item, and so on, in a mirror-image structure that turns back on itself.[218] Such extended chiasms or palistrophes may be especially appropriate for narrating a flood story because the literary structure resembles the real-life situation. The account falls naturally into halves, framed by Noah's entering and exiting the ark, the rising and falling of the flood waters, etc.[219]

Several of these attempts to explain the unity of the flood story are helpful, but all must admit the complexity of the text as it now stands, presumably with original strands of Yahwistic and priestly traditions behind it. Nonetheless, a text such as Gen 6:9–9:29 is more than the sum of its parts. A thorough reading of the flood narrative requires studying each account of the deluge separately before undertaking an exegesis of the final, canonical form of the text to see how the two sources are combined and what new meanings are developed.[220] In the commentary that follows, I have attempted to pay attention to the so-called "final form" of the text while also taking note of the passage's "*intra*textuality"; that is, the way priestly and non-priestly earlier strands have acquired new meaning in their current context.

Our story begins with the third *tōlĕdôt* clause of Genesis (6:9a): "These are *the descendants* of Noah." The first one introduced the Eden narrative plus the Cain

---

[217] Ibid., 49–50.

[218] E.g., Bernhard W. Anderson, "From Analysis to Synthesis: The Interpretation of Gen 1–11," *JBL* 97 (1978): 23–39:37–39; repr. in R. S. Hess and D. T. Tsumura, eds., *I Studied Inscriptions from Before the Flood* (1994), 416–35; Gordon J. Wenham, "The Coherence of the Flood Narrative," *VT* 28 (1978): 336–48, esp. 336–39; Robert E. Longacre, "The Discourse Structure of the Flood Narrative," *JAAR* 47 (1979; supplement B): 89–133.

[219] G. J. Wenham, *Genesis 1–15* (1987), 157.

[220] Thus, an interpretation that uses both diachronic and synchronic approaches is sensitive to the stages of composition in the history of the text *and* the complete story as we now possess it; see P. J. Harland, *The Value of Human Life: A Study of The Story of The Flood (Genesis 6–9)* (VTSup 64; Leiden: Brill, 1996), esp. 6–19; David L. Petersen, "The Formation of the Pentateuch," in *Old Testament Interpretation: Past, Present, and Future. Essays in Honor of Gene M. Tucker*, eds. James L. Mays, David L. Petersen, and Kent H. Richards (Nashville: Abingdon Press, 1995), 31–45, esp. 41–44.

and Abel episode (2:4a); the second began the genealogy of Adam (5:1a). This time the *tôlĕdôt* clause precedes an extended narration of the flood, after only a brief genealogical notation on the three sons of Noah (6:10, perhaps reflecting 5:32). Verses 9–12 characterize Noah fully and vindicate the decision to send a flood. After establishing both Noah's character and the irrefutable need for the flood, the narrator moves to divine speech giving detailed instructions to Noah (6:13–21).

Noah has been introduced previously as one who may provide relief for humanity, although the specifics were rather vague (5:29). In addition to the earlier mention of his three sons (5:32), the previous paragraph concluded with a brief characterization of Noah from the perspective of Yahweh (6:8): "Noah found favor in the sight of the Lord." Here Noah is described more extravagantly, in three expressions that are most likely formulaic priestly phraseology. First, he is a "righteous man," which emphasizes his essential moral innocence (as confirmed by Yahweh in 7:1). This is the Bible's first description of anyone as "righteous," and serves to illustrate the quality of life hoped for and made possible through Israel's later covenant relationship with God. Second, he is "blameless" among his contemporaries (NRSV's "in his generation," a plural term in Hebrew denoting people of Noah's era). This expression borrows from Israel's priestly description of sacrificial animals that are free of blemishes, and emphasizes Noah's acceptance before God. Third, as with Enoch before him, Noah "walked with God" (cf. 5:22, 24), which highlights the consistent intimacy of Noah's relationship with God and exemplifies the Old Testament ideal of piety. Noah is a character to be admired and emulated, especially in light of the extreme wickedness of his generation, with which he is contrasted (6:5).

This characterization of Noah in 6:9b is a narrative expansion on the *tôlĕdôt* clause. Now vv. 11–12 present another expansion after the notation on Shem, Ham, and Japheth in v. 10, in order to justify God's decision to flood the earth. As 6:5 presented Yahweh's perception of humankind's depravity (cf. "The Lord saw"), so now the text presents a priestly description of God's view (cf. "And God saw" in v. 12). Together, these two justifications for the deluge (6:5–6 and 6:11–12) create a binocular effect, bringing into focus for the reader the divine view of the state of affairs and making it impossible to deny the need for punitive action. The earth is "corrupt" (repeated three times, and again in v. 13), and full of violence. These verses create a suspenseful tension for the reader. On the one hand, Noah stands before God as one who brings a smile to God's face and fulfills the purpose for humanity's existence. On the other hand, the inevitability of the flood is not to be denied, as has been stated so clearly both before (vv. 6–7) and after the characterization of Noah (vv. 11–12). Noah's righteous presence changes everything and nothing; that is, it changes *nothing* about the need for an expression of God's justice, but it changes *everything* about our understanding of God's mercy. The justice of God demands that a flood occur, but the grace of God allows an escape for Noah.

Noah will be given a brief explanation for the impending disaster (6:13) but the reader is given more detail (6:11–12). These verses anticipate God's speech to

Noah with a summary of the problem: corruption and violence in full measure. As in 6:5, the divine perception here (6:12) is a reversal of the positive evaluation of everything God created (1:31): "God saw everything that he had made, and indeed, it was very good." Such divine appraisal makes the sorry conclusion inescapable for the reader, as it was for Noah; indeed, the earth is full of violence because humankind ("all flesh") has corrupted it. The narrative verses (vv. 11–12) anticipate God's brief explanation to Noah (v. 13) by adroitly using the same verb in different verbal patterns (or derived stems).

"The earth *was corrupt* in God's sight" (*šḥt*, in the Niphal, v. 11)
"God saw that the earth *was corrupt*" (*šḥt*, in the Niphal, v. 12)
"all flesh *had corrupted* its ways" (*šḥt*, in the Hiphil, v. 12)
"I am *going to destroy* them" (*šḥt*, in the Hiphil, v. 13)

In a way difficult to express in English, the use of this Hebrew verb illustrates that God's actions are both unavoidable and just. Humanity has corrupted itself and therefore God declares humanity corrupt (i.e., "destroyed"). The Old Testament often uses such word plays to illustrate a sort of "poetic justice," meaning the penalty inflicted matches repayment in kind for the harm done, or a sort of commensurate form of justice. Thus in the Bible, divine punishment matches the crime. God's actions are measured and just, never reckless or unmerited, and God's punishment does not go beyond the ability of God's grace to restore.[221]

God's speech to Noah (6:13–21) is the first of four in the flood story (the others are 7:1–4; 8:15–17; and 9:1–17, the last being a cluster of three subspeeches).[222] Interestingly, after each divine speech, the narrative states succinctly that Noah quietly obeyed all that God commanded: "Noah did this" (6:22); "And Noah did all ... " (7:5); "So Noah went out ... " (8:18); and less dramatically yet nonetheless obediently, "The sons of Noah who went out of the ark were Shem, Ham, and Japheth" (9:18). Noah does not speak until all is said and done (9:25–27). His actions reflect the righteous and blameless character we have been prepared to meet, and which found favor with God (6:8–9).

This first divine speech of the narrative reveals God's intentions and relates detailed instructions to Noah (6:13–21). In a remarkably succinct statement, God informs Noah of the plan to destroy all flesh because of excessive human violence (6:13). God then gives Noah detailed instructions (6:14–16): a plan for the ark, including details of its building materials, design, and dimensions. After itemizing Noah's responsibilities ("Make yourself an ark ... "), God continues with an emphatic statement of his own imminent actions: God himself will bring the flood waters and establish a covenant with Noah (6:17–18a).[223]

---

[221] P. D. Miller, Jr., *Sin and Judgment in the Prophets* (1982), esp. 121–39.
[222] V. P. Hamilton, *The Book of Genesis, Chapters 1–17* (1990), 280.
[223] The beginning of 6:17 might be translated "I myself am about to bring a flood ... "

With this promise of a covenant between God and Noah, we have arrived at one of the most important concepts in biblical thought. This is the Bible's first use of "covenant" (*bĕrît*). Unfortunately, our English "covenant" is inadequate to connote the essence of the Hebrew concept, both in its narrower understanding of a binding relationship between two parties and in the much richer significance the concept acquires elsewhere in biblical theology (see Closer Look at "Covenants in the Hebrew Scriptures," p. 101). In this passage the covenant emphasizes the commitment of God to save Noah and his family from death in the floodwaters, while it implies certain obligations of Noah as well, contained in the imperatives to build the ark and follow God's directives (more obligations will be stated when the covenant is formally instituted, 9:4–6).

We have long understood this covenant concept as an important priestly concern, and the specific phraseology and linguistic formulas of this statement will occur later in Genesis in another important priestly context (Gen 17:7, 19, 21).[224] In this first occurrence of the Bible, God assures that he "will establish" a covenant with Noah, although the specific verb used (Hiphil of *qwm*) may connote confirmation of a covenant already in existence.[225] Since a different verb is used for initiating an entirely new covenant ("cut, make" a covenant, *kārat*, e.g., Gen 15:18; 21:27, 32), the implication is that Noah is already in a covenant relationship with God, which further explains that his righteousness (6:9–10) is derivative of that relationship. This interpretation may be confirmed by the syntax of 6:17–18, which can be taken sequentially rather than NRSV's disjunctive: "I am going to bring a flood of waters on the earth, . . . *and then* I will confirm my covenant with you."[226]

If in fact this theme of a covenant between God and Noah (in promise, 6:18, and in realization, 9:8–17) was originally part of Israel's ancient priestly traditions, it has been given new theological significance by its present location in the canon. The final editors of the book of Genesis have retained the theme, no doubt because Noah's covenantal righteousness resulted in salvation for him, his family, and the animals, and probably also because this theme was already widely accepted and venerated as an authoritative explanation of the events. But the editors have also

---

[224] Julius Wellhausen, *Prolegomena to the History of Israel* (Atlanta: Scholars Press, 1994), 338–39; repr. of *Prolegomena to the History of Israel*, trans. J. Sutherland Black and Allan Enzies (Edinburgh: Adam & Charles Black, 1885), although Wellhausen's identification of four covenants in the Priestly Code has required serious revision.

[225] Moshe Weinfeld, "*bĕrît*," *TDOT* 2:253–79: esp. 260, and see William J. Dumbrell, *Covenant and Creation: An Old Testament Covenantal Theology* (Exeter, Devon, Flemington Markets, N.S.W.: Paternoster Press. Lancer Books, 1984), 25–26, although I believe Dumbrell overreaches when he assumes the covenant being reestablished is the broken universal covenant of creation (p. 32).

[226] The imminent action of the active participle in v. 17 yields a sequential "and then" translation for the perfect plus the *waw* consecutive of v. 18; B. T. Arnold and J. H. Choi, *A Guide to Biblical Hebrew Syntax* (2003), 88.

amplified the covenant theme by including it soon after the narratives of human origins (sin in the Garden of Eden, and Cain's murder of Abel, Gen 2:4–4:16) and after the descriptions of the sinful human condition (6:5 and 6:11–12). By means of contrast with the unrighteousness of humanity at large, Noah's covenant with God is given fuller meaning. Covenant-living is not only the means of survival (i.e., salvation) from the flood, but also the Bible's answer to humanity's sinful nature more generally. In this, and in other ways, Noah's covenant anticipates and previews the covenant between God and Abraham, as we shall see. Righteous covenant-living will be highlighted as Israel's hope for salvation, nationally and individually.

A CLOSER LOOK – COVENANTS IN THE HEBREW SCRIPTURES

Ancient Near Eastern covenants were agreements between two parties binding them to relationship where no such relationship existed previous to the agreement. Such bilateral and mutual agreements could be between individuals or national groups. The parties could be social equals, a "parity covenant," or of different status, reflected in "suzerain–vassal" terminology, a "suzerainty covenant."

Biblical covenants, like their ancient Near Eastern counterparts, are binary, and most are asymmetrical. By "binary" I mean not simply that they are mutual agreements between at least two parties, but rather that the agreements themselves consist of two components: promise and obligation. Some emphasize the promises while hardly mentioning the obligations of the parties involved, so these are sometimes referred to as "promissory" covenants. By contrast, some leave the promissory element implicit, and are primarily "obligatory" covenants. But these designations are misleading because all covenants are both promissory and obligatory by definition, although either component may be left entirely implicit in the language describing the covenant. In the first covenant of the Bible (between God and Noah, Gen 6:18; 9:9, 11, 17), the covenant appears at first sight to be only promissory. But the obligatory component is implicit in Noah's responsibilities to build the ark, and to avoid blood guilt in the future (9:5–6). Similarly, the Abrahamic covenant (Gen 17) is predominantly promissory. By contrast, the Mosaic covenant, so central to the rest of the Pentateuch, details the obligations of the Israelites in the numerous commandments, while even the promissory elements become clear in the book of Deuteronomy.

A few covenants of the Bible are symmetrical, meaning they emphasize the promises and obligations of both parties equally (e.g., Abraham and Abimelech, Gen 21:25–34; Jacob and Laban, Gen 31:44–54). Most, however, emphasize the responsibilities of one party more than the other. So the covenant with Noah highlights God's commitment to save Noah from the floodwaters and never again to destroy the earth by flood (9:8–17). In this case the covenant is asymmetrical, emphasizing

the promises of the stronger party – God. Conversely, the asymmetry is most evident in the opposite direction in the Mosaic covenant, where the obligations of the
weaker party are detailed in the elaborate Israelite legal system.[227]

The second speech of God to Noah (7:1–4) announces a precise chronology for the
imminent disaster, and commands Noah to enter the ark with all his "household."
Noah's household is defined repeatedly in the flood story as Noah, his sons, his
wife, and his daughters-in-law (6:18; 7:7, 13; 8:16, 18). The religious, social, and
economic focus of life in ancient Israel was the joint family, a multiple-family
household of blood relatives plus the women connected by marriage and their
children.[228] Salvation from the floodwaters for Noah alone, without his extended
family, would hardly have been genuine deliverance, nor in any way would it be
deemed as real salvation by Israelite readers. While unfamiliar to readers more
accustomed to today's nuclear family (husband, wife, and unmarried children), the
concept, as evident in the flood story, is the basic family unit of Israelite society, and
illustrates the "corporate reality" of Old Testament times: "The principle involved is
the religious solidarity of the family: its members are saved for the righteousness of
its head."[229] This family unit, the "father's household," will be an important theme
elsewhere in Genesis.

Instructions for preservation of the animals, seven pairs of all clean animals
and birds together with one pair of unclean (7:2–3), and the precise chronology
for the flood (7:4), create a literary dissonance with other portions of the flood
story, where we find "two of every kind" of animals (6:19–20) and a flood of 150
days (7:24; 8:3). Such differences disrupt our literary sensibilities, and many have
offered explanations, harmonizing the account in an effort to remove the disjointed
quality of the story.[230] But as we have seen, the best explanation still seems to
be the traditional source approach, which assumes the two sources or traditions
combined in the canonical flood story were already widely accepted as authoritative,

---

[227] On "symmetry" and "asymmetry" in biblical covenants, see Gary N. Knoppers, "Ancient
Near Eastern Royal Grants and the Davidic Covenant: A Parallel?" *JAOS* 116/4 (1996):
670–697, esp. 695–96.

[228] Rarely exceeding three generations; Philip J. King and Lawrence E. Stager, *Life in Biblical
Israel* (Library of Ancient Israel; Louisville, Ky.: Westminster John Knox Press, 2001), 39–
40; J. D. Schloen, *The House of the Father as Fact and Symbol: Patrimonialism in Ugarit and
the Ancient Near East* (Studies in the Archaeology and History of the Levant 2; Winona
Lake, Ind.: Eisenbrauns, 2001).

[229] J. Skinner, *A Critical and Exegetical Commentary on Genesis* (1910), 152; and see Joel S.
Kaminsky, *Corporate Responsibility in the Hebrew Bible* (JSOTSup 196; Sheffield: Sheffield
Academic Press, 1995).

[230] John E. Hartley, *Genesis* (NIBCOT 1; Peabody, Mass.: Hendrickson Publishers, 2000),
100–1 and 107; John H. Sailhamer, "Genesis," in *The Expositor's Bible Commentary*, ed.
Frank E. Gaebelein (Grand Rapids, Mich.: Zondervan, 1976), 2:1–284, esp. 86–87; and J.
H. Walton, *Genesis* (2001), 315–16.

and therefore the editor accepted the details of both without making changes to coordinate or synchronize them. The resulting disjointedness was not considered problematic in ancient literature. As with the conclusion to the first divine speech (6:22), Noah was thoroughly obedient to God's instructions (7:5): "Noah did all that the Lord had commanded him."

As we have seen, the linear genealogy of Gen 5 branched into a segmented genealogy at the tenth generation, Noah (5:32). The recurring genealogical formula was modified slightly in order to present Enoch (5:21–24) but has been altered more radically with Noah in order to narrate the flood story (see 9:28–29). The editor of the story has borrowed from this genealogical framework in order to fill in chronological details for the flood, basing it on the day, month, and year of Noah's age (7:6, 11; 8:4–5, 13–14).

On the very day of Noah's obedience, the flood waters came upon the earth (7:10, 13). The cosmic phenomena described in 7:11–24 are not some banal punishment for the sin of that ancient generation, but they represent a reversal of creation, or "uncreation" as it has been called. The priestly creation account of Gen 1 portrayed creation as a series of separations and distinctions, whereas Gen 6:9–7:24 portrays the annihilation of those distinctions.[231] As the sky dome was created to keep the heavenly waters from falling to earth (1:6–7), here the opened "windows of the heavens" reverse that created function (7:11). When the "fountains of the great deep [*těhôm*]" burst forth (7:11), the cosmic order that had been fashioned from watery chaos returns to watery chaos (1:2, 9). Strikingly the sequence of annihilation, "birds, domestic animals, wild animals, all swarming creatures that swarm on the earth, and all human beings" (7:21), follows closely that of creation itself in Gen 1:1–2:3.[232]

This account of entering the ark and the beginning of the flood, joining as it does two sources or traditions, seems redundant and repetitive to us. But the resulting composite text serves to highlight an important message. The final form of the text invites the reader to pay especially close attention, through detailed repetition, to the occupants of the ark, as Noah and his family members accompanied by the assorted animals enter the ark (7:7–9), and then enter it again (7:13–16). The second time they enter the ark, Noah's sons are named one by one, to dramatize the events (7:13): " . . . with his sons, Shem and Ham and Japheth." This grand processional, so prosaic for modern readers, intentionally pauses the action in order to highlight the salvific effects.[233] The significance of the moment is emphasized again by another dramatic if subtle feature of v. 16: after Noah, his family, and the animals enter as God commanded, the Lord Himself battened them down safely in the ark. The statement

---

[231] David J. A. Clines, "Theme in Genesis 1–11," *CBQ* 38 (1976): 483–507, esp. 499–500; repr. in R. S. Hess and D. T. Tsumura, eds., *I Studied Inscriptions from Before the Flood* (1994), 285–309.

[232] Ibid., 500.

[233] J. H. Sailhamer, "Genesis," in *The Expositor's Bible Commentary* (1976), 88.

retains the intimate anthropomorphism of the old epic tradition (the Yahwist) in order to combine a "near-childlike simplicity" with theological profundity.[234] Whereas in the Babylonian version, Uta-napishti shut the hatch himself, here only the Lord can deliver from the flood.[235]

When only Noah was left upon the earth (7:23), along with those with him in the ark, "God remembered" (8:1). The Hebrew word for "remember" (*zākar*) denotes more than mere intellectual process but often results in action.[236] So here God remembers *and* sends a wind to drive back the flood waters, *and* closes the fountains of the deep and the windows of heaven (8:1b–2). Revolutionary acts of salvation and deliverance often ensue when God remembers someone in the midst of their pain or crisis, as with Abraham (Gen 19:29) and Israel (Exod 2:24). When God remembers, promises are kept, salvation delivered, old covenants renewed. God's remembering may well be the literary centerpiece of the flood story and its theological fulcrum.[237] As the first part of the story moves toward chaos (6:9–7:24), from this point forward it moves toward a new creation (8:1–9:19). Indeed, a re-creation is signaled by the renewed separation of sea and land, the receding of waters, and the gradual reappearance of dry ground in a way reminiscent of Gen 1, making complete the theme of creation – uncreation – re-creation (8:3, 7, 13).[238]

After the waters abated, the ark came to rest on the mountains of Ararat (8:4). The picture of the ark resting creates an interesting word play, since the verb used here ("rest," *nwḥ*) is the same from which Noah's name is derived. In a similar play on his name, he brings "relief" to humanity (*yĕnaḥămēnû*, 5:29), and now Noah, whose name itself means "rest," rides the ark to its resting place. Noah's righteousness blesses humanity with relief and preserves its remnant, along with the animals, in the resting ark in Ararat. The location "on the mountains" of Ararat indicates not a specific mountain by that name, but rather the mountainous region of the land of Ararat. The name is the Hebrew spelling of the ancient kingdom of Urartu, which was centered at the eastern bank of the upper Euphrates River near Lake Van extending into modern Iran, Iraq, Russia, and Turkey, and which was a powerful state in the ancient Near East during the eighth and seventh centuries BCE.[239] The

---

[234] G. von Rad, *Genesis* (1961), 120.

[235] A. George, *The Epic of Gilgamesh* (2003), 91.

[236] And is often so closely associated with action that it functions as a synonym for action itself; Leslie C. Allen, "*zkr*," *NIDOTTE* 1:1100–6; Hermann Eising, "*zākar*," *TDOT* 4:64–82, esp. 66.

[237] B. W. Anderson, "From Analysis to Synthesis: The Interpretation of Gen 1–11," 37–39; repr. in R. S. Hess and D. T. Tsumura, eds., *I Studied Inscriptions from Before the Flood* (1994), 416–35. See G. J. Wenham, *Genesis 1–15* (1987), 156–57, and W. Brueggemann, *Genesis* (1982), 85–87.

[238] D. J. A. Clines, "Theme in Genesis 1–11," 500.

[239] Paul E. Zimansky, *Ancient Ararat: A Handbook of Urartian Studies* (Anatolian and Caucasian Studies; Delmar, N.Y.: Caravan Books, 1998); Paul E. Zimansky, *Ecology and Empire: The Structure of the Urartian State* (SAOC 41; Chicago: Oriental Institute of the University of Chicago, 1985); R. D. Barnett, "Urartu," *CAH²* 3/1:314–71.

specific mountain now known as Mount Ararat in Armenia has been associated with the Genesis flood story only since the eleventh–twelfth centuries CE. Since the ancient kingdom of Ararat/Urartu was much more extensive geographically than this isolated location in Armenia, modern attempts to find remnants of Noah's ark here are misguided. The "mountains of Ararat" of 8:4 most likely refers to the foothills where the Mesopotamian plains in the north yield to the highlands near the sources of the Tigris and Euphrates rivers. A site of long tradition is Qardu(n), identified as the landing place in the Quran (11:44).[240]

The episode of the birds (8:6–12) – the raven and the dove – is one of the best known elements of the flood story. The assumption is that the birds can reveal something to humans locked up in the ark that the humans cannot discern for themselves. The use of birds by ancient sailors to find land was a common practice.[241] Here, of course, Noah is not locating land, since his ark has been grounded by the mountains of Ararat. Rather the text emphasizes Noah's care for his family and the animals in his charge by determining the readiness of the land for habitation.[242] The Babylonian version of the flood story includes a similar event, although with dove, swallow, and raven in a different sequence, but the genetic connections are undeniable (see Closer Look, "Excerpts from the Babylonian Flood Story" at p. 106). Noah does not open "the door of the ark in its side" (6:16), which could cause disaster if opened prematurely, but rather a window (*hallôn*, here perhaps "skylight") presumably in its roof, which we have not been told about until now. The view from this skylight apparently did not allow an accurate assessment of the condition of earth (implied also by v. 13), and thus Noah relies on birds to help. But in the first case, he receives no help at all! The raven is a scavenger, feeding on carrion, and was therefore independent of both the food in the ark or fresh meat on the ground. In the flood's aftermath, the raven has plenty of floating corpses to feed upon, and needs no "place to set its foot" upon, as the dove will need (8:9). NRSV's "went to and fro" until the waters were dried up may instead indicate "took off, flying thither and back," indicating in fact that the raven kept coming back to the ark and leaving it until the earth was dry.[243] Thus the raven was of no value in determining whether the earth was now hospitable to human life! On the other hand, the three trips of the dove illustrate the degrees of readiness of earth. Noah's unhindered care of the dove ("he put out his hand and took it and brought it into the ark with him," 8:9) reflects the idealist connection between humans and the animal kingdom, just as the dove's help signaled the time for a rebirth of God's created order. Humanity's role as ecological caretaker (Gen 1:26–30) has been restored after the violence of the pre-flood generation.

[240] For discussion and an alternative site, see Lloyd R. Bailey, "Ararat," *ABD* 1:351–53, esp. 353.

[241] N. M. Sarna, *Genesis* (1989), 57.

[242] J. H. Walton, *Genesis* (2001), 314; V. P. Hamilton, *The Book of Genesis, Chapters 1–17* (1990), 303–5.

[243] H. C. Brichto, *The Names of God* (1998), 114–6.

A CLOSER LOOK — EXCERPTS FROM THE BABYLONIAN FLOOD STORY

The older dictum of a Wilfred G. Lambert is still true: "The flood remains the clearest case of dependence of Genesis on Mesopotamian legend."[244] Consider the following excerpts from the Gilgamesh Epic. Gilgamesh asked Uta-napishti how he found eternal life. Uta-napishti, the so-called 'Babylonian Noah,' tells of a divine plan to send a flood. However, one of the gods revealed the plan to him with instructions to build a boat. Uta-napishti built the boat in seven days and loaded everything he owned.[245]

> Everything I owned I loaded aboard:
> all the silver I owned I loaded aboard,
> all the gold I owned I loaded aboard,
> all the living creatures I had I loaded aboard.
> I sent on board all my kith and kin,
> the beasts of the field, the creatures of the wild, and members of every skill and
>   craft.

On the day when the storm began, even the gods were terrified. For six days and seven nights, the storm raged. In the calm after the storm, Uta-napishti saw the entire landscape completely leveled and "all the people had turned to clay." Through a vent, he felt sunlight for the first time since the rains, and then his boat came to rest on a mountain. After seven days, he attempted to learn the extent of the flood.

> The seventh day, when it came,
> I brought out a dove, I let it loose:
> off went the dove but then it returned,
> there was no place to land, so back it came to me.
> I brought out a swallow, I let it loose:
> off went the swallow but then it returned,
> there was no place to land, so back it came to me.
> I brought out a raven, I let it loose:
> off went the raven, it saw the waters receding,
> finding food, bowing and bobbing, it did not come back to me.
> I brought out an offering, to the four winds made sacrifice,
> incense I placed on the peak of the mountain.
> Seven flasks and seven I set in position,
> reed, cedar and myrtle I piled beneath them.
> The gods did smell the savour,
> the gods did smell the savour sweet,
> the gods gathered like flies around the man making sacrifice.

---

[244] W. G. Lambert, "A New Look at the Babylonian Background of Genesis," esp. 291.

[245] Excerpts are from A. George, *The Epic of Gilgamesh* (2003), 88–100; cf. also S. Dalley, *Myths from Mesopotamia* (2000), 109–120; and B. R. Foster, "Epic of Creation."

George Smith stunned the world in 1872 by announcing his discovery of the Babylonian parallel, and published it four years later in a popular translation.[246] The story itself likely arose from a specific historical flood that took place in parts of southern Mesopotamia around 2900 BCE.[247]

The eleventh tablet of the Gilgamesh Epic is not the only Mesopotamian flood account. The alluvial plain of the Tigris–Euphrates valley flooded frequently, unlike Syria–Palestine and Anatolia, making it all the more likely that early Mesopotamian traditions are at the source of the biblical flood story. Indeed, the Sumerian King List considers one such flood so catastrophic that it stood between the remote primordial past and more recent history.[248] We also have a Sumerian flood account involving a single human survivor, Ziusudra, which account may have been the model or inspiration for the sequence of creation, antediluvian ancestors, and the flood in Genesis 1–9.[249] On the other hand, the Epic of Atra-ḫasis, dated to around 1700 BCE, although its composition may have been centuries earlier, also presents in sequence the creation of humanity and its near extinction in the flood.[250]

Ten and one-half months after the flood began (7:11), Noah uncovered the ark and saw for himself that the ground was drying (8:13).[251] His salvation complete, earth is now ready for new life. The age of a new world order is about to begin, and will be consecrated with new laws and a covenant in Gen 9.[252] The importance of the occasion is dutifully marked with elaborate dates (8:13–14), presumably worked out by priestly editors and authors early in Israel's history. As the text now stands, the progression over the ensuing month and a half is from "drying" ground to "dry"

---

[246] George Smith, *The Chaldean Account of Genesis Containing the Description of the Creation, the Fall of Man, the Deluge, the Tower of Babel, the Times of the Patriarchs, and Nimrod; Babylonian Fables, and Legends of the Gods; From the Cuneiform Inscriptions* (New York: Scribner, Armstrong & Co, 1876).

[247] William W. Hallo, "Antediluvian Cities," *JCS* 23 (1970–1971): 57–67, esp. 61–62.

[248] Jean-Jacques Glassner, *Mesopotamian Chronicles*, ed. Benjamin R. Foster (SBLWAW 19; Atlanta: Society of Biblical Literature, 2004), 117–26.

[249] Miguel Civil, "The Sumerian Flood Story," in W. G. Lambert, A. R. Millard, and M. Civil, *Atra-ḫasīs: The Babylonian Story of The Flood* (1999), 138–45; Thorkild Jacobsen, "The Eridu Genesis," *COS* 1.158:513–15; and Thorkild Jacobsen, "The Eridu Genesis," *JBL* 100 (1981): 513–29.

[250] W. G. Lambert, A. R. Millard, and M. Civil, *Atra-ḫasīs: The Babylonian Story of The Flood* (1999); S. Dalley, *Myths from Mesopotamia* (2000), 1–38; Benjamin R. Foster, "Atra-ḫasis," *COS* 1.130:450–453.

[251] The differing dates of vv. 13 and 14 may have to do with coordinating the solar and lunar years, but they most likely result from an editor's combination of different sources; compare Umberto Cassuto, *A Commentary on the Book of Genesis* (Publications of the Perry Foundation for Biblical Research; Jerusalem: Magnes Press, Hebrew University, 1972), 2:43–45 and 113–14, and Niels P. Lemche, "The Chronology in the Story of the Flood," *JSOT* 18 (1980): 52–62.

[252] C. Westermann, *Genesis 1–11* (1984), 450.

earth, the long process of recovery now complete. The divine command of 8:16 ("Go out of the ark") begins the third speech of God to Noah, and is the counterpoint to "Go into the ark" of 7:1, bringing closure to the flood event proper. The animals disembark "by families (or "clans," *mišpāḥâ*, 8:19) just as Noah is surrounded by his extended family (8:18), illustrating that life in the new creation begins in community and must necessarily be so.

As in the Babylonian flood story, sacrifice and worship follow immediately after disembarkation. The differences, however, are profound, since in the Gilgamesh Epic, the gods are so famished in the absence of humans to feed them, they gather over the sacrifice like flies (see Closer Look at p. 106). By contrast, here the proper sacrifice on a proper altar of Yahweh results in salutary effects. Yahweh resolves (says "in his heart") not to repeat such a terrible catastrophe, even though the "inclination of the human heart is evil from youth" (8:21). The etiological interests of the Primeval History (Gen 1–11) return here as the narrative culminates in an explanatory limerick, presumably a poem well-known in Israelite culture. As long as earth endures, and as surely as God has set the seasons in unalterable motion ("seedtime and harvest, cold and heat, summer and winter, day and night"),[253] surely also he will never again inflict such catastrophic destruction on humanity, despite the evil of the human heart. Such is the mercy of God! As Yahweh revels in the worship of Noah, he commits himself to overlook the basic depravity of the human condition, driven as he is by passion to celebrate sacrificial fellowship with humans, and to smell "the pleasing odor" of human devotion (8:21). In Israel's version, the story of the flood "has been made a witness to the judgment and grace of the living God" and bespeaks "a gracious will that is above all [humankind] and is effective and recognizable in the changeless duration of nature's order."[254]

The fourth speech of God to Noah (9:1–17) is really a cluster of three sub-speeches.[255] The first of these in 9:1–7 is replete with echoes of Gen 1. The new, post-diluvian cosmic order begins as the old had done, reverting essentially to a pre-creation state. Now that the cosmic waters are tamed again, God blesses the humans and commissions them to take dominion over all creatures (9:1–2, see the commentary at Gen 1:26–28).[256] In Gen 1, divine blessing distinguished all "living creatures," animals and humans alike, from sun, moon, stars, and other parts of the

---

[253] The narrative and poem combined in 8:20–22 may explain Israel's customary sacrificial offerings, indicating the occasions for these recurrent offerings, especially the last couplet of the poem (8:22), "day and night," which may provide the etiology for the twice-daily sacrifice at the temple in Jerusalem (Exod 29:28–42 and Num 28:2–8); Alan Cooper and Bernard R. Goldstein, "The Development of the Priestly Calendars (I): The Daily Sacrifice and the Sabbath," *HUCA* 74 (2003): 1–20, esp. 7.

[254] G. von Rad, *Genesis* (1961), 123–24.

[255] V. P. Hamilton, *The Book of Genesis, Chapters 1–17* (1990), 280.

[256] On the especially close connections between the priestly materials here and the creation of Gen 1, see David L. Petersen, "The Yahwist on the Flood," *VT* 26 (1976): 438–46, esp. 441.

universe; reproduction is the unique blessing of "living creatures." Like his ancestors in Gen 1, Noah and his family are commanded to perpetuate God's life-giving creativity by filling up and inhabiting the new world. And like Gen 1, that blessing is articulated as a command to "be fruitful and multiply" (the same verbal play as in 1:22, 28, *pĕrû ûrĕbû*). As illocutionary utterances, "the pronouncement of the benediction in itself is the act of blessing."[257] The blessing of God declares that God is favorably disposed toward Noah and his family, and expresses God's will that they represent him on earth by exercising dominion. The blessing is repeated at the conclusion of the divine speech, as a literary *inclusio* (9:7).

However, the new order is not altogether the same as the old, since it also involves an alteration of the food chain (9:3). Many readers assume this text implies something inherently virtuous in vegetarianism, since it was the original cosmic order ("plan A"), or inversely, something innately blameworthy in meat-eating. Others have assumed the change in human diet is a concession to humanity's weakness. But in reality, the only implication of the text is that the new order is also accompanied by a change in the animals' relationship to humans (9:2). The fear of humans is new, since pre-flood animals enjoyed a primitive fellowship with humans, now lost in the new natural order of things. Rather than placing value on either vegetarianism or meat-eating, this supplement of Noah's deity with meat is part of a biblical progression toward holiness for humanity.[258] By incremental steps, the biblical dietary laws bring humans from vegetarianism, to unrestricted meat-eating, and finally, to a dietary law that distinguishes Israelites from their neighbors (Lev 11). "[T]he dietary law represented the culmination of a progression in holiness, by which God had brought a people by steps to enjoy unprecedented proximity to himself."[259]

The prohibition on eating flesh "with its life, that is, its blood" (9:4) is likely an ancient proscription that the priestly tradition used to restrict the new dietary freedom of v. 3. Such intratextuality means the ancient ban has acquired new meaning, associated as it is with the blessing of God in the new natural order of things (vv. 1–2). The ban against consumption of blood rests on the priestly conviction, stated frequently in the Bible, that the blood is the life, and that life is sacred (Lev 17:11, 14; Deut 12:23; see also Lev 3:17; 7:26–27; 19:26; Deut 12:15–16).[260] The conviction respects all animal life but becomes especially emphatic when applied to the

---

[257] C. W. Mitchell, *The Meaning of* brk *"to bless" in the Old Testament* (1987), 62.

[258] Edwin Firmage, "The Biblical Dietary Laws and the Concept of Holiness," in *Studies in the Pentateuch*, ed. John A. Emerton (VTSup 41; Leiden: E.J. Brill, 1990), 177–208, esp. 196–97.

[259] Ibid., 197. For a unique proposal on the provision of meat-eating, see J. H. Walton, *Genesis* (2001), 341–42.

[260] Note more narrowly that the life is identical with the rhythmic, pulsating blood, and therefore the prohibition is only on eating an animal immediately after wounding or killing; see C. Westermann, *Genesis 1–11* (1984), 464–65; and for objections, see G. J. Wenham, *Genesis 1–15* (1987), 193.

taking of human life, homicide (9:5). The concise poetic line of 9:6a, a chiastic word play, underlines the crime–punishment correspondence of Old Testament thought, here in the form of the ancient *lex talionis* principle (that is, the offending party is sentenced to the same harm experienced by the injured party, see Exod 21:12; Lev 24:21).[261] Those who try to apply this text to capital punishment in contemporary societies miss the subtle ambiguities of 9:6 due to the concise poetry, fail to understand the inappropriateness of modern nation states to execute this principle, and miss the thrust of the *imago Dei* ("image of God") statement of 9:6b (and 1:27).[262] The value of all animal life but especially human life is at the highest premium in God's economy. Those who shed innocent human blood will suffer mightily by the nature of God's ordering of the universe.[263]

Like the speech in 9:1–7, which begins and ends with the blessing of God, the speech of 9:8–17 (really, two speeches) begins and ends with the covenant of God as literary *inclusio* (9:8–9 and 9:17). This covenant fulfills the promise God made to Noah prior to the flood (see commentary at 6:18, and Closer Look at "Covenants in the Hebrew Scriptures" at p. 101). "Covenant" (*běrît*) occurs seven times in ten verses (9:8–17), and the very density of the term itself makes the point: God's covenant with Noah is central to the post-diluvian world order. The verb used to "establish" the covenant is the same as that in 6:18 (Hiphil of *qwm*, 9:9,11,17). The immediacy of the active participle in 9:9 ("I am establishing . . . ") underscores the moment: as God promised (6:18), so now he delivers. We have seen that the verb in question (Hiphil of *qwm*, as opposed to *kārat*, typically used for initiating an entirely new covenant) connotes confirming or ratifying an existing covenant, implying that Noah was already in a covenant relationship with God. God has delivered Noah from the flood, fulfilling the promise of his pre-flood statement, and now God extends Noah's covenant to his descendants, the animals (9:10), "all future generations" (9:12), and "all flesh" on the earth (9:17). Noah's righteousness resulted in a covenant with God that saved him and his family during the flood, and now God extends that salvation-covenant to all the living as a second chance for the world. These themes are forward looking, since all of this will recur in a crucial text of the Abrahamic narrative (Gen 17), including specific terminology. Just as covenant defines God's relationship

---

[261] Attested also in other ancient Semitic cultures, illustrated by the laws of Hammurapi; see Bill T. Arnold, *Who Were the Babylonians?* (SBLABS 10; Boston/Atlanta: Brill/Society of Biblical Literature, 2004), 56. For possible origins of the talionic principle in early Amorite culture, see Samuel Greengus, "Biblical and Mesopotamian Law: An Amorite Connection?" in *Life and Culture in the Ancient Near East*, eds. Richard E. Averbeck, Mark W. Chavalas, and David B. Weisberg (Bethesda, Md.: CDL Press, 2003), 63–81, esp. 67–79.

[262] V. P. Hamilton, *The Book of Genesis, Chapters 1–17* (1990), 315; C. Westermann, *Genesis 1–11* (1984), 469.

[263] The text does not justify capital punishment today because God is the final arbiter of such justice, and modern nation states are incapable of serving as infallible executors of God's will; compare Terence E. Fretheim, "The Book of Genesis," *NIB* 1:319–674, esp. 399–401.

with post-flood humanity generally, so covenant will define God's relationship with Israel's ancestors, and by extension, with Israel.

Covenants may bear a "sign" (*'ôt*) to signify the faithfulness of the covenant-makers and to remind them of their obligations. Here the rainbow serves as just such a sign (9:12, 13, 17), but with a surprise. In most contexts in which signs are important in the Bible, they are intended to remind humans of their obligations to God. Here, the rainbow becomes a sign seen by *humans* but intended to remind *God* of his obligations (9:15–16).[264] Such a gracious and unexpected turn, no doubt, still inspires confidence in God as a covenant-keeping God. Such confidence is inspired further by the assertion that this agreement is an "everlasting covenant" (*bĕrît 'ôlām*, 9:16), a phrase used to describe the most important covenants of the Old Testament (Abrahamic, Gen 17:7, 13, 19; Mosaic, Exod 31:16; Lev 24:8; Davidic, 2 Sam 23:5).[265] This technical term has parallels in ancient Near Eastern legal contracts with no anticipated terminus point, and which therefore exist in perpetuity. God's perpetual covenant is "of long duration" although it is not necessarily unconditional, which, as we have said, would not be the nature of a bilateral covenant.[266] In perpetuity *from God's perspective* is all that one needs when living in covenant relationship with God, while also remembering the human conditions of all such covenants.

The genealogical framework of Gen 5 returns at 9:18–19, although the exact phraseology is only used at 9:28–29. The tenth generation in the linear genealogy of humanity was segmented at Noah (5:32) and the genealogical template was placed aside in order to narrate the justification for the flood and the flood story itself. This genealogical pattern holds the Primeval History together, using an elaborate first-order intertextuality.[267] As we have seen, Gen 1 and Gen 5 were intended to be read together, after the Eden and Cain–Abel narratives fleshed out details. Similarly here, the repetitive resumption of 9:18–19, "the sons of Noah . . . Shem, Ham, and Japheth" (compare 5:32; 6:10; 7:13; 10:1) prepares the reader for the concluding genealogical notation of 9:28–29. But the news in 9:19 that "Ham was the father of Canaan" also prepares the reader for one last note on the life of Noah (9:20–27). This illustrates again a common literary pattern for Genesis: the conclusion to each episode is often etiological, and resumes the genealogical links to the entire book structure, preparing the reader to move on to the next section (see discussion of the

---

[264] Michael V. Fox, "The Sign of the Covenant: Circumcision in the Light of the Priestly *'ôt* Etiologies," *RB* 81 (1974): 557–96.

[265] See also 1 Chron 16:17; Ps 105:10; Isa 24:5; 55:3; 61:8; Jer 32:40; 50:5; Ezek 16:60; 37:26, and see also Num 18:19; 25:13.

[266] See Closer Look on "Covenants in the Hebrew Scriptures" at p. 101, and Matitiahu Tsevat, "The Steadfast House: What Was David Promised in 2 Samuel 7?" in *The Meaning of the Book of Job and Other Biblical Studies: Essays on the Literature and Religion of the Hebrew Bible*, ed. M. Tsevat (New York: Ktav, 1980), 101–17, esp. 106–7; repr. from *HUCA* 34 (1963): 71–82.

[267] K. Nielsen, "Intertextuality and the Hebrew Bible," in *Congress Volume, Oslo 1998* (2000), and see commentary above at Gen 5.

tôlĕdôt clause in the introduction). Gen 4 concluded with key features in the origins of human civilization: urbanization (4:17), pastoral nomadism (4:20), musical arts (4:21), metallurgy (4:22), and religion (4:26). Now the origins of viticulture, an important agricultural innovation, are explained and linked to a development related to the blessings and curses of post-flood humanity: the curse of Canaan vis-à-vis the blessings of Shem and Japheth.

The description of Noah as "a man of the soil" (9:20) who first cultivated grapes is likely connected to Lamech's hopes that Noah would bring relief "out of the ground that the Lord has cursed" (5:29).[268] Noah became not only the first viticulturist, but also the first to practice viniculture, the cultivation of grapes specifically for wine (9:21). Elsewhere in the ancient world, the arts of human civilization were routinely credited to the gods rather than explained as human achievements as in the Bible (compare 4:17–22).[269] It is most unlikely that this text condemns Noah for drinking wine, and even his drunkenness is not lifted for critique. The only offensive behavior of this episode is revealed by the contrast between Ham's response to Noah's inebriation (9:22) when compared to the response of Shem and Japheth (9:23). On the one hand, Ham "saw" and "told," while on the other hand, his brothers went to great lengths to avoid any indiscretion, and we are told specifically, they "did *not* see their father's nakedness." Interpreters have offered many explanations of the offense involved, particularly voyeurism, castration, paternal incest, or maternal incest.[270] Although there are enough uncertainties in the text to give us reason to consider the other options, the most likely solution begins with the so-called voyeurism theory, combined with the cultural indiscretions of failure to care for Noah and talking to his brothers about what Ham had done. An important parallel may be found in the list of a son's duties for his father in the Ugaritic "'Aqhatu Legend," which includes "to take his hand when he is drunk, to bear him up when he is full of wine."[271] Ham's offense was more than simple voyeurism, although it began there. He also failed to honor his father, which was a serious offense in ancient northwestern Semitic culture, as is also clear in Israel's official legislation (Exod 20:12; Deut 5:16).

However, two other features of this paragraph have perplexed readers for generations, for which we have less satisfying solutions. First, Noah's curse is clearly directed against Canaan (9:25), although it was Ham who committed the offense. Second, Ham is identified as Noah's "youngest son" (9:24), while the order is "Shem, Ham, and Japheth" elsewhere. The text is clearly interested in the source of the curse on Canaan, and thus Ham is identified twice as the father of Canaan (9:18, 22). The sons of Noah personify their subsequent descendants in a way that gives

---

[268] U. Cassuto, *A Commentary on the Book of Genesis* (1972), 2:158–60.

[269] N. M. Sarna, *Genesis* (1989), 65.

[270] John S. Bergsma and Scott W. Hahn, "Noah's Nakedness and the Curse on Canaan (Genesis 9:20–27)," *JBL* 124/1 (2005): 25–40.

[271] Dennis Pardee, "The 'Aqhatu Legend," *COS* 1.103:343–56, esp. 344.

explanation for the blessings of Shem and Japhet but cursing for Canaan.[272] Thus the event narrated here is the occasion for the pronouncement of cursing, not necessarily the reasons for the curse *per se*, which are more to be found in the subsequent actions of the Canaanites themselves. A solution for the second problem may be simpler. Perhaps Ham actually *was* the youngest in birth order, and the familiar list "Shem, Ham, and Japhet" simply reflects the Hebrew fondness for placing the shortest words first in a list.[273]

After the curse of Canaan and the blessings for Shem and Japheth, the entire unit is concluded with the genealogical pattern of Gen 5, reporting in the usual way the death of Noah (9:28–29): "all the days of Noah were nine hundred fifty years; and he died." We encounter one subtle and interesting difference here, however. Instead of marking the number of years the patriarch lived after the birth of his firstborn son, we are told Noah lived 300 years "after the flood," emphasizing once more the central importance of this event in human history.

GENESIS 10:1–32 TABLE OF NATIONS

(10:1) *These are the descendants of Noah's sons, Shem, Ham, and Japheth; children were born to them after the flood.*

(10:2) *The descendants of Japheth: Gomer, Magog, Madai, Javan, Tubal, Meshech, and Tiras.*

(10:3) *The descendants of Gomer: Ashkenaz, Riphath, and Togarmah.*

(10:4) *The descendants of Javan: Elishah, Tarshish, Kittim, and Rodanim.*

(10:5) *From these the coastland peoples spread. These are the descendants of Japheth in their lands, with their own language, by their families, in their nations.*

(10:6) *The descendants of Ham: Cush, Egypt, Put, and Canaan.*

(10:7) *The descendants of Cush: Seba, Havilah, Sabtah, Raamah, and Sabteca. The descendants of Raamah: Sheba and Dedan.*

(10:8) *Cush became the father of Nimrod; he was the first on earth to become a mighty warrior.*

(10:9) *He was a mighty hunter before the LORD; therefore it is said, "Like Nimrod a mighty hunter before the LORD."*

(10:10) *The beginning of his kingdom was Babel, Erech, and Accad, all of them in the land of Shinar.*

(10:11) *From that land he went into Assyria, and built Nineveh, Rehoboth-ir, Calah, and*

(10:12) *Resen between Nineveh and Calah; that is the great city.*

(10:13) *Egypt became the father of Ludim, Anamim, Lehabim, Naphtuhim,*

(10:14) *Pathrusim, Casluhim, and Caphtorim, from which the Philistines come.*

(10:15) *Canaan became the father of Sidon his firstborn, and Heth,*

[272] G. J. Wenham, *Genesis 1–15* (1987), 201–2.
[273] U. Cassuto, *A Commentary on the Book of Genesis* (1972), 2:164–65.

(10:16) *and the Jebusites, the Amorites, the Girgashites,*

(10:17) *the Hivites, the Arkites, the Sinites,*

(10:18) *the Arvadites, the Zemarites, and the Hamathites. Afterward the families of the Canaanites spread abroad.*

(10:19) *And the territory of the Canaanites extended from Sidon, in the direction of Gerar, as far as Gaza, and in the direction of Sodom, Gomorrah, Admah, and Zeboiim, as far as Lasha.*

(10:20) *These are the descendants of Ham, by their families, their languages, their lands, and their nations.*

(10:21) *To Shem also, the father of all the children of Eber, the elder brother of Japheth, children were born.*

(10:22) *The descendants of Shem: Elam, Asshur, Arpachshad, Lud, and Aram.*

(10:23) *The descendants of Aram: Uz, Hul, Gether, and Mash.*

(10:24) *Arpachshad became the father of Shelah; and Shelah became the father of Eber.*

(10:25) *To Eber were born two sons: the name of the one was Peleg, for in his days the earth was divided, and his brother's name was Joktan.*

(10:26) *Joktan became the father of Almodad, Sheleph, Hazarmaveth, Jerah,*

(10:27) *Hadoram, Uzal, Diklah,*

(10:28) *Obal, Abimael, Sheba,*

(10:29) *Ophir, Havilah, and Jobab; all these were the descendants of Joktan.*

(10:30) *The territory in which they lived extended from Mesha in the direction of Sephar, the hill country of the east.*

(10:31) *These are the descendants of Shem, by their families, their languages, their lands, and their nations.*

(10:32) *These are the families of Noah's sons, according to their genealogies, in their nations; and from these the nations spread abroad on the earth after the flood.*

*T*he fourth *tôlĕdôt* clause of Genesis occurs in 10:1, introducing a new unit: "These are *the descendants of* Noah's sons, Shem, Ham, and Japheth."[274] At 6:9, the *tôlĕdôt* clause was followed by a descriptive nominal clause, characterizing Noah fully ("Noah was a righteous man . . ."). Then, after a brief genealogical notation on the three sons of Noah (6:10), the *tôlĕdôt* of Noah introduced a narrative expansion on the flood (6:11–9:29). This time the clause is followed, not by a temporal or nominal clause like the ones we have seen elsewhere (e.g., 2:4a; 5:1; 6:9), but by a narrative verbal clause introducing the children born to Noah's three sons (10:1b): " . . . children were born to them after the flood." Thus, instead of a narrative expansion, as in the case of the flood story, this *tôlĕdôt* is followed by a genealogical expansion in order to develop further the note at 9:19: "These three were the sons

---

[274] The occurrences thus far have been in 2:4a, 5:1, and 6:9. See introduction for discussion.

of Noah; and from these the whole earth was peopled." By listing the descendants of Noah's sons, according to their families, languages, lands, and nations (vv. 5, 20, and 31), this chapter presents a snapshot of the human race in the post-flood era.

As we have seen, genealogies in Genesis are either linear or segmented, their form being dependent upon their function (see introduction and Closer Look at p. 82). Rather than unfortunate necessities, such genealogical lists comprise an integral component in ancient Israel's story. The genealogy of Gen 10 is "segmented" or horizontal, in that it branches out in order to trace various descendants. Such ancient lists provided a powerful social identification, especially for its explanatory value. In this case, Gen 10 locates Israel in relationship to all other people groups by highlighting the ancestor Eber (related to "Hebrew," vv. 21 and 24–25). As a medium of special relevance for ancient authors, such genealogical assertions of identity and territory define Israel's position in relation to others.

The names included in this list are viewed at times as individuals (Japheth, Ham, Shem, etc.), locations (Egypt, Canaan, Sidon, etc.), or people groups (complete with gentilic endings, Caphtorim, Jebusites, Amorites, etc.). Each is the progenitor of other children who are not part of the Israelite ancestry and who become the ancestors of other people groups in the known world. As we have observed (see commentary at Gen 4), by means of this process of genealogical differentiation ("divergence") Genesis gives explanation to other populations in a kind of ethnic map of the world, and explains further the way Israel related to those populations. While the world's populations are described through this process of branching, Israel's lineage is traced in distinction to these through a straight line, from Adam to Jacob. In each generation, only one son continues the Israelite ancestry. This process is used routinely in Genesis to present and discuss each of the "other" descendants of Israel's ancestors first, before picking up the descent line of interest. So in Gen 4, Cain and his son, Enoch, are discussed and in a way, placed aside before taking up the account of Seth. In Gen 10, Japheth and Ham are included, as well as Shem's "other" close relatives. This list brings the reader all the way up to Eber, and even covers Eber's two sons Peleg and Joktan, to which the list in 11:10–26 will return before narrowing the line down to Abram's immediate family. This process of both diverging from the descent line of interest while also tracing Israel's patriarchs linearly ("invergence") continues in Genesis until we reach the twelve sons of Jacob, at which point segmentation becomes primary in order to amplify the tribes of Israel.[275]

Post-diluvian humanity is divided into three parts following the three sons of Noah, each sub-unit concluding with a nearly identical summarizing statement (vv. 5, 20, 31): "These are the descendants of X, by their families, their languages,

---

[275] K. R. Andriolo, "A Structural Analysis of Genealogy and World View in the Old Testament," esp. 1657–63.

their lands, and their nations."[276] Many attempts have been made to explain this tripartite division as primarily related to geography, although it may be better to think in terms of the sociocultural position of the perceived groups: those who were seafarers (Japheth), those who were pastoral nomads (Shem), and those responsible for urban civilization (Ham).[277] The chapter ends with a summary statement for the whole (v. 32), which uses *tôlĕdôt,* although not in the familiar introductory formula, "according to *their genealogies.*"[278]

The birth-order of the three sons of Noah is left ambiguous. Depending on how one reads v. 21 together with 9:24, the order may have been Shem, Japheth, and Ham (see commentary at 9:20–27). The sequence of Japheth, Ham, and Shem in Gen 10 is clearly part of the divergence–invergence pattern at work in the genealogies. Japheth and Ham are being presented in order to be placed aside (divergence), so the primary line of descent, Shem, may be continued (invergence). The only note of expansion for the descendants of Japheth is that they became the "coastland peoples" (v. 5), thus distinguishing Israel from the numerous islanders and seafaring peoples of the East along the Mediterranean Sea. "Javan" is to be identified with Ionia, while "Elishah" is Alashiya (= Crete) and Kittim is Cyprus,[279] illustrating that the Mediterranean islands and coastlands were viewed as geographic extremes for ancient Israel.

The list of Ham's descendants includes two expansions critical to Israel's understanding of the ancient world. First, Nimrod is the world's quintessential "mighty warrior," and is credited with building the first urban empires, Babylon, Uruk (= Erech), Akkad, and Nineveh, among others. This note also gives the etiological understanding of an early aphorism in ancient Israel (v. 9): "Like Nimrod a mighty hunter before Yahweh." This presumably hints that post-flood humanity has already reverted to pre-flood despotism. Attempts to identify Nimrod in ancient Mesopotamian civilization have considered humans, deities, and demigods, or have considered Nimrod an archetypal ideal rather than an historical figure. Although far from certain, the best explanation is that Nimrod is a composite Hebrew equivalent of Sargon of Akkad, the twenty-third-century BCE founder of the Old Akkadian Empire, and his son Naram-Sin.[280] It is also possible that the Nimrod tradition of 10:8–12 reflects the non-Semitic origins of the earliest city builders in third

---

[276] In the summaries of Ham and Shem, the difference is only an insignificant preposition (*lĕ-* rather than *bĕ-* on the last word of v. 31), while the differences for Japheth in v. 5 are more substantial.

[277] Bustenay Oded, "The Table of Nations (Genesis 10) – A Socio-Cultural Approach," *ZAW* 98 (1986): 14–31.

[278] One of only two times in Genesis the term is used other than its use in the formula; compare 25:13.

[279] David W. Baker, "Javan," *ABD* 3:650.

[280] Yigal Levin, "Nimrod the Mighty, King of Kish, King of Sumer and Akkad," *VT* 52 (2002): 350–366.

millennium Mesopotamia, which may explain the surprising Hamitic connections for a predominantly Semitic culture in Mesopotamia.[281]

A second expansion of Ham's descendants is the important note on the "territory" of the Canaanites (v. 19). The list of Canaanite people groups will reappear in variant forms later in Genesis, and plays an important role in subsequent Israelite history (Gen 15:19–21; Deut 7:1; Josh 3:10; 24:11). The importance of this expansion, therefore, is that the boundaries of the Canaanite territory outlined in v. 19 constitute the first portrait of the "Promised Land" later to be promised to Israel's ancestors but as yet undefined in the text.[282] This land will become the focus of attention in the ancestral narratives. The fact that the geographical boundaries given here roughly correspond to later Israel's homeland, and the fact that this land is inhabited by numerous Canaanite groups prepares the reader for significant features of the ancestral narratives of Genesis, and indeed, for the Pentateuch and Joshua as well.

Thus far, the expansions in the genealogy relate to the Mesopotamians, Egyptians, Canaanites, and Philistines (counting the brief note at v. 14), people groups who will play important roles in the subsequent history of ancient Israel. The names and geographic details of Shem's list are quite obscure (vv. 21–31). His great-grandson, Eber, is given pride of place in the opening verse ("To Shem also, the father of all the children of Eber," v. 21), and is the putative ancestor of Israel, as well as of the Moabites, Ammonites, Arameans, and Arabs, (as is clear from 11:16–26; 19:30–38; 22:20–24; 25:1–4, 12–15).[283] One would expect all these people groups to be known as "Hebrew" (*'ibrî*), and yet only descendants traced through Shem, Arpachshad, Shelah, Eber, and Peleg, all the way down to Abraham, Isaac, and Jacob, are designated "Hebrews." By so tracing the line of Jacob, in a careful invergence of direct descent, and at the same time defining carefully the origins of all other people groups of Israel's world, this genealogy defines and clarifies what it means to be an ancient Israelite. Gen 10 thus prepares ancient Israelites to embrace their identity as the people of God. Similarly, it prepares today's readers for the rest of the Genesis account, and therefore, for the rest of biblical literature, as a means of embracing one's own identity in the ongoing saga of God's story.[284]

---

[281] D. J. Wiseman, "Genesis 10: Some Archaeological Considerations," *Faith and Thought* 87 (1955): 14–24; repr. in R. S. Hess and D. T. Tsumura, eds., *I Studied Inscriptions from Before the Flood* (1994), 254–65.

[282] G. J. Wenham, *Genesis 1–15* (1987), 226–27.

[283] N. M. Sarna, *Genesis* (1989), 78. The caution sounded by Westermann about identifying Eber as the ancestor of Israel, relying on Cassuto, seems unfounded; C. Westermann, *Genesis 1–11* (1984), 526; U. Cassuto, *A Commentary on the Book of Genesis* (1972), 2:217–18 and 302–3.

[284] The primeval blessing, renewed for Noah after the flood (9:1, cf. 1:28), is in the *process* of being realized in this text. But the Table of Nations also establishes an expectation of *future* fulfillment that will be taken up in the Shemite genealogy (11:10–26), continued in Abraham's progeny, and ultimately fulfilled in the children of Israel; Carol M. Kaminski, *From Noah to Israel: Realization of the Primaeval Blessing after the Flood* (JSOTSup 413; London/New York: T & T Clark International, 2004), 43–59.

GENESIS 11:1–9 THE TOWER OF BABEL

(11:1) Now the whole earth had one language and the same words.

(11:2) And as they migrated from the east, they came upon a plain in the land of Shinar and settled there.

(11:3) And they said to one another, "Come, let us make bricks, and burn them thoroughly." And they had brick for stone, and bitumen for mortar.

(11:4) Then they said, "Come, let us build ourselves a city, and a tower with its top in the heavens, and let us make a name for ourselves; otherwise we shall be scattered abroad upon the face of the whole earth."

(11:5) The LORD came down to see the city and the tower, which mortals had built.

(11:6) And the LORD said, "Look, they are one people, and they have all one language; and this is only the beginning of what they will do; nothing that they propose to do will now be impossible for them.

(11:7) Come, let us go down, and confuse their language there, so that they will not understand one another's speech."

(11:8) So the LORD scattered them abroad from there over the face of all the earth, and they left off building the city.

(11:9) Therefore it was called Babel, because there the LORD confused the language of all the earth; and from there the LORD scattered them abroad over the face of all the earth.

*A*lthough quite different in style and general outlook, these nine verses share similar themes with the Table of Nations in Gen 10. Indeed, if we read the book strictly according to the *tôlĕdôt*-structuring device, this little narrative serves as the conclusion to the genealogical list of Noah's sons begun at 10:1 (see introduction). The next *tôlĕdôt* clause of Genesis occurs at 11:10 ("These are the descendants of Shem"), making 10:1–11:9 a self-contained literary unit. The Table of Nations follows the three sons of Noah out of the ark and throughout the inhabited world. Here, the Tower of Babel demonstrates that the rebellious inclinations of pre-flood humanity have exited the ark with Noah's family, and have now spread around the world. It matters little whether humans are in the Garden of Eden, east of the Garden, or settled in the plain of Shinar. The problem is not geography, but humanity itself.

With this paragraph, we have returned to Israel's national epic account of early human history, normally identified as part of the Yahwist's history, or the J document. In addition to using Yahweh ("the LORD" of vv. 5, 6, 8, 9, instead of Elohim, "God"), this material also evinces an intimacy between Yahweh and the world ("The LORD came down, . . . " v. 5), and is especially interested in etiological etymologies, such as the origin of the name Babel (v. 9). As we have seen elsewhere in the Primeval History of Gen 1–11, careful attention to the history of the tradition adds depth of theological perception, because new and richer meaning is created by the canonical shape of the materials. In this case, a story of general hubris and prideful human rebellion takes on even more profound significance because of its location after the Table of Nations and in the Primeval History overall.[285]

The opening statement about "one language" for all humanity (v. 1) needs explanation, coming as it does immediately after the many various languages of Noah's descendants (10:5, 20, 31).[286] Instead of the present arrangement, the ethnic map of chapter 10 with its multifarious families and languages seems more naturally to *follow* the Tower of Babel episode as effect follows cause. God has destroyed the tower, scattered the humans across the face of the earth, and given them different languages (11:1–9). Therefore humanity is spread across the earth in three branches, and many sub-families (Gen 10). The best explanation is that these materials have been intentionally dischronologized in order to arrange them thematically. The purpose of the arrangement is to highlight a "spread of sin, spread of grace" theme throughout Gen 1–11, which in turn is part of a larger creation–uncreation–recreation theme of the Pentateuch.[287] The Table of Nations in its current location fulfills the divine command to "be fruitful and multiply, and fill the earth" (9:1, reflecting also 1:28), and is therefore predominantly a positive appraisal of human dispersion.[288] The sons of Noah were fulfilling their purpose by bringing God's blessing to fruition. Had it been placed *after* 11:1–9, the Table of Nations in Gen 10 would of necessity been transformed into a sign of God's judgment. As these two units stand, the division of humanity and multiplicity of languages are evaluated both positively (Gen 10) and negatively (Gen 11). Humanity stands under both the blessing and the curse of God, and this ambivalence in the relationship between God and humanity brings the Primeval History to a conclusion.[289] The judgment of God upon humanity is clear, although humans also experience his grace. Together these traditions as they are now arranged lead the reader forward in expectation of a better way.

---

[285] It has recently been argued that this text is not about pride and punishment at all, but about the origins of cultural difference and the world's diverse cultures; Theodore Hiebert, "The Tower of Babel and the Origin of the World's Cultures," *JBL* 126/1 (2007): 29–58. Although this may have been the intent of an earlier version of this episode, the canonical meaning generated by the final editor when it was placed alongside other accounts of crime and punishment (Garden of Eden, Cain and Abel, the Great Flood) seem clearly to give it this meaning of divine punishment of human pride.

[286] Although it is true that different Hebrew terms are used (*lāšôn* for "language" in Gen 10 and *śāpâ* in 11:1), the interpretation of 11:1 as the official diplomatic *lingua franca* for international communication vis-à-vis the "languages" of Gen 10 as local dialects for family and ethnic communication has not been persuasive; see, e.g., V. P. Hamilton, *The Book of Genesis, Chapters 1–17* (1990), 350–51.

[287] D. J. A. Clines, "Theme in Genesis 1–11," 494.

[288] Albeit only a partial fulfillment, see C. M. Kaminski, *From Noah to Israel* (2004).

[289] Ibid.; Jack M. Sasson, "The 'Tower of Babel' as a Clue to the Redactional Structuring of the Primeval History (Genesis 1:1–11:9)," in *The Bible World: Essays in Honor of Cyrus H. Gordon*, ed. Gary A. Rendsburg (New York: Ktav, 1980), 211–19; repr. in R. S. Hess and D. T. Tsumura, eds., *I Studied Inscriptions from Before the Flood* (1994), 448–57.

The correspondence of vv. 1 and 9 – one language giving way to many languages – gives the paragraph an impressive unity.[290] The migration of humans vaguely "from the east" into the plain of Shinar, or southern Mesopotamia (v. 2), is consonant with numerous features of the narrative. It is generally assumed that the city and tower in view is Babylon with its Marduk temple, *Esagil*, the "House of the Uplifted Head," which stood along a processional route adjacent to an enclosure incorporating the temple-tower (*ziggurat*), *E-temen-an-ki*, the "House of the Foundation of Heaven and Earth."[291] The fired bricks and bitumen (v. 3) are building materials native to Babylonia, and in fact the *Enuma Elish* reports the making of bricks for Marduk's temple, *Esagil*.[292] The editorial note that these were used instead of stone and mortar undoubtedly explains the custom as unfamiliar to Israelite readers (v. 3b). Unlike the flood story (Gen 6–9), we have no precise literary parallel from ancient Babylonia to this text, although there is a general parallel in the Sumerian tradition of a united people who have one universal language.[293]

But this text is no mere curiosity about the confusing array of languages. The speeches of humans and of Yahweh both contain a grammatical feature that sets in opposition the rebellious human behavior and the acts of God. The exhortation cohortative is used of plural speakers determined to encourage each other into decisive action, and is intensified here with a preceding interjection, *hābâ*, ("Come!" in the NRSV, vv. 3, 4, 7).[294] As the descendants of Noah in Babylonia were resolute and unified in burning bricks, building impressive architecture and a lasting reputation, Yahweh was just as resolute in bringing their rebellion to an end. Indeed, we may wonder what precisely was the sin of these human ancestors at Babel. As I have suggested, the original Israelite tradition behind this text appears to have been a story of general hubris and prideful human rebellion. But its location after the Table of Nations, together with certain other literary echoes, gives it a more profound significance. The canonical location of 11:1–9 highlights the severity of the crime because it included an attempt to avoid scattering across the face of the whole earth in deliberate rebellion of the commands of Gen 1:28 and 9:1, to be fruitful and multiply, and to fill the earth.[295]

---

[290] C. Westermann, *Genesis 1–11* (1984), 534; some would say an elaborate inverted structural unity; see J. P. Fokkelman, *Narrative Art in Genesis: Specimens of Stylistic and Structural Analysis* (SSN 17; Assen: Van Gorcum, 1975), 19–32; G. J. Wenham, *Genesis 1–15* (1987), 235. Studies dissecting the text into as many as four layers of transmission history have been unsuccessful; Hermann Gunkel, *Genesis: Translated and Interpreted*, trans. Mark E. Biddle (Macon, Ga.: Mercer University Press, 1997), 94–95; Christoph Uehlinger, *Weltreich und "eine Rede": Eine neue Deutung der sogenannten Turmbauerzählung (Gen 11, 1–9)* (OBO 101; Freiburg, Schweiz: Universitätsverlag, 1990), 308–583.

[291] *Esagil* was described in the *Enuma Elish* as built with its top raised as high as Apsu [heaven]; S. Dalley, *Myths from Mesopotamia* (2000), 262. The *E-temen-an-ki* was built much later, however, and was probably not specifically in view here.

[292] Ibid.

[293] For translation and further bibliography, see *RANE* 71.

[294] B. T. Arnold and J. H. Choi, *A Guide to Biblical Hebrew Syntax* (2003), 66.

[295] P. J. Harland, "Vertical or Horizontal: The Sin of Babel," *VT* 48 (1998): 515–33.

The divine judgment is a logical corollary of the crime committed, comparing v. 4 with v. 8.

Verse 4: "... otherwise we shall be scattered abroad upon the face of the whole earth."

Verse 5: "So the LORD scattered them abroad from there over the face of all the earth."

As we have seen elsewhere, divine punishment in the Hebrew Scriptures mirrors precisely the sin being punished (see commentary at 3:14–19 and 6:11–13). In this case, the punishment matches the crime in grammatical and lexical detail. Yahweh speaks with the exhortation cohortative, just as the humans did: "Come, let us go down..."[296] Lexically, the ironic use of "scattered" in v. 8 and repeated in v. 9, corresponds precisely to the very result the humans were trying to avoid in v. 4.[297] Such word plays often illustrate divine justice, in which the penalty inflicted matches repayment in kind for the harm done, or a sort of commensurate form of justice.[298] With what we may call "poetic justice," the humans got what they deserved, which was, however, precisely what they tried desperately to avoid, albeit through illicit means.

Etiological interests appear again at the conclusion, with the naming of Babel (v. 9). The earliest form of the name appears to have been *babil(a)*, the origin and meaning of which are lost to antiquity.[299] Akkadian speakers, through popular etymology, contrived a lofty meaning for the city's name, *bāb-ilim*, "Gate of God," which assumed also a Sumerian equivalent, *ka-dingirra*, also meaning "Gate of God." The ingenious word play of Gen 11:9 refutes this haughty claim and, in fact, turns the tables on the city's name: "therefore it was called Babel (*bābel*), because there the LORD confused (*bālal*) the language of all the earth" (Gen 11:9). Far from being the gate of God, Babylon stands for humanity's rebellion against heaven, and is therefore marked by confusion. The "gate of heaven" has been turned into "confusion of speech" and the dispersion of humanity.

GENESIS 11:10–26 GENEALOGY OF SHEM

(11:10) **These are the descendants of Shem. When Shem was one hundred years old, he became the father of Arpachshad two years after the flood;**

(11:11) **and Shem lived after the birth of Arpachshad five hundred years, and had other sons and daughters.**

(11:12) **When Arpachshad had lived thirty-five years, he became the father of Shelah;**

---

[296] On the use of divine plurals, see commentary at 1:26–27.

[297] The verb is *pûṣ*, occurring in the Qal in v. 4, and in the Hiphil in vv. 8 and 9.

[298] P. D. Miller, Jr., *Sin and Judgment in the Prophets* (1982), esp. 121–39.

[299] B. T. Arnold, *Who Were the Babylonians?* (2004), 2 and 32–33.

(11:13) and Arpachshad lived after the birth of Shelah four hundred three years, and had other sons and daughters.

(11:14) When Shelah had lived thirty years, he became the father of Eber;

(11:15) and Shelah lived after the birth of Eber four hundred three years, and had other sons and daughters.

(11:16) When Eber had lived thirty-four years, he became the father of Peleg;

(11:17) and Eber lived after the birth of Peleg four hundred thirty years, and had other sons and daughters.

(11:18) When Peleg had lived thirty years, he became the father of Reu;

(11:19) and Peleg lived after the birth of Reu two hundred nine years, and had other sons and daughters.

(11:20) When Reu had lived thirty-two years, he became the father of Serug;

(11:21) and Reu lived after the birth of Serug two hundred seven years, and had other sons and daughters.

(11:22) When Serug had lived thirty years, he became the father of Nahor;

(11:23) and Serug lived after the birth of Nahor two hundred years, and had other sons and daughters.

(11:24) When Nahor had lived twenty-nine years, he became the father of Terah;

(11:25) and Nahor lived after the birth of Terah one hundred nineteen years, and had other sons and daughters.

(11:26) When Terah had lived seventy years, he became the father of Abram, Nahor, and Haran.

*T*his unit opens with the *tôlĕdôt*-structuring clause of v. 10, "These are the descendants of Shem," and is framed by another in v. 27, making it the smallest such literary panel in the Primeval History and one of the smallest in the book (compare also 25:12–18 and 36:1–8). In the distinctive priestly style we expect of the genealogies, this unit resumes the list of Shem's descendants, some of whom were included already in 10:21–31. It is possible to take this list as introducing the ancestral narratives, providing a structural and thematic unity in the stories of Abraham, Isaac, and Jacob.[300] Although it clearly stands as a transitional marker between human history and Israelite history, numerous affinities with Gen 5 and 10 make 11:10–26 more natural as a concluding note for the Primeval History than as an introduction to the ancestral history. In either case, these verses mark a new era in world history, and therefore serve a Janus-like function, facing both backward to Adam and Noah, but also forward to Abraham and the Israelite nation.

The list of Shem's descendants uses the same distinctive style as that of Seth's genealogy in Gen 5: "When A had lived *x*-years, he became the father of B; and A lived after the birth of B *y*-years, and had other sons and daughters." In Gen

---

[300] Naomi A. Steinberg, "The Genealogical Framework of the Family Stories in Genesis," *Semeia* 46 (1989): 41–50; but see also D. M. Carr, *Reading the Fractures of Genesis* (1996), 122–23.

5, this is followed by an additional sentence omitted here: "Thus all the days of A were z-years; and he died." Israelite genealogies tend to highlight especially noteworthy ancestors by placing them in the seventh position in the list, and at times in the fifth or tenth positions of a genealogical order (see commentary at Gen 5). Such a literary convention allowed ancient authors to focus didactic efforts on one or sometimes two positions in the genealogical tree, which often changed from linear to segmented at the point of emphasis (see Closer Look at p. 82). Thus Cain's genealogy was segmented at the seventh generation, Lamech (4:19–24), while Seth's genealogy moves Lamech to the ninth position, placing Enoch in the seventh position and Noah in the tenth position (5:1–32). Here, in an obviously critical juncture in the Bible's telling of salvation history, Shem's descendants culminate in the tenth position at a segmented list of Terah's sons: Abram, Nahor, and Haran (v. 26). It would not have escaped ancient readers that these three were born to Terah after he lived seventy years, showing again the significance of the numbers seven and ten. Taking all the priestly genealogies together, Abraham is counted as the seventh since Eber (by whose name the Hebrews became known, Eber "Hebrew," *'ibrî*, 10:21), the tenth since Shem, and the twentieth since Adam.[301]

When the Table of Nations traced the line of post-flood humanity through the sons of Noah, the line of Shem's middle son, Arpachshad stopped at the fifth generation, Peleg and Joktan (10:21–25). As Genesis typically does, the line of Joktan was included in order to be laid aside and discussed no more (10:26–30). In 11:10–26, the most important branch of the family tree, that of Shem through Arpachshad, Eber, Peleg, etc., is taken up again in order to carry it down to the tenth generation, that of Abram. Just as Noah was the tenth generation of the human family, now Abram is the tenth from Noah. The line of Seth linked Adam to Noah (Gen 5), the beginning of a new post-flood humanity, and similarly, the line of Shem links Noah to Abram, the beginning of Israel, the people of God.

BRIDGING THE HORIZONS: GOD OF ISRAEL AND LORD OF ALL

Of the two components of Genesis – Primeval History and ancestral narratives – it is the ancestral narratives that define for Israel its identity and chart its destiny (see introduction). At critical junctures in the Pentateuchal narrative (Exod 2:24) and at certain other confessions of faith (sometimes called "creeds," Deut 26:5; Josh 24:2–4), it is Abraham, Isaac, and Jacob who are honored as the patriarchs of the nation Israel. And that is as it should be.

However, the literary structure of Genesis has quite intentionally drawn a distinct line connecting the God of Israel's ancestors and the God of creation through the use of genealogies. The Primeval History that concludes in Gen 11 makes a profound

---

[301] J. M. Sasson, "A Genealogical 'Convention' in Biblical Chronology?" 176–77.

theological statement by equating Yahweh – the God of Israel – with the sovereign creator of the cosmos. The Pentateuch in general establishes continuity between the God of Sinai and the God of Moriah (Gen 22); that is, between the God of the Mosaic covenant and the God who established covenant with Abraham (Exod 2). The Lord, Yahweh of the exodus and of the Sinai covenant, is the very same Yahweh God who forged a relationship with Abraham (Exod 6:2–8). In a similar way, Gen 1–11 ties Israel's ancestral covenant to the Creator of the universe. Yahweh is not simply the God of Jerusalem, nor of geographic Israel, nor is Yahweh only the God of the exodus plagues, nor of the Sinai desert. In a remarkable theological move that transcends most of ancient Near Eastern speculative thought, Yahweh of Israel, the God of the exodus and Sinai covenant as well as the God of the ancestral covenant, becomes also the sovereign Lord of all. The God of Sinai and Zion is thus also the God of Eden and Ararat.

This is central to the legacy of the Hebrew Scriptures. The concept of one God, sovereign over all becomes an important theme in Deuteronomic thought (Deut 4:35,39, and compare Deut 6:4) and in the classical prophets, especially Second Isaiah (Isa 44:8; 45:5, 6, 14, 18, 21, 22; 46:9, and compare Isa 42:8). Yahweh is not a typical ancient Near Eastern deity, tied to and defined by a natural phenomenon, such as sun, moon, or storm, nor was he limited to a geographical or national entity. Whether Israel moved through evolutionary steps to arrive at this conviction is a moot question (henotheism, monolatry, etc.). Irrespective of the outcome of that debate, it remains clear that Israel believed Yahweh was supreme in the cosmos, and as we have seen, at times Israelite theologians expressed the conviction that only Yahweh was real, all other deities were pretenders. And this conviction opened the door for further reflection. As sovereign Lord, Yahweh alone is capable of providing a new beginning for humanity (Gen 6–9) as he provides a new beginning in Abram for the Israelite people (Gen 12:1–3). The covenants with Abraham and Moses, and later with David, each provide new beginnings of salvation history, which at the same time continue Yahweh's plan for salvation of humanity. This legacy of monotheistic faith is indeed a bridge to our contemporary times, as one of the most important concepts in the history of human thought.

IV. Commentary Part Two: Ancestral Narratives – Genesis 12–50

GENESIS 11:27–12:9 CALL OF ABRAM

(11:27) Now these are the descendants of Terah. Terah was the father of Abram, Nahor, and Haran; and Haran was the father of Lot.

(11:28) Haran died before his father Terah in the land of his birth, in Ur of the Chaldeans.

(11:29) Abram and Nahor took wives; the name of Abram's wife was Sarai, and the name of Nahor's wife was Milcah. She was the daughter of Haran the father of Milcah and Iscah.

(11:30) Now Sarai was barren; she had no child.

(11:31) Terah took his son Abram and his grandson Lot son of Haran, and his daughter-in-law Sarai, his son Abram's wife, and they went out together from Ur of the Chaldeans to go into the land of Canaan; but when they came to Haran, they settled there.

(11:32) The days of Terah were two hundred five years; and Terah died in Haran.

(12:1) Now the LORD said to Abram, "Go from your country and your kindred and your father's house to the land that I will show you.

(12:2) I will make of you a great nation, and I will bless you, and make your name great, so that you will be a blessing.

(12:3) I will bless those who bless you, and the one who curses you I will curse; and in you all the families of the earth shall be blessed."[a]

(12:4) So Abram went, as the LORD had told him; and Lot went with him. Abram was seventy-five years old when he departed from Haran.

(12:5) Abram took his wife Sarai and his brother's son Lot, and all the possessions that they had gathered, and the persons whom they had acquired in Haran; and they set forth to go to the land of Canaan. When they had come to the land of Canaan,

(12:6) Abram passed through the land to the place at Shechem, to the oak of Moreh. At that time the Canaanites were in the land.

[a] Or by you all the families of the earth shall bless themselves.

(12:7) Then the LORD appeared to Abram, and said, "To your offspring I will give this land." So he built there an altar to the LORD, who had appeared to him.

(12:8) From there he moved on to the hill country on the east of Bethel, and pitched his tent, with Bethel on the west and Ai on the east; and there he built an altar to the LORD and invoked the name of the LORD.

(12:9) And Abram journeyed on by stages toward the Negeb.

OVERVIEW OF CHAPTERS 12–50

The book of Genesis takes a dramatic turn at 11:27 with the *tôlĕdôt*–structuring clause, "these are *the descendants of* Terah." So far, this literary device has introduced genealogical lists with occasional brief explanatory glosses, or narrative expansions that covered only a few chapters.[1] At Gen 11:27, however, "the descendants of Terah" phrase introduces a much larger portion of narrative, extending all the way to Gen 25:11. The sheer size of this narrative expansion reflects the importance of Terah's family, as though Genesis fast-forwards through the generations of human history to arrive at Abram of Ur, the son of Terah. It is without question a great moment in the biblical storyline when Abram arrives on the scene.

The rest of the book of Genesis traces pertinent details in the lives of Abram/ Abraham (Gen 12–25), Jacob/Israel (Gen 26–36), and Joseph (Gen 37–50). The *tôlĕdôt*–structuring clauses link them all together to the Primeval History of Gen 1–11, suggesting that the diverse stories collected here are really only one story. As the generations of the heavens and the earth reflect the grandeur and glory of God, so the generations of Terah manifest the glory of God through the promises fulfilled in Israel's ancestors. Beyond the specific *tôlĕdôt* device, the genealogies themselves link Israel's ancestors with the primordial events of Gen 1–11. This is done deliberately at the nexus of the tenth generation. Noah, in the tenth generation from Adam, brings comfort to a suffering humanity (Gen 5:29; compare 3:17), and in the tenth generation from Noah, Abram receives promises of land, descendants, and blessing, together constituting a "typological reversal of the primordial curses in Eden."[2] Cosmic beginnings and Israel's national beginnings are tied together theologically as one story. God created the universe and forged a covenant relationship with a single righteous individual, Noah, as a means of salvation from the flood waters. Now in Gen 12–50, God creates a nation, Israel, and establishes a covenant with a single righteous individual, Abraham, as a solution to humanity's sinful dilemma.

---

[1] So genealogies are introduced with *tôlĕdôt* at 5:1, 10:1, and 11:10, and for examples of the smaller glosses in these genealogies, see 5:22–24 or 10:8b–12. Narrative expansions are introduced by the clause at 2:4a (Garden of Eden and Cain–Abel episodes), and at 6:9a (the flood story). See Introduction for more.

[2] Michael A. Fishbane, *Biblical Interpretation in Ancient Israel* (Oxford: Clarendon Press, 1988), 372–73.

This ingenious book-structure, made possible by the genealogies and the *tôlĕdôt*–structuring device, make God's relationship with Abraham and the nation Israel the means of salvation for all humanity. "It is as though God, having tried once, twice, and a third time with humankind as a whole, concludes that his hopes were too ambitious. He will start again, this time with one man and his family, one people, slowly emerging into history, perhaps to succeed where mankind as a whole has failed."[3]

Thus the unity of the book of Genesis has impressive theological significance. The Primeval History (Gen 1–11) and the ancestral narratives (Gen 12–50) are in dialogue with each other, the former posing a question or problem, ultimately answered only by the latter. Now we must ask about the relationship in the opposite direction. How do the ancestral accounts of Gen 12–50 relate to what follows in the rest of the Pentateuch? The stories of Abraham, Isaac, and Jacob look back to, and are in dialogue with, the cosmic beginnings of Gen 1–11. How then do they relate to Exodus, Leviticus, Numbers, and Deuteronomy, and indeed, how do they relate to the rest of the Bible?

The ancestral narratives of Gen 12–50 have been called "the Old Testament of the Old Testament," meaning this portion of Genesis relates to the rest of the Old Testament in a way analogous to the relationship of the Old Testament as a whole to the New Testament.[4] The Christian Bible contains Old and New Testaments with two different periods of salvation history portraying one God revealed in two different periods. As the New Testament considers Jesus of Nazareth the fulfillment of the divine promises of the Old Testament, so God's deliverance of Israel from Egypt, the covenant at Sinai, the conquest of the Promise Land, etc., all fulfill the promises made to Abraham in the ancestral covenant of Gen 12–50. Or to turn the direction of influence around, just as the Old Testament anticipates and prefigures the New, so the ancestral narratives prefigure the events of the Mosaic era and the rest of Israel's history. In the commentary that follows, I will draw on this analogy occasionally in order to emphasize the Janus-qualities of the ancestral narratives, which look both backward to the Primeval History and forward to the rest of Israel's Scriptures.

COMMENTS ON 11:27–12:9

The genealogies of Adam (5:1–32) and Seth (11:10–26) repeated incessantly the verb translated by the NRSV "became the father of" or simply "had" (causative Hiphil of

---

[3] Herbert C. Brichto, *The Names of God: Poetic Readings in Biblical Beginnings* (New York: Oxford University Press, 1998), 184.

[4] R. W. L. Moberly, *The Old Testament of the Old Testament: Patriarchal Narratives and Mosiac Yahwism* (OBT; Minneapolis: Fortress Press, 1992), 126, and for this discussion in general, pages 105–46. For helpful critique of Moberly's "supersessionism," see J. G. Janzen, *Abraham and All the Families of the Earth: A Commentary on the Book of Genesis 12–50* (ITC; Grand Rapids, Mich.: Eerdmans, 1993), 6–12.

yālad, "bear, bring forth").[5] This verbal root is related to the noun form *tôlĕdôt*, "line of descendants," so central as a structuring device in Genesis, as well as another noun in 11:28 and 12:1, "land of one's birth" or "land of one's kindred" (*môledet*, cf. 24:4, 7). At the beginning of Terah's family tree, this verb returns in the clauses "Terah *was the father of* Abram" and "Haran *was the father of* Lot" (both in 11:27). The next verse explains that Haran died in Ur of the Chaldeans, his *môledet* or birthplace, prior to his father. Preceding one's father in death is an unusual circumstance in itself, but in this case Haran's death is also an important detail for the rest of the narrative. Additionally we are informed in 11:29 for the first time in these genealogical lists the names of wives: Abram married Sarai and Nahor married Milcah.[6]

The most important background information in Terah's family tree is reserved for the painfully brief 11:30: "Now Sarai was barren; she had no child." This detail is reported twice, in parallel clauses for dramatic effect. Nothing like this has happened in Genesis before. Indeed, the book is structured by fecundity, by the fertility and (re)productivity of humanity as a result of God's blessing "be fruitful and multiply" (1:28 and 9:1). The articulation of that blessing was itself the benediction because it made it true; it was an announcement as much as an imperative, a statement of what *will* be as much as what *must* be.[7] And Adam's descendants have indeed been especially fruitful, as the book of Genesis makes clear. The genealogies and *tôlĕdôt* clauses have meticulously recorded birth after birth in the universal story of God's relationship with humanity. But here stands Sarai, an exception to the cosmic rule. She has no "child," an extremely rare spelling of an otherwise very common noun, preserved here most likely in an archaic form, fossilized by its use in a formulaic expression of infertility.[8] The root of that rare term, the "child" (*wālād*) that Sarai lacks, is the same root as *tôlĕdôt*, "descendants," and *môledet*, "birth place." The abrupt news that Sarai has no "child" brings the reader up short. Instead of birthing-places and long lines of fruitful progeny, we read for the first time of barrenness. Sarai's sterility immediately creates a suspenseful tension in the genealogical details of 11:27–32, and therefore in the narrative that follows. Terah's family line will not require much ink. With the death of one son, Haran, and the barrenness of a daughter-in-law, Sarai, Terah's list will be succinct indeed! And the reader presumes there will be no literary catch phrase "these are the descendants of Abram." His genealogical line will be discontinued we assume, leaving no doubt

---

[5] Twenty-eight times in 5:1–32 (imperfect plus *waw* consecutive nineteen times and the infinitive construct nine) and twenty-five times in 11:10–26 (imperfect plus *waw* consecutive seventeen times and the infinitive construct eight).

[6] On the importance of endogamy, marriage within a specific kinship, ethnic, or religious community as a means of ensuring continuity of cultural values, see Closer Look at 24:1–9, p. 219.

[7] See commentary at 1:28 and 9:1, and Christopher W. Mitchell, *The Meaning of* brk *"to bless" in the Old Testament* (SBLDS 95; Atlanta: Scholars Press, 1987), 62.

[8] Compare 2 Sam 6:23; Claus Westermann, *Genesis 12–36: A Commentary* (Minneapolis: Augsburg Pub. House, 1985), 138–39.

that Abram is a minor character, and of necessity, the story will continue along other avenues. But to assume so much is to get ahead of the narrative, which contains, of course, a few surprises.

The reason for Terah's sojourn from Ur of the Chaldeans is not given, and we can only speculate about its causes (11:31). Famine was a common reason for such travels in the ancient world (12:10; 41:57 and Ruth 1:1), and climatic changes may have made such relocation necessary. Patriarchal culture is reflected in the news that Terah brought his childless son, Abram, his orphaned grandson, Lot, and his barren daughter-in-law, Sarai, all part of his responsibility as *paterfamilias*. Presumably his remaining son, Nahor, also traveled to the region of Haran, as his own family will reappear later in the story in central roles (22:20–23; 24:10–61; 29:5).[9] We are told with no explanation that the family traveled to the edge of Canaan and settled in the region of Haran rather than their original destination, the land of Canaan itself. Terah died in Haran, leaving Abram bereaved of his father, his brother, and now responsible for his nephew and barren wife (11:32). As we have seen, the Table of Nations (Gen 10) and the Tower of Babel narrative immediately following it (11:1–9) were intentionally dischronologized in order to arrange them thematically (see commentary at 11:1–9). Similarly, the chronological figures here (11:26, 32, and 12:4) suggest that the genealogical data are being presented first in order to place Terah aside and focus the reader's attention solely on Abram in the ensuing narrative. Terah was 70 at Abram's birth (11:26), and so when Terah died at age 205, Abram would have been 135 (11:32). We learn a few verses later that Abram was 75 when he left Haran for Canaan (12:4), and therefore the reader is to surmise that Terah was 145 when Abram left for Canaan, and that Terah lived in Haran another 60 years before his death at age 205. The formulaic death announcement for Terah (11:32) is therefore tying off the genealogical material rhetorically in preparation for the narrative to follow. The sequence is for rhetorical effect, not chronological.[10]

The narratival beginning "Now the Lord said to Abram" has an arresting familiarity (12:1). Divine speech introduced in such a way in the Primeval History marks significant benchmarks (e.g., 1:3, 29; 2:18; 6:13; 7:1), and here it marks the transition from genealogical background to the narrative itself. The effect is a telescoping of attention, from the overview of Terah's family tree generally to specific words spoken to individual characters at a given place and time. The text fast forwards

---

[9] The identical spellings in English of the personal name, Haran, and a geographical location of the same name are strictly coincidental (11:31–32). The Hebrew spellings differ in one tiny phoneme, which unfortunately is not indicated in most translations (Terah's son is *hārān*, and the place in northern Syria–Palestine is *ḥārān*).

[10] Stephen's speech has a different chronology, stating that Abram left Haran "after his father died" (Acts 7:4), probably relying on the textual variant of the Samaritan Pentateuch at 11:32, which has Terah's age at death as 145 rather than 205. Attempts at harmonization have not been convincing; Victor P. Hamilton, *The Book of Genesis, Chapters 1–17* (NICOT; Grand Rapids, Mich.: Eerdmans, 1990), 366–68.

through Terah's family tree (11:27–32), pausing only to note critical background information, and now the rhetorical effect of "Now the Lord said . . . " narrows the focus and demands careful attention. As God was the subject of the first verb of the Bible ("God created"), so now Yahweh "is the subject of the first verb at the beginning of the first statement and thus the subject of the entire subsequent sacred history."[11]

"Go" is the vaguest of commands, and the three qualifiers provided by the series of prepositional phrases are little help in clarification ("from your . . . and your . . . and your" 12:1). Moreover the precise diction of God's command is of interest. The otherwise exceedingly common verb ("go") is here attached to a prepositional phrase rightly omitted in NRSV and most other translations.[12] The semantic force of the additional phrase is in question,[13] but it is at least of interest that this collocation occurs only twice in the Hebrew Bible, here and in Gen 22:2: "*go* to the land of Moriah." As we shall see, this is one of several lexical links between Gen 12 and 22, the first and last times Yahweh speaks to Abram.[14] These chapters serve as bookends framing the Abrahamic stories, and throw into bold relief the motif of divine command followed by radical obedience so important to the narrative as a whole.

Abram is called to leave three things – country, kindred, and his father's house – and to go unto one thing: "the land that I will show you" (12:1). The three things he is to abandon are interrelated as a threefold summation of "homeland," and we should not make too fine a distinction between them. On the other hand, the "father's house" (*bêt 'āb*) has a more specific denotation as one of the most important features of Israelite society, the extended or "joint family" of up to three generations, which was the center of religious, social, and economic life in ancient Israel.[15] It is

---

[11] Gerhard von Rad, *Genesis: A Commentary* (OTL; Philadelphia: Westminster Press, 1961), 159.

[12] Wenham's "go by yourself," while laudable as an attempt to include the additional phrase, gives the wrong impression at least in American English, since Abram was certainly not being called to leave Sarai, Lot, and his other dependents behind; Gordon J. Wenham, *Genesis 1–15* (WBC 1; Waco, Tex.: Word Books, 1987), 265.

[13] The phrase in question is *lek-lĕkā*, the simple imperative *lek* followed by the prepositional phrase "to you" (*lĕkā*), a reflexive use of the preposition *lĕ*, common with imperatives or verbs of motion. The so-called "ethical dative" is less likely here; Bill T. Arnold and John H. Choi, *A Guide to Biblical Hebrew Syntax* (Cambridge: Cambridge University Press, 2003), 114, and see 112 for the ethical dative.

[14] In both instances the specific destination is withheld from Abram/Abraham, creating a Canaan-land/Moriah-land comparison; H. C. Brichto, *The Names of God* (1998), 283.

[15] Perhaps better translated "family household." On this important concept, see Lawrence E. Stager, "The Archaeology of the Family in Ancient Israel," *BASOR* 260 (1985): 1–35, esp. 20–22; Oded Borowski, *Daily Life in Biblical Times* (SBLABS 5; Atlanta: Society of Biblical Literature, 2003), 22; Carol L. Meyers, "The Family in Early Israel," in *Families in Ancient Israel*, eds. Leo G. Perdue, Joseph Blenkinsopp, John J. Collins, and Carol L. Meyers (Family, Religion, and Culture; Louisville, Ky.: Westminster John Knox Press, 1997), 1–47, esp. 19; J. D. Schloen, *The House of the Father as Fact and Symbol: Patrimonialism in*

possible that such a call would have been received as quite natural for a pre-sedentary nomad, even as a divine offer of salvation for Abram.[16] If so, an earlier meaning has been enriched by its canonical location and becomes a definite crisis of faith, nuanced by editors who spoke from a different social context. As we have seen, the chronology of the context means Terah was still alive when Abram departed (11:26, 32; 12:4), which adds another dimension to the call to abandon the "father's house." Abram must launch out as a new *paterfamilias*, even while still childless, and indeed, without any assurance that he himself would in fact become a father, thereby establishing a new "house." Yahweh required Abram to give up the security of his social sanctuary and familial support – so central to ancient tribal sensibilities – in order to depend on Yahweh alone while following this directive. In this way, the call of Abram also echoes Israel's later experiences as a people called from Egypt in a great faith experiment in order to travel to an unknown land.

Canaan is the land to which Abram is called. This was Terah's original destination (11:31) although we are not told the reasons for his detour in Haran. Noah pronounced a curse against the Canaanites because of the offense of their father, Ham (9:25), and the Table of Nations detailed the various descendants of Canaan and where they settled, explaining how the urbanite children of Ham came to inhabit this land of promise (10:15–19). However, the reader is not to suppose that Abram knows so much. The relative clause in 12:1, "to the land *that I will show you*" makes it clear that Abram is without certainty, if not completely clueless about his destination. Abram must depend on Yahweh's divine decree rather than his own ability to navigate his journey (Heb 11:8). Without societal, familial support – even without knowledge of his destination – this nomadic Abram must launch out relying solely and exclusively on Yahweh for direction and sustenance.

But God does not leave Abram completely adrift and rudderless. In the divine speech, the command to leave three things and go unto one is followed immediately by a series of six clauses, traditionally identified as "promises" (12:2–3). These interrelated and overlapping clauses are hardly more specific than the vague "Go" imperative but together they provide all that Abram needs for obedience. Indeed, the specific ways in which these promises will become a reality remain somewhat nebulous until another revelatory speech in 12:7 – *after* Abram's obedience.

The syntax of the six clauses in 12:2–3 may well express purpose following the imperative of 12:1: "Go . . . *so that* I may make of you a great nation, *so that* I may bless you and make your name great, and *so* you may be a blessing" (and similarly in 12:3).[17] The first assertion is that Yahweh will make Abram "a great nation,"

Ugarit and the Ancient Near East (Studies in the Archaeology and History of the Levant 2; Winona Lake, Ind.: Eisenbrauns, 2001).

[16] C. Westermann, *Genesis 12–36* (1985), 148.

[17] On "intended result" or "purpose" in verbal sequences using *waw* conjunctive with volitives, as in five of these six clauses, see B. T. Arnold and J. H. Choi, *A Guide to Biblical Hebrew Syntax* (2003), 92. Nevertheless, purpose in these cases is not marked lexically

imagining a future political entity taking its place among the nations of Gen 10, which the reader no doubt understands as Israel. Second, Yahweh intends to "bless" Abram, which most interpreters accept as the elemental core of the other promises, due largely to the repetition of the root "bless" (*brk*) five times in 12:2–3.[18] God blesses Abram in order to motivate him to obey the command "go," and to draw him to a close relationship with himself, subsequently defined as "covenant."[19] Such divine blessing in the ancestral narratives has God as its source and is an expression of his good will. Third, Yahweh will make Abram's name "great," which is more than a promise of renown or acclaim. Rather, in contrast to the tower-builders at Babel, who pathetically strove for permanence themselves by building a name in their own strength (11:4), to have a great name given to one by God in the Hebrew Scriptures is to be viewed as a royal figure (2 Sam 7:9). In the fourth clause, Yahweh states not only that he will bless Abram, but that indeed, Abram himself will become a blessing. The syntax is awkward here and often debated, but the particular verbal form probably connotes Abram's passivity: it is beyond his power to become a blessing although it is a certainty of the future.[20]

The theme of blessing returns in the fifth clause in which Yahweh intends to bless those who are on good terms with Abram and inversely to curse those who are not. "Blessing" in this case is to "bestow benefits" generally.[21] Finally, in the sixth and final clause, the theme of blessing is complete in the assertion that all the families of humanity will be blessed in Abram. These statements pull a curtain back on the central theological convictions of Genesis, and bring to light the themes and ideological convictions that bind the ancestral narratives to the earlier Primeval History while also driving the narrative forward to Israel's role in the world. More than promises of security and greatness for Abram, when read in the context of Gen 1–11, these promises reveal a divine plan to extend blessing to all the families of the earth. The word translated "families" (*mišpĕḥôt*, also "clans") is that social sphere in Israelite culture between the smaller "father's house" and the larger tribe.[22] However, its use to denote all clans "of the earth" in 12:3 transcends Israelite society and has in mind all the nations in a way reminiscent of the Table of Nations in its

---

or explicitly by syntax, and so caution is in order; see Takamitsu Muraoka, "The Alleged Final Function of the Biblical Hebrew Syntagm <*WAW* + A Volitive Verb Form>," in *Narrative Syntax and the Hebrew Bible: Papers of the Tilburg Conference 1996*, ed. Ellen J. van Wolde (Biblical Interpretation Series 29; New York: Brill, 1997), 229–41.

18 G. von Rad, *Genesis* (1961), 159.

19 C. W. Mitchell, *The Meaning of* brk *"to bless" in the Old Testament* (1987), 29–36.

20 So we have here the "imperative of promise," and emendation to a perfect with *waw* consecutive is unnecessary; B. T. Arnold and J. H. Choi, *A Guide to Biblical Hebrew Syntax* (2003), 64.

21 C. W. Mitchell, *The Meaning of* brk *"to bless" in the Old Testament* (1987), 30. Also it may be noted that the twin nature of this clause leads some interpreters to count seven promises rather than six.

22 L. E. Stager, "The Archaeology of the Family in Ancient Israel," esp. 22.

recurring description of the descendants of Noah's sons, according to their *families,* languages, lands, and nations (10:5, 20, 31). Yahweh's plan is not merely to bless Abram for Abram's sake, nor for his family's sake, but to make Abram a mediator of blessing for the world.

This final assertion contains, however, an interesting translation problem that has perplexed interpreters for generations: "in you all the families of the earth *shall be blessed.*" A few modern scholars as well as the great medieval Jewish scholar, Rashi, have argued that the promise should be rendered reflexively, which is possible grammatically: "by you all the families of the earth *shall bless themselves*" as in the NRSV footnote. Although a mixed approach is also possible, it has been shown recently that the reflexive is unlikely in this context, and that the traditional passive "shall be blessed" is to be preferred.[23]

"So Abram went" is one of the most remarkable statements of the Bible (12:4). We might expect any manner of dialogue or debate between verses 3 and 4, or hesitation on Abram's part motivated by confusion, self-doubt, or stubbornness. But this text is not interested in such things. Rather the simplicity of "so Abram went" portrays a picture of bold and radical dependence on God's word, the diametric opposite of Adam's and Eve's rationalization (3:1–7), which makes Abram's obedience a model of faith for the rest of the Bible. "Went" (*wayyēlek*) is an unadorned, almost nonchalant response, corresponding to the imperative of the same word in 12:1, "go" (*lek*). It is as though everything in the text has been stripped away in order to reveal just how perfectly Abram's obedience matches Yahweh's command. Indeed, the degree to which his response is precisely what the Bible (and Yahweh) desires is illustrated by the qualifying clause "as the Lord had told him." Even the additional note that "Lot went with him" contributes to Abram's character, since he was fulfilling his patriarchal responsibility to his deceased brother by providing for the orphaned nephew. The news of Lot's presence also establishes the "presumed heir" motif, leading the reader to assume that Lot will inherit the childless Abram. But this nephew will be the first of a series of candidates identified as potential heirs, only to be unceremoniously placed aside as unqualified to inherit Abram.

Abram took all that he had and traveled to Canaan (12:5–6). He traversed the land all the way to Shechem, in the heart of the central highlands, located along the pass between Mt. Ebal to its north and Mt. Gerizim to its south. The city flourished in the early Middle Bronze age as an unfortified open settlement, shortly after 1900 BCE.[24]

---

[23] Keith N. Grüneberg, *Abraham, Blessing, and the Nations: A Philological and Exegetical Study of Genesis 12:3 in its Narrative Context* (BZAW 332; Berlin: de Gruyter, 2003); for the reflexive sense, which is expressed more clearly later in Genesis, see David M. Carr, *Reading the Fractures of Genesis: Historical and Literary Approaches* (Louisville, Ky.: Westminster John Knox Press, 1996), 155–58, as well as Carr's review of Grüneberg in *JBL* 123/4 (2004): 741–44 (and cf. Gen 22:18 and 26:4). For a defense of the middle meaning, see C. W. Mitchell, *The Meaning of* brk *"to bless" in the Old Testament* (1987), 31–33.

[24] Joe D. Seger, "Shechem," *OEANE* 5:19–23.

Abram arrives in Shechem not as a settler, but as a visitor to the sacred site ("the place"), positioned presumably just outside the city, "the oak of Moreh." The word "Moreh" is "teacher" (*môreh*), and it seems most likely this particular tree was noted as a worship center where one could expect to receive divine oracles and revelations (cf. 35:4; Deut 11:30; Josh 24:26; Judg 9:6, 37).[25] While seeking another word from Yahweh, perhaps hoping for assurance of the rather vaguely stated promises in 12:2–3, Abram is reminded of his non-immigrant status in Canaan by the presence of Canaanites "in the land." He may have arrived in the land of promise, but "at that time" it was occupied by others.

Here at Shechem, at the oak of Moreh, Abram received a revelation from Yahweh that confirmed the promises of 12:2–3 by stating specifically what they involved (12:7). The verb "appeared" occurs twice in 12:7, both with the sense of special revelation – an act of divine self-introduction to humans. This particular form of the verb becomes important in the Old Testament for occasions when Yahweh pulls back the curtain on himself, allowing himself to be seen in revelatory theophanies.[26] What Abram actually saw is not the issue here, but rather what he heard (see Closer Look "Divine Revelation in the Hebrew Scriptures" at p. 135). In fact, the substance of the appearance or revelation is contained in the words "to your offspring I will give this land."[27] Here, finally, the specifics of the promise are unambiguous. The blessing and fame of Abram will come through "seed" (*zera'*, NRSV's "offspring") and "land" (*'ereṣ*). After Abram's obedient sojourn from Haran to Shechem, Yahweh confirms the promises by fleshing out their details. Abram will become a great nation and a blessing for the world through children and land inheritance, despite his currently hopeless circumstances. This promise of "seed" and "land" is enough for Abram, and so he builds an altar to Yahweh who appeared to him at Shechem. The patriarchs never use existing cult sites, but rather build new altars or reuse ones they themselves built previously (see Closer Look at "Ancestral Religion," p. 142).[28] The rest of the Abrahamic narrative will develop the promises of seed and land, as our main character learns new ways to trust them and wait for them to become a reality.

---

[25] Probably the evergreen Kermes oak (*Quercus coccifera*), which in antiquity covered considerable areas of the central hill country; F. N. Hepper, *Baker Encyclopedia of Bible Plants* (Grand Rapids, Mich.: Baker Book House, 1992), 34–35. Trees held religious significance throughout the ancient Near East as physical symbols of divine presence and holy sites; Othmar Keel, *Goddesses and Trees, New Moon and Yahweh: Ancient Near Eastern Art and The Hebrew Bible* (JSOTSup 261; Sheffield: Sheffield Academic Press, 1998), 20–48.

[26] The verb in question is *r'h*, "to see," which in the causative-reflexive use of the Niphal is "appear, become visible"; B. T. Arnold and J. H. Choi, *A Guide to Biblical Hebrew Syntax* (2003), 41. See Closer Look at "Divine Revelation in the Hebrew Scriptures," p. 135.

[27] The "and said" of 12:7 is for epexegesis or specification, fleshing out the details of the appearance of Yahweh itself in the words spoken to Abram; B. T. Arnold and J. H. Choi, *A Guide to Biblical Hebrew Syntax* (2003), 87.

[28] Nahum M. Sarna, Genesis: *The Traditional Hebrew Text with the New JPS Translation* (JPS Torah Commentary; Philadelphia: Jewish Publication Society, 1989), 92.

Abram's nomadic lifestyle remained the same, as he moved further south, pitching his tent between Bethel and Ai (12:8). Here he built another altar to Yahweh, and "invoked the name of the Lord." Using the same phraseology as in Gen 4:26 for the institution of Yahweh worship among humanity generally, this invoking or "calling upon" the name of Yahweh is most likely a reference to formal, public worship (cf. 13:4). There is no indication how long Abram remained in Bethel, but he clearly sets up camp, using Yahweh-worship and yet another altar, to make himself at home. His subsequent journey "by stages" as far as the southern reaches of later Judah, "the Negeb," means Abram has now traversed the "promised land" itself.

A CLOSER LOOK – DIVINE REVELATION IN THE HEBREW SCRIPTURES

The extraordinary statement that Yahweh "appeared" to Abram (12:7) is important in Old Testament theology. Yahweh is frequently thought of anthropomorphically in early Israelite traditions, that is, as having a form like that of a man, or to turn it around more appropriately, humans were considered theomorphically, creatures made in the image of God.[29] So on the one hand, God is transcendent, all-powerful, and far removed from the created order. On the other hand, the common verb "to see" in a causative–reflexive (Niphal) form is used for divine self-disclosure at times when Yahweh makes himself known to humans in dramatic fashion and for revelatory communiqués.[30] Such uses of the verb transcend the visual–sensory domain to that of a personal encounter with Yahweh. So in the ancestral narratives of Genesis, Yahweh God appears to Abram at critical junctures of his faith journey (12:7; 17:1; 18:1), as did to Isaac (26:2, 24) and Jacob (35:1, 9; 48:3; cf. 28:13–15; 35:7; 46:2–4). For the patriarchs, these theophanies, or appearances, were times for learning more about Yahweh and for making critical, life-altering decisions. The emphasis is not on the physical appearance of that which is seen, but rather on the content of the truth revealed or communicated. In most cases, the "appearance" is followed by divine speech, which gives direction or comfort to the patriarch, or which reveals more of the character of God. Divine revelation is not given in order to satisfy human curiosity about God, but rather to deepen the human–God relationship and to inspire the patriarch to press forward in obedience.

Not surprisingly, then, the same concept is important later when Yahweh reveals himself to Moses at a critical juncture in Israel's story. The angel of Yahweh "appeared" to Moses in a burning bush (Exod 3:2, and compare 4:1, 5), although thereafter, the angel is simply Yahweh, "the Lord." Moreover, in a passage that deliberately links this new Mosaic revelation together with the earlier ancestral covenant,

---

[29] Gerhard von Rad, *Old Testament Theology* (New York: Harper, 1962–1965), 1.145 and 219.

[30] Non-theophanic examples of this verbal form occur, as for example, when the dry land *appears* from the primordial waters (1:9), and again when the tops of the mountains *appear* after the flood waters subside (8:5), or when Joseph *presented himself* to his father, Jacob (46:29).

God declares that he "appeared" to the patriarchs as God Almighty (Exod 6:3). Subsequently, the glory of Yahweh "appeared" in the cloud (Exod 16:10). And, beyond this particular verbal form, God continues to reveal himself to Israel through pillars of cloud and fire (Exod 13:21–22; Num 9:15–23), theophanies of thunder and lightning and trumpet blast (Exod 19:16), or through divinely approved Urim and Thummim (Exod 28:30; Lev 8:8; Num 27:21; 1 Sam 23:1–6). In subsequent generations, the Hebrew prophets became the instruments of divine self-disclosure, and during the pain of the Babylonian exile, Jews turned increasingly to the written word as the medium of revelation. The God of the Hebrew Scriptures is paradoxically a hidden God who reveals himself, a transcendent God of self-revelation, whose desire is to make himself known to humanity.

GENESIS 12:10–20 SOJOURN IN EGYPT

(12:10) Now there was a famine in the land. So Abram went down to Egypt to reside there as an alien, for the famine was severe in the land.

(12:11) When he was about to enter Egypt, he said to his wife Sarai, "I know well that you are a woman beautiful in appearance;

(12:12) and when the Egyptians see you, they will say, 'This is his wife'; then they will kill me, but they will let you live.

(12:13) Say you are my sister, so that it may go well with me because of you, and that my life may be spared on your account."

(12:14) When Abram entered Egypt the Egyptians saw that the woman was very beautiful.

(12:15) When the officials of Pharaoh saw her, they praised her to Pharaoh. And the woman was taken into Pharaoh's house.

(12:16) And for her sake he dealt well with Abram; and he had sheep, oxen, male donkeys, male and female slaves, female donkeys, and camels.

(12:17) But the LORD afflicted Pharaoh and his house with great plagues because of Sarai, Abram's wife.

(12:18) So Pharaoh called Abram, and said, "What is this you have done to me? Why did you not tell me that she was your wife?

(12:19) Why did you say, 'She is my sister,' so that I took her for my wife? Now then, here is your wife, take her, and be gone."

(12:20) And Pharaoh gave his men orders concerning him; and they set him on the way, with his wife and all that he had.

*F*amine was often a cause for travel in the biblical world (12:10; 26:1; 41:54–57; 42:5; 43:1–2, and Ruth 1:1). Ancient Canaan was susceptible to famine because its fragile agrarian economy depended on rainfall, whereas Egypt and Mesopotamia relied largely on river-irrigation. For the most part, climatic changes were not responsible for long-term famines in ancient history, except perhaps at the close of the Early Bronze and beginning of the Middle Bronze Ages (ca. 2200–2000 BCE), for which ample Egyptian inscriptions complain about severe famine.[31] The severity of the famine in Abram's day is emphasized by repetition in the opening verse (v. 10). He needs to find sustenance elsewhere beyond Canaan. Unlike his visits to Shechem, Bethel, and the Negeb in the previous paragraph, Abram builds no altars, nor does he experience divine revelations or call upon the name of Yahweh. He has descended to Egypt as a sojourner, "to reside there as an alien" (*gûr*). Whereas he formerly pitched his tent in the Promised Land and received confirmation of the divine promises, now those promises themselves seem in jeopardy, as Abram pulls up stakes, leaves the Promised Land itself, and turns to Egypt to find food for his family.

Famine is not the only threat to the ancestral promises. As he enters Egypt, Abram understands that his life is in mortal peril, and he takes preemptive steps, which however put Israel's matriarch, Sarai, also at risk (vv. 11–13).[32] This episode contains a number of confusing features, for which we have no satisfying answers. First, Sarai, at age sixty-five, is a woman of such alluring beauty as to inspire the murder of a husband. Second, Abram's character, upheld as righteous elsewhere in the narrative, is tarnished (to say the least) by his plot to enlist his wife in a ruse to save his own neck. Third, Sarai apparently colludes with Abram without objection. Fourth, the acquisition of great wealth as a result of the collusion is nowhere condemned (v. 16). Fifth, and perhaps most confusing of all, quite similar episodes occur on two other occasions in Genesis. Abraham and Sarah use the ruse again in their dealings with Abimelech of Gerar, as if they were incapable of learning a lesson from their mistakes in Egypt (Gen 20), and the same King Abimelech, as if he also cannot learn from the past, was victimized by the scam again, this time by Isaac and Rebekah (Gen 26:1–16). The three accounts of the "wife–sister" theme share many similar lexical and phraseological connections, making it impossible to assume they are independent of each other.[33]

Such intractable problems have led to an enormous amount of scholarly literature on the "Matriarch in Danger" literary topos, or type-scene. Source critics have

---

[31] William H. Shea, "Famine," *ABD* 2:769–73, esp. 770–71.

[32] Other Semites migrated to the eastern Delta during times of drought and famine, but for Israelites, Egypt was always a detour away from the land of milk and honey, and always considered dangerous; F. V. Greifenhagen, *Egypt on the Pentateuch's Ideological Map: Constructing Biblical Israel's Identity* (JSOTSup 361; London: Sheffield Academic Press, 2002), 24–45.

[33] One theory made popular by Ephraim Speiser over forty years ago had it that this custom was paralleled in Hurrian culture and preserved in Nuzi texts: an individual could adopt his wife as a sister in a unique high-status marriage to provide security and safety for the whole family. However, the theory has rightly been abandoned for several reasons; see Samuel Greengus, "Sisterhood Adoption at Nuzi and the 'Wife-Sister' in Genesis," *HUCA* 46 (1975): 5–31; Thomas L. Thompson, *The Historicity of The Patriarchal Narratives: The Quest for the Historical Abraham* (BZAW 133; Berlin: de Gruyter, 1974), 234–47.

typically separated the three ancestral wife–sister stories into J and E variations, two stemming from an original Yahwistic, or J source (12:10–20 and 26:1–16) and the other from E (20:1–18).[34] Other interpreters have theorized how one of the episodes may have been midrashic commentary or exegetical development of the others, such as the possibility that 26:1–16 is a theological reworking of 20:1–18, which in turn may be a revision of 12:10–20.[35] But it may be just as likely that all three derive from an oral tradition – a formulary topos of the Endangered Matriarch – the standardized features of which would have been widely known in ancient Israel, and which was adapted variously in our three texts. The final editors of Genesis saw no need to fill in the gaps, to answer all the questions raised by this text, because apparently it was assumed the first readers and hearers of Genesis would have enough cultural context to understand the literary topos.[36] And in this case, the traditional form of the story has been turned to emphasize God's intervention for deliverance (v. 17): "But the Lord afflicted Pharaoh. . . . " The lesson here is that Israel's forebears, despite their vulnerability as aliens in Egypt and their failures in the face of peril, were under Yahweh's protection and that God was nevertheless at work to bring about the fulfillment of the ancestral promises.[37]

Regardless of the original form of this literary type-scene, it has been edited in order to anticipate Israel's subsequent exodus from Egypt, not only in despoiling the Egyptians (Exod 3:21–22; 11:1–3; 12:35–36), but also by Yahweh's intervention and the sending of plagues.[38] Sarai's role also, as a slave in Pharaoh's house, may foreshadow Israel's bondage in Egypt. Great comfort can be derived from identifying with the ancestors, whether one is reflecting on Israel's bondage and deliverance from Egypt, or the later exilic period and its deliverance from Babylon.

GENESIS 13:1–18 ABRAM AND LOT SEPARATE

(13:1) So Abram went up from Egypt, he and his wife, and all that he had, and Lot with him, into the Negeb.

(13:2) Now Abram was very rich in livestock, in silver, and in gold.

---

[34] E. A. Speiser, *Genesis: Introduction, Translation, and Notes* (AB 1; Garden City, N.Y.: Doubleday, 1964), xxxi–xxxii, and 150–52.

[35] For discussion and critique of this approach, see M. A. Fishbane, *Biblical Interpretation in Ancient Israel* (1988), 11–12.

[36] On the other hand, it is also possible the narrator was just as uncomfortable with the topos, and may no longer have understood it; Tikva S. Frymer-Kensky, "Sarah 1/Sarai," in *Women in Scripture: A Dictionary of Named and Unnamed Women in the Hebrew Bible, the Apocryphal/Deuterocanonical Books, and the New Testament*, eds. Carol L. Meyers, Toni Craven, and Ross S. Kraemer (Boston: Houghton Mifflin, 2000), 150–51.

[37] H. C. Brichto, *The Names of God* (1998), 270.

[38] Thomas C. Römer, "Recherches actuelles sur le cycle d'Abraham," in *Studies in the Book of Genesis: Literature, Redaction and History*, ed. André Wénin (BETL 155; Leuven/Sterling, Va.: Leuven University Press/Uitgeverij Peeters, 2001), 179–211, esp. 196.

(13:3) He journeyed on by stages from the Negeb as far as Bethel, to the place where his tent had been at the beginning, between Bethel and Ai,

(13:4) to the place where he had made an altar at the first; and there Abram called on the name of the LORD.

(13:5) Now Lot, who went with Abram, also had flocks and herds and tents,

(13:6) so that the land could not support both of them living together; for their possessions were so great that they could not live together,

(13:7) and there was strife between the herders of Abram's livestock and the herders of Lot's livestock. At that time the Canaanites and the Perizzites lived in the land.

(13:8) Then Abram said to Lot, "Let there be no strife between you and me, and between your herders and my herders; for we are kindred.

(13:9) Is not the whole land before you? Separate yourself from me. If you take the left hand, then I will go to the right; or if you take the right hand, then I will go to the left."

(13:10) Lot looked about him, and saw that the plain of the Jordan was well watered everywhere like the garden of the LORD, like the land of Egypt, in the direction of Zoar; this was before the LORD had destroyed Sodom and Gomorrah.

(13:11) So Lot chose for himself all the plain of the Jordan, and Lot journeyed eastward; thus they separated from each other.

(13:12) Abram settled in the land of Canaan, while Lot settled among the cities of the Plain and moved his tent as far as Sodom.

(13:13) Now the people of Sodom were wicked, great sinners against the LORD.

(13:14) The LORD said to Abram, after Lot had separated from him, "Raise your eyes now, and look from the place where you are, northward and southward and eastward and westward;

(13:15) for all the land that you see I will give to you and to your offspring[b] forever.

(13:16) I will make your offspring like the dust of the earth; so that if one can count the dust of the earth, your offspring also can be counted.

(13:17) Rise up, walk through the length and the breadth of the land, for I will give it to you."

(13:18) So Abram moved his tent, and came and settled by the oaks of Mamre, which are at Hebron; and there he built an altar to the LORD.

*T*his chapter is largely preparatory for what follows in the narrative of the Battle of Siddim Valley in the next chapter (Gen 14), and ultimately for Gen 18–19, the destruction of Sodom and Gomorrah. Thus we learn why Abram and Lot separate, how Lot came to live in the plain of Jordan so near Sodom, and how Abram came to live by the oaks of Mamre near Hebron (18:1). Along the way, however, we also learn

---

b Heb "seed."

much about each man's character, and the Lord dramatically restates and reaffirms his promises to Abram (vv. 15–17).

The phraseology of v. 1 clearly takes up the narrative thread of 12:20, with this additional note as reminder: Lot was still with Abram. He had been absent in the previous episode in Egypt (12:10–20), but a passing circumstantial clause, "and Lot with him," confirms that they are still together, and indeed, that Lot was returning with Abram and the rest of the family to the promised land. The several geographical references – the Negeb, Bethel, Ai (v. 3) – give the impression that Abram is returning home, to the land where he had formerly pitched his tent, built altars, and worshiped Yahweh (12:1–9) prior to the famine and his detour in Egypt (12:10–20). Indeed, when he arrives at the altar he built at Bethel previously (v. 4, cf. 12:8), he once again calls "on the name of the Lord."[39] Abram has resumed the devout practices he observed on his first excursion in the promised land, indicating perhaps that he has returned home in ways other than physical.

Abram and Lot have both acquired great possessions, which is most easily measured among pastoral nomads in flocks and herds (vv. 2 and 5). A dilemma thus presents itself when their respective shepherds are unable to avoid conflict, presumably over water (vv. 6–7), which is a persistent problem in the region at this time (cf. 21:25–31; 26:17–22). That the land was incapable of supporting both Abram and Lot, along with their considerable livestock, seems problematic until we recall that they are not alone. After all, the Canaanites and Perizzites also live in the land (v. 7).

Abram and Lot decide to go their separate ways (vv. 8–13). With typical ancient Near Eastern obsequiousness, Abram defers to his nephew to decide which portion of the land to take. Courtesy demands that Lot defer to his uncle, but shockingly, he agrees to make the selection himself. He promptly (and discourteously) chooses the Jordan valley, leaving the dry and rocky hill country to his uncle. The process by which Lot made his decision was distinctly sensory (v. 10, "Lot looked about him, and saw . . . "), which of itself is not alarming. But the expression is preparing the reader for comparison with Abram (v. 14, see commentary below), which leaves Lot looking rather greedy and selfish. In a geographical context in which water is at a premium, Lot saw that the Jordan valley was "well watered" like the Garden of Eden and the Nile valley. He chose the best for himself without hesitation or apology. A directional comment locates Lot's choice as "in the direction of Zoar," a city in the vicinity of the southernmost part of the Jordan valley (cf. 14:2, 8; 19:20–23, 30).[40] Another ominous note reminds the reader this portion of the Jordan valley was beautiful and well watered because these events took place "before the Lord had destroyed Sodom and Gomorrah." Abram stayed in the "land of Canaan,"

---

[39] Same phraseology as in 12:8, although NRSV translates differently; "invoked" versus "called on" the name of Yahweh.

[40] Michael C. Astour, "Zoar," *ABD* 6:1107; Anson F. Rainey and R. S. Notley, *The Sacred Bridge: Carta's Atlas of the Biblical World* (Jerusalem: Carta, 2006), 113.

a reference that perhaps approves his location in the Promised Land, while Lot moved his tent "as far as Sodom" (v. 12). The text subtly reflects the suspicions Israelites shared about Canaanite urban life (Lot settled "among the cities of the Plain"), and condemns the duplicity of moving his nomadic domicile so close, in fact as close as possible, to Sodom. Subtlety, however, is cast to the wind in the narrator's description of the inhabitants of Sodom as wicked and exceedingly sinful against Yahweh, terminology reminiscent of earlier texts on sin (4:7; 6:5). Lot chose association with sinners among the cities of the plain, while Abram remained in the land of promise.

The Hebrew word order of v. 14 marks a change of subject, shifting scenes from Lot's tent at Sodom back to Abram in the land of Canaan. Having learned how Lot came to live at Sodom, we learn in this last paragraph that Abram came to live near Hebron. More important than geography, however, is the content of Yahweh's speech in vv. 14–17, restating and confirming in dramatic fashion the promises of 12:1–9. The Lord begins with an imperative, using the same words the narrator used in the indicative to describe Lot's decision (obscured by nearly all translations, including NRSV):

v. 10 – Lot lifted up his eyes and saw . . .
v. 14 – Lift up your eyes and see . . .

The ironic contrast between Lot's sensory-based selfishness and Abram's visionary-based promises may also have a connection to the assertion that "the land could not *support*" them both (v. 6). A single verb (*nāśā'*, "lift up, carry, support") ties all of this together. Lot hungrily desires the best his eyes can see, while Yahweh charges Abram to see more than he could otherwise imagine. From Hebron, looking in all directions, Yahweh ties "land" and "seed" (see NRSV's note) together, once again with the verb "give," as he had done originally in 12:7. God himself will bestow all the land Abram can see to his descendants, and this time he adds "forever."[41] In the next verses, God substantiates the claim by adding tangible, concrete reality to the promises of land and seed. Abram's offspring will become innumerable as dust (v. 16) and the length and breadth of the land will be given to him, as far as he can mark it out on foot (v. 17). These are still only promises, but stated more and more emphatically and with graphic imagery to bring home their reality.

Whereas Lot "moved his tent" near the depraved city-life of Sodom (v. 12), Abram moved his to the oaks of Mamre near Hebron (v. 18). The origin and meaning of

---

[41] Although "forever" is misleading because the notion of temporal absoluteness is foreign to the Hebrew Bible; Matitiahu Tsevat, "The Steadfast House: What Was David Promised in 2 Samuel 7?" in *The Meaning of the Book of Job and Other Biblical Studies: Essays on the Literature and Religion of the Hebrew Bible*, ed. M. Tsevat (New York: Ktav, 1980), 101–17, esp. 106–7.

the name "Mamre" is much in doubt, but it may be Hittite for "friendship, peaceful relations, alliance," especially interesting in light of the presence of Hittites in the area of Hebron (cf. Gen 23).[42] As we saw in 12:6, trees held religious significance in the ancient Near East as physical symbols of divine presence and holy sites.[43] We may assume this particular site seemed appropriate for Abram to pause, once again, and build another altar to Yahweh (cf. 12:7–8; 13:4). Now that the promises have been confirmed, Abram moves to another holy site in the heart of the land of promise, and strengthens his resolve to worship Yahweh. Much speculation has gone into the nature of Abram's worship practices (see Closer Look at "Ancestral Religion"), but none can question its sincerity.

A CLOSER LOOK – ANCESTRAL RELIGION

Genesis *shows* Israel's ancestors at worship – building altars, praying, offering sacrifices, planting trees, pouring oil on standing-stones, etc. – but it expressly *tells* us little about their religious beliefs. According to the older influential theory of Albrecht Alt, the patriarchs worshiped three separate and anonymous deities, identified simply as the "Shield of Abraham" (based loosely on Gen 15:1), the "Fear of Isaac" (Gen 31:42), and the "Mighty One of Jacob" (Gen 49:24; Ps 132:2, 5; Isa 49:26; 60:16).[44] In Alt's view, these deities were worshiped by disparate tribes in Israel's early preconquest period. After settlement in Canaan, these clan-based deities took on Canaanite-style "El names," such as "El, the God of Israel" (Gen 33:20), "El Shaddai" (Gen 17:1), etc. As the tribes of Israel became more unified politically, these gods eventually converged and were identified with each other, giving rise to "the God of Abraham, the God of Isaac, and the God of Jacob" (Exod 3:6, 15–16; 4:5, and cf. Gen 28:13). Yahwism, or Mosaic religion, was secondarily introduced, in Alt's reconstruction, so that Yahweh was identified as the God of the Fathers and the national God of all Israel (Exod 6:3; Josh 24:14).

Alt's assumption about the original anonymity of these deities has been severely criticized, as well as his reliance on late comparative materials (Nabataean and Palmyrene from the first century BCE and fourth century CE). Frank Moore Cross

---

[42] Yoël L. Arbeitman, "The Hittite Is Thy Mother: An Anatolian Approach to Genesis 23," in *Bono Homini Donum: Essays in Historical Linguistics in Memory of J. Alexander Kerns,* eds. Yoël L. Arbeitman and Allan R. Bomhard (Amsterdam: John Benjamins, 1981), 889–1026, esp. 959–1002.

[43] O. Keel, *Goddesses and Trees, New Moon and Yahweh* (1998), 20–48. Hebron appears to be the southernmost limit of the kind of vegetation in which the evergreen Kermes oak (*Quercus coccifera*) can grow; F. N. Hepper and Shimon Gibson, "Abraham's Oak of Mamre: The Story of a Venerable Tree," *PEQ* 126 (1994): 94–105.

[44] Albrecht Alt, *Essays on Old Testament History and Religion,* trans. R. A. Wilson (Oxford: Blackwell, 1966), 3–86; trans. of *Kleine Schriften zur Geschichte des Volkes Israel* (München: Beck, 1953–1959), 1.1–78; repr. of *Der Gott der Väter: Ein Beitrag zur Vorgeschichte der israelitischen Religion* (BWANT 3/12; Stuttgart: Kohlhammer, 1929).

agreed with Alt's assessment of ancestral practices as a type of personal clan religion, but as a partial correction, he argued that the ancestors worshiped the high god of Canaan, namely "El." Rather than secondary elements added after the settlement, Canaanite El-type names were the original name of the God worshiped by Israel's ancestors.[45] By emphasizing continuity between Canaanite El and later Israelite Yahwism, Cross attempted to explain certain features of later Yahwism, even proposing that the name Yahweh was an abbreviated form of a primitive cultic name for El, which in time became a divine name itself: *'ēl zū yahwī ṣaba'ōt*, "El, who creates the heavenly armies," and later simply "El who causes to be," or "El the Creator." Subsequent scholarship has focused on the differentiation of Israelite religion from this Canaanite heritage.[46]

Thus, Israel's ancestors worshiped the ancient Near Eastern high god, El, who is described as revealing himself to the leaders of their clans, promising land, descendants, and divine protection, and eventually calling them to a special relationship, defined in Gen 15 and 17 as a covenant (see commentary below).[47] They are men and women of faith, who accepted God's promises, obeyed his commands (with a few notable exceptions), and engaged in traditional acts of piety and devotion, such as sacrifice, vows and libations, tithes, and prayers. Because of the way Genesis has been heavily edited from a later perspective (that is, from the perspective of later Mosaic Yahwism), we will likely never be able to discern precisely how similar ancestral religion was to later Israelite practices. However, there are at least four features that distinguish ancestral religion from that of later Israel.[48] First, the exclusive, almost sectarian nature of Mosaic religion is absent here. Because of the shared Canaanite name of God, "El," and other common religious practices, the ancestors enjoyed an early form of ecumenism that later Israelite Yahwism (and especially the prophets) condemned vigorously. Second, there is a complete absence of the Baal cult, so soundly critiqued and condemned by the rest of the Hebrew Scriptures. Third, Israel's ancestors enjoyed a certain unmediated intimacy in their relationship with God. They communicated with God directly, at times in dreams and visions,

---

[45] Frank M. Cross, *Canaanite Myth and Hebrew Epic: Essays in the History of the Religion of Israel* (Cambridge, Mass.: Harvard University Press, 1973), 3–75.

[46] Especially in the important work of Mark S. Smith; e.g., Mark S. Smith, *The Early History of God: Yahweh and the Other Deities in Ancient Israel* (Grand Rapids, Mich.: Eerdmans, 2002); and for review of these developments, Bill T. Arnold, "Religion in Ancient Israel," in *The Face of Old Testament Studies: A Survey of Contemporary Approaches,* eds. David W. Baker and Bill T. Arnold (Grand Rapids, Mich.: Baker Books, 1999), 391–420, esp. 392–404.

[47] Wolfgang Herrmann, "El," *DDD*[2] 274–80, esp. 277–79.

[48] For more than these, with introductory discussion, see Richard S. Hess, *Israelite Religions: An Archaeological and Biblical Survey* (Grand Rapids, Mich.: Baker Academic, 2007), 149–51; and Gordon J. Wenham, "The Religion of the Patriarchs," in *Essays on the Patriarchal Narratives,* eds. A. R. Millard and D. J. Wiseman (Leicester, England: InterVarsity Press, 1980), 161–95, esp. 194–95.

but at others through unannounced spoken words, and no prophets were needed to mediate or interpret the revelation, nor were priests required to offer sacrifices for them. Finally, the ancestors worshiped freely at sanctuaries near Shechem, Bethel, Hebron, and Beersheba, while there is no mention of Jerusalem, which contrasts with the Deuteronomic mandate for central worship (e.g., Deut 12:2–7).

GENESIS 14:1–24 THE BATTLE OF SIDDIM VALLEY AND ITS AFTERMATH

(14:1) In the days of King Amraphel of Shinar, King Arioch of Ellasar, King Chedorlaomer of Elam, and King Tidal of Goiim,

(14:2) these kings made war with King Bera of Sodom, King Birsha of Gomorrah, King Shinab of Admah, King Shemeber of Zeboiim, and the king of Bela (that is, Zoar).

(14:3) All these joined forces in the Valley of Siddim (that is, the Dead Sea).

(14:4) Twelve years they had served Chedorlaomer, but in the thirteenth year they rebelled.

(14:5) In the fourteenth year Chedorlaomer and the kings who were with him came and subdued the Rephaim in Ashteroth-karnaim, the Zuzim in Ham, the Emim in Shaveh-kiriathaim,

(14:6) and the Horites in the hill country of Seir as far as El-paran on the edge of the wilderness;

(14:7) then they turned back and came to En-mishpat (that is, Kadesh), and subdued all the country of the Amalekites, and also the Amorites who lived in Hazazon-tamar.

(14:8) Then the king of Sodom, the king of Gomorrah, the king of Admah, the king of Zeboiim, and the king of Bela (that is, Zoar) went out, and they joined battle in the Valley of Siddim

(14:9) with King Chedorlaomer of Elam, King Tidal of Goiim, King Amraphel of Shinar, and King Arioch of Ellasar, four kings against five.

(14:10) Now the Valley of Siddim was full of bitumen pits; and as the kings of Sodom and Gomorrah fled, some fell into them, and the rest fled to the hill country.

(14:11) So the enemy took all the goods of Sodom and Gomorrah, and all their provisions, and went their way;

(14:12) they also took Lot, the son of Abram's brother, who lived in Sodom, and his goods, and departed.

(14:13) Then one who had escaped came and told Abram the Hebrew, who was living by the oaks of Mamre the Amorite, brother of Eshcol and of Aner; these were allies of Abram.

(14:14) When Abram heard that his nephew had been taken captive, he led forth his trained men, born in his house, three hundred eighteen of them, and went in pursuit as far as Dan.

(14:15) He divided his forces against them by night, he and his servants, and routed them and pursued them to Hobah, north of Damascus.

(14:16) Then he brought back all the goods, and also brought back his nephew Lot with his goods, and the women and the people.

(14:17) After his return from the defeat of Chedorlaomer and the kings who were with him, the king of Sodom went out to meet him at the Valley of Shaveh (that is, the King's Valley).

(14:18) And King Melchizedek of Salem brought out bread and wine; he was priest of God Most High.

(14:19) He blessed him and said, "Blessed be Abram by God Most High, maker of heaven and earth;

(14:20) and blessed be God Most High, who has delivered your enemies into your hand!" And Abram gave him one tenth of everything.

(14:21) Then the king of Sodom said to Abram, "Give me the persons, but take the goods for yourself."

(14:22) But Abram said to the king of Sodom, "I have sworn to the LORD, God Most High, maker of heaven and earth,

(14:23) that I would not take a thread or a sandal-thong or anything that is yours, so that you might not say, 'I have made Abram rich.'

(14:24) I will take nothing but what the young men have eaten, and the share of the men who went with me – Aner, Eshcol, and Mamre. Let them take their share."

*A*bram and Lot become embroiled in international politics, as a war between opposing coalitions, "four kings against five" (v. 9), results in a battle in their area, the Siddim Valley. Abram seems little affected at first, presumably because of his location near the less strategic city of Hebron, while Lot, who is now said to be living "*in* Sodom" (v. 12), is captured. Abram musters a small contingent of fighting men from his own resources, and together with two allies from near Hebron, they rescue Lot and others from the hostile coalition. Afterward, Abram is blessed by King Melchizedek of Salem but comes to an uneasy peace with the king of Sodom. This chapter is important in the progression of thought in the book of Genesis, not so much for the geopolitical developments narrated here, as for Abram's encounter with Melchizedek at the conclusion.

Attempts have failed to identify positively any of the nine kings of vv. 1–2 with historical figures, in spite of enormous scholarly effort.[49] A few of the place names are known, but it is uncertain whether these ancient polities are really in view here. "Shinar" occurs elsewhere in the Bible (Gen 10:10; 11:2; Josh 7:21; Isa 11:11; Dan 1:2;

---

[49] For summary of the efforts, see C. Westermann, *Genesis 12–36* (1985), 193–95; and G. J. Wenham, *Genesis 1–15* (1987), 308–10. The relationship of Gen 14 with the so-called "Chedorlaomer Texts" of the second century BCE is still very much in doubt; Michael C. Astour, "Chedorlaomer," *ABD* 1:893–95.

Zech 5:11) and from these uses, and others in Egyptian and cuneiform sources, it is clear that Shinar is an ancient term for southern Mesopotamia. Its etymology seems to derive from the name of a Kassite tribe, which was in power when the term began to appear in the middle of the second millennium BCE.[50] Elam also is well known from extra-biblical sources as a country of international weight, although its location in the Iranian plateau east of Mesopotamia made it of little consequence throughout most of biblical history.[51] Other geographical identifications for the places mentioned here are extremely uncertain. Admah and Zeboiim are points marking the southern border of Canaan (10:19), and were presumably destroyed with Sodom and Gomorrah, and later became proverbial symbols of divine wrath (Deut 29:22 [Eng. 29:23]; Hos 11:8).[52] Curiously, the ninth king is not named as the others, but instead is simply "the king of Bela" (and cf. v. 8), identifying the place name as Zoar, the city somewhere in the southernmost portion of the Jordan valley (see commentary at 13:10, and cf. 19:18–23). So in general, four kings from the east, under the general leadership of Chedorlaomer (vv. 4–5 and 17), were aligned against five from the west, predominantly from the southern Jordan valley.

The chapter has two clear components: the account of the Battle of Siddim Valley and the subsequent actions of Abram. It is unclear whether these two portions originated as separate sources, although we may speak of a campaign report typical of ancient Near Eastern kings (vv. 1–11) and a narrative on the heroic actions of Abram (vv. 12–24), to which the Melchizedek fragment may have been added later (vv. 18–20).[53] It is also possible to argue that the kings of the east were not among the most powerful rulers of the time, but were instead lesser potentates of approximately the eighteenth century BCE, who were attempting to control the copper mines south of the Dead Sea, and that therefore the text "has all the ingredients of historicity."[54]

The details of the campaign report have the markings of typical military engagements in the ancient world. Chedorlaomer's victories in vv. 4–7 are anterior action in a parenthetical background paragraph, preparing for the Battle of Siddim Valley by describing the impressive initial victories of the eastern alliance. Thus vv. 1–3 introduce the Battle of Siddim Valley generally, vv. 4–7 relate the first part of the campaign of Chedorlaomer and his allies, which was highly successful, and vv. 8–12 narrate the Battle of Siddim Valley itself.[55] Twelve years of hegemony over the region is followed by one year of rebellion against Chedorlaomer and his allies, followed by

---

[50] Ran Zadok, "The Origin of the Name Shinar," *ZA* 74 (1984): 240–244.

[51] I. M. Diakonoff, "Elam," *Cambridge History of Iran* 2:1–24, esp. 16–18; and René Labat, "Elam and Western Persia, *c.* 1200–1000 B.C.," *CAH*³ 2/2:482–506.

[52] On the location of Sodom, see commentary at 19:1.

[53] J. A. Emerton, "Some False Clues in the Study of Genesis XIV," *VT* 21 (1971): 24–47; J. A. Emerton, "The Riddle of Genesis XIV," *VT* 21 (1971): 403–39.

[54] E. A. Speiser, *Genesis* (1964), 108–9.

[55] It is not necessary to assume two separate conflicts, one in vv. 1–4 and another in vv. 5–12, as in G. J. Wenham, *Genesis 1–15* (1987), 307–13, nor to take vv. 5b–7 as an unconnected insertion about a separate campaign, as in C. Westermann, *Genesis 12–36* (1985), 196–97.

a year of campaign to reassert his dominance (vv. 4–5). The eastern alliance quickly restores rule over all of Syria–Palestine, which is implied by the wide geographical references in vv. 5–7.

The Siddim coalition is defeated quickly and decidedly (vv. 8–11). Some of their forces fall victim to the valley's "bitumen pits" (v. 10, and cf. 11:3), no doubt a reference to the region's abundant tar supply just below ground level, while others escape to the hills. The eastern coalition plundered Sodom and Gomorrah, and we are told unceremoniously, "they also took Lot, the son of Abram's brother" and his property as well (vv. 11–12). The last words of v. 12 form in Hebrew a circumstantial clause, reminding us that Lot "lived in Sodom," and is a subtle reminder of Lot's choice in 13:10–13. His decisions, based as they were on selfishness and sensory gratification, have placed Lot and his family in jeopardy. Lot's capture as a prisoner-of-war also threatens to cost Abram his "presumed heir" and the ancestral promises of land and descendants are suspended.

Abram learns of Lot's plight and moves into action, rescuing Lot and recovering the property (vv. 13–16). Abram is "the Hebrew," which may be intended to distinguish him from Mamre "the Amorite" (v. 13).[56] "Hebrew" (*'ibrî*) is probably not related etymologically to the Akkadian term *abiru/apiru*, which may mean "fugitive, refugee," and which occurs in texts throughout the ancient Near East in the second millennium BCE, although at times the two terms exhibit sociological similarities.[57] In the Old Testament, "Hebrew" is frequently used by non-Israelites to describe an Israelite, as when Egyptians call Joseph a Hebrew (Potiphar's wife, 39:14, 17; Pharaoh's cupbearer, 41:12), or when the Philistines refer to the Israelites in Samuel's day (1 Sam 4:6). Here, the narrator's "Abram the Hebrew" seems to refer to our hero as though for the first time, and as I say, distinguishes him from Mamre the Amorite and all other peoples appearing so far in this text. For this and other reasons, this chapter appears to have had an independent history from its context, and is likely older than the other sources used in the composition of Genesis. The addition that Abram was "living by the oaks of Mamre" is also more than a simple reminder of 13:18, but was probably originally part of the introduction of Abram into the narrative. These three companions of Abram – Mamre, Eshcol, and Aner – were on friendly terms with him, and we learn at the conclusion of the story, they joined forces with him to defeat Chedorlaomer (v. 24).[58] In its current canonical

---

Both miss the nature of vv. 4–7 as parenthetical background information for the Battle of Siddim Valley.

[56] "Mamre" is both a personal name and a place name (13:18), suggesting an individual by the name was, like Abram, an influential tribalist of the region, giving his name to the location.

[57] Nadav Na'aman, "Ḥabiru and Hebrews: The Transfer of a Social Term to the Literary Sphere," *JNES* 45 (1986): 271–88.

[58] Lipiński speaks of the four allies as literary personifications of the four clans of the area, whose union gave rise to the municipality called Kiriath-arba or Hebron; Edward Lipiński, "ʿAnaq-Kiryat ʾArbaʿ-Hebron et ses sanctuaires tribaux," *VT* 24 (1974): 41–55.

location, v. 13 also serves to show Abram's continued nomadic life style, i.e., living by the oaks of Mamre, in contrast to his city-dwelling nephew.[59]

On his return from pursuing Chedorlaomer and the kings of his coalition in the far north (Dan and Hobah, vv. 14–15), Abram encounters two more kings. The king of Sodom, having narrowly escaped the enemy as well as the tar pits (v. 10) and King Melchizedek of Salem (most likely Jerusalem/Zion, cf. Ps 76:3 [Eng. 76:2]), of whom we have heard nothing prior to this point (vv. 17–24). One treats Abram with great deferential gratitude, while the other struggles even to be civil. Melchizedek's name itself, "My King is Righteousness," signals a figure of outstanding personal character, a worthy ally for Abram, in contradistinction to the literary names Bera and Birsha, kings of Sodom and Gomorrah, which denote "evil" and "wickedness" respectively. Melchizedek presented himself before Abram, acknowledging the latter's superior status, offering bread and wine, and blessing Abram.[60] That Melchizedek blesses Abram is perhaps the first fulfillment of the ancestral promises of 12:3. Melchizedek himself will be the recipient of blessing, and the three occurrences of the verb "bless" (*brk*) in vv. 19–20 invite the reader to reflect on ways in which the "families of the earth" are already finding blessing through Abram.

Melchizedek is also a priest of "God Most High" (*'ēl 'elyôn*), he blesses Abram in the name of God Most High, and finally, he invokes blessing for God Most High, who is credited with delivering the enemy into Abram's hands. The divine epithet "Most High" (*'elyôn*) is attested in numerous extra-biblical inscriptions in Aramaic, Phoenician, Ugaritic, and Greek, reflecting its widespread use in ancient West Semitic religion in diverse times and places to exalt any god thought to be supreme.[61] Melchizedek also worships his God Most High as "maker [*qōnēh*] of heaven and earth," an archaic title attested in abbreviated form in the Canaanite world for the high god El as early as the Late Bronze Age.[62] Abram is at ease with this blessing, and indeed gives a tithe of the war plunder to Melchizedek. Later, in a speech to the much more surly king of Sodom, Abram equates Yahweh with Melchizedek's God Most High, even co-opting the exact phraseology of the creation formula (v. 22): "I have sworn to the Lord [Yahweh], God Most High, *maker of heaven and earth.*" This association certainly legitimizes the cult in (Jeru)salem and its much later national cult of David and Solomon. Melchizedek, King of Salem, is "the prototype and precursor" of the Davidic monarchs (Ps 110:1–4), and thus even

---

[59] C. Westermann, *Genesis 12–36* (1985), 200.

[60] All establishing a treaty, a pact in which Abram enjoyed superior status, according to one interpretation; David Elgavish, "The Encounter of Abram and Melchizedek King of Salem: A Covenant Establishing Ceremony," in *Studies in the Book of Genesis: Literature, Redaction and History*, ed. André Wénin (BETL 155; Leuven/Sterling, Va.: Leuven University Press/Uitgeverij Peeters, 2001), 495–508. Abram's tithe may also be explained as a gift accompanying such a treaty ceremony.

[61] Eric E. Elnes and Patrick D. Miller, Jr, "Elyon," *DDD²* 293–99, esp. 293–96.

[62] F. M. Cross, *Canaanite Myth and Hebrew Epic* (1973), 15–16, 50–52.

Israel's venerable patriarch, Abram, gives a tithe and submits to the one who holds the place for the future anointed one, and all this in a story full of other kings and potentates.[63]

By contrast, the king of Sodom seems rude (vv. 21–22). He offers Abram nothing and speaks to him brusquely (v. 21): "Give me the persons, but take the goods for yourself." As returning conqueror, Abram was entitled to keep all the war plunder, and the king of Sodom expected he would do precisely that. Without the customary friendly ancient Near Eastern civilites, his proposal pleads for the freedom of the people, while acknowledging the animals and captured property are rightfully Abram's, even if stated begrudgingly. Abram had not been above accepting the wealth of Egypt (12:16). But this was different! After donating one-tenth of the spoils to Melchizedek, Abram forfeits all profit, accepting only enough to cover his expenses and those of his allies, Aner, Eshcol, and Mamre (v. 24). This is more than a simple refusal to profit from the vagaries of warfare, but is also a rejection of zero-sum economics, as his stated motivation makes clear (vv. 22–23): "I have sworn . . . that I would not take, . . . so that you might not say, 'I have made Abram rich.'"[64] Abram knows that the source of his blessing is not dependent upon the losses of another. The blessings of God are infinitely expandable, and whatever Abram acquires will be by the hand of the God who called him from Mesopotamia, rather than at the expense of his neighbors in the Jordan Valley.

BRIDGING THE HORIZONS: MELCHIZEDEK

In a book like Genesis, driven as it is by genealogies and focused on the origins of things, it is remarkable that Melchizedek appears on the scene with so little background information. Surprisingly, his mystique – as both king of Salem and priest of God Most High – was seldom picked up elsewhere in the Old Testament; the only other reference being Ps 110:4, where he is the human archetype of the ideal priest-king of Jerusalem.

However, Melchizedek came to hold a place of esteem in subsequent Jewish and Christian traditions. In early Judaism, Melchizedek is a heavenly savior engaged in an eschatological struggle against the sons of Belial. In his only appearance in texts from the Judean Desert (11QMelch),[65] he is likely not a human figure but the archangel Michael in another form, with royal and high priestly characteristics, and accompanied by one bringing good news, the anointed one, probably the Teacher of Righteousness known from other Qumran texts.[66] But mainstream Judaism did not always consider Melchizedek a heavenly figure. Both Josephus and Philo know

---

[63] G. von Rad, *Genesis* (1961), 180–81.
[64] H. C. Brichto, *The Names of God* (1998), 196–97.
[65] Although the story of Gen 14:18–20 is translated closely in 1QapGen 22, which also includes mention of Melchizedek.
[66] George J. Brooke, "Melchizedek (11QMelch)," *ABD* 4:687–88.

Melchizedek as a historical priest and king. True, Philo perceived him as the embodiment of the divine "right reason" (*orthos logos*), and therefore transcending history, but Melchizedek is nevertheless a historical person for both Philo and Josephus.[67]

The book of Hebrews, the New Testament's letter to Jewish Christians, contains a number of references to Melchizedek. In three of these references, the author of Hebrews applies to Christ the words of Ps 110:4, "You are a priest forever, according to the order of Melchizedek" (Heb 5:6; 6:20; 7:17). In an elaborate treatise, Heb 7:1–19 argues that (1) since Abram gave a tithe to Melchizedek, and (2) since Melchizedek is the righteous king of (Jeru)salem, and (3) since we know that Melchizedek was superior to Abram because he received the tithe and blessed Abram, and only the superior can bless an inferior, then finally, therefore, (4) Melchizedek's priesthood takes precedence over that of Abram's descendants, the Levitical priests. The conclusion is that the priesthood of Christ is "according to the order of Melchizedek" rather than "according to the order of Aaron," and is therefore superior to the levitical priesthood. The use of Ps 110:4 also links Melchizedek with David and the Davidic dynasty, as the prototype of the ideal king of Israel. Therefore, Melchizedek's blessing and Abram's tithe make Abram "mysteriously open to that salvation which God would later unite with David's throne in Nathan's prophecy."[68]

GENESIS 15:1–21 PROMISES CONFIRMED BY WORD AND COVENANT

(15:1) After these things the word of the LORD came to Abram in a vision, "Do not be afraid, Abram, I am your shield; your reward shall be very great."

(15:2) But Abram said, "O Lord GOD, what will you give me, for I continue childless, and the heir of my house is Eliezer of Damascus?"

(15:3) And Abram said, "You have given me no offspring, and so a slave born in my house is to be my heir."

(15:4) But the word of the LORD came to him, "This man shall not be your heir; no one but your very own issue shall be your heir."

(15:5) He brought him outside and said, "Look toward heaven and count the stars, if you are able to count them." Then he said to him, "So shall your descendants be."

(15:6) And he believed the LORD; and the LORD[c] reckoned it to him as righteousness.

(15:7) Then he said to him, "I am the LORD who brought you from Ur of the Chaldeans, to give you this land to possess."

(15:8) But he said, "O Lord GOD, how am I to know that I shall possess it?"

---

[67] Jannes Reiling, "Melchizedek," *DDD*[2] 560–563.
[68] G. von Rad, *Genesis* (1961), 181.

[c] Heb he

(15:9) He said to him, "Bring me a heifer three years old, a female goat three years old, a ram three years old, a turtledove, and a young pigeon."

(15:10) He brought him all these and cut them in two, laying each half over against the other; but he did not cut the birds in two.

(15:11) And when birds of prey came down on the carcasses, Abram drove them away.

(15:12) As the sun was going down, a deep sleep fell upon Abram, and a deep and terrifying darkness descended upon him.

(15:13) Then the LORD said to Abram, "Know this for certain, that your offspring shall be aliens in a land that is not theirs, and shall be slaves there, and they shall be oppressed for four hundred years;

(15:14) but I will bring judgment on the nation that they serve, and afterward they shall come out with great possessions.

(15:15) As for yourself, you shall go to your ancestors in peace; you shall be buried in a good old age.

(15:16) And they shall come back here in the fourth generation; for the iniquity of the Amorites is not yet complete."

(15:17) When the sun had gone down and it was dark, a smoking fire pot and a flaming torch passed between these pieces.

(15:18) On that day the LORD made a covenant with Abram, saying, "To your descendants I give this land, from the river of Egypt to the great river, the river Euphrates,

(15:19) the land of the Kenites, the Kenizzites, the Kadmonites,

(15:20) the Hittites, the Perizzites, the Rephaim,

(15:21) the Amorites, the Canaanites, the Girgashites, and the Jebusites."

*I*n previous chapters, God has promised to bless Abram as the father of a great nation, to give him a great name, and to make him a blessing to all families of the earth (12:2–3). These general and somewhat ambiguous blessings have been specifically identified as gifts of "seed" (*zeraʿ*, or "offspring") and "land" (*ʾereṣ*), and they have been tied together as dual gifts: the land will be given to the seed (12:7; 13:15). The two gifts, seed and land, are inextricably bound together as a matched set. Subsequently, Yahweh confirmed these two promises, emphasizing that Abram's seed will become as innumerable as the dust of the earth and that the land will be given to them (13:15–17). So far in the narrative, however, Abram has had little tangible confirmation of these promises, as wonderful as they are. In this text, the promises of seed and land are confirmed again, stated even more emphatically, and yet God's restatements of the promises raise questions that drive the narrative forward. Specifically, the promised seed is developed further as a biological son rather than merely a slave born in Abram's household, and the land promise is confirmed in a solemn covenant.

Genesis 15 has long been the focus of scholarly attention, standing as it does at the center of critical studies of Genesis, and therefore of the whole Pentateuch. The promises of "seed" and "land" are picked up in two parallel portions (vv. 1–6 and vv. 7–21, respectively), with many disjointed features reflecting a composite nature. Although the unity of the chapter has been forged from disparate original sources, a century and a half of scholarship has not been able to determine the nature or approximate date of those sources.[69] Whereas it was once assumed that vv. 1–6 came from an early Elohist source and vv. 7–21 from a Yahwist source, few today would be so bold or confident, and several scholars have argued for origins much later. At most we can assume that earlier materials of unreconstructable nature have been reworked by a Yahwistic editor, and were thus part of what I have called Israel's old epic narrative (see introduction).

The chapter may also be viewed as a "theological compendium," in which major themes of the Pentateuch are drawn together and interpreted theologically.[70] Thus the text uses Abram's story to reflect on the exodus and wilderness (vv. 13–14), the Sinai covenant (vv. 17–18), and Israel's subsequent encounters with other peoples in and near the Promised Land (vv. 19–21). Such theological interpretation of other portions of the Pentateuch, and in some opinions, connections to deuteronomic and prophetic thought as well, may reflect the lateness of the text. On the other hand, Gen 15 could just as easily be the source as the deposit of later pentateuchal, deuteronomic, and prophetic traditions.[71]

In Gen 15, the promises of "seed" and "land" are each in turn confirmed by a divine predicate nominative for identification, signifying Yahweh's nature and identity: "I am your shield" (v. 1) and "I am the Lord" (v. 7).[72] Each divine assertion prompts a question from Abram (vv. 2 and 8), which then leads to dialogical resolution and confirmation of the promises. In the first dialogue, the "seed" promise is confirm by a restatement and elaboration of the promise, as well as dramatic symbolism ("count the stars"), which results in Abram's faith (v. 6). In the second dialogue, the "land" promise is confirm by a call for a solemn covenant between Abram and Yahweh, which prefigures and authenticates Israel's later covenant at Sinai (vv. 7–21). The two parallel portions of the chapter – or "scenes" to follow the dramatic nature of the literature – begin with gracious, divine self-disclosure, "I am your shield" and "I am Yahweh"; this is who I am by name and you know me by my actions ("who brought you up," v. 7). Each dialogue is instigated by Yahweh's revelation of his nature and purposes, which leads the patriarch to new levels of theological understanding and commitment.

---

[69] C. Westermann, *Genesis 12–36* (1985), 214–16. Brichto's "synoptic-resumptive" solution, in which he assumes the second episode (vv. 7–17) returns to the previous event's beginning as a synoptic expansion, is ingenious but not entirely convincing; H. C. Brichto, *The Names of God* (1998), 203–212.

[70] John Ha, *Genesis 15: A Theological Compendium of Pentateuchal History* (BZAW 181; Berlin: W. de Gruyter, 1989).

[71] G. J. Wenham, *Genesis 1–15* (1987), 326.

[72] Another revelatory predicate nominative occurs in 17:1, "I am God Almighty."

In the first scene, "the word of the Lord" came to Abram in a vision (v. 1). The "vision" (*maḥăzeh*) occurs only four times in the Old Testament, and denotes revelatory communications of a word from God, although these are not necessarily visual images (Gen 15:1; Num 24:4, 16; Ezek 13:7). The stylized collocation "the word of Yahweh came to [personal name]" is used in prophetic literature generally (e.g., 1 Sam 15:10; Hos 1:1), and found only here in all the Pentateuch (and v. 4). Abram is plainly thought of here as a prophet, which anticipates God's description of him to King Abimelech of Gerar as a prophet, who can pray effectual prayers for Abimelech (20:7). As the recipient of the word of Yahweh, Abram thus becomes the "father of the faith" even for those in ancient Israel who were messengers of the salvific and living word of prophecy. Elsewhere in the historical and prophetic books of the Old Testament, the word of Yahweh functioned in history to judge and to save by means of a creative and active "word," which is decisive for the life and death of Israel.[73] God's words to Abram of comfort, assurance, and self-revelation in vv. 1–6 are thus prophetic not only for the individual patriarch, but for his promised progeny, the nation Israel, who would also experience the word of Yahweh in all its judging and saving force.

The depiction of God as a "shield" (*māgēn*) is rare in the Pentateuch and historical books (only here, Deut 33:29; and 2 Sam 22:3, 31) but common in the Psalter (e.g., Pss 3:4; 7:10; 18:3, 31; and Prov 2:7, etc.). The shield is a common instrument of weaponry for defensive purposes and is used of God metaphorically for protection and refuge.[74] Abram was in particular need of refuge since this assurance comes "after these things," a transition marker noting the passage of some time since the encounter with Melchizedek and the King of Sodom (14:17–24). The military actions of Gen 14 prove Abram is living in a dangerous time and place, and the less than cordial interchange with the King of Sodom likely left Abram in need of Yahweh's opening words here, "Do not be afraid."[75] In fact, we may assume this divine speech was precisely what Abram needed at the time, since it comes in the narrative immediately after the military action in which he was victorious, and yet he magnanimously refused all personal gain from the victory (14:22–24). The words of God play on the words of Melchizedek in order to emphasize the cause and effect relationship: "blessed be God Most High, who has *delivered* (*miggēn*) your enemies into your hand" (14:20) and "I am your *shield* (*māgēn*)" (15:1).[76] As

[73] Bill T. Arnold and Paul M. Cook, "Word of God," *DOTHB* 999–1003.

[74] Various attempts have been made to read "shield" as a verb instead; e.g., Martin Kessler, "The 'Shield' of Abraham?" *VT* 14 (1964): 494–97. However, in light of the metaphoric parallels in Israelite poetry and several other reasons, the best reading is the simple noun "shield."

[75] Stated here in a form that stresses the immediacy of the prohibition ("Stop being afraid!") rather than its permanency; B. T. Arnold and J. H. Choi, *A Guide to Biblical Hebrew Syntax* (2003), 130 and 137.

[76] On the possibility of *māgēn* as both "shield" and "benefactor" in Janus parallelism, see Gary A. Rendsburg, "Word Play in Biblical Hebrew: An Eclectic Collection," in *Puns and*

God has delivered and protected Abram in the past, so now he will continue to be a shield; and because Abram declined the spoils of war, God will provide wealth.

For the first time in our narrative, Abram addresses God in response, which may reflect the depth of this dialogue. His response may at first sound unrelated (v. 2): "what will you give me, for I continue childless." By stressing seed over reward, Abram's response illustrates the primacy of the promise of seed or descendants over that of land (12:7; 13:16–17), or anything else for that matter. What good is wealth without an heir? At his age, it matters little if Abram has great reward or even protection, if he has no descendants. God delivered Abram's enemies into his hand, but would he also deliver a son into Abram's household?[77] His anguished "for I continue childless" is a causal clause underscoring his current conditions and the incongruence of any gift other than a son.

Abram's statement about Eliezer contains awkward syntax (v. 2b). While the subtleties of the text escape us, we have no doubt that Abram is referring to inheritance customs of the ancient Near East, as the parallel statement in v. 3 makes clear: "a slave born in my house is to be my heir." We have evidence from Ugarit, Nuzi, and Alalakh of the firstborn son's inheritance being legally transferred to another.[78] Various attempts have been made to understand Abram's comments in vv. 2–3 as denoting ancient adoption practices, whereby a childless man would adopt a son, perhaps a slave, to provide for him during his waning years, and to mourn and bury him properly at the time of his death. In exchange, the adopted son becomes the heir of the estate. Various examples of such adoptions have been proposed as parallels to Abram and Eliezer, none of which are convincing as exact parallels.[79] Yet the principle is that normally only a relative could serve as one's heir (Num 27:8–11; and see Prov 17:2). Whether or not formal adoption is in view here, Abram is concerned that someone other than a biological descendant will serve as his heir.[80]

The first presumed heir of the extended narrative, Abram's nephew Lot, proved to be unsuitable (Gen 13), and now the next presumed heir, Eliezer, is not even a blood relative. Abram's words reflect the incongruity of a tribal leader who has no tribe. His query is completely understandable. What good is protection and

---

Pundits: Word Play in the Hebrew Bible and Ancient Near Eastern Literature, ed. Scott B. Noegel (Bethesda, Md.: CDL Press, 2000), 137–62, esp. 138–39.

[77] V. P. Hamilton, *The Book of Genesis, Chapters 1–17* (1990), 420.

[78] For an example from Alalakh, see Richard S. Hess, "Marriage Customs," *COS* 3.101B:251–2; and compare Gen 25:31–33; 48:13–14, 22; and 49:3–4.

[79] For critique of the parallels, see T. L. Thompson, *The Historicity of The Patriarchal Narratives* (1974), 203–230.

[80] Another interpretation assumes Eliezer is not the same individual as the "son of my house" in v. 3 (NRSV's "slave born in my house" is misleading); Laurence A. Turner, *Genesis: Readings, A New Biblical Commentary* (Sheffield, England: Sheffield Academic Press, 2000), 73. In this interpretation, Eliezer is a senior servant of the house in v. 2, who perhaps returns to the story in 24:2, and Lot himself is the "son of my house" in v. 3. However, parallels between vv. 2 and 3 make it more likely that Eliezer is the one in mind in both verses; C. Westermann, *Genesis 12–36* (1985), 220–21.

wealth if he has no legitimate heir? His response merely pushes the dialogue in the direction of God's promise of descendants, as illustrated by the recurrence of "seed" and "inherit" in these verses: "seed" (*zeraʿ*, or "offspring; descendant") in vv. 3 and 5, and the verbal root "inherit" (*yrš*, "be heir") in v. 3 and twice in v. 4. Abram is not challenging God's sincerity (3:5) but seeking clarity and understanding on that which God has promised – descendants (12:2, 7; 13:15–16).

The Lord responded succinctly to Abram's request, first with an assertion (v. 4) and then with an invitation (v. 5). The assertion carries prophetic certainty ("the word of Yahweh came to him"); a biological descendant will function as Abram's heir ("your very own issue") rather than the slave Eliezer. Next, God's invitation employs symbolism and dramatic imagery to convince Abram that his children will indeed be numerous. Counting his descendants is like trying to number the stars of heaven, a metaphor reminiscent of the earlier "seed like the dust of the earth" (13:16). The obvious inability to fulfill this invitation overwhelms the senses. One simply cannot count the stars, which is inversely related to certitude about the promise of God. As the first is certainly *not* true (Abram's ability to count the stars), the second certainly *is* true (God's ability to give Abram enumerable descendants). Abram is certain that he cannot count the stars, and so he can now be assured that his descendants will be countless. And God's conclusion, "so shall your seed be," perfectly matches Abram's concern "you have given me no seed."[81]

Verse 6 is one of the most remarkable verses of the Bible, its simplicity surpassed by its profundity. Although only five words in Hebrew, the notion expressed here becomes the standard of faith in Israel's Scriptures and central to early Christian formulations of faith (see Bridging the Horizons at p. 157). The verse contains two clauses.

v. 6a – And he believed the Lord;
v. 6b – and he reckoned it to him as righteousness.[82]

The verse begins with no specific causal marker (such as "Therefore he believed . . . "), yet the context implies that v. 6a is Abram's unadorned and unconditional acceptance of God's promise in vv. 4–5. Similarly, the movement to v. 6b has no particular marker other than the usual conjunction "and," yet a simple cause and effect movement is implied, making v. 6b the result of Abram's faith. The first line is the simple faith of a humble man, and the second is God's response.

The assertion "he believed Yahweh" employs a precise collocation denoting both that Abram accepted Yahweh's word as true and also that he accepted Yahweh as trustworthy (i.e., he "believed *in*" Yahweh).[83] The particular temporal form of this

---

[81] "Seed" in both clauses (vv. 3 and 5) is singular in the Hebrew; the NRSV's "descendants" represents the plurality of the stars but misses the correspondence between Abram's request in v. 3 and Yahweh's response in v. 5.

[82] NRSV's "and the Lord reckoned it" supplies the logical change of subject for the Hebrew's ambiguous "he" (see Levenson's critique below).

[83] R. W. L. Moberly, "*ʾmn*," *NIDOTTE* 1:427–33, esp. 431.

word may also imply repeated action in the past ("he kept on believing").[84] This episode is not singly exceptional in Abram's life but is instead an example of the way Abram routinely responded to God; his life was characterized by such belief.

God's response is succinctly summarized in the words "he reckoned it" to Abram as righteousness (v. 6b). Using a computational accounting metaphor ("count, calculate, reckon" *ḥšb*), the narrator asserts that Abram's faith counts in God's economy as that moral quality so greatly needed – righteousness, or a right relationship with God.[85] The subject of the verb is ambiguous in Hebrew (simply "*he* reckoned," see NRSV's footnote), as is the antecedent of the pronoun "it." Who reckoned what to whom? Did Yahweh reckon something to Abram or vice versa? The "it" may refer to Abram's act of faith (v. 6a), resulting in Abram's righteousness in Yahweh's sight, or to Yahweh's word (vv. 4–5), resulting in Yahweh's favor in Abram's sight. Some interpreters have concluded that *Abram* reckoned God's word of promise as an expression of *God's* righteousness; Abram now assumes God is worthy of trust.[86] Although possible grammatically, the context favors the interpretation adopted in the main text of the NRSV: Yahweh accredited Abram's faith as righteousness.[87]

Verse 6, then, is a narrative intrusion into the dialogue between Abram and Yahweh. It interrupts the conversation in order to draw the reader's attention to this most important theological reflection: here we read of a human who had faith in God, which resulted in righteousness.[88] In the scope of the book of Genesis as a whole, we have finally reached the answer to the problem of unbelief so prevalent in the Primeval History (3:6; 4:8; 6:5; 11:4).

Yet even without the macrostructural context, the sheer philosophical import of this verse should not be missed. Why should the narrator feel compelled to highlight Abram's faith?[89] The reality is that Abram's faith (v. 6) is the result of divine self-disclosure, of a particular revelation of God (vv. 1–5). This narrative intrusion, therefore, highlights revelation and faith, and the relation between the two. The narrator is compelled to insert this theological reflection because revelation itself

---

[84] The perfect aspect of the verb implying continuing action in the past; GKC 112ss; or perhaps present/habitual action; Bruce K. Waltke and Michael P. O'Connor, *An Introduction to Biblical Hebrew Syntax* (Winona Lake, Ind.: Eisenbrauns, 1990), 485.

[85] For semantic details, see Klaus Seybold, "*ḥāšab*," *TDOT* 5:228–45, esp. 241–44.

[86] Levenson critiques Gerhard von Rad's interpretation of Gen 15:6, which he assumes von Rad has forced into a Pauline straightjacket according to Lutheran theology; Jon D. Levenson, *The Hebrew Bible, the Old Testament, and Historical Criticism: Jews and Christians in Biblical Studies* (Louisville, Ky.: Westminster/John Knox Press, 1993), 56–61; and see G. von Rad, *Genesis* (1961), 184–85.

[87] Thus the "it" in "he reckoned it" refers to Abram's act of faith (v. 6a), which results in his righteousness in Yahweh's eyes.

[88] But not a simplistic, legalistic righteousness, since Abram comes prior to the giving of the law. This is a genuine meritorious acceptance of Abram on God's part (Deut 6:25; 24:13; Ps 106:31).

[89] For some of what follows in this paragraph, see H. C. Brichto, *The Names of God* (1998), 211–12.

is not enough, or at least, divine revelation is not alone sufficient for the narrator's purpose. Faith in God is the goal, and faith itself cannot be compelled by God, even through dramatic self-disclosure of God's nature and purpose. Revelation can either be relegated to general insignificance, or it can be accepted as a basis for faith in God. After each self-revealing event, God can be accepted or reject by humanity, and in this case at least, Israel's father in faith, Abram, believed and became righteous. And of course, the narrator is also urging the reader to overcome and reject the tendency to assign Abram's faith to some unattainable realm of yesteryear's spiritual giants, long since unattainable. Indeed, revelation and faith are repeatable events, as this text would have us believe.

BRIDGING THE HORIZONS: ABRAM'S FAITH

Echoes of the faith of Abram, as articulated in Gen 15:6, may be heard elsewhere in Israel's Scriptures. The specific terminology of v. 6b is used in Ps 106:31 to elucidate the implications of Phinehas's faithful intercession (compare Num 25:6–13). The lexical specifics of Hab 2:4b may also be related to Abram's faith: "the righteous live by their faith." Much later in Israelite history, this verse and the covenant God made with Abram in the rest of Gen 15 were central in defining faith for the postexilic community in its moment of national confession (Neh 9:7–8).

Genesis 15:6 finds more than echoes in the New Testament, where it is quoted five times (Rom 4:3, 9, 22; Gal 3:6; Jas 2:23). For the Apostle Paul, Abra(ha)m serves as the example of justifying faith, defined first in Rom 3:21–31 and then illustrated in Rom 4 with liberal references to Abraham. The point in both Romans and Galatians is that justifying faith is a matter of grace, not works, so that Abraham is "the ancestor of all who believe without being circumcised and who thus have righteousness reckoned to them, and likewise the ancestor of the circumcised who are not only circumcised but who also follow the example of the faith that our ancestor Abraham had before he was circumcised" (Rom 4:11–12). The assertions in the Epistle of James that Abraham was justified by his works (Jas 2:21, 23) have been famously overstated as contradicting Paul's emphasis on faith alone. But surely we have here a difference of degree or emphasis and not substance. When James avers that Abraham's faith "was active along with his works," and that "faith was brought to completion by the works" (Jas 2:22), he is making a point about the *evidence* of justification, not its *means*. James sets out to show that faith without works is dead (Jas 2:17, 26), and unlike Paul's use of Abraham as an example, James is interested in showing that Abraham's works demonstrate that his faith was genuine. (See further Bridging the Horizons at 25:7–11, p. 227.)

The second portion of this two-part chapter describes a ceremony of covenant ratification (vv. 7–21). Like the first portion in vv. 1–6, we have here a dialogue between God and Abram, and again this dialogue is initiated by God in a statement of self-revelation ("I am the Lord . . . ," v. 7, similar to "I am your shield" in v. 1). The driving theme of the second dialogue is Abram's need for assurance about the "land" (*'ereṣ*) promise. Yet "seed" (*zera'*, NRSV's "offspring," v. 13) recurs again here as it did in vv. 1–6. This time Yahweh establishes a covenant with Abram, binding together the promises of "seed" and "land," and assuring the patriarch that these promises will be fulfilled. This covenant has a literary Janus quality, looking both back to Noah's covenant (6:18; 9:8–17) and forward to the covenant with Abram's descendants at Mount Sinai (Exod 19:5; 24:7–8).

The dialogue opens with another divine self-revelation, "I am Yahweh. . . . " (v. 7) Like the more general "I am your shield . . . " of v. 1, this predicate nominative for identification is a more specific declaration of Yahweh's identity and nature (and compare another at 17:1, "I am God Almighty"). Each of these revelations takes Abram's understanding of Yahweh to a new level, and with greater understanding comes greater commitment to Yahweh's promises. In order for Abram to serve as Yahweh's instrument of blessing for the nations (12:3), the patriarch needs more insight and commitment to Yahweh's identity. Similarly, later Israelites will receive revelatory "I am" statements as a means of illumination and encouragement to follow Yahweh's calling ("I am who I am," "I am Yahweh," Exod 3:14; 6:2). This movement from revelation to faith (see v. 6 above) does not always use such explicit "I am" terminology but is repeated elsewhere in the Pentateuch as the underlying motivational ethic for the whole. The ultimate revelation that Yahweh "is one" results straight away in the injunction to love Yahweh wholeheartedly (Deut 6:4–5). In Gen 15:7, divine self-disclosure moves the narrative forward, illustrating Abram's growing understanding of and trust in Yahweh.

Moreover, the specific phraseology of this revelation in v. 7 is familiar: "I am Yahweh, . . . who brought you *out of the land of Egypt* [from Ur of the Chaldeans]" (Exod 20:2; Lev 25:38; Deut 5:6). The similarities can hardly be coincidental. The narrative intentionally offers Abram as a paradigm for future Israelite experiences. Just as this covenant between Abram and God foreshadows the Mosaic covenant, so the great patriarch's journey of revelation-to-faith generally becomes a paradigm for all Israelites. Abram's encounters with Yahweh resulted in faith and commitment, and so Yahweh's later theophany on Mount Sinai should result in faith and obedience among his children.

Verse 7 closes with a purpose clause that sets the theme for the rest of the chapter. Yahweh brought Abram from Ur of the Chaldeans *in order to give* the land as a possession. Specific words here echo earlier important texts in the Abrahamic narrative: "give" (*nātan*), "land" (*'ereṣ*; Gen 12:7; 13:15, and see also Exod 6:4). And like the first paragraph of this chapter, the emphasis is on inheritance (*yrš*; NRSV's "possess" is essentially "possess as inheritance"; compare "heir" in vv. 3–4). As a childless, seminomadic tribesman, Abram's lack of heir and inheritance necessarily remains the fulcrum point of this narrative.

As before, divine revelation leads Abram to ask for assurances, this time specifically for cognitive certainty ("how am I to *know*," *yd'*, v. 8, and compare v. 2).[90] God's charge to bring an assortment of animals, apparently sacrificial animals, is *prima facie* perplexing for contemporary readers (v. 9). The significance of such a request escapes us, especially in the details of how it might possibly relate to Abram's need for certainty. However, Abram's response (vv. 10–11) shows that he himself understood perfectly well. His dividing and arranging of the animals can only be thought of as ritual preparation for a covenant between Yahweh and Abram, and in fact, the entire event is termed a "covenant" in v. 18. In light of examples from the ancient Near East and at least one reference in the Bible, we understand this ritual as a solemn covenant oath.[91] Passage between the divided corpses invokes a curse upon oneself should one later violate the promise. Such a conditional self-curse has here been transferred to Yahweh in the form of the smoking fire pot and flaming torch (v. 17), by which Yahweh enacts his own death should he fail to fulfill his promises to Abram. In response to Abram's need for assurance, Yahweh has said, in effect, "in order that I may commit myself completely to you, bring these animals to prepare for a covenant. . . . "[92] God has no other deity or higher authority by which to swear an oath, and so he symbolically assumes the role of covenant partner in order to swear upon his own death. It is an extraordinary summit in the narrative; the creator God of Israel desires to swear an oath of fidelity to Abram.

At dusk, when all is ready, Abram assumes a dutiful passivity (v. 12). Yahweh's speech clarifies specifically what Abram should learn from the solemn ceremony; that which he should know beyond doubt (vv. 13–16). He had asked for knowledge ("how am I to *know*") and now Yahweh assures him emphatically of four things ("*Know* this for certain").[93] First, Abram will indeed have offspring but they will be aliens in another country for a period of time (v. 13). Rather than addressing the land promise directly, Yahweh returns to the topic of the first portion of the chapter, the seed promise (vv. 3 and 5). Using the collective of the word "seed," Yahweh asserts succinctly that Abram's seed will be a sojourner (NRSV's "your offspring shall be aliens"). However, the "land" in which they dwell will be the wrong one, because it will not belong to them and they will be forced into submission in that foreign land for four hundred years. Second, Yahweh will in due season pass sentence on that nation, and Abram's seed will be liberated with great possessions (v. 14).

---

[90] Another curious link between the two portions of Gen 15 is the use of an unusual spelling for "O Lord God" here and in v. 2, which may be reserved for contexts of complaint or intercession; for details see N. M. Sarna, *Genesis* (1989), 113.

[91] Billie Jean Collins, "The 'Ritual between the Pieces,'" *COS* 1.61:160–61; Joseph A. Fitzmyer, "The Inscriptions of Bar-ga'yah and Mati'el from Sefire," *COS* 2.82:213–17, esp. 214; and compare Jer. 34:18–20.

[92] C. Westermann, *Genesis 12–36* (1985), 225.

[93] The same verb, "to know," (*yd'*) is used here as in v. 8, this time in the Infinitive Absolute for emphasis.

Third, Abram himself will have a long and peaceful life, not himself being forced to endure the bondage and suffering of his descendants. And finally, Abram's seed will indeed "come back here" in the fourth generation, after the iniquity of the Amorite inhabitants has come to full fruition (thereby justifying their removal from the land, see Deut 9:4–5). Yahweh pulled back the curtain on Abram's future that he might have confidence in his present.

In all likelihood, both the smoking stove and flaming torch represented God's movement between the pieces, while Abram remained passive (v. 17).[94] In case the reader is uncertain about the symbolism or significance of this event, the narrator's voice returns in v. 18a to remove all doubt: "On that day Yahweh made a covenant (*bĕrît*) with Abram." It is commonly asserted that this covenant, unlike the Mosaic/Sinaitic covenant, is a unilateral promissory oath made by God alone, reducing Abram to a recipient of promises.[95] Similarly, some interpret the Abrahamic and Davidic covenants as promissory covenants based on ancient Near Eastern royal grants, in distinction to the obligatory Mosaic covenant based on political treaties. The former obligated the master to the servant, in this case Yahweh to Abram, while the latter was an obligation of the servant (vassal Israel) to the master, Yahweh.[96] But ancient Near Eastern covenants were, by definition, both bilateral (involving two parties) and binary (having two components, consisting of both promises and obligations; review Closer Look "Covenants in the Hebrew Scriptures," p. 101). Covenants were always asymmetrical, emphasizing the role of one party over the other (either promise or obligation), but never totally unilateral. Implicitly, the passive party always had some obligation or promise to uphold, otherwise we have only a promise and no real covenant at all. In the Bible, the covenants of Abraham and David stress the promises of the powerful party (God), while the Mosaic stresses the responsibilities of the weaker party (Israel).[97] But none is totally unilateral.

The first covenant in the Bible was God's commitment to save Noah and his family from death in the floodwaters. This second covenant is God's commitment to Abram to provide land to his descendants. The canonical location of the first covenant in the Bible (Noah's, 6:17–18; 9:8–17) was instructive (see commentary there). Covenant-living was not only Noah's means of salvation from the flood, but the Bible's solution to the sin problem defined earlier in the Primeval History (Gen 2:4–4:16; 6:5, 11–12). Noah's covenantal righteousness resulted in salvation, and it therefore anticipates and previews Yahweh's covenant with Abram. The great

---

[94] Although it is at least possible to take fire pot and torch as representing Abram and God as two parties; see J. G. Janzen, *Abraham and All the Families of the Earth* (1993), 40.

[95] E.g., G. J. Wenham, *Genesis 1–15* (1987), 333; V. P. Hamilton, *The Book of Genesis, Chapters 1–17* (1990), 437.

[96] Moshe Weinfeld, "The Covenant of Grant in the Old Testament and in the Ancient Near East," *JAOS* 90 (1970): 184–203.

[97] Gary N. Knoppers, "Ancient Near Eastern Royal Grants and the Davidic Covenant: A Parallel?" *JAOS* 116/4 (1996): 670–697, esp. 696.

patriarch's righteousness (v. 6) has resulted in salvation from a life of barrenness, and therefore hopelessness. Once again, righteous covenant-living is Israel's hope for salvation, as illustrated in father Abram.

In the dramatic conclusion, Yahweh ties all the pieces together by declaring that he has given the land to Abram's seed (v. 18b). All the lexical components are here: verb "give" (*nātan*), with nouns "land" (*'ereṣ*) and "seed" (*zeraʿ*). The verbal form of "*I give* this land . . ."* is a performative perfect, denoting an action that occurs by means of speaking.[98] The Creator who spoke the cosmos into being has also, by means of this covenant, declared the land belongs to Abram's seed. The covenant reaffirms the original promises to Abram (12:7; 13:15) and drives the narrative forward for a future day (Exod 6:4). There being no further questions or objections, Abram seems content now to live in the covenant assurances of God.

The idealized dimensions of the promised land, from the river of Egypt (most likely the modern Wadi el-ʿArish) to the northwest bend of the Euphrates, were seldom a reality in ancient Israel.[99] The ten nations inhabiting the promised land are also given to Abram's descendants at this time (vv. 19–21). This is the most comprehensive list we have of nations inhabiting the land (see commentary at 10:15–20).[100] All ten in the list are marked as simple objects of Yahweh's giving, making the NRSV's addition of the words "the land of" at the head of v. 19 somewhat misleading. All are simple objects, like the land itself.

GENESIS 16:1–16 HAGAR AND ISHMAEL

(16:1)   Now Sarai, Abram's wife, bore him no children. She had an Egyptian slave-girl whose name was Hagar,

(16:2)   and Sarai said to Abram, "You see that the LORD has prevented me from bearing children; go in to my slave-girl; it may be that I shall obtain children by her." And Abram listened to the voice of Sarai.

(16:3)   So, after Abram had lived ten years in the land of Canaan, Sarai, Abram's wife, took Hagar the Egyptian, her slave-girl, and gave her to her husband Abram as a wife.

(16:4)   He went in to Hagar, and she conceived; and when she saw that she had conceived, she looked with contempt on her mistress.

(16:5)   Then Sarai said to Abram, "May the wrong done to me be on you! I gave my slave-girl to your embrace, and when she saw that she had conceived,

---

[98]   B. T. Arnold and J. H. Choi, *A Guide to Biblical Hebrew Syntax* (2003), 56.

[99]   A. F. Rainey and R. S. Notley, *The Sacred Bridge: Carta's Atlas of the Biblical World* (2006), 35 and 164.

[100]   Edwin C. Hostetter, *Nations Mightier and More Numerous: The Biblical View of Palestine's Pre-Israelite Peoples* (BIBAL dissertation series 3; N. Richland Hills, Tex.: BIBAL Press, 1995), 14–15; William H. C. Propp, *Exodus 19–40: A New Translation with Introduction and Commentary* (AB 2A; New York: Doubleday, 2006), 746–53.

she looked on me with contempt. May the LORD judge between you and me!"

(16:6) But Abram said to Sarai, "Your slave-girl is in your power; do to her as you please." Then Sarai dealt harshly with her, and she ran away from her.

(16:7) The angel of the LORD found her by a spring of water in the wilderness, the spring on the way to Shur.

(16:8) And he said, "Hagar, slave-girl of Sarai, where have you come from and where are you going?" She said, "I am running away from my mistress Sarai."

(16:9) The angel of the LORD said to her, "Return to your mistress, and submit to her."

(16:10) The angel of the LORD also said to her, "I will so greatly multiply your offspring that they cannot be counted for multitude."

(16:11) And the angel of the LORD said to her, "Now you have conceived and shall bear a son; you shall call him Ishmael, for the LORD has given heed to your affliction.

(16:12) He shall be a wild ass of a man, with his hand against everyone, and everyone's hand against him; and he shall live at odds with all his kin."

(16:13) So she named the LORD who spoke to her, "You are El-roi"; for she said, "Have I really seen God and remained alive after seeing him?"[d]

(16:14) Therefore the well was called Beer-lahai-roi; it lies between Kadesh and Bered.

(16:15) Hagar bore Abram a son; and Abram named his son, whom Hagar bore, Ishmael.

(16:16) Abram was eighty-six years old when Hagar bore him Ishmael.

*T*he previous chapter made it clear that Abram would have a biological heir (15:4). Gen 16 now introduces a new character, Hagar the Egyptian slave-girl, as the solution to Sarai's barrenness according to ancient custom. The result is not a happy outcome. When Hagar runs away, she is met by the "angel of Yahweh," who ministers to her directly and extends promises to her that rival the covenant promises given to Abram. The etiological interests of Genesis continue in the conclusion, where we learn the origins of the names of Ishmael and Beer-lahai-roi.

The first presumed heir of the extended narrative, Abram's nephew Lot, proved to be unsuitable (Gen 13). God has now ruled out the slave Eliezer, for Abram will have a biological heir (15:4). Elsewhere, God has promised Abram children in great abundance (like the dust of the earth and the stars of the sky, 13:16 and 15:5). Yet the reader has also been informed early in the narrative that Abram's wife, Sarai, is barren (11:30). Now the narrator returns in 16:1 to pick up this thread in a brief description of Sarai, "Abram's wife," who is unable to bear children. The Hebrew word order marks a change of subject introducing a new unit, and signaling that

---

[d] Meaning of Heb uncertain.

the narrative is moving forward. But the logical dissonance between the promises of great progeny and Sarai's infertility is now unavoidable. The reader encounters a deliberate literary antinomy between God's promises and Abram's reality. We simply cannot move forward without resolving the tension. How can Abram have numerous children if his wife is barren?

Verse 1a, then, is resumptive. It introduces a new unit and reminds the reader that Sarai is still barren. This is followed immediately by what appears to be the solution: "She had an Egyptian slave-girl" (v. 1b). The Hebrew word order implies a disjunctive relationship with v. 1a ("Sarai . . . bore him no children, *but* she had an Egyptian slave-girl"), which assumes Hagar was an easy solution to Sarai's dilemma.[101] Sarai's instruction, "go in to my slave-girl" (v. 2), has an unmistakably sexual meaning, which v. 4 confirms: "He went in to Hagar, and she conceived." Sarai's motivation is to "obtain children by her" (literally: "perhaps I may be built up because of her").

The summary statement at v. 3 describes the surrogate role for Hagar: the barren wife presented (i.e., "took . . . and gave . . . ") the slave-girl to her husband "as a wife." In the ancient world generally, monogamy was the rule and concubines entered the family for childbearing purposes only when the wife was barren (Gen 30:1–4, 9). Ancient Near Eastern parallels confirm that a wife's slave-girl could reasonably be supplied to compensate for a barren womb.[102] In fact, we should probably assume that Sarai was obligated to provide for Abram in this way, and none of the characters in the story so far are to be indicted for less than noble behavior. This was not only an acceptable solution to Sarai's barrenness but a reasonable and righteous one.

After years of barrenness, Sarai's surrogate conceived immediately (v. 4). Resentment and conflict were perhaps inevitable, as happened in other similar cases (Gen 30:1). However justified all the characters must be thus far, the narrator now implies something less in Hagar's contempt for Sarai (v. 4b). The Hebrew implies that Hagar now considered Sarai less significant or no longer needed ("her mistress was lowered in her esteem"). As a surrogate wife who now bears the next presumed heir of the divine promise, Hagar's feeling of superiority was misplaced confidence and the delicate roles of ancient family life were at risk. Sarai perceives the result as a "wrong" (lit.: "violence") and calls for divine justice, assuming Abram's toleration of such disrespect of his primary wife is inexcusable (v. 5).

As we have seen, the social custom of supplying a slave-girl in concubinage to compensate for a barren womb is acceptable behavior in that ancient culture, and therefore the three primary characters have been entirely innocent of wrongdoing.

---

[101] Gordon J. Wenham, *Genesis 16–50* (WBC 2; Dallas, Tex.: Word Books, 1994), 1; V. P. Hamilton, *The Book of Genesis, Chapters 1–17* (1990), 441.

[102] E.g., Richard S. Hess, "Marriage Customs," *COS* 3.101B:251–2. For many other examples, and thorough discussion, see T. L. Thompson, *The Historicity of the Patriarchal Narratives* (1974), 252–69; Martin J. Selman, "Comparative Customs and the Patriarchal Age," in *Essays on the Patriarchal Narratives,* eds. A. R. Millard and D. J. Wiseman (Leicester, England: InterVarsity Press, 1980), 91–139, esp. 119 and 137.

However, suddenly now all are guilty; Hagar of failure to respect her mistress, Abram of failure to maintain a balance between primary and secondary wives, and Sarai of failure to treat Hagar appropriately. NRSV's "Sarai *dealt harshly* with her" (v. 6) is an aggressive humiliation, an intentional oppression of Hagar, which caused her to run away. Ironically, this is the same word used only a few verses earlier to describe the Egyptian oppression of Abram's children (15:13; Piel stem of *'nh*), while here Abram's wife oppresses an Egyptian slave-girl. Sarai's treatment of Hagar is not to be equated with the Egyptian oppression of Israel, but her behavior is indefensible nonetheless.

Hagar was not running away in order to find God, but an "angel of Yahweh" found her running. This is the first appearance in the Bible of the Messenger of Yahweh (*mal'ak yhwh*). It typically represents the appearance of an unspecified supernatural envoy sent from Yahweh, which however is often perplexingly identified with Yahweh himself.[103] So here, the angel speaks for Yahweh in the first person (v. 10) and is later identified by the narrator as Yahweh himself (v. 13). We may be tempted to assume the angel of Yahweh is dispatched to address Hagar in order to maintain a sense of transcendence or distance with her, especially in light of other contexts thus far in Genesis in which Yahweh addressed characters directly (2:16; 3:9, 14, 16, 17; 12:1, etc.). But the encounter should nevertheless be understood as entirely gracious in light of Hagar's identity as an Egyptian slave-girl who presumably has no prior experience with Yahweh, and who is running under duress. Yahweh finds her alone in the desert, tenderly addresses her with rhetorical questions, leading her along and directing her to return to the safety of her mistress's supervision, and even extends the ancestral promises to her and her son. This surprising turn of events confirms how deeply Yahweh is committed to the covenant promises to Abram's offspring.

Hagar had apparently set out to return to Egypt. Although we do not know the precise location of Beer-lahai-roi (v. 14), which will appear again in the Isaac narratives (24:62; 25:11), the "way to Shur" was a southern route to Egypt from Beer-sheba west of Kadesh-barnea (20:1; 25:18). The wilderness of Shur is the desert region in the northwestern Sinai bordering the Egyptian Delta (Exod 15:22).[104]

Whatever her intended destination, Hagar was able to answer only one portion of the angel's two-part question (v. 8). Now destitute and unlikely to arrive safely in Egypt on her own, her destination hardly seems pertinent in light of this encounter with the angel of Yahweh. Her answer is itself an admission of her plight: "I am running away from my mistress."

In a series of three speeches, introduced with identical statements, the angel of Yahweh commands Hagar what to do and assures her of her future. First, she is told

---

[103] Samuel A. Meier, "Angel of Yahweh," *DDD*[2] 53–59; C. Westermann, *Genesis 12–36* (1985), 242–44.

[104] A. F. Rainey and R. S. Notley, *The Sacred Bridge: Carta's Atlas of the Biblical World* (2006), 114.

to return to Sarai and "submit to her" (v. 9). The command is ironic because the same verb is used in v. 6, "*dealt harshly* with her" to describe Sarai's treatment of Hagar (ʿnh, here in Hithpael rather than Piel derived stem). The angel says Hagar is to humble herself by submitting to Sarai's role as primary wife. This could have been a dangerous prospect for Hagar, which leads to the next two speeches. Second, with terminology directly and intentionally reminiscent of the promises to Abram, the angel says he will multiply Hagar's "seed" (*zeraʿ*, NRSV's "offspring") beyond number (v. 10, cf. 13:16 and 15:5).[105] Miraculously and graciously, this Egyptian slave-girl is now the recipient of the wondrous covenant promises of God through Abram. Third, the angel announces the birth of Ishmael in stylized language used in the Bible to introduce the birth of a blessed individual who brings salvation or a turning point in a crisis (Judg 13:3–5; Isa 7:14–16, Luke 1:28–32).[106]

One ingredient of such birth announcements is the proclamation of the child's name, which typically uses popular etymology to ascribe significance to the individual. "Ishmael" means "God hears" and is not at all an unusual name, although the etymology given here is expanded. In the interpretation of the name itself, the angel of Yahweh has fittingly changed the divine element of the name (i.e., the theophoric) from El, "God," to Yahweh in the causal clause "Yahweh has given heed to your affliction." Presumably that which is heard by God is also changed, from the parents' cry for a son to Hagar's cry from her oppression. Verse 12 is a promise of strength for the unborn lad. The promise that he will be a "wild ass of a man," while certainly sounding enigmatic today, was a promise of independent defiance and strength, as the rest of v. 12 explains. Ishmael will be his own man, a freedom-loving nomad, independent of the rest of Abram's descendants and free to chart his own course. On the sons of Ishmael, see commentary at 25:12–18.

Hagar's response personalizes her experience with God: Yahweh is the "God who sees (me)" (v. 13; El-roi). Unlike Abram, who receives the names of God ("I am Yahweh," "I am God Almighty," 15:7; 17:1), Hagar is honored to *give* God a name. She does not attempt to change Yahweh's name or give him a new name for all time, but merely to assert that whatever other name he may have, he will always be for her the God who saw her affliction.[107] The rest of v. 13 has largely been reconstructed in the NRSV because the Hebrew text is untranslatable as it stands (see note to NRSV). The assumption in the reconstructed translation is that ancient popular theology lies at the root of her comment, assuming that one cannot see God and live (32:30 [Heb 32:31]; Exod 33:20). However, something like "I have seen face-to-face the one who appeared to me" is also possible, which seems supported also by the Septuagint.

---

[105] J. A. Emerton concluded that this is one of the promises original to the J complex; J. A. Emerton, "The Origin of the Promises to the Patriarchs in the Older Sources of the Book of Genesis," *VT* 32 (1982): 14–32, esp. 32.

[106] C. Westermann, *Genesis 12–36* (1985), 245.

[107] Ibid., 247.

The etiological interests of the book of Genesis continue in the conclusion of this unit. The spring of water of v. 7 received the name Beer-lahai-roi, "Well of the Living One who has seen me" (v. 14). It lay somewhere between Kadesh(-barnea) and Bered along the road to Shur, as we know from this episode (vv. 7 and 14). Beyond this we cannot speculate about the location, although we will encounter it again in the Isaac narrative (24:62; 25:11).

Verse 15 concludes the episode with the birth of a son to Abram, at long last! He dutifully names the son Ishmael, as Hagar was instructed to do. The occasion is marked by Abram's advanced age (v. 16), hinting at the significance of this event. Indeed, the entire book of Genesis is focused on "descendants" (or "generations," in the macrostructuring *tôlĕdôt*–clause), and the book has valued being fruitful and multiplying from the beginning (1:22, 28; 8:17; 9:1, 7). Yet barrenness and the need to know who will serve as Abram's heir have been the overarching problems of the Abram narrative thus far (11:30; 15:2–3). As this text closes, the reader is satisfied with another presumed heir for Abram, this time a biological son.

GENESIS 17:1–27 COVENANTAL DETAILS

(17:1) When Abram was ninety-nine years old, the LORD appeared to Abram, and said to him, "I am God Almighty; walk before me, and be blameless.

(17:2) And I will make my covenant between me and you, and will make you exceedingly numerous."

(17:3) Then Abram fell on his face; and God said to him,

(17:4) "As for me, this is my covenant with you: You shall be the ancestor of a multitude of nations.

(17:5) No longer shall your name be Abram, but your name shall be Abraham; for I have made you the ancestor of a multitude of nations.

(17:6) I will make you exceedingly fruitful; and I will make nations of you, and kings shall come from you.

(17:7) I will establish my covenant between me and you, and your offspring after you throughout their generations, for an everlasting covenant, to be God to you and to your offspring after you.

(17:8) And I will give to you, and to your offspring after you, the land where you are now an alien, all the land of Canaan, for a perpetual holding; and I will be their God."

(17:9) God said to Abraham, "As for you, you shall keep my covenant, you and your offspring after you throughout their generations.

(17:10) This is my covenant, which you shall keep, between me and you and your offspring after you: Every male among you shall be circumcised.

(17:11) You shall circumcise the flesh of your foreskins, and it shall be a sign of the covenant between me and you.

(17:12) Throughout your generations every male among you shall be circumcised when he is eight days old, including the slave born in your house and the one bought with your money from any foreigner who is not of your offspring.

(17:13) Both the slave born in your house and the one bought with your money must be circumcised. So shall my covenant be in your flesh an everlasting covenant.

(17:14) Any uncircumcised male who is not circumcised in the flesh of his foreskin shall be cut off from his people; he has broken my covenant."

(17:15) God said to Abraham, "As for Sarai your wife, you shall not call her Sarai, but Sarah shall be her name.

(17:16) I will bless her, and moreover I will give you a son by her. I will bless her, and she shall give rise to nations; kings of peoples shall come from her."

(17:17) Then Abraham fell on his face and laughed, and said to himself, "Can a child be born to a man who is a hundred years old? Can Sarah, who is ninety years old, bear a child?"

(17:18) And Abraham said to God, "O that Ishmael might live in your sight!"

(17:19) God said, "No, but your wife Sarah shall bear you a son, and you shall name him Isaac. I will establish my covenant with him as an everlasting covenant for his offspring after him.

(17:20) As for Ishmael, I have heard you; I will bless him and make him fruitful and exceedingly numerous; he shall be the father of twelve princes, and I will make him a great nation.

(17:21) But my covenant I will establish with Isaac, whom Sarah shall bear to you at this season next year."

(17:22) And when he had finished talking with him, God went up from Abraham.

(17:23) Then Abraham took his son Ishmael and all the slaves born in his house or bought with his money, every male among the men of Abraham's house, and he circumcised the flesh of their foreskins that very day, as God had said to him.

(17:24) Abraham was ninety-nine years old when he was circumcised in the flesh of his foreskin.

(17:25) And his son Ishmael was thirteen years old when he was circumcised in the flesh of his foreskin.

(17:26) That very day Abraham and his son Ishmael were circumcised;

(17:27) and all the men of his house, slaves born in the house and those bought with money from a foreigner, were circumcised with him.

God appears to Abram again, this time to expand upon the nature of their covenant relationship. Gen 17 bears a structural resemblance to the two episodes of Gen 15, which described encounters between God and Abram. Each such encounter is initiated by God in self-revelatory disclosures and continues in dialogue between God and Abram. So this unit opens with a revelatory proclamation followed by dialogue. This time, however, Abram speaks hardly at all but hears five divine speeches, in which God emphasizes again how vast will be Abram's offspring, changes his and Sarai's names, institutes circumcision as a sign of their covenant relationship, and announces the birth of Isaac.

Genesis 17 is full of themes, phraseology, and literary features commonly associated with Israel's priestly school. I am not inclined to assume the existence of a priestly source behind the chapter, but rather assume it was composed whole cloth by a priestly redactor of the holiness school. The intent of Gen 17 is to supplement much of the surrounding narrative about Abram/Abraham, which comes from the earlier national epic.[108] Specifically, this chapter circles back around to the covenant themes of Gen 15 to supplement and nuance them, in much the same way Gen 1 related to Gen 2–4. This chapter also has 18:9–15 in view, in part intending to prepare the reader by presenting a different perspective on the prediction of Sarah's conception and the birth of Isaac. These themes and literary features, therefore, reflect the theological contributions central to the work of the redactor (see Introduction, where I also argue there is no need to posit a postexilic date for this redaction).

The narrator opens the chapter using the only occurrence of "Yahweh" in this unit, which carefully makes the point that the God who revealed himself to the Israelites in the Mosaic covenant is the same God who revealed himself to Israel's ancestors as El, El Elyon, and El Shadday (cf. 16:13 and Exod 6:3).[109] The verb "appeared" is a causative-reflexive term for "become visible (Niphal of *r'h*, "to see") used in Genesis at critical junctures in the ancestral narratives (12:7; 17:1; 18:1; 26:2, 24; 35:1, 9; 48:3). God thus causes himself to be seen, pulling back the curtain on himself as it were, allowing himself – even presenting himself – in theophanic certainty. What one *sees* in such revelatory appearances of divine self-disclosure is not the issue, but rather what one *hears* (see Closer Look "Divine Revelation in the Hebrew Scriptures" at p. 135). In most cases, the substance of the appearance or revelation is contained in a speech, as here where the words "and said to him" mark the beginning of the revelation itself.

The revelation of God in vv. 1–2 is introduced with another notation on the age of Abram, highlighting the significance of this event (v. 1a, and cf. 12:4; 16:16). The revelation itself is the first of five speeches of God in Gen 17. Highly structured and carefully detailed, each speech is punctuated by literary focus markers, achieved in most cases by simple word order, to emphasize the role of everyone related to the covenant: first God, then Abraham, followed by Sarah and Ishmael.[110]

---

[108] More specifically, Westermann takes vv. 3b–21 as a late theological expansion of vv. 1–3a, which he assumes was an ancient patriarchal promise being expounded upon by a priestly author; C. Westermann, *Genesis 12–36* (1985), 255–57.

[109] G. J. Wenham, *Genesis 16–50* (1994), 19–20.

[110] Verse 1 is a predicate nominative of identification, but the rest are examples of *casus pendens*; B. K. Waltke and M. P. O'Connor, *An Introduction to Biblical Hebrew Syntax* (1990), 76–77. "As for Ishmael" in v. 20 is complex because it also uses a lamed of specification; B. T. Arnold and J. H. Choi, *A Guide to Biblical Hebrew Syntax* (2003), 113.

vv. 1b–2 – General declaration ("I am God Almighty," v. 1)
vv. 4–8 – God's covenant obligations ("As for me, . . ." v. 4)
vv. 9–14 – Abraham's covenant obligations ("As for you, . . ." v. 9)
vv. 15–16 – Sarah's blessing ("As for Sarah, . . . " v. 15)
vv. 19–21 – Ishmael's blessing ("As for Ishmael, . . . " v. 20)

1. *First Divine Speech* (vv. 1–2). "God Almighty" (*ʾēl šadday*) occurs seven times in the Hebrew Scriptures, although it occurs many more times abbreviated simply as "Almighty" (*šadday*), especially in the book of Job.[111] A deity by the name Shadday is attested elsewhere in the ancient Near East, but we have no convincing etymology for the name, most assuming it means "God of the mountain."[112] It is likely we will never know the origins of this archaic name for God, and the traditional translation used in NRSV, "God Almighty," is appropriate in the context here, and elsewhere in the Bible. While "Yahweh" was the distinctive name by which God revealed himself to later Israel, "God Almighty" was taken as the special revelatory name for the ancestors (Exod 6:3). Similar to "I am your shield" (15:1) and "I am Yahweh" (15:7), this revelatory speech begins with a divine predicate nominative for identification, signifying God's nature and identity as Shadday.

The imperatives "walk before me, and be blameless" (v. 1) hint that Abram has important covenant obligations. These obligations will, in fact, be elucidated in the third speech (vv. 9–14), this first speech being more general, while the other four are the particulars. The verbal sequencing here may imply a purpose clause: "walk before me, *in order to* be blameless," but hendiadys seems more likely: "walk blamelessly before me."[113] The walking-metaphor relates to the way one lives life, while "blameless" denotes unobjectionable acceptability; one stressing positive action and the other calling for the absence of negative characteristics.[114] A good translation might be "Conduct yourself according to my will, and so sustain your integrity."[115]

Divine revelations in Gen 15 ("I am your shield," "I am Yahweh") introduce assurances of God's promises of seed and land. Similarly here, the "I am God Almighty" revelation is followed immediately by God's intent to establish the covenant and make Abram fruitful (v. 2), buttressing the themes of Gen 15. This first speech of God reintroduces the "covenant" (*bĕrît*), which is clearly central to all the speeches in vv. 1–22, shown simply by the sheer repetition of this term thirteen times in just

---

[111] Gen 17:1; 28:3; 35:11; 43:14; 48:3; Exod 6:3; Ezek 10:5.
[112] Knauf has proposed a different etymology yielding "God of the field/steppe," which would identify the deity as "lord of the animals;" Ernst Axel Knauf, "Shadday," *DDD*² 749–753.
[113] B. T. Arnold and J. H. Choi, *A Guide to Biblical Hebrew Syntax* (2003), 92 and 148, respectively.
[114] "Blameless" (*tāmîm*) is used in constructions with "walk" (*hlk*, here in the Hithpael) to characterize a way of life marked by uprightness and probity; Benjamin Kedar-Kopfstein, "*tāmîm*," *TDOT* 15:699–711, esp. 708–9.
[115] Adapted from H. C. Brichto, *The Names of God* (1998), 223.

twenty-two verses.[116] The covenant with Abram first established in 15:7–21 is now explained in great detail (see discussion of covenant there, and review Closer Look at "Covenants in the Hebrew Scriptures," p. 101). While many have assumed this particular biblical covenant is unilateral or unconditional, Abram's obligations are clearly explained in this passage ("walk blamelessly before me," "keep my covenant," "circumcise your males," etc.). The first speech is followed immediately by an act of submission (v. 3a, "Abram fell on his face").[117]

2. *Second Divine Speech* (vv. 4–8). The second speech details God's covenant obligations, as marked by the opening words, "As for me. . . . " These include, first, making Abram the "father of a multitude of nations" (v. 4). Originally, of course, before Ishmael was born (Gen 16), God had promised to make Abram "a great nation" (singular; 12:2). But Ishmael will become a great nation in his own right (17:20; 21:13, 18). As a sign of this covenant obligation, God also declares the name change from Abram to Abraham, which is substantiated by the repetition of the phrase "father of a multitude" (v. 5).[118] The name change signals a new era and status for Abra(ha)m, whose new name is used consistently throughout the rest of Genesis, and therefore from this point forward in this commentary. The name is most likely a simple dialectical variant, and has little to do with the actual etymological explanation provided in v. 5.[119] Hebrew narrators often use names as a means of direct characterization, revealing the kernel of character and dramatizing individuals, so name changes imply a change of character or circumstances (32:28; 41:45; Num 13:16; 2 Kgs 23:34; 24:17; Dan 1:7).[120] While some name changes in the Bible are introduced by pharaohs or kings, God has changed Abraham's name himself, assuring the change of status for this patriarch and his multitudinous descendants.

A second covenant obligation listed in this speech is yet another occurrence of the promise to make Abraham exceedingly fruitful (v. 6). New on this occasion is

---

[116] One of many *leitwörter* in this chapter illustrating its independent transmission history, although Warning has overstated the intentionality with which such terminological "patterns" associates this passage with older portions of the Primeval History; Wilfried Warning, "Terminological Patterns and Genesis 17," *HUCA* 70/71 (1999–2000): 93–107.

[117] On the similarities between vv. 1–3a and 12:1–4a, see C. Westermann, *Genesis 12–36* (1985), 257.

[118] As elsewhere in the Hebrew Bible, this is not an actual etymology, as '*ab hămôn*, "chief of a multitude" has nothing to do with the new syllable in Abra(ha)m. Hebrew names typically use paronomasia for theological effect rather than actual etymology.

[119] For more on the names, their popular etymologies, and significance, see T. L. Thompson, *The Historicity of the Patriarchal Narratives* (1974), 22–36; and D. J. Wiseman, "Abraham Reassessed," in *Essays on the Patriarchal Narratives,* eds. A. R. Millard and D. J. Wiseman (Leicester, England: Inter-Varsity Press, 1980), 141–60, esp. 158–60.

[120] Meir Sternberg, *The Poetics of Biblical Narrative: Ideological Literature and the Drama of Reading* (Indiana Studies in Biblical Literature; Bloomington, Ind.: Indiana University Press, 1985), 328–31. On the dangers of reading too much into biblical names, as though name etymologies contain a certain magical virtue or priestly divination, see Herbert Marks, "Biblical Naming and Poetic Etymology," *JBL* 114/1 (1995): 21–42, esp. 23–24.

the announcement that "kings" will come from Abraham (cf. v. 16), which follows a pattern of expanding the promises slightly as the narrative progresses. A third obligation is God's commitment to make this "an everlasting covenant" (*bĕrît 'ôlām*, v. 7, and cf. vv. 13 and 19), which is used to describe the most important covenants in the Bible (cf. 9:16; Exod 31:16; Lev 24:8; 2 Sam 23:5). The phrase is employed here to clarify that this covenant is not just for Abraham, but for his "seed" (NRSV's "offspring") to follow him "throughout their generations." Such a covenant is of indefinite long duration although it is not necessarily unconditional, which, as we have said, would not be the nature of a bilateral agreement.[121] An "enduring covenant," then, does not denote quantitative infinitude, but rather stresses God's qualitative commitment to Abraham.

In a fourth and final obligation listed in this speech, God once again links Abraham's "seed" and the "land" of Canaan (v. 8). Although Abraham is currently "an alien" in the land, God will eventually make Canaan a lasting property for his offspring. The commitment to "be their God" is covenant terminology, assuring Abraham that his descendants can also enter into this agreement with God.

3. *Third Divine Speech* (vv. 9–14). Abraham's covenant obligations are now the focus, connoted by the word order, "As for you...." (v. 9) His responsibilities are also clear from the collocation using "keep" (*šmr*) with "covenant" (*bĕrît*) in v. 9, and again in v. 10 to urge faithfulness (cf. Exod 19:5).[122] The emphasis in this third speech leaves off any references to "land," and focuses instead on Abraham's "seed" as future recipients of the covenant. Accordingly, circumcision is now instituted as the sign of the covenant for all Abraham's descendants, whether house-born or purchased slaves (vv. 12–13). Repetition is the hallmark of this speech, as a means of emphasizing the importance of this new covenant rite. Indeed, "every male" (v. 10) must be circumcised or he has forfeited his membership in Israel's covenant community by neglect (v. 14). God's covenant "in your flesh" (v. 13) is both the sign of the covenant and the covenant itself.[123] Circumcision was well known in the ancient Near East (see Closer Look "Circumcision as a Sign of the Covenant" at p. 172), although it was certainly unique to Israel as a sign of one's relationship to God. Like other facets of its own society, ancient Israel has transformed a custom otherwise known by its neighbors and given it new religious significance. Rather than instituting a new ritual to signify the covenant, circumcision has been adapted and invested with new meaning.

---

[121] See Closer Look "Covenants in the Hebrew Scriptures" at p. 101, and M. Tsevat, "The Steadfast House: What Was David Promised in 2 Samuel 7?" in *The Meaning of the Book of Job and Other Biblical Studies* (1980), esp. 106–7; repr. from *HUCA* 34 (1963): 71–82.

[122] F. García López, "*šāmar*," *TDOT* 15:279–305, esp. 284, 289–91, and 298.

[123] Thus it is said of circumcision, both "this is my covenant" (v. 10) and "it shall be a sign of the covenant" (v. 11); John Skinner, *A Critical and Exegetical Commentary on Genesis* (ICC 1; New York: Scribner, 1910), 294.

A CLOSER LOOK – CIRCUMCISION AS A SIGN OF THE COVENANT

Male circumcision was practiced widely in the ancient Near East, administered at puberty or as a prenuptial ceremony, and presumably as a fertility rite or for apotropaic effect. The origins of the practice are obscure. It appears first in Upper Syria in the early third millennium BCE and moved from there to the south, where it is attested at Egypt.[124] Many of Israel's neighbors used the practice (Jer 9:25–26), although the Babylonians and Greeks were notable exceptions. Of course, another notable exception was Israel's perennial enemies, the Philistines, for which "uncircumcised" could be used as a derogatory descriptor (Judg 14:3; 1 Sam 17:26).[125]

Israel's use of circumcision is transformed, not only in the timing of the rite to much earlier in life ("when he is eight days old," rather than at puberty, 17:12), but also in the use of circumcision as a "sign" (*'ôt*, or "token," 17:11, cf. KJV, JPS) of the covenant relationship with God. Thus for Israel, the magical or mythical significance of an ancient practice has been converted into a mnemonic "cognition sign," to remind Abraham's descendants to keep the covenant, and perhaps also to remind God to keep his promise of posterity.[126] Thus the appropriation of circumcision in Gen 17 as a sign of the Abrahamic covenant imbued it with new religious significance because it linked future generations of Abraham's descendants with the promises of the ancestral covenant.

Famously, it has been assumed for many decades that circumcision and the Sabbath law reflect exilic and postexilic times, and are therefore important for establishing the date of the priestly materials devoted to these topics (see introduction). This assumption must be called into question in light of the overwhelming religious significance attributed to circumcision prior to the exile, along with our failure to demonstrate that circumcision acquired any new emphasis during the exile.[127] The prescribed use of flint knives for the procedure may also suggest ancient origins for the rite among the Israelites (Exod 4:25; Josh 5:2–3). It is more likely that circumcision and the Sabbath were characteristic topics of the priestly circles that produced these materials, rather than results of a slow progression of thought from the secular to the sacred culminating in the exile, as is commonly thought.

---

[124] Jack M. Sasson, "Circumcision in the Ancient Near East," *JBL* 95 (1966): 473–76.

[125] The terra-cotta model of a circumcised phallus was discovered at Gezer in 1969, but in a Canaanite/Egyptian stratum rather than a Philistine stratum, confirming that circumcision was a cultural marker distinguishing the Israelites from the Philistines; Philip J. King, "Gezer and Circumcision," in *Confronting the Past: Archaeological and Historical Essays on Ancient Israel in Honor of William G. Dever*, eds. Seymour Gitin, J. E. Wright, and J. P. Dessel (Winona Lake, Ind.: Eisenbrauns, 2006), 333–40.

[126] Michael V. Fox, "The Sign of the Covenant: Circumcision in the Light of the Priestly 'ôt Etiologies," *RB* 81 (1974): 557–96, esp. 586–96. On problems related to the gender exclusivity of the practice, and the concept that male circumcision implies it is the males who embody spiritual unfitness to belong to the covenant community, see John Goldingay, "The Significance of Circumcision," *JSOT* 88 (2000): 3–18.

[127] For evidence on circumcision prior to the exile, see Moshe Weinfeld, *The Place of the Law in the Religion of Ancient Israel* (VTSup 100; Leiden: E. J. Brill, 2004), 119–120.

4. *Fourth Divine Speech* (vv. 15–16). The focus now switches to Sarai's role in the covenant, marked by similar word order as that used in vv. 4 and 9: "As for Sarai. . . . " (v. 15). Like Abraham, she is given a new name, making the covenant relationship a family affair. The difference between the two, Sarai and Sarah, is probably limited again to dialectical variation, both meaning "princess." We are given no etymological explanation for the name change (cf. v. 5b), it being sufficient that both names bear the same meaning.

Whereas the previous two divine speeches focused on covenant obligations, God's (vv. 4–8) and Abraham's (vv. 9–14), this one is only about a blessing. Perhaps the prohibition against calling Sarah by her former name is a hint of obligation, but the verb "bless" is repeated twice in v. 16 for emphasis.[128] The blessing itself is a son that God will provide for Sarah; moreover, she will become the mother of nations and kings of peoples (cf. v. 6). The covenant promises are being expanded again. The promise of multitudinous offspring given to Abraham is now extended to elderly Sarah, whose womb has been closed heretofore (16:1). And for the first time, the question of the presumed heir is settled. God had promised to "bless" Abraham (12:2–3), and now the same verb is used to denote specifically the means for that blessing: it will be Sarah. The one who inherits Abraham will not be Lot (13:8–13), Eliezer (15:1–6), or Ishmael (16:7–12), but a son born to Sarah.

Abraham's response is understandable (vv. 17–18). The first portion of the response is said inaudibly, "to himself," in which Abraham doubts the blessing because of their advanced age (v. 17). His laughter ironically becomes the foundation for the lad's name (v. 19) and anticipates Sarah's laughter in 18:12–15 (a passage with much affinity to this one). Although falling upon one's face before theophanic revelation is an act of submission (cf. vv. 3 and 17), Abraham's laughter and silent questions interrupt the divine speech and raise rather serious doubts about what God has just said. Rare in priestly materials, such an abrupt interruption allows the narrator to respond to the reader's doubts too, and merely restates the promises more emphatically.[129]

Thus far in Gen 17, Abraham has not spoken. He breaks his silence now in order to propose that Ishmael may serve as a means of God's covenant blessings. He doubts the blessing God has promised through Sarah. The statement itself is nothing more than a prayer for Ishmael's wellbeing (v. 18): "O that Ishmael might live in your sight!" But in the context of God's promise of a son to Sarah, and as a response to that promised blessing, this is tantamount to an objection.[130]

5. *Fifth Divine Speech* (vv. 19–21). God answers Abraham's protest with a firm, "No" (*'ăbāl*, "on the contrary"). Despite Abraham's skepticism, Sarah *will* have a

---

[128] Divine blessings are illocutionary or performative utterances (cf. v. 20, and see 1:28; 2:3; 9:1; 12:2–3), in which the pronouncement of benediction is itself the act of blessing. The articulation of the blessing is the benediction because it makes it true; C. W. Mitchell, *The Meaning of* brk *"to bless" in the Old Testament* (1987), 7–8, and 62.

[129] C. Westermann, *Genesis 12–36* (1985), 267–68.

[130] H. C. Brichto, *The Names of God* (1998), 228.

son and the lad's name will remind Abraham of his first response, "he laughs."[131] In an assertion more clearly and emphatically stated than any so far, God announces that he will establish the covenant with Sarah's son, Isaac, and with Isaac's seed (v. 19). The speech now adopts the punctuating word order characteristic of the other divine addresses in this text to emphasize the role of Ishmael in the covenant family (v. 20): "As for Ishmael. . . . " God has "heard" Abraham, a word play on Ishmael's name ("God hears," see 16:11). God will "bless" Ishmael too, as he blessed Sarah (v. 16), and he will grow into a nation mirroring Isaac's own descendants, "fruitful and exceedingly numerous." Indeed, like Isaac's descendants, Ishmael will become a "great nation," with twelve princes paralleling the twelve tribes of Israel. (The twelve chiefs of Ishmael are named in 25:12–18.) Far from being cast aside, Ishmael too will benefit from the covenant promises of blessings to Abraham.

The speech concludes with a strong disjunctive: God will bless Ishmael, *but* the covenant itself is for Isaac alone, whom Sarah will bear (v. 21). An additional detail is now provided: the baby will be born "this season next year," which again anticipates the narrative in Gen 18 (18:10, 14, and cf. 21:2). God cuts across Abraham's doubt with a stronger assertion and a resolute announcement about the boy's birth date. The speeches are ended and after the final word, God "went up" from Abraham. The expression implies a theophanic burden in which God has encountered Abraham for special divine revelation (cf. 35:13). Since this chapter began with "Yahweh appeared to Abram" (v. 1), it is fitting to translate this "God disappeared from Abraham's sight."[132]

The narrator concluded the chapter with a postscript on Abraham's obedience (vv. 23–27). As a response to the theophany, Abraham immediately circumcised every male in his household, whether house-born or purchased slave, including his son Ishmael. The latter received the sign of the covenant even though not the son of the covenant.[133] Abraham's obedience was instant ("that very day," vv. 23 and 26) and complete ("every male," v. 23), and is therefore reminiscent of his exemplary action in 12:4. The significance of the occasion was marked once again by recording the ages of Abraham (v. 24) and Ishmael (v. 25).

GENESIS 18:1–19:38 YAHWEH VISITS HEBRON, THEN SODOM AND GOMORRAH

(18:1) The LORD appeared to Abraham by the oaks of Mamre, as he sat at the entrance of his tent in the heat of the day.

---

[131] On the name "Isaac," see also 18:12–15 and 21:6. The Hebrew verb "laugh" may be onomatopoeic, making the word play easier; Rüdiger Bartelmus, "*ṣāḥaq/śāḥaq*," *TDOT* 14:58–72, esp. 61.

[132] V. P. Hamilton, *The Book of Genesis, Chapters 1–17* (1990), 479.

[133] The inclusion of Ishmael implies that Yahweh's covenantal commitment extends to Ishmael's descendants and thus to Arab peoples, providing a foundation for Jewish–Christian–Islamic dialogue; John Goldingay, *Old Testament Theology: Volume 1, Israel's Gospel* (Downers Grove, Ill.: InterVarsity Press, 2003), 203 and 225–26.

(18:2) He looked up and saw three men standing near him. When he saw them, he ran from the tent entrance to meet them, and bowed down to the ground.

(18:3) He said, "My lord, if I find favor with you, do not pass by your servant.

(18:4) Let a little water be brought, and wash your feet, and rest yourselves under the tree.

(18:5) Let me bring a little bread, that you may refresh yourselves, and after that you may pass on– since you have come to your servant." So they said, "Do as you have said."

(18:6) And Abraham hastened into the tent to Sarah, and said, "Make ready quickly three measures of choice flour, knead it, and make cakes."

(18:7) Abraham ran to the herd, and took a calf, tender and good, and gave it to the servant, who hastened to prepare it.

(18:8) Then he took curds and milk and the calf that he had prepared, and set it before them; and he stood by them under the tree while they ate.

(18:9) They said to him, "Where is your wife Sarah?" And he said, "There, in the tent."

(18:10) Then one said, "I will surely return to you in due season, and your wife Sarah shall have a son." And Sarah was listening at the tent entrance behind him.

(18:11) Now Abraham and Sarah were old, advanced in age; it had ceased to be with Sarah after the manner of women.

(18:12) So Sarah laughed to herself, saying, "After I have grown old, and my husband is old, shall I have pleasure?"

(18:13) The LORD said to Abraham, "Why did Sarah laugh, and say, 'Shall I indeed bear a child, now that I am old?'

(18:14) Is anything too wonderful for the LORD? At the set time I will return to you, in due season, and Sarah shall have a son."

(18:15) But Sarah denied, saying, "I did not laugh"; for she was afraid. He said, "Oh yes, you did laugh."

(18:16) Then the men set out from there, and they looked toward Sodom; and Abraham went with them to set them on their way.

(18:17) The LORD said, "Shall I hide from Abraham what I am about to do,

(18:18) seeing that Abraham shall become a great and mighty nation, and all the nations of the earth shall be blessed in him?

(18:19) No, for I have chosen him, that he may charge his children and his household after him to keep the way of the LORD by doing righteousness and justice; so that the LORD may bring about for Abraham what he has promised him."

(18:20) Then the LORD said, "How great is the outcry against Sodom and Gomorrah and how very grave their sin!

(18:21) I must go down and see whether they have done altogether according to the outcry that has come to me; and if not, I will know."

(18:22) So the men turned from there, and went toward Sodom, while Abraham remained standing before the LORD.[e]

(18:23) Then Abraham came near and said, "Will you indeed sweep away the righteous with the wicked?

(18:24) Suppose there are fifty righteous within the city; will you then sweep away the place and not forgive it for the fifty righteous who are in it?

(18:25) Far be it from you to do such a thing, to slay the righteous with the wicked, so that the righteous fare as the wicked! Far be that from you! Shall not the Judge of all the earth do what is just?"

(18:26) And the LORD said, "If I find at Sodom fifty righteous in the city, I will forgive the whole place for their sake."

(18:27) Abraham answered, "Let me take it upon myself to speak to the Lord, I who am but dust and ashes.

(18:28) Suppose five of the fifty righteous are lacking? Will you destroy the whole city for lack of five?" And he said, "I will not destroy it if I find forty-five there."

(18:29) Again he spoke to him, "Suppose forty are found there." He answered, "For the sake of forty I will not do it."

(18:30) Then he said, "Oh do not let the Lord be angry if I speak. Suppose thirty are found there." He answered, "I will not do it, if I find thirty there."

(18:31) He said, "Let me take it upon myself to speak to the Lord. Suppose twenty are found there." He answered, "For the sake of twenty I will not destroy it."

(18:32) Then he said, "Oh do not let the Lord be angry if I speak just once more. Suppose ten are found there." He answered, "For the sake of ten I will not destroy it."

(18:33) And the LORD went his way, when he had finished speaking to Abraham; and Abraham returned to his place.

(19:1) The two angels came to Sodom in the evening, and Lot was sitting in the gateway of Sodom. When Lot saw them, he rose to meet them, and bowed down with his face to the ground.

(19:2) He said, "Please, my lords, turn aside to your servant's house and spend the night, and wash your feet; then you can rise early and go on your way." They said, "No; we will spend the night in the square."

(19:3) But he urged them strongly; so they turned aside to him and entered his house; and he made them a feast, and baked unleavened bread, and they ate.

(19:4) But before they lay down, the men of the city, the men of Sodom, both young and old, all the people to the last man, surrounded the house;

(19:5) and they called to Lot, "Where are the men who came to you tonight? Bring them out to us, so that we may know them."

---

[e] Another ancient tradition reads while the LORD remained standing before Abraham.

(19:6) Lot went out of the door to the men, shut the door after him,

(19:7) and said, "I beg you, my brothers, do not act so wickedly.

(19:8) Look, I have two daughters who have not known a man; let me bring them out to you, and do to them as you please; only do nothing to these men, for they have come under the shelter of my roof."

(19:9) But they replied, "Stand back!" And they said, "This fellow came here as an alien, and he would play the judge! Now we will deal worse with you than with them." Then they pressed hard against the man Lot, and came near the door to break it down.

(19:10) But the men inside reached out their hands and brought Lot into the house with them, and shut the door.

(19:11) And they struck with blindness the men who were at the door of the house, both small and great, so that they were unable to find the door.

(19:12) Then the men said to Lot, "Have you anyone else here? Sons-in-law, sons, daughters, or anyone you have in the city – bring them out of the place.

(19:13) For we are about to destroy this place, because the outcry against its people has become great before the LORD, and the LORD has sent us to destroy it."

(19:14) So Lot went out and said to his sons-in-law, who were to marry his daughters, "Up, get out of this place; for the LORD is about to destroy the city." But he seemed to his sons-in-law to be jesting.

(19:15) When morning dawned, the angels urged Lot, saying, "Get up, take your wife and your two daughters who are here, or else you will be consumed in the punishment of the city."

(19:16) But he lingered; so the men seized him and his wife and his two daughters by the hand, the LORD being merciful to him, and they brought him out and left him outside the city.

(19:17) When they had brought them outside, they said, "Flee for your life; do not look back or stop anywhere in the Plain; flee to the hills, or else you will be consumed."

(19:18) And Lot said to them, "Oh, no, my lords;

(19:19) your servant has found favor with you, and you have shown me great kindness in saving my life; but I cannot flee to the hills, for fear the disaster will overtake me and I die.

(19:20) Look, that city is near enough to flee to, and it is a little one. Let me escape there – is it not a little one? – and my life will be saved!"

(19:21) He said to him, "Very well, I grant you this favor too, and will not overthrow the city of which you have spoken.

(19:22) Hurry, escape there, for I can do nothing until you arrive there." Therefore the city was called Zoar.

(19:23) The sun had risen on the earth when Lot came to Zoar.

(19:24) Then the LORD rained on Sodom and Gomorrah sulfur and fire from the LORD out of heaven;

(19:25) and he overthrew those cities, and all the Plain, and all the inhabitants of the cities, and what grew on the ground.

(19:26) But Lot's wife, behind him, looked back, and she became a pillar of salt.

(19:27) Abraham went early in the morning to the place where he had stood before the LORD;

(19:28) and he looked down toward Sodom and Gomorrah and toward all the land of the Plain and saw the smoke of the land going up like the smoke of a furnace.

(19:29) So it was that, when God destroyed the cities of the Plain, God remembered Abraham, and sent Lot out of the midst of the overthrow, when he overthrew the cities in which Lot had settled.

(19:30) Now Lot went up out of Zoar and settled in the hills with his two daughters, for he was afraid to stay in Zoar; so he lived in a cave with his two daughters.

(19:31) And the firstborn said to the younger, "Our father is old, and there is not a man on earth to come in to us after the manner of all the world.

(19:32) Come, let us make our father drink wine, and we will lie with him, so that we may preserve offspring through our father."

(19:33) So they made their father drink wine that night; and the firstborn went in, and lay with her father; he did not know when she lay down or when she rose.

(19:34) On the next day, the firstborn said to the younger, "Look, I lay last night with my father; let us make him drink wine tonight also; then you go in and lie with him, so that we may preserve offspring through our father."

(19:35) So they made their father drink wine that night also; and the younger rose, and lay with him; and he did not know when she lay down or when she rose.

(19:36) Thus both the daughters of Lot became pregnant by their father.

(19:37) The firstborn bore a son, and named him Moab; he is the ancestor of the Moabites to this day.

(19:38) The younger also bore a son and named him Ben-ammi; he is the ancestor of the Ammonites to this day.

*T*he passage consists of two visitations of God to mortals, and the results of each. Yahweh appears to Abraham at the oaks of Mamre near Hebron, and their conversation continues along the road to Sodom (Gen 18). Then Yahweh's emissaries visit Lot at Sodom, which results in the conflagration destroying Sodom and Gomorrah, and the ensuing incestuous conception and birth of Lot's grandsons, Moab and Ben-ammi (Gen 19). The contrast between Abraham and his nephew, Lot, was the topic of an earlier narrative (13:8–18). There we learned how Abraham and Lot came to live in separate locations, Lot in the plain of Jordan so near Sodom, and Abraham by the oaks of Mamre near Hebron. Gen 13 also taught us much about each man's character. The contrast between them comes to full fruition here.

Genesis 18–19 is particularly interested in etiology, a literary feature designed to provide explanation for a situation or name that exists at the time the narrative is written (see introduction). Often in Genesis, an episode is concluded with an etiological connection that helps the reader understand why something *is as it is*, and secondarily prepares the reader for the next unit of the book.[134] So here we learn the origins of the name "Zoar" (19:22), are reminded of the meaning of "Isaac" (18:12–15, cf. 17:19), the ancestral origins of the Moabites and Ammonites (19:37–38), as well as how Sodom and Gomorrah were destroyed and perhaps why the plain of Jordan has humanoid pillars of salt or stone (19:26). But the unit is not *primarily* etiological. Although these chapters have gone through a long transmission history, they stand now as an integrated narrative, contrasting the integrity of father Abraham with the less than exemplary behavior of Lot.[135]

Yahweh has "appeared" to Abraham at critical junctures of his faith journey (12:7; 17:1), and does so again here (18:1), preparing us for another important theophanic revelation.[136] What one *sees* in such revelatory appearances of God is not usually as important as what one *hears* (cf. 17:1, and see Closer Look "Divine Revelation in the Hebrew Scriptures" at p. 135). Like other appearances of God, the substance of the revelation here is in what is said (especially in 18:9–15). On the other hand, most other examples move immediately from "Yahweh/God *appeared*" to "and he *said*," introducing a divine promise (12:7) or a speech of self-disclosure (17:1). In this text, there is neither promise nor self-disclosure but a surprising switch to what Abraham actually sees: "He [Abraham] looked up and saw..." (18:2). This raises, of course, the problem of the relationship between Yahweh and the "three men" Abraham saw.[137] The narrator has informed us from the outset that Yahweh is at least *among* them (18:1, cf. 18:13, 14, etc.). And apparently when "the men" turned to go to Sodom (19:1), two messengers (NRSV's "angels") went ahead and served as emissaries to Lot. The one staying behind was Yahweh himself, as the continued use of the tetragrammaton in 18:22–33 makes clear. But the narrator's point of view, and therefore our informed position as readers, is not Abraham's perception. The Hebrew phraseology of 18:2 specifies Abraham's "participant perspective," which is

---

[134] E.g., so far Genesis has used etiologies to explain at least the following: sabbath law (2:1–3), marriage (2:24), serpentine locomotion (3:14), human hatred of snakes (3:15), pain in childbirth (3:16), inextricability of life and work (3:17–18), inevitability of death (3:19), human cultural institutions, including urbanization, pastoral agriculture, music, and metallurgy (vv. 17–22), Nephilim (6:4), seasons of the year (8:22), viticulture (9:20–21), the name Babel (11:9), the name Ishmael (16:11), and the name Beer-lahai-roi (16:14).

[135] On the unity of these chapters, see Robert I. Le Tellier, *Day in Mamre, Night in Sodom: Abraham and Lot in Genesis 18 and 19* (Biblical Interpretation Series 10; Leiden, New York: E.J. Brill, 1995), 30–70.

[136] Cf. also the appearances of God to Isaac (26:2, 24) and Jacob (35:1,9; 48:3). In all these texts, the verb "appeared" is a causative-reflexive term for "become visible" (Niphal of r'h, "to see").

[137] On ways this has been interpreted, see G. von Rad, *Genesis* (1961), 204–6.

an untranslatable way of switching the scene from the narrator's perspective in 18:1 to the character's point of view.[138] The narrator and reader understand this to be Yahweh who is appearing, but Abraham sees "three men." (On the "oaks of Mamre" near Hebron, see 13:18 and commentary there.)

Abraham seems to have grasped immediately that these three men, by all appearances *only* men, were in fact *numina* representing Yahweh himself.[139] Abraham left his tent entrance, ran forward to meet them, and prostrated himself before them, going considerably beyond the requirements of conventional etiquette. The Masoretic Text of the Bible, preserving the tradition of rabbinical interpretation, spells "My lord" in 18:3 as "My LORD," meaning "Yahweh," indicating some early Jewish interpreters suspected Abraham understood these were more than mere men.[140] Regardless of how much Abraham understood about his hosts at this point in the encounter, his offer for bread, water, and refreshment before they continue their journey was accepted (18:3–5). His gracious hospitality, humbly stated at first, becomes in reality a feast, requiring Sarah's help with the baking (18:6), a servant's help with preparing a calf (18:7), and his own presentation complete with curds and milk (18:8).

Abraham stands nearby serving as a waiter while the men eat. Quite suddenly the question arises, "Where is your wife Sarah?" The bald declaration in the first person singular, "I will surely return, . . . " means one of the three "men" has taken the lead in announcing that Sarah will give birth to a son (18:10). NRSV's "in due season" (recurring in 18:14) means roughly "about this time next year."[141] This narrative adds a detail not specifically stated in the parallel announcement in 17:15–17: "it had ceased to be with Sarah after the manner of women" (18:11), making it all the more understandable that Sarah would silently laugh, especially in the seclusion of her place at the tent door behind the guests. Sarah may no longer have monthly periods, but she can at least enjoy a good laugh at the expense of these visitors. Or can she? The seemingly omniscient visitor, identified simply as "Yahweh" by the narrator, seemed to have heard Sarah's every thought and snicker (18:13). The prediction is repeated, and when Sarah denies having laughed, the divine visitor rejoins, "Oh yes, you did laugh" (18:15). The exchange confirms implicitly what 17:19 had stated plainly. Abraham's and Sarah's laughter provides the etiological word play using the verb "laugh" (*ṣāḥaq*) for the lad's name, Isaac, *yiṣḥāq*, "he laughs."[142]

---

[138] The use of *wĕhinnēh* for perception; B. T. Arnold and J. H. Choi, *A Guide to Biblical Hebrew Syntax* (2003), 159.

[139] H. C. Brichto, *The Names of God* (1998), 230–31.

[140] So we have *'ădōnāy*, the distinct spelling for the tetragrammaton, Yahweh, rather than *'ădōnî*, "my lord," or "sir." If this is correct, there is no need to read "unwitting double entendre" into Abraham's elaborate speech; contra G. J. Wenham, *Genesis 16–50* (1994), 46.

[141] GKC §118u; and now confirmed by an Akkadian parallel, *AHw* 99a.

[142] The name "Isaac" most likely meant something like "God laughs (as a sign of favor over the newborn child)." On the complexities of the name and its use in the Bible, see Rüdiger Bartelmus, "*ṣāḥaq/śāḥaq*," *TDOT* 14:58–72, esp. 61–63.

After dinner, the men depart toward Sodom. Abraham accompanies them a good distance along the way, as is ancient Near Eastern custom (18:16). As they walk, the omniscient narrator reveals the inner life of Yahweh, who ponders whether or not he should hide his intentions from Abraham (18:17–19). Yahweh's musings reflect on Abraham's future as a great and mighty nation, through whom all peoples of the earth shall be blessed, relying on the promises of 12:2–3. Eventually, Yahweh decides "No, for I have chosen him" (18:19) and reveals to Abraham his intentions for the excursion to Sodom. "Chosen" is simply the word "know" ("I have known him" or "I know him"). In this context (and in the Perfect aspect), it means Yahweh decides to reveal his intentions to Abraham because of prior revelatory experiences with him and because of the closeness of his prior relationship with Abraham.[143] In Yahweh's inner dialogue, he decides to confide in Abraham partly because the patriarch will instruct his descendants "to keep the way of the LORD by doing righteousness and justice" (18:19). Appropriately, it is Abraham's concern for justice and righteousness that leads him to intercede for Sodom (18:25).

Having decided to disclose all to Abraham, Yahweh states succinctly his reason for the mission to Sodom (18:20–21). NRSV's "the outcry *against* Sodom and Gomorrah" is more precise than the original, where the literal "cry of Sodom and Gomorrah" could more naturally imply the cities have raised an alarm, a plaintive cry for God's aid. But the next phrase is epexegetical, explaining and interpreting further the initial assertion: "how very grave their sin!" The outcry, in this context therefore, is the lament of those oppressed by the wickedness of the cities. This reconnaissance mission will discern if things are as bad as they appear. If so, the implications cannot be positive for the citizens of Sodom, including Lot who now lives close to Sodom (13:12). The phraseology implies there is no hope, that Yahweh has decided upon punishment.[144] And yet the final " . . . and if not, I will know" leaves the door open for Abraham.

What follows in the rest of the chapter has become a classic text on the righteousness and justice of God, and the responsibility of God's servants. The circumstantial clause in 18:22, "while Abraham remained standing before the LORD," is one of the rare occasions when the earliest Jewish scribes altered the text. We have reason to believe the text originally said "while the LORD remained standing before Abraham," (as in the NRSV footnote), which seemed irreverent to the scribes. They presumably thought it inappropriate for Yahweh to stand before Abraham, so they reversed the order, leaving Abraham before Yahweh.[145] In either case, the reference clarifies that

---

[143] The idea of election is often overstated, as in G. Johannes Botterweck, *"yāda'," TDOT* 5:448–481, esp. 468. The idea is really the fullness and intimacy of relationship; Terence E. Fretheim, *"yd'" NIDOTTE* 2: 409–14, esp. 410–11. On the Perfect of Experience; B. T. Arnold and J. H. Choi, *A Guide to Biblical Hebrew Syntax* (2003), 55.

[144] G. J. Wenham, *Genesis 16–50* (1994), 50.

[145] Some scholars, however, doubt that these "corrections of the scribes" (*tiqqûnê sōpĕrîm*) reflect a genuine textual history but were midrashic interpretations, so that the original here would have been as it stands in the NRSV text (and perhaps supported by 19:27);

two of the original three visitors now go on to Sodom (19:1), while the one lagging behind to chat with Abraham is unquestionably identified as Yahweh. The chapter to this point has not always been clear about which of the three was speaking when representing Yahweh, and what his relationship was to the other two visitors. But 18:22 settles that question, and the effect of the imprecision to this point may have been deliberate in order to help the reader appreciate how difficult it is for mortals to comprehend the divine world.[146]

Regardless of the original word order – Abraham standing before Yahweh or vice versa – the narrator's voice here creates a slight pause in the action, as though Abraham were pondering whether or not to speak up. On previous occasions when Abraham addressed God (15:2, 8; 17:17), he did so always on behalf of his own needs or concerns. For the first time, Abraham speaks on behalf of another, revealing a deeply compassionate and moral character (cf. Gen 14).[147] He has just received assurances that a son, Isaac, will be born to Sarah (18:9–15). But how can he abandon his nephew Lot to the awful fate of Sodom! Having been informed by Yahweh of the impending disaster, Abraham decides to take up the task of defending God's own righteousness for the sake of Lot and the citizens of Sodom. And so "Abraham came near" or approached God to engage him in dialogue (18:23).

The oft-repeated assumption that the exchange in 18:23–33 is an example of bargaining, bartering, or even haggling, has been overstated, or at least misunderstood. Of course, such bartering was expected in that part of the world, then as now. Abraham no doubt *began* with the expectation that his offer of fifty righteous would be countered with a higher number.[148] His offer anticipates a counter offer, which would be followed by a socially prescribed bidding custom proceeding from the initial offers (fifty in this case, and presumably a much higher number, such as one hundred, for example) with back-and-forth offers until the two parties converge upon an agreed-upon number. Abraham's speech about the need for justice and righteousness at the beginning of the encounter (18:23–25) even presumes to instruct Yahweh in the ways of righteousness and justice, as Abraham is indeed supposed to do for his descendants and household (18:19). His appeal for the Judge of all the earth to do what is just surely anticipates the bartering custom; he is appealing for his interlocutor to counter with a reasonable number, within his bidding range, so the haggling can begin. The expected response would be for a high number, yet one close enough to Abraham's fifty to begin negotiations for a reasonable agreement.

Israel Yeivin, *Introduction to the Tiberian Masorah,* trans. E. J. Revell (Masoretic Studies 5; Missoula, Mont.: Scholars Press, 1980), 49–51; Emanuel Tov, *Textual Criticism of the Hebrew Bible* (Minneapolis, Assen/Maastricht: Fortress Press/Van Gorcum, 1992), 64–67.

[146] G. J. Wenham, *Genesis 16–50* (1994), 51.

[147] N. M. Sarna, *Genesis* (1989), 132–33. Sarna assumes Abraham is driven by pure altruism and his compassion for the anonymous strangers of Sodom, while I rather assume he is also thinking about his nephew, Lot.

[148] Nathan MacDonald, "Listening to Abraham – Listening to YHWH: Divine Justice and Mercy in Genesis 18:16–33," *CBQ* 66/1 (2004): 25–43, esp. 30–35.

What happens next surprises. Yahweh refuses to play the game, and his answer is subversive.[149] He agrees to forgive "the whole place" for the sake of Abraham's fifty. Breaking all patterns of socially agreed-upon haggling, Yahweh has cut across Abraham's opening salvo but at the same time acquiesced to his intent. Abraham's next offer takes an entirely different stance. Rather than instructing Yahweh in the ways of justice, Abraham obsequiously embraces his "dust and ashes" identity before the Judge of all the earth (18:27). Without having a true counteroffer from Yahweh, all he can do is tentatively lower his opening bid to see if Yahweh's grace will extend that far. Thus we move from fifty, to forty-five, to forty, and then down by increments of ten (18:28–32). Instead of Abraham teaching Yahweh about justice, Abraham has learned about the mercy of Yahweh. Abraham boldly stepped up to barter with the Judge of all the earth but his strategy is turned upside down, as he learns instead that he has underestimated the mercy of God. In the end, Yahweh is more merciful than Abraham could have imagined, and the encounter becomes a lesson in intercession for Israel's model ancestor.

Having reached the limit of Abraham's imagination, the reverse bidding stops at ten. I do not believe the tone between Yahweh and Abraham cools as the negotiations proceed, nor that the change in phraseology has anything to do with an awkward tone between them.[150] Rather the increasing brevity of offers and counteroffers relates to this surprising reversal of the normal haggling rules. Yahweh has introduced a new way of looking at grace and forgiveness by pushing Abraham to the limits of his own imagination, whereas Abraham at first thought he was pushing the limits of Yahweh. After Abraham's limit of ten, Yahweh went his way, while Abraham returned to Mamre, no doubt to contemplate the lesson he had just learned (18:33).

The scene shifts at 19:1 and so do the characters. Abraham has a minimal role in Gen 19, only in the aftermath of the destruction (vv. 27, 29), and Yahweh only in the destruction itself (vv. 24–25). Here Lot comes to center stage for the first time, as he graciously greets "the two angels" when they arrive at Sodom that evening. Whatever questions were raised by the vague relationship between Yahweh and the other two "men" who visited Abraham in Gen 18 have been answered here, where the two are messengers or representatives of Yahweh.

Lot's presence "in the gateway of Sodom" is an ominous sign, since the narrator informed us earlier that Sodom and Gomorrah are doomed cities (13:10). An opening scene at the gates of Sodom, and with Lot playing a prominent role, can only signal trouble again (cf. Gen 14). A city's gate was the prominent place for commerce and city government, a place to "meet and greet," and conduct business. Lot has apparently become a city leader since moving to Sodom (13:12; 14:12).

The location of Sodom and Gomorrah is impossible to determine. We have seen that these ancient polities played an important role among the cities of the southern

149 Ibid., 35.
150 Contra G. J. Wenham, *Genesis 16–50* (1994), 51–53.

Jordan valley, along with Admah, Zeboiim, and Zoar, a kind of "pentapolis" along the southern coast of the Dead Sea (see commentary at 14:1–2). While it is possible this text has in view a geographical location at the northern end of the Dead Sea, a southern location is more likely. Remains of a large Early Bronze Age (3300–2000 BCE) city southeast of the Dead Sea in Jordan have most often been identified with Sodom.[151]

Lot's hospitality is impressive (19:1–3). He is sufficiently obsequious, insists on providing food and shelter, which is appropriate given the hour, "in the evening." Guests traveling through an ancient city had the option of spending the night in an open square, although citizens were expected to provide overnight lodging (Judg 19:15).[152] Sodom's two visitors opted to spend the night in the square, but Lot appears to understand the danger to their wellbeing, either in the square or in the home of other citizens of Sodom.

What happens next in the narrative may seem appalling to today's reader, and indeed, this text has evoked an enormous amount of scholarly literature attempting to understand it. All the men of Sodom come to Lot's residence that evening and demand he turn the visitors over to them, in order that they may "know" them (19:5). Having taken the two guests into this abode, Lot is obligated to protect them and so he attempts to negotiate with the men of Sodom. His solution is equally appalling, in that he offers his two virgin daughters to the rogues to do with as they see fit (19:8). They rebuff his offer and turn violent (19:9). Traditionally, of course, the sexual connotations of "know" (*yd*ʿ) have led interpreters to assume the offense of the men of Sodom is homosexuality (or homosexual gang rape), which gave rise to our English term "sodomy." Other options have been offered, such as the citizens' violation of hospitality laws, compounded by Lot's offer of his daughters as the most deplorable treatment of women.[153] However, the use of "know" with an undeniably sexual denotation in the same context (19:8) makes it difficult to deny homosexual intent on the part of the men of Sodom, whether it is taken as the most serious offense of the text or not.[154] Attempts to deny this are driven more by today's sensibilities rather by the text before us. Yet it cannot be denied that the citizens of Sodom are also guilty of brutish treatment of Lot and his guests, and that Lot himself has continued to make horrible decisions, as we have come to expect of him (13:10–11; 14:13).

The curious description of the "men of the city, the men of Sodom," young and old alike, every last one of them ("to the last man," 19:4) surely has in view

[151] R. Thomas Schaub, "Bab edh-Dhraʿ," *OEANE* 1:248–51; R. Thomas Schaub, "Southeast Dead Sea Plain," *OEANE* 5:62–64.

[152] Lot's hospitality shares much in common with Abraham's and the differences are probably related to the different time of day (18:1–8).

[153] For an attempt to explain the problems as general failure of the rule of law, justifying the destruction of the city, see Scott N. Morschauser, "'Hospitality', Hostiles and Hostages: On the Legal Background to Genesis 19:1–9," *JSOT* 27/4 (2003): 461–85.

[154] Bruce Vawter, *On Genesis: A New Reading* (Garden City, N.Y.: Doubleday, 1977), 233–35.

Abraham's intercession on their behalf (18:22–33). Yahweh's emissaries enter the city to determine whether there might be ten righteous in it, while the narrator finds none. Lot's guests rescue him and strike the men of Sodom with blindness (19:10–11). They reveal to Lot the imminent danger and advise him to get his extended family out of the city (19:12–13). We learn at this point that Lot's virgin daughters are betrothed to be married. His attempt to save his future sons-in-law fails because they cannot take him seriously (19:14).

Amazingly, the next morning, when Lot's guests announce that doomsday has arrived, he dallies and has to be forcibly removed (19:15–16). It is only because of "the pity of Yahweh" that the angels seize Lot, his wife, and their two daughters by the hand and deposit them safely outside the city.[155] These four are saved, despite the lack of ten righteous in the city, illustrating for the reader what Abraham has learned: Yahweh's mercy is impossible to quantify.

Yet even in the moment of catastrophe and undeserved mercy, Lot cannot restrain himself. Hearing strict instructions to run to the hills and not look back, Lot objects (19:17–20). He does not want the hills, but prefers the cities of the plain (cf. 13:10), and therefore makes a presumptuous request at this, a most inopportune moment. He prefers the little city of Zoar, in the vicinity of the southernmost point of the Jordan valley (14:2, 8). As we have seen, Zoar was one of the five cities of the Jordan valley along the southern coast of the Dead Sea (and one of the five cities of the west aligned against the four kings from the east, Gen 14). Lot rejects salvation in the hills and requests instead to be saved in Zoar. Surprisingly, one of the angels sounds a little worn down, "Oh, all right," as he agrees not to include Zoar in the devastation (19:21). Zoar is thus spared, and the etiological aspect of the account explains the contrast between the desolate west shore of the Dead Sea and the immediately adjacent lush oasis of Zoar.[156]

The Hebrew word order marks a change of subject at 19:24–25. Yahweh returns to the narrative to rain "sulfur and fire," which is nominal hendiadys ("sulfurous fire," NJPS) and a fixed image for God's judgment in action.[157] Hebrew narrative is not interested in secondary causes, so that whatever natural phenomena might have been perceived as contributing to the disaster is irrelevant. It only matters that the rain of fire was "from the LORD out of heaven."

Lot's wife acted foolishly, giving no heed to the angels' prohibition about looking back at the carnage behind them (19:17). Many have observed the interesting parallel with Greek mythology, in which Orpheus is helping his wife Eurydice escape the underworld. They had been given permission to do so under one condition: Orpheus must allow her to walk behind him and he must not look back until reaching the land of the living. Just before reaching the upper world, Orpheus looked back in anxiety

---

[155] NRSV's "the LORD being merciful to him"; Matitiahu Tsevat, "*ḥāmal*," *TDOT* 4:470–72.
[156] Michael C. Astour, "Zoar," *ABD* 6:1107.
[157] C. Westermann, *Genesis 12–36* (1985), 306.

and Eurydice vanished again from his sight.[158] In this case, she has only herself to blame rather than her husband, for she looked back and was overcome by the conflagration. She also leaves behind two daughters, who in the same moment lose their mother and their betrothed husbands, and are left to ponder their prospects for children (19:31). The narrator is most likely aware of the etiological tradition preserved also in the Apocrypha and Josephus, linking Lot's wife with the presence of grotesquely humanlike rock formations in the salt cliffs of the Dead Sea area (Wis. 10:7; *Ant.* 1.11.4).[159]

Abraham witnessed the devastation from his observation deck near the spot where he had interceded for the city (19:27–28, cf. 18:22–33). In a carefully phrased summary, the narrator makes it clear that Lot's salvation is because "God remembered Abraham," perhaps referring to Abraham's intercession (19:29). Lot was saved, in spite of the fact that Lot himself had chosen to settle in the cities of the Plain. Perhaps also the reader is invited to recall that his salvation was conditioned upon finding ten righteous people in the city, reminding us again of the boundless mercy of Yahweh.

After the annihilation of Sodom and Gomorrah, Lot discovers that Zoar did not prove to be what he had expected. Whatever the nature or source of his fear, Lot is driven to leave Zoar and settle – ironically enough – in the hills, living in a cave with his two daughters (19:30).[160] The daughters themselves are left destitute without their betrothed husbands, who were killed in the destruction of Sodom. Their driving motivation for using their intoxicated (and pitiful) father to conceive children is not simply because other males were unavailable (as implied in 19:31), for marriageable men would have survived in Zoar. Rather, we may assume they feared their father would remain a widower ("our father is old"), and would therefore be unable to continue his own line. Their actions are motivated by a desire to preserve offspring ("seed," *zeraʿ*, 19:32 and 34), not for their own sakes, but for their father's sake. They used wine presumably because they believed he would not approve their plan.

While this text is not *predominantly* etiological, it clearly shows an interest in explaining the origins of things, and as elsewhere in Genesis, these explanations are often at the conclusion of a narrative. The daughters give birth to Moab and Ben-ammi, yet the emphasis is not on their names *per se* but on the origin of Moab and Ammon (19:37–38).[161] Thus the text concludes by explaining where two

---

[158] On the so-called "turn-around-and-everything-is-lost" motif, see Karin R. Andriolo, "A Structural Analysis of Genealogy and World View in the Old Testament," *AA* 75 (1973): 1657–69, esp. 1660.

[159] Victor P. Hamilton, *The Book of Genesis, Chapters 18–50* (NICOT; Grand Rapids, Mich.: Eerdmans, 1995), 48; for photograph, see R. Lansing Hicks, "Lot," *IDB* 3:162–63.

[160] Ironic, because he had been told to seek refuge in the hills and had rejected that plan (19:17).

[161] C. Westermann, *Genesis 12–36* (1985), 314.

of Israel's transjordanian neighbors came from, and how they came to settle in their approximate geographical locations. The familial relationship of Moab and Ammon through Abraham's nephew explains their linguistic and ethnic affinity with Israel. The recurrence of "to this day" reflects the presence of the Moabites and Ammonites in the transjordan at the time of the narrator, so that the etiology explains his current situation by means of an event from the distant past. Whether "to this day" is part of a later Deuteronomistic redaction remains to be determined, but it at least reflects the eyewitness perspective of someone living in the land some considerable amount of time after the events.[162]

GENESIS 20:1–18 ABRAHAM AND ABIMELECH, KING OF GERAR

(20:1) From there Abraham journeyed toward the region of the Negeb, and settled between Kadesh and Shur. While residing in Gerar as an alien,

(20:2) Abraham said of his wife Sarah, "She is my sister." And King Abimelech of Gerar sent and took Sarah.

(20:3) But God came to Abimelech in a dream by night, and said to him, "You are about to die because of the woman whom you have taken; for she is a married woman."

(20:4) Now Abimelech had not approached her; so he said, "Lord, will you destroy an innocent people?

(20:5) Did he not himself say to me, 'She is my sister'? And she herself said, 'He is my brother.' I did this in the integrity of my heart and the innocence of my hands."

(20:6) Then God said to him in the dream, "Yes, I know that you did this in the integrity of your heart; furthermore it was I who kept you from sinning against me. Therefore I did not let you touch her.

(20:7) Now then, return the man's wife; for he is a prophet, and he will pray for you and you shall live. But if you do not restore her, know that you shall surely die, you and all that are yours."

(20:8) So Abimelech rose early in the morning, and called all his servants and told them all these things; and the men were very much afraid.

(20:9) Then Abimelech called Abraham, and said to him, "What have you done to us? How have I sinned against you, that you have brought such great guilt on me and my kingdom? You have done things to me that ought not to be done."

(20:10) And Abimelech said to Abraham, "What were you thinking of, that you did this thing?"

(20:11) Abraham said, "I did it because I thought, There is no fear of God at all in this place, and they will kill me because of my wife.

---

[162] Jeffrey C. Geoghegan, "Additional Evidence for a Deuteronomistic Redaction of the 'Tetrateuch'," *CBQ* 67/3 (2005): 405–21, esp. 410–11 for the six occurrences in Genesis.

(20:12) Besides, she is indeed my sister, the daughter of my father but not the daughter of my mother; and she became my wife.

(20:13) And when God caused me to wander from my father's house, I said to her, 'This is the kindness you must do me: at every place to which we come, say of me, He is my brother.' "

(20:14) Then Abimelech took sheep and oxen, and male and female slaves, and gave them to Abraham, and restored his wife Sarah to him.

(20:15) Abimelech said, "My land is before you; settle where it pleases you."

(20:16) To Sarah he said, "Look, I have given your brother a thousand pieces of silver; it is your exoneration before all who are with you; you are completely vindicated."

(20:17) Then Abraham prayed to God; and God healed Abimelech, and also healed his wife and female slaves so that they bore children.

(20:18) For the LORD had closed fast all the wombs of the house of Abimelech because of Sarah, Abraham's wife.

*A*braham abandons his long held encampment near Hebron at the oaks of Mamre and travels south. The text does not explain why, although we may assume another famine is the reason (12:10). During these sojourns in the south, Abraham meets King Abimelech of Gerar. Abraham once again struggles to relate properly to a foreign king, as he had done with the Pharaoh while he sojourned in Egypt (12:10–20), and with similar results. He acquires more wealth, settles in a location that will eventually become Beer-sheba (21:25–34), and proves himself a prophet with abilities to pray for blessings for his new neighbors. Abimelech shows himself to be an upstanding, honorable character, who will be important in this chapter and the next (and again in Gen 26).

Thus the chapter continues the epic narrative of Abraham and explains how he came to live in the Negeb at Beer-sheba, which becomes an important location elsewhere in the ancestral narratives (22:19; 26:23–25, 33; 28:10; 46:1). God is everywhere called "Elohim" in this chapter except the last verse, and this preference over "Yahweh" here and in the next two chapters has led to speculation that Gen 20–22 as a unit had an early independent tradition.[163]

The opening words of v. 1, "from *there* Abraham journeyed," remind the reader that for a long time Abraham's home encampment has been at the oaks of Mamre near Hebron (13:18; 14:13; 18:1). The specific vocabulary used implies "breaking camp" and moving forward, and reminds us of Abraham's identity as a semi-nomadic tribesman, living in tents, moving about as needed, and reminds us further that he is, after all, an alien in the land of Canaan, looking forward to the fulfillment

---

[163] G. J. Wenham, *Genesis 16–50* (1994), 69, and for the older understanding of Gen 20 as the first connected narrative of E, see E. A. Speiser, *Genesis* (1964), 150–52. For the idea that Gen 20–22 serve as a conclusion to a unified Yahwistic Abraham narrative, see T. D. Alexander, *Abraham in the Negev: A Source-Critical Investigation of Genesis 20:1–22:19* (Carlisle, Cumbria: Paternoster, 1997).

of the promised country of his own.[164] The geographical references in v. 1 indicate that Abraham traversed through the Negeb all the way to the Sinai Peninsula, between Kadesh and Shur.[165] Along the way, he "sojourned in Gerar" using a word play on the verb "sojourn" and the name "Gerar" (v. 1b).[166]

Abraham once again tells a foreign ruler that Sarah is his sister (v. 2, and cf. 12:13). Immediately Abimelech "sent and took" Sarah, raising the question whether she and the ancestral promises themselves may be in jeopardy. This is the second of three accounts of the "wife–sister" theme, otherwise known as the Endangered Matriarch literary topos or type-scene (see commentary at 12:10–20, and cf. 26:1–16). This account has the added detail that Sarah is, in fact, Abraham's half-sister (v. 12, see below). Whatever the source of the literary formula, each of these three accounts has been edited to emphasize God's intervention for deliverance and blessing for the patriarch.

The threat, and along with it the suspense created in the narrative, is resolved almost immediately. NRSV's disjunctive at the beginning of v. 3 goes straightaway to the heart of the matter: "But God came. . . . " God intervenes to protect Sarah and Abraham, and preserves the ancestral promises.

God's presence with Abimelech in a dream (vv. 3–7) is different from the revelatory appearances of God to Israel's ancestors elsewhere in Genesis (12:7; 17:1; 18:1; etc.).[167] Those are occasions when Yahweh reveals himself ("appears") in divine self-disclosure in order to make himself known and to inspire the patriarch at critical, life-altering moments in the narrative. In contrast, God comes to Abimelech in a dream by night to warn him of impending doom and give him an opportunity to avert disaster. Although different in many ways, the coming of God to Abimelech is equally gracious as a theophanic means of preventing judgment.[168]

The vital piece of information missing for Abimelech is that Sarah "is a married woman" (v. 3). God gives Abimelech what Abraham has withheld – the truth. Before we read Abimelech's response, the narrator interjects to remove all doubt of impropriety. The king of Gerar had not yet approached Sarah (v. 4) and later we learn that God prevented Abimelech from even touching her (v. 6). With Isaac's

---

[164] The same verb ("break camp, journey on," *nsʿ*) is used in 12:9; 33:17; 35:5, 16, 21; 46:1, and compare Heb 11:8–10. Whether or not the verb was originally "pull out (tent pegs)" is uncertain; Menahem Zvi Kaddari and Helmer Ringgren, "*nāsāʿ*" *TDOT* 9:461–64, esp. 461, and Cornelis Van Dam, "*nsʿ*," *NIDOTTE* 3:117–19.

[165] A. F. Rainey and R. S. Notley, *The Sacred Bridge: Carta's Atlas of the Biblical World* (2006), 114.

[166] NRSV's "while residing in Gerar as an alien" is *wayyāgor bigrār*, which is homonymous word play; Jack M. Sasson, "Wordplay in the OT," *IDBSup* 968–70. On the verse division of v. 1, followed by NRSV, see E. A. Speiser, Genesis (1964), 148. The modern identification of Gerar appears now to have been settled; Eliezer D. Oren, "Gerar," *ABD* 2:989–91; Eliezer D. Oren, "Haror, Tel," *OEANE* 2:474–76.

[167] See Closer Look "Divine Revelation in the Hebrew Scriptures" at p. 135 and Closer Look "Dreams in the Hebrew Scriptures" at p. 322.

[168] Bill T. Arnold, "*bwʾ*," *NIDOTTE* 1:615–18.

birth narrative around the corner (Gen 21), it seemed imperative to make clear that Abraham was indeed Isaac's father.

Abimelech's response to the news is admirable (vv. 4b–5). He raises three issues: the justice of God, the guilt of Abraham and Sarah, and his own innocence. His concern for the justice of God ("will you destroy an innocent people?") is ironically similar to Abraham's intercession on behalf of Sodom (18:23). Indeed, Abimelech's objection focuses on "an innocent people," which implies he has the wicked of Sodom and Gomorrah in mind. Will God destroy the people of Gerar as he did the people of Sodom and Gomorrah?[169] Is Gerar next? Abimelech's declaration of innocence and appeal for mercy set him in contrast with the people of Sodom and Gomorrah. His relationship with Abraham and Sarah has put him at risk, but his response to God's dream shows him to be upright and honorable. Abimelech's behavior is marked by a good heart and innocent hands. Moreover, the narrator has already implied that Abraham is the guilty party, not Abimelech (v. 2a).

God confirms Abimelech's innocence (v. 6). In fact, God himself has graciously prevented a worse situation by not allowing Abimelech to touch Sarah. God next instructs Abimelech what to do in order to rectify the situation. If the king chooses to return Sarah, he may gain the favor of Abraham, who is a "prophet" (*nābî'*, v. 7). This is the first occurrence of "prophet" in the biblical canon. In the ancient Near East generally, prophecy was a branch of divination, or consultation of the divine, in which the prophet transmitted divine messages as a mouthpiece for the deity.[170] While Old Testament prophets also served as mouthpieces for Yahweh, their function was broader as illustrated by Abraham's role here: "he will pray for you and you shall live." The intercessory role of Abraham in 18:22–33 is in view here, for he prayed for the righteous of Sodom and therefore Lot survived. If Abimelech does what is right and returns Sarah, Gerar will escape the fate of Sodom and Gomorrah. But moreover, he will discover the fount of blessing for himself and his people.

The rest of the chapter moves quickly from confrontation (vv. 8–13) to resolution (vv. 14–18). Abimelech "rose early in the morning," which connotes his resolve to take action without delay (19:27; 21:14; 22:3; etc.).[171] In two passionate speeches, the king confronts Abraham with the "great guilt" that he has brought upon Gerar (vv. 9–10). Abimelech asks three accusatory questions, the last of which ("What were you thinking of . . . ?") is literally "What did you see, that you should do this thing?" Perhaps the use of "see" relates to Abimelech's understanding of what it means for Abraham to be a prophet. What could Abraham have possibly observed that could

---

[169] The use of *gam*, "also, even" in his question may be for "addition" rather than "assevera-
tive" as in most translations, so that the meaning is: Will you also kill an innocent people
(Gerar) as you did the wicked (Sodom and Gomorrah)? B. T. Arnold and J. H. Choi, *A
Guide to Biblical Hebrew Syntax* (2003), 132–33.

[170] Martti Nissinen, *Prophets and Prophecy in the Ancient Near East* (SBLWAW 12; Atlanta,
Ga.: Society of Biblical Literature, 2003), 1–8.

[171] Rüdiger Bartelmus, "*škm*," *TDOT* 14:681–88, esp. 687–88.

lead him to take such action? The first two questions in Abimelech's accusations were rhetorical, leaving Abraham with no reply, while this one was real and demands an answer.[172]

Abraham's explanation is a montage of excuses. First, he assumed Abimelech and the people of Gerar were irreverent, violent, and lustful (v. 12). Those assumptions, he must now admit, were unfair and inaccurate, especially so in light of the fact that God has revealed the truth about Sarah to King Abimelech in a dream and the good king has chosen to act appropriately.

Second, Abraham confesses the truth about his kinship with Sarah, who is both wife and half-sister (v. 13). His lie is a half-truth. He has touted Sarah's sibling status while concealing her matrimonial status. In the ancestral period, marriages were arranged by parents and preferably between cousins (see Closer Look "Endogamy in Ancient Israel" at p. 219). Abraham's marriage to his half-sister was exceptional in that it was closer in kinship than most. Such marriages probably ensured provision and protection for female children of second marriages who needed a social safety-net.[173] Later texts in the Bible clearly condemn marriage to one's half-sister (Lev 18:6–11; 20:17; Deut 27:22; Ezek 22:11). When social norms in the ancestral traditions are so at odds with later biblical law, it may suggest the great antiquity of the traditions behind the current book of Genesis.[174]

Third, Abraham explains that this is a previously arranged stratagem that he and Sarah have used since the time they left his "father's house" (v. 13). The "father's house" (*bêt'āb*) was the center of religious, social, and economic life in ancient Israel (see commentary at 12:1). When Abraham and Sarah left behind the security of this familial sanctuary, they committed to depending upon God alone with no assurances that they would be capable of establishing a new "house" of their own because of her barrenness. Yet they relied on this ruse to protect themselves against the presumed evil of whatever hosts they encountered, and it fell to the unfortunate Gerarites to be their next victims.[175] Whereas God affirmed Abimelech's innocence in vv. 6–7, there is only silence after Abraham's defense. The explanation for his actions is no vindication; he can explain but he cannot justify his actions. Abimelech is innocent, but Abraham is not.[176]

Without further word, Abimelech restores Sarah and adds to Abraham's considerable wealth (cf. 12:16; 13:2). Furthermore, he graciously offers Abraham the right to dwell wherever he chooses in his land, perhaps recalling that Abraham is a prophet who could bring benefits to Gerar (v. 15). Indeed, after the king duly

---

172 C. Westermann, *Genesis 12–36* (1985), 325.

173 Although it is peculiar we were not given this datum at 11:27–29, where the genealogical connections are explained. As Nahor married his niece Milcah, whose father, Haran, had died (11:29), we now learn that Abram had married Sarai, whose father, Terah, had died.

174 G. J. Wenham, *Genesis 16–50* (1994), 73.

175 H. C. Brichto, *The Names of God* (1998), 266.

176 C. Westermann, *Genesis 12–36* (1985), 327.

exonerates Sarah as well (v. 16), Abraham prays and Gerar finds healing (vv. 17–18). The barrenness of all the wombs of the kingdom was attributable to Sarah, which is ironic in light of her own sterility. She too is barren (11:30) and will remain so until the next verses (21:1–2).

The closing verses of the chapter have been called "an illuminating epilogue" because they answer several questions left unanswered in earlier portions of the narrative.[177] Abimelech's complaint that Abraham has brought "great guilt" (or "great affliction," v. 9) upon Gerar may now be understood as a threat of extinction due to widespread barrenness, which explains the king's fear that the entire nation ("an innocent people") was at risk (v. 4). It also explains why the king included all his servants in the news about Abraham's deception, and the depth of their great fear (v. 8). Abraham's prayer brought healing and restoration to a suffering nation, just as these closing verses fill in the missing gaps of the narrative.

GENESIS 21:1–34 ISAAC, ISHMAEL, AND THE COVENANT AT BEER-SHEBA

(21:1) The LORD dealt with Sarah as he had said, and the LORD did for Sarah as he had promised.

(21:2) Sarah conceived and bore Abraham a son in his old age, at the time of which God had spoken to him.

(21:3) Abraham gave the name Isaac to his son whom Sarah bore him.

(21:4) And Abraham circumcised his son Isaac when he was eight days old, as God had commanded him.

(21:5) Abraham was a hundred years old when his son Isaac was born to him.

(21:6) Now Sarah said, "God has brought laughter for me; everyone who hears will laugh with me."

(21:7) And she said, "Who would ever have said to Abraham that Sarah would nurse children? Yet I have borne him a son in his old age."

(21:8) The child grew, and was weaned; and Abraham made a great feast on the day that Isaac was weaned.

(21:9) But Sarah saw the son of Hagar the Egyptian, whom she had borne to Abraham, playing with her son Isaac.[f]

(21:10) So she said to Abraham, "Cast out this slave woman with her son; for the son of this slave woman shall not inherit along with my son Isaac."

(21:11) The matter was very distressing to Abraham on account of his son.

(21:12) But God said to Abraham, "Do not be distressed because of the boy and because of your slave woman; whatever Sarah says to you, do as she tells you, for it is through Isaac that offspring shall be named for you.

[177] H. C. Brichto, *The Names of God* (1998), 263–64.

f Gk Vg: Heb lacks "with her son Isaac."

(21:13) As for the son of the slave woman, I will make a nation of him also, because he is your offspring."

(21:14) So Abraham rose early in the morning, and took bread and a skin of water, and gave it to Hagar, putting it on her shoulder, along with the child, and sent her away. And she departed, and wandered about in the wilderness of Beer-sheba.

(21:15) When the water in the skin was gone, she cast the child under one of the bushes.

(21:16) Then she went and sat down opposite him a good way off, about the distance of a bowshot; for she said, "Do not let me look on the death of the child." And as she sat opposite him, she lifted up her voice and wept.

(21:17) And God heard the voice of the boy; and the angel of God called to Hagar from heaven, and said to her, "What troubles you, Hagar? Do not be afraid; for God has heard the voice of the boy where he is.

(21:18) Come, lift up the boy and hold him fast with your hand, for I will make a great nation of him."

(21:19) Then God opened her eyes and she saw a well of water. She went, and filled the skin with water, and gave the boy a drink.

(21:20) God was with the boy, and he grew up; he lived in the wilderness, and became an expert with the bow.

(21:21) He lived in the wilderness of Paran; and his mother got a wife for him from the land of Egypt.

(21:22) At that time Abimelech, with Phicol the commander of his army, said to Abraham, "God is with you in all that you do;

(21:23) now therefore swear to me here by God that you will not deal falsely with me or with my offspring or with my posterity, but as I have dealt loyally with you, you will deal with me and with the land where you have resided as an alien."

(21:24) And Abraham said, "I swear it."

(21:25) When Abraham complained to Abimelech about a well of water that Abimelech's servants had seized,

(21:26) Abimelech said, "I do not know who has done this; you did not tell me, and I have not heard of it until today."

(21:27) So Abraham took sheep and oxen and gave them to Abimelech, and the two men made a covenant.

(21:28) Abraham set apart seven ewe lambs of the flock.

(21:29) And Abimelech said to Abraham, "What is the meaning of these seven ewe lambs that you have set apart?"

(21:30) He said, "These seven ewe lambs you shall accept from my hand, in order that you may be a witness for me that I dug this well."

(21:31) Therefore that place was called Beer-sheba; because there both of them swore an oath.

(21:32) When they had made a covenant at Beer-sheba, Abimelech, with Phicol the commander of his army, left and returned to the land of the Philistines.
(21:33) Abraham planted a tamarisk tree in Beer-sheba, and called there on the name of the LORD, the Everlasting God.
(21:34) And Abraham resided as an alien many days in the land of the Philistines.

*A*t long last, the promised son is born. The arrival of Isaac in the biblical storyline is a momentous occasion. The portion of the text immediately following the birth announcement is needed to explain Ishmael's role now that Isaac has entered the picture. The narrative has several affinities with Gen 16 when Hagar ran away from the ancestral family to the desert, where the angel of Yahweh assured her of Ishmael's bright future. The chapter also shows the denouement of God's declaration that he would establish the ancestral covenant with Isaac while Ishmael would be richly blessed (17:19–21). So the theme of the presumed heir continues. Ishmael is placed aside as Lot and Eliezer before him, and now Isaac is taken up as the line of promise. The chapter concludes by returning to Abraham's relationship with Abimelech in the Negeb, which ties this chapter together with Gen 20.

Although impossible to capture in translation, the Hebrew word order at the beginning of v. 1 marks the beginning of a new scene and takes up again a previous subject that has been suspended momentarily.[178] That previous subject is God's promise of a son for Sarah (17:16–21; 18:9–15). Several intervening episodes have created distance between those promises and the birth of Isaac: Abraham's intercession (18:22–33), the destruction of Sodom and Gomorrah (19:1–29), Lot and his daughters (19:30–38), and Abraham's sojourn in Gerar (20:1–18). Thus the word order of the opening clause ("The LORD dealt with Sarah . . . ") reactivates the topic, closing the distance between the promise and its fulfillment, in order to emphasize the faithfulness of Yahweh to Sarah. That faithfulness is further emphasized by recurrence to ensure the reader understands Yahweh's gracious actions: "as he had said . . . as he had promised."

And God was on time. Isaac is born late in his parents' lives, so much so that he is a son of Abraham's "old age," and yet he is nevertheless born at precisely the appointed time (*môʿēd*), of which God had spoken (v. 2, and cf. 17:21; 18:14). As God was faithful to Sarah and Abraham, so Abraham remembers the covenant. He gives the boy a name long anticipated in the narrative, and by now quite unavoidable, "He laughs," and fulfills the covenant obligation on the eighth day (vv. 3–4, cf. 17:10–14, 19; 18:12–15).

---

[178] The topic of a child for Sarah is not "discourse active" and therefore "fronting" reactivates the topic; Christo H. J. van der Merwe, Jackie A. Naudé, and Jan H. Kroeze, *A Biblical Hebrew Reference Grammar* (Biblical Languages, Hebrew 3; Sheffield: Sheffield Academic Press, 1999), 346–48.

The NRSV of v. 3 smoothes over a rather awkward syntax, which has an extra relative clause repeating the verbal root *yālad*, "give birth" in two voices, one passive, the other active; literally "Abraham called the name of his son who *was born* to him, whom Sarah *bore* for him, Isaac." The awkward grammar is understandable in light of this long-awaited birth anticipated since the beginning of the Abraham narrative, and especially in a book structured wholly by the same verbal root in the form of the *tôlĕdôt*–structuring clauses (Hiphil noun pattern of the same root, see Introduction). The happy occasion is commemorated by Abraham's age again (v. 5, cf. 12:4; 16:16; 17:1, 24), using the verbal root *yālad* once more: "when his son Isaac *was born* to him."[179]

The word plays on Isaac's name continue in v. 6. The name "Isaac" is the source of other word play associations in this narrative (17:17–19; 18:12–15), none of them strictly etymological.[180] The connotations of Sarah's statement are open for interpretation because the little prepositions used with "laugh" in both Hebrew and English change the nuance significantly. Is this laughter "for/with" Sarah or "at" her? The NRSV reflects the majority opinion that Sarah is rejoicing over motherhood so late in life rather than complaining that she has become the object of mockery and joking. The Hebrew uses the same preposition (*lî*) twice in v. 6 in "laughter *for* me" and "laugh *with* me," but this preposition could also mean laugh *at* or *about* me.[181] Some interpreters, therefore, take this as derisive laughter: "God has made a joke of me; whoever hears will laugh at me."[182] Yet Sarah expresses sheer astonishment over what has happened (v. 7) and the general tone of this paragraph is rejoicing and celebration at the birth of Isaac.

The next paragraphs explain how Ishmael comes to have a life separate from Isaac and the ancestral family (vv. 8–21). With the exception of his list of descendants in 25:12–18, this brings to a close the narration of Ishmael.[183] This process is part of the inexorable movement of Genesis, as it traces Israel's ancestry in a straight line through a process of divergence, in which each generation has only one son continuing the line. Other sons born to Abraham and Isaac are declared the ancestors of various peoples, but each one diverges from the descent line of ancient Israel.[184] Although tragic in the familial and personal conflict surrounding Ishmael's

---

[179] And again in v. 7: "Yet I have born him a son in his old age."

[180] Rüdiger Bartelmus, "*ṣāḥaq/śāḥaq*," *TDOT* 14:58–72, esp. 61–63. Hebrew narrative is rich in such word play associations using personal names.

[181] B. T. Arnold and J. H. Choi, *A Guide to Biblical Hebrew Syntax* (2003), 112; *HALOT* 2:508–9; *DCH* 4:482.

[182] V. P. Hamilton, *The Book of Genesis, Chapters 18–50* (1995), 72; and cf. B. Vawter, *On Genesis: A New Reading* (1977), 246.

[183] There remain only passing references, at the burial of Abraham (25:9) and as the father-in-law of Esau (28:9, and cf. 36:3).

[184] The process is suspended finally with the segmentation of Jacob's line; cf. K. R. Andriolo, "A Structural Analysis of Genealogy and World View in the Old Testament," esp. 1657–60.

abandonment, the text is not disparaging of him or his descendants, rather there is only the promise of a bright future as a descendant of Abraham (vv. 13, 18).

The natural joy of a festive occasion (v. 8) turns to conflict when Sarah grows protective and defensive, as she has done once before (v. 9, cf. 16:5–6). The meaning of "playing with her son Isaac" is ambiguous, and we are probably best served by making no attempt to fill the narrative gaps.[185] It may be enough to assume that Sarah saw proleptically into the future and took drastic action to protect her son's inheritance (v. 10).[186] Her proposal displeases Abraham but God assures him all will be well (vv. 11–13). We hear again that it is through Isaac that "seed" (*zeraʿ*, NRSV's "offspring") will be named for Abraham, and yet Ishmael will also become a great nation because he too is Abraham's seed. Isaac is the son of the covenant and the promises, and yet Ishmael will also be greatly blessed (16:10–12; 17:19–21, and cf. 25:12–18).

Abraham sends Hagar and Ishmael off the next morning to the desert of Beer-sheba with provisions of food and water (v. 14). NRSV's "along with the child" leaves ambiguous a difficulty related to Ishmael's age at this time. In a sequential reading of the extended narrative, he is certainly a teenager, perhaps around fourteen years old (17:25; and compare 16:16 with 21:5), making it unlikely Abraham placed him on Hagar's shoulders along with the provisions. On the other hand, this particular text at times gives the impression Ishmael is an infant,[187] in which case "along with the child" might denote placing the baby on Hagar's shoulders. Attributing this text to a separate source than that of Gen 17 may be a partial solution, but ultimately the text stands now to emphasize the compassionate concern Abraham has for Ishmael. Translating "and to the child" rather than "along with the child" conveys Abraham's reluctance to let Ishmael go (and see v. 11), and leaves open the possibility he placed the provisions on her back so her hands were free to take Ishmael by the hand (cf. 18).[188]

When the water failed, Hagar lapsed into despair and longed only to avoid seeing her son suffer (vv. 15–16). As the angel of Yahweh found Hagar once before in the desert of Shur (16:7–10), so the "angel of God" hears the boy crying in the desert of Beer-sheba, and comes with comfort and assurances that Ishmael will become a great nation (vv. 17–18). Unlike the previous occasion when Yahweh instructed Hagar to return to her role as a servant in the ancestral household, here God simply

---

[185] The NRSV is right to restore the Greek variant "with her son Isaac," which probably dropped from the text by homoioteleuton. On the various options for "playing," see V. P. Hamilton, *The Book of Genesis, Chapters 18–50* (1995), 78–79.

[186] Hermann Gunkel, *Genesis: Translated and Interpreted,* trans. Mark E. Biddle (Macon, Ga.: Mercer University Press, 1997), 226.

[187] He is either the "boy" (*naʿar,* vv. 12, 17 [twice], 18, 19, 20) or the "child" (*yeled,* vv. 14, 15, 16), and he languishes helplessly under the bush (v. 15). The "son of Hagar" is nowhere called by name in this text.

[188] G. J. Wenham, *Genesis 16–50* (1994), 78 and 84.

provides for their needs in the desert (v. 19), which provision confirms his promise to make Ishmael a great nation.

The narrator's conclusion to the episode (vv. 20–21) relates the final and definitive separation of Ishmael from Isaac and the rest of the ancestral family, both geographically and socially. Ishmael's dwelling in the "wilderness of Paran" locates him further south among the expanses of the Sinai Peninsula, far away from Abraham, Sarah, and Isaac.[189] His marriage to an Egyptian, although not condemned in any way, nevertheless distinguishes him further from the ancestral family through exogamous marriage, much the more so once Isaac marries endogamously (Gen 24, and see Closer Look "Endogamy in Ancient Israel" at p. 219). Moreover, God was "with" Ishmael, which often connotes God's protection and provision for well-being and prosperity (v. 20, cf. v. 22; 39:23, etc.).

Having settled Hagar and Ishmael in the wilderness of Paran, the chapter concludes with an explanation of how Abraham came to be associated with Beer-sheba (vv. 22–34). His relationship with Abimelech, king of Gerar, had been the focus of Gen 20. Now Abraham has grown so strong that Abimelech fears for the future of his kingdom. As God was "with" Ishmael so that he grew up to be prosperous (v. 20), so now Abimelech acknowledges that God is "with" Abraham. The presence of Abimelech's army general, Phicol, is ominous, perhaps threatening. Abimelech requests that Abraham swear an oath of fealty and make a covenant, in order to ensure the safety of Abimelech's posterity (vv. 22–24).

Abraham agrees to the oath (v. 24), but before entering a formal covenant, he needs to clear the air. Water rights were a perennial problem in the Negeb (cf. 13:5–7). Abraham complains that Abimelech's men had taken a well his men had dug (v. 30), and were apparently restricting access to it. The king denies prior knowledge of the problem, implying he will act to rectify the dispute (v. 26). Having satisfied that question, Abraham initiates the covenant with gifts of sheep and oxen, perhaps returning a profit on Abimelech's initial investment (cf. 20:14). Since Abraham is the only one giving gifts, he may be somewhat weaker of the two parties, and is ensuring the good will of the king of Gerar and perhaps even purchasing the rights to live at Beer-sheba. (On the nature of "covenant," *bĕrît*, see commentary at 6:18, and Closer Look "Covenants in the Hebrew Scriptures" at p. 101)

The setting apart of the seven ewe lambs as an additional gift was to enlist Abimelech as a witness that Abraham dug the well (vv. 29–30). It also introduces the homonymous sounds of "seven" (*šebaʿ*) and "swear" (*šābaʿ*), which prepares for the etiological conclusion of v. 31: "Therefore that place was called Beer-sheba." As a kind of double word play, the place name is associated both with the swearing of an oath and the number seven. Abraham and Abimelech swear a covenant *oath* to each

---

[189] A. F. Rainey and R. S. Notley, *The Sacred Bridge: Carta's Atlas of the Biblical World* (2006), 120; Jeffries M. Hamilton, "Paran," *ABD* 5:162.

other and Abraham is giving *seven* ewe lambs to seal the deal, so the name is doubly appropriate, as both "well of oath" and "well of seven."[190] Some interpreters assume "seven" and "swear" are etymologically related, so that oath-taking in the ancient world is somehow "to seven oneself" in an act of affirmation of the oath.[191] But this goes beyond our evidence.[192] It is just as likely the words came to be associated secondarily in word play, as in our text and in the naming of Beer-sheba, because of their similarity in sound.

After the covenant, Abimelech and Phicol return "to the land of the Philistines" (v. 32). The reference to Gerar as the land of the Philistines is not likely a simple anachronism, because there are too many dramatic differences between the people of Gerar and the later Philistines.[193] More likely, the narrator is making a proleptical reference to the general region that would one day become the land of the Philistines; he does not assume the people of Gerar are the same as the much later Philistines proper.[194]

As at other important occasions, especially when Abraham has settled after a journey or conflict, he offers acts of worship and praise (v. 33). We should not look for meaning in the use of a tamarisk tree rather than oak (12:6–8; 13:18; 14:13; 18:1), because the tamarisk was likely more robust in the southern regions.[195] Trees had religious significance in the ancient Near East as physical symbols of divine presence and holy sites.[196] We have seen that invoking the name of Yahweh is to establish an institution of public worship (see commentary at 4:26), and it seems likely that Abraham is initiating a new Yahweh cult at Beer-sheba (cf. 12:8; 13:4; 26:25). He also

---

[190] For a summary of the long and complicated debate among scholars about two layers of this text, partly to explain the two meanings for "Beer-sheba," see C. Westermann, *Genesis 12–36* (1985), 346–49. For an interesting solution to take the second part of v. 31b as a temporal clause, thus eliminating at least some of the need for two strata in the text ("when there the two of them swore to each other"), see V. P. Hamilton, *The Book of Genesis, Chapters 18–50* (1995), 92–93.

[191] E.g., A. F. Rainey and R. S. Notley, *The Sacred Bridge: Carta's Atlas of the Biblical World* (2006), 114.

[192] For etymological precision, see Ingo Kottsieper, "šābaʿ," *TDOT* 14:311–36, esp. 312–13.

[193] For excellent summary, see N. M. Sarna, *Genesis* (1989), 390. Nor is it necessary to insist the presence of Philistines in Gerar is indication of a late, Iron II date of composition; Israel Finkelstein, "The Philistines in the Bible: A Late-Monarchic Perspective," *JSOT* 27/2 (2002): 131–67, esp. 152–54.

[194] Another approach is to assume Abimelech and the Gerarites may have been Kaphtorians or other groups from, or otherwise linked with, the Aegean region, and were therefore precursors to the later "Philistines," and/or that the text simply uses "land of the Philistines" to update a term obsolete by the time of the author; Kenneth A. Kitchen, *On the Reliability of the Old Testament* (Grand Rapids, Mich.: Eerdmans, 2003), 339–341.

[195] Hebrew *ʾēšel* is likely the Athel tamarisk, or Tamarix aphylla, which is drought resistant and well suited to arid and semi-arid regions; F. N. Hepper, *Baker Encyclopedia of Bible Plants* (1992), 64. On the possibility that this should be emended according to the Septuagint and Vulgate readings to refer to plotting a strip of land at Beer-sheba rather than planting a tree, see V. P. Hamilton, *The Book of Genesis, Chapters 18–50* (1995), 93–94.

[196] O. Keel, *Goddesses and Trees, New Moon and Yahweh* (1998), 20–48.

calls Yahweh "the Everlasting God" (*'ēl 'ôlām*), a name as old as Canaanite worship in the fifteenth century BCE, and meaning "the eternal (or ancient) god."[197] These acts of worship may reflect that finally, after all these years, Abraham has received the promised son, Isaac, and he owns a single well in the southernmost part of the promised land. It appears the covenant promises are coming to reality, and yet Abraham's faith is about to be tested as never before.

GENESIS 22:1–24 THE TESTING OF ABRAHAM

(22:1) After these things God tested Abraham. He said to him, "Abraham!" And he said, "Here I am."

(22:2) He said, "Take your son, your only son Isaac, whom you love, and go to the land of Moriah, and offer him there as a burnt offering on one of the mountains that I shall show you."

(22:3) So Abraham rose early in the morning, saddled his donkey, and took two of his young men with him, and his son Isaac; he cut the wood for the burnt offering, and set out and went to the place in the distance that God had shown him.

(22:4) On the third day Abraham looked up and saw the place far away.

(22:5) Then Abraham said to his young men, "Stay here with the donkey; the boy and I will go over there; we will worship, and then we will come back to you."

(22:6) Abraham took the wood of the burnt offering and laid it on his son Isaac, and he himself carried the fire and the knife. So the two of them walked on together.

(22:7) Isaac said to his father Abraham, "Father!" And he said, "Here I am, my son." He said, "The fire and the wood are here, but where is the lamb for a burnt offering?"

(22:8) Abraham said, "God himself will provide the lamb for a burnt offering, my son." So the two of them walked on together.

(22:9) When they came to the place that God had shown him, Abraham built an altar there and laid the wood in order. He bound his son Isaac, and laid him on the altar, on top of the wood.

(22:10) Then Abraham reached out his hand and took the knife to kill his son.

(22:11) But the angel of the LORD called to him from heaven, and said, "Abraham, Abraham!" And he said, "Here I am."

(22:12) He said, "Do not lay your hand on the boy or do anything to him; for now I know that you fear God, since you have not withheld your son, your only son, from me."

---

[197] Albert de Pury, "El-Olam," *DDD*[2] 290–91; F. M. Cross, *Canaanite Myth and Hebrew Epic* (1973), 46–50.

(22:13) And Abraham looked up and saw a ram, caught in a thicket by its horns. Abraham went and took the ram and offered it up as a burnt offering instead of his son.

(22:14) So Abraham called that place "The LORD will provide";[g] as it is said to this day, "On the mount of the LORD it shall be provided."[h]

(22:15) The angel of the LORD called to Abraham a second time from heaven,

(22:16) and said, "By myself I have sworn, says the LORD: Because you have done this, and have not withheld your son, your only son,

(22:17) I will indeed bless you, and I will make your offspring as numerous as the stars of heaven and as the sand that is on the seashore. And your offspring shall possess the gate of their enemies,

(22:18) and by your offspring shall all the nations of the earth gain blessing for themselves, because you have obeyed my voice."

(22:19) So Abraham returned to his young men, and they arose and went together to Beer-sheba; and Abraham lived at Beer-sheba.

(22:20) Now after these things it was told Abraham, "Milcah also has borne children, to your brother Nahor:

(22:21) Uz the firstborn, Buz his brother, Kemuel the father of Aram,

(22:22) Chesed, Hazo, Pildash, Jidlaph, and Bethuel."

(22:23) Bethuel became the father of Rebekah. These eight Milcah bore to Nahor, Abraham's brother.

(22:24) Moreover, his concubine, whose name was Reumah, bore Tebah, Gaham, Tahash, and Maacah.

*T*his text has been the object of much study for centuries, and rightly so.[198] Here the narrator ties together several important strands that would have remained disconnected otherwise. First, he has explained the significance of an axiomatic saying that was presumably common in his day, "On Yahweh's mount, He is revealed" (see commentary below at v. 14). We may take this as an adage that was repeated often in later Israel without literary context. Here the narrator has used this ancestral ordeal to give the saying a framework with theological gravitas. Second, the narrator has explained, by means of this episode, why Israelites do not practice child sacrifice, as other people did in the ancient world. Third, the text continues the characterization of Abraham as the father of faith, exemplary in every way. Indeed, this text is associated with previous ones in several ways, and serves in the extended narrative as the culminating episode of Abraham's obedience and

---

g Or "will see;" Heb traditionally transliterated *Jehovah Jireh.*

h Or "he shall be seen."

198 On Jewish and Christian interpretations of Gen 22, see Kenneth A. Mathews, *Genesis 11:27–50:26* (NAC 1B; Nashville: Broadman & Holman Publishers, 2005), 300–6. Gen 20–22 have been intensively studied from the perspective of the E document. But on the impossibility of tracing the early history of Gen 22, through either Elohistic (E) or Yahwistic (J) traditions, see D. M. Carr, *Reading the Fractures of Genesis* (1996), 196–202.

faithfulness. Having tied all these strands together, the result is a classic for the ages, as rich in theological reflection as it is in rhetorical power.

This text is also shocking. If we could imagine reading through the Abraham narrative for the first time, as though we were somehow unaware of this famous text, the opening verses of Gen 22 would be jarring. The divine imperative to sacrifice Isaac in v. 2 creates a narrative reversal, risking everything that the extended narrative has accomplished thus far. The ancestral promises, so central to the narrative as a whole, are absorbed in the life of this one child. Without Isaac, the promises of land and progeny are meaningless. God has slowly shown Abraham that no other child would do, that in fact, a biological child of his old age, born to his nonagenarian wife, would be the child of promise. Surely Isaac's presence in the ancestral family was an unrepeatable miracle of God's promises. Moreover, in the preceding chapter, everything seemed to be working out beautifully. Isaac had been born to Sarah, Ishmael had been dutifully blessed but separated from the ancestral family, and Abraham had come into possession of a well in the southern reaches of the promised land. Suddenly, this call to sacrifice Isaac creates a literary dissonance that is difficult to process. With regard to the personal trauma such a divine command caused for the patriarch, Ephraim A. Speiser said it best.

> Isaac was to Abraham more than a child of his old age, so fervently hoped for yet so long denied. Isaac was also, and more particularly, the only link with the far-off goal to which Abraham's life was dedicated (see 21:12). To sacrifice Isaac, as God demanded, was to forego at the same time the long-range objective itself.[199]

More shocking still is the philosophical and theological antinomy created by v. 2.[200] The reader of the book of Genesis has so far discovered much about Yahweh, the God of national Israel. He is the all-powerful creator of the universe, the sustainer of human life after the loss of the Garden of Paradise. God graciously preserved a faithful line of devotees through Seth, kept Noah and his family alive while the rest of the world was evil, and prevented the spread of human rebellion at the Tower of Babel. Yahweh has also called and nurtured Abraham by a series of self-revelations, covenant promises, and miraculous interventions. On the other hand, this is the same deity who expelled Adam and Eve from the garden, sent a massive flood destroying all but a small family, dispersed humanity creating confusion through different languages, and destroyed Sodom and Gomorrah in a massive conflagration. The reader has learned much about this God while watching father Abraham relate to him. This Yahweh, God of Heaven, is not to be taken lightly, nor can Abraham afford to presume upon his grace. The Abraham narrative is about a

---

[199] E. A. Speiser, *Genesis* (1964), 164.
[200] Immanuel Kant's skepticism that v. 2 could have been a command from God illustrates the conceptual problems, see summary in C. Westermann, *Genesis 12–36* (1985), 353–54.

journey, learning more about God with each step. Perhaps now Abraham is about to learn something new about God, which the reader would rather avoid.[201]

And yet the reader is privileged at the outset with information Abraham does not have. The opening verse is unique in the Abraham narrative. It uses specific Hebrew word order, not translatable into English, to introduce a new topic and set the theme for vv. 1–19 as a whole.[202] And so we learn from the beginning that Gen 22 is about a test (v. 1). Several titles are possible for this text, "the (near) sacrifice of Isaac," "the binding of Isaac," and so forth, but "Abraham's Test" is the theme based on this lead verse. The idea is not to torture Abraham, but to demonstrate a truth that can be observed, in contrast to a truth that is only asserted.[203] In other words, the assertion "Abraham fears God" may be accepted as true on no other basis than the assertion itself. But having passed this test, Abraham has demonstrated tangibly his fear of God, and God accepts the truth of that assertion experientially ("now I know," v. 12).[204] The heading in v. 1a that God is testing Abraham removes for the reader the question of whether Isaac might be sacrificed and puts in its place another question, that of whether Abraham will pass the test.[205]

"After these things" marks an indefinite length of time between this episode and the previous ones, and introduces a new episode (cf. v. 20; and 15:1; 39:7; 40:1). Abraham's response to God's call, "Here I am," denotes focused attention, and when spoken to one's superior (as here), is more like "At your service, sir."[206] The

---

[201] From the perspective of this narrator, child sacrifice has long since been abolished and replaced with animal sacrifice. Gen 22 partially seeks to explain why Israelites do not practice child sacrifice, although the text as it now stands is no simple etiological polemic against the practice. Since ancestral religion bears many features in common with Canaanite religious practices (see Closer Look on "Ancestral Religion" at p. 142), an earlier form of Gen 22 may have represented a rejection of this feature assumed to be widespread among the Canaanites and others. The narrator assumes Abraham would have been aware of the deplorable cult ritual for some deities, and this is simply a new aspect of his understanding of Yahweh. The substitution of an animal in place of the first-born son is therefore also exemplary for future Israelites (Exod 22:28–29[Eng. 29–30]; 34:20; Deut 15:19). The Bible has few specific examples of human sacrifice (Judg 11:30–40; 2 Kgs 3:27), but to these may be added references to making a child "pass through the fire" (2 Kgs 23:10; Jer 7:31–32); Hans-Peter Müller, "*mōlek*," *TDOT* 8:375–388; idem, "Malik," *DDD*² 538–42; George C. Heider, "Molech," *DDD*² 581–85.

[202] Barry L. Bandstra, "Word Order and Emphasis in Biblical Hebrew Narrative: Syntactic Observations on Genesis 22 from a Discourse Perspective," in *Linguistics and Biblical Hebrew*, ed. Walter R. Bodine (Winona Lake, Ind.: Eisenbrauns, 1992), 109–23, esp. 117 and 120; and cf. C. Westermann, *Genesis 12–36* (1985), 354.

[203] Franz-Josef Helfmeyer, "*nissâ*," *TDOT* 9:443–455, esp. 445 and 449–50.

[204] Such speech about God is more than anthropomorphic (describing God in human forms), but is anthropopathic (ascribing human thoughts, emotions, or inner-life to God).

[205] G. J. Wenham, *Genesis 16–50* (1994), 103.

[206] H. C. Brichto, *The Names of God* (1998), 282; Speiser's translation "Ready," is poignant; E. A. Speiser, *Genesis* (1964), 161–62. Wenham observes that it occurs three times in this text, and each time signals a tense new development; G. J. Wenham, *Genesis 16–50* (1994), 104.

chapter's introduction is already unique, but this call formula as a prelude to divine speech is striking (cf. 12:1; 13:14; 15:1, 7; 17:1, etc.). God formally calls upon Abraham (the reader knows for purposes of a test), and Abraham declares his readiness. Something momentous is about to happen. The reader can only read further to learn if Abraham is up to the test, if he really is at God's disposal. Then comes the awful command (v. 2).

The divine speech consists of three imperatives: "take ... go ... offer."[207] Each merits additional comment.

1. *"Take. . . . "* The first imperative has a spelling that may denote politeness ("take, please"), which is rare when God addresses humans.[208] Nothing disturbing has yet been requested, but clearly something difficult is in store for Abraham. Then, in a grammatical surprise, the imperative has three direct objects, each marked separately in Hebrew, and yet each referring to the same person, Isaac.[209] The three objects, which are really only one, move from the general to the specific: "take, please (a) your son, (b) your only son, whom you love, (c) Isaac." The NRSV and most English translations relocate Isaac's name before the relative clause for stylistic purposes, which also however obscures the telescoping and particularizing effect. With astonishing and unmistakable clarity, God makes it impossible to misunderstand or redirect the imperative.[210]

The term "only son" (*yāḥîd*) conveys the idea of sole descent, or only begotten child. Some deny its numerical aspect, preferring instead "precious one" or "beloved child," which it denotes in Prov 4:3. But its repeated use here (vv. 2, 12, 16) and elsewhere (Ps 25:16; Jer. 6:26; Amos 8:10) supports the idea of sole descent, without brothers or sisters.[211] The loss of the only son explains how this is a test of Abraham's faith. The afterlife for an Israelite depended on leaving behind a son to continue one's life in one's ancestral land. This is not a test of Abraham's readiness to take

---

[207] Literary studies have noted the unity and progressive intensity of "take ... go ... offer" as theme words in verses 1–19; Jean L. Ska, "Gn 22, 1–19: Essai sur les niveaus de lecture," *Bib* 69 (1988): 324–37.

[208] Paul Joüon and Takamitsu Muraoka, *A Grammar of Biblical Hebrew* (SubBi 14; Roma: Editrice Pontificio Istituto Biblico, 1993), 350–51.

[209] The untranslatable definite direct object marker (*'et-*) is rarely used to mark the same object three times, which probably indicates God is aware of the enormity of the request.

[210] Midrashic interpretation imagines a dialogue between God and Abraham illustrating the particularizing impact of the three objects. After "your son," Abraham reminds God that he has two sons, Isaac and Ishmael, to which God replies "your only son." The patriarch answers that Ishmael is the only son of Hagar, and Isaac the only son of Sarah. When God clarifies "whom you love," Abraham says that he loves them both. Finally and solemnly, God says "Isaac." Jacob Neusner, *Genesis Rabbah, the Judaic Commentary to the Book of Genesis: A New American Translation* (BJS 104–106; Atlanta, Ga.: Scholars Press, 1985), 2:271–72, ¶55:7.

[211] Heinz-Josef Fabry, "*yāḥad*," *TDOT* 6:40–48, esp. 46; contra V. P. Hamilton, *The Book of Genesis, Chapters 18–50* (1995), 97. The Septuagint's consistent use of "beloved" (*agapētos*) for this word in vv. 2, 12, 16 probably means the translator misread the word as *yādîd*, "beloved," or had a consistently different text.

Isaac's life only, but of his readiness to sacrifice his own life as well. Isaac's future is Abraham's immortality.[212]

2. *"Go...."* The specific spelling of this second imperative would have had a familiar ring in Abraham's ears. It occurs only once elsewhere in the Bible spelled in precisely this fashion, that of God's initial call to *"go from your country and your kindred and your father's house..."* (12:1).[213] This close lexical link between 12:1 and 22:2 draws attention to a more general literary association between these passages that is deliberate. As the call of Abram in Gen 12 begins his journey of faith, so this passage concludes it, being the last divine speech to the great patriarch. These chapters, Gen 12 and 22, serve as bookends for the Abraham narrative, throwing into bold relief the motif of divine command followed by radical obedience so important to the narrative as a whole. In both, the patriarch receives a command: there to leave his father's house and forsake his past, here to forsake his future. In both, Abraham responds in radical obedience (12:4 and 22:3), which "encases the biography of Abraham within a framework of unwavering faith."[214] In both, the ultimate destination is withheld from the patriarch; "to the land that I will show you," and "on one of the mountains that I will show you." In both, the commands involve Hebrew triads, building in each case to the most important at the end: "country... kindred... father's house," and "son,... only son,... Isaac." Both culminate in promises of great offspring (12:2–3; 22:17–18).

The "land of Moriah" is not known. The name itself, Moriah, may anticipate a word play on an important verb in the text: God/Yahweh will "provide" (vv. 8, 14). If so, the verb "here in the name of the place to which Abraham must take his son... is the first hint of salvation."[215] The only other Moriah in the Bible connects it with Jerusalem, where Solomon built the temple (1 Chr 3:1). We have no reason to assume this is the same place as Abraham's Moriah.

3. *"Offer...."* If there were any hope of diverting the worst, this last imperative dispels it all. What God wants is Isaac as a burnt offering. The imperative verb itself and its product, "offer... as a burnt offering," are technical terms defined in Lev 1 and elsewhere in the Hebrew Bible. We are not certain whether the 'offering up' (Hiphil of *ʿālâ*) of a sacrifice denotes the lifting of the sacrifice upon the altar or its rising into the air in smoke. We are certain, however, that the burnt offering itself (*ʿōlâ*) was slaughtered, dismembered, and wholly consumed in fire upon an altar.[216]

---

[212] On this text as the martyrdom of Abraham instead of Isaac, see H. C. Brichto, *The Names of God* (1998), 285.

[213] The imperative of an otherwise exceedingly common verb (*hlk*, "go") is attached to a prepositional phrase rightly omitted in NRSV and most other translations. See the commentary at 12:1.

[214] For this quote and more on the parallels between the two, see N. M. Sarna, *Genesis* (1989), 150.

[215] G. J. Wenham, *Genesis 16–50* (1994), 105; James R. Davila, "Moriah," *ABD* 4:905.

[216] Hans Ferdinand Fuhs, "*ʿālâ*," *TDOT* 11:76–95; Diether Kellermann, "*ʿōlâ*," *TDOT* 11:96–113, esp. 99–100.

As we have seen, rising "early in the morning" connotes resolve to take action without delay (v. 3; cf. 19:27; 20:8; 21:14; etc.).[217] Abraham brings along on the journey all that is needed for sacrificial worship: servants to assist, kindling for the immolation, and the victim himself, although at this juncture this last detail is presumably known only to Abraham. His silence is baffling, especially from one who contended so passionately for the lives of ten righteous in Sodom (18:22–33). Why not plead for the boy's life? Here again, the parallels with 12:1–4 are most instructive. "So Abraham rose early . . ." corresponds to "So Abram went . . ." (12:4) and rounds off our understanding of the kind of faith this patriarch represents. When God first called Abram to leave all for a new life, the simply worded response "So Abram went" (12:4) corresponded perfectly and lexically to the divine imperative "Go" (12:1). Similarly, v. 3 narrates the fulfillment of two of the three imperatives in the divine command of v. 2: "Abraham . . . *took* . . . his son Isaac, . . . and *went* . . ." (corresponding to "take," and "go"). There remains only the act of offering the sacrifice to complete the divine requirement. So the text is silent about whatever angst and debate went on in Abraham's mind between verses 2 and 3, and is focused instead on his outrageous trust in the divine Voice. We have come far from Adam's and Eve's rationalizing blame-game (3:1–7), through Abram's initial reckless abandonment into the amorphous, divine Voice, all the way now to the mature Abraham, whose obedience looks almost like insanity, but is meritorious nonetheless.[218]

The designation of the sacrificial victim as "his son Isaac" in v. 3 is one of numerous uses of possessive pronouns on familial words, "father" and "son," in this passage.[219] The universally understood affection between father and son makes the tension palpable, as the two of them walk along together on their way to worship God on yonder mountain. The divine command is confusing and the action excruciating to watch, but we thus far have no reason to think that Isaac is aware of the plan.

Nearing the destination, Abraham instructs his two workmen to stay behind with the provisions, while he and Isaac walk on together (vv. 4–5). The repetition of the phrase "the two of them walked on together" (vv. 6 and 8) creates a drumbeat of inevitability in the narrative. Abraham's words to his servants, "the boy and I will go over there," add similarly to the tone: this is something he and Isaac must do alone. We are left only to wonder at his statement "we will worship, and then we will come back to you." Jewish and Christian interpreters through the ages have attempted various ways of understanding what he meant. The Talmud suggests Abraham's prophetic gifts came to the foreground in this statement, and that he

---

217 Rüdiger Bartelmus, "*škm*," *TDOT* 14:681–88, esp. 687–88.
218 Indeed, his trancelike adherence to this revelatory voice has been interpreted as a metaphorical madness; H. C. Brichto, *The Names of God* (1998), 279–90.
219 "His son" (vv. 3, 6, 9, 10, 13), "his father" (v. 7), "my father" (v. 7), "my son" (vv. 7, 8), and "your son" (vv. 2, 12, 16).

knew he would not have to carry out the command, while medieval Jewish sources claim that Isaac was killed and resurrected from the ashes of the altar.[220] The author of the Letter to the Hebrews assumed Abraham trusted God to raise Isaac from the dead (Heb 11:17–19), and the church fathers routinely read the episode typologically as the redemption story of Christ's crucifixion.[221] Perhaps Abraham was simply deceiving Isaac and the workmen, or perhaps he intended to bring Isaac's charred remains back down the mountain with him.[222] Ultimately it is best to resist any attempts to understand this statement, "we will come back to you," with certainty because of our limitations as readers, and because of the intentional gaps left in the account by the narrator. The only thing that seems to matter here is that Abraham is obeying.

Abraham carried the fire and knife but laid the firewood on Isaac (v. 6). Everything is accounted for except one thing, of course – the animal for the sacrifice. This leads to the obvious question that no one has yet dared to ask (v. 7): "where is the lamb for a burnt offering?" Ironically, it is the intended victim himself who asks, while the dismayed reader and Abraham alone know the cold truth. Midrashic interpretation observes that laying the firewood for the offering on Isaac's back is "like one who carries his own cross on his shoulder."[223] It also chillingly foreshadows Isaac's lying on the wood ready for death (v. 9). [224]

Abraham's answer is pregnant with meaning and yet still ambiguous (v. 8): "God himself will provide." To his credit, this has been Abraham's watchword from the beginning of this spiritual odyssey. God has and will provide because he must, because he promised. "Provide" or "furnish" is a secondary meaning of the common verb "see,"[225] and so conveniently works in an English idiom that matches this Hebrew clause almost perfectly, "God will see to it, my son." With this, the two of them walked on together, leaving us open to the interpretation that Isaac now understood and accepted his role in the act of worship. This is now a job the two of them own and understand, a test for Isaac as much as it is for Abraham.[226]

With cold precision, the sonorous verbal actions in vv. 9–10 bring the narrative to heartstricken breaking point. Having arrived at the destination, Abraham builds an altar, as he has done on other occasions (12:7, 8; 13:18). He prepares the pyre, binds

[220] On Abraham as prophet, cf. *b. Moʿed Qaṭ.* 18a and Rashi; on resurrection, cf. *Pirqe R. El.* 31:3, and for discussion, K. A. Mathews, *Genesis 11:27–50:26* (2005), 301.

[221] K. A. Mathews, *Genesis 11:27–50:26* (2005), 303–4.

[222] On the latter interpretation by Bachya ben Asher, see Jon D. Levenson, *The Death and Resurrection of the Beloved Son: The Transformation of Child Sacrifice in Judaism and Christianity* (New Haven: Yale University Press, 1993), 131.

[223] J. Neusner, *Genesis Rabbah, the Judaic Commentary to the Book of Genesis* (1985), 2:280, ¶56:3.

[224] G. J. Wenham, *Genesis 16–50* (1994), 108.

[225] Although "choose" or "select" may also work in this context; *HALOT* 3:1159, ¶12; BDB 907, ¶ 6,g.

[226] J. D. Levenson, *The Death and Resurrection of the Beloved Son* (1993), 133–34.

Isaac on top the wood and altar, and seizes the knife to do the deed.[227] The verb for binding of Isaac (ʿāqad) is used only here in the Hebrew Scriptures, so that Jewish tradition uses the corresponding noun, Akedah, for the entire episode.

With equal conciseness, the action is halted by the sudden appearance of the "angel of the LORD" (v. 11). The Messenger of Yahweh (malʾak yhwh) appeared to Hagar in the desert of Shur (cf. commentary at 16:7–10) and the "angel of God" helped Hagar again in the desert of Beer-sheba (21:17–18). This is the angel's one and only appearance to Abraham. In most cases, the messenger is an unspecified supernatural envoy sent from Yahweh, who is interchangeably identified with Yahweh. Here the angel calls "from heaven," and his speech in v. 12 is clearly God himself (". . . you have not withheld your son . . . from me"). Great relief is the call, "Abraham, Abraham," repeated for urgency's sake, and its response, "At your service, sir." As the first call in v. 1 brought a sense of foreboding, this one sounds a note of joy. Abraham has passed the test. Now God knows that Abraham is a God-fearer (v. 12), not that God's prior knowledge was somehow incomplete. Abraham's enactment has dramatized the reality of obedience experientially and qualitatively for God. Moreover, as we shall see, Isaac does not return with Abraham to Beer-sheba but begins a life on his own, independent and ready to receive the covenant promises for himself. In a real sense, Abraham *has* sacrificed his son, although the young man's life was spared. Now God knows that Abraham qualifies as a God-fearer, whose future is thereby secured as one who hears the "voice" of God (v. 19), transcending even the earthly promises of the covenant, which are now ready for the next generation.[228]

A ram, previously unnoticed on the mountain and now caught by its horns, serves as a substitute burnt offering (v. 13). It is unlikely that this episode establishes the Israelite principle of redemption of the first-born son through the death of a sheep, for several reasons.[229] Yet this substitution does confirm the use of animals in place of humans more generally, and assumes that once the command to make sacrifice has been given, it must be fulfilled. The Hebrew stresses the immediacy of the ram's appearance, implying the providential provision of a sacrifice, as hoped for by Abraham (v. 8).

As Abraham named Beer-sheba (21:31), so he names this spot where he passed his test (v. 14). The place name, "The LORD will provide" or "Yahweh sees," is a response to Abraham's plaintive longing in v. 8, now turned to a joyful cry, relieved of all despair. The name is said to be related to the dictum in v. 14b, which was well-known in the narrator's day. The dictum itself, "On the mount of the LORD it

---

[227] "To kill his son" is a purpose clause ("in order to kill") with the verb "slaughter" (šāḥaṭ) commonly used for ritual killing of sacrificial animals for the cult: "in order to slaughter his son."

[228] Hugh C. White, *Narration and Discourse in the Book of Genesis* (Cambridge: Cambridge University Press, 1991), 197.

[229] The paschal lamb of the tenth plague served that role (Exod 12–13); J. D. Levenson, *The Death and Resurrection of the Beloved Son* (1993), 13 and 111–42.

shall be provided," introduces the passive of "see," and is therefore more likely "On the mount of Yahweh, he/it is seen." In other words, a word play is introduced at this point in the narrative, playing on the active voice "provides" and the passive "be seen," albeit using the same Hebrew verb.[230] Moreover, this passive "be seen" is the term used several times in Genesis for "appear" in divine self-disclosure at times when God makes himself known in revelatory communications (Closer Look, "Divine Revelation in the Hebrew Scriptures," p. 135). Thus this well-known maxim in the narrator's day was something like "On Yahweh's mount, He appears," or "He is revealed." Perhaps this connection in v. 14 hints at the meaning of the entire bizarre episode in vv. 1–19, in that God's provision is also God's self-disclosure. God is revealed in his act of providing. The mount of Yahweh's revelation is the spot where he providentially provided for the ancestral family and the continuation of the promised line. All hopes of connecting the location to Jerusalem or any other specific locale should be abandoned.[231]

Implicit in Abraham's name for the place – Yahweh Provides – is a paradigmatic principle for readers of the ancestral narrative. The paradigm offered to ancient readers by this text would certainly have included an appreciation for the importance of sacrificial worship, and an understanding of the use of animals rather than people. It also added new depth of meaning to the everyday expression, "On Yahweh's mount, He is revealed," in that it personalized the revelation of God as provision for one's profoundest needs. But for willing readers, the paradigmatic principle extends to today, because the experience of our father Abraham is the experience of all Israelites. Or at least, it *should* be the experience of all "the present heirs of the biblical (or Judeo–Christian) tradition, and to all who in the future will lay claim to constituting the ideal Israel."[232] As such, this text continues to offer a paradigm of unwavering faith in the Voice from heaven; or more poignantly, a disposition to say "At your service, sir."

The angel of Yahweh calls a second time to Abraham (v. 15), and reaffirms the ancestral promises to him for the last time (vv. 16–18, and cf. 12:2–3; 13:14–17; 15:1–21; 17:7–8).[233] This last elocution of the blessing contains new components.[234] First,

---

[230] Metaphonic word play depends on the same verbal root in different derived stems, in this case Qal (sees/provides) and Niphal (is seen/appears).

[231] C. Westermann, *Genesis 12–36* (1985), 362–63;

[232] H. C. Brichto, *The Names of God* (1998), 288–89. In a sense, later Israel owes its very existence to mimicking the faithfulness of the great patriarch; R. W. L. Moberly, "The Earliest Commentary on the Akedah," *VT* 38 (1988): 302–23, esp. 320–21.

[233] On the older consensus that these verses are a later addition to the text, see C. Westermann, *Genesis 12–36* (1985), 363; now however, see G. J. Wenham, *Genesis 16–50* (1994), 101–3 and 111; V. P. Hamilton, *The Book of Genesis, Chapters 18–50* (1995), 114–16.

[234] I am overlooking the new use of the Hithpael of "bless" (v. 18) instead of the Niphal we have seen earlier (12:3; 18:18), assuming there is no measurable distinction between their meanings; B. K. Waltke and M. P. O'Connor, *An Introduction to Biblical Hebrew Syntax* (1990), 395.

Yahweh introduces a solemn oath formula, "by myself I have sworn," adding certain numinous weight to the statement. Second, the "sand on the seashore" is a new metaphor, complementing the earlier stars-of-heaven and dust-of-earth metaphors. Third, Abraham's "seed" (*zera'*, NRSV's "offspring") will possess the gate of their enemies, implying military victory over adversaries.[235]

Having passed his test, Abraham reunites with his two workmen and they return to Beer-sheba (v. 19). Where is Isaac? The phrase "the two of them walked on together" (vv. 6, 8) is conspicuous by its absence, or we might expect some corresponding variation. The next we hear of Isaac's location, he has settled in the Negeb at Beer-lahai-roi (24:62). Much has been made of Isaac's absence in v. 19, including some who think Isaac was present but unmentioned due to a return of focus to Abraham. But a convincing case has been made for Gen 22 as having origins in the intergenerational context of an ancient rite of initiation, involving the symbolic murder of a child.[236] In this interpretation, the child is required to face his own imminent death and to accept it emotionally in order to pass into independence and manhood. Isaac does not return again to Beer-sheba to live with his father, not because of a dispute between them like that of Abram and Lot, but because the parent–child bond has been severed naturally, and a transition is being enacted from the first generation of the promise to the second. The binding of Isaac was a strategy to sever the psychological bonds connecting the generations, producing an Isaac who is not simply Abraham's son physically but a patriarch in his own right spiritually, with wife Rebekah (Gen 24) and ancestral promises of his own (26:1–5). Abraham's obedience lifts him above the unfolding biological process. As a God-fearer, Abraham's future rests only with the "voice" he must follow as in the last divine word spoken to him (v. 18): " . . . because you have obeyed my voice." Abraham the God-fearer has arrived. From this point forward, the narrative turns slowly but irrevocably to Isaac, heir to the covenant promises.

Another indefinite length of time is marked by "after these things" (v. 20, cf. v. 1), and the chapter concludes with a summary statement of Nahor's genealogy (vv. 20–24). Nahor is identified as the remaining brother of Abraham, and context reminds us Milcah is Nahor's wife. Both are details presented at the heading of the narrative in 11:27–29. The list is a segmented genealogy, presenting eight sons by Milcah and four by the concubine Reumah. Reading the list of names, twelve sons and one granddaughter, after so many chapters of barrenness and only two births in Abraham's family, highlights the dilemma of Abraham's journey. But more to

---

[235] Hamilton also notes the conditionality of this statement, based as it is on Abraham's obedience; V. P. Hamilton, *The Book of Genesis, Chapters 18–50* (1995), 116. But I have argued in this commentary that the covenant itself and all its promises are by nature conditional since all covenants are bilateral and typically asymmetrical, and therefore I have not counted this as a new component; see commentary at 6:18; 15:17–18; and 17:1–2 and Closer Look at "Covenants in the Hebrew Scriptures" at Gen 6, p. 101.

[236] H. C. White, *Narration and Discourse in the Book of Genesis* (1991), 186–203.

the point, the genealogy is important because it introduces Rebekah, daughter of Bethuel, granddaughter of Nahor, and we learn later, brother of Laban (24:29). The genealogy prepares the reader for Gen 24. Now that Isaac has survived Abraham's test, it is time to find him a wife.

GENESIS 23:1–20 DEATH OF SARAH

(23:1) Sarah lived one hundred twenty-seven years; this was the length of Sarah's life.

(23:2) And Sarah died at Kiriath-arba (that is, Hebron) in the land of Canaan; and Abraham went in to mourn for Sarah and to weep for her.

(23:3) Abraham rose up from beside his dead, and said to the Hittites,

(23:4) "I am a stranger and an alien residing among you; give me property among you for a burying place, so that I may bury my dead out of my sight."

(23:5) The Hittites answered Abraham,

(23:6) "Hear us, my lord; you are a mighty prince among us. Bury your dead in the choicest of our burial places; none of us will withhold from you any burial ground for burying your dead."

(23:7) Abraham rose and bowed to the Hittites, the people of the land.

(23:8) He said to them, "If you are willing that I should bury my dead out of my sight, hear me, and entreat for me Ephron son of Zohar,

(23:9) so that he may give me the cave of Machpelah, which he owns; it is at the end of his field. For the full price let him give it to me in your presence as a possession for a burying place."

(23:10) Now Ephron was sitting among the Hittites; and Ephron the Hittite answered Abraham in the hearing of the Hittites, of all who went in at the gate of his city,

(23:11) "No, my lord, hear me; I give you the field, and I give you the cave that is in it; in the presence of my people I give it to you; bury your dead."

(23:12) Then Abraham bowed down before the people of the land.

(23:13) He said to Ephron in the hearing of the people of the land, "If you only will listen to me! I will give the price of the field; accept it from me, so that I may bury my dead there."

(23:14) Ephron answered Abraham,

(23:15) "My lord, listen to me; a piece of land worth four hundred shekels of silver – what is that between you and me? Bury your dead."

(23:16) Abraham agreed with Ephron; and Abraham weighed out for Ephron the silver that he had named in the hearing of the Hittites, four hundred shekels of silver, according to the weights current among the merchants.

(23:17) So the field of Ephron in Machpelah, which was to the east of Mamre, the field with the cave that was in it and all the trees that were in the field, throughout its whole area, passed

(23:18) to Abraham as a possession in the presence of the Hittites, in the presence of all who went in at the gate of his city.

(23:19) After this, Abraham buried Sarah his wife in the cave of the field of Machpelah facing Mamre (that is, Hebron) in the land of Canaan.

(23:20) The field and the cave that is in it passed from the Hittites into Abraham's possession as a burying place.

*T*he spiritual odyssey of father Abraham is over. The previous chapter serves as fitting closure. The remaining portions of the *tôlĕdôt* ("descendants") of Terah begun in 11:27 are devoted to preparations for Isaac to assume his place in the patriarchal line. These include the death and burial of Sarah (Gen 23), Isaac's marriage to Rebekah (Gen 24), and the death of Abraham followed by the genealogy of Ishmael (25:1–18).

We have Sarah's obituary in vv. 1–2, the first in a series of such ancestral death-and-burial notations that serve purposes of closure for the book of Genesis (25:7–11; 35:27–29; 49:29–33; 50:13). In this case, Sarah's obituary also introduces the narration of Abraham's purchase of the ancestral burial cave and field near Hebron.[237] The number of years of Sarah's lifespan, "one hundred twenty-seven," may have symbolic significance, such as the number of years of a life well-lived (120, cf. Deut 34:7) plus the sacred number seven.[238] Her death at Hebron (also known as Kiriath-arba), rather than Beer-sheba is not explained (22:19), other than Hebron's proximity to an earlier encampment of the ancestral family, by the oaks of Mamre (13:18; 14:13; 18:1, and cf. vv. 17, 19).

Abraham enters into negotiations with the Hittites, the dominant inhabitants of the region ("the people of the land," v. 7), for a family burial ground (vv. 3–16). The moment is driven by a common need that everyone in the conversation understands, that of burying one's dead (vv. 4, 6, 8, 11, 13, 15, 19). Abraham requests "property...for a burying place," a simple genitive construction (property-of-grave), which may be either genitive of purpose ("property used for burial") or of species ("land, more specifically, burial property").[239] In either case, Abraham is requesting permanent ownership of a portion of land in the area of his semi-permanent encampment at the oaks of Mamre.

The closest ancient Near Eastern parallels are the so-called Neo-Babylonian Dialogue Documents, in which negotiations are related in first-person discursive texts, and the verb "hear" plays a prominent role (*šemû* in the Babylonian records; *šāmaʿ*

---

[237] On failed attempts to date the text based on parallels with Late Bronze Age Hittite law, see C. Westermann, *Genesis 12–36* (1985), 372; T. L. Thompson, *The Historicity of The Patriarchal Narratives* (1974), 295–96. Land transactions from Ugarit may present better parallels; Raymond Westbrook, "Purchase of the Cave of Machpelah," *Israel Law Review* 6 (1971): 29–38. See further below for references to the Neo-Babylonian dialogue documents of sale, and the common social customs at work here, most of which were in practice for centuries in the ancient world making it impossible to locate this text in any particular historical timeframe.

[238] Nahum M. Sarna, *Understanding Genesis* (New York: Schocken Books, 1966), 83–84.

[239] Waltke and O'Connor prefer the latter; B. K. Waltke and M. P. O'Connor, *An Introduction to Biblical Hebrew Syntax* (1990), 153.

in Hebrew, vv. 6, 8, 11, 13, 15, 16).[240] NRSV's "Abraham agreed with Ephron" is simply "Abraham heard Ephron" (v. 16). The Babylonian texts include the following parallels: proposal (v. 15), agreement (v. 16), weighing out of silver (v. 16), declaration of transfer of ownership of property and description of property (v. 17), and witnesses (v. 18).

Recent anthropological research on bazaar economies around the world sheds light on this text, especially as this relates to the technical rules of "haggling," with its social customs of extravagant expressions of affection and trust (e.g., "you are a mighty prince among us") and elaborate gestures of subservience, such as bowing low before the other party (vv. 7, 12).[241] Abraham is at a distinct disadvantage in these negotiations with his Hittite neighbors. In the ancient Near East, such bargaining for the exchange of a field or other items was dependent upon a delicate balance of favors given and returned between two parties, especially based upon existing relationships (of "brotherhood" or "love") between the potential partners.[242] These rules for bartering were socially established and binding, and well-understood by all parties. Yet Abraham had no previous relationships with the Hittites, and had no reason to expect them to grant his request. His proposal (v. 4b) is prefaced by an acknowledgement of the social distance between himself and the Hittites; he is "a stranger and an alien" residing among them (v. 4a).

In such negotiations, when no previous relationship exists to which one may appeal, the one making the request might also appeal to the potential damage to follow if the favor is not granted.[243] In Abraham's case, his proposal only hints at the implied damage, which is that he would have no place to bury Sarah. Yet, as we have said, proper burial of the dead is the obvious common social need that drives the negotiations. The complicating factor is that Abraham is semi-nomadic without provisions for burial of his dead and he is negotiating with settled urbanites near Hebron.

Ephron's offer to make the field and cave a gift is something of a *crux interpretum* in this passage (v. 11). Was his offer a genuine offer of gift-exchange? Was it an opening volley in an assumed haggling procedure, which surprisingly never occurred because no alternative price was countered by Abraham? Both assumptions are simplistic. It seems more likely that Ephron's offer was an invitation into a socially embedded

---

[240] David B. Weisberg, "A Neo-Babylonian Dialogue Document," *COS* 3.123:271–2; idem, *Neo-Babylonian Texts in the Oriental Institute Collection* (OIP 122; Chicago: Oriental Institute of the University of Chicago, 2003), 13–14.

[241] Nathan MacDonald, "Driving a Hard Bargain? Genesis 23 and Models of Economic Exchange," in *Anthropology and Biblical Studies: Avenues of Approach,* eds. Louise J. Lawrence and Mario I. Aguilar (Leiden: Deo, 2004), 79–96, esp. 81–90.

[242] For example, see Oded Tammuz, "Do Me a Favor! The Art of Negotiating according to Old Babylonian Letters," in *Intellectual Life of the Ancient Near East: Papers Presented at the 43rd Rencontre assyriologique international, Prague, July 1–5, 1996,* ed. Jiří Prosecký (Prague: Oriental Institute, 1998), 379–88.

[243] Ibid., esp. 382–83.

relationship (i.e., a "balanced reciprocity") in which Abraham would have assumed a closer social affinity with the local Hittites, and would have been expected to reciprocate with more gifts later. Instead, Abraham preferred a commercial exchange in which the social distance is maintained (a "negative reciprocity").[244] This would have been less desirable to the Hittites, which probably explains the price, "four hundred shekels of silver." The cost was probably exorbitant, although we have no way of estimating the price of the property beyond doubt.

The chapter concludes with a two-tiered summary (vv. 17–20). The first summary announces the formal transaction, with dimensions of the property, giving the impression of a legal text (perhaps a source for the chapter). There follows the burial of Sarah in this new property (v. 19).[245] The second-level summary repeats the transaction of the field and cave, and brings the episode to final closure (v. 20). Abraham's covenant with Abimelech had secured his own well, where he was privileged to plant a tree, and perhaps claimed one small piece of property as his own (21:28–33). Now at Machpelah, he has purchased a field near Hebron, with its cave and all its trees, which will become the family burial plot (25:9; 49:29–30; 50:13). The promised land is still in view, but Abraham has come into all that will be his during his lifetime.

GENESIS 24:1–67 THE MARRIAGE OF ISAAC AND REBEKAH

(24:1) Now Abraham was old, well advanced in years; and the LORD had blessed Abraham in all things.

(24:2) Abraham said to his servant, the oldest of his house, who had charge of all that he had, "Put your hand under my thigh

(24:3) and I will make you swear by the LORD, the God of heaven and earth, that you will not get a wife for my son from the daughters of the Canaanites, among whom I live,

(24:4) but will go to my country and to my kindred and get a wife for my son Isaac."

(24:5) The servant said to him, "Perhaps the woman may not be willing to follow me to this land; must I then take your son back to the land from which you came?"

(24:6) Abraham said to him, "See to it that you do not take my son back there.

(24:7) The LORD, the God of heaven, who took me from my father's house and from the land of my birth, and who spoke to me and swore to me, 'To your

---

[244] For anthropological background, see N. MacDonald, "Driving a Hard Bargain? Genesis 23 and Models of Economic Exchange," in *Anthropology and Biblical Studies: Avenues of Approach* (2004).

[245] Which leads to the speculation that v. 19 originally followed immediately after vv. 1–2 as part of the priestly framework; C. Westermann, *Genesis 12–36* (1985), 371 and 375.

offspring I will give this land,' he will send his angel before you, and you shall take a wife for my son from there.

(24:8) But if the woman is not willing to follow you, then you will be free from this oath of mine; only you must not take my son back there."

(24:9) So the servant put his hand under the thigh of Abraham his master and swore to him concerning this matter.

(24:10) Then the servant took ten of his master's camels and departed, taking all kinds of choice gifts from his master; and he set out and went to Aram-naharaim, to the city of Nahor.

(24:11) He made the camels kneel down outside the city by the well of water; it was toward evening, the time when women go out to draw water.

(24:12) And he said, "O LORD, God of my master Abraham, please grant me success today and show steadfast love to my master Abraham.

(24:13) I am standing here by the spring of water, and the daughters of the townspeople are coming out to draw water.

(24:14) Let the girl to whom I shall say, 'Please offer your jar that I may drink,' and who shall say, 'Drink, and I will water your camels'– let her be the one whom you have appointed for your servant Isaac. By this I shall know that you have shown steadfast love to my master."

(24:15) Before he had finished speaking, there was Rebekah, who was born to Bethuel son of Milcah, the wife of Nahor, Abraham's brother, coming out with her water jar on her shoulder.

(24:16) The girl was very fair to look upon, a virgin, whom no man had known. She went down to the spring, filled her jar, and came up.

(24:17) Then the servant ran to meet her and said, "Please let me sip a little water from your jar."

(24:18) "Drink, my lord," she said, and quickly lowered her jar upon her hand and gave him a drink.

(24:19) When she had finished giving him a drink, she said, "I will draw for your camels also, until they have finished drinking."

(24:20) So she quickly emptied her jar into the trough and ran again to the well to draw, and she drew for all his camels.

(24:21) The man gazed at her in silence to learn whether or not the LORD had made his journey successful.

(24:22) When the camels had finished drinking, the man took a gold nose-ring weighing a half shekel, and two bracelets for her arms weighing ten gold shekels,

(24:23) and said, "Tell me whose daughter you are. Is there room in your father's house for us to spend the night?"

(24:24) She said to him, "I am the daughter of Bethuel son of Milcah, whom she bore to Nahor."

(24:25) She added, "We have plenty of straw and fodder and a place to spend the night."

(24:26) The man bowed his head and worshiped the LORD

(24:27) and said, "Blessed be the LORD, the God of my master Abraham, who has not forsaken his steadfast love and his faithfulness toward my master. As for me, the LORD has led me on the way to the house of my master's kin."

(24:28) Then the girl ran and told her mother's household about these things.

(24:29) Rebekah had a brother whose name was Laban; and Laban ran out to the man, to the spring.

(24:30) As soon as he had seen the nose-ring, and the bracelets on his sister's arms, and when he heard the words of his sister Rebekah, "Thus the man spoke to me," he went to the man; and there he was, standing by the camels at the spring.

(24:31) He said, "Come in, O blessed of the LORD. Why do you stand outside when I have prepared the house and a place for the camels?"

(24:32) So the man came into the house; and Laban unloaded the camels, and gave him straw and fodder for the camels, and water to wash his feet and the feet of the men who were with him.

(24:33) Then food was set before him to eat; but he said, "I will not eat until I have told my errand." He said, "Speak on."

(24:34) So he said, "I am Abraham's servant.

(24:35) The LORD has greatly blessed my master, and he has become wealthy; he has given him flocks and herds, silver and gold, male and female slaves, camels and donkeys.

(24:36) And Sarah my master's wife bore a son to my master when she was old; and he has given him all that he has.

(24:37) My master made me swear, saying, 'You shall not take a wife for my son from the daughters of the Canaanites, in whose land I live;

(24:38) but you shall go to my father's house, to my kindred, and get a wife for my son.'

(24:39) I said to my master, 'Perhaps the woman will not follow me.'

(24:40) But he said to me, 'The LORD, before whom I walk, will send his angel with you and make your way successful. You shall get a wife for my son from my kindred, from my father's house.

(24:41) Then you will be free from my oath, when you come to my kindred; even if they will not give her to you, you will be free from my oath.'

(24:42) "I came today to the spring, and said, 'O LORD, the God of my master Abraham, if now you will only make successful the way I am going!

(24:43) I am standing here by the spring of water; let the young woman who comes out to draw, to whom I shall say, "Please give me a little water from your jar to drink,"

(24:44) and who will say to me, "Drink, and I will draw for your camels also" – let her be the woman whom the LORD has appointed for my master's son.'

(24:45) "Before I had finished speaking in my heart, there was Rebekah coming out with her water jar on her shoulder; and she went down to the spring, and drew. I said to her, 'Please let me drink.'

(24:46) She quickly let down her jar from her shoulder, and said, 'Drink, and I will also water your camels.' So I drank, and she also watered the camels.

(24:47) Then I asked her, 'Whose daughter are you?' She said, 'The daughter of Bethuel, Nahor's son, whom Milcah bore to him.' So I put the ring on her nose, and the bracelets on her arms.

(24:48) Then I bowed my head and worshiped the LORD, and blessed the LORD, the God of my master Abraham, who had led me by the right way to obtain the daughter of my master's kinsman for his son.

(24:49) Now then, if you will deal loyally and truly with my master, tell me; and if not, tell me, so that I may turn either to the right hand or to the left."

(24:50) Then Laban and Bethuel answered, "The thing comes from the LORD; we cannot speak to you anything bad or good.

(24:51) Look, Rebekah is before you, take her and go, and let her be the wife of your master's son, as the LORD has spoken."

(24:52) When Abraham's servant heard their words, he bowed himself to the ground before the LORD.

(24:53) And the servant brought out jewelry of silver and of gold, and garments, and gave them to Rebekah; he also gave to her brother and to her mother costly ornaments.

(24:54) Then he and the men who were with him ate and drank, and they spent the night there. When they rose in the morning, he said, "Send me back to my master."

(24:55) Her brother and her mother said, "Let the girl remain with us a while, at least ten days; after that she may go."

(24:56) But he said to them, "Do not delay me, since the LORD has made my journey successful; let me go that I may go to my master."

(24:57) They said, "We will call the girl, and ask her."

(24:58) And they called Rebekah, and said to her, "Will you go with this man?" She said, "I will."

(24:59) So they sent away their sister Rebekah and her nurse along with Abraham's servant and his men.

(24:60) And they blessed Rebekah and said to her, "May you, our sister, become thousands of myriads; may your offspring gain possession of the gates of their foes."

(24:61) Then Rebekah and her maids rose up, mounted the camels, and followed the man; thus the servant took Rebekah, and went his way.

(24:62) Now Isaac had come from Beer-lahai-roi, and was settled in the Negeb.

(24:63) Isaac went out in the evening to walk[i] in the field; and looking up, he saw camels coming.

---

[i] Meaning of Heb word is uncertain.

(24:64) And Rebekah looked up, and when she saw Isaac, she slipped quickly from the camel,

(24:65) and said to the servant, "Who is the man over there, walking in the field to meet us?" The servant said, "It is my master." So she took her veil and covered herself.

(24:66) And the servant told Isaac all the things that he had done.

(24:67) Then Isaac brought her into his mother Sarah's tent. He took Rebekah, and she became his wife; and he loved her. So Isaac was comforted after his mother's death.

*A*braham has become a God-fearer and Isaac is prepared to become a patriarch in his own right (Gen 22). Sarah has died and been buried in the new ancestral burial plot in the field of Machpelah near Hebron (Gen 23). There remains only the need to find Isaac a suitable wife. Yet the theme of the narrative is not simply finding a suitable wife, but that of divine guidance for Israel's ancestors, a theme that has been central to the extended narrative since Abraham's call in Gen 12.[246] This chapter is the longest in Genesis and among the longest in the Bible, leading early Jewish interpreters puzzled over why it demanded so much space.[247] Interpreters have also most often assumed a late composition for this chapter when compared to other ancestral narratives, although the basis for this argument has been overstated.[248]

The opening verse is comprised of two circumstantial clauses, one for Abraham and one for Yahweh (v. 1). The Hebrew word order marks the beginning of a new scene and provides pertinent background information for the episode to follow in vv. 2–67.[249] Abraham has reached an advanced age, which sounds as though the narrator is preparing to announce his death and burial. This, however, is delayed until 25:7–11, and his age becomes background information for the intervening episode.

The second clause of v. 1 is the narrator's assertion that Yahweh has blessed Abraham in every way, illustrated most immediately by his relationship with the Hittites (Gen 23). The theme of blessing has, of course, been constant in Genesis since the fifth day of creation (1:20–23, where see commentary). Specifically the blessing of

---

[246] Evidently as part of Israel's national epic literature; John Van Seters, *Prologue to History: The Yahwist as Historian in Genesis* (Louisville, Ky.: Westminster/John Knox Press, 1992), 267.

[247] Compared to more important legal matters that seem to rely on a single word or consonant; J. Neusner, *Genesis Rabbah, the Judaic Commentary to the Book of Genesis* (1985), 2:322, ¶60:8.

[248] Alexander Rofé, "An Enquiry into the Betrothal of Rebekah," in *Die Hebräische Bibel und ihre zweifache Nachgeschichte: Festschrift für Rolf Rendtorff zum 65. Geburtstag*, eds. Erhard Blum, Christian Macholz, and Ekkehard Stegemann (Neukirchen-Vluyn: Neukirchener Verlag, 1990), 27–39; for objections, see Gary A. Rendsburg, "Some False Leads in the Identification of Late Biblical Hebrew Texts: The Cases of Genesis 24 and 1 Samuel 2:27–36," *JBL* 121 (2002): 23–46.

[249] The first clause reactivates Abraham as the lead character and the second clause affirms his quality; C. H. J. van der Merwe, J. A. Naudé, and J. H. Kroeze, *A Biblical Hebrew Reference Grammar* (1999), 346–48.

Abraham has included direct blessing of the patriarch himself, blessings continued diachronically through his line, and blessings to others through Abraham's descendants.[250] In this passage, the narrator asserts that Yahweh has blessed Abraham "in all things" (v. 1), and the servant's voice explains that Yahweh has blessed Abraham with great wealth and a son in his old age (vv. 35–36).

The servant who undertook this errand for his master is anonymous throughout, even though commentaries through the ages have identified him with Eliezer (cf. 15:2).[251] The origins of the idiom "to place one's hand under another's thigh" (vv. 2 and 9) are obscure, but it seems to enact or ritualize the oath by the organ of procreation.[252] Oath-taking is often accompanied by solemn gestures, but it is difficult to know how placing one's hand under another's thigh should confirm the oath. Nevertheless, even without origins or cultural background, the significance of this particular gesture is explained in v. 3 because it accompanies the swearing of a solemn oath. Elsewhere in the chapter, the sworn commitment, together with its ratifying gesture, is an "oath" (v. 8, šĕbûʿâ) and a curse under which the servant has been placed (v. 41, ʾālâ).

The oath is taken in the name of Yahweh, God of heaven and earth (v. 3). Israel's national God is thus identified as the Sovereign of the observable cosmos (Hebrew merism "heaven and earth"), for which there is no separate word in Biblical Hebrew. While this cannot be said to be strict, philosophical monotheism, such claims already mark out the contours of Israel's exclusive worship and the extent of Yahweh's dominion, features essential to the thought of the Hebrew Scriptures.

The oath itself consists of a commitment to avoid marriage to the local women for Isaac, but to find a suitable wife instead from among Abraham's kinship group in northwestern Mesopotamia at Haran (vv. 3b–4). "Canaanite" here is not only ethnic, since the region had Hittites and other ethnic groups (Gen 23), but is a geographical designation for the entire region in the southern Levant (cf. 12:6; Num 34:1–12; Ezek 47:15–20).[253] Instead of marriage to the Canaanites, Abraham is rather insistent that the servant find a wife for Isaac from his "country" (or "land," ʾereṣ), his "kindred" (môledet, v. 4; or "land of birth," v. 7), and from his "father's house" (bêt ʾāb, v. 7). These, of course, are the very things Abraham is called to leave in 12:1, and represent the center of religious, social, and economic life in ancient Israel (cf. commentary at 12:1). When he began his spiritual odyssey, Abraham set out

---

[250] C. W. Mitchell, *The Meaning of* brk *"to bless" in the Old Testament* (1987), 67–68.

[251] E.g., J. Neusner, *Genesis Rabbah, the Judaic Commentary to the Book of Genesis* (1985), 2:309 ¶59:9.

[252] Gottfried Vanoni, "*śîm*," *TDOT* 14:89–112, esp. 104. An oath symbolized by touching the genitals may have entailed a threat of sterility if the servant failed to keep the commitment, especially since children issued from their father's thigh (46:26; Exod 1:5); E. A. Speiser, *Genesis* (1964), 178. For a Sumerian parallel, see Yitschak Sefati, "The Women's Oath," *COS* 1.169A:540–41.

[253] A. F. Rainey and R. S. Notley, *The Sacred Bridge: Carta's Atlas of the Biblical World* (2006), 33–36.

to establish a new "father's house" and to become a new *paterfamilias*. But he did so while yet childless. Now that Yahweh has proven his faithfulness in the birth of Isaac, it is now imperative to choose the future matriarch from the same social and religious infrastructure. Marriage within one's kinship group, or "endogamy," was considered necessary to ensure continuity of cultural and religious values (see Closer Look "Endogamy in Ancient Israel").

A CLOSER LOOK — ENDOGAMY IN ANCIENT ISRAEL

Endogamy is the social custom of marrying within one's own clan or tribe, while exogamy is the custom of marrying outside one's clan or tribe.[254] Preexilic biblical texts reflect a distinct preference for endogamy, which was important for community identity in ancient Israel, as in other traditional peoples. Toward the end of the biblical period, when the people of God ceased to exist as a political identity, endogamy was even more important as a means of ensuring religious and ethnic identity. It has been observed that the prohibition of exogamy was asymmetrical; that is, only marriages between Israelite men and local non-Israelite women were forbidden whereas the postexilic ban included both sexes.

It seems likely the prohibition had predominantly cultural roots rather than a religious origin. Perhaps the motivation for endogamy is to be found in the crucial roles of women in household life, which would have made it a risk to Israelite cultural identity if local non-Israelite women were to become wives in Yahwistic households.[255]

In the ancestral period narrated here, endogamous marriages were the norm for the patriarchal family. Marriages were typically arranged by parents as was standard in the ancient Near East, and preference appears to have been given to marriage between cousins: Isaac and Esau married cousins, Rebekah and Mahalath respectively (24:15, 24, 47 and 28:2, 5, 9), and Jacob married his cousins Rachel and Leah (29:12). On the other hand, Abraham married his half-sister Sarah (20:12) and Nahor married his niece Milcah (11:29). Endogamy was preferred in the ancestral period but not mandated. Several married outside the group, and at times with no repercussions (38:2; 41:45; and cf. Exod 2:21; Num 12:1).

Jacob's marriages to two of his cousins are different because his sons are the first in the ancestral narratives to be unanimously included among the ancestors of the people of Israel. Both Abraham and Isaac had sons who were not included in the line

[254] Victor P. Hamilton, "Marriage (Old Testament and Ancient Near East)," *ABD* 4:559–69, esp. 563–64.

[255] Carol L. Meyers, "Daughters of the Inhabitants of the Land as Marriage Partners (Exod 34:16; Gen 24:3; 27:46; 28:1,6,8; Deut 7:3; Josh 23:12–13; Judg 3:5–6)," in *Women in Scripture: A Dictionary of Named and Unnamed Women in the Hebrew Bible, the Apocryphal/Deuterocanonical Books, and the New Testament*, eds. Carol L. Meyers, Toni Craven, and Ross S. Kraemer (Boston: Houghton Mifflin, 2000), 200–201.

of promise (Ishmael and Esau respectively), but not so of Jacob.[256] The genealogies of Genesis are linear from Abraham to Jacob, but then Jacob's segments. Thus it appears the sons of the direct line of the ancestral promises were required to marry endogamously.

Before locking himself in to the oath, the servant wisely and logically raises a question. Suppose no suitable woman will return with him, should he then take Isaac back to the ancestral homeland to find a wife (v. 5)? Abraham's primary concern comes to the surface in his answer – the servant is not to take Isaac back there, ever (v. 6)! Having survived the ordeal at Moriah (22:1–19), Abraham does not want Isaac to risk treacherous travel or other potential threats. Isaac is, after all, the only living son of the covenant promises.

Instead of taking Isaac back to Haran, the great patriarch gives his servant another way of looking at the mission (v. 7). Abraham's answer uses particularly striking word order to emphasize Yahweh's role in the search for Isaac's wife.[257] It is Yahweh, "God of heaven" (again emphasizing God's universality, important when traveling to such a distant land) who will send his angel before the servant. Yahweh is further characterized by three relative clauses in the original word order: Yahweh is the God (1) who called Abraham from that homeland, (2) who commanded him to leave it (NRSV's "spoke to me"), and (3) who linked together for Abraham the promises of "seed" (*zeraʿ*, NRSV's "offspring") and "land" (*ʾereṣ*). In making these assurances for the servant, Abraham has so recalled his own experiences of leaving Haran, relying even on the same terminology for the covenant promises repeated frequently in Gen 12–25, he has associated this mission and task with his own spiritual odyssey. Yahweh will send his angel before the servant just as Yahweh has consistently directed, protected, and guided Abraham thus far. In this way, Abraham's faith is passed along to the servant, to Isaac, and ultimately to Rebekah, just as it has been articulated for us by the narrator (15:6).

Abraham is so confident that Yahweh will direct the mission, he releases the servant from the oath altogether if either Yahweh's angel or the young woman should fail to cooperate (v. 8). After hearing one final admonition against taking Isaac back to the ancestral homeland, the servant agrees to take the oath (v. 9).

---

[256] Robert A. Oden, Jr, "Jacob as Father, Husband, and Nephew: Kinship Studies and the Patriarchal Narratives," *JBL* 102/2 (1983): 189–205, esp. 195. On the ideal nature of "cross-cousin marriage," see C. L. Meyers, "The Family in Early Israel," in *Families in Ancient Israel* (1997), esp. 36.

[257] The use of *casus pendens* highlights the subject, Yahweh, and characterizes Yahweh with three relative clauses before actually getting to the verbal action: Yahweh, God of heaven, who took me, . . . who commanded me, . . . and who swore to me, saying, . . . He Himself will send his messenger before you. . . . "; B. T. Arnold and J. H. Choi, *A Guide to Biblical Hebrew Syntax* (2003), 7.

A long and artful narrative mirrors the servant's long trip and the eventual success of his mission. After arriving at his destination, he first encounters Rebekah at a well outside the city (vv. 10–27) and then the family at home (vv. 28–61). Aram-naharaim ("Aram of two rivers") refers in general to the region between the upper Euphrates River and the Habur River triangle in northwest Mesopotamia, and includes the city of Haran (11:31–32).[258] The "city of Nahor" may be Haran itself, simply as the city occupied by Nahor. Alternatively, early cuneiform texts mention a city name Naḫur, also located near the Habur River just east of Haran.[259] The appearance of camels in the ancestral narratives (v. 10), whether for transportation or as pack animals, has long been considered anachronistic. We have no widespread evidence of domesticated camels in Syria–Palestine prior to the Late Bronze Age (ca. 1550–1200 BCE).[260] On the other hand, Abraham's camels were said to be a gift from Egypt (12:16), and in any case, the lack of evidence about their domestication has been over-interpreted.[261]

One evening, the servant arrived at the city of his destination, whether Haran or Nahor, and positioned himself beside the city's water supply just at the time when the women go out to draw water (v. 11). The local well was apparently the proper place to find a suitable wife (29:1–14; Exod 2:15b-22).[262] Now that all is ready, the servant prays to Yahweh, God of his master Abraham, for a specific sign that he has found the right woman for Isaac. The critical piece of the sign will be, not only her kindness to help the stranger asking for a drink, but her kindness to the camels.[263] If Yahweh will help in this specific way, the servant will then know that Yahweh has been faithful (NRSV's shown "steadfast love," *ḥesed*, vv. 12, 14) to Abraham. This important concept – "loyalty, faithfulness, kindness, love,

---

[258] See Deut 23:4; Ps 60:2 [Eng. 60:1]; 1 Chron 19:6, and it was known in both Egyptian and Akkadian sources; Bill T. Arnold, "Mesopotamia," *NIDB*, forthcoming; Wayne T. Pitard, "Aram-naharaim," *ABD* 1:341.

[259] Richard S. Hess, "Nahor," *ABD* 4:997.

[260] Philip J. King and Lawrence E. Stager, *Life in Biblical Israel* (Library of Ancient Israel; Louisville, Ky.: Westminster John Knox Press, 2001), 117–18; Juris Zarins, "Camel," *ABD* 1:824–26; Paula Wapnish, "Camels," *OEANE* 1:407–8.

[261] Alan R. Millard, "Methods of Studying the Patriarchal Narratives as Ancient Texts," in *Essays on the Patriarchal Narratives*, eds. A. R. Millard and D. J. Wiseman (Leicester, England: InterVarsity Press, 1980), 35–51, esp. 42–43.

[262] Finding an eligible bride at a well appears to have been a stock scene in antiquity; J. Van Seters, *Prologue to History* (1992), 266–67. Beyond the specific scene at the well, more general parallels have been explored with the Ugaritic Kirta Epic. King Kirta, after the loss of his family, goes on a mission to the city of Udmu to request the princess Hurraya's hand in marriage; the expedition for a wife includes delicate negotiations leading finally to marriage and childbirth; Dennis Pardee, "The Kirta Epic," *COS* 1.102:333–343, esp. 333–39.

[263] It has been estimated that such a generous act of watering ten camels would have required dozens of trips between the spring and the trough taking hours to perform, testing not only Rebekah's social fitness for marriage, but also her physical and mental fitness; Jack M. Sasson, "The Servant's Tale: How Rebekah Found a Spouse," *JNES* 65/4 (2006): 241–65, esp. 251 and 254.

mercy,"[264] – is often linked to Yahweh's covenant with humans, but more generally denotes "a responsible keeping of faith with another with whom one is in a
relationship."[265] Such kindness implies that one member in the relationship is in
a position to render help or aid to the other, who is for one reason or another in
need and unable to help himself.[266] The servant's prayer is therefore specific and
urgent. Abraham (and the servant!) need Yahweh's help this evening, right now, at
this watering hole, in order to find the right woman for Isaac.

Before the servant finishes praying, Rebekah appears (v. 15). We have been prepared for her genealogical qualifications by 22:20–24 (and cf. 11:27–29). Those qualifications, together with her unmarried status and good looks (v. 16) meet all the
prerequisites, which are known to the narrator and reader, but not to Abraham's
servant, of course, who needs to rely completely on Yahweh's guidance. The servant's
request for a simple drink of water leads immediately to confirmation that Rebekah
is the one (vv. 17–20). Her words are the very words he sought to hear, and her
quick and generous care is amazing confirmation that she is indeed the one Yahweh
has designated as Isaac's wife. The servant appears stunned; he stands gazing at her
silently (v. 21). The narrator exposes his inner thoughts in a purpose clause: in order
"to learn" (*yd*ʿ, "to know," or "to discern") whether or not Yahweh had indeed made
the journey successful.

Having apparently decided that Yahweh has indeed gone before him and made
the trip successful, the servant produces impressive gifts (v. 22). Slyly, he enquires
about her genealogical specifics, especially about her "father's house" (*bêt ʾāb*, cf. v.
7; and see commentary at 12:1 and 20:13) so that he might learn what the narrator
has already revealed to the reader (v. 23, cf. v. 15). His request also assumes the
hospitality rules of the ancient world, in that a stranger relied upon the hospitality
of others for overnight lodging.[267] Her suitable genealogy and generosity (vv. 24–25)
appear to be too much for Abraham's servant. His response is a prayer of grateful
praise, celebrating Yahweh's faithfulness and fidelity, acknowledging that Yahweh
has led him to Abraham's immediate kinship group (vv. 26–27).[268]

Rebekah ran quickly to "her mother's household" to report what had happened
(v. 28). We cannot be certain why her home is so designated, except it may reflect the
dominant role of the senior woman in a family household, presumably referring to

---

[264] *HALOT* 1:336–37; *DCH* 3:277–81; BDB 338–39.

[265] Katharine D. Sakenfeld, *The Meaning of Ḥesed in the Hebrew Bible: A New Inquiry*
(HSM 17; Missoula, Mont.: Published by Scholars Press for the Harvard Semitic Museum,
1978), 233. See also Gordon R. Clark, *The Word Ḥesed in the Hebrew Bible* (JSOTSup 157;
Sheffield: JSOT Press, 1993); Nelson Glueck, *Ḥesed in the Bible* (New York: Ktav Pub.
House, 1975).

[266] G. R. Clark, *The Word Ḥesed in the Hebrew Bible* (1993), 267.

[267] P. J. King and L. E. Stager, *Life in Biblical Israel* (2001), 186.

[268] The last clause, "As for me, . . . " is an objective *casus pendens*, stressing Yahweh's faithfulness to him as well as to his master; P. Joüon and T. Muraoka, *A Grammar of Biblical
Hebrew* (1993), 586–87.

her grandmother, Milcah.[269] Rebekah's brother Laban now appears in the extended narrative for the first time, taking decisive action and perhaps attempting to take credit (vv. 29–31). His motives are exposed by the narrator, who implies that Laban is impressed by the appearance of the gifts: " . . . as soon as he had seen the nose-ring, and the bracelets. . . . " Much of Laban's actions and motives here anticipate his role later in the narrative.

The customary meal was provided for the stranger, yet he refused to eat, asking instead permission to explain his mission for such a trip (v. 33). When his host, presumably Laban, said "speak on," the servant launches into a lengthy speech that repeats much from the chapter thus far (vv. 34–49). Repetition is a dominant literary technique in Hebrew narrative rhetoric, and has long since been understood as something other than redundancy. Rather, such repetition, especially as illustrated in the servant's speech, elevates and intensifies the suspense of the narrative and anticipates a resolution.[270] He also diplomatically avoids all theological and social details that may have sounded offensive to his Mesopotamian audience, such as any references to the God of heaven and earth, and covenantal promises of divine gifts of land to Abraham's seed.[271] The speech is, in essence, an elaborate and diplomatically stated proposal of marriage between Rebekah and Isaac, culminating in the forceful "Now then," of v. 49, which marks a shift in the argument and places the burden of decision on Rebekah and the family.[272] The servant has upheld his part of the commitment and declares himself free of his oath to his master, Abraham. It now rests with Rebekah's family to deal loyally and faithfully with Abraham – from the servant's perspective – or to reject the proposal of marriage.

Their answer comes quickly and decisively (vv. 50–51). Rebekah's father and brother speak on the family's behalf: How can one argue with such clear guidance and direction from Yahweh?[273] Abraham's servant responded with appropriate

---

[269] Carol L. Meyers, "Rebekah in the Hebrew Bible," in *Women in Scripture: A Dictionary of Named and Unnamed Women in the Hebrew Bible, the Apocryphal/Deuterocanonical Books, and the New Testament,* eds. Carol L. Meyers, Toni Craven, and Ross S. Kraemer (Boston: Houghton Mifflin, 2000), 143–44.

[270] M. Sternberg, *The Poetics of Biblical Narrative* (1985), 365–440; Adele Berlin, *Poetics and Interpretation of Biblical Narrative* (Bible and Literature Series 9; Sheffield: Almond Press, 1983), 72–80; Robert Alter, *The Art of Biblical Narrative* (New York: Basic Books, 1981), 47–62.

[271] Robert Alter, *Genesis: Translation and Commentary* (New York: W.W. Norton, 1996), 119.

[272] The logical adverb shifts an argument without changing topics, and shifts also from the past events to present action; B. T. Arnold and J. H. Choi, *A Guide to Biblical Hebrew Syntax* (2003), 140.

[273] Rebekah exhibits both of two types of status assumed by women in the Bible; i.e., as an "object of exchange" and an "agent of exchange." She is the object of give-and-take when she is given by Laban and Bethuel as a wife for Isaac, but later in the narrative, she becomes an agent – an active partner in transaction – when she, by means of deceit, exchanges Jacob for the firstborn Esau. See Karin R. Andriolo, "Myth and History: A General Model and Its Application to the Bible," *AA* 83 (1981): 261–84, esp. 270, and see pages 278–79 for many other examples from the Bible.

expressions of praise and with even more extravagant gifts for Rebekah, Laban, and Milcah (vv. 52–53). The mission complete and the matter settled, the servant and his men agree to eat and lodge with Milcah's family (v. 54). The next morning, Laban and Milcah seemed to demur, a technique that elevates the rhetorical suspense further (v. 55).[274] On the other hand, the servant's request to leave may have been a break in marriage protocol, in which a set number of days of betrothal was expected during which there would be a formal banquet and the bride would have time to make her final preparations.[275] This would explain why Rebekah is called upon to settle the matter, which she does at once (vv. 57–58).

Rebekah's family sends her forth with a blessing that she would become the mother of myriads (v. 60). Of course, blessing is an important theme in the book of Genesis, and this passage particularly has emphasized the blessing of Abraham (v. 1, where see commentary, and cf. v. 35). Now at the conclusion of the text, Rebekah's family prays for fertility in what may have been a customary blessing for brides. The particular use of "they blessed" her (Piel of *brk*) connotes a prayer requesting benefits from God that have not been already promised.[276] Yet its language echoes the ancestral promises ("may your offspring [lit. seed, *zera'*] gain possession of the gates of their foes"), and in this sense, Rebekah's family did not realize they were praying that Yahweh would fulfill one of the ancestral promises (cf. 22:17).

The concluding paragraph is full of uncertainties (vv. 62–67). Why was Isaac in Beer-lahai-roi, a place more often associated with Ishmael (cf. 16:14; 25:11)? What was Isaac doing in the field in the evening? The NRSV's "to walk" is admittedly as much guesswork as other translations.[277] How could Rebekah have slipped quickly from a moving camel, especially in light of the Hebrew text, which implies something more like "she *fell* from the camel"? What is the symbolism behind covering herself with the veil? Interpreters have offered considerably more answers than we can possibly cover here.[278] It seems best to allow the narrator to leave these gaps unfilled, and to accept the gist of the conclusion as an act of marriage. This is certainly the intent of the clause "he took Rebekah, and she became his wife," the customary idiom for marriage. And this was most likely the meaning behind the veiled covering, which was probably an ancient signal of betrothal.[279] It is enough to conclude with the thought that this new love comforted Isaac in the wake of the loss of his mother.

---

[274] The narrator leaves gaps in the story, without informing the reader whether Laban and Milcah were delaying in order to take advantage of the generous servant, or whether they were genuinely sorry to see Rebekah leave. The nature of Laban's character later in the narrative perhaps suggests the former option.

[275] Samuel Greengus, "Old Babylonian Marriage Ceremonies and Rites," *JCS* 20/2 (1966): 55–72, esp. 62.

[276] C. W. Mitchell, *The Meaning of* brk *"to bless" in the Old Testament* (1987), 101–2.

[277] The word in question, "Isaac went out in the evening to walk in the field," does not occur elsewhere and is obscure; *HALOT* 3:1311–12. BDB reconstructs the text as a different root, "rove about"; BDB 1001–2.

[278] J. M. Sasson, "The Servant's Tale: How Rebekah Found a Spouse," esp. 264–65.

[279] J. M. Sasson, "The Servant's Tale: How Rebekah Found a Spouse," 265.

GENESIS 25:1–18 DEATH OF ABRAHAM

(25:1) Abraham took another wife, whose name was Keturah.

(25:2) She bore him Zimran, Jokshan, Medan, Midian, Ishbak, and Shuah.

(25:3) Jokshan was the father of Sheba and Dedan. The sons of Dedan were Asshurim, Letushim, and Leummim.

(25:4) The sons of Midian were Ephah, Epher, Hanoch, Abida, and Eldaah. All these were the children of Keturah.

(25:5) Abraham gave all he had to Isaac.

(25:6) But to the sons of his concubines Abraham gave gifts, while he was still living, and he sent them away from his son Isaac, eastward to the east country.

(25:7) This is the length of Abraham's life, one hundred seventy-five years.

(25:8) Abraham breathed his last and died in a good old age, an old man and full of years, and was gathered to his people.

(25:9) His sons Isaac and Ishmael buried him in the cave of Machpelah, in the field of Ephron son of Zohar the Hittite, east of Mamre,

(25:10) the field that Abraham purchased from the Hittites. There Abraham was buried, with his wife Sarah.

(25:11) After the death of Abraham God blessed his son Isaac. And Isaac settled at Beer-lahai-roi.

(25:12) These are the descendants of Ishmael, Abraham's son, whom Hagar the Egyptian, Sarah's slave-girl, bore to Abraham.

(25:13) These are the names of the sons of Ishmael, named in the order of their birth: Nebaioth, the firstborn of Ishmael; and Kedar, Adbeel, Mibsam,

(25:14) Mishma, Dumah, Massa,

(25:15) Hadad, Tema, Jetur, Naphish, and Kedemah.

(25:16) These are the sons of Ishmael and these are their names, by their villages and by their encampments, twelve princes according to their tribes.

(25:17) (This is the length of the life of Ishmael, one hundred thirty-seven years; he breathed his last and died, and was gathered to his people.)

(25:18) They settled from Havilah to Shur, which is opposite Egypt in the direction of Assyria; he settled down alongside of all his people.

*T*he extended narrative on Abraham, begun with the *tôlĕdôt*–structuring clause at 11:27 ("these are *the descendants of* Terah"), comes to a close with a report of Abraham's other children by Keturah, and his death and burial in the cave of Machpelah. As elsewhere in Genesis, a record of those descendants not included in the covenant ancestral line ties off a portion of the narrative before proceeding with the line of promise (cf. 4:17–24; 36:1–37:1). Thus Terah's family story concludes not only with Keturah's children, but also returns to finish the account of Ishmael's descendants in yet another *tôlĕdôt*–structuring clause (vv. 12–18). Genesis uses these concurrently contrasting processes of divergence and invergence, setting aside those descendants not in the line of the covenant promises and at the same time tracing the line of promise through a single line down to Jacob, where the genealogy will segment at the sons of Israel (29:31 – 30:24, where see commentary).[280]

The announcement that Abraham "took another wife" occurs after the death of Sarah in the narrative, but should be understood as occurring many years before (v. 1).[281] Keturah is also called a "concubine" in v. 6 indicating her secondary status, along with Hagar, to the primary wife, Sarah. The children of Keturah are listed succinctly in a segmented genealogy, highlighting only the children of Jokshan and Midian (vv. 2–4). Such genealogies, as also in vv. 13–16, define Israel's relationships with many of its neighbors, and the common descent back to father Abraham shows close affinity with them.[282]

The inclusion of Keturah's children raises again the question of inheritance, and the nature of Isaac's relationship with his siblings. So the text adds that Abraham gave "all he had" to Isaac, while also giving gifts to Hagar's and Keturah's children and sending them far away "to the east country." The operative idea here is that Isaac's siblings are all far from him (cf. 21:8–21); Isaac is the sole descendant of the promise. Thus Abraham was not constrained by later Israelite laws of *primogeniture*, in which the firstborn son receives a double portion of the inheritance regardless of which wife was his mother (Deut 21:15–17). There is no condemnation of Abraham's actions here, illustrating that later Israelite legal and social boundaries were not applicable to the ancestral family.

Abraham's obituary is introduced with a standard formula (v. 7a), followed by his age at death (v. 7b, cf. 23:1–2, 9; 35:28–29). Since the great patriarch was seventy-five years old when he first traveled from Haran to Canaan (12:4), he lived in the Promised Land precisely one hundred years. Abraham was fully sated with life and was "gathered to his people," idioms for a life well-lived and full of success (v. 8). Advanced age for the patriarchs was viewed as reward for serving as a God-fearer (22:12), and since they had no expectation for life in the hereafter, a death such as Abraham's was considered ideal, after a long life and at the right moment just as one's vital powers were declining.[283] Abraham was reunited with Sarah in burial when Isaac and Ishmael interred him in the cave of Machpelah, which he had purchased from the Hittites for Sarah's burial (vv. 9–10; Gen 23). The mention of Ishmael, once again raises the need to state that subsequent to Abraham's death, God carried forward the entirety of the covenant promises and beneficent actions with Isaac as the new recipient (v. 11).[284]

---

[280] K. R. Andriolo, "A Structural Analysis of Genealogy and World View in the Old Testament."

[281] N. M. Sarna, *Genesis* (1989), 172; so the use of the English pluperfect is preferable, "Abraham had taken another wife"; V. P. Hamilton, *The Book of Genesis, Chapters 18–50* (1995), 165.

[282] G. J. Wenham, *Genesis 16–50* (1994), 161.

[283] Heinz-Josef Fabry, "*śêbâ*," *TDOT* 14:79–85, esp. 82.

[284] C. W. Mitchell, *The Meaning of brk "to bless" in the Old Testament* (1987), 68–69.

The *tôlĕdôt* clauses in Genesis, as we have seen, introduce either genealogical lists with occasional brief explanatory glosses, or larger narrative expansions. The one in v. 12 introduces the descendants of Ishmael, and takes the standard form for those introducing genealogies (cf. 10:1; and see the introduction). The genealogy itself is segmented, with twelve sons, who are themselves twelve princes, indicating the greatness of the descendants of Ishmael (cf. 17:20).[285] The narrator appears to have had two separate lists originally, one naming the sons "by the order of their birth," and the other listing them "by their villages and encampments." The narrator has conflated the two, omitting the second and including only its heading "these are the sons of Ishmael . . . " (v. 16). Later we learn there was also a daughter, Mahalath, who became the wife of Esau (28:9).

Ishmael's obituary mirrors that of his father, yet dropping the idioms for exceptional long life and prosperity, "in a good old age, an old man and full of years," (v. 17, cf. vv. 7–8). We have seen "the way to Shur" as the southern route to Egypt from Beer-sheba west of Kadesh-barnea, where Ishmael's mother, Hagar, encountered the angel of Yahweh (16:7, and cf. 20:1; 1 Sam 15:7). The wilderness of Shur is the desert region in the northwestern Sinai bordering the Egyptian Delta (Exod 15:22), and Havilah was presumably a location in the northern Arabian peninsula.[286] The description "in the direction of Assyria" is sensible in light of references in later Assyrian documents.[287] The point, once again of course, is that Ishmael's descendants are far removed from Isaac's. Similarly, Yahweh has been faithful to fulfill his promises to Hagar and Abraham concerning Ishmael (16:12; 17:20). "If God did not overlook his promises to Ishmael, how much more certainly will he fulfill those guaranteed by oath to Abraham about Isaac and his descendants."[288]

BRIDGING THE HORIZONS: ABRAHAM, FATHER OF US ALL

We have seen that specific echoes of Abraham's faith, articulated in Gen 15:6, are heard elsewhere in Israel's Scriptures and in the New Testament (see Bridging Horizons at p. 157). Beyond the specifics of that observation, it should also be noted here, at the conclusion of the Abraham narrative, that the traditions contained in Gen 12–25 are unique in the extent of their influence throughout the remainder of the Old Testament, into the New Testament, the Mishnah and Talmud, and the Koran.[289]

---

[285] The inclusion of twelve princes implies a tribal confederation similar to Israel's twelve tribes, which is confirmed by the appearance of some of the names as eponyms for Arab tribes. On the names themselves and theories about historical origins, see Ernst Axel Knauf, "Ishmaelites," *ABD* 3:513–20, esp. 514–15.

[286] Walter W. Müller, "Havilah," *ABD* 3:82.

[287] E. A. Knauf, "Ishmaelites," 515.

[288] G. J. Wenham, *Genesis 16–50* (1994), 166.

[289] C. Westermann, *Genesis 12–36* (1985), 403–4; Ronald S. Hendel, *Remembering Abraham: Culture, Memory, and History in the Hebrew Bible* (New York: Oxford University Press, 2005), 41–43.

The multifarious interpretations of the Abraham narrative make it impossible to limit our understanding of the great patriarch to any one portrait. But the most enduring picture, one that continues to contribute to the taproot of Western culture to one degree or another, is the picture of Abraham, the Father of Faith. As "father," he certainly did become the progenitor of a great nation, traced ahead in the rest of the ancestral narratives, through his son Isaac and grandson Jacob, whose genealogy will be segmented to narrate the twelve tribes of Abraham's descendants. These children come to be the ancestral figureheads for the nation Israel, and the focus of the rest of the Hebrew Bible (Exod 1:1–7). But more than the biological father of Israel, Abraham also became the father of "faith." What has been constant throughout this Abraham narrative is the theme of his progressively deepening relationship with his revelatory God, his acceptance of God's covenant and promises, and his willingness to live his life with an eye to the future fulfillment and culmination of that faith. Surely the Apostle Paul has it right when he identifies Abraham as the "father of us all" (Rom 4:16, and cf. vv. 11–12). Abraham is more than the father of Jews, the father of Christians, or the father of Muslims. He is the father of all who believe.

GENESIS 25:19–34 JACOB AND ESAU

(25:19) These are the descendants of Isaac, Abraham's son: Abraham was the father of Isaac,

(25:20) and Isaac was forty years old when he married Rebekah, daughter of Bethuel the Aramean of Paddan-aram, sister of Laban the Aramean.

(25:21) Isaac prayed to the LORD for his wife, because she was barren; and the LORD granted his prayer, and his wife Rebekah conceived.

(25:22) The children struggled together within her; and she said, "If it is to be this way, why do I live?"[j] So she went to inquire of the LORD.

(25:23) And the LORD said to her, "Two nations are in your womb, and two peoples born of you shall be divided; the one shall be stronger than the other, the elder shall serve the younger."

(25:24) When her time to give birth was at hand, there were twins in her womb.

(25:25) The first came out red, all his body like a hairy mantle; so they named him Esau.

(25:26) Afterward his brother came out, with his hand gripping Esau's heel; so he was named Jacob. Isaac was sixty years old when she bore them.

(25:27) When the boys grew up, Esau was a skillful hunter, a man of the field, while Jacob was a quiet man, living in tents.

(25:28) Isaac loved Esau, because he was fond of game; but Rebekah loved Jacob.

(25:29) Once when Jacob was cooking a stew, Esau came in from the field, and he was famished.

---

[j] Syr: Meaning of Heb uncertain.

(25:30) Esau said to Jacob, "Let me eat some of that red stuff, for I am famished!" (Therefore he was called Edom.)

(25:31) Jacob said, "First sell me your birthright."

(25:32) Esau said, "I am about to die; of what use is a birthright to me?"

(25:33) Jacob said, "Swear to me first." So he swore to him, and sold his birthright to Jacob.

(25:34) Then Jacob gave Esau bread and lentil stew, and he ate and drank, and rose and went his way. Thus Esau despised his birthright.

OVERVIEW OF THE JACOB NARRATIVE, CHAPTERS 25–36[290]

The book of Genesis took a dramatic turn with Terah's genealogy at 11:27 (that is, with Terah's *tôlĕdôt*-structuring clause, "These are *the descendants of* Terah"). There the book transitioned from the Primeval History of Gen 1–11 to the ancestral narratives of Abraham, Isaac, Jacob, and Joseph (Gen 12–50). Cosmic beginnings and Israel's national beginnings are thus tied together theologically as one story in Genesis. The book is organized into eleven panels of material by the *tôlĕdôt* clauses to introduce either genealogies or narratives (see my introduction above). This ingenious macrostructure is made possible by five occurrences in the Primeval History (2:4; 5:1; 6:9; 10:1; 11:10), and five more in the ancestral narratives (11:27; 25:12; 25:19; 36:1; 37:1; plus an extra one in 36:9). In Terah's panel, Gen 12–25, God establishes a covenant with Israel's ancestor Abraham as a solution to humanity's sinful dilemma in Gen 1–11. By tying all of it together through the genealogies and *tôlĕdôt*-structuring device, Abraham and the nation Israel serve as the means of salvation for all humanity, indeed, for the entire cosmos. The unity created by the *tôlĕdôt*-clause creates a dialogue between the Primeval History (Gen 1–11) and the ancestral narratives (Gen 12–50), in which the former poses questions or problems, answered eventually by the latter.

The *tôlĕdôt*-clause of 25:19, "These are *the descendants of* Isaac," is the eighth *tôlĕdôt*-clause of the book. Like those introducing the Eden narrative (2:4a), the flood narrative (6:9a), and the Abraham narrative (11:27a), this one introduces an extended narrative (25:19–35:29) rather than a genealogical list.[291] As Terah's *tôlĕdôt*-clause is not really about Terah at all, but rather about his son Abraham, so Isaac's *tôlĕdôt*-clause is really about Jacob. This third overall section of Genesis, the Jacob narrative, is concluded by the ninth *tôlĕdôt*-clause, the descendants of Esau (36:1).

[290] The chapter and verse breaks in Gen 25 are unfortunate. For the sake of convenience, I will refer to the Jacob narrative (25:19–35:29) simply as Gen 25–35. The genealogical list of Esau (Gen 36) serves to conclude the Jacob narrative, just as Ishmael's list concluded the Abraham narrative (25:12–18), and thus occasionally I will treat the extended Jacob narrative simply as Gen 25–36.

[291] Those introducing lists are 5:1; 10:1; 11:10; 25:12; and 36:1.

The Jacob narrative, more so than any other portion of Genesis, is an artful chiasm or palistrophically structured unit (i.e., arranged in concentric rings, such as ABCDCBA), using a reversal in the plot line in which Jacob flees to the ancestral homeland in northern Mesopotamia, sojourns there, and eventually returns to the Promised Land.[292] The passage at the heart of the concentric structure is the birth of Jacob's sons (29:31–30:24), and especially the birth of Joseph to Rachel (30:22–24). The symmetry of structure is more convincing here than elsewhere in Genesis, and the original observations of Fokkelman and Fishbane especially have been followed by many subsequent commentators. I take the lexical and thematic associations contributing to the chiasm as undeniable.[293] However, I find less convincing the same organization in several other biblical units, and believe that the concentric pattern may even be secondary here except for the central chapters, Gen 29–31 (see below).

The literary structure may be relatively clear in the so-called Jacob Cycle, but scholarship is less settled on its origins and composition. It seems likely the final literary form of the text is a variation of a long and rich oral epic with roots in old Canaanite epic traditions.[294] Most assume a relatively modest amount of secondary priestly insertions into the older materials.[295] It is possible to interpret the three chief themes of the Jacob Narrative as birth, blessing, and land, corresponding to the threefold promises to Abraham, and each marked by a fundamental polarity.[296] Birth functions together with its opposite, barrenness, and creates the angst of Rebekah and Rachel and the interpersonal struggles between Rachel and Leah. Blessing also functions with its contrastive theme, the curse of nonblessing, which is

---

[292] Observed by numerous scholars, but see especially Michael A. Fishbane, *Biblical Text and Texture: A Literary Reading of Selected Texts* (Oxford: Oneworld, 1998), 40–58; adapted and repr. from *JJS* 26 (1975): 15–38; and simultaneously J. P. Fokkelman, *Narrative Art in Genesis: Specimens of Stylistic and Structural Analysis* (SSN 17; Assen: Van Gorcum, 1975), 86–241. See my comments on Gen 29–31 below for further observations about this structure.

[293] Gary A. Rendsburg, *The Redaction of Genesis* (Winona Lake, Ind.: Eisenbrauns, 1986), 56–59.

[294] Frank M. Cross, *Canaanite Myth and Hebrew Epic: Essays in the History of the Religion of Israel* (Cambridge, Mass.: Harvard University Press, 1973), 293; Ronald S. Hendel, *The Epic of the Patriarch: The Jacob Cycle and the Narrative Traditions of Canaan and Israel* (HSM 42; Atlanta: Scholar Press, 1987). The amount of secondary literature on the Jacob Cycle is enormous, and it is enough here to observe simply that most assume these accounts are among the earliest of the ancestral narratives of Genesis put into writing; Erhard Blum, *Die Komposition der Vätergeschichte* (WMANT 57; Neukirchen-Vluyn: Neukirchener Verlag, 1984), 202–3.

[295] David M. Carr, *Reading the Fractures of Genesis: Historical and Literary Approaches* (Louisville, Ky.: Westminster John Knox Press, 1996), 256–71. Yet even the priestly insertions may be organized concentrically, together with all the priestly materials in Gen 25–50; Peter Weimar, "Aufbau und Struktur der priesterschriftlichen Jakobsgeschichts-darstellung," *ZAW* 86 (1974): 174–203, esp. 200–3.

[296] For this assessment, see M. A. Fishbane, *Biblical Text and Texture* (1998), 60–61; repr. from *JJS* 26 (1975): 15–38.

at the heart of the actions and motive of the characters here, Rebekah, Isaac, Jacob, Esau, and even Laban. Finally, land functions here in the binary pair exile and homeland. Jacob flees the Promised Land, and stays in Paddan-aram until Rachel gives birth, after which he returns to his homeland. He encounters God going and coming, at the border both times (Gen 28 and 32), marking the transition from sacred to profane space.[297]

COMMENTS ON 25:19–34

The form of the *tôlĕdôt*-clause of 25:19, "These are the descendants of Isaac," is unique in that the object of the construction "descendants of X" is further qualified as "Abraham's son," before the narrative continues. The relationship with Abraham is further highlighted by the redundancy, "Abraham was the father of Isaac." The narrator clearly wanted to underline the biological lineage from Abraham to Isaac. Perhaps in light of the covenant promises and the long struggle of barrenness that preceded Isaac's birth, it seemed worthy of emphasis here at the beginning of Isaac's *tôlĕdôt*: he is Abraham's son!

The problem of the barren matriarch will not go away. Abraham fathered Isaac (v. 19b), and the obvious need and expectation is that Isaac will now father a son to carry on the promised line. But Isaac was forty years old (v. 20) and we learn in this text that it was only after twenty years of marriage before Rebekah conceived and bore children (v. 26). This is a compact and succinct narrative, but the reality of twenty years of barrenness is an excruciatingly long delay after Sarah's turmoil.

Yet unlike the Abraham narrative, this text moves quickly to resolution. The expression "Isaac *prayed* to the Lord . . . and the Lord *granted his prayer*" (v. 21) is the only place in the Bible the verbal root *ʿtr*, "pray, plead, entreat," is used in both active and passive voices in such a deliberate word play: Isaac *entreated* . . . and Yahweh *was entreated*.[298] I propose this turn-of-phrase denotes that Yahweh was emotively stirred into action, not against his will, but precisely to accomplish his will through the urging of his servant. As such, this passage contributes to the biblical understanding of intercessory prayer, in which the efficacy of intercession is linked to a deep-seated expectation on God's part. There is an openness in God to the intercession of his servant and a commensurate expectation that the intercession will have results.[299]

---

[297] Fishbane further explores how these three themes of the Jacob narrative are related not only to the Abraham narrative, but also to the Primeval History before it, and to much later covenantal texts, such as the Book of Deuteronomy; M. A. Fishbane, *Biblical Text and Texture* (1998), 61–62.

[298] Such metaphonic word play depends on the use of a verbal root in different derived stems, in this case Qal and Niphal; J. J. Glück, "Paronomasia in Biblical Literature," *Semitics* 1 (1970): 50–78, esp. 61–66; Jack M. Sasson, "Wordplay in the OT," *IDBSup* 968–70.

[299] Patrick D. Miller, Jr., *They Cried to the Lord: The Form and Theology of Biblical Prayer* (Minneapolis: Fortress Press, 1994), 275–76.

At breathtaking pace, this text moves through barrenness, answered prayer, conception, and troubled pregnancy (vv. 21–22). The assertion "the children struggled together within her" assumes the presence of twins, which is not actually stated until their birth (v. 24). The pregnancy is so difficult Rebekah questions whether she will survive, although the word for "life" appears to have dropped from the Hebrew text (see NRSV note). She too prays and Yahweh responds with poetic assurances of both good news and bad news: she is carrying two nations but the two will have conflict (v. 23). The younger will be stronger than the elder, reflecting the common Old Testament pattern of a younger son displacing the firstborn (cf. 1 Chr 5:1–2; see Joseph and Reuben, Ephraim and Manasseh, Moses and Aaron, David and Eliab, Solomon and Adonijah, and perhaps even Cain and Abel).[300] Thus Jacob will prevail over Esau, anticipating Israel's domination of Edom in early Israel's history.[301]

When the twins are born, they are given names that serve as proleptic epithets, revealing their character and anticipating their roles in the family and national history (vv. 25–26).[302] The word plays on the names "Jacob" and "Esau" are complex, relying on physical features, personality traits, and in Esau's case, two variants of his name, Esau/Edom.[303] In true Hebrew narrative fashion, the names reflect the character of each boy, and the die is cast for the rest of the Jacob narrative.

Their differences at birth continue into their young adulthood (vv. 27–28). Esau was an outdoorsman, Jacob a homebody, although "living in tents" probably implies no more than a fondness for what might be thought of as a more civilized lifestyle.[304] Isaac loved Esau because of the fruits of his hunting prowess, while Rebekah preferred Jacob. The narrator omits Rebekah's motives for loving Jacob more. The parental favoritism shown to the boys is not condemned in the text, although it presents a problem that is gradually critiqued in the extended narrative by the family

---

[300] Israel as Yahweh's firstborn received a position of honor and privilege, although youngest and least among the nations (Exod 4:22; Jer 31:9).

[301] There may also be several lexical resonances with the names "Jacob" and "Esau" in the divine proclamation; Gordon J. Wenham, *Genesis 16–50* (WBC 2; Dallas, Tex.: Word Books, 1994), 176.

[302] Meir Sternberg, *The Poetics of Biblical Narrative: Ideological Literature and the Drama of Reading* (Indiana Studies in Biblical Literature; Bloomington: Indiana University Press, 1985), 328–31; Stanley Gevirtz, "Of Patriarchs and Puns: Joseph at the Fountain, Jacob at the Ford," *HUCA* 46 (1975): 33–54, esp. 33–34.

[303] For specifics, see Kenneth A. Mathews, *Genesis 11:27–50:26* (NAC 1B; Nashville: Broadman & Holman Publishers, 2005), 388–90, and on naming in the Hebrew Scriptures and the ancient Near East generally, Bill T. Arnold, "Word Play and Characterization in Daniel 1," in *Puns and Pundits: Word Play in the Hebrew Bible and Ancient Near Eastern Literature*, ed. Scott B. Noegel (Bethesda, Md.: CDL Press, 2000), 231–48, esp. 243–46.

[304] Claus Westermann, *Genesis 12–36: A Commentary* (Minneapolis: Augsburg Pub. House, 1985), 414–15. The polarity between nature and culture, in which culture is valued and nature is seen as unstable, is a common theme in the ancient world. For parallels between Jacob/Esau and Gilgamesh/Enkidu, see R. S. Hendel, *The Epic of the Patriarch* (1987), 116–21,

discord resulting from such partiality. The love expressed to each does not imply the other was unloved, but connotes the imbalance of preferential treatment.[305]

The differences between the twins come immediately to the foreground when Jacob's skill as a cook presents a temptation too great for Esau, the ravenous hunter (v. 29). Deliberate and artful word plays are used again, as the narrator associates the meaty red stew (*ʾādōm*) with Esau's alternate name, Edom (*ʾĕdôm*, v. 30). Esau's request is somewhat obscured by NRSV's "Let me eat some of that red stuff," because of a reduplication of "red stuff" in the original; lit. "the red stew, this red stew." The effect, combined with a rare word for "swallow," gives the impression of an uncouth and abrasive request: "Let me chow-down some of the red – that red stuff there!"[306] Without delay, Jacob moves to strike a deal (vv. 31–34). The Israelite reader would see nothing wrong with this proposal, and would instead appreciate the wiser and more cunning Jacob over the shortsighted Esau. The "right of firstborn" (*bĕkōrâ*) was the privilege of receiving a double portion of inheritance (Deut 21:15–17), and this episode shows that such a right was transferable, although Esau's actual rank and position in the family was not forfeited by his decision (cf. 1 Chr 5:1–2).[307] Esau sealed the deal with a verbal oath, the elocution of which made the trade irrevocable. The closing clause, "Esau despised his birthright," solidifies him in the narrative as the thoughtless and coarse one, while Jacob is shrewd and calculating. Jacob's and Esau's birth-names already appear appropriate.

GENESIS 26:1–35 ISAAC THE PATRIARCH

(26:1) Now there was a famine in the land, besides the former famine that had occurred in the days of Abraham. And Isaac went to Gerar, to King Abimelech of the Philistines.

(26:2) The LORD appeared to Isaac and said, "Do not go down to Egypt; settle in the land that I shall show you.

(26:3) Reside in this land as an alien, and I will be with you, and will bless you; for to you and to your descendants I will give all these lands, and I will fulfill the oath that I swore to your father Abraham.

(26:4) I will make your offspring as numerous as the stars of heaven, and will give to your offspring all these lands; and all the nations of the earth shall gain blessing for themselves through your offspring,

---

[305] Elsewhere in the Hebrew Bible, Edom is distinguished from the other transjordanian neighbors, Ammon and Moab, as closer in kin to Israel (Deut 23:8, cf. Gen 19:37–38). The prophet Malachi developed this further (Mal 1:2–3), and for the New Testament appropriation of this theme, see Victor P. Hamilton, *The Book of Genesis, Chapters 18–50* (NICOT; Grand Rapids, Mich.: Eerdmans, 1995), 187–88.

[306] John Skinner, *A Critical and Exegetical Commentary on Genesis* (ICC 1; New York: Scribner, 1910), 361–62.

[307] Matitiahu Tsevat, "*bĕkôr*," *TDOT* 2:121–127, esp. 126; Bill T. Arnold, "*bkr*," *NIDOTTE* 1:658–59.

(26:5)   because Abraham obeyed my voice and kept my charge, my commandments, my statutes, and my laws."

(26:6)   So Isaac settled in Gerar.

(26:7)   When the men of the place asked him about his wife, he said, "She is my
sister"; for he was afraid to say, "My wife," thinking, "or else the men of
the place might kill me for the sake of Rebekah, because she is attractive
in appearance."

(26:8)   When Isaac had been there a long time, King Abimelech of the Philistines
looked out of a window and saw him fondling his wife Rebekah.

(26:9)   So Abimelech called for Isaac, and said, "So she is your wife! Why then did
you say, 'She is my sister'?" Isaac said to him, "Because I thought I might
die because of her."

(26:10) Abimelech said, "What is this you have done to us? One of the people
might easily have lain with your wife, and you would have brought guilt
upon us."

(26:11) So Abimelech warned all the people, saying, "Whoever touches this man
or his wife shall be put to death."

(26:12) Isaac sowed seed in that land, and in the same year reaped a hundredfold.
The LORD blessed him,

(26:13) and the man became rich; he prospered more and more until he became
very wealthy.

(26:14) He had possessions of flocks and herds, and a great household, so that the
Philistines envied him.

(26:15) (Now the Philistines had stopped up and filled with earth all the wells that
his father's servants had dug in the days of his father Abraham.)

(26:16) And Abimelech said to Isaac, "Go away from us; you have become too
powerful for us."

(26:17) So Isaac departed from there and camped in the valley of Gerar and settled
there.

(26:18) Isaac dug again the wells of water that had been dug in the days of his
father Abraham; for the Philistines had stopped them up after the death
of Abraham; and he gave them the names that his father had given them.

(26:19) But when Isaac's servants dug in the valley and found there a well of spring
water,

(26:20) the herders of Gerar quarreled with Isaac's herders, saying, "The water is
ours." So he called the well Esek,[k] because they contended with him.

(26:21) Then they dug another well, and they quarreled over that one also; so he
called it Sitnah.[l]

(26:22) He moved from there and dug another well, and they did not quarrel over
it; so he called it Rehoboth,[m] saying, "Now the LORD has made room for
us, and we shall be fruitful in the land."

---

[k] That is *Contention*
[l] That is *Enmity*
[m] That is *Broad places* or *Room*

(26:23) From there he went up to Beer-sheba.

(26:24) And that very night the LORD appeared to him and said, "I am the God of your father Abraham; do not be afraid, for I am with you and will bless you and make your offspring numerous for my servant Abraham's sake."

(26:25) So he built an altar there, called on the name of the LORD, and pitched his tent there. And there Isaac's servants dug a well.

(26:26) Then Abimelech went to him from Gerar, with Ahuzzath his adviser and Phicol the commander of his army.

(26:27) Isaac said to them, "Why have you come to me, seeing that you hate me and have sent me away from you?"

(26:28) They said, "We see plainly that the LORD has been with you; so we say, let there be an oath between you and us, and let us make a covenant with you

(26:29) so that you will do us no harm, just as we have not touched you and have done to you nothing but good and have sent you away in peace. You are now the blessed of the LORD."

(26:30) So he made them a feast, and they ate and drank.

(26:31) In the morning they rose early and exchanged oaths; and Isaac set them on their way, and they departed from him in peace.

(26:32) That same day Isaac's servants came and told him about the well that they had dug, and said to him, "We have found water!"

(26:33) He called it Shibah;[n] therefore the name of the city is Beer-sheba to this day.

(26:34) When Esau was forty years old, he married Judith daughter of Beeri the Hittite, and Basemath daughter of Elon the Hittite;

(26:35) and they made life bitter for Isaac and Rebekah.

*T*his is Isaac's chapter. After the twins are born in 25:24–26, the ancestral narratives focus almost immediately upon the relationship of Jacob and Esau, and Jacob's role as a patriarch. Isaac plays a secondary role in the next chapter, mistakenly blessing Jacob rather than Esau, and then he practically disappears until his death in 35:28–29. Yet in Gen 26, the twins make no appearance until Esau's Hittite wives are mentioned in the last verses (vv. 34–35). This is the sole chapter devoted exclusively to Isaac as patriarch.

In fact, this text is devoted to making Isaac look as much like Abraham as possible. Echoes and direct allusions to the Abraham narrative permeate the whole, inviting the reader to relive many of those episodes through Abraham's son. The effect is to confirm Isaac as the true heir of Abraham's covenant blessing, the legitimate successor in the ancestral line and therefore the true patriarch of Israel.[308] The following list of common themes illustrates the intentional literary connection between Gen 26 and the Abraham narrative.

---

[n] A word resembling the word for *oath*

[308] Most of those echoes are to Yahwistic portions of Gen 12–25, leading most source critics to take Gen 26 as Yahwistic as well.

	Isaac	Abraham
Famine	26:1	12:10
Sojourn in Gerar	26:1,6	20:1
"Appearance" theophany	26:2,24	12:7; 17:1; 18:1
Journey to unspecified destination,		
"... the land that I will show you. .."	26:2	12:1
Promises of land and seed (general)	26:3-5,24	12:1-3; 13:14-17; 15:1-6;
		15:7-16; 17:1-8; 22:16-18
Covenant promises (specific)		
– blessing	26:3,24	12:2; 22:17
– seed like the stars	26:4	15:5; 22:17
– means of blessing for the nations	26:4	12:3; 22:18
Wife-sister ploy	26:6-11	12:11-16; 20:1-16
Acquisition of wealth	26:12-13	13:2; 24:35
Conflict with Philistines over water rights	26:14-33	22:25-32
New altar and public worship	26:25	12:8; 13:4; 21:33
Tent-dwelling	26:25	12:8; 13:18; 18:1-10
Digging and naming wells	26:18-33	21:25,30
Covenant with Abimelech	26:28-31	21:27-32
Naming of Beer-sheba	26:33	21:31

As the list illustrates, the general promises of land and seed have three specific reflexes in this chapter as sub-categories of the covenant promises: God will bless Isaac, his seed will become like the stars of heaven, and Isaac will become a means of blessing for the nations. Gen 26 is something of a compendium of patriarchal experiences, repeating for Isaac in rapid succession the events that made Abraham the great patriarch that he is. That Isaac is made to look so much like Abraham is a tribute to the importance of his father as the first patriarch of Israel.

A new topic is introduced when another famine occurs in the land (v. 1). Like his father Abraham, Isaac is forced to sojourn in search of water on the fringes of the Promised Land, which was proving difficult to occupy because of lack of water (cf. 12:10).[309] The modern identification of the city of Gerar appears now to have been settled as Tel Haror in the western Negeb, but the "valley of Gerar" (v. 17) implies also the name for an area or region (cf. 2 Chr 14:13–14).[310] And again, like his father Abraham, Isaac encounters there a king with a Semitic name, Abimelech

---

[309] The expression, "now there was a famine in the land," is an embedded intertextual comparison to 12:10, implying the narrator has used it as a signifier pointing the reader to 12:10–22 as a specific intertext; Kirsten Nielsen, "Intertextuality and the Hebrew Bible," in *Congress Volume, Oslo 1998*, eds. André Lemaire and Magne Sæbø (VTSup 80; Leiden: Brill, 2000), 17–31, esp. 18–19; see also John Barton, "Intertextuality and the 'Final Form' of the Text," in the same volume (pages 33–37).

[310] Anson F. Rainey and R. S. Notley, *The Sacred Bridge: Carta's Atlas of the Biblical World* (Jerusalem: Carta, 2006), 114; Eliezer D. Oren, "Gerar," *ABD* 2:989–91; Eliezer D. Oren, "Haror, Tel," *OEANE* 2:474–76.

(20:1–18; 21:22–34). The reference to "Philistines" in Gerar is problematic because the Philistines of later biblical times certainly did not occupy any portion of this region during any purported ancestral period. Their appearance here has at times been taken as a simple historical anachronism, assuming they are indeed the same people-group and that the narrator simply has them in the wrong time period, suggesting perhaps this is evidence of a late date of composition.[311] But the narrator understands the many dramatic differences between the early Philistines of Gerar and the later Philistines, and it seems more likely that such references are proleptical, referring to the general region that would one day become the land of the Philistines (see commentary at 21:32).

And so in a time of famine, when Isaac is vulnerable as a sojourner in another's territory, Yahweh "appeared" to him as he had to Abraham. Yahweh's appearances to Abraham occurred at critical junctures of his faith journey (12:7; 17:1; 18:1). The verb "appeared" is a causative-reflexive term for "become visible" or "make oneself visible" (Niphal of *r'h*, "to see") and is used as a technical term for divine revelation in the ancestral narratives (see Closer Look "Divine Revelation in the Hebrew Scriptures" at p. 135). God thus causes himself to be seen, pulling back the curtain on himself as it were, allowing himself – even presenting himself – in theophanic certainty. What one *sees* in such revelatory appearances of divine self-disclosure is not the issue, but rather what one *hears*. In most cases, the substance of the appearance or revelation is contained in a speech, as here where the words "and said" mark the beginning of the revelation itself. Usually the revelation moves immediately from "Yahweh/God *appeared*" to a speech introducing divine promises (12:7) or announcing self-disclosure (17:1).

In this case, the divine revelation to Isaac reiterates the covenant promises to Abraham, made afresh for Isaac personally (vv. 2–5). Isaac is the heir to his father's covenant promises, including of course the central promises of "seed" (*zera'*, NRSV's "descendants" in v. 3 but "offspring" elsewhere) and "land" (*'ereṣ*, here plural, "lands," for the first time).[312] As before Yahweh promises increased offspring, like the stars of heaven, and blessings for all nations through Isaac's seed.[313] Yahweh refers to the oath he swore to father Abraham (v. 3), which is almost certainly an allusion to 22:16 when Abraham passed his test by his willingness to sacrifice Isaac. One new feature in the promises is the assurance of God's protecting presence

[311] Israel Finkelstein, "The Philistines in the Bible: A Late-Monarchic Perspective," *JSOT* 27/2 (2002): 131–67, esp. 152–54.

[312] The plural may broaden the promise to include the southern stretches of territory, especially perhaps Gerar or Philistia themselves; G. J. Wenham, *Genesis 16–50* (1994), 189.

[313] As at 22:18, the nations of the earth "gain blessing for themselves" (v. 4), employing the Hithpael of "bless" instead of the Niphal used earlier (12:3; 18:18). I am assuming no measurable distinction between their meanings; Bruce K. Waltke and Michael P. O'Connor, *An Introduction to Biblical Hebrew Syntax* (Winona Lake, Ind.: Eisenbrauns, 1990), 395.

(v. 3): "I will be with you." Since ancients typically associated a certain deity with a specific locale, and since Isaac had relocated because of famine to the fringes of the Promised Land, he needed assurances that Yahweh would be with him wherever he went, even while residing as an alien in Gerar.

These promises are sure because Abraham obeyed Yahweh, keeping his commandments, statutes, and laws (v. 5).[314] Later Israelite readers would no doubt have heard in these words the specifics of the Mosaic law, the Torah, as given at Mount Sinai. But the reader is also to assume that Abraham's faith and obedience were so exemplary that he kept Yahweh's mandate without needing the specifics of the complete revelation. Abraham's faith is the fountain, from which flows the covenant promises to his offspring. For the first time in the ancestral narratives, those covenant promises must be handed down to the next generation in a step toward their fulfillment. The question arises, will Isaac be up to the challenge? Will his obedience match that of his father's?

The text moves quickly to an answer. The promises in vv. 2–5 were prefaced with three divine directives: "Do not go down to Egypt, . . . settle in the land, . . . reside in this land. . . . " The simplicity of v. 6 – only three words in Hebrew – make the point eloquently: "So Isaac settled in Gerar."[315] This is Isaac's fulcrum moment. Abraham had been called upon twice to obey Yahweh's voice in radical abandonment, and in both instances, the simplicity of "so Abram went," or "so Abraham rose early in the morning . . . and went," confirmed his character and moved his journey with God forward (12:4; 22:3). Now is Isaac's time. His obedience proves Isaac as the legitimate successor of father Abraham and the worthy recipient of the covenant promises.

Once again, fear drives the patriarch to deceive his host about the true identity of his wife (vv. 7–11). The reader is aware that Rebekah is Isaac's cousin (Closer Look "Endogamy in Ancient Israel" at p. 219), whereas Sarah was Abraham's half-sister (20:12). Like Abraham before him, Isaac benefits from the ruse, when disaster is narrowly averted and the matriarch's honor preserved (12:10–20; 20:1–28).[316] The exact nature of Isaac's "fondling" of Rebekah is unclear, but the text uses a word play on Isaac's name to denote sexual play, which happens to work well in a similar English idiom: Isaac was "fooling around" with Rebekah (v. 8).[317] Whatever the

---

[314] Phraseology commonly cited as Deuteronomistic; Bruce Vawter, *On Genesis: A New Reading* (Garden City, N.Y.: Doubleday, 1977), 291. But this list of "commandments, statutes, and laws" is more priestly than deuteronomistic; G. J. Wenham, *Genesis 16–50* (1994), 190.

[315] In fact, the promises after the directives could be translated as purpose clauses, "Do not go down, but settle and reside here, . . . *in order that* I might be with you, and bless you, . . . " Bill T. Arnold and John H. Choi, *A Guide to Biblical Hebrew Syntax* (Cambridge: Cambridge University Press, 2003), 91–92. Thus the promises are conditioned on Isaac's obedience.

[316] On the "Matriarch in Danger" literary topos, see commentary at 12:10–20.

[317] The sound play is unmistakable in the original: *yiṣḥāq mĕṣaḥēq*, Abimelech saw *Isaac fondling* his wife. Rüdiger Bartelmus, "*ṣāḥaq/śāḥaq*," *TDOT* 14:58–72, esp. 68. Hamilton

precise meaning, the truth was exposed. During the ensuing confrontation, we learn that no one laid a hand on Rebekah, so that our matriarch's honor is ensured and Abimelech warns all under his charge to leave Isaac and his family alone (vv. 9–11).

The next portion of the text continues the comparison between Isaac and Abraham by narrating the conflict with the Philistines of Gerar over water rights in the Negeb (vv. 12–33, cf. 21:22–34). As we have seen, this is the setting for several other comparisons between Isaac and Abraham, including another revelatory theophany, the acquisition of great wealth, altar-building, well-digging, covenant-making, and the naming of Beer-sheba. In all these ways, Isaac is his father's son!

The conflict arises due to the drought causing the famine (v. 1) combined with Isaac's dramatic success and wealth (vv. 12–14). Remarkably, Isaac reaps a hundredfold during a famine, a sign of Yahweh's blessing indeed! Isaac does not purchase agricultural property but grows prosperous as a small-cattle pastoralist, who was given permission to invest in the local agricultural economy. But prosperity leads to jealousy. The word order of NRSV's parenthetical v. 15 emphasizes the wells that Abraham's servants had built: "Now as for the wells, . . . the Philistines had stopped them up. . . . "[318] Their motive for doing so, especially during a time of drought, is presumably to be found in their jealousy (v. 14). More fundamentally, such strategies were employed by mobile pastoralists or seminomads during land disputes, when one group would expel another from a certain territory by stopping up the wells while the offended party needed to dig out the wells again in order to find sustenance.[319] Ultimately, Isaac's prosperity was too much for the Gerarites. As Abram and Lot were forced to separate because of their great individual wealth, so now Isaac is forced to relocate (v. 16, cf. 13:6–7).

Adequate water supply was a perennial problem in the southern reaches of the Promised Land. The most common sources were running springs, wells, and cisterns or reservoirs, in descending order of preference.[320] In a region where there are almost no rivers and streams, the purity and convenience of flowing spring water was optimal. Short of a spring, the most dependable option was well water drawn from a subterranean source, while cisterns, of course, were useless in times of prolonged drought. This text reflects the territory disputes between Isaac and the Gerarites and local herders loosely associated with Gerar. Isaac was forced to relocate, and find new water supplies in the unknown region "the valley of Gerar" (v. 17). Verse 18 is a general statement, preparing for the re-digging and re-naming of several wells, which had been dug and named earlier by Abraham, but which now need to be reclaimed from the Philistines of Gerar.

cleverly explains it as "Isaac was 'Isaacing' with Rebekah"; V. P. Hamilton, *The Book of Genesis, Chapters 18–50* (1995), 190, n. 9.

[318] An objective *casus pendens*; Paul Joüon and Takamitsu Muraoka, *A Grammar of Biblical Hebrew* (SubBi 14; Roma: Editrice Pontificio Istituto Biblico, 1993), 586–87.

[319] C. Westermann, *Genesis 12–36* (1985), 426.

[320] John P. Oleson, "Water Works," *ABD* 6:883–93, esp. 884–88.

Isaac's servants found the most desirable source of water available, outside an actual perennial stream; that is, "a well of spring water" (v. 19, lit. "a well of living water"). Ownership of the spring was immediately contested by the local herders, so Isaac turned it over to them and named it Esek ("Contention," see NRSV note). A second well continued to cause animosity between them, and so it was turned over and named Sitnah ("Enmity," see NRSV note). When he finally came to a more remote region, where the herders did not contest their well, Isaac called it Rehoboth ("Broad Places," see NRSV note). Successful wells remained in use over many centuries, and these narratives trace their etiological origins to Israel's earliest ancestors.

From Rehoboth, Isaac moved on to a familiar site, which presumably also needed renaming, Beer-sheba (v. 23, cf. v. 33, and cf. 21:31). There Isaac received a second theophany, with the familiar words, "the LORD appeared to him and said" (see commentary at v. 2 above). Most such revelatory speeches introduce divine promises (12:7) or announce self-disclosure ("I am. . . . " statements, 17:1). This one combines the two (v. 24). First, "I am the God of your father Abraham" is an important self-disclosure for Isaac, confirming that he is indeed the heir to the covenant promises.[321] Isaac is in right relationship with God and in the right lineage from Abraham. Second, the covenant promises are repeated for Isaac, perhaps reflecting his need to be assured that all is well in light of his recent struggles with the surrounding inhabitants of the Promised Land. Since being banished from Gerar itself (v. 16), Isaac has struggled to find space and adequate provisions for his family, flocks and herds. His relationship with the Gerarites continued to hold great danger, as we shall soon see (vv. 26–31).

After the theophany, Isaac looks quite patriarchal. He builds an altar, invokes the name of Yahweh in worship, pitches his tent, and digs a well (v. 25). The patriarchs never use existing cult sites, preferring instead to build new altars or reuse ones they themselves built previously (13:4). Typically, the actions of (1) moving the tent, (2) building an altar, and (3) invoking the name of Yahweh, occur together as features of a formal move from one temporary nomadic residence to another (12:7–8; and cf. 13:4, 18; 35:1). Calling upon Yahweh's name is most likely a reference to formal, public worship (4:26; 13:4), and is part of setting up camp in a new location, using Yahweh-worship to make oneself at home. In such a way, the patriarch stakes out Yahweh-worship for himself and his family at Beer-sheba.

The final scene of the chapter is a threatening visit from King Abimelech, and two of his top officers (vv. 26–33). The failure of the Gerarites to contest ownership of the third well, Rehoboth ("Broad Places"), is likely because Isaac had by that point moved out of their territory and was considered now beyond their boundaries or territorial sphere. Isaac has now moved even beyond Rehoboth to Beer-sheba, which he would have considered uncontested territory, and his question to Abimelech and

---

[321] Another revelatory predicate nominative of identification, cf. 15:1; 15:7; 17:1; B. T. Arnold and J. H. Choi, *A Guide to Biblical Hebrew Syntax* (2003), 6.

his entourage seems reasonable (v. 27): Why now, after driving me out of your jurisdiction, have you come out to me in my bailiwick?[322] But Isaac is in a position of strength. King Abimelech acknowledges the blessing of Yahweh as the source of Isaac's prosperity, and wishes only for peace in the form of a covenant, such as the one he made with Abraham (vv. 28–29, cf. 21:25–34). The NRSV misses an interesting purpose clause at v. 28, which is more likely, "let there be an oath between you and us, *in order that* we may make a covenant with you."[323] Accordingly, Isaac prepared a meal for Abimelech and his entourage that evening as part of the covenant agreement (v. 30). Common meals were occasionally associated with sealing a pact of nonaggression, as later between Jacob and Laban (31:43–54, and cf. 18:12; 24:11). As we have seen, rising early in the morning connotes resolve to take action without delay (19:27; 21:14; 22:3, etc.).[324] So Isaac and Abimelech rose early the next morning to exchange covenant oaths and agree to part ways peaceably (v. 31).

Ironically, on the very day Abimelech leaves Isaac to the dry southern portions of the Promised Land, Isaac's servants succeed in reaching well water (vv. 32–33). The occasion merits yet another naming, so that Isaac named the place Shibah ("Oath," see NRSV footnote) or Beer-sheba, providing yet another way in which Isaac is like his father Abraham, who named Beer-sheba at 21:33. Beer-sheba's name is still in use "to this day" so that the etiology explains for the narrator his current realities by means of an event from the distant past. Whether "to this day" is part of a later Deuteronomistic redaction remains to be determined, but it at least reflects the eyewitness perspective of someone living in the land some considerable amount of time after the events.[325]

The coda on Esau's Hittite wives prepares the reader for Rebekah's proposal to find a suitable wife for Jacob (vv. 34–35, cf. 27:46). Similarly, the genealogy of Rebekah (22:20–24) had prepared for the search for a suitable wife for Isaac (Gen 24), illustrating that closing summary statements in Genesis often prepare for subsequent narratives. Esau's Hittite wives made life bitter for his parents because of the preference for endogamous marriages in that ancient society (Closer Look "Endogamy in Ancient Israel" at p. 219).

GENESIS 27:1–46 JACOB STEALS ESAU'S BLESSING

(27:1) When Isaac was old and his eyes were dim so that he could not see, he called his elder son Esau and said to him, "My son"; and he answered, "Here I am."

(27:2) He said, "See, I am old; I do not know the day of my death.

---

[322] Herbert C. Brichto, *The Names of God: Poetic Readings in Biblical Beginnings* (New York: Oxford University Press, 1998), 372–73.

[323] B. T. Arnold and J. H. Choi, *A Guide to Biblical Hebrew Syntax* (2003), 92.

[324] Rüdiger Bartelmus, "*škm*," *TDOT* 14:681–88, esp. 687–88.

[325] Jeffrey C. Geoghegan, "Additional Evidence for a Deuteronomistic Redaction of the 'Tetrateuch,'" *CBQ* 67/3 (2005): 405–21, esp. 410–11 for the six occurrences in Genesis.

(27:3) Now then, take your weapons, your quiver and your bow, and go out to the field, and hunt game for me.

(27:4) Then prepare for me savory food, such as I like, and bring it to me to eat, so that I may bless you before I die."

(27:5) Now Rebekah was listening when Isaac spoke to his son Esau. So when Esau went to the field to hunt for game and bring it,

(27:6) Rebekah said to her son Jacob, "I heard your father say to your brother Esau,

(27:7) 'Bring me game, and prepare for me savory food to eat, that I may bless you before the LORD before I die.'

(27:8) Now therefore, my son, obey my word as I command you.

(27:9) Go to the flock, and get me two choice kids, so that I may prepare from them savory food for your father, such as he likes;

(27:10) and you shall take it to your father to eat, so that he may bless you before he dies."

(27:11) But Jacob said to his mother Rebekah, "Look, my brother Esau is a hairy man, and I am a man of smooth skin.

(27:12) Perhaps my father will feel me, and I shall seem to be mocking him, and bring a curse on myself and not a blessing."

(27:13) His mother said to him, "Let your curse be on me, my son; only obey my word, and go, get them for me."

(27:14) So he went and got them and brought them to his mother; and his mother prepared savory food, such as his father loved.

(27:15) Then Rebekah took the best garments of her elder son Esau, which were with her in the house, and put them on her younger son Jacob;

(27:16) and she put the skins of the kids on his hands and on the smooth part of his neck.

(27:17) Then she handed the savory food, and the bread that she had prepared, to her son Jacob.

(27:18) So he went in to his father, and said, "My father"; and he said, "Here I am; who are you, my son?"

(27:19) Jacob said to his father, "I am Esau your firstborn. I have done as you told me; now sit up and eat of my game, so that you may bless me."

(27:20) But Isaac said to his son, "How is it that you have found it so quickly, my son?" He answered, "Because the LORD your God granted me success."

(27:21) Then Isaac said to Jacob, "Come near, that I may feel you, my son, to know whether you are really my son Esau or not."

(27:22) So Jacob went up to his father Isaac, who felt him and said, "The voice is Jacob's voice, but the hands are the hands of Esau."

(27:23) He did not recognize him, because his hands were hairy like his brother Esau's hands; so he blessed him.

(27:24) He said, "Are you really my son Esau?" He answered, "I am."

(27:25) Then he said, "Bring it to me, that I may eat of my son's game and bless you." So he brought it to him, and he ate; and he brought him wine, and he drank.
(27:26) Then his father Isaac said to him, "Come near and kiss me, my son."
(27:27) So he came near and kissed him; and he smelled the smell of his garments, and blessed him, and said, "Ah, the smell of my son is like the smell of a field that the LORD has blessed.
(27:28) May God give you of the dew of heaven, and of the fatness of the earth, and plenty of grain and wine.
(27:29) Let peoples serve you, and nations bow down to you. Be lord over your brothers, and may your mother's sons bow down to you. Cursed be everyone who curses you, and blessed be everyone who blesses you!"
(27:30) As soon as Isaac had finished blessing Jacob, when Jacob had scarcely gone out from the presence of his father Isaac, his brother Esau came in from his hunting.
(27:31) He also prepared savory food, and brought it to his father. And he said to his father, "Let my father sit up and eat of his son's game, so that you may bless me."
(27:32) His father Isaac said to him, "Who are you?" He answered, "I am your firstborn son, Esau."
(27:33) Then Isaac trembled violently, and said, "Who was it then that hunted game and brought it to me, and I ate it all before you came, and I have blessed him? – yes, and blessed he shall be!"
(27:34) When Esau heard his father's words, he cried out with an exceedingly great and bitter cry, and said to his father, "Bless me, me also, father!"
(27:35) But he said, "Your brother came deceitfully, and he has taken away your blessing."
(27:36) Esau said, "Is he not rightly named Jacob? For he has supplanted me these two times. He took away my birthright; and look, now he has taken away my blessing." Then he said, "Have you not reserved a blessing for me?"
(27:37) Isaac answered Esau, "I have already made him your lord, and I have given him all his brothers as servants, and with grain and wine I have sustained him. What then can I do for you, my son?"
(27:38) Esau said to his father, "Have you only one blessing, father? Bless me, me also, father!" And Esau lifted up his voice and wept.
(27:39) Then his father Isaac answered him: "See, away from[o] the fatness of the earth shall your home be, and away from[p] the dew of heaven on high.
(27:40) By your sword you shall live, and you shall serve your brother; but when you break loose,[q] you shall break his yoke from your neck."

[o] Or *See, of*
[p] Or *and of*
[q] Meaning of Heb uncertain.

(27:41) Now Esau hated Jacob because of the blessing with which his father had blessed him, and Esau said to himself, "The days of mourning for my father are approaching; then I will kill my brother Jacob."

(27:42) But the words of her elder son Esau were told to Rebekah; so she sent and called her younger son Jacob and said to him, "Your brother Esau is consoling himself by planning to kill you.

(27:43) Now therefore, my son, obey my voice; flee at once to my brother Laban in Haran,

(27:44) and stay with him a while, until your brother's fury turns away –

(27:45) until your brother's anger against you turns away, and he forgets what you have done to him; then I will send, and bring you back from there. Why should I lose both of you in one day?"

(27:46) Then Rebekah said to Isaac, "I am weary of my life because of the Hittite women. If Jacob marries one of the Hittite women such as these, one of the women of the land, what good will my life be to me?"

*H*aving shown Isaac to be a worthy patriarch and child of the covenant promises (Gen 26), the narrative now begins to focus immediately on the question of succession. The theme of the presumed heir, so prevalent in the Abraham narrative continues here. Isaac was the child of promise rather than Ishmael or Abraham's other children. And so, which of Isaac's twins would be heir to the covenant promises? The narrator has reported the differences in Esau's and Jacob's personalities (25:23–27), the problematic favoritism of their parents (25:28), and the strife between them (25:29–34). Jacob has already taken Esau's birthright. In this chapter, the parental favoritism and family dysfunction will result in cheating Esau of his blessing as well. Full-fledged animosity between the brothers is the outcome.

This text illustrates a type of repetition popular in Hebrew narrative, in which a speech is delivered to one character, and then repeated almost verbatim to a second character, and at times repeated yet again to other characters.[326] Rebekah overhears Isaac planning to bless Esau, she repeats the plan to Jacob, and the narrator repeats the plan again in the enactment of it (vv. 3–4, 7, 9–10, 31, 33). Such repetition emphasizes the key messages of a text, and in this case brings to focus the ancient concept of the testamental blessing, a blessing at or near the end of the patriarch's life. In Hebrew thought, there is an associative power in the spoken word, especially in such a formal benedictory setting. Once spoken, the word of blessing cannot be undone. There is a perceived finality especially in deathbed blessings. In this case, the father regrets having blessed the wrong son, but he cannot reverse or undo what has been said (v. 33): "... yes, and blessed he shall be!" Similarly, the idea of

---

[326] See the commentary at 24:34–49; M. Sternberg, *The Poetics of Biblical Narrative* (1985), 365–440; Adele Berlin, *Poetics and Interpretation of Biblical Narrative* (Bible and Literature Series 9; Sheffield: Almond Press, 1983), 72–80; Robert Alter, *The Art of Biblical Narrative* (New York: Basic Books, 1981), 47–62.

pronouncing such a blessing in the strength of a meal prepared by the recipient of that blessing may be particularly suitable and meaningful.[327]

Besides emphasizing the key messages of a text, such repetition also suggests an oral history behind the text.[328] Many have speculated about the length of such an oral tradition, and whether that tradition allows us to know anything about the historicity of the Jacob narrative.[329] But there are conflicting views on the reliability of orally transmitted traditions, and we are not likely ever to settle the issue. It is enough here simply to agree that this chapter, and to some degree the Jacob cycle itself, is the product of a complex oral tradition that was at the heart of ancient Israel's old epic accounts.[330]

As the chapter opens, we know that Esau is the eldest, that he is a skillful hunter, and that Isaac favors him (25:27–28). Isaac's instructions vv. 1–4 come as no surprise. The value of a patriarchal blessing was preeminent, and receiving the blessing at or near the end of the patriarch's life made it a legally binding will. Such "testamental blessings" were illocutionary or performative utterances, in that the pronouncement of the words in itself accomplished the act of blessing.[331] Meat dishes were not daily fare in ancient Israel, and hunted animals rather than domesticated animals were considered a delicacy.[332] Isaac evidently thought it especially meaningful to bless Esau, while sustained by food Esau has prepared himself in this particular manner (vv. 19, 25, 31).

---

[327] It seems unlikely to me that the "savory food" (*maṭʿām*) in this passage is a sacrificial meal and that Jacob's wearing of animal skins is a vestige of ritual practices; R. S. Hendel, *The Epic of the Patriarch* (1987), 83–86. Rather, the savory food is probably nothing more than Isaac's favorite dish, served up in order to give him energy and nourishment for the blessing, and the skins are simply part of Rebekah's ruse.

[328] An "oral register" used to create an oral aesthetic quality in Israelite literature consists of repetition, formulas and formula patterns, and conventionalized patterns of content. These do not necessarily demonstrate that such a text was an "oral composition," composed extemporaneously without the aid of writing; Susan Niditch, *Oral World and Written Word: Ancient Israelite Literature* (Library of Ancient Israel; Louisville, Ky.: Westminster John Knox Press, 1996), 8–24. For similar conclusions based on the rhythmic-verbal style of the ancestral narratives, see Frank H. Polak, "Linguistic and Stylistic Aspects of Epic Formulae in Ancient Semitic Poetry and Biblical Narrative," in *Biblical Hebrew in Its Northwest Semitic Setting: Typological and Historical Perspectives*, eds. Steven E. Fassberg and Avi Hurvitz (PAIS 1; Winona Lake, Ind./Jerusalem: Eisenbrauns/Hebrew University Magnes Press, 2006), 285–304, esp. 301–2.

[329] E.g., Wahl's conclusions are negative about the possibility of investigating the early history of Israel on the basis of the Jacob narrative, based on his understanding of oral traditions; Harald-Martin Wahl, *Die Jakobserzählungen: Studien zu ihrer mündlichen Überlieferung, Verschriftung und Historizität* (BZAW 258; Berlin: de Gruyter, 1997), 311.

[330] Rather than a free composition of the Yahwist editing together strands of Canaanite and Israelite traditions, much less a late literary composition drawing on little or no oral tradition; R. S. Hendel, *The Epic of the Patriarch* (1987), 24–32.

[331] Christopher W. Mitchell, *The Meaning of* brk *"to bless" in the Old Testament* (SBLDS 95; Atlanta: Scholars Press, 1987), 79.

[332] Oded Borowski, *Daily Life in Biblical Times* (SBLABS 5; Atlanta: Society of Biblical Literature, 2003), 67.

Having overheard Isaac's instructions to Esau, Rebekah decided to give a few instructions of her own (vv. 5–17). An important subplot in the narrative is the dysfunction caused by parental favoritism (cf. 25:28). Rebekah suspected her husband's fondness for the firstborn would result in cheating the younger son, which in fact, Isaac believed he was doing when he blessed Esau (v. 37). Isaac intended from the outset to leave nothing for Jacob. His favoritism for Esau led him to call only one son in for the testamental blessing, while social convention dictated that both boys receive blessings at the same time (48:8–9; 49:1, 28). Conversely, Rebekah's favoritism for Jacob drove her to assume he would not get a fair blessing, and to take matters into her own hands.[333]

Jacob's objection to his mother's proposed subterfuge is not *whether* to do it, but *how* to get by with it (vv. 11–12). Because of their physical differences, the plan could fail and he would be cursed rather than blessed. Rebekah's response offers the answer immediately to his object, which she has apparently worked out in her plans (v. 13). She says only that she will bear whatever guilt may befall them, and that Jacob must "obey" her word (or "do what I say," lit. "hear my voice"), an urgent command repeated twice in this dialogue (vv. 8 and 13). Rebekah has taken charge of the situation. Her plans for the ruse include elaborate disguises and calculated deception. She leaves nothing to chance.

The treachery is made possible because Isaac's aged eyes are too dim to distinguish between his sons. Initially, he inquires only as to how his son has managed to prepare the food so quickly (vv. 18–20). The disguised Jacob responds with a disingenuous but pious sounding "Oh, Yahweh made it happen!" Perhaps growing increasingly suspicious, Isaac asks his son to draw closer because "the voice is Jacob's voice" (vv. 21–22). But Jacob's (Rebekah's!) disguise works. Isaac makes Jacob articulate the lie twice, "I am Esau your firstborn" (v. 19, and cf. v. 24) escalating Jacob's own culpability. Convinced by the treacherous disguise, Isaac eats the food and prepares to pronounce the blessing (vv. 23–27a).

The blessing itself is induced by Isaac's senses at the moment he embraces his son (v. 27b). The aroma of Esau's clothes sets off the beginning of the blessing: "Ah, the smell of my son is like the smell of a field that the LORD has blessed." The blessing has four components (vv. 27b–29): the abundance of nature's best gifts, dominance over nations, lordship of siblings, and the covenantal promise of proportional blessings or curses for others. The third of these elements, "lord" over one's brothers, is a term that occurs only here in the Bible (*gĕbîr*, vv. 29 and 37), and implies that Isaac thinks he is restoring Esau as the head of the family perhaps overcoming Esau's loss of the birthright.[334] Of course, the reader understands what Isaac fails to see: that he is

---

[333] In this sense, she anticipates the actions and character of her brother Laban.

[334] Hans Kosmala, "*gābar*," *TDOT* 2:367–81, esp. 373. The expression, "may your mother's sons *bow down* to you," also reflects a conventional formula of epic language common to epic poetry and to ancient Hebrew narrative; F. H. Polak, "Linguistic and Stylistic Aspects of Epic Formulae in Ancient Semitic Poetry and Biblical Narrative," in *Biblical Hebrew in Its Northwest Semitic Setting* (2006), esp. 297–98.

really only confirming Jacob as his true successor and as the patriarch of the family. The final component of the blessing further solidifies Jacob's position by continuing the original ancestral promise of blessing for those who bless Abram and curses for those who curse Abram (12:3). There is a particularizing or telescoping movement in these four benedictory elements from the most general to the specific: from the gifts of nature, to dominion over all nations, even over one's brothers, and finally, to a more particular pronouncement of Jacob as the next patriarch designate. Isaac has unwittingly given him the whole package.

The ruse was quickly discovered (vv. 30–33). Esau's reaction is predictably one of despair, marked by his initial derisive, almost maniacal cry (v. 34). This is followed by a desperate appeal for another blessing; one pronounced for him instead of his brother. But as we have noted, blessings once spoken are irrevocable, and Isaac's answer shows that he cannot rescind the blessing intended for Esau but pronounced over Jacob (v. 35).[335] Isaac's words "he has taken away your blessing" ring with finality; Jacob has stolen Esau's blessing.

Esau's response in v. 36 contains a double word play. His anguished question requires a positive answer: "Is he not rightly named Jacob?" Surely, Esau exclaims, the name is suitable because Jacob (*ya'ăqōb*) has "supplanted" (*'āqab*) Esau twice, once in stealing the birthright and now the blessing. But even this last assertion has an ironic word play, in that "birthright" (*běkōrâ*) and "blessing" (*běrākâ*) are so similar in sound. Esau's complaint is that the two offenses are equally criminal. Then, as though in disbelief, he appeals to his father once more for whatever blessing may be leftover. But as Rebekah suspected he would do, Isaac had compressed all the patriarchal blessings into one pronouncement for Esau (v. 37), which had now been spoken over Jacob. With one final appeal, Esau urged his father to bless him as well (v. 38), and Isaac responds with what may be understood as an inverted version of Jacob's blessing (vv. 39–40). In place of the abundance, lordship, and blessing–curse pattern of the first blessing (vv. 28–29), this one states that Esau will not have ready access to nature's gifts, will live in violence and servitude, and will struggle to free himself from his brother's lordship.[336]

Isaac's and Rebekah's preferential love – his love for Esau and her love for Jacob (25:28) – results in hatred (v. 41): "Esau hated Jacob because of the blessing." The word "hated" is not the common verb "hate" (*śānē'*) but a rare term that connotes extended hostility over time, or harboring animosity (*śāṭam*).[337] Esau devised a plot of his own to answer the plot of Rebekah and Jacob. Theirs was deceptive, but his was murderous. Rebekah learns of Esau's plan to kill his twin, and she again

---

[335] Such testamental blessings were spoken shortly before the patriarch's death, so there was no socially accepted procedure for rescinding them; C. W. Mitchell, *The Meaning of* brk *"to bless" in the Old Testament* (1987), 83.

[336] The Hebrew of Esau's blessing is somewhat obscure (see NRSV's footnotes). It almost reads more like a curse than a blessing, confirming that Isaac had intended to leave Jacob out entirely.

[337] Bruce Baloian, "*śṭm*" *NIDOTTE* 3:1230–31; *HALOT* 3:1316; BDB 966.

takes control (vv. 42–45). In her instructions to Jacob, she once again insists that Jacob must "obey" her word (or "do what I say," lit. "hear my voice," cf. vv. 8 and 13).[338] And as before, Rebekah leaves nothing to chance. She intends to save the lives of both her sons by sending her younger one to her brother Laban, back to the ancestral homeland, where he will be safe. And where coincidentally, the reader understands, endogamous marriage will be possible for Jacob (cf. 26:34–35; and see Closer Look "Endogamy in Ancient Israel" at p. 219).

This time, Rebekah's plot is not complete trickery as before. The narrator has informed us of the anguish caused by Esau's Hittite wives (26:34–35). She need not detail the entire plan to Isaac, but merely rehearse the unsatisfactory nature of marriage outside the ancestral family for Jacob as well (v. 46). Social custom and the religious values of the culture dictate that Jacob should return to Haran to find a suitable wife, and Isaac fully agrees (28:1–2). The fact that the younger twin has received the blessing, it matters not by what means, confirms that he will be the legitimate heir of the covenant promises. It is now necessary to find a suitable wife for Jacob, as it was for Isaac before him (Gen 24). Thus at the conclusion of this text, Rebekah and Isaac are together on this one point, at least. And the reader is prepared for yet another blessing of Jacob and the beginning of his long sojourn in the ancestral homeland.

GENESIS 28:1–22 JACOB AT BETHEL

(28:1) Then Isaac called Jacob and blessed him, and charged him, "You shall not marry one of the Canaanite women.

(28:2) Go at once to Paddan-aram to the house of Bethuel, your mother's father; and take as wife from there one of the daughters of Laban, your mother's brother.

(28:3) May God Almighty bless you and make you fruitful and numerous, that you may become a company of peoples.

(28:4) May he give to you the blessing of Abraham, to you and to your offspring with you, so that you may take possession of the land where you now live as an alien – land that God gave to Abraham."

(28:5) Thus Isaac sent Jacob away; and he went to Paddan-aram, to Laban son of Bethuel the Aramean, the brother of Rebekah, Jacob's and Esau's mother.

(28:6) Now Esau saw that Isaac had blessed Jacob and sent him away to Paddan-aram to take a wife from there, and that as he blessed him he charged him, "You shall not marry one of the Canaanite women,"

(28:7) and that Jacob had obeyed his father and his mother and gone to Paddan-aram.

---

[338] NRSV inexplicably translates "obey my voice" here but "obey my word" in vv. 8 and 13 for the same Hebrew idiom.

(28:8) So when Esau saw that the Canaanite women did not please his father Isaac,

(28:9) Esau went to Ishmael and took Mahalath daughter of Abraham's son Ishmael, and sister of Nebaioth, to be his wife in addition to the wives he had.

(28:10) Jacob left Beer-sheba and went toward Haran.

(28:11) He came to a certain place and stayed there for the night, because the sun had set. Taking one of the stones of the place, he put it under his head and lay down in that place.

(28:12) And he dreamed that there was a ladder^r set up on the earth, the top of it reaching to heaven; and the angels of God were ascending and descending on it.

(28:13) And the LORD stood beside him^s and said, "I am the LORD, the God of Abraham your father and the God of Isaac; the land on which you lie I will give to you and to your offspring;

(28:14) and your offspring shall be like the dust of the earth, and you shall spread abroad to the west and to the east and to the north and to the south; and all the families of the earth shall be blessed^t in you and in your offspring.

(28:15) Know that I am with you and will keep you wherever you go, and will bring you back to this land; for I will not leave you until I have done what I have promised you."

(28:16) Then Jacob woke from his sleep and said, "Surely the LORD is in this place – and I did not know it!"

(28:17) And he was afraid, and said, "How awesome is this place! This is none other than the house of God, and this is the gate of heaven."

(28:18) So Jacob rose early in the morning, and he took the stone that he had put under his head and set it up for a pillar and poured oil on the top of it.

(28:19) He called that place Bethel; but the name of the city was Luz at the first.

(28:20) Then Jacob made a vow, saying, "If God will be with me, and will keep me in this way that I go, and will give me bread to eat and clothing to wear,

(28:21) so that I come again to my father's house in peace, then the LORD shall be my God,

(28:22) and this stone, which I have set up for a pillar, shall be God's house; and of all that you give me I will surely give one tenth to you."

*I*n the previous chapter, Jacob stole the patriarchal blessing of his brother, Esau. Whatever may have been wrong about that theft and about Jacob's actions there, Isaac and Rebekah now agree on what should happen next. Jacob must return to the ancestral homeland to acquire a suitable wife (cf. 27:46). This chapter narrates an additional blessing for Jacob, an additional wife for Esau, and the departure of

---

^r Or *stairway* or *ramp*
^s Or *stood above it*
^t Or *shall bless themselves*

Jacob for northern Mesopotamia to seek a suitable wife. At an overnight rest stop along the way, Jacob experiences a revelation of God, which is as sensational as any in Genesis. Jacob is on his way to becoming the legitimate heir to the ancestral promises, although as we will see, the narrative has many twists and turns along the way and not a few questions about whether Jacob is a worthy patriarch.[339]

The first half of v. 1 is something of a superscription, introducing another blessing for Jacob (a first blessing came at 27:27b–29).[340] Such patriarchal blessings were highly valued, and Jacob's receiving a *second* blessing is ironic in light of Esau's need for a first one for himself (27:38).[341] A patriarchal blessing bestowed at or near the end of the patriarch's life became a legally binding will (on the nature of the "testamental blessing," see commentary for Gen 27). Isaac begins his blessing, not with the customary elocution of benefits, but with a charge (vv. 1b–2).

"Canaanite women" is not an ethnically precise designation; Esau's wives were Hittites who lived in Canaan (Gen 23; 26:34–35; 27:46). Rather "Canaan" is used here to distinguish the Promised Land from the ancestral homeland in northern Mesopotamia. This ancestral homeland is known as Paddan-aram (v. 2), a name used only in Genesis and particularly in Gen 28–31, where it is likely an alternate name for Aram-naharaim (cf. 24:10).[342] Thus Isaac charges Jacob to travel to the ancestral homeland to acquire a wife, as Abraham's servant had done for Isaac himself (Gen 24). Specifically, he should return to the house of Bethuel, his maternal grandfather, and find a wife from among his cousins, the daughters of Laban (cf. 11:27–29; 22:20–24; 27:43). In the ancestral period, marriages within one's kinship group were preferable in order to ensure continuity of cultural and religious values and societal infrastructure (see Closer Look "Endogamy in Ancient Israel" at p. 219).

Isaac's blessing of Jacob in vv. 3–4 is different in several ways from the testamental blessing of 27:27–29. Rather than the abundance of nature's gifts and general dominance of nations and siblings, this blessing is more specifically related to the

---

[339] It is generally assumed that vv. 1–9 were part of the priestly materials of ancient Israel, while vv. 10–22 were part of the old epic narratives; D. M. Carr, *Reading the Fractures of Genesis* (1996), 80–81.

[340] The opening clause may be consequential rather than NRSV's narratival translation, which would connect it logically to 27:46: "Rebekah said to Isaac . . . *and so* Isaac called Jacob and blessed him . . ." Many interpreters assume the new unit begins at 27:46 rather than 28:1; J. Skinner, *A Critical and Exegetical Commentary on Genesis* (1910), 374–75.

[341] Of course, source critics have long since identified this as the priestly version of Jacob's blessing and Gen 27 as the Yahwist's version; E. A. Speiser, *Genesis: Introduction, Translation, and Notes* (AB 1; Garden City, N.Y.: Doubleday, 1964), 215, and on the further difficulty of the chronology of Gen 27–28, see S. R. Driver, *The Book of Genesis, with Introduction and Notes* (Westminster Commentaries 1; London: Methuen, 1943), 262.

[342] On the area of Canaan, see A. F. Rainey and R. S. Notley, *The Sacred Bridge: Carta's Atlas of the Biblical World* (2006), 33–36 and 113–116; and on Paddan-aram, see Wayne T. Pitard, "Paddan-aram," *ABD* 5:55.

ancestral promises of Genesis.[343] Isaac confirms Jacob as the rightful heir of the Abrahamic and Isaac covenant. And the blessing itself is more of a prayer than other blessings, uttered as a perlocutionary speech act, seeking to persuade, convince, or otherwise affect another. Such blessings are used for a desired effect upon the human recipient, not because of their effect upon God, and they typically ask God to bless in a way God has already promised to do. So in this case, Jacob is reminded and reassured of his place in the ancestral line and of his calling to marry within the kinship group.[344] On his way to Paddan-aram to find a wife, Jacob is thus bolstered by his status as heir of the covenant promises of Abraham and Isaac.

"God Almighty" (*'ēl šadday*, v. 3) is an archaic, revelatory name of God for the ancestors, as opposed to "Yahweh," the name by which God revealed himself to later Israel (Exod 3:14–15; 6:3; and see commentary at 17:1). The word order of the utterance stresses that it is none other than God Almighty who blesses Jacob, making him heir to Abraham's revelation from God. That birthright is borne out by the specifics of the blessing, "make you fruitful and numerous," which fulfills not only Abraham's promises (17:2, 6) but the creation mandate itself (1:22, 28). Fittingly, the Almighty's blessing is identified as "the blessing of Abraham," used only here in the Bible, to tie together once again the promises of "seed" (*zeraʿ*, NRSV's "descendants") and "land" (*'ereṣ*), so central to the ancestral promises.

Having dutifully blessed Jacob, Isaac sends him away to Paddan-aram (v. 5). Esau observes that Jacob was off to find a suitable wife, and that Jacob had in fact "obeyed" his parents ("Esau saw" is repeated for emphasis, vv. 6–8). He now understands that his own Canaanite wives were problematic. In order to remedy his offense, he goes off on a journey like his brother, in order to marry again, this time within the kinship group (v. 9). But his selection of Mahalath, daughter of Ishmael, only solidifies his position as the son who has squandered his birthright, and the one outside the line of the covenant promises (25:31–34).

Jacob sets out from his father's house at Beer-sheba (26:33) to travel to the ancestral city of Haran, in northwestern Mesopotamia (v. 10; cf. 11:31–32). Along the way, he stops in "a certain place" to spend the night outdoors sleeping with a stone for a makeshift headrest (v. 11).[345] Jacob is clearly vulnerable, alone as he is, running for his life, away from the murderous plot of Esau, and unsure how he will accomplish his mission. His vulnerability, or genuine helplessness, is heightened by his nature

---

[343] See 12:1–3; 13:14–17; 15:1–6; 15:7–16; 17:1–8; 22:16–18; 26:3–5, 24, and the commentary for each.

[344] C. W. Mitchell, *The Meaning of* brk *"to bless" in the Old Testament* (1987), 7–8, 99–100.

[345] The Hebrew definite article, "*the* place," is imperfect determination, meaning it denotes a place not defined for the moment but specifically determinate in itself, and therefore "a certain place"; P. Joüon and T. Muraoka, *A Grammar of Biblical Hebrew* (1993), 511. Of course, in this text, the narrator has reserved for a surprise ending the identity of the "certain place" as Bethel (v. 19).

as a homebody, a quiet man who prefers more civilized activities to hunting and camping. Ironically, it is his brother who prefers the outdoors (25:27).

During the night, Jacob has a dream (v. 12). Dreams in antiquity were routinely regarded as portents revealing future events, but they were occasionally also a means of seeing into other worlds.[346] Such dreams of course are a central feature of the Joseph narrative, but thus far in Genesis, Jacob is the first patriarch to encounter God in such a dream. God visited King Abimelech of Gerar in a dream, but the text relates none of the visual effects of that dream, only the content of the divine speech (20:3–7). Unlike Abraham and Isaac, this would-be patriarch observes a theatrical display, complete with ladder stretching from heaven to earth, with God's messengers (the "angels of God," *mal'ăkê 'ĕlōhîm*) moving up and down.[347] The effect is a sense of divine imminence, of God's presence with Jacob in the unnamed place. He is not alone at all, but simply unaware of the divine highway connecting the stone where he sleeps on the ground and the celestial realms above.

The "ladder" (or "stairway," *sullām*) occurs nowhere else in the Bible, and does not have obvious parallels in other ancient Semitic languages. The most persuasive theory assumes the term is a loan word from the Akkadian for "stair(case)."[348] If so, we may have here an allusion to the dominant feature of temple complexes in ancient Mesopotamia, the ziggurat, or stepped tower of three to seven stages. Such stepped pyramids were central to religious conceptions in ancient Babylonia, and may therefore add to the *mysterium tremendum* or numinous aura of Jacob's dream. Yet the association with stepped pyramids is uncertain, and even without it, the loan word itself may imply a simple staircase, reaching all the way to the sky and full of traffic. That alone would create the desired effect for the sleeping Jacob.

---

[346] Jeremy A. Black and Anthony R. Green, *Gods, Demons, and Symbols of Ancient Mesopotamia: An Illustrated Dictionary* (Austin: University of Texas Press, 1992), 71–72. On the need for interpretation of most dreams, see Scott B. Noegel, *Nocturnal Ciphers: The Allusive Language of Dreams in the Ancient Near East* (AOS 89; New Haven, Conn.: American Oriental Society, 2007), 46–50. Jacob records another revelatory dream in 31:11–13 in his speech to Leah and Rachel. See Closer Look "Dreams in the Hebrew Scriptures" at p. 322.

[347] The divine messenger (*mal'āk*) comes to correct injustices, appearing to Hagar in the desert of Shur and again in the desert of Beer-sheba (16:7–10; 21:17–18). The angel appeared once to Abraham in a slightly different role (22:11, 15), but in all cases the messenger is an unspecified supernatural envoy sent from God (or Yahweh), who becomes interchangeably identified with God in the narrative. The plural is used here and at 32:1 [Heb 32:2].

[348] Even though the term (*selimmiltu*) would have gone through several changes in transition from one language to another, Benno Landsberger, "Lexikalisches Archiv," *ZA* 41 (1933): 218–33, esp. 230–31. See the cautious discussion of Mankowski, who argues that the loan must have been in the opposite direction (i.e., from early Semitic *sullām* to Akkadian *simmiltu*) if it is truly a loanword at all; Paul V. Mankowski, *Akkadian Loanwords in Biblical Hebrew* (HSS 47; Winona Lake, Ind.: Eisenbrauns, 2000), 114–18. For the Akkadian word, see *CDA* 323.

But this is not all Jacob sees. Yahweh also appears, standing "beside him" (NRSV), "beside it" (i.e., beside the staircase), "above him," or "above it" (v. 13). All are possible, the Hebrew being ambiguous at this point (see NRSV note). Whatever the precise spatial relationship, Yahweh makes his presence known to Jacob. We do not have in this text the verb "appear, become visible" as a technical term for divine revelation, which we have come to expect in the ancestral narratives (Niphal of *r'h*; see commentary at 12:7, and Closer Look "Divine Revelation in the Hebrew Scriptures" at p. 135). But the term *does* occur in 35:1 to describe this event. Therefore, as in other theophanies to patriarchs, Yahweh presents himself in this dream, pulling back the curtain on his majesty, allowing himself to be presented in theophanic certainty. Typically in such appearances, what one *sees* is less important than what one *hears*. Each is followed almost immediately by divine speech in which God states the nature of his self-disclosure: "Yahweh/God appeared, . . . and said." But in Jacob's dream, the theophany is more theatrical. In his dream, he sees a staircase, the angels, and Yahweh standing, and then Yahweh speaks.

Yahweh's speech follows a similar pattern as other revelatory appearances in the ancestral narratives (vv. 13b-15).[349] First comes the divine self-disclosure, "I am Yahweh,"[350] signifying God's nature and identity, similar to "I am your shield" (15:1), or "I am God Almighty" (17:1). In this case, however, Yahweh is further characterized with a new descriptor, "the God of Abraham your father and the God of Isaac." This theophany thus characterizes Yahweh as a God who keeps faith with Israel's ancestors, and further confirms for Jacob that he is indeed the heir to their covenant promises.

God's self-disclosure is followed immediately by the familiar list of covenant promises: land, seed (NRSV's "offspring"), blessing for all nations, divine presence, and protection. There are a few surprises, however. The opening promise in v. 13b uses particularly striking word order to link together "land" (*'ereṣ*) and "seed" (*zera'*).[351] The syntax highlights the land as an object, which Yahweh will give to Jacob's unborn seed.[352] In this way, the covenant promises, which may now be called the promises of the fathers, are being explained to a new generation and promised afresh to the rightful heir.

The "seed-like-dust" metaphor has occurred previously (13:16), as has the four-corners directional extent of the patriarch's offspring (13:14). This version of the

---

[349] See 15:1; 15:7; 17:1; 26:24; 35:9–12, and cf. 12:7; 26:2; 48:3.

[350] Predicate nominative for identification; B. T. Arnold and J. H. Choi, *A Guide to Biblical Hebrew Syntax* (2003), 6.

[351] In addition to simple word order, NRSV's "*the land* on which you lie . . . " is likely a demonstrative article, connoting something like "*this very land* . . . "; B. T. Arnold and J. H. Choi, *A Guide to Biblical Hebrew Syntax* (2003), 32.

[352] "Land" is an objective *casus pendens*, which places great emphasis on the promised land as the object of Yahweh's gift to Jacob's seed; P. Joüon and T. Muraoka, *A Grammar of Biblical Hebrew* (1993), 586–87.

promises has the interesting translation problem related to the expression "all the families of the earth *shall be blessed* in you." As we have seen, a reflexive denotation is possible, "all the families of the earth *shall bless themselves*" (see NRSV footnote), although this is less likely than the traditional passive "shall be blessed" (see commentary at 12:3 and bibliography there). On the word translated "families" (*mišpĕḥôt*, "clans"), see also the commentary at 12:3. The assurance of divine presence, "I am with you," was new with Isaac, who needed assurances that Yahweh's personal, protecting aura was transportable, when Isaac was forced to move about in different locations in the Negeb during a drought (26:3, 24, and see commentary there). Similarly Jacob is on the move, and he needs assurances that Yahweh is not a deity restricted to any particular locale. This God will be with Jacob whether at home in Beer-sheba, on the road at a rocky overnight rest stop, or all the way to Paddan-aram. Finally, the promise that Yahweh will "keep" Jacob and bring him back home safely is a significant expansion of the promises, important to Jacob especially in light of Esau's vendetta (27:41).

The rest of the chapter contains two responses to the dream-revelation, one during the night (vv. 16–17) and one the next morning (vv. 18–22). During the night, Jacob is awakened by the dream and acknowledges the awe-inspiring presence of Yahweh in the place, a presence Jacob was not previously aware of until the dream itself. The revelation made Jacob aware for the first time of the numinous and frightening attendance of Yahweh, and Jacob associates the inspiration to "the place" as much as to the personhood of God: "How awesome is this place!" His conclusion that this place is "none other than the house of God" prepares for the naming of the place the next morning. The concept that a particular location may be supernaturally endowed as "the gate of heaven" is not unlike the Mesopotamian claim in the name of "Babylon," which by popular etymology came to mean "Gate of the Gods."[353] The image of a stairway linking heaven and earth, with divine emissaries marching to and fro, may also reflect the widespread ancient conception of a cosmic navel connecting the divine and human realms, such as the Greeks thought of ancient Delphi. Whatever the details of his beliefs, Jacob is clearly impressed by what he saw and heard.

The next day, Jacob "rose early in the morning," which connotes his resolve to take action without delay (19:27; 20:8; 21:14; 22:3, etc.).[354] As appropriate acts of worship in response to the dream-revelation, Jacob sets up the stone he had used as a headrest, poured oil on it, and gave the place a new name (vv. 18–19; on patriarchal religion generally, see Closer Look "Ancestral Religion" at p. 142). The early Israelites used standing stones in a variety of ways: as markers for territorial boundaries (31:44–49) or tombs (35:19–20), to symbolize the twelve tribes of Israel

[353] Bill T. Arnold, *Who Were the Babylonians?* (SBLABS 10; Atlanta: Society of Biblical Literature, 2004), 2–3.

[354] Rüdiger Bartelmus, "*škm*," *TDOT* 14:681–88, esp. 687–88.

(Exod 24:4; Josh 4:1–9) or the lack of a male heir (2 Sam 18:18), or to commemorate a great military victory (1 Sam 7:12). At times, as in this text, Israel appears also to share a common religious assumption in ancient Syria–Palestine that one is permitted to represent the deity visually but without pictorial images (known as "aniconism"). The use of standing stones or stone pillars to represent deity is "material aniconism," which was considered acceptable in the ancestral period but rejected later because of associations with Canaanite fertility worship (e.g., Exod 23:24; Deut 16:22).[355] Thus the stone is likely more than merely commemorative, but also marks the sacred spot where the numinous presence of Yahweh seemed especially prevalent, the stone representing that presence hypostatically.[356]

We are prepared for Jacob's name for the place, Bethel ("House of God"), because of his observation during the night that the numinous place is the house of God (v. 17). Yet the narrator has reserved articulation of the name until now, suspending the surprise ending since the reference to "a certain place" at v. 11. Bethel, located approximately ten miles north of Jerusalem on what later became a border between Israel and Judah, is the most frequently occurring place name in the Old Testament, next to Jerusalem itself.[357] Its identification here as an ancestral place of worship (cf. also 12:8) makes Bethel one of the most important sites of the Hebrew Scriptures, along with its important political role later in the northern kingdom of Israel.[358] As with Abraham's and Isaac's naming of Beer-sheba, the book of Genesis continues its etiological interest in explaining the origins for a name existing at the time the narrative is written (21:31; 26:33; and see Introduction).

---

[355] Thus the use of such a stone as "a pillar" (*maṣṣēbâ*) by Jacob may suggest the great antiquity of this tradition. For more on "material aniconism," and on "empty-space aniconism" as illustrated in Israel's ark of the covenant, where the cherubim serve as a throne for the invisible Yahweh (1 Sam 4:4; Exod 25:22), see Tryggve N. D. Mettinger, *No Graven Image? Israelite Aniconism in Its Ancient Near Eastern Context* (ConBOT 42; Stockholm: Almqvist & Wiksell International, 1995), esp 18–20; and Theodore J. Lewis, "Divine Images and Aniconism in Ancient Israel," *JAOS* 118 (1998): 36–53. See further on the origins of aniconism, Nathan MacDonald, "Aniconism in the Old Testament," in *The God of Israel*, ed. Robert P. Gordon (University of Cambridge Oriental Publications 64; Cambridge, New York: Cambridge University Press, 2007), 20–34.

[356] It is also possible, although quite hypothetical, that Jacob's vow (vv. 20–22) would have been taken as commentary on an inscription placed on the pillar itself, making this stone pillar something like the Babylonian entitlement monuments, displayed before the gods to solicit divine protection of the privileges granted; cf. Kathryn E. Slanski, *The Babylonian Entitlement* narûs (kudurrus): *A Study in Their Form and Function* (ASOR Books 9; Boston: American Schools of Oriental Research, 2003).

[357] Located at the Arab village of Beitîn; Anson F. Rainey, "Looking for Bethel: An Exercise in Historical Geography," in *Confronting the Past: Archaeological and Historical Essays on Ancient Israel in Honor of William G. Dever*, eds. Seymour Gitin, J. E. Wright, and J. P. Dessel (Winona Lake, Ind.: Eisenbrauns, 2006), 269–73.

[358] The honor accorded to Bethel in the ancestral narratives may suggest these traditions about the city are ancient in light of the reproach it bore later during the Josianic reforms (2 Kgs 23:4, 15–17).

Jacob's final act of worship is a vow, containing an elaborate conditional sentence (vv. 20–22).[359] Such vows follow a fixed literary pattern: the introductory formula ("Jacob made a vow"), the conditions of the vow (the protasis of the conditional clause introduced by "if"), and the promise (the apodosis, or the "then . . . " clause).[360] The conditions of Jacob's vow are completely logical in light of what Yahweh promised in the dream. Jacob hopes for and expects God's presence with him, protection on his journey, adequate provisions, resulting in a safe return to the promised land (vv. 20–21a).[361] In return Jacob commits that Yahweh will be his God, the stone will be God's house, and he will return one tenth of his gain to Yahweh (vv. 21b–22). Jacob accepts the reality of the dream, and embraces it enthusiastically as his future.[362]

Readers may be tempted to critique Jacob's conditional vow as a reflection of his calculating and manipulative personality.[363] However, his vow and its commitments are not specifically condemned or even vaguely critiqued in the text itself. The most that can be said about Jacob here is that his faith is not mature, like Abraham's before him or even Isaac's. Rather than a radical and exemplary act of obedience, we see here a timid and cautious patriarch, one who is willing to go as far with Yahweh as Yahweh is willing to go with him, but no farther. His actions and faith are patriarch-esque; he is close to fulfilling the role of "father of faith" but not quite there. We still have many miles to travel with Jacob before he takes his position in the distinguished line of patriarchs of ancient Israel.

GENESIS 29:1–31:55 JACOB IN PADDAN-ARAM

(29:1) Then Jacob went on his journey, and came to the land of the people of the east.

(29:2) As he looked, he saw a well in the field and three flocks of sheep lying there beside it; for out of that well the flocks were watered. The stone on the well's mouth was large,

---

[359] This is a "real conditional clause" in that it specifies situations that have the potential of being fulfilled; B. T. Arnold and J. H. Choi, *A Guide to Biblical Hebrew Syntax* (2003), 173–74.

[360] Otto Kaiser, "*nādar*," *TDOT* 9:242–255, esp. 247–49.

[361] The Hebrew leaves open some question about where the protasis ends and the apodosis begins. Because Yahweh assures Jacob in the dream that he will bring him back to the promised land (v. 15), I take v. 21a as part of the protasis, and therefore agree with NRSV's result clause, "so that I come again to my father's house in peace." Contra Hamilton, who extends the protasis through v. 21, and begins the apodosis only at v. 22, "then this stone . . . shall be God's abode," V. P. Hamilton, *The Book of Genesis, Chapters 18–50* (1995), 238 and 248.

[362] Walter Brueggemann, *Genesis: A Bible Commentary for Teaching and Preaching* (IBC; Atlanta: John Knox Press, 1982), 246.

[363] E.g., Leon Kass, *The Beginning of Wisdom: Reading Genesis* (New York: Free Press, 2003), 417; John H. Walton, *Genesis* (NIV Application Commentary; Grand Rapids, Mich.: Zondervan, 2001), 573–74.

(29:3) and when all the flocks were gathered there, the shepherds would roll the stone from the mouth of the well, and water the sheep, and put the stone back in its place on the mouth of the well.

(29:4) Jacob said to them, "My brothers, where do you come from?" They said, "We are from Haran."

(29:5) He said to them, "Do you know Laban son of Nahor?" They said, "We do."

(29:6) He said to them, "Is it well with him?" "Yes," they replied, "and here is his daughter Rachel, coming with the sheep."

(29:7) He said, "Look, it is still broad daylight; it is not time for the animals to be gathered together. Water the sheep, and go, pasture them."

(29:8) But they said, "We cannot until all the flocks are gathered together, and the stone is rolled from the mouth of the well; then we water the sheep."

(29:9) While he was still speaking with them, Rachel came with her father's sheep; for she kept them.

(29:10) Now when Jacob saw Rachel, the daughter of his mother's brother Laban, and the sheep of his mother's brother Laban, Jacob went up and rolled the stone from the well's mouth, and watered the flock of his mother's brother Laban.

(29:11) Then Jacob kissed Rachel, and wept aloud.

(29:12) And Jacob told Rachel that he was her father's kinsman, and that he was Rebekah's son; and she ran and told her father.

(29:13) When Laban heard the news about his sister's son Jacob, he ran to meet him; he embraced him and kissed him, and brought him to his house. Jacob told Laban all these things,

(29:14) and Laban said to him, "Surely you are my bone and my flesh!" And he stayed with him a month.

(29:15) Then Laban said to Jacob, "Because you are my kinsman, should you therefore serve me for nothing? Tell me, what shall your wages be?"

(29:16) Now Laban had two daughters; the name of the elder was Leah, and the name of the younger was Rachel.

(29:17) Leah's eyes were lovely,[u] and Rachel was graceful and beautiful.

(29:18) Jacob loved Rachel; so he said, "I will serve you seven years for your younger daughter Rachel."

(29:19) Laban said, "It is better that I give her to you than that I should give her to any other man; stay with me."

(29:20) So Jacob served seven years for Rachel, and they seemed to him but a few days because of the love he had for her.

(29:21) Then Jacob said to Laban, "Give me my wife that I may go in to her, for my time is completed."

(29:22) So Laban gathered together all the people of the place, and made a feast.

(29:23) But in the evening he took his daughter Leah and brought her to Jacob; and he went in to her.

---

[u] Meaning of Heb uncertain

(29:24) (Laban gave his maid Zilpah to his daughter Leah to be her maid.)

(29:25) When morning came, it was Leah! And Jacob said to Laban, "What is this you have done to me? Did I not serve with you for Rachel? Why then have you deceived me?"

(29:26) Laban said, "This is not done in our country – giving the younger before the firstborn.

(29:27) Complete the week of this one, and we will give you the other also in return for serving me another seven years."

(29:28) Jacob did so, and completed her week; then Laban gave him his daughter Rachel as a wife.

(29:29) (Laban gave his maid Bilhah to his daughter Rachel to be her maid.)

(29:30) So Jacob went in to Rachel also, and he loved Rachel more than Leah. He served Laban for another seven years.

(29:31) When the LORD saw that Leah was unloved, he opened her womb; but Rachel was barren.

(29:32) Leah conceived and bore a son, and she named him Reuben;[v] for she said, "Because the LORD has looked on my affliction; surely now my husband will love me."

(29:33) She conceived again and bore a son, and said, "Because the LORD has heard[w] that I am hated, he has given me this son also"; and she named him Simeon.

(29:34) Again she conceived and bore a son, and said, "Now this time my husband will be joined[x] to me, because I have borne him three sons"; therefore he was named Levi.

(29:35) She conceived again and bore a son, and said, "This time I will praise[y] the LORD"; therefore she named him Judah; then she ceased bearing.

(30:1) When Rachel saw that she bore Jacob no children, she envied her sister; and she said to Jacob, "Give me children, or I shall die!"

(30:2) Jacob became very angry with Rachel and said, "Am I in the place of God, who has withheld from you the fruit of the womb?"

(30:3) Then she said, "Here is my maid Bilhah; go in to her, that she may bear upon my knees and that I too may have children through her."

(30:4) So she gave him her maid Bilhah as a wife; and Jacob went in to her.

(30:5) And Bilhah conceived and bore Jacob a son.

(30:6) Then Rachel said, "God has judged me, and has also heard my voice and given me a son"; therefore she named him Dan.[z]

(30:7) Rachel's maid Bilhah conceived again and bore Jacob a second son.

---

[v] That is *See, a son*
[w] Heb *shama*
[x] Heb *lawah*
[y] Heb *hodah*
[z] That is *He judged*

(30:8) Then Rachel said, "With mighty wrestlings I have wrestled[aa] with my sister, and have prevailed"; so she named him Naphtali.

(30:9) When Leah saw that she had ceased bearing children, she took her maid Zilpah and gave her to Jacob as a wife.

(30:10) Then Leah's maid Zilpah bore Jacob a son.

(30:11) And Leah said, "Good fortune!" so she named him Gad.[bb]

(30:12) Leah's maid Zilpah bore Jacob a second son.

(30:13) And Leah said, "Happy am I! For the women will call me happy"; so she named him Asher.[cc]

(30:14) In the days of wheat harvest Reuben went and found mandrakes in the field, and brought them to his mother Leah. Then Rachel said to Leah, "Please give me some of your son's mandrakes."

(30:15) But she said to her, "Is it a small matter that you have taken away my husband? Would you take away my son's mandrakes also?" Rachel said, "Then he may lie with you tonight for your son's mandrakes."

(30:16) When Jacob came from the field in the evening, Leah went out to meet him, and said, "You must come in to me; for I have hired you with my son's mandrakes." So he lay with her that night.

(30:17) And God heeded Leah, and she conceived and bore Jacob a fifth son.

(30:18) Leah said, "God has given me my hire[dd] because I gave my maid to my husband"; so she named him Issachar.

(30:19) And Leah conceived again, and she bore Jacob a sixth son.

(30:20) Then Leah said, "God has endowed me with a good dowry; now my husband will honor[ee] me, because I have borne him six sons"; so she named him Zebulun.

(30:21) Afterwards she bore a daughter, and named her Dinah.

(30:22) Then God remembered Rachel, and God heeded her and opened her womb.

(30:23) She conceived and bore a son, and said, "God has taken away my reproach";

(30:24) and she named him Joseph,[ff] saying, "May the LORD add to me another son!"

(30:25) When Rachel had borne Joseph, Jacob said to Laban, "Send me away, that I may go to my own home and country.

(30:26) Give me my wives and my children for whom I have served you, and let me go; for you know very well the service I have given you."

(30:27) But Laban said to him, "If you will allow me to say so, I have learned by divination that the LORD has blessed me because of you;

(30:28) name your wages, and I will give it."

[aa] Heb *niphtal*
[bb] That is *Fortune*
[cc] That is *Happy*
[dd] Heb *sakar*
[ee] Heb *zabal*
[ff] That is *He adds*

(30:29) Jacob said to him, "You yourself know how I have served you, and how your cattle have fared with me.

(30:30) For you had little before I came, and it has increased abundantly; and the LORD has blessed you wherever I turned. But now when shall I provide for my own household also?"

(30:31) He said, "What shall I give you?" Jacob said, "You shall not give me anything; if you will do this for me, I will again feed your flock and keep it:

(30:32) let me pass through all your flock today, removing from it every speckled and spotted sheep and every black lamb, and the spotted and speckled among the goats; and such shall be my wages.

(30:33) So my honesty will answer for me later, when you come to look into my wages with you. Every one that is not speckled and spotted among the goats and black among the lambs, if found with me, shall be counted stolen."

(30:34) Laban said, "Good! Let it be as you have said."

(30:35) But that day Laban removed the male goats that were striped and spotted, and all the female goats that were speckled and spotted, every one that had white on it, and every lamb that was black, and put them in charge of his sons;

(30:36) and he set a distance of three days' journey between himself and Jacob, while Jacob was pasturing the rest of Laban's flock.

(30:37) Then Jacob took fresh rods of poplar and almond and plane, and peeled white streaks in them, exposing the white of the rods.

(30:38) He set the rods that he had peeled in front of the flocks in the troughs, that is, the watering places, where the flocks came to drink. And since they bred when they came to drink,

(30:39) the flocks bred in front of the rods, and so the flocks produced young that were striped, speckled, and spotted.

(30:40) Jacob separated the lambs, and set the faces of the flocks toward the striped and the completely black animals in the flock of Laban; and he put his own droves apart, and did not put them with Laban's flock.

(30:41) Whenever the stronger of the flock were breeding, Jacob laid the rods in the troughs before the eyes of the flock, that they might breed among the rods,

(30:42) but for the feebler of the flock he did not lay them there; so the feebler were Laban's, and the stronger Jacob's.

(30:43) Thus the man grew exceedingly rich, and had large flocks, and male and female slaves, and camels and donkeys.

(31:1) Now Jacob heard that the sons of Laban were saying, "Jacob has taken all that was our father's; he has gained all this wealth from what belonged to our father."

(31:2) And Jacob saw that Laban did not regard him as favorably as he did before.

(31:3) Then the LORD said to Jacob, "Return to the land of your ancestors and to your kindred, and I will be with you."

(31:4) So Jacob sent and called Rachel and Leah into the field where his flock was,

(31:5) and said to them, "I see that your father does not regard me as favorably as he did before. But the God of my father has been with me.

(31:6) You know that I have served your father with all my strength;

(31:7) yet your father has cheated me and changed my wages ten times, but God did not permit him to harm me.

(31:8) If he said, 'The speckled shall be your wages,' then all the flock bore speckled; and if he said, 'The striped shall be your wages,' then all the flock bore striped.

(31:9) Thus God has taken away the livestock of your father, and given them to me.

(31:10) During the mating of the flock I once had a dream in which I looked up and saw that the male goats that leaped upon the flock were striped, speckled, and mottled.

(31:11) Then the angel of God said to me in the dream, 'Jacob,' and I said, 'Here I am!'

(31:12) And he said, 'Look up and see that all the goats that leap on the flock are striped, speckled, and mottled; for I have seen all that Laban is doing to you.

(31:13) I am the God of Bethel, where you anointed a pillar and made a vow to me. Now leave this land at once and return to the land of your birth.'"

(31:14) Then Rachel and Leah answered him, "Is there any portion or inheritance left to us in our father's house?

(31:15) Are we not regarded by him as foreigners? For he has sold us, and he has been using up the money given for us.

(31:16) All the property that God has taken away from our father belongs to us and to our children; now then, do whatever God has said to you."

(31:17) So Jacob arose, and set his children and his wives on camels;

(31:18) and he drove away all his livestock, all the property that he had gained, the livestock in his possession that he had acquired in Paddan-aram, to go to his father Isaac in the land of Canaan.

(31:19) Now Laban had gone to shear his sheep, and Rachel stole her father's household gods.

(31:20) And Jacob deceived Laban the Aramean, in that he did not tell him that he intended to flee.

(31:21) So he fled with all that he had; starting out he crossed the Euphrates, and set his face toward the hill country of Gilead.

(31:22) On the third day Laban was told that Jacob had fled.

(31:23) So he took his kinsfolk with him and pursued him for seven days until he caught up with him in the hill country of Gilead.

(31:24) But God came to Laban the Aramean in a dream by night, and said to him, "Take heed that you say not a word to Jacob, either good or bad."

(31:25) Laban overtook Jacob. Now Jacob had pitched his tent in the hill country, and Laban with his kinsfolk camped in the hill country of Gilead.

(31:26) Laban said to Jacob, "What have you done? You have deceived me, and carried away my daughters like captives of the sword.

(31:27) Why did you flee secretly and deceive me and not tell me? I would have sent you away with mirth and songs, with tambourine and lyre.

(31:28) And why did you not permit me to kiss my sons and my daughters farewell? What you have done is foolish.

(31:29) It is in my power to do you harm; but the God of your father spoke to me last night, saying, 'Take heed that you speak to Jacob neither good nor bad.'

(31:30) Even though you had to go because you longed greatly for your father's house, why did you steal my gods?"

(31:31) Jacob answered Laban, "Because I was afraid, for I thought that you would take your daughters from me by force.

(31:32) But anyone with whom you find your gods shall not live. In the presence of our kinsfolk, point out what I have that is yours, and take it." Now Jacob did not know that Rachel had stolen the gods.

(31:33) So Laban went into Jacob's tent, and into Leah's tent, and into the tent of the two maids, but he did not find them. And he went out of Leah's tent, and entered Rachel's.

(31:34) Now Rachel had taken the household gods and put them in the camel's saddle, and sat on them. Laban felt all about in the tent, but did not find them.

(31:35) And she said to her father, "Let not my lord be angry that I cannot rise before you, for the way of women is upon me." So he searched, but did not find the household gods.

(31:36) Then Jacob became angry, and upbraided Laban. Jacob said to Laban, "What is my offense? What is my sin, that you have hotly pursued me?

(31:37) Although you have felt about through all my goods, what have you found of all your household goods? Set it here before my kinsfolk and your kinsfolk, so that they may decide between us two.

(31:38) These twenty years I have been with you; your ewes and your female goats have not miscarried, and I have not eaten the rams of your flocks.

(31:39) That which was torn by wild beasts I did not bring to you; I bore the loss of it myself; of my hand you required it, whether stolen by day or stolen by night.

(31:40) It was like this with me: by day the heat consumed me, and the cold by night, and my sleep fled from my eyes.

(31:41) These twenty years I have been in your house; I served you fourteen years for your two daughters, and six years for your flock, and you have changed my wages ten times.

(31:42) If the God of my father, the God of Abraham and the Fear of Isaac, had not been on my side, surely now you would have sent me away empty-handed.

God saw my affliction and the labor of my hands, and rebuked you last night."

(31:43) Then Laban answered and said to Jacob, "The daughters are my daughters, the children are my children, the flocks are my flocks, and all that you see is mine. But what can I do today about these daughters of mine, or about their children whom they have borne?

(31:44) Come now, let us make a covenant, you and I; and let it be a witness between you and me."

(31:45) So Jacob took a stone, and set it up as a pillar.

(31:46) And Jacob said to his kinsfolk, "Gather stones," and they took stones, and made a heap; and they ate there by the heap.

(31:47) Laban called it Jegar-sahadutha:[gg] but Jacob called it Galeed.[hh]

(31:48) Laban said, "This heap is a witness between you and me today." Therefore he called it Galeed,

(31:49) and the pillar Mizpah,[ii] for he said, "The LORD watch between you and me, when we are absent one from the other.

(31:50) If you ill-treat my daughters, or if you take wives in addition to my daughters, though no one else is with us, remember that God is witness between you and me."

(31:51) Then Laban said to Jacob, "See this heap and see the pillar, which I have set between you and me.

(31:52) This heap is a witness, and the pillar is a witness, that I will not pass beyond this heap to you, and you will not pass beyond this heap and this pillar to me, for harm.

(31:53) May the God of Abraham and the God of Nahor" – the God of their father – "judge between us." So Jacob swore by the Fear of his father Isaac,

(31:54) and Jacob offered a sacrifice on the height and called his kinsfolk to eat bread; and they ate bread and tarried all night in the hill country.

(31:55[jj]) Early in the morning Laban rose up, and kissed his grandchildren and his daughters and blessed them; then he departed and returned home.

*T*his text is about the approximately twenty years that Jacob lived outside the Promised Land (31:38). It begins with his arrival in Paddan-aram, and concludes with a sacrifice and covenant meal in the hills of Gilead, with Jacob on the verge of reentry into the Promised Land. The three chapters form a continuous, relatively self-contained unit devoted to Jacob's sojourn in Paddan-aram and his relationship with his uncle Laban and his family.

As I have stated in the introduction to the Jacob narrative (see commentary at Genesis 25:19–34), the arguments for a symmetrical, chiastic structure in Gen 25–35

[gg] In Aramaic *The heap of witness*
[hh] In Hebrew *The heap of witness*
[ii] That is *Watchpost*
[jj] Ch 32.1 in Heb.

are more convincing than elsewhere in Genesis.[364] However, the most convincing evidence of all for such a palistrophic arrangement is in Gen 29–31 at the core of the overall pattern. The chapters are framed by Jacob's arrival in Paddan-aram (29:1–14) and his departure from there (31:1–31:55). Within this frame is a set of matching accounts in which Laban outmaneuvers Jacob in the marriage of his daughters (29:15–30) but Jacob bests Laban in the acquisition of wealth in livestock (30:25–43). Finally, at the center of the concentric pattern, is the birth of Jacob's sons, culminating especially in the birth of Joseph to Rachel (29:31–30:24).

> A 29:1–14, Jacob arrives in Paddan-aram
>   B 29:15–30, Laban gains an advantage over Jacob
>   C 29:31–30:24, Birth of Jacob's children
>   B' 30:25–43, Jacob gains an advantage over Laban
> A' 31:1–55, Jacob departs from Paddan-aram

While many have argued that the birth accounts at the core are secondary and added at a later time,[365] the dominance of the chiastic pattern here and the importance of the central component within it suggest otherwise.[366]

The "land of the people of the east" (29:1) is Paddan-aram, as we know from 28:5, which is the name of the ancestral homeland in the Jacob and Joseph narratives. The expression "went on his journey, and came . . . " (lit. "lifted his feet and went . . . ") is an idiom used in early epic narrative traditions, and probably reflects the antiquity of this account.[367] Jacob came first to a well (29:2). As the city gate was the place for men to gather, often for judicial decisions, so women and eligible girls gathered at the well, which was the place to find a suitable wife (Gen 24; Exod 2:15b–22).

Information about the use of this particular well is given in 29:2b–3, where the word order introduces background needed to understand the paragraph.[368] The well was protected by a large stone, large enough to require more than one shepherd to move it. The custom, therefore, was to water all the flocks together to save moving the stone more than was necessary, its size and weight apparently significant enough to merit joint efforts. It is also likely that several families shared rights to this well with Laban, so that the stone was an impediment to unsupervised use of the water.

---

[364] See the admission of such by Wenham, a scholar generally favorable to chiastic structures at every turn in Genesis; G. J. Wenham, *Genesis 16–50* (1994), 169–70.

[365] C. Westermann, *Genesis 12–36* (1985), 471–72.

[366] In fact, the primacy of the pattern in Gen 29–31 may have led ultimately to the use of such a pattern for the entire Jacob narrative.

[367] F. H. Polak, "Linguistic and Stylistic Aspects of Epic Formulae in Ancient Semitic Poetry and Biblical Narrative," in *Biblical Hebrew in Its Northwest Semitic Setting* (2006).

[368] Fronting is used to begin a subparagraph (29:2b–3) providing the background information; Christo H. J. van der Merwe, Jackie A. Naudé, and Jan H. Kroeze, *A Biblical Hebrew Reference Grammar* (Biblical Languages, Hebrew 3; Sheffield: Sheffield Academic Press, 1999), 347–48.

Only the entire group of co-owners would be able to roll the stone away and gain access to the water.[369]

Jacob wastes no time with his inquiries (29:4–6). With the answer to each of his questions, the shepherds take Jacob closer to his desired goal: they are from Haran, they know Laban, he is well, and in fact, here is his daughter coming just now. Jacob has only just arrived but has already identified a cousin who can at least lead him to his uncle's household. The shepherds have supplied the needed information, but they have not been particularly helpful or courteous.[370] Jacob apparently concludes they are lazy, since they are neither watering their flocks nor leading them out for more grazing (29:7). Their response explains to Jacob something the narrator has already revealed: these flocks are watered together with others using the well, and they are obligated to wait (29:8).

While this discourse is taking place, Rachel arrives. (29:9). When Jacob sees her and the flock of his kinsman, Laban, he immediately rolls the stone away from the well, apparently by himself (29:10). Jacob accomplished alone what it normally took two or three shepherds to do as a group, and this Herculean action appears to be motivated by the mere appearance of Rachel and the flock of his uncle.[371] The threefold repetition of "his mother's brother Laban" surely highlights the irony of finding his kinsfolk so quickly. He is overwhelmed with emotion, greets Rachel appropriately and identifies himself as her cousin, whereupon she runs to inform her father (29:11–12). Many of the details of this meeting are similar to Abraham's servant meeting Rebekah, including now the young maiden running home to report the details of what seems like a providential encounter (24:28). As he did on that occasion, Laban runs to meet the stranger at the well to bring him into the household (cf. 24:29–32). The "my bone and my flesh" idiom (29:14), the so-called kinship formula, stresses an existing blood relationship, the suitability of that relationship, and the responsibilities implied by it (cf. 2:23).[372] They rightly celebrate their kinsman relationship but Laban will shortly attempt to take advantage of it.

Laban's offer is not harmless or innocent (29:15). He exploits the kinsman relationship by offering to turn it into a work-for-hire arrangement. Laban understands that Jacob has every right to own property, and to return to his father's house in Canaan at any time. Yet Jacob's problem is that he has no bride-price, such as Abraham's servant paid in 24:53, and which was expected to be paid to the bride's

---

[369] J. P. Oleson, "Water Works," *ABD* 6:883–93, esp. 886.

[370] Their monosyllabic answers may, in fact, indicate a rather surly treatment of Jacob, and when they quickly point Rachel out, they may have been suggesting, "here's his daughter; go ask her!" See G. J. Wenham, *Genesis 16–50* (1994), 230.

[371] Although Rachel is described as good-looking in 29:17, the text at this point emphasizes only the kinsman-connection. Jacob has miraculously and quickly found his uncle's household.

[372] N. P. Bratsiotis, "*bāśār*," *TDOT* 2:317–332, esp. 327–38; Karl-Martin Beyse, "*'eṣem*," *TDOT* 11:304–9, esp. 306.

father as a form of compensation for the loss of one's daughter.[373] In order to take full advantage of Jacob's need to find a suitable wife, Laban proposes hiring him for "wages" (*maśkōret*), which will become a point of bitter contention between them later (31:41).[374]

A "tale of two daughters" is introduced as more background information (29:16–17).[375] Translations of the word "weak" to describe Leah's eyes should be reconsidered (e.g., RSV, NJPS, NIV), because the word, rare as it is, more naturally means "delicate" or "soft" in this context.[376] It seems unlikely that the matriarch of six of Israel's tribes should be described in unattractive terms. On the other hand, NRSV's "lovely" is probably too generous. More likely, Leah had "appealing" or "pleasant" eyes. More importantly, the contrast between Leah and her younger sister is still valid; NRSV should be "*but* Rachel was graceful and beautiful." In other words, Leah was attractive enough in her own way, but Rachel was stunning! This contrast between sisters sets up a symmetrical inversion of the Jacob–Esau story, in which the theme of competition between siblings highlights the goal of each sibling to participate in the continuation of the covenant promises; that is, to become the legitimate patriarch or matriarch of the ancestral family.[377] Only one of the brothers can continue the lineage, so Jacob defeats Esau to become the legitimate patriarch in a linear genealogy. But in the case of the competing sisters, they both become matriarchs in their own right, and the segmentation of Israel's genealogy is introduced into the ancestral narratives (see 29:31–30:24 below).

---

[373] O. Borowski, *Daily Life in Biblical Times* (2003), 82; Samuel Greengus, "Old Babylonian Marriage Ceremonies and Rites," *JCS* 20/2 (1966): 55–72.

[374] This region of northern Mesopotamia had a long history of pastoralists tending flocks of sheep and goats on the fringes of settled society, and occasionally hiring themselves out on contract as shepherds to villagers. This economic principle seems to be in view here, although precisely how Laban and Jacob may have been perceived as relating to such specialized mobile pastoralism is not clear; Daniel E. Fleming, *Democracy's Ancient Ancestors: Mari and Early Collective Governance* (Cambridge: Cambridge University Press, 2004), 34–39.

[375] Again fronting, by means of word order that introduces new characters and identifies their defining traits; C. H. J. van der Merwe, J. A. Naudé, and J. H. Kroeze, *A Biblical Hebrew Reference Grammar* (1999), 347–48.

[376] *HALOT* 3:1230; BDB 940; V. P. Hamilton, *The Book of Genesis, Chapters 18–50* (1995), 258–59; Tikva Frymer-Kensky, "Leah," in *Women in Scripture: A Dictionary of Named and Unnamed Women in the Hebrew Bible, the Apocryphal/Deuterocanonical Books, and the New Testament*, eds. Carol L. Meyers, Toni Craven, and Ross S. Kraemer (Boston: Houghton Mifflin, 2000), 108–9. Leah's and Rachel's names, "wild cow" and "ewe lamb" respectively, are grist for the punning mill throughout the passage, and are particularly useful in the hands of a narrator gifted at word plays (and see especially Gen 32); Scott B. Noegel, "Drinking Feasts and Deceptive Feats: Jacob and Laban's Double Talk," in *Puns and Pundits: Word Play in the Hebrew Bible and Ancient Near Eastern Literature*, ed. Scott B. Noegel (Bethesda, Md.: CDL Press, 2000), 163–79.

[377] Karin R. Andriolo, "A Structural Analysis of Genealogy and World View in the Old Testament," *AA* 75 (1973): 1657–69: esp. 1666–69.

Jacob's love for Rachel drove him to accept her father's proposal (29:18–20). Having no means of paying the customary bride-price, Jacob agrees to work in Laban's employ for seven years for Rachel, which seemed to him "but a few days." When his service was complete, Laban had the wedding banquet and all seemed in order. But Jacob's uncle got the better of him by switching his daughters in the cover of darkness ("in the evening") presumably hiding Leah's identity under a bridal veil.[378] With the acquisition of Leah comes the maid Zilpah as well, thus providing half of the matriarchal quadrumvirate for Israel's genealogy (29:24).

Jacob's response to the scam is understandably vigorous (29:26). His own words, however, draw out the irony of the situation: the deceiver himself has now been deceived (cf. 27:35).[379] Jacob has been outwitted by his uncle, who used the same bait-and-switch techniques of disguise and deception Jacob himself had used so effectively against Esau. The text has no sympathy for Laban's actions, but the irony engenders little for Jacob either. Laban's answer reveals his motives, if they were in doubt for the reader (29:26–27). His appeal to custom ("it's just not done here") rings hollow in light of Jacob's seven years of service. Might such a custom have been mentioned during that time? Laban's demand for yet another seven years makes clear his dependence upon Jacob, or at least his perceived dependence, for continued prosperity. Jacob is trapped, and agrees to an additional seven years of service. During the week, he takes another wife, Rachel, and she is given yet another maid, Bilhah, completing the set of matriarchs for ancient Israel (29:28–29). The episode closes with the observation that Jacob loved Rachel more than Leah (29:30), raising the specter of favoritism once more and warning of trouble ahead, just as parental favoritism was the source of conflict earlier (cf. 25:28).[380]

In the next unit, Jacob's two primary wives and their handmaidens, who are given to him as additional wives, have twelve children in rapid succession, eleven boys and one girl (29:31–30:24). In a book structured by genealogical tag lines tracing lineal descendants (the *tôlĕdôt*-structuring clauses) and driven by a subplot of barrenness, we have finally come to the place of abundance and fertility. With the birth of Jacob's children, we have clearly reached an important moment in the biblical drama. These, of course, are the distant ancestors of what will become the tribes of Israel. They thus reflect early Israel's tribal league or federation, which united the tribes based on kinship, religious, and military ideology and organization.[381] More importantly

---

378 On the veil, see 24:65. A woman's entry into the groom's home (or tent) was the significant moment, at which point she was considered his wife; Philip J. King and Lawrence E. Stager, *Life in Biblical Israel* (Library of Ancient Israel; Louisville, Ky.: Westminster John Knox Press, 2001), 55–56.

379 Isaac had described Jacob's trickery as "deception" (*mirmâ*), and now Jacob's own verb, "you deceived me" uses the same Hebrew root (Piel of *rmh*).

380 The closing note may additionally be the narrator's subtle condemnation of polygyny.

381 And that gave rise to later Israel's covenant ideology; Frank M. Cross, *From Epic to Canon: History and Literature in Ancient Israel* (Baltimore: Johns Hopkins University Press, 1998),

for the book of Genesis itself, they represent the initial fulfillment of the ancestral promise of "seed" (12:7, and repeated often since).

As we have seen, this is the central point of a symmetrical structure for this unit and perhaps for the entire Jacob narrative.[382] This is also the point at which the book changes from lineal genealogies to segmented genealogies. Up to this point in Genesis, genealogies have been used to distinguish ancient Israel's ancestors from all other people groups of the world and at the same time to trace Israel's ancestry through a singular line of descendant, from Adam to Noah, to Abraham, and now to Jacob.[383] Now that the promised seed is multiplying, the lineal descent gives way to twelve sub-units in a single generation. We now speak of branches of the family, all considered *within* the covenant blessing of Israel's ancestry, rather than certain branches that are excluded (e.g., Ishmael, Esau). By this means of segmentation, all branches are equally part of the Israelite nation, which itself illustrates that the covenant blessings are becoming a reality.

Barrenness is the general rule for Israel's matriarchs (11:30; 16:1; 25:21). Leah's sudden fertility is credited to Yahweh, who apparently did not approve the favoritism Jacob showed Rachel (29:31). As usual, Israelite authors are not interested in secondary causes but are quick to credit Yahweh as the ultimate reason for most events. God's blessing enables Leah to give birth to four sons, Reuben, Simeon, Levi, and Judah (29:32–35). Naming the newborn is often the mother's prerogative, and women outnumber men in naming newborns nearly two-to-one in the Bible.[384] Birth narratives in the Hebrew Scriptures commonly use paronomasia, or word plays, in announcing the name of a child. Etymological precision is not expected in these "naming" contexts, but rather association by assonance (similarity of sound) is the norm, in order to give new significance to the birth.[385] So, for example, Reuben's name most likely means simply "behold a son," (*rĕʾûbēn*) as the most

---

19–21. On taking these "sons of Jacob" as eponymous tribal chieftains, see Nahum M. Sarna, *Understanding Genesis* (New York: Schocken Books, 1966), 196–99.

[382] Cf. the introduction to the Jacob narrative at 25:19–34 above, and for more on the composition and structure of this specific pericope, see K. A. Mathews, *Genesis 11:27–50:26* (2005), 472–78.

[383] Through the processes of divergence and invergence, which both come to an end with the genealogical segmentation here with Jacob's children; K. R. Andriolo, "A Structural Analysis of Genealogy and World View in the Old Testament," esp. 1657–63.

[384] Naming the child may have been a ritual act as part of women's religious culture; Carol L. Meyers, "From Household to House of Yahweh: Women's Religious Culture in Ancient Israel," in *Congress Volume: Basel, 2001*, ed. André Lemaire (VTSup 92; Leiden: Brill, 2002), 277–303, esp. 291–92.

[385] These naming passages also serve the etiological purposes of the book of Genesis generally. With the exception of Dinah, the narrator has given punning etymologies to all the children's names; Robert Alter, *Genesis: Translation and Commentary* (New York: W.W. Norton, 1996), 156–62. On the dangers of reading too much into biblical names, see Herbert Marks, "Biblical Naming and Poetic Etymology," *JBL* 114/1 (1995): 21–42, esp. 23–24.

natural parental exclamation at the birth itself, especially of a firstborn.[386] But in this passage, the name is associated with two different assertions by sound-alike word plays: "Yahweh has looked upon my affliction" and "my husband will love me."[387] Similar word plays will be used throughout this text for naming the children, and the reader is advised to note the NRSV footnotes where appropriate.[388]

The birth of Leah's sons intensified the pain of Rachel's barrenness, and caused friction with Jacob (30:1–2). Rachel's solution, as was Sarah's before her, is surrogate motherhood through the use of a slave-girl as a substitute wife (16:1–3). As in the case of Hagar in Gen 16, secondary wives, sometimes called "concubines," may enter the family for childbearing purposes when the primary wife is barren. Ancient Near Eastern parallels confirm that a wife's slave-girl could reasonably be supplied to compensate for a barren womb.[389] Rachel, therefore, cannot be condemned for presenting her maid, Bilhah, to her husband for purposes of surrogate motherhood (30:3). Her desire for Bilhah to bear children "upon my knees" is partly explained in the remainder of the statement, "that I too may have children through her." This is likely not formal adoption, as often assumed, but rather an ancient Near Eastern custom (attested in Hurrian and Neo-Assyrian texts) in which a surrogate mother welcomes and receives the newborn into the family by acts of attending at birth, naming, and breast-feeding.[390]

This new union with Bilhah results in two more sons, Dan and Naphtali (30:4–8).[391] Not to be outdone, Leah presents her own maid, Zilpah, to Jacob as a wife for surrogate motherhood, now that she herself has stopped bearing children (30:9; cf. 29:35). Cohabitation with Bilhah results in two more sons, luckily and happily named Gad and Asher (30:9–13).

The competition between Leah and Rachel only escalates with the birth of these four by secondary wives. Rachel has continued childless and now Leah has become barren as well, so when a perceived fertility drug becomes available in the form

---

[386] *HALOT* 3:1162; BDB 910.

[387] Which sound like *rāʾâ* [*yhwh*] *bĕʿonyî* and *yeʾĕhābanî*, respectively, creating loose associations with the sounds in the name "Reuben." Thus the name "Look a son!" has been given additional significances through triple entendre.

[388] There may also be a progression in the names of the first four children, from seeing to hearing to union with Leah's husband, and finally, to the praise of Yahweh; L. Kass, *The Beginning of Wisdom: Reading Genesis* (2003), 428.

[389] E.g., Richard S. Hess, "Marriage Customs," *COS* 3.101B:251–2. For many other examples, and thorough discussion, see Thomas L. Thompson, *The Historicity of The Patriarchal Narratives: The Quest for the Historical Abraham* (BZAW 133; Berlin: de Gruyter, 1974), 252–69.

[390] Martin J. Selman, "Comparative Customs and the Patriarchal Age," in *Essays on the Patriarchal Narratives*, eds. A. R. Millard and D. J. Wiseman (Leicester, England/Downers Grove, Ill.: InterVarsity Press, 1980), 91–139, esp. 136–37.

[391] Dan is listed fifth here but seventh in Gen 49 and 1 Chr 2:1–2, perhaps as part of a genealogical convention to honor individuals deemed worthy in the seventh or fifth position. However, it is not entirely clear why Dan is so honored; Jack M. Sasson, "A Genealogical 'Convention' in Biblical Chronology?" *ZAW* 90 (1978): 171–85, esp. 181–83.

of mandrakes, open conflict results. The mandrake (Heb pl. *dûdāʾîm*, scientifically called *Mandragora officinarum*) grows wild in the Mediterranean countries, often around the edges of cultivated fields. Thus here, the lad Reuben finds them during the harvest season "in the field" and brought them to his mother Leah (30:14). A small fruit, yellow and tomato-like, grows from the plant's clump of dark leaves and spreads out on the ground, which fruit has been regarded as an aphrodisiac from ancient times, often used in fertility rites.[392] Leah exchanges the mandrakes for the right to sleep with Jacob that night (30:15–16). The agreement assumes Rachel has the upper hand among the wives in that she controls who has time alone with Jacob, perhaps reflecting again her position as his favorite. She has Jacob's love (29:20, 30), a love Leah desperately wants (29:32), while Leah has the children Rachel needs.

If indeed conjugal rights were being withheld from Leah, she had a legitimate and serious complaint against Jacob and Rachel.[393] The confrontation over the mandrakes appears to have brought the injustice to light and so Jacob resumes treating Leah as a wife. She gives birth to three more children, making her previously noted barrenness look more like Jacob's and Rachel's fault than her own. The narrator notes simply that Leah bore more children because "God heeded" her (lit. "heard her"), once again showing more interest in ultimate causes. The births of Issachar, Zebulun, and a daughter, Dinah, could only have exacerbated the family dysfunction (30:17–21).

Finally, God heeds Rachel as well (30:22–24). God "remembered" and "heard" Rachel, verbs for divine favor extended to someone just before God's action on their behalf.[394] So the narrator states succinctly, God "opened her womb," stressing again the primary cause for Rachel's sudden fertility, and her contribution in the burgeoning ancestral family.[395] As Reuben's name is given two nuances by means of sound-alike word plays (29:32), so the naming of Joseph has two applications, with typical disregard for precise etymology. Rachel states that God has "taken away" (*ʾāsap*) her reproach and appeals to Yahweh to "add" (*yōsēp*) another son, making Joseph's name (*yôsēp*) fitting for her situation. The child's name often reflects the faith of the parent, so that Rachel is putting her scorned life behind her and pressing on in the expectations of more of Yahweh's blessings.

The arrival of twelve children – eleven boys and one girl – is a sign of abundance and proof of God's blessing.[396] Almost immediately after the birth of Joseph, Jacob

---

[392] *HALOT* 1:215–16; *DCH* 2:424; F. N. Hepper, *Baker Encyclopedia of Bible Plants* (Grand Rapids, Mich.: Baker Book House, 1992), 151.

[393] G. J. Wenham, *Genesis 16–50* (1994), 247.

[394] E.g., Exod 2:24–25; Hermann Eising, "*zākar*," *TDOT* 4:64–82, esp. 69–70; Udo Rüterswörden, "*šāmaʿ*," *TDOT* 15:253–79, esp. 262. And for the possibility that such language stands at the center of two palistrophes, the Jacob narrative (39:22) and the flood narrative (8:1), see Gordon J. Wenham, *Genesis 1–15* (WBC 1; Waco, Tex.: Word Books, 1987), 156–57 and G. J. Wenham, *Genesis 16–50* (1994), 170.

[395] Even while the mandrakes are the presumed secondary cause for Rachel's opened womb.

[396] Ishmael became the father of twelve princes (17:20; 25:16). Eventually, Jacob will be the father of twelve sons (35:22–26; 49:28), Dinah standing in temporarily in this list.

senses a need to return to the Promised Land and establish his own household rather than to continue in Paddan-aram as an employee of his uncle. His request to return to his "land" (*'ereṣ*, NRSV's "country") reminds the reader that abundant fulfillment of one patriarchal promise (that is, "seed") is no fulfillment of all (30:25–26). The promised seed of Abraham has arrived, but the Promised Land is still far distant.

Not surprisingly, Laban demurs (30:27–28), and the rest of this text is devoted to the complex relationship between Jacob and Laban, culminating in a covenant between them and their amicable separation (31:43–55). In a sense, Jacob's departure from the ancestral homeland in northern Mesopotamia to Canaan mirrors the trek of his grandfather Abraham many years earlier. He is abandoning the certainty and security of the life he has known for two decades, and departing for a land where he will certainly meet animosity and perhaps danger. Jacob's assurances of successful return to Canaan have the advantage over his grandfather only in that those assurances were actually stated within the Promised Land itself (28:15, cf. "the land that I will show you," 12:1). His initial attempt to depart Paddan-aram seems to flow from his instinctive drive to do what he knows he must, to return to his home and land (30:25). But then Jacob hears the command of Yahweh, tantamount to Abraham's own call (31:3): "Return to the land of your ancestors and to your kindred, and I will be with you." As Isaac grew into the role of patriarch, son of Abraham (Gen 26), so now Jacob has a need to grow too. But this journey has more twists and turns.

While Jacob stresses that his "service" to Laban is complete, his uncle simply counters with an offer to increase his wages (30:27–28). The nature of Laban's "divination" is not given, but most types of divination are proscribed in the Hebrew Bible. The particular term employed here is used elsewhere without condemnation for divining the truth about a particularly needed item,[397] and the point here is the content of the divination, "that Yahweh has blessed me because of you."[398] Jacob quickly agrees with his uncle that Yahweh's blessing is evident in the increase in livestock since Jacob began his service (30:29–30). His final concern is that the time has arrived for Jacob to provide for his own household rather than contributing to Laban's household. Nearly all interpreters take "house(hold)" (*bayit*) to denote the wealth of one's estate, so that Jacob's concern is to build his own wealth rather than Laban's. In fact, the result of the new arrangement Jacob proposes results in considerable wealth for Jacob (30:43). But it seems just as likely that Jacob is raising the issue of how to establish his "house" denoting clan or tribe. His arrangement with Laban has been a work-for-hire relationship, which does not endow his "house" for the future, and Laban continues to press the issue of "wages" (*maśkōret*, 29:15, or

---

[397] Especially by pre-Yahwistic (that is, pre-Torah) ancestors or by pagans (Gen 44:5, 15; Num 24:1; 1 Kgs 20:33) but not by later Israelites; G. André, "*kāšap*," *TDOT* 7:360–366, esp. 365.

[398] The epexegetical clause, "Yahweh has blessed me," supplements the main verb, that of divination; GKC ¶120f.

śākār, 30:28, 32). Thus the impasse is about whether Laban will continue to employ Jacob as a hired hand or whether Jacob will be allowed to build his own personal wealth in preparation for supporting his own house.

Once more Laban asks what he can give to persuade Jacob to stay, and Jacob replies, "nothing!" Apparently in a concession to Laban's persistence, Jacob proposes a new arrangement, one that had modest potential for his own success as well as Laban's but one that involved great risk (30:31–33). Among the caprine family of sheep and goats so central in this ancient economy, the sheep were generally white and the goats black or dark brown.[399] Thus, in return for shepherding Laban's flocks, Jacob would receive as his own possession and in place of wages, all those animals that were not of a solid color. Both knew that speckled, spotted, or striped lambs or kids among the flocks would be a relatively small percentage. Contracts from ancient Mesopotamia suggest that shepherds sometimes received as much as twenty percent of the new births, while Jacob would most likely receive a far smaller amount using this arrangement.[400] Laban was quick to agree (30:34). As an added precaution, apparently as a trust-but-verify measure, Laban separated the flocks himself, putting sheep and goats of mixed color-patterns in the charge of his sons, and putting a three days' journey between them and the black goats and white sheep in Jacob's care (30:35–36). Thus he believes he is ensuring a minimal return on Jacob's investment.

Jacob, however, outwits his uncle, relying on his superior knowledge of the breeding cycles of his animals (30:37–42). The techniques he uses (e.g., placing visual aids before the animals while they mate) will not hold up to modern genetics, and yet he understood that breeding strong animals would result in stronger offspring and weak animals in weaker offspring (30:41–42). So although he held to the superstitious use of striped and streaked breeding rods, Jacob nonetheless was able to outmaneuver his uncle in acquiring more sheep and goats that anyone thought possible. The result was that Jacob became exceedingly wealthy, acquiring numerous flocks, slaves, camels, and donkeys (30:43). The phraseology is reminiscent of Abram's acquisition of wealth at the hands of the Pharaoh (12:16), so that Jacob became as rich in exile in Paddan-aram as his grandfather did in Egypt.[401]

Jacob's successes led naturally to jealousy and further problems with Laban's family (31:1–2). Laban's sons were mentioned in 30:35, where they were given charge over the sheep and goats of mixed color-patterns, and sent away from Jacob. Their jealousy was not simply because Jacob had done well, but because he had done well at their father's expense and presumably at the expense of their own inheritance.

---

[399] The sheep were the fat-tailed Awassi (*Ovis aries*) and the goats known as the Maʿaz Jebali (*Capra hircus*); Edwin Firmage, "Zoology," *ABD* 6:1109–1167, esp. 1126–27.

[400] Jacob J. Finkelstein, "An Old Babylonian Herding Contract and Genesis 31:38f," *JAOS* 88/1 (1968): 30–36.

[401] G. J. Wenham, *Genesis 16–50* (1994), 257–58.

Jacob's initial request to leave Paddan-aram and return to the Promised Land was thwarted by his avaricious uncle (30:25–36). Now however, Jacob receives divine direction to return to Canaan, the land of his ancestor, and his kindred (31:3). The assurance of Yahweh's protecting presence had been new in the list of patriarchal promises with Isaac (26:3) and had been repeated to Jacob in the Bethel dream (28:15). The means by which this directive from Yahweh comes to Jacob is not stated, but it is essentially the same as that revealed to him earlier in a dream and summarized in his speech to Leah and Rachel (31:13): "return to the land of your ancestors/birth."[402] Now Jacob is under divine mandate to return. Yahweh has spoken, and his uncle must not stand in his way again.

In order to be free of Laban's grip, Jacob needs the agreement and support of Leah and Rachel. He called them "into the field" for a private heart-to-heart, in which he made his case (31:4–13). In his appeal to his wives, Jacob makes three points. First, he has experienced a change in his relationship with Laban, who no longer views his son-in-law favorably as he once did (31:5). Second, Laban has been unfair in his treatment of Jacob. While Jacob has served his uncle diligently these many years, Laban has persistently attempted to cheat him, changing his wages ten times. Third, God has protected Jacob and, in fact, favored him by miraculously increasing his livestock holdings at the expense of Laban's flocks (thereby confirming to some degree the complaint of Laban's sons, 31:1). God's protecting presence is a recurring them in Jacob's speech (31:5, 7, 9).

To buttress this last point about God's protection, Jacob describes to his wives a dream revelation received earlier (31:10–13). The "angel of God" appeared in a dream and assured Jacob that God sees the injustice of his situation and that God will superintend the success of Jacob's unorthodox breeding techniques among the flocks.[403] The angel or messenger of God ($mal'ak\ h\bar{a}'\check{e}l\bar{o}h\hat{i}m$) usually comes to correct injustices. The angel appeared to Hagar in the desert of Shur with a similar mission (16:7–10), and again to Hagar in the desert of Beer-sheba (21:17–18).[404] The angel appeared once to Abraham in a slightly different role (22:11, 15), but in all cases the messenger is an unspecified supernatural envoy sent from God/Yahweh, who becomes interchangeably identified with God in the narrative.

---

[402] Yahweh simply spoke in 31:3 but in Jacob's report to his wives of an earlier encounter, "the angel of God" appeared to him in a dream (31:10–13). The source critical implications of these references have been duly noted, and may reflect the differences between priestly and non-priestly sources for the Jacob narrative (see introduction); D. M. Carr, *Reading the Fractures of Genesis* (1996), 212–13. As the text stands now, the two utterances of God complement each other in adding weight to the necessity for Jacob to travel back to Canaan.

[403] Jacob was the only patriarch (in the narrow use of that term) to receive dream-revelations; see commentary at 28:10–15. The dream in 31:10–13 has little of the theatrical effects of the ladder dream in Gen 28, until the angel of God appears. Such dreams of course will become a central feature of the Joseph narrative; see Closer Look "Dreams in the Hebrew Scriptures" at p. 322.

[404] Assuming no substantial difference between the angel of Yahweh and the angel of God.

The dream theophany culminates in the revelatory predicate nominative, "I am *the God of Bethel*," which elsewhere introduces divine promises or further divine self-disclosure.[405] Here, however, the revelation is a reminder of Jacob's commitments at Bethel, represented in the pillar and vow, and thereby also reminding him of the promise that he would return to Canaan safely.[406] In the strength of this revelation, Jacob is commanded to return now to Canaan, and by relating the dream's message to his wives, he hopes Leah and Rachel will agree.

Jacob's wives are in complete agreement with his new resolve to return to Canaan (31:14–16). Their father's treatment of them has been boorish and self-serving. And so having agreed, Jacob takes his entire family, wives and children, and his possessions in livestock, and sets out from Paddan-aram to return "to his father Isaac in the land of Canaan" (31:17–18). Having been thwarted by Laban once before in his attempt to return home (30:25–36), and separated from Laban by a three days' journey, Jacob decides against attempting to negotiate further with his dodgy father-in-law (31:19–20). It seems better simply to leave.

While departing Paddan-aram, Jacob and Rachel each steal something. Jacob steals Laban's heart, the idiom for deception in "Jacob deceived Laban the Aramean" (31:20), and Rachel steals her father's "household gods" (31:19).[407] These gods (or "household idols," *tĕrāpîm*) have long been a source of curiosity. All indications are that these were real objects (that is, physical, tangible objects rather than something indeterminate), most likely statuettes in human form, and in this case small enough to hide in a saddle-bag (31:34). Their function is equally obscure but these figurines appear to have represented one's ancestors and were used for divination.[408] Why exactly Rachel would steal them is not clear, although we may take a clue from the complaint that Laban has not provided a suitable inheritance for her and Leah (31:14–16), assuming they were somehow associated with one's estate. But in general, we cannot be certain why Rachel stole them.[409]

---

[405] Cf. also 15:1; 15:7; 17:1; 26:24; and 28:13. On the predicate nominative of identification, see B. T. Arnold and J. H. Choi, *A Guide to Biblical Hebrew Syntax* (2003), 6.

[406] The designation "the God of Bethel" is textually uncertain, and should probably be reconstructed based on the Septuagint as "the God *who appeared to you at* Bethel." If so, this is another example of the verb "appeared," a causative-reflexive term for "become visible (Niphal of *r'h*, "to see") used in Genesis at critical junctures in the ancestral narratives for divine self-disclosure (12:7; 17:1; 18:1; 26:2, 24; 35:1,9; 48:3), and see Closer Look "Divine Revelation in the Hebrew Scriptures" at p. 135, and commentary at 12:7.

[407] The verb "steal" (*gānab*) is a *leitwort* in 31:19–32, occurring six times in close proximity (vv. 19, 20, 26, 27, 30, 32). On the idiom, "to steal one's heart" as "cheat" or "deceive one," and on the semantic field of "steal" evolving from "remove (secretly)" to "cheat" generally, see Vinzenz Hamp, "*gānab*," *TDOT* 3:39–45, esp. 41.

[408] Note that Laban calls them his "gods" in 31:30. Additional evidence suggests these were kept in one's bedchamber in the rear of the house, near the door or doorpost of the bedchamber; Karel van der Toorn and Theodore J. Lewis, "*tĕrāpîm*," *TDOT* 15:777–789, esp. 781–88; Theodore J. Lewis, "Teraphim," *DDD*² 844–50.

[409] Perhaps the "household gods" were a sort of good luck charm; G. J. Wenham, *Genesis 16–50* (1994), 273–74; see also V. P. Hamilton, *The Book of Genesis, Chapters 18–50* (1995), 294–95.

So Jacob absconded with everything he had, crossed the Euphrates River, and headed for the hills of Gilead (31:21). The latter is a mountainous region in central Transjordan, and although not considered part of Canaan proper (Josh 22:9), it was eventually occupied by the tribes of Gad and Manasseh, with the Jabbok River as a natural border between them (Josh 13:24–31).[410] Laban learns of their departure and he sets out after them with "his kinsfolk," which hints at trouble (31:22–23). Jacob has a three-day lead, so it takes Laban seven days to catch up to him in the hills of Gilead. The text implies that military conflict would have ensued immediately, had God not warned Laban that night in a dream against precipitous actions (31:24).[411] They meet at an unspecified location in the hills of Gilead, which will be named later in the narrative, Galeed (31:25, cf. v. 47).[412]

Laban's opening complaint lists several grievances, culminating in his central concern – the theft of his household idols, which he calls simply "my gods" (31:26–30). Jacob is succinct in his reply, compared to his garrulous uncle; he feared Laban would use force to detain Leah and Rachel (31:31–32). Jacob is unaware the idols have indeed been stolen, as the narrator states, and so he indignantly vows to use capital punishment on anyone who has taken them.

The search for the missing idols is full of suspense (31:33–35). Laban enters each tent, one by one, Jacob's, Leah's, Bilhah's, Zilpah's, reserving Rachel's for last. When he finally goes into Rachel's tent, the narrator maintains the suspense until the last moment before revealing that Rachel has hidden the idols in the camel's saddle-bag where she is sitting. Rachel's ruse succeeds, showing she is every bit as resourceful as her father or husband. Her words to her father, "I cannot rise before you, for the way of women is upon me," appear to contain a *double entendre*. On the one hand, she is referring to her menstrual period, and on the other hand, her words imply she cannot prevail against him legally because of her status as a woman.[413] Thus the text neither condemns nor condones Rachel's actions, but rather admires her resourcefulness in seeking justice in a powerless situation.

Being unable to prove the accusation of theft, Laban is now on the defensive. Jacob's anger is palpable in his speech, now longer than before because of the list of grievances against his uncle (31:36–42). Laban has now falsely accused him of theft (so Jacob thinks), after abusing him for twenty years. Laban's flocks have faired well

---

[410] A. F. Rainey and R. S. Notley, *The Sacred Bridge: Carta's Atlas of the Biblical World* (2006), 41.

[411] Unlike Jacob's dreams (28:12–15; 31:10–13) the details of this dream theophany are left vague, although one is reminded of God's communication to King Abimelech in a dream; cf. 20:6.

[412] Thus following the same pattern as Gen 28 when Jacob settles for the night at "a certain place," which later receives the name Bethel (28:11 and 19).

[413] The expression "way of women" is not used elsewhere to refer to menstruation, while to "rise before" someone is language of confrontation; Jacqueline E. Lapsley, "The Voice of Rachel: Resistance and Polyphony in Gen 31:14–35," in *Genesis*, ed. Athalya Brenner (FCB² 1; Sheffield: Sheffield Academic Press, 1998), 233–48.

under Jacob's care, and in fact, Jacob sacrificed personal comforts to ensure their well-being.[414] Jacob's rebuke culminates in his central complaint, which succinctly summarizes his dilemma (31:41). He has "served" (another theme word in this text) twenty years in Laban's house, making it impossible for Jacob to build up his own house, and all that time he has done so for mere "wages," which in fact Laban has changed ten times. He closes with a faith statement: it is only divine intervention that has prevented Jacob from returning home empty-handed (31:42). The description of God as "the Fear of Isaac" occurs only here (and cf. 31:53), and is somewhat mysterious, generating several options for its meaning.[415] Perhaps the best we can do is understand the name as part of Jacob's attempt to reason with Laban, so that Laban might respect Isaac's side of the family by acquiescing to the dream warning he received from God (31:24).

At first, Laban sounds as though he will not acquiesce at all, insisting rather that Leah and Rachel belong to him, along with the children and livestock (31:43). Finally, however, Laban accepts the inevitable reality before him, and proposes a covenant to initiate a new relationship of peace between them (31:44). A few covenants in the Bible are symmetrical, emphasizing the obligations of both parties equally, which appears to be the case here (on the nature of "covenant," *běrît*, see commentary at 6:18, and Closer Look "Covenants in the Hebrew Scriptures" at p. 101). Jacob agrees, taking another stone and setting it up as a pillar, as he had done at Bethel (28:18), this time to commemorate the covenant with his uncle. He also orders the creation of a mound of other, presumably smaller stones, which he names Galeed in Hebrew and which Laban names Jegar-sahadutha in Aramaic, both meaning "Head of Witness" (31:46–48). The pillar they also name, calling it Mizpah, or "Watchpost," to watch over the peaceful relationship between them (31:49–50). The mound of stones and the single pillar, Galeed and Mizpah, perhaps constituted a boundary between two peoples, the Israelites and the Arameans, at Mount Gilead, thus also explaining the origins of its name.[416] Besides explaining the amicable separation between Jacob and Laban, the passage has clear etiological motives, providing background for several geographical names. In addition, the reference to Gilead three times leading up to this episode (31:21, 23, 25) prepares for the naming of the place as Galeed, and offers by popular etymology an explanation for the name of Mount Gilead.[417]

---

[414] Note an additional use of the *leitwort* "steal" (*gānab*) in 31:39. In this text, Rachel steals, Jacob steals, and wild animals steal, all in a context in which Laban is trying to steal everything.

[415] For convenient survey of the options, see Matthias Köckert, "Fear of Isaac," *DDD*[2] 329–331.

[416] Although Arameans may be a more general term including Ammonites; Roland de Vaux, *The Early History of Israel* (London: Darton, Longman, and Todd, 1978), 170–71, and 572–74. North Mesopotamia contained a mixture of ethnic groups, and the use of Aramaic on Laban's lips is not unexpected.

[417] Magnus Ottosson, "Gilead," *ABD* 2:1020–22, esp. 1020.

In one final speech, Laban stresses the covenant agreement as a pact of nonaggression (31:51–52). The covenant is ratified in solemn oaths, appealing to the God of Abraham, of Nahor, and the Fear of Isaac (31:53). The phraseology of this verse is difficult, and we may have here a reflex of henotheism or monolatry, in that Jacob is swearing by the only God he acknowledges, that of Abraham and Isaac, while Laban swears by the God of Nahor. Whether or not these deities are perceived as the same god is unclear.[418] There follows the ceremonial covenant meal beside the mound of stones (31:54, mentioned proleptically in 31:46). Laban rose "early in the morning," which connotes resolve to take action without delay (31:55).[419] His return to Paddan-aram opens a new door of opportunity for Jacob, who now must return to the unfinished business with his brother in the Promised Land.

GENESIS 32:1–32 JACOB AT THE JABBOK

(32:1) Jacob went on his way and the angels of God met him;

(32:2) and when Jacob saw them he said, "This is God's camp!" So he called that place Mahanaim.[kk]

(32:3) Jacob sent messengers before him to his brother Esau in the land of Seir, the country of Edom,

(32:4) instructing them, "Thus you shall say to my lord Esau: Thus says your servant Jacob, 'I have lived with Laban as an alien, and stayed until now;

(32:5) and I have oxen, donkeys, flocks, male and female slaves; and I have sent to tell my lord, in order that I may find favor in your sight.' "

(32:6) The messengers returned to Jacob, saying, "We came to your brother Esau, and he is coming to meet you, and four hundred men are with him."

(32:7) Then Jacob was greatly afraid and distressed; and he divided the people that were with him, and the flocks and herds and camels, into two companies,

(32:8) thinking, "If Esau comes to the one company and destroys it, then the company that is left will escape."

(32:9) And Jacob said, "O God of my father Abraham and God of my father Isaac, O LORD who said to me, 'Return to your country and to your kindred, and I will do you good,'

(32:10) I am not worthy of the least of all the steadfast love and all the faithfulness that you have shown to your servant, for with only my staff I crossed this Jordan; and now I have become two companies.

(32:11) Deliver me, please, from the hand of my brother, from the hand of Esau, for I am afraid of him; he may come and kill us all, the mothers with the children.

---

[418] Especially since the Masoretic Text uses a plural verb, may the gods "judge between us," which is corrected to singular in the Septuagint and Samaritan Pentateuch (31:53).

[419] Cf. 19:27; 21:14; 22:3, 26:31; Rüdiger Bartelmus, "*škm*," *TDOT* 14:681–88, esp. 687–88.

[kk] Here taken to mean *Two camps*.

(32:12) Yet you have said, 'I will surely do you good, and make your off-spring as the sand of the sea, which cannot be counted because of their number.'"

(32:13) So he spent that night there, and from what he had with him he took a present for his brother Esau,

(32:14) two hundred female goats and twenty male goats, two hundred ewes and twenty rams,

(32:15) thirty milch camels and their colts, forty cows and ten bulls, twenty female donkeys and ten male donkeys.

(32:16) These he delivered into the hand of his servants, every drove by itself, and said to his servants, "Pass on ahead of me, and put a space between drove and drove."

(32:17) He instructed the foremost, "When Esau my brother meets you, and asks you, 'To whom do you belong? Where are you going? And whose are these ahead of you?'

(32:18) then you shall say, 'They belong to your servant Jacob; they are a present sent to my lord Esau; and moreover he is behind us.'"

(32:19) He likewise instructed the second and the third and all who followed the droves, "You shall say the same thing to Esau when you meet him,

(32:20) and you shall say, 'Moreover your servant Jacob is behind us.'" For he thought, "I may appease him with the present that goes ahead of me, and afterwards I shall see his face; perhaps he will accept me."

(32:21) So the present passed on ahead of him; and he himself spent that night in the camp.

(32:22) The same night he got up and took his two wives, his two maids, and his eleven children, and crossed the ford of the Jabbok.

(32:23) He took them and sent them across the stream, and likewise everything that he had.

(32:24) Jacob was left alone; and a man wrestled with him until daybreak.

(32:25) When the man saw that he did not prevail against Jacob, he struck him on the hip socket; and Jacob's hip was put out of joint as he wrestled with him.

(32:26) Then he said, "Let me go, for the day is breaking." But Jacob said, "I will not let you go, unless you bless me."

(32:27) So he said to him, "What is your name?" And he said, "Jacob."

(32:28) Then the man said, "You shall no longer be called Jacob, but Israel, for you have striven with God and with humans, and have prevailed."

(32:29) Then Jacob asked him, "Please tell me your name." But he said, "Why is it that you ask my name?" And there he blessed him.

(32:30) So Jacob called the place Peniel, saying, "For I have seen God face to face, and yet my life is preserved."

(32:31) The sun rose upon him as he passed Penuel, limping because of his hip.

(32:32) Therefore to this day the Israelites do not eat the thigh muscle that is on the hip socket, because he struck Jacob on the hip socket at the thigh muscle.

I n Gen 28, Jacob was on the road, running away from his past in the Promised Land, and especially running away from his irate brother, Esau. Headed for the ancestral homeland, Paddan-aram, Jacob came to a rest stop along the way, and there encountered Yahweh in a dream. The Lord assured Jacob of his role in the ancestral lineage, promised that one day he would return to his home, and that he would not be alone while in exile. Yahweh would be with him for protection and guidance. Jacob named the placed Bethel, "house of God." Now Jacob is on the road again, finally free of uncle Laban and poised on the border of the Promised Land, ready for reentry. At another rest stop on the border, he encounters God again, this time on a more personal level. He limps away a different man, ready to face his past, including especially his disgruntled brother.

As we have seen several times in Genesis, the book's etiological interests lead to explanations of why things are the way they are, and in this case, why important locations in later Israel are named as they are. Gen 12–36 are especially interested in associating these places with the ancestors (e.g., Bethel in Gen 28), giving the locales a unique significance. This text, together with Gen 33, has three such places in view, Mahanaim, Penuel (aka Peniel), and Succoth (33:17). Before going further in this text, it will be necessary to sort out what we know about these places, as much as possible. On his way back from Paddan-aram, Jacob followed a corridor of seasonal seminomadic migration connecting the warm Jordan Valley lowlands, where shepherds would spend the winters, with the relatively cool transjordanian highlands during the summers.[420] The migration corridor appears to have ended at Succoth (modern Tell Deir ʿAllā), near where the Jabbok River issues onto the plain of the Jordan Valley (33:17). East of Succoth, further upstream in the Jabbok Valley, are found two sites across the stream from each other.[421] As one moves westward into the Promised Land, these twin cities defended the last feasible crossing-point of the Jabbok River, and in some senses may be said to rest on the border of the Promised Land itself. The larger of the two, Mahanaim, is situated on the northern bank of the river, which meanders in such a way as to run north–south precisely at the ford between Mahanaim, and the smaller site, Penuel.[422] Mahanaim's location

---

[420] Jeremy M. Hutton, "Mahanaim, Penuel, and Transhumance Routes: Observations on Genesis 32–33 and Judges 8," *JNES* 65/3 (2006): 161–78, esp. 173–78.

[421] A. F. Rainey and R. S. Notley, *The Sacred Bridge: Carta's Atlas of the Biblical World* (2006), 115, and for confirmation of these site identifications, see J. M. Hutton, "Mahanaim, Penuel, and Transhumance Routes: Observations on Genesis 32–33 and Judges 8." See also H. J. Franken, "Deir ʿAlla, Tell," *OEANE* 2:137–38; and Diana V. Edelman, "Mahanaim," *ABD* 4:472–73.

[422] Known today as Tulūl aḏ-Ḏahab al-Ġarbīya, "the western hills of gold," and Tulūl aḏ-Ḏahab aš-Šarqīya, "the eastern hills of gold," respectively. So the western site, Mahanaim, is on the north bank, but an S-shaped bend in the Jabbok loops around between the twin cities, so that Penuel, the eastern city, is on its south bank. Mahanaim later became the administrative seat of Gilead during the United Monarchy (2 Sam 2:9; 1 Kgs 4:14), and Penuel was a military outpost for Jeroboam I (1 Kgs 12:25).

on the northern bank made it the natural point for movement from Paddan-aram as one moves westward toward the promised land.

The Hebrew word order of v. 1[2][423] marks a change of subject introducing a new unit, and signaling that the narrative is moving forward.[424] The "angels of God" (*mal'ăkê 'ĕlōhîm*) were not in motion, ascending and descending, as they had been in Jacob's ladder-dream (28:12), but were apparently stationary here, as though encamped.[425] Their appearance at the beginning of this text implies that the "man" Jacob wrestled in v. 24[25] may be one of these angels, as was apparently the interpretation of the prophet Hosea (Hos 12:4 [Heb 12:5]). Their appearance also prompts the first of two etiological explanations of the place name, Mahanaim ("two camps"), since the angels appeared to Jacob as a divine encampment (v. 2[3]).[426] Having now arrived safely at the portal to the Promised Land, the sudden appearance of these "angels of God" must surely be intended to bring to the foreground the promises and commitments of their former appearance at Bethel (28:10–22).

The next portion of the chapter focuses on initiating contact with Jacob's brother Esau, and preparing for the encounter with him (vv. 3–21[4–22]).[427] This is Jacob's unavoidable task. After twenty years, he cannot avoid facing the fact that he deceived his father Isaac and stole the blessing of his brother, who has vowed to repay him violently (27:41). Life in the promised land cannot and will not be a fulfillment of the divine mandate until Jacob has come to terms with his treatment of Esau in the past. The beginning of the action in v. 3a[4a] has an ironic feature unmistakable in the Hebrew original, but obscured in almost all translations. Jacob's "messengers" sent to Esau in Seir correspond to the "angels" of God who met Jacob at Mahanaim

---

[423] The Bible's chapter breaks and verse numbers follow the medieval Vulgate translation, and are sometimes at odds with the most natural unit markers for the Hebrew text. Hebrew editions put the chapter break at 31:55 (see NRSV's footnote), and so the English verse numbers of the NRSV for Gen 32 are off by one. Numbers in brackets in the commentary will indicate the Hebrew versification.

[424] On the other hand, placing the chapter break at 31:55 means the word order contrasts Laban and Jacob: "Laban rose up,... then he departed and returned home, *but* Jacob went on his way."

[425] Such divine messengers have appeared in Genesis to correct injustices (16:7–10; 21:17–18), or to execute punishment (Gen 19), but always as unspecified supernatural envoys sent from God (or Yahweh). The exact expression "angels of God" occurs only here and at 28:12 in the Hebrew Scriptures (but cf. similarly, 2 Chr 36:16).

[426] The dual suffix may not have been primary in the name, but lends itself beautifully to the word play in the second etiology explaining the name, in which Jacob divides his company into "two camps" (vv. 7 and 10 [8, 11]). *HALOT* 2:570–71; *DCH* 5:225.

[427] Most are agreed we have a composite text here, made up of two sources, whether we take them as the conventional J and E sources (vv. 2b–22[3b–23] and vv. 1–2a, 23–29[2–3a, 24–30] respectively), or as "survival" and "gift" traditions, distinguishing sources based on the reasons for Jacob's division of his possessions. For the first approach, see Tzemah Yoreh, "Jacob's Struggle," *ZAW* 117/1 (2005): 95–97, and for the second, J. M. Hutton, "Mahanaim, Penuel, and Transhumance Routes: Observations on Genesis 32–33 and Judges 8," esp. 166–67.

(the same word is used, *mal'ākîm*).[428] Jacob takes his cue from God. As God has sent messengers to Mahanaim, perhaps to protect Jacob as promised in the Bethel theophany (28:15), so now Jacob sends messengers to find Esau, to tell him of his great successes in Paddan-aram, and perhaps to soften the effect of Jacob's return (vv. 3–5[4–6]).

Thus far in Gen 32, we have seen a creative word play to explain the name of Mahanaim and the artful use of "angels/messengers" to transition from God's angels to Jacob's messengers. This reflects a dominant feature of the chapter impossible to communicate in translation; that of the literary artistry and interpretive power of word plays.[429] The three geographical locations, Mahanaim, Penuel, and Succoth (including 33:17) are given punning names, and obviously Jacob's name change to Israel uses word play. But in addition, and less obvious in translation, Jacob's name sounds similar to both "Jabbok" and "wrestle" in Hebrew, and there are other subtler word plays in the narrative. The narrator uses such techniques to draw out ironic connections, and sometimes to stimulate the reader's memory in order to associate contrasting figures, themes, or events.[430] The final effect is a wonderfully textured narrative that highlights God's sovereign but subtle role in the events, and links Israel's later customs and geopolitical realities with the far distant ancestors.

Jacob's speech to Esau, mediated through his messengers, is marked by the submissive rhetoric of the ancient Near East (vv. 4–5[5–6]). The uses of "lord" for Esau and "servant" for Jacob are self-designations of subservience reflecting more than cultural courtesy, but acknowledging Jacob's dependence upon Esau, and seeking his favor.[431] Jacob also calls attention to the great wealth he has acquired while away, hoping this too will assuage Esau's ill feelings. The news that Esau is, in fact, on his way to meet Jacob with a company of four hundred men hints at trouble, and elevates the suspense in the narrative (v. 6[7]). Such a large escort implies military conflict may be imminent, especially when one remembers that Abram needed only 318 men to rescue Lot from the four kings from the east (together with two allies from near Hebron, 14:13–14). The narrator exposes Jacob's inner life as full of fear and distress, which is only reasonable (vv. 7–8[8–9]). He divides all that he has into "two companies [lit. camps]," which is a defensive strategy for Jacob, and another opportunity for word play on the name Mahanaim, "two camps," for the narrator (cf. v. 2[3]).

---

[428] The "land of Seir" is located nebulously somewhere in the south in the Arabah valley; A. F. Rainey and R. S. Notley, *The Sacred Bridge: Carta's Atlas of the Biblical World* (2006), 115.

[429] See the classic study of this topic in S. Gevirtz, "Of Patriarchs and Puns: Joseph at the Fountain, Jacob at the Ford," esp. 50–53; and also the list in G. J. Wenham, *Genesis 16–50* (1994), 288–89.

[430] For these techniques, see S. B. Noegel, "Drinking Feasts and Deceptive Feats: Jacob and Laban's Double Talk," in *Puns and Pundits* (2000), esp. 163.

[431] Helmer Ringgren, Udo Rüterswörden, and Horacio Simian-Yofre, "*ābad*," *TDOT* 10:376–405, esp. 392.

Division of the family and goods into two camps is the first of three precautionary measures, taken in order to prepare for Jacob's meeting with Esau. The second is an eloquent prayer, in which Jacob appeals for deliverance from Esau's hand (vv. 9–12[10–13]). With several allusions to Gen 28, Jacob identifies God as Yahweh, the God of his fathers, recalls that he is traveling back to the Promised Land in response to God's own command, recalls too that God has promised to protect him, and humbly acknowledges that he does not deserve God's steadfast love and faithfulness, which has resulted in his rags-to-riches life so far. His desperate cry for help, "deliver me, please, . . . for I am afraid," stands at the center of the prayer, and is made more compelling by the real possibility that Esau might kill not only Jacob, as he has threatened to do (27:41), but the entire family as well. The threat of annihilation of Jacob's family directly negates God's promises to make Jacob's "seed" (*zeraʿ*, NRSV's "offspring") like "the sand of the sea," an image of fecundity used only here for Jacob, and only at 22:17 for Abraham.

Jacob's third and final preparation is a generous gift for Esau, together with the instructions he gives his servants for delivering the gift (vv. 13–21[14–22]). The purpose for the gift is clearly to pacify Esau, but it may also be variously understood as a sign of obsequious courtesy, or as a return of the blessing Jacob stole from Esau.[432] The size of the gift in livestock is staggering, five hundred fifty animals in all (vv. 14–15[15–16]). He divided the animals into droves and sent them ahead to meet Esau in separate groups, spaced from each other so they will encounter Esau *seriatim* (vv. 16–21[17–22]). Each time Esau meets another drove, Jacob's servants are to use the servant–lord obsequious tone again: these belong to "your servant Jacob" and are sent as a present to "my lord Esau." By so doing, Jacob hopes to "appease" Esau (lit. "atone his face"), which will then result in reconciliation, "I shall see his face" and "he will accept me" (v. 20[21]).[433] The attempt to "appease" someone (*kipper*, "make amends," "atone") is a term used frequently in ritual texts in the Bible for the removal of an impediment to the divine–human relationship, which is prerequisite to reconciliation.[434] Here, the use is nonritual because it involves two humans, Jacob

---

[432] This "gift" (*minḥâ*) is called a "blessing" (*bĕrākâ*) in 33:11, implying that Jacob is giving back to Esau the blessing he stole from him before his escape to Paddan-aram; C. Westermann, *Genesis 12–36* (1985), 510.

[433] Although the NRSV translation of v. 20(21) has the word "face" only once, the Hebrew uses the term three times in three separate idioms: "I will atone his face," "I will see his face," and "he will lift up my face" (four times, counting the compound preposition *lĕpānāy*, "ahead of me"). The first addresses the direct result of Jacob's gifts, which he hopes will atone for his treatment of Esau, but the other two occurrences connote reconciliation, favor, and acceptance. These recurring uses of "face" (*pāneh*) also prepare the reader for the next pericope in which the place is named Peniel, "the face of God" (v. 30[31]), as well as for the occasion when Jacob sees Esau's face again (33:10, where see commentary). On the idioms using "face," see Horacio Simian-Yofre, "*pānîm*," *TDOT* 11:589–615, esp. 597–605.

[434] *HALOT* 2:494; *DCH* 4:455–56; Roy Gane, *Cult and Character: Purification Offerings, Day of Atonement, and Theodicy* (Winona Lake, Ind.: Eisenbrauns, 2005), 194.

and Esau, and yet it illustrates the principle. Jacob is attempting to take away Esau's ground for hatred of him, which is something Jacob can accomplish because it is in his control. Reconciliation itself, however, is not assured because it depends entirely on Esau's ability to extend grace.[435]

That night, Jacob forded the river with his family and all that he had (vv. 22–23[23–24]).[436] Left alone in his fear and distress, and having finished his final preparations to meet Esau, Jacob wrestles there during the night with "a man" (v. 24[25]). The verb "wrestle" (*'ābaq*) almost certainly plays on the name of the river, Jabbok (*yabbōq*) as well as on the name Jacob (*ya'ăqōb*).[437] These sound-alike associations work together to portray Israel's ancestor at a critical moment in life's journey, restlessly spending the night on the border of the promised land, struggling with God in a way that echoes both his name and the land he will inherit. As a patriarch for all who would count themselves among his descendants, "Jacob at the Jabbok *'ābaq*-ing with God" becomes the paradigm for all who would struggle with God.

Although Jacob's nocturnal opponent is "a man," he blesses Jacob (v. 29[30]), he represents the face of God (v. 30[31]), and by implication even identifies himself as supernatural ("you have striven with God," v. 28[29]).[438] This mysterious encounter with a supernatural being, at night and alone, in which the attacker needs to escape before the rising sun and needs to retain his anonymity, has obviously generated a enormous amount of reflection and commentary. Since the days of Hermann Gunkel over a century ago, many have assumed the text reflects an original oral tradition relating a local legend of a night-time battle, in which a deity impedes the human from crossing the river but is compelled to give him a gift.[439] Based on similar legends in other cultures in which a god, demon, or monster guards a river-crossing, Gunkel proposed that this Israelite version originally had the patriarch delivering the blow against the deity but a later redactor attributed the blow to God. It is unlikely we will ever trace such origins of this episode, and yet the wrestling scene may indeed have roots in an older version in which the patriarch wrestled with a human stranger during the night, not unlike Gilgamesh wrestling with Enkidu and

---

[435] Similarly, cultic atonement does not automatically result in reconciliation with God, which rests entirely on Yahweh's volition; R. Gane, *Cult and Character* (2005), 195.

[436] It is not a simple matter to sort out the chronology, or even geography, of this text. While the separate references to "that night" (vv. 13 and 21–22[14 and 22–23]) have been used as a criterion for source distinction, this is likely resumptive repetition, a necessary tool used by ancient authors and redactors; Moshe Anbar, "La 'Reprise'," *VT* 38/4 (1988): 385–98.

[437] S. Gevirtz, "Of Patriarchs and Puns: Joseph at the Fountain, Jacob at the Ford," esp. 51.

[438] The eighth century prophet Hosea called Jacob's foe an angel; Hos 12:4 [Hebrew 12:5].

[439] Gunkel takes Yahweh's attack of Moses in Exod 4:24–26 as an instructive parallel, and draws comparisons with many extrabiblical examples of the literary motif of nocturnal battle with demons, monsters, phantoms, or the devil; Hermann Gunkel, *Genesis: Translated and Interpreted*, trans. Mark E. Biddle (Macon, Ga.: Mercer University Press, 1997), 349 and 352–53.

other ancient heroic literature.[440] This human stranger may at some point have been identified with the celestial patron of Esau, but was subsequently transformed by the editor into God himself, as shown by the narrative's conclusion in which "Peniel" ("the face of God") plays central etiological role.[441] Also, it has been suggested that parallels with heroic literature in the ancient Near East illuminate this text in that the hero is defined by one's adversary, and therefore the greater the adversary, the greater the hero.[442] The fact that Jacob wrestles with God gives the patriarch unparalleled stature.

Adding to the uncertainty of this text is the curious wound Jacob received during the struggle (v. 25[26]): "he struck him on the hip socket." The narrator's conclusion to the text draws an etiological application (v. 32[33]). This explains why later Israelites, those living in the narrator's time, do not eat "the thigh muscle that is on the hip socket." Yet this dietary restriction is mentioned nowhere else in the Bible, and the specific words used for "thigh muscle" and "hip socket" are full of translation difficulties.[443] Whatever the precise nature of the wound, Jacob is able to continue the fight, and the reader is left to marvel at Jacob's nearly superhuman strength, especially once we know the identity of this adversary as God.[444]

For the first time in the wrestling match, words are spoken and a dialogue ensues (vv. 26–29[27–30]). The nocturnal foe cannot risk tarrying until dawn, which adds to the mystery and contributes to the theories that he was originally a Canaanite river deity or demon in the earliest versions of this text.[445] Whatever the foe's

---

[440] Andrew George, *The Epic of Gilgamesh: The Babylonian Epic Poem and Other Texts in Akkadian and Sumerian* (London: Penguin, 2003), 16–17 (Standard Version) and 106–7 (Old Babylonian Version).

[441] Nahum M. Sarna, *Genesis: The Traditional Hebrew Text with the New JPS Translation* (JPS Torah Commentary; Philadelphia: Jewish Publication Society, 1989), 403–4. Thus the text may be explained diachronically in a sort of *intra*textuality; that is, an older account has been corrected in redaction to reflect Israel's monotheism.

[442] R. S. Hendel, *The Epic of the Patriarch* (1987), 101–2.

[443] For this discussion, see S. Gevirtz, "Of Patriarchs and Puns: Joseph at the Fountain, Jacob at the Ford," 51–53. Gevirtz proposes taking "the hip socket" as a euphemism for *membrum virile*, and supported by S. H. Smith, "'Heel' and 'Thigh': The Concept of Sexuality in the Jacob-Esau Narratives," *VT* 40 (1990): 464–73, esp. 466–69. If so, God asserted his sovereignty over Jacob's procreative power, perhaps in rebuke of his polygamous relationships upon returning to the Promised Land, or perhaps to underscore the divine promise of land-inheritance and its interconnectedness with the promise of procreativity. It is also possible to interpret the Jabbok episode as a divine condemnation of Jacob's polygamy, and that hereafter in the Jacob narrative, only Rachel is considered his wife; Richard M. Davidson, *Flame of Yahweh: Sexuality in the Old Testament* (Peabody, Mass.: Hendrickson Publishers, 2007), 188–89.

[444] Jacob's herculean strength was also a theme at the well near Haran, when he rolled away a well-stone that normally required two or three men (29:10); see V. P. Hamilton, *The Book of Genesis, Chapters 18–50* (1995), 255 and 330.

[445] So the demon is powerful only at night because his strength slips away with the rising sun. Many have also observed the similarities of this text with Exod 4:24–26, in which the hostile demon or evil spirit has secondarily been changed to Yahweh; C. Westermann, *Genesis 12–36* (1985), 516–17; H. Gunkel, *Genesis: Translated and Interpreted* (1997), 349.

limitations, Jacob recognizes he has the upper hand and refuses to release him until he receives a blessing. His request for a departing benediction most likely denotes simply an expression of friendship, signifying that the stranger is no longer hostile but has become an ally.[446] Although the same word is used, "bless" (*brk*), one simply cannot equate this blessing with the all-important patriarchal blessing (whether formal testamental blessings or not, cf. 27:27b–29; 28:1b–4; 48:15–49:32). However, in a text so rich in word plays and literary allusions, we should not miss the irony of Jacob's request for a blessing. Having stolen Isaac's testamental blessing intended for Esau, and having benefited from the blessing of Yahweh while in exile (30:27), Jacob nevertheless still needs a blessing. The need is heightened, of course, by the imminent meeting with his aggrieved brother, to whom he will offer a blessing (33:11, and see commentary below).

The nighttime foe – perhaps now a friend – changes Jacob's name, which may be a result of Jacob's request for a blessing (vv. 27–28[28–29]).[447] Names in Hebrew narrative portray the individual, revealing a kernel of character, so that name changes imply a change of character, life circumstances, or status.[448] Joseph and Daniel receive new names from foreign kings (41:45; Dan 1:7). But Jacob's name is changed by the mysterious riverside visitor, who is identified later as God himself, and therefore more like God's change of "Abram" to "Abraham" (17:5).

To the simple query about his name, the patriarch replies with a single word, "Jacob." When asked a similar question once before, Jacob had flatly lied, "I am Esau your firstborn" (27:18–19). This time his abrupt response was honest, "Jacob," and something of a confession, since it echoes "deceiver." The explanation of the new name uses a sound-alike word play so common in Genesis, "you have striven with God" (*śārîtā 'im-'ĕlōhîm*), and echoes the name "Israel" (*yiśrā'ēl*). The NRSV denotes that Jacob has successfully striven with both God and humans, but another interpretation breaks the sentence differently: "you have striven with God, and with humans you have prevailed."[449] The name "Israel" itself likely employs a word meaning "rule, judge" rather than "strive," and is thus "God rules" or "God judges."[450] The geopolitical implications of Jacob's new name are undeniable. As Esau is also Edom (25:30), so now Jacob will become Israel.[451] Now with a new

---

[446] C. W. Mitchell, *The Meaning of* brk *"to bless" in the Old Testament* (1987), 109.

[447] As in the consequential imperfect plus *waw*-consecutive assumed at v. 27(28) in NRSV's "*So* he said to him. . . . "

[448] See commentary at 17:5; and M. Sternberg, *The Poetics of Biblical Narrative* (1985), 328–31.

[449] S. Gevirtz, "Of Patriarchs and Puns: Joseph at the Fountain, Jacob at the Ford," 51.

[450] Robert B. Coote, "The Meaning of the Name *Israel*," *HTR* 65/1 (1972): 137–42, esp. 140. The matter remains unsettled; Hans-Jürgen Zobel, "*yiśrā'ēl*," *TDOT* 6:397–420, esp. 399–401.

[451] However, it is counterintuitive to take "Israel" in this text as reflecting a change in the loyalties of a nomadic group, forebears to ancient Israel itself, who renounced their ancestral deity when they migrated to Canaan in favor of the indigenous god, El. For critique of such a rigidly traditio-historical methodology, see H. Marks, "Biblical Naming and Poetic Etymology," 34.

name, the patriarch Jacob, representing the nation Israel, is soon to cross the Jordan River and claim the land promised to his grandfather many years ago.

Jacob's interlocutor refuses to reveal his name, confirming the idea that the name of God is ineffable. As in other contexts in which someone asks the divine emissary for a name, the response is a question, "why is it that you ask my name?" (cf. Judg 13:18). The response itself confirms the supernatural status of the "man" wrestling with Jacob, and prepares for the assumption of ancient popular theology that one cannot see God and live (v. 30[31]; 16:13; cf. Exod 33:20). The exchange closes with the simple assertion, "he blessed him," although we are not given the contents or articulation of the blessing itself.

The text closes with the narrator's summary, containing two important etiological conclusions (vv. 30–32[31–33]). First, Jacob named the place Peniel, "the face of God," which occurs only here and again uses word play to associate the event just narrated with the important city, Penuel.[452] Jacob has survived an encounter with the face of God, against the common understanding of God–human interaction. So he commemorates the event, as patriarchs often do, by pronouncing a new name for the location (as he had done at Bethel, 28:19; cf. also 21:31; 22:14; 26:33). Jacob forded the Jabbok expecting to see Esau's face and fearing death as a result.[453] Instead, he saw God's face, and lived! It seemed only right to commemorate the event and the spot as Peniel, before moving on to face his brother.

The second etiological note is prompted by the image of Jacob limping as he passes Penuel, which resumes the odd topic of "the thigh muscle that is on the hip socket." We have no unequivocal explanation of dietary restriction related to it, since it is not mentioned elsewhere in the Bible. It may be enough to note that this practice was current in the life of the narrator, since "to this day" reflects the eyewitness perspective of life in the land some considerable amount of time after the events.[454] It is also possible, in a text so rich in word play and sound-alike associations, that "the thigh muscle" is an artificial but intentional articulation of a surprise ending to this episode. The phrase appears to contain an allusion through word plays to the names Gad and Manasseh.[455] If so, the geopolitical relationship between the transjordanian tribes of Gad and the half-tribe of Manasseh are intentionally associated with this event at the very place that will one day form a border between

---

[452] For the location of Penuel, see discussion of Mahanaim at v. 2(3).

[453] On seeing Esau's face, note the commentary at v. 20(21), and for Jacob's concern that Esau might kill him and his entire family, see his prayer at v. 11(12).

[454] Whether the phrase is part of a later Deuteronomistic redaction remains open for debate; Jeffrey C. Geoghegan, "Additional Evidence for a Deuteronomistic Redaction of the 'Tetrateuch,'" *CBQ* 67/3 (2005): 405–21, esp. 411–13.

[455] S. Gevirtz, "Of Patriarchs and Puns: Joseph at the Fountain, Jacob at the Ford," 53–54. The "thigh muscle" is *gîd hannāšeh*, while Gad and Manasseh are *gād* and *měnaššeh* respectively.

the tribes (Josh 12:2–6; 13:24–31), and thereby also linking these tribes closer to father Jacob.

GENESIS 33:1–20 JACOB AND ESAU MEET

(33:1) Now Jacob looked up and saw Esau coming, and four hundred men with him. So he divided the children among Leah and Rachel and the two maids.

(33:2) He put the maids with their children in front, then Leah with her children, and Rachel and Joseph last of all.

(33:3) He himself went on ahead of them, bowing himself to the ground seven times, until he came near his brother.

(33:4) But Esau ran to meet him, and embraced him, and fell on his neck and kissed him, and they wept.

(33:5) When Esau looked up and saw the women and children, he said, "Who are these with you?" Jacob said, "The children whom God has graciously given your servant."

(33:6) Then the maids drew near, they and their children, and bowed down;

(33:7) Leah likewise and her children drew near and bowed down; and finally Joseph and Rachel drew near, and they bowed down.

(33:8) Esau said, "What do you mean by all this company that I met?" Jacob answered, "To find favor with my lord."

(33:9) But Esau said, "I have enough, my brother; keep what you have for yourself."

(33:10) Jacob said, "No, please; if I find favor with you, then accept my present from my hand; for truly to see your face is like seeing the face of God – since you have received me with such favor.

(33:11) Please accept my gift that is brought to you, because God has dealt graciously with me, and because I have everything I want." So he urged him, and he took it.

(33:12) Then Esau said, "Let us journey on our way, and I will go alongside you."

(33:13) But Jacob said to him, "My lord knows that the children are frail and that the flocks and herds, which are nursing, are a care to me; and if they are overdriven for one day, all the flocks will die.

(33:14) Let my lord pass on ahead of his servant, and I will lead on slowly, according to the pace of the cattle that are before me and according to the pace of the children, until I come to my lord in Seir."

(33:15) So Esau said, "Let me leave with you some of the people who are with me." But he said, "Why should my lord be so kind to me?"

(33:16) So Esau returned that day on his way to Seir.

(33:17) But Jacob journeyed to Succoth, and built himself a house, and made booths for his cattle; therefore the place is called Succoth.

(33:18) Jacob came safely to the city of Shechem, which is in the land of Canaan, on his way from Paddan-aram; and he camped before the city.

(33:19) And from the sons of Hamor, Shechem's father, he bought for one hundred
         pieces of money the plot of land on which he had pitched his tent.
(33:20) There he erected an altar and called it El-Elohe-Israel[ll].

O ur hero ran away from the Promised Land as Jacob but returns as Israel. He
     acquired a family and great wealth while away in Paddan-aram, and was given
a new name while encamped at Penuel, the gateway to Canaan. There remains one
final requirement, however: reconciliation with his estranged brother, Esau. This
text narrates their meeting, the outcome of which was by no means clear until the
last moment. The chapter closes with Jacob's reentry into the Promised Land.

Verse 1 resumes the previous chapter's tension and anxiety with the reminder
that Esau is approaching with "four hundred men" (cf. 32:6[32:7]). The wrestling
episode at the Jabbok ford suspended this topic momentarily, but v. 1 takes up once
again the question of whether Esau will forgive or exact the vengeance he has vowed
(27:41). Jacob is in a most precarious position, exposed with his entire family, both
women and children, plus livestock, facing an approaching battalion of Esau's men.
Fear of the unknown leads him to divide his family again, this time not into two
camps as before (32:7–8[32:8–9]), but into three groups organized according to their
mothers: Bilhah and Zilpah's group first, then Leah's, and finally Rachel and Joseph
(vv. 1b-2). The order of march is determined by Jacob's favoritism, so that the degree
of risk corresponds to his order of preference: least loved at the front line, most
loved at the rear.

Jacob also, however, takes personal responsibility by going on ahead of his family
to face Esau himself (v. 3).[456] The Jacob we see now attempting to make amends
for his past crimes is not focused simply on self-preservation as the old pre-Jabbok
patriarch. His strategy designed for self-protection and defense (32:7–8[32:8–9])
has now become one of complete submission, as a guilty servant stands before
an overlord waiting for punishment. Jacob appears truly to have become Israel.[457]
Bowing "seven times" before another is one of the most obsequious expressions of
submission possible in the ancient world.[458] The concept is that Jacob bowed seven

---

[ll] That is *God, the God of Israel.*

[456] The Hebrew word order of "*he himself* went on ahead of them" highlights Jacob's own
       personal role in taking responsibility for what happens next; C. H. J. van der Merwe, J.
       A. Naudé, and J. H. Kroeze, *A Biblical Hebrew Reference Grammar* (1999), 347.

[457] Transformation of the scheming Jacob into the submissive Israel is advanced quite subtly
       in the text. I do not find entirely convincing some of the evidence garnered for the argu-
       ment that the text contrasts the pre-Peniel Jacob with the new, post-Peniel Israel; Stephen
       A. Geller, "The Struggle at the Jabbok: The Uses of Enigma in a Biblical Narrative,"
       JANESCU 14 (1982): 37–60; V. P. Hamilton, *The Book of Genesis, Chapters 18–50* (1995),
       343–45. The gifts Jacob sent ahead to meet Esau (v. 8, cf. Gen 32) were different from
       the arrangement of his family, and the idea that Jacob was attempting to hide behind his
       family in Gen 32 but marched boldly in front of his family in Gen 33 is forced.

[458] The Amarna correspondence has numerous examples of bowing seven times. The most
       servile of all is prostration at another's feet "seven times and seven times, on the back and

times, the first while Esau was visible but at a great distance, and the seventh before Esau at his feet. Ironically, Jacob's obeisance forfeits the blessing of Isaac (27:29): "Be lord over your brothers, and may your mother's sons bow down to you."

The denouement at v. 4 is dense with verbal action: Esau ran,... and embraced,... and fell on,... and kissed,... and they wept."[459] The emotional scene is similar to Laban's reaction when he unexpectedly hears news of his sister after many years of distance between them (29:13): "he ran,... embraced,... and kissed." Esau's magnanimous response is the warm and forgiving greeting of a brother. By contrast, Jacob's elaborate behavior is the formal greeting of submission, which one would expect of a subject before his king. His ceremonial manner of bowing and gift-giving, marked by repeated references to himself as "servant" and to Esau as "lord," contrasts dramatically with Esau's warm and natural expression of relief and joy at seeing his brother again.[460] The dread and fear marking Jacob's preparations for this reunion are relieved quickly and emotionally, as the brothers join in weeping.[461]

When Esau inquires about the family, each group is presented *seriatim* in the order arranged previously: Bilhah and Zilpah and their children, then Leah and her children, and finally Joseph and Rachel (vv. 5–7). All dutifully bow before Esau, assuming the same obsequious manner as Jacob. Next Esau inquires about the company sent in advance of their meeting, an enormous gift in livestock numbering five hundred fifty animals in all (v. 8, cf. 32:13–21[14–22]). Jacob refers to the livestock as a "gift" in v. 10 (*minḥâ*, NRSV's "present") and so it is consistently in the previous chapter (NRSV's "present," 32:13, 18, 20, 21 [32:14, 19, 21, 22]). But in the very next breath, Jacob uses "blessing" to describe the gift (v. 11, *běrākâ*, NRSV's "gift"). This is, in fact, the same word used for "blessing" in 27:36, and is what Jacob stole from Esau.[462] In this context, this is not the genuine blessing of the patriarch; Jacob

---

on the stomach," that is both supine and prone; Ellen F. Morris, "Bowing and Scraping in the Ancient Near East: An Investigation into Obsequiousness in the Amarna Letters," *JNES* 65/3 (2006): 179–95, esp. 180 and 184–85.

[459] The concentration of verbs used to show the reconciliation of Jacob and Esau corresponds to the initial break between the two, also narrated with an intense succession of five verbs (25:34): Jacob gave, Esau ate, drank, rose up, and went away. See N. M. Sarna, *Genesis* (1989), 229. The words "and kissed him" have mysterious Masoretic dots above each letter, possibly marking them as an erasure, in which case the earliest scribes intended them to be omitted; GKC ¶5n; Emanuel Tov, *Textual Criticism of the Hebrew Bible* (Minneapolis, Assen/Maastricht: Fortress Press/Van Gorcum, 1992), 55–57; Israel Yeivin, *Introduction to the Tiberian Masorah*, trans. E. J. Revell (Masoretic Studies 5; Missoula, Mont.: Scholars Press, 1980), 44–46.

[460] C. Westermann, *Genesis 12–36* (1985), 524–25.

[461] The editors of *BHS* propose reading "they wept" as a singular, "he wept." There is no textual support for the emendation, and although it is unusual, Hebrew grammar allows the change of subjects to a plural in such a context.

[462] R. S. Hendel, *The Epic of the Patriarch* (1987), 130. Fishbane sees the use of *běrākâ*, "blessing," as a theme word linking Gen 33 with 27:1–28:9 in the narrative's chiastic structure, and states further that the guilt of Jacob's wealth, acquired through the beneficence of a

cannot return something it is not his right to bestow. Rather, this is Jacob's best attempt at restoring what he took, and is his last, best hope for reconciliation.

The dialogue about the gift/blessing is marked by ancient Near Eastern deference, in which the giver insists his gift is justified but inadequate, while the recipient refuses to accept because the gift is too generous (vv. 8–11). Eventually the recipient will accept, as Esau does at the conclusion in v. 11, but he must be forced to appear reluctant. Jacob is sincere in his giving because seeing his brother again is "like seeing the face of God."[463] To "see one's face" denotes access to someone's presence or permission to have an audience with a person of exalted status.[464] Jacob has been in God's presence at Peniel and now in Esau's presence, and in both cases he has been received favorably. Taken together with the immediately preceding Peniel episode, one cannot fail to miss the irony of Jacob's words. Jacob saw God at Peniel and survived, surprisingly. Now he has seen Esau and survived again. Reconciliation with God is followed by reconciliation with brother.[465]

Now reconciled, the brothers need only to sort out how they will relate to each other from this point forward. Esau assumes Jacob will journey with him to Seir and live with him there (v. 12, cf. v. 14). But Jacob's continued use of "servant–lord" terminology for their relationship, despite Esau's "my brother" in v. 9, denotes his desire for continued distance between them. Jacob uses the differences between their two caravans to illustrate the separate directions in which they must go: he leads a caravan of women, children, and livestock, while Esau's is a caravan of four hundred men (vv. 13–14).[466] Esau accepts the differences. When his counteroffer to leave behind a protective battalion is also rebuffed, both understand they are officially parting company (v. 15). Their parting is polite, Esau returning to Seir and Jacob heading toward Canaan (vv. 16–17).

Moving westward toward the Jordan Valley, Jacob comes to Succoth (v. 17).[467] In another etiological notation, the text explains the name "Succoth" (*sukkôt*) as a place where Jacob built a house for himself and "booths" (*sukkōt*) for his livestock.

---

stolen blessing, lies heavily upon his tongue. Jacob's use of "blessing" therefore acknowledges his guilt in crimes of the past. M. A. Fishbane, *Biblical Text and Texture* (1998), 52.

[463] Literally, "for therefore I have seen [or 'I see'] your face as one sees the face of God." The unusual syntax of this clause uses an impersonal subject of the infinitive construct, which makes it possible to allude obliquely to Jacob's having seen the face of God at Peniel without stating it in so many words. Cf. P. Joüon and T. Muraoka, *A Grammar of Biblical Hebrew* (1993), 439.

[464] Horacio Simian-Yofre, "*pānîm*," *TDOT* 11:589–615, esp. 604–5.

[465] Hamilton cleverly ties this together as Peni-El followed by Peni-Esau, the "face-of-God" and the "face-of-Esau;" V. P. Hamilton, *The Book of Genesis, Chapters 18–50* (1995), 346.

[466] His promise to come to Seir is a veiled way of marking their official separation. They need no covenant or treaty to mark their parting, as with Jacob and Laban, because they remained brothers; C. Westermann, *Genesis 12–36* (1985), 526–27.

[467] On the location of Succoth (modern Tell Deir ʿAllā) on the migration corridor near where the Jabbok River issues onto the plain of the Jordan Valley, see the commentary at 32:2.

This is the only time an Israelite patriarch builds a house (*bayit*) for himself, and since Jacob is depicted living again in the familiar patriarchal tent (*'ōhel*) in the next verses, the reference is striking and requires comment. This may reflect what cultural anthropologists have learned in recent decades about the small-livestock economy of ancient Semitic groups in the transjordan and elsewhere in northern Mesopotamia, which was a prevalent way of life for millennia.[468] Such tribes often lived on the fringes of the desert, sometimes moving among grazing regions in the steppes, migrating seasonally, and returning during the off-seasons to permanent towns and villages. If so, perhaps Succoth was one of the permanent villages on the fringes of the grazing region, which might explain Jacob's "house" as a semi-permanent dwelling on his way back into Canaan.[469]

From Succoth, Jacob came safely across the Jordan River into Canaan (v. 18). The notation that he arrived "peaceably" (*šālēm*, NRSV's "safely") is not insignificant in light of the dangers of travel in the ancient world, and potential threats from both Laban and Esau. The many geographic references in this verse, especially the mention of "the land of Canaan," illustrate the faithfulness of God, who promised protection and guidance, and a safe return (28:15).[470] Like his father Abraham, who purchased a field and cave from the local inhabitants (23:17–18), Jacob purchased the plot of land on which he had pitched his tent (v. 19). The reference to "the sons of Hamor" prepares for the next chapter, and the unusual characterization of Hamor as "Shechem's father" is particularly important for establishing the characters for that episode. Finally, Jacob sets up an altar and gives it a name, again looking very much like his father and grandfather (12:7–8; 13:18; 26:15; and see Closer Look "Ancestral Religion" at p. 142). The name of the altar, "El, God of Israel," preserves an ancient Canaanite tradition, but one that Jacob now makes quite personal.[471] Its original Canaanite form likely had henotheistic overtones, naming a local Canaanite deity El, as the one named "God of Israel." Later Israelite monotheism would have understood the name differently, turning it into an identifying predication: "God *is* the God of Israel."[472]

---

[468] Ilse Köhler-Rollefson, "A Model for the Development of Nomadic Pastoralism on the Transjordanian Plateau," in *Pastoralism in the Levant: Archaeological Materials in Anthropological Perspectives*, eds. Ofer Bar-Yosef and Anatoly M. Khazanov (Monographs in World Archaeology 10; Madison, Wis.: Prehistory Press, 1992), 11–18, esp. 13–14.

[469] And might further explain Mahanaim as an irregularly used encampment in the grazing zone itself.

[470] On the role of Shechem, see commentary at 34:1–4 below.

[471] For the Canaanite background, see Wolfgang Herrmann, "El," *DDD*² 274–80, esp. 277–78.

[472] My proposal is that "God, the God of Israel" (*'ēl 'ĕlōhê yiśrā'ēl*) is not a construct chain, since "El" itself has no construct form. The entire phrase would have originally been understood as an explicative apposition, in which "El" is a general category and "God of Israel" is a particular member of that category, yielding a name that assumes henotheism. In later Israelite history, the name would have become a predicate nominative for identification, transforming it into a monotheistic polemic. On the explicative apposition and predicate nominative, see B. T. Arnold and J. H. Choi, *A Guide to Biblical Hebrew Syntax* (2003), 6 and 24, respectively.

GENESIS 34:1–31 SHECHEM AND DINAH

(34:1) Now Dinah the daughter of Leah, whom she had borne to Jacob, went out to visit the women of the region.

(34:2) When Shechem son of Hamor the Hivite, prince of the region, saw her, he seized her and lay with her by force.

(34:3) And his soul was drawn to Dinah daughter of Jacob; he loved the girl, and spoke tenderly to her.

(34:4) So Shechem spoke to his father Hamor, saying, "Get me this girl to be my wife."

(34:5) Now Jacob heard that Shechem had defiled his daughter Dinah; but his sons were with his cattle in the field, so Jacob held his peace until they came.

(34:6) And Hamor the father of Shechem went out to Jacob to speak with him,

(34:7) just as the sons of Jacob came in from the field. When they heard of it, the men were indignant and very angry, because he had committed an outrage in Israel by lying with Jacob's daughter, for such a thing ought not to be done.

(34:8) But Hamor spoke with them, saying, "The heart of my son Shechem longs for your daughter; please give her to him in marriage.

(34:9) Make marriages with us; give your daughters to us, and take our daughters for yourselves.

(34:10) You shall live with us; and the land shall be open to you; live and trade in it, and get property in it."

(34:11) Shechem also said to her father and to her brothers, "Let me find favor with you, and whatever you say to me I will give.

(34:12) Put the marriage present and gift as high as you like, and I will give whatever you ask me; only give me the girl to be my wife."

(34:13) The sons of Jacob answered Shechem and his father Hamor deceitfully, because he had defiled their sister Dinah.

(34:14) They said to them, "We cannot do this thing, to give our sister to one who is uncircumcised, for that would be a disgrace to us.

(34:15) Only on this condition will we consent to you: that you will become as we are and every male among you be circumcised.

(34:16) Then we will give our daughters to you, and we will take your daughters for ourselves, and we will live among you and become one people.

(34:17) But if you will not listen to us and be circumcised, then we will take our daughter and be gone."

(34:18) Their words pleased Hamor and Hamor's son Shechem.

(34:19) And the young man did not delay to do the thing, because he was delighted with Jacob's daughter. Now he was the most honored of all his family.

(34:20) So Hamor and his son Shechem came to the gate of their city and spoke to the men of their city, saying,

(34:21) "These people are friendly with us; let them live in the land and trade in it, for the land is large enough for them; let us take their daughters in marriage, and let us give them our daughters.

(34:22) Only on this condition will they agree to live among us, to become one people: that every male among us be circumcised as they are circumcised.

(34:23) Will not their livestock, their property, and all their animals be ours? Only let us agree with them, and they will live among us."

(34:24) And all who went out of the city gate heeded Hamor and his son Shechem; and every male was circumcised, all who went out of the gate of his city.

(34:25) On the third day, when they were still in pain, two of the sons of Jacob, Simeon and Levi, Dinah's brothers, took their swords and came against the city unawares, and killed all the males.

(34:26) They killed Hamor and his son Shechem with the sword, and took Dinah out of Shechem's house, and went away.

(34:27) And the other sons of Jacob came upon the slain, and plundered the city, because their sister had been defiled.

(34:28) They took their flocks and their herds, their donkeys, and whatever was in the city and in the field.

(34:29) All their wealth, all their little ones and their wives, all that was in the houses, they captured and made their prey.

(34:30) Then Jacob said to Simeon and Levi, "You have brought trouble on me by making me odious to the inhabitants of the land, the Canaanites and the Perizzites; my numbers are few, and if they gather themselves against me and attack me, I shall be destroyed, both I and my household."

(34:31) But they said, "Should our sister be treated like a whore?"

*J*acob returned to Canaan from the ancestral homeland in northern Mesopotamia, and arrived "safely" at Shechem, near where he purchased a plot of land and set up camp for the family (33:18–19). Unfortunately his peaceful return, having avoided violent confrontation with both Laban and Esau, ends abruptly at Shechem. The chapter narrates a series of events that culminate in the slaughter of the inhabitants of Shechem in one of the most violent texts of the Bible. This chapter raises a number of questions for which we have no convincing answers, such as whether or not the motives and actions of the man named Shechem in vv. 2–3 constitute rape (see below). But central to all other questions is why such a text as this is even included in the Bible? I am most persuaded by those interpretations that place Gen 34 in the larger context of the Jacob narrative, seeing in this text a critique of marriages outside the ancestral family, especially when those marriages assume assimilation with the polytheistic inhabitants of Canaan. The narrator is arguing for marriages such as Jacob's, over against Esau's marriages to Hittite/Canaanite women (26:34, 46; 36:2, and see Closer Look "Endogamy in Ancient Israel" at p. 219).[473]

---

[473] Gen 34 is framed by the theological understanding of the altar's name in 33:20, El-Elohe-Israel, and the apparent monotheistic text of 35:1–4. The polytheism of the Shechemites is buried in the same grave as "the foreign gods" in Jacob's household. See Ellen J. van Wolde,

A text with as many peculiarities as this one will likely contain several cultural features far removed from our times. In general, it may be assumed the text is a polemic against cultural assimilation with the inhabitants of the land. Secondarily, it explains why Simeon and Levi were not given pride of place among their brothers, especially in light of their birth order as the second and third sons (29:33–34), and explains why Israelite royalty would come through the fourth son, Judah, instead. In this way, the text carries etiological weight and prepares for Jacob's deathbed blessing in 49:5–7. It has also been suggested that Jacob's association with the city of Shechem reflects one of the oldest portions of the Jacob narrative, and elevates Jacob's role as a patriarch because Shechem was the place where the Israelite tribes established their central covenantal cult (Josh 24).[474]

The first paragraph narrates a problem that Jacob will need to address (vv. 1–4). There are a number of potential solutions open to him, but the reader is left in suspense about which solution will be followed. Dinah is the lone sister of eleven brothers and half-brothers (30:21). She plays no role in the narrative outside this chapter, which contributes to the puzzlement about why the text is included in Genesis at all (cf. 46:15). Dinah "went out," presumably from Jacob's encampment, "to see" (NRSV's "to visit") the local women, which sets up an ironic word play of reversal in the next verse when Shechem "saw her." Shechem is the son of Hamor, identified in 33:19 as a local landowner and further characterized here as a Hivite, and "prince of the region."[475] The Hivites appear to have inhabited portions of the central hill country from Gibeon to Shechem, and further northward to Mount Hermon (Josh 9:1–7; 11:3; Judg 3:3, cf. Gen 10:17). They were said to be related to either the Hurrians or Hittites, and were likely non-Semitic peoples, despite having Semitic names at times.[476]

The problem is that Shechem and Dinah have intercourse before the proper arrangements are made between the families and before marriage is agreed upon

---

"Love and Hatred in a Multiracial Society: The Dinah and Shechem Story in Genesis 34 in the Context of Genesis 28–35," in *Reading from Right to Left: Essays on the Hebrew Bible in Honour of David J.A. Clines,* eds. J. C. Exum and H. G. M. Williamson (JSOTSup 373; London, New York: Sheffield Academic Press, 2003), 435–49, esp. 444–47. It is not necessary to assume such a prohibition against marriage to idolatrous gentiles reflects a late, postexilic perspective, as done again recently by Alexander Rofé, "Defilement of Virgins in Biblical Law and the Case of Dinah (Genesis 34)," *Bib* 86/3 (2005): 369–75.

[474] For summary of these issues, see R. S. Hendel, *The Epic of the Patriarch* (1987), 14–15.

[475] And later identified as progenitor of the Shechemites (Josh 24:32; Judg 9:28). Hamor is "donkey" and Shechem is "shoulder" in Hebrew, names that may have symbolic significance in this text, beyond the obvious connection between the city Shechem and the eponymous individual Shechem. I remain unconvinced by the proposed connections between "sons of Hamor" and covenant communities formed by the ritual slaughter of donkeys at Mari; V. P. Hamilton, *The Book of Genesis, Chapters 18–50* (1995), 349.

[476] Edwin C. Hostetter, *Nations Mightier and More Numerous: The Biblical View of Palestine's Pre-Israelite Peoples* (BIBAL dissertation series 3; N. Richland Hills, Tex.: BIBAL Press, 1995), 72–76.

by all parties. Precisely what happened between Shechem and Dinah has become a topic of debate in recent years. The verbs in v. 2 – he took her, he slept with her, and he humiliated her – are more ambiguous than implied by the NRSV's "seized her and lay with her by force." While this particular sequence of verbs, or one very similar to it, clearly connotes rape in another context (cf. 2 Sam 13:14), the intent here is not as clear as it first appears. The last of the three verbs (Piel of *'nh*, "oppress, humiliate") is the only one that might imply rape specifically, but more likely refers either to defloration or forbidden (though consensual) intercourse, and in this context connotes further the act of debasement in a social–judicial perspective.[477] The series of verbs in v. 3 likewise portray the couple's relationship as that of love and affection, and even Dinah's continued presence in Shechem's house (v. 26) is no indication of some sort of captivity or house-arrest. The relationship appears consensual.

Rather Shechem and Dinah have been interpreted as a tragic love story, not unlike Romeo and Juliet, whose fate as lovers depends upon their families to come to terms with their love.[478] Indeed, Israelite law prescribes a solution for this very situation. When a man seduces a virgin who is not engaged and they have sexual intercourse prior to the proper arrangements between their families, he must marry her and pay the bride-price to the girl's father. If the father is unwilling to give his daughter in marriage, a fine must be paid nonetheless (Exod 22:16–17 [Hebrew 22:15–16]; and cf. Deut 22:28–29). The problem posed by Shechem's seduction of Dinah is the intertwining of these families across lines that are not only tribal, but across ethnic, cultural, and religious lines as well. The problem may find solution in the laws of Exodus and Deuteronomy, but those are for later Israelites to settle disputes among themselves. Marriage between Shechem and Dinah raises a different set of questions.

Apparently aware of the potential dangers, Jacob waited to take action until his sons could return from the field (v. 5). That Shechem "had defiled" (*ṭimmē*), "dishonored") Dinah is clearly a central concern for her father and brothers, as well as for the narrator (vv. 5, 13, 27). Such ritual impurity was not ordinarily a

---

[477] When used with a woman as object, the term points to social debasement of the men related to her, and therefore does not describe Shechem's rape or sexual abuse of Dinah in this context; Ellen J. van Wolde, "Does *'innâ* Denote Rape? A Semantic Analysis of a Controversial Word," *VT* 52/4 (2002): 528–44; Nicolas Wyatt, "The Story of Dinah and Shechem," *UF* 22 (1990): 433–58, esp. 436. For the opposite view, see Yael Shemesh, "Rape is Rape is Rape: The Story of Dinah and Shechem (Genesis 34)," *ZAW* 119/1 (2007): 2–21.

[478] E. J. van Wolde, "Love and Hatred in a Multiracial Society: The Dinah and Shechem Story in Genesis 34 in the Context of Genesis 28–35," in *Reading From Right to Left: Essays on the Hebrew Bible in Honour of David J.A. Clines* (2003), esp. 437–39. For the view that this chapter should be read strictly as a rape story, see Susanne Scholz, *Rape Plots: A Feminist Cultural Study of Genesis 34* (Studies in Biblical Literature 13; New York: Peter Lang, 2000), and on the use of the verbs, see esp. 136–38. For discussion of the use of prepositions in this narrative (and a different conclusion than held here) plus full bibliography, see R. M. Davidson, *Flame of Yahweh* (2007), 512–18.

consequence of sexual intercourse for an unmarried woman. Something else is in view here. Defilement in this case is most likely the result of intercourse with a man perceived to be outside the ancestral family, especially with an uncircumcised partner.[479] As Hamor and Shechem make their way to Jacob to propose a solution, the sons of Jacob return from the fields (vv. 6–7). Hamor and Shechem seem oblivious to any indiscretion. It is only the Jacobites who are outraged because of the code of morality assumed by the group, which is obviously different than the Shechemite code. If a marriage were to occur, the sons of Jacob fully expected an arrangement between the fathers, Jacob and Hamor, and then there would be appropriate gifts, ceremonies, and only then the giving of the daughter, who enters the home of the groom.[480] Dinah's brothers are outraged at the insult caused by Shechem's behavior, which the narrator agrees is something that "ought not to be done" in Israel (v. 7).

Hamor, unaware of the complexities of the situation created by his son, only speaks of Shechem's deep love for Dinah and proposes marriage (vv. 8–10). Not only so, but Hamor proposes two further changes in the relationship between the inhabitants of the city of Shechem and Jacob's family. First, he proposes intermarriage generally between the groups, offering complete assimilation between the Semitic Jacobites and the Hivite Hamorites. As we have seen, the ancestral ideal is marriage within one's kinship group in order to ensure continuity of cultural and religious values and societal infrastructure (see Closer Look "Endogamy in Ancient Israel" at p. 219). Thus Abraham sends a servant back to the ancestral homeland (Gen 24) and Isaac sends Jacob there as well (28:2) in order to acquire a suitable wife. Conversely, Ishmael's Egyptian wife and Esau's Hittite/Canaanite wives mark them as outside the official ancestral line of descent (21:21; 26:34–35; 27:46; 36:2).

Hamor's second proposal is for a different economic arrangement between Jacob and the city, suggesting a land-sharing agreement that would facilitate complete assimilation between the two groups (v. 10). The specific word order of Hamor's offer highlights the "land" (*'ereṣ*) as a particularly attractive feature of this new arrangement: "... as for the land, it is before you."[481] Whatever the details of his previous arrangement, in which Jacob purchased only a plot of land where he pitched his tent (33:19), this was a proposal to expand that agreement. As we saw in Gen 29–31, Israel's ancestors are perceived in these texts as pastoralists tending flocks of

---

[479] Rofé's general arguments are correct, although his conclusion is a *non sequitur*. Rather than the postexilic concept of defilement resulting from the impurity of the nations of the land, I take this as an offense related to exogamous relationships and the centrality of circumcision in the ancestral covenant. Cf. A. Rofé, "Defilement of Virgins in Biblical Law and the Case of Dinah (Genesis 34)." The nature of the defilement is no help in dating the text.

[480] The weddings of Leah and Rachel to Jacob illustrate the customs expected in such a situation (29:21–24).

[481] So a *casus pendens*, cf. GKC ¶143b; B. T. Arnold and J. H. Choi, *A Guide to Biblical Hebrew Syntax* (2003), 7.

sheep and goats on the fringes of settled society, and occasionally hiring themselves out as shepherds to villagers. Isaac also does not purchase agricultural property but grows prosperous as a small-cattle pastoralist, who was given permission to invest in the local agricultural economy (26:12–14). But Hamor proposes a departure from mobile pastoralism in a way that would also require assimilation with the local inhabitants. This was a question of the land! Jacob was invited to "live with" the Hamorites of Shechem, to live and trade in the land, and to acquire portions of the land. But the land itself is, of course, the ancestral right, the object of covenant promises – not just a field near Shechem, nor portions of it acquired through economic cooperation with the inhabitants, but all of it by God's grace and in his timing (cf. the restatement of the covenant promises in 35:12).[482]

Hamor's proposal is followed by Shechem's own speech, in which he essentially offers to pay any bride-price, as high as Jacob would ask (vv. 11–12). In a way that Hamor and Shechem could not understand, their proposals were not only unattractive to Jacob's family, they were insulting and actually at odds with their own cultural and religious values. Accepting Hamor's offer would be tantamount to forfeiting the ancestral covenant and the promises that sustained Jacob while in exile in Paddan-aram. Surprisingly, Jacob allows his sons to speak for him, and they counter Hamor's proposal with an offer of their own (vv. 13–17).[483] They will allow the marriage if all male Hamorites become circumcised, just as all Jacob's sons are circumcised, and only then will they agree to become "one people" living together with the inhabitants of Shechem (v. 16). Assimilation as a single, unified people is precisely the risk that must be avoided at nearly all cost for the children of Jacob, while the Shechemites assume it is a positive prospect. Thus the sons of Jacob use the sign of their covenant with God, circumcision, as a condition of the marriage, although the narrator has informed us of their subterfuge (v. 13). The sons have learned well the lessons in deception taught by their father and grandmother (Gen 27).

Hamor and Shechem agree at once (v. 18). The unusual request saved having to pay the bride-price and seemed a mere cultural concession to the children of Jacob. Since Shechem was "the most honored of all his family" (v. 19), his opinion together with Hamor's counsel, would hold sway in the gate of the city (v. 20). Their speech at the city gate rehearses the original proposals for intermarriage and the

---

482 Thus Hamor's proposal would have made Jacob's family permanent residents, who hoped slowly to acquire portions of the land, rather than transhumant pastoralists living in the expectation that their descendants would some day be the rightful and sole inhabitants of the land. The text therefore presents a critique of those in the north during the monarchy who would compromise with the Canaanites in a symbiotic relationship (cf. 1 Kgs 12:26–33; 16:24–28).

483 It seems likely we are to assume Jacob's apparent indifference to Dinah's humiliation is related to her brothers' violent overreaction; G. J. Wenham, *Genesis 16–50* (1994), 308 and 310.

economic arrangements, and then explains circumcision as the single requirement for becoming "one people" with the children of Jacob (vv. 21–22). However, Hamor and Shechem add a feature, which reveals their own calculating and shrewd motives: they intend to acquire the livestock and personal wealth of Jacob's children (v. 23). All the able-bodied men of Shechem agree to the surgery (v. 24).

Simeon and Levi take the lead in exterminating all the males of the city, including Hamor and Shechem themselves (vv. 25–26). They enter the city "unawares" while the Shechemites are "still in pain," taking full advantage of a surprise attack against weakened opponents. The "other sons of Jacob" plunder the city and its inhabitants thoroughly (vv. 27–29). The feeble response of Jacob is less than noble (v. 30). He is concerned only about a counter-offensive from an alliance of other Canaanites in the region. There is no challenge to the strategy of Simeon and Levi, or even a question about the need for decisive action. Jacob's rebuke, if it can even be called that, seems focused only on the *extent* of the massacre. He assumed only Hamor and Shechem were to be killed, and that the ruse of circumcision had been used only to prevent the rest of the city from protecting these two. But now the entire male population has been exterminated, raising the prospects of reprisals from the other inhabitants in the region.

Simeon and Levi defend themselves only with a rhetorical question, implying that their actions were justified and necessary because of Shechem's offense (v. 31): "Should our sister be treated like a whore?"[484] Surprisingly, the text has no formal conclusion or appropriate closure. The final question is open-ended and prepares the reader for Jacob's deathbed blessing of Simeon and Levi, the brothers of violence, condemned for their inhumanity and cruelty (49:5–7).

GENESIS 35:1–29 JACOB'S RETURN TO BETHEL AND TO ISAAC

(35:1) God said to Jacob, "Arise, go up to Bethel, and settle there. Make an altar there to the God who appeared to you when you fled from your brother Esau."

(35:2) So Jacob said to his household and to all who were with him, "Put away the foreign gods that are among you, and purify yourselves, and change your clothes;

(35:3) then come, let us go up to Bethel, that I may make an altar there to the God who answered me in the day of my distress and has been with me wherever I have gone."

(35:4) So they gave to Jacob all the foreign gods that they had, and the rings that were in their ears; and Jacob hid them under the oak that was near Shechem.

(35:5) As they journeyed, a terror from God fell upon the cities all around them, so that no one pursued them.

---

484 Reminding one of another text ending in a rhetorical question, Jonah 4:11.

(35:6) Jacob came to Luz (that is, Bethel), which is in the land of Canaan, he and all the people who were with him,

(35:7) and there he built an altar and called the place El-bethel,[mm] because it was there that God had revealed himself to him when he fled from his brother.

(35:8) And Deborah, Rebekah's nurse, died, and she was buried under an oak below Bethel. So it was called Allon-bacuth.[nn]

(35:9) God appeared to Jacob again when he came from Paddan-aram, and he blessed him.

(35:10) God said to him, "Your name is Jacob; no longer shall you be called Jacob, but Israel shall be your name." So he was called Israel.

(35:11) God said to him, "I am God Almighty: be fruitful and multiply; a nation and a company of nations shall come from you, and kings shall spring from you.

(35:12) The land that I gave to Abraham and Isaac I will give to you, and I will give the land to your offspring after you."

(35:13) Then God went up from him at the place where he had spoken with him.

(35:14) Jacob set up a pillar in the place where he had spoken with him, a pillar of stone; and he poured out a drink offering on it, and poured oil on it.

(35:15) So Jacob called the place where God had spoken with him Bethel.

(35:16) Then they journeyed from Bethel; and when they were still some distance from Ephrath, Rachel was in childbirth, and she had hard labor.

(35:17) When she was in her hard labor, the midwife said to her, "Do not be afraid; for now you will have another son."

(35:18) As her soul was departing (for she died), she named him Ben-oni; but his father called him Benjamin.

(35:19) So Rachel died, and she was buried on the way to Ephrath (that is, Bethlehem),

(35:20) and Jacob set up a pillar at her grave; it is the pillar of Rachel's tomb, which is there to this day.

(35:21) Israel journeyed on, and pitched his tent beyond the tower of Eder.

(35:22) While Israel lived in that land, Reuben went and lay with Bilhah his father's concubine; and Israel heard of it. Now the sons of Jacob were twelve.

(35:23) The sons of Leah: Reuben (Jacob's firstborn), Simeon, Levi, Judah, Issachar, and Zebulun.

(35:24) The sons of Rachel: Joseph and Benjamin.

(35:25) The sons of Bilhah, Rachel's maid: Dan and Naphtali.

(35:26) The sons of Zilpah, Leah's maid: Gad and Asher. These were the sons of Jacob who were born to him in Paddan-aram.

(35:27) Jacob came to his father Isaac at Mamre, or Kiriath-arba (that is, Hebron), where Abraham and Isaac had resided as aliens.

[mm] That is *God of Bethel*
[nn] That is *Oak of weeping*

(35:28) Now the days of Isaac were one hundred eighty years.

(35:29) And Isaac breathed his last; he died and was gathered to his people, old and full of days; and his sons Esau and Jacob buried him.

*T*his chapter narrates the final episodes of Isaac's *tôlĕdôt*-clause, begun in 25:19, "these are the descendants of Isaac," and ended with the *tôlĕdôt* of Esau (36:1). Isaac's son Jacob eradicates the "foreign gods" from his family brought with them from Paddan-aram, returns to Bethel, and eventually back to Hebron to be reunited with his father. Along the way, Rachel dies giving birth to Benjamin, and Jacob has two more theophanies. In a variety of ways, each concluding episode narrated here points to the faithfulness of God in fulfilling the covenant promises to Jacob, bringing him back safely to the Promised Land (28:15) and to Isaac, who dies at the narrative's conclusion at a good old age.

The sons of Jacob have jeopardized the ancestral family by their ruthless slaughter of the inhabitants of Shechem (Gen 34). Jacob is rightfully frightened at the possibility of military reprisals from the surrounding Canaanites (34:30). Hamor, the Hivite prince at Shechem, had proposed that Jacob and his family "live" (*yšb*, 34:10) in a semi-permanent lifestyle near Shechem. The Shechemite proposal had raised an important question since Jacob's return to Paddan-aram: Where should they settle? Not at Mahanaim-Penuel (Gen 32), nor Succoth (Gen 33), and now life at Shechem is tenuous (Gen 34). Thus God's speech in the opening verse of this chapter brings comforting relief and guidance.[485] He is ordered to go up to Bethel and "settle" (*yšb* again) there, answering definitively the question raised by Hamor whether he might settle near Shechem. Furthermore, God reminds him of the promises of the place Jacob himself had named Bethel, where God had assured him he would protect him while he was away in Mesopotamia and one day bring him back home (32:15). That is the place where God had "appeared" to him (Niphal of *r'h*, "to see," and see v. 9 below) when he was running for his life from Esau. Surely it would be good to return there, settle there, and build an altar to God there, as his fathers had done before him in other locations (12:7, 8; 13:8; 26:25) and as Jacob had done at Shechem (33:20).

Jacob then calls upon his family to purify themselves and put away their "foreign gods" (vv. 2–3, *'ĕlōhê hannēkār*, lit. "the gods of the foreign land").[486] There is no mention of these in God's address to Jacob in v. 1, nor did God call for greater purity

---

[485] Unlike several other divine speeches in Genesis, this one is not prefaced with revelatory-diction, "God appeared to him," or theatrical accoutrements, such as a dream. With no introduction, God simply spoke to Jacob.

[486] Thus an attributive genitive. The phrase is possibly intended to clarify the nature of the "household idols" (*tĕrāpîm*) that Rachel stole from Laban (31:19). Their precise nature might have been already perplexing to ancient readers, and so Jacob's extirpation of them is placed here to explain them further. See Bernhard Lang and Helmer Ringgren, "*nkr*," *TDOT* 9:423–432, esp. 430.

and clean clothes. But the trip back to Bethel to build a new altar there seemed naturally to require these actions. The foreign gods may have consisted of idols carried with them upon their return from Mesopotamia, stolen from Laban (31:19), taken in the plunder at Shechem, or a combination of all these. Whatever their origin or nature, such vestiges of foreign worship were inconsistent with the service of Yahweh. The foreign gods must be placed aside before reentry of the Promised Land was considered complete.

That these idols were physical objects is shown by their being buried near the oak tree at Shechem (v. 4). The earrings must also have been used in the adoration or service of foreign gods, and so they too must go.[487] Trees had religious significance in the ancient Near East as physical symbols of divine presence and holy sites, and could also lend their names to places or serve as markers for graves (as at v. 8).[488] NRSV's "oak" was likely the Atlantic terebinth (*'ēlâ*, also known as pistachio or teil tree, *Pistacia atlantica*), and was common in the drier mountains from Dan to the central Negeb desert in the south.[489]

The trip from Shechem to Bethel was uneventful because "a terror from God" fell upon the surrounding inhabitants (v. 5). Such fear seems reasonable in light of the violence inflicted on Shechem by Jacob's sons. Yet the narrator is stressing the miraculous origin of this fear. Jacob's safe return to Bethel, "he and all the people who were with him," is carefully worded to emphasize God's faithfulness to Jacob (v. 6). He came to Luz, a place elaborately described – in the land of Canaan (that is, Bethel) – highlighting the fulfillment of God's promises to Jacob (28:15). Correspondingly, Jacob fulfilled the command to build an altar there and named the place El-Bethel, "The God of Bethel" (v. 7).[490] Presumably Jacob's acts of faith and worship fulfill the vow he made on his first trip to Bethel to make

---

[487] Perhaps the rings were part of the plunder captured from the Shechemites, along with outer garments and foreign gods; G. J. Wenham, *Genesis 16–50* (1994), 324.

[488] See 21:33; Josh 24:26; and cf. 12:6; 13:18; Deut 11:30; Judg 9:6,37; Othmar Keel, *Goddesses and Trees, New Moon and Yahweh: Ancient Near Eastern Art and The Hebrew Bible* (JSOTSup 261; Sheffield: Sheffield Academic Press, 1998), 20–48. If this passage is textually related to Josh 24 and refers to a well-known shrine near Shechem, as Martin Noth suggests, then perhaps this is the same tree; Martin Noth, *The History of Israel* (New York: Harper & Row, 1960), 94–95; trans. of *Geschichte Israels* (2d ed.: Göttingen: Vandenhoeck & Ruprecht, 1954).

[489] F. N. Hepper, *Baker Encyclopedia of Bible Plants* (1992), 32–33.

[490] Jacob's name for the place, El-Bethel, was the original long-form of a Canaanite deity; Wolfgang Röllig, "Bethel," *DDD²* 173–75. Most likely, the original name had henotheistic overtones, understood as an explicative apposition, in which "El" is a general category and "Bethel" is a particular member of that category (not unlike *'ēl 'ĕlōhê yiśrā'ēl* at 33:20): "Deity, the one known as Bethel." Later Israelite usage would have understood the name differently, as apparently on the lips of Jacob, turning it into a genitive of location, the God at Bethel. Thus the name as used here does not yet reflect later monotheism, but is a step in that direction. On the explicative apposition, see B. T. Arnold and J. H. Choi, *A Guide to Biblical Hebrew Syntax* (2003), 24, and for the genitive of location, B. K. Waltke and M. P. O'Connor, *An Introduction to Biblical Hebrew Syntax* (1990), 147–48.

Yahweh his personal God (28:20–22).[491] The vow had revealed a timid and cautious patriarch, willing to go as far with God as God went with him, but no farther (see commentary at 28:20–22). The faith expressed in the vow itself is not mature faith, as we saw in Abraham or Isaac, and the Jacob who left Bethel that day was not quite ready to fulfill the role of "father of faith." Now, however, the text presents the full-orbed Jacob/Israel, returning to this place of commitment, and ready to assume his position in the distinguished line of patriarchs of ancient Israel. Thus the narrator reminds us that it was in this place that God "had revealed himself" to Jacob, one of several direct allusions to 28:10–22 linking these texts in order to round off the story of Jacob.[492]

Rebekah's nurse, Deborah, who left Mesopotamia with her mistress to return with Abraham's servant (24:59), is mentioned again here in a passing death and burial notice (v. 8). She plays no role in the narrative and is named only here.[493] But the record of her death is the first of three in this chapter, which together serve to bring closure to the Jacob narrative generally. The naming of the tree marking her grave, "Oak of Weeping" (see NRSV footnote), is one of several etiological notations in the text, also indicating closure to the extended narrative.

The text has already made specific references to the dream theophany of Gen 28 (vv. 1, 3, 7), and now the narrator states that God appeared to Jacob "again" at Bethel (v. 9), making the dream theophany the first appearance. The use of "appeared" (causative-reflexive Niphal of *r'h*, "to see") is by now quite familiar in the ancestral narratives as a technical term for divine revelation (see Closer Look at p. 135, and commentary at 12:7). God's appearances to Abraham and Isaac occurred at critical junctures of their faith journeys (12:7; 17:1; 18:1; 26:2, 24). God thus causes himself to be seen, pulling back the curtain on himself as it were, allowing himself – even presenting himself – in theophanic certainty. Here, as frequently elsewhere in Genesis, what one actually *sees* in such revelatory appearances of divine self-disclosure is not the issue, but rather what one *hears*. In most cases, the substance

---

[491] "Yahweh" is nowhere mentioned by name in Gen 35, resulting in the identification of the chapter as mostly priestly material; D. M. Carr, *Reading the Fractures of Genesis* (1996), 120–29.

[492] The use of the Niphal of *glh* for divine revelation, like the more common use of "appear" (Niphal of *r'h*) in Genesis (see Closer Look "Divine Revelation in the Hebrew Scriptures" at p. 135), denotes a coming forth out of seclusion or becoming visible. And yet Gen 28 and 35 together articulate the revelation as more than a visible appearance, but also in terms of the promises and faithfulness of God to Jacob. See Hans-Jürgen Zobel, "*gālâ*," *TDOT* 2:476–88, esp. 484.

[493] Neo-Babylonian dowries sometimes include the awarding of a female slave as a personal nurse to the bride, most likely intended to help the bride adjust to her new surroundings, which fleshes out the meager references to this practice in Genesis. This certainly fits Rebekah's needs especially, as she returned to Canaan to marry Isaac, but may also explain Laban's gifts of Zilpah and Bilhah, who became mothers of Israelite tribes (29:24, 29). See Martha T. Roth, "Deborah, Rebekah's Nurse," in *Hayim and Miriam Tadmor Volume*, eds. Israel Eph'al, Amnon Ben-Tor, and Peter Machinist (ErIsr 27; Jerusalem: Israel Exploration Society, 2003), 203–7, who however only makes the application to Deborah.

of the appearance or revelation is contained in a speech, moving immediately from "Yahweh/God *appeared*" to a speech introducing divine promises (12:7) or announcing self-disclosure (17:1). In this case, the speech is a divine blessing, in which the pronouncement of benediction is itself the act of blessing.[494]

The blessing consists of two independent divine utterances, the first of which announces the name change from Jacob to Israel (v. 10).[495] Of course, Jacob has already been renamed in 32:27–28 [Heb 32:28–29], which raises an interesting tension in the narrative. The problem of a second naming of Jacob/Israel is handled variously, and some would suggest that the naming of Gen 32 was only done by a messenger and done so beyond the traditional borders of the Promised Land, which leaves doubt or uncertainty, while here God is doing the naming at Bethel, leaving no doubt or question in Jacob/Israel's mind.[496] However, the traditional source approach seems the best explanation, assuming that Gen 32 is the non-priestly version, which has been assumed and built upon here by the priestly account. The two were not developed independently, at least as they stand before us now. This naming episode clearly has several earlier passages in view, as we have seen (especially Gen 17, 28, and 32), and so no explanation of the meaning of Jacob's new name is offered here. The reader is invited to take this episode together with Gen 32, as a reaffirmation of the new name.[497]

The second divine utterance announces God's self-disclosure as "God Almighty," commands Jacob to "be fruitful and multiply," and recites the now familiar ancestral promises of land and seed (vv. 11–12). The speech follows the pattern of revelatory appearances used elsewhere in the ancestral narratives.[498] First comes the divine self-disclosure, in this case, "I am God Almighty,"[499] signifying God's nature and identity.[500] Then comes the familiar list of covenant promises, especially that of land and seed (NRSV's "offspring"). The command to be fruitful and multiply is

---

[494] On divine blessings as illocutionary or performative utterances, in which the articulation of the blessing *is* the benediction because it makes it true, see C. W. Mitchell, *The Meaning of* brk *"to bless" in the Old Testament* (1987), 7–8, and 62.

[495] On the significance of name changes, see the commentary at 17:5 and 32:27–28 [Hebrew 32:28–29].

[496] N. M. Sarna, *Genesis* (1989), 241–42.

[497] Of all the intertexts in view in vv. 9–15, the most important appears to be 17:1–8, in which Abram's name is changed and the promises of the covenant are detailed. So perhaps, along the lines suggested in my introduction, a Holiness redactor has developed his priestly materials in Gen 35 in order to update and clarify previous texts. In this case, the Holiness editor may be tying loosely organized materials together – materials well known to his reader, both priestly and non-priestly – into a continuous and meaningful whole in the final form of Genesis.

[498] See 15:1; 15:7; 17:1; 26:24; 28:13b–15; and cf. 12:7; 26:2; 48:3.

[499] Predicate nominative for identification; B. T. Arnold and J. H. Choi, *A Guide to Biblical Hebrew Syntax* (2003), 6.

[500] Similar to "I am your shield" (15:1), or "I am Yahweh" (28:13). On "God Almighty" (*'ēl šadday*) as an archaic, revelatory name of God for the ancestors, as opposed to "Yahweh," the name by which God revealed himself to later Israel (Exod 3:14–15; 6:3), see commentary at 17:1.

commonly used in priestly contexts, such as the first creation account (1:22, 28) and is especially associated with "God Almighty" (17:2, 6; 28:3, and cf. 9:1–7).[501] We may assume the priestly materials being woven into this text originally placed this command to be fruitful before the birth of Jacob's many children (29:31–30:24), as we have similarly for Abraham in 17:6. As the text now stands, the reader is invited to apply the command to be fruitful and multiple to Jacob's children themselves, so that they will be greatly numerous (as indeed is reported later, 46:8–28; Exod 1:1–7).

God's promises to Israel's ancestors in Genesis are remarkably consistent.[502] Their recurrence throughout the ancestral narrative creates a literary continuity that testifies to God's faithfulness to the covenant. In this case (vv. 11b–12), the narrator has combined and summarized the theologically relevant components of 28:10–22 and 32:22–32 [Hebrew 32:23–33], and repeated almost verbatim those promises stated to Abraham in 17:1–8, in order "to show that the promise to Abraham was renewed completely to Jacob."[503] And once again, the promises of "land" (*'ereṣ*) and "seed" (*zera'*, NRSV's "offspring") are tied together in v. 12, as at 12:7 and frequently thereafter. The syntax here highlights the land as an object, which Yahweh will give to Jacob and his seed.[504]

The narrator's notation that the theophany is officially over at v. 13, "God went up from him," is repeated almost verbatim from 17:22, which closed that important covenant theophany to Abraham. This revelatory appearance of God in vv. 9–15 makes Jacob essentially another Abraham. In a sense, this passage is Jacob's covenant renewal. It relates to Jacob at the Jabbok (Gen 32), as Abraham's covenant chapter (Gen 17) relates to the establishment of the covenant (Gen 15). Jacob is fittingly Abraham's successor as "father of the faith."[505]

Jacob's worshipful response is similar to 28:18–19. His pillar of stone, and various acts of anointing are reminiscent of the first Bethel encounter, and he (re)names the place Bethel (vv. 14–15). Thus, the final revelatory theophany to Jacob rounds off the ancestral narratives, and clears the way for the final unit of the book – the Joseph narrative. It ties together into a single, final appearance of God several important themes recurring in the ancestral narratives: name changes, divine self-disclosure, covenant promises of land and descendants, and suitable worship. There remain in this text only a few details about Jacob to be tidied up.

---

[501] C. W. Mitchell, *The Meaning of* brk *"to bless" in the Old Testament* (1987), 62.

[502] Cf. 12:1–4; 13:14–17; 15:1–21; 17:4–14; 22:16–18; 26:2–5; 28:11–16; 31:12–13.

[503] Gerhard von Rad, *Genesis: A Commentary* (OTL; Philadelphia: Westminster Press, 1961), 338–39. Note, for example, the reference to "kings" in the line of Jacob, cf. 17:6.

[504] "Land" is an objective *casus pendens*, which places great emphasis on the Promised Land as the object of Yahweh's gift to Jacob's seed; P. Joüon and T. Muraoka, *A Grammar of Biblical Hebrew* (1993), 586–87.

[505] In addition to parallels between Gen 17 and 35, both Abraham and Jacob have terrifying night encounters with the divine (15 and 32), and both have subsequent covenant events with name changes (17 and 35); David W. Cotter, *Genesis* (Berit Olam; Collegeville, Minn.: Liturgical Press, 2003), 257–59.

The route from Bethel southward toward Hebron, where Jacob would be reunited with his father, followed the central hills across the saddle connecting what would later be identified as the hill country of Ephraim and the hill country of Judah.[506] In the zone between the two, Rachel died giving birth to Benjamin, making it appropriate that this region became the inheritance of the tribe of Benjamin (vv. 16–18). The midwife's role in comforting Rachel in her moment of crisis suggests that such midwives offered what might be termed holistic care, addressing one's emotional needs as well as assisting in the birth process.[507] The name Benjamin is based on similar word play as the names of Jacob's other children, using similarity of sound between Ben-oni and Ben-jamin (see commentary at 29:31–30:24). One significant difference, however, is that Israelite "Benjamin" matches exactly the form and meaning of the name of other ancient Semitic tribes, especially as attested in cuneiform texts from the city of Mari on the middle Euphrates.[508] Recent reevaluation of these second millennium BCE texts suggests an association between the Rachel tribes of ancient Israel and the tribal culture of Syria; that is, northern Mesopotamia.[509] Of course, no specific historical connections can be traced for ancient Israel to this Syrian heritage, but the cuneiform evidence is at least suggestive of the possibility that the Bible preserves authentic and ancient memories of Israel's origins in tribal pastoralists ancestry in northern Mesopotamia.

Jacob memorialized Rachel by placing a stone pillar at her gravesite, somewhere along the road to Bethlehem (vv. 19–20). The site was known to the narrator (since it "is there to this day"), which reflects the eyewitness perspective of someone living in the land some considerable amount of time after the events.[510] Jacob, who for the first time is called "Israel" by the narrator, moves on from near Bethlehem, pitching his tent near Migdal-Eder, or the "tower of Eder [i.e., the flock]" (v. 21). This locale must be in the vicinity of Jerusalem (Mic. 4:8), but identification of the site is uncertain.[511] The use of "Israel" as the official name of the patriarch marks a subtle but significant transition in the narrative. Jacob has finally become

---

[506] A. F. Rainey and R. S. Notley, *The Sacred Bridge: Carta's Atlas of the Biblical World* (2006), 115. Thus the birth of Benjamin brings the Jacob narrative to a close on what would later become the border between Israel and Judah.

[507] Carol L. Meyers, "Midwife (Gen 35:17; 38:28)," in *Women in Scripture: A Dictionary of Named and Unnamed Women in the Hebrew Bible, the Apocryphal/Deuterocanonical Books, and the New Testament,* eds. Carol L. Meyers, Toni Craven, and Ross S. Kraemer (Boston: Houghton Mifflin, 2000), 182–83.

[508] Daniel E. Fleming, "Genesis in History and Tradition: The Syrian Background of Israel's Ancestors, Reprise," in *The Future of Biblical Archaeology: Reassessing Methodologies and Assumptions,* eds. James K. Hoffmeier and A. R. Millard (Grand Rapids, Mich.: Eerdmans, 2004), 193–232, esp. 216–19.

[509] Ibid., esp. 223–26.

[510] Jeffrey C. Geoghegan, "Additional Evidence for a Deuteronomistic Redaction of the 'Tetrateuch'," *CBQ* 67/3 (2005): 405–21, esp. 410–11 for the six occurrences in Genesis.

[511] For the possibilities, see Dale C. Liid, "Eder, Tower of," *ABD* 2:284.

Israel in the narrative. His transformation from "Deceiver" to "God-striver" is complete.[512]

While the family was encamped at Migdal-Eder, Reuben fell into an incestuous relationship with Bilhah, which did not escape Jacob's attention (v. 22). His first three sons are now tainted, Reuben by this sexual wrongdoing, and Simeon and Levi because of their atrocities in the Shechem massacre (Gen 34). The brief note about Reuben is included here in the appendices of the Jacob narrative in order to prepare the reader for Jacob's deathbed blessing at 49:4.

Another feature concluding the Jacob narrative is the list of twelve sons, summarizing especially the birth narratives of 29:31–30:24, and arranged according to their mothers (vv. 22b–26). This list may illustrate the honor accorded the seventh position in genealogies, placing Joseph there by narrating Rachel's and Bilhah's sons, before returning to Leah's sons through Zilpah.[513]

The closing notice of Isaac's *tôlĕdôt*-section, begun in 25:19, records Jacob's reunion with his father at Hebron, and Isaac's death and burial (vv. 27–29). The narration of Jacob's return to the place "where Abraham and Isaac had resided as aliens" is an understated assertion on the faithfulness of God, who promised to bring Jacob back to the Promised Land (28:15). Like Abraham before him, Isaac was fully sated with life and was "gathered to his people," idioms for a life well-lived and full of success (cf. 25:8).[514] Isaac is the only patriarch born in the Promised Land, who lives his whole life in the Promised Land, and who dies in the Promised Land, which authenticates his descendants' rights to the land.[515]

GENESIS 36:1–43 ESAU THE FATHER OF EDOM

(36:1) These are the descendants of Esau (that is, Edom).

(36:2) Esau took his wives from the Canaanites: Adah daughter of Elon the Hittite, Oholibamah daughter of Anah son of Zibeon the Hivite,

(36:3) and Basemath, Ishmael's daughter, sister of Nebaioth.

(36:4) Adah bore Eliphaz to Esau; Basemath bore Reuel;

(36:5) and Oholibamah bore Jeush, Jalam, and Korah. These are the sons of Esau who were born to him in the land of Canaan.

(36:6) Then Esau took his wives, his sons, his daughters, and all the members of his household, his cattle, all his livestock, and all the property he had

---

[512] That an original priestly source used "Israel" consistently after the name change in v. 10 remains possible, along the line of the Abraham narrative, in which "Abraham" is used consistently after 17:5. But the Jacob narrative does not reflect such editorial consistency, and the composite nature of the narrative is therefore dominant, as seen in the presence of two (re)naming texts, 32:27–28 [Hebrew 32:28–29] and 35:10.

[513] J. M. Sasson, "A Genealogical 'Convention' in Biblical Chronology?" 183.

[514] Also like Abraham, Isaac was buried by his two sons (cf. 25:9).

[515] Jean L. Ska, *Introduction to Reading the Pentateuch* (Winona Lake, Ind.: Eisenbrauns, 2006), 205.

acquired in the land of Canaan; and he moved to a land some distance from his brother Jacob.

(36:7) For their possessions were too great for them to live together; the land where they were staying could not support them because of their livestock.

(36:8) So Esau settled in the hill country of Seir; Esau is Edom.

(36:9) These are the descendants of Esau, ancestor of the Edomites, in the hill country of Seir.

(36:10) These are the names of Esau's sons: Eliphaz son of Adah the wife of Esau; Reuel, the son of Esau's wife Basemath.

(36:11) The sons of Eliphaz were Teman, Omar, Zepho, Gatam, and Kenaz.

(36:12) (Timna was a concubine of Eliphaz, Esau's son; she bore Amalek to Eliphaz.) These were the sons of Adah, Esau's wife.

(36:13) These were the sons of Reuel: Nahath, Zerah, Shammah, and Mizzah. These were the sons of Esau's wife, Basemath.

(36:14) These were the sons of Esau's wife Oholibamah, daughter of Anah son of Zibeon: she bore to Esau Jeush, Jalam, and Korah.

(36:15) These are the clans[oo] of the sons of Esau. The sons of Eliphaz the firstborn of Esau: the clans Teman, Omar, Zepho, Kenaz,

(36:16) Korah, Gatam, and Amalek; these are the clans of Eliphaz in the land of Edom; they are the sons of Adah.

(36:17) These are the sons of Esau's son Reuel: the clans Nahath, Zerah, Shammah, and Mizzah; these are the clans of Reuel in the land of Edom; they are the sons of Esau's wife Basemath.

(36:18) These are the sons of Esau's wife Oholibamah: the clans Jeush, Jalam, and Korah; these are the clans born of Esau's wife Oholibamah, the daughter of Anah.

(36:19) These are the sons of Esau (that is, Edom), and these are their clans.

(36:20) These are the sons of Seir the Horite, the inhabitants of the land: Lotan, Shobal, Zibeon, Anah,

(36:21) Dishon, Ezer, and Dishan; these are the clans of the Horites, the sons of Seir in the land of Edom.

(36:22) The sons of Lotan were Hori and Heman; and Lotan's sister was Timna.

(36:23) These are the sons of Shobal: Alvan, Manahath, Ebal, Shepho, and Onam.

(36:24) These are the sons of Zibeon: Aiah and Anah; he is the Anah who found the springs in the wilderness, as he pastured the donkeys of his father Zibeon.

(36:25) These are the children of Anah: Dishon and Oholibamah daughter of Anah.

(36:26) These are the sons of Dishon: Hemdan, Eshban, Ithran, and Cheran.

(36:27) These are the sons of Ezer: Bilhan, Zaavan, and Akan.

(36:28) These are the sons of Dishan: Uz and Aran.

(36:29) These are the clans of the Horites: the clans Lotan, Shobal, Zibeon, Anah,

oo Or *chiefs*

(36:30) Dishon, Ezer, and Dishan; these are the clans of the Horites, clan by clan
in the land of Seir.

(36:31) These are the kings who reigned in the land of Edom, before any king
reigned over the Israelites.

(36:32) Bela son of Beor reigned in Edom, the name of his city being Dinhabah.

(36:33) Bela died, and Jobab son of Zerah of Bozrah succeeded him as king.

(36:34) Jobab died, and Husham of the land of the Temanites succeeded him as
king.

(36:35) Husham died, and Hadad son of Bedad, who defeated Midian in the
country of Moab, succeeded him as king, the name of his city being Avith.

(36:36) Hadad died, and Samlah of Masrekah succeeded him as king.

(36:37) Samlah died, and Shaul of Rehoboth on the Euphrates succeeded him as
king.

(36:38) Shaul died, and Baal-hanan son of Achbor succeeded him as king.

(36:39) Baal-hanan son of Achbor died, and Hadar succeeded him as king, the
name of his city being Pau; his wife's name was Mehetabel, the daughter
of Matred, daughter of Me-zahab.

(36:40) These are the names of the clans of Esau, according to their families and
their localities by their names: the clans Timna, Alvah, Jetheth,

(36:41) Oholibamah, Elah, Pinon,

(36:42) Kenaz, Teman, Mibzar,

(36:43) Magdiel, and Iram; these are the clans of Edom (that is, Esau, the father of
Edom), according to their settlements in the land that they held.

*T*he Jacob narrative concluded with the genealogy of Jacob's children (35:22b–
26) and the death and burial of Isaac (35:27–29). Before continuing with the
story of Jacob's family (37:2a), the text follows a pattern we have observed elsewhere
in Genesis. All secondary lines of Israel's ancestry (that is, brothers of the promised
seed) must also be narrated, and then properly placed aside as ancillary in the
overall narration.[516] We have observed the theme of the presumed heir throughout
the ancestral narratives, which has now been settled. Lot proved to be unsuitable as
Abraham's heir (13:8–13), and God ruled out the slave Eliezer as a legitimate heir in
favor of a biological descendant (15:1–5). Ishmael was a biological son, and so was
blessed, but he too was placed aside by the narrative (16:7–12; 17:20–21). Esau was the
firstborn son, but not the recipient of the ancestral covenant and promises (28:3–4).
So as we saw at the conclusion of the Abraham narrative and before the story of
Isaac began, Ishmael's descendants were listed, their role in history explained, and

---

[516] So additional children born in the ancestral family become the progenitors of various
people groups of the ancient world through a process of divergence, while Israel's descent
continues along a straight line from Adam to Jacob, with only one son continuing
the covenant promises in a process of invergence. All of this ends with the segmented
genealogy of Jacob, whose twelve sons become the twelve tribes of Israel; K. R. Andriolo,
"A Structural Analysis of Genealogy and World View in the Old Testament," 1657–63.

their homeland placed far away from the Promised Land (25:12–18). Now Esau is given his proper place in history – important but far distant from Jacob and his children. This text is perhaps the ultimate closure on any presumed heir. Now that Jacob/Israel and his sons are on the scene, the narrative will move forward without detours.

Unlike other *tôlĕdôt*-panels in the book of Genesis, this one has two *tôlĕdôt*-structuring clauses, both translated "these are the descendants of Esau" (vv. 1 and 9). The first one addresses Esau's immediate family and their relocation to Edom in the hill country of Seir, while the second one goes far beyond Esau's first-generation children, as we shall see. The materials combined in the second of these (vv. 9–43) are collected from a wide range of lists, assorted "independent files" so to speak, and have been collected here as a means of bringing closure to the Esau story, while serving at the same time an etiological function for later readers who are interested in the nation Edom.[517]

The first *tôlĕdôt*-clause repeats the assertion that Esau and his descendants became the later nation of Edom, Israel's neighbor to the southeast (v. 1, cf. 25:30).[518] That Esau took wives "from the Canaanites" continues to be an indictment of his character (vv. 2–4; cf. 26:34–35; 27:46). Jacob's sons are enumerated according to their four mothers, all acquired by Jacob while in exile in the ancestral homeland and all suitable as wives for the patriarch (35:22b–26). By contrast, Esau had married exogamously, outside the ancestral family (a Hittite, a Hivite, and an Ishmaelite), which served to distinguish sharply between Jacob and Esau.[519] The wives' names do not match what has been said earlier about Esau's wives, leaving us with traditions in tension with each other.[520] The record of Esau's five sons is succinctly organized according to their mothers, as Jacob's had been in 35:22b–26. Ironically, these were the five sons born to Esau "in the land of Canaan," while all but one of Jacob's sons were born in Paddan-aram.

The reasons for the separation of Jacob and Esau are economic, using phrases similar to the separation of Abram and Lot (vv. 6–8; cf. 13:5–7). However, the

---

[517] On the identification of these genealogical materials as priestly, see D. M. Carr, *Reading the Fractures of Genesis* (1996), 96. On the materials gathered here as "independent files" edited with little supervision, see E. A. Speiser, *Genesis* (1964), 281–82.

[518] Edom's western border is somewhat vague, but the territory was generally east of the Arabah, north of the Gulf of Aqabah, and south of Moab; A. F. Rainey and R. S. Notley, *The Sacred Bridge: Carta's Atlas of the Biblical World* (2006), 41. See also Kenneth G. Hoglund, "Edomites," in *Peoples of the Old Testament World*, eds. Alfred J. Hoerth, Gerald L. Mattingly, and Edwin M. Yamauchi (Grand Rapids, Mich.: Baker Books, 1994), 335–47.

[519] See Closer Look "Endogamy in Ancient Israel" at p. 219.

[520] Cf. 26:34 and 28:9. It is likely the tension modern readers feel was not a problem for the ancients, who used genealogies in more fluid and flexible ways than we generally imagine and who would have considered each list accurate in its own particular sphere; Robert R. Wilson, *Genealogy and History in the Biblical World* (Yale Near Eastern Researches 7; New Haven: Yale University Press, 1977), 180–81.

narrator's primary interest is in the result of the separation; that is, Esau and his family, livestock and all property, have relocated to "a land some distance from his brother Jacob." The precise location is not named until v. 8. It is almost incidental where Esau goes, as long as it is far from Jacob. "Seir" is a name used occasionally for a mountainous region that became part of the nation Edom, as in vv. 20–21, and at other times synonymously for all Edom, as in vv. 8–9.[521]

The second of the two *tôlĕdôt*-structuring clauses introduces the rest of the chapter (vv. 9–43), which itself appears to be a secondary insertion into a text that flows more naturally from 36:1–8 directly to 37:1. "Esau settled in the hill country of Seir" (36:8) matches perfectly and prepares for "but Jacob settled in . . . the land of Canaan" (37:1).[522] This *tôlĕdôt*-panel goes considerably beyond the first one by listing more than Esau's first generation sons, but rather combines (1) a segmented genealogy, vv. 9–14, including the grandsons for Eliphaz and Reuel, but not Oholibamah, (2) a repetition of the sons and grandsons, vv. 15–19, according to their roles as tribal chieftains in ancient Edom, (3) the sons of Seir the Horite, vv. 20–30, inhabitants of the land who became part of ancient Edom, (4) the kings of the nation Edom, vv. 31–39, who ruled before monarchy in ancient Israel, and (5) a final list of Esau's tribal chiefs, vv. 40–43, according to their land allotments, perhaps after the Edomite monarchy has ceased to exist. Thus the purpose for a second *tôlĕdôt*-clause may be apparent in the subtle characterization of Esau as "ancestor [lit. father] of the Edomites." These lists go beyond the simple enumeration of Esau's sons by their mothers as in vv. 2–5 (and 35:22b–26 for Jacob), but use genealogies and lists to present a history of Esau/Edom. The subsequent history of Jacob/Israel will be narrated in the rest of the Bible, but that of Esau/Edom is dispatched rather quickly here.

Esau's sons and grandsons (partial) are listed again in vv. 15–19, this time according to their clans, or "chiefs" (see NRSV's footnote). The term (*'allûp, 'allūp*) designates the chief of a clan, tribe, or region, but also occurs in this passage as a title for a personal name, "Chief Teman, Chief Omar, Chief Zepho," and so forth (often represented only by "clans" in NRSV before the string rather than being translated in each case).[523] Because of the switch to "kings" (*mĕlākîm*) in vv. 31–39 and back to "clans, chiefs" again in vv. 40–43, it is possible that the text is somewhat chronological, moving from a premonarchic period in vv. 10–30 to the Edomite monarchy in vv. 31–39, and finally back to a postmonarchic period in vv. 40–43.[524] The appearance of Amalek should be noted, especially since the list has been

---

[521] Ernst Axel Knauf, "Seir," *ABD* 5:1072–73.

[522] Most interpreters agree on this observation, although Westermann goes even further by proposing that the insertion itself is from the royal archives of Edom; C. Westermann, *Genesis 12–36* (1985), 561.

[523] *HALOT* 1:54; *DCH* 1:288–89.

[524] Gordon H. Johnston, "*'allûp*," *NIDOTTE* 1:406–10, esp. 408. If so, this text illustrates the movement from pastoralism, to monarchy, and back to pastoralism, while also showing that seminomadic pastoralist groups may easily come to see their corporate leadership

expanded at v. 16 in order to place Amalek in the seventh position, probably giving him a prominent place because of the ominous role of the Amalekites in Israel's history.[525]

The sons of Seir are included next, presumably because they were considered inhabitants of the land prior to the arrival of Esau's family, and came to be included in the nation Edom. Genealogies may be used fluidly as a means of representing shifting political realities in order to explain the author's present historical situation.[526] So national Edom may have been a combination of Esau's descendants together with the former inhabitants of the hill country of Seir.

The kings of Edom (vv. 31–39) are not known from any other source, and yet it seems likely that this paragraph is based on what has been called "the only historical document" in Genesis.[527] None of these eight kings is attested in extrabiblical sources, and yet we can discern that this was not a continuous dynasty. Each king appears to have arisen on his own family's strength and in his own city. This was not likely a monarchy in the strict sense of the word, with standing armies, central capitals, with building projects of palaces and temples. Rather this was likely an early experimental form of tribal-leader rising to kingship, perhaps even temporarily, not unlike Israel's first attempts with Abimelech and Saul (Judg 9 and 1 Sam 9–15 respectively). The chapter closes with a list of the chiefs again, this time according to their settlements in the land (vv. 40–43). Although not a verifiable theory, it is again quite plausible that this list was drawn up for the purpose of Israelite administration of occupied Edom during the Davidic monarchy (cf. 2 Sam 8:14).[528] The overall effect of the chapter shows the fulfillment of God's promise to Abraham that great nations would come from his children (17:4).

GENESIS 37:1–36 JOSEPH AND HIS BROTHERS

(37:1) Jacob settled in the land where his father had lived as an alien, the land of Canaan.

(37:2) This is the story of the family of Jacob. Joseph, being seventeen years old, was shepherding the flock with his brothers; he was a helper to the sons of

---

as a "king" without an elaborate monarchy as such. The archaeology does not support large monarchies in Edom. On the possibilities for a tribal chiefdom society in Edom and helpful bibliography, see Robert D. Miller, *Chieftains of the Highland Clans: A History of Israel in the 12th and 11th Centuries B.C.* (Grand Rapids, Mich.: Eerdmans, 2005), 107–8.

[525] The Amalekites were the first people to oppose the Israelites after the Exodus and played a particularly insidious role in Israel's history (Exod 17:8–16; Deut 25:17–19; 1 Sam 15:2). On the seventh position in a genealogy for persons deemed worthy of attention, see J. M. Sasson, "A Genealogical 'Convention' in Biblical Chronology?" esp. 178–79.

[526] R. R. Wilson, *Genealogy and History in the Biblical World* (1977), 29.

[527] C. Westermann, *Genesis 12–36* (1985), 565; whether or not Westermann is correct that the list came from the Edomite chancery at the time of David (p. 561), it remains a fascinating glimpse into early Semitic monarchy as it evolved from pastoralism.

[528] C. Westermann, *Genesis 12–36* (1985), 566.

Bilhah and Zilpah, his father's wives; and Joseph brought a bad report of them to their father.

(37:3) Now Israel loved Joseph more than any other of his children, because he was the son of his old age; and he had made him a long robe with sleeves.^{PP}

(37:4) But when his brothers saw that their father loved him more than all his brothers, they hated him, and could not speak peaceably to him.

(37:5) Once Joseph had a dream, and when he told it to his brothers, they hated him even more.

(37:6) He said to them, "Listen to this dream that I dreamed.

(37:7) There we were, binding sheaves in the field. Suddenly my sheaf rose and stood upright; then your sheaves gathered around it, and bowed down to my sheaf."

(37:8) His brothers said to him, "Are you indeed to reign over us? Are you indeed to have dominion over us?" So they hated him even more because of his dreams and his words.

(37:9) He had another dream, and told it to his brothers, saying, "Look, I have had another dream: the sun, the moon, and eleven stars were bowing down to me."

(37:10) But when he told it to his father and to his brothers, his father rebuked him, and said to him, "What kind of dream is this that you have had? Shall we indeed come, I and your mother and your brothers, and bow to the ground before you?"

(37:11) So his brothers were jealous of him, but his father kept the matter in mind.

(37:12) Now his brothers went to pasture their father's flock near Shechem.

(37:13) And Israel said to Joseph, "Are not your brothers pasturing the flock at Shechem? Come, I will send you to them." He answered, "Here I am."

(37:14) So he said to him, "Go now, see if it is well with your brothers and with the flock; and bring word back to me." So he sent him from the valley of Hebron. He came to Shechem,

(37:15) and a man found him wandering in the fields; the man asked him, "What are you seeking?"

(37:16) "I am seeking my brothers," he said; "tell me, please, where they are pasturing the flock."

(37:17) The man said, "They have gone away, for I heard them say, 'Let us go to Dothan.'" So Joseph went after his brothers, and found them at Dothan.

(37:18) They saw him from a distance, and before he came near to them, they conspired to kill him.

(37:19) They said to one another, "Here comes this dreamer.

(37:20) Come now, let us kill him and throw him into one of the pits; then we shall say that a wild animal has devoured him, and we shall see what will become of his dreams."

---

^{PP} Traditional rendering (compare Gk): *a coat of many colors*; Meaning of Heb uncertain.

(37:21) But when Reuben heard it, he delivered him out of their hands, saying, "Let us not take his life."

(37:22) Reuben said to them, "Shed no blood; throw him into this pit here in the wilderness, but lay no hand on him" – that he might rescue him out of their hand and restore him to his father.

(37:23) So when Joseph came to his brothers, they stripped him of his robe, the long robe with sleeves that he wore;

(37:24) and they took him and threw him into a pit. The pit was empty; there was no water in it.

(37:25) Then they sat down to eat; and looking up they saw a caravan of Ishmaelites coming from Gilead, with their camels carrying gum, balm, and resin, on their way to carry it down to Egypt.

(37:26) Then Judah said to his brothers, "What profit is it if we kill our brother and conceal his blood?

(37:27) Come, let us sell him to the Ishmaelites, and not lay our hands on him, for he is our brother, our own flesh." And his brothers agreed.

(37:28) When some Midianite traders passed by, they drew Joseph up, lifting him out of the pit, and sold him to the Ishmaelites for twenty pieces of silver. And they took Joseph to Egypt.

(37:29) When Reuben returned to the pit and saw that Joseph was not in the pit, he tore his clothes.

(37:30) He returned to his brothers, and said, "The boy is gone; and I, where can I turn?"

(37:31) Then they took Joseph's robe, slaughtered a goat, and dipped the robe in the blood.

(37:32) They had the long robe with sleeves taken to their father, and they said, "This we have found; see now whether it is your son's robe or not."

(37:33) He recognized it, and said, "It is my son's robe! A wild animal has devoured him; Joseph is without doubt torn to pieces."

(37:34) Then Jacob tore his garments, and put sackcloth on his loins, and mourned for his son many days.

(37:35) All his sons and all his daughters sought to comfort him; but he refused to be comforted, and said, "No, I shall go down to Sheol to my son, mourning." Thus his father bewailed him.

(37:36) Meanwhile the Midianites had sold him in Egypt to Potiphar, one of Pharaoh's officials, the captain of the guard.

OVERVIEW OF THE JOSEPH NARRATIVE, CHAPTERS 37–50[529]

The *tôlĕdôt*–structuring clause of Jacob (37:2), "this is *the story of* the family of Jacob," is the final one of the book, and introduces the last portion of Genesis. I

---

[529] The *tôlĕdôt* clause is in 37:2, making the chapter break at 37:1 awkward. For the sake of convenience, I will refer to the Joseph narrative (37:2–50:26) simply as Gen 37–50.

will call these last fourteen chapters of Genesis "the Joseph narrative," although the label is somewhat awkward. While "Joseph narrative" works well in balancing out the Abraham and Jacob narratives, the label for Gen 37–50 is not perfect because (1) Joseph is technically not a patriarch in the same way that the heroes of the Abraham and Jacob narratives are, and (2) Gen 37–50 is not the same kind of narrative as Gen 12–36. The first point is simple to explain. Joseph is not in the line of royal descent for ancient Israel. In terms of tracing the genuine fathers of Israel's national history, Joseph should be a peripheral figure in many ways. The future kings came through Judah rather than Ephraim or Manasseh, the tribes of Joseph. So when later biblical passages list the patriarchs, they are without fail Abraham, Isaac, and Jacob/Israel (Exod 2:24). But Joseph's story is simply too good to miss. The power of the drama makes many of the points the editors and compilers of Genesis want to make, and so it has been adapted as part of the last major portion of the book. The second reason the label "Joseph narrative" for Gen 37–50 is awkward needs a bit more explanation.

Simply said, the differences between Gen 37–50 and the Abraham and Jacob narratives in Gen 12–36 are sufficient enough to make the term "narrative" some-what awkward for both. The literary characteristics of 12–36, as we have seen, are genealogies used either to introduce descendants or narrative segments, which were then tied together into a continuous narrative thread. These threads were interspersed with traditions often associated with oral societies, such as etiological name-giving episodes, but especially itineraries of the patriarchs' travels (Abram from Ur to Shechem, Bethel, Egypt, and Beer-sheba, Isaac to Gerar and Beer-sheba, Jacob to Paddan-aram and back again, etc.). Such traditional materials have been tied together and worked into a continuous history by priestly editors, as I have argued in the introduction. By contrast, Gen 37–50 is not composed of narrative segments but is primarily a continuous whole, especially that portion called "the Joseph story in the stricter sense" by Claus Westermann.[530] This Joseph story in the narrower sense is preserved in chapters 37, 39–45, and portions of 46–50, which has none of the traditional materials, such as genealogies, etiologies, journey-tales, and so forth.[531] Rather than a series of narrative segments sown together, as in Gen 12–36, this portion is a continuous storyline with multiple scenes, carefully plotted suspense, and an artfully crafted denouement.

---

[530] Claus Westermann, *Genesis 37–50: A Commentary* (Minneapolis: Augsburg Pub. House, 1986), 22–26.

[531] The Joseph story has goings-and-comings to and from Egypt, of course, but these trips have nothing of the sense of patriarchal pilgrimage so characteristic of Gen 12–36. For discussion of the beginning and ending of the *Novella* proper, see Roy L. Heller, *Narrative Structure and Discourse Constellations: An Analysis of Clause Function in Biblical Hebrew Prose* (HSS 55; Winona Lake, Ind.: Eisenbrauns, 2004), 33–41. Heller accepts as portions of the original Joseph story 37:1–36; 39:1–46:8a; 46:26–47:27, assuming that none of 48–50 were original to it.

There is also a very different role for God in the Joseph story in the narrower sense. We have no theophanic appearances, revelations, or speeches of God, no *deus ex machina*, or devices of divine intervention to drive the narrative forward. Rather we have the subtleties of dialogue portraying characters and conflicts that build suspense to a dramatic conclusion, at which time we learn an important lesson intended from the start (see below at 45:5–8 and 50:20). These techniques are unique in Genesis, and indeed, in this form, they are rare in the Bible generally. For this reason and others, this portion of Genesis (chapters 37, 39–45, and bits of 46–50) has been identified as an independent source – a so-called *Novella*, or short story.[532] As such, the Novella was not comprised originally of the various sources we have seen elsewhere in Genesis, the older epic narrative of Israel's national history, often associated with the Yahwist, and the later priestly materials (see introduction). Although some scholars continue to speculate about Yahwistic and priestly strands in the Novella itself, I am of the opinion it stood alone as an independent, self-contained short story, which has been broken apart, especially at its conclusion (Gen 46–50) and adapted as the final portion of the book of Genesis.[533] Thus I will use "Joseph Novel" for the remnants of this original *Novella* (37, 39–45, and portions of 46–50), and "Joseph narrative" for all of Gen 37–50 in order to preserve its continuity with the ancestral story begun in Gen 12, which was certainly also intended by the final editors of Genesis. So although there are significant differences in the narratives of 12–36 and 37–50, the book of Genesis may conveniently be sorted into four portions: the Primeval History (1–11), the Abraham narrative (12–25), the Jacob narrative (25–36), and the Joseph narrative (37–50).[534]

[532] The literary observations and identification of these chapters as a *Novella* goes back to Hermann Gunkel and his student Hugo Gressmann, who first used the word. Gunkel admitted he could not call the Joseph narrative a "legend" or "saga," as he had the Abraham and Jacob narratives, and Gressmann used "Novella," which has been widely adopted in the secondary literature, including by Gunkel himself in subsequent editions of his commentary; Hermann Gunkel, *Genesis: Translated and Interpreted*, trans. Mark E. Biddle (Macon, Ga.: Mercer University Press, 1997), xliv–xlvii and 381–83; Hugo Gressmann, "Ursprung und Entwicklung der Joseph-Sage," in *EUCHARISTĒRION: Studien zur Religion und Literatur des Alten und Neuen Testaments*, ed. Hans Schmidt (FRLANT 36; Göttingen: Vandenhoeck & Ruprecht, 1923), 1–55.

[533] In this sense, Gen 37–50 illustrates the principle of "*intra*textuality" in which an ancient literary piece has been adapted and incorporated into a new composition, as opposed to "*inter*textuality," in which a text builds upon another text existing outside itself. Intra-textuality calls attention to the ways a text wraps itself around an older text, reproducing it, co-opting its authority and power, and in most cases, altering its original intent. For introduction to this topic, see David M. Carr, *Reading the Fractures of Genesis: Historical and Literary Approaches* (Louisville, Ky.: Westminster John Knox Press, 1996), 12–15.

[534] Gen 25 is split in two by the *tôlĕdôt*-structuring clauses, and must necessarily serve twice in this simplified schematic. Brueggemann relates the four sections of the book to "the call of God": (1) the sovereign call of God, (2) the embraced call of God, (3) the conflicted call of God, and (4) the hidden call of God; Walter Brueggemann, *Genesis: A Bible Commentary for Teaching and Preaching* (IBC; Atlanta: John Knox Press, 1982), 8–10.

The Joseph Novel is "the work of an artist, not the product of oral tradition," which again calls attention to certain distinct differences between it and the Abraham and Jacob narratives (Gen 12–36).[535] Many interpreters have observed the narrator's masterful use of characterization, plot development, and suspenseful drama, in what is some of the best prose ever written.[536] Many also assume such ancient short stories are complete works of fiction, or that everything in them is an invention of the author. Indeed, this is often assumed in the definition of "Novella" itself. However, such an assumption is not necessary, and it is entirely possible to think in terms of an "historical" novel for these chapters.[537] Nor does the identification of the literary nature and distinctiveness of the Joseph Novel settle the date of composition, which ranges from suggestions in the late second millennium BCE, to the so-called Solomonic Enlightenment, down to the sixth–fifth centuries BCE.[538]

A final question about the Joseph narrative is its function in Genesis and the Pentateuch as a whole. The covenant and the ancestral promises of land and seed – so central throughout Gen 12–36 – are absent entirely, nor do we encounter any further revelatory theophanies.[539] This theological uniqueness combines with the literary distinctiveness we have discussed to illustrate the role of the Joseph narrative in the Bible. The great tradition complexes of ancient Israel tell us none of the details of Israel's centuries-long sojourn in Egypt, which is said variously to have lasted "four hundred years" or "four hundred thirty years" (Gen 15:13; Exod 12:40). Similarly, the Bible's summaries of Israel's history include extensive periods of sojourn in Egypt, showing awareness of Israel's long period of slavery but without providing

---

[535] George W. Coats, *Genesis, with an Introduction to Narrative Literature* (FOTL 1; Grand Rapids, Mich.: Eerdmans, 1983), 266. Many interpreters have observed the literary artistry of the Joseph Novel in particular, and I will refer to several recent studies of its artistry in the commentary below.

[536] Gary A. Rendsburg, *The Redaction of Genesis* (Winona Lake, Ind.: Eisenbrauns, 1986), 79–80; Meir Sternberg, *The Poetics of Biblical Narrative: Ideological Literature and the Drama of Reading* (Indiana Studies in Biblical Literature; Bloomington: Indiana University Press, 1985), 285–308.

[537] Roland de Vaux, *The Early History of Israel*, trans. David Smith (Philadelphia: Westminster, 1978), 296; and for the Egyptian elements in the Joseph Novel, see de Vaux's pages 297–310, and James K. Hoffmeier, *Israel in Egypt: The Evidence for the Authenticity of the Exodus Tradition* (New York: Oxford University Press, 1997), 83–95.

[538] Respectively, Kenneth A. Kitchen, "Review of Donald B. Redford, *A Study of the Biblical Story of Joseph (Genesis 37–50)*, VTSup 20, 1970," *OrAnt* 12 (1973): 223–42; Gerhard von Rad, *Genesis: A Commentary* (OTL; Philadelphia: Westminster Press, 1961), 433–40; Donald B. Redford, *A Study of the Biblical Story of Joseph (Genesis 37–50)* (VTSup 20; Leiden: E. J. Brill, 1970). For evidence that the present form of the Joseph Novel took shape shortly after the split of the United Monarchy, see Yigal Levin, "Joseph, Judah and the 'Benjamin Conundrum,'" *ZAW* 116/2 (2004): 223–41.

[539] The single occurrence of the ancestral promises at the conclusion of the book (50:24) is the editorial work of tying the Joseph Novel into the rest of the ancestral narratives; G. von Rad, *Genesis* (1961), 433 and 439.

any narratives or details of the sojourn itself (Deut 6:21–23; 26:5–9; Josh 24:4–5; 1 Sam 12:8). The Israelites simply preserved no traditions about their long sojourn in Egypt. Rather the Bible skips from ancestral life in and around Canaan (Gen 12–36) to the exodus from Egypt (Exod 1–15). Thus the Joseph Novel has been incorporated into the Joseph narrative as the conclusion of Genesis in order to serve as a bridge, theologically and structurally, between the ancestors and the exodus.[540]

COMMENTS ON 37:1–36

The medieval chapter division (inherited from the Vulgate translation) has stranded v. 1 at the beginning of this text immediately prior to the beginning of the Jacob genealogical notation. In all likelihood, it once followed immediately after 36:8, assuming 36:9–43 was inserted secondarily (see commentary above). Thus the conclusion to Esau's first genealogical notation, begun at 36:1, ended in a contrast between Esau and Jacob: "So Esau settled in the hill country of Seir, . . . but Jacob settled in . . . the land of Canaan."[541] The proximity of the verses emphasized the contrast between the brothers, especially the important notion that Esau moved far away from Jacob and his family, who remained in the Promised Land. That Jacob "settled" in the land where his fathers had only "sojourned" marks another progression in the ancestral narrative, so that Jacob/Israel came to occupy the Promised Land, just as Esau came to occupy Edom (Gen 36).[542]

Verse 2a is the last *tôlĕdôt*-structuring clause of Genesis. Several of these have introduced a narrative or genealogy by repeating the proper name immediately after the clause; e.g., "These are the descendants of Noah – Noah was a righteous man" (6:9, cf. Shem in 11:10; Terah in 11:27). The surprising juxtaposition of *different* names in v. 2, "the story of the family of Jacob – Joseph, . . . " probably reflects the adaptation of the genealogical structuring technique to introduce the Joseph Novel.[543] In this way, the Joseph Novel has been combined with additional materials

---

[540] Martin Noth, *A History of Pentateuchal Traditions*, trans. Bernhard W. Anderson (Englewood Cliffs, N.J.: Prentice-Hall, 1972), 208–13; George W. Coats, *From Canaan to Egypt: Structural and Theological Context for the Joseph Story* (CBQMS 4; Washington: Catholic Biblical Association of America, 1976), 1–5.

[541] Grammatical parallelism of the Hebrew makes the original juxtaposition of these two verses, 36:8 and 37:1, virtually certain.

[542] The contrast between Esau and Jacob is undeniable, and because of the two genealogical lists of Gen 36, one added secondarily, the *waw*-consecutive beginning of v. 1 should now be taken as narratival, "Now let's get back to the story . . . "; Robert E. Longacre, *Joseph, a Story of Divine Providence: A Text Theoretical and Textlinguistic Analysis of Genesis 37 and 39–48* (Winona Lake, Ind.: Eisenbrauns, 2003[1989]), 20. Yet such a reading was created only when the insertion of 36:9–43 took place, the *waw*-consecutive originally being simply disjunctive. Longacre assumes the sentence stands now as a summary of Gen 36.

[543] R. E. Longacre, *Joseph, a Story of Divine Providence* (2003[1989]), 20.

on Jacob's family to extend the Jacob narrative far beyond Gen 25–36. Indeed, in some ways, this last portion of Genesis is an extension of the Jacob narrative.[544]

The opening verses of this text are an elaborate general introduction to the Joseph Novel in three parts, providing all the background information needed for the beginning of the Novel itself in v. 5.[545] First, the settling of Jacob in Canaan (v. 1) and the *tôlĕdôt*–clause (v. 2a) place the Joseph Novel in the context of the book of Genesis as a whole.[546] Second, v. 2b provides pertinent background information concerning the characters of Joseph and his brothers generally. Joseph was the last son born in Paddan-aram (30:23–24), and is characterized here as young in comparison to his half-brothers. He is also, however, shepherding "with" his half-brothers, and "a helper" for the sons of Bilhah and Zilpah, the primary herders responsible for the flocks. The narrator seems intent on portraying Joseph's equal status among his half-brothers.[547] Third, the introduction also sets the stage by providing the background actions and attitudes of the characters of the Joseph Novel (vv. 2c–4). Joseph's "bad report" concerned only the brothers born to Jacob's secondary wives (Dan, Naphtali, Gad, and Asher, 30:3–13), and must have related to their work among the flocks.[548] But his father's favoritism produced hatred in all his brothers (vv. 3–4).[549]

The precise nature of Joseph's "long robe with sleeves" (*kĕtōnet passîm*) is rather famously impossible to identify (see NRSV's footnote). The leading noun is easy enough, "tunic" or "long shirt-like garment" (*kĕtōnet*), but the modifying noun occurs only in this phrase and leaves us in the dark.[550] In the only other occurrence of the phrase, it denotes a garment of royal presence (2 Sam 13:18–19), and so probably indicates exceptional length, color, or both. Regardless of the details, we can assume the garment was a luxury item that only those who did not have to work could think of having.[551] In a story as old and tragic as human history itself, the

---

544 The interchange between "Jacob" (vv. 1–2) and "Israel" (v. 3) occurs throughout the Joseph narrative, and defies simple explanation. Longacre's proposal that "Jacob" emphasizes his suffering, feeling human side, while "Israel" reflects his office and dignity seems unlikely to me; R. E. Longacre, *Joseph, a Story of Divine Providence* (2003[1989]), 147–48.

545 For discourse-linguistic details, see R. L. Heller, *Narrative Structure and Discourse Constellations* (2004), 59–62.

546 Heller assumes v. 1 parallels "Thus Israel settled in the land of Egypt, in the region of Goshen" (47:27), forming an *inclusio* tying the Joseph Novel together as a unit; R. L. Heller, *Narrative Structure and Discourse Constellations* (2004), 62.

547 The inclusion of details, such as Joseph's age and attendant circumstances, and the fact that he is characterized by means of the attitudes of others to him (his father and brothers) marks him as the central character in the narrative; R. E. Longacre, *Joseph, a Story of Divine Providence* (2003[1989]), 139–42.

548 Wenham speculates that Joseph misrepresented his brothers, returning a report that was untrue; Gordon J. Wenham, *Genesis 16–50* (WBC 2; Dallas, Tex.: Word Books, 1994), 350. But this goes beyond the evidence; see C. Westermann, *Genesis 37–50* (1986), 36.

549 Note that the sons of Leah are also present in the subsequent narrative, vv. 21, 22, 26, 29.

550 *HALOT* 3:946; BDB 509 and 821.

551 H. Gunkel, *Genesis: Translated and Interpreted* (1997), 390.

robe represented ill-advised love, or at least love tainted by favoritism, resulting in brotherly hatred and a lack of peace (v. 4).

Dreams and the interpretation of dreams were viewed as a means of divine communication throughout the ancient Near East (see Closer Look "Dreams in the Hebrew Scriptures" at p. 322). Dreams have already occurred in Genesis as a means of divine revelation. At times, God simply appeared and communicated directly through the dream (20:3–7; 31:24). At other times, the dream contained a vision followed immediately by an interpretation provided by God (Jacob's ladder, 28:12–17, and the vision of the mating flocks, 31:10–13). Joseph's dreams are different in that they are metaphorical visions without interpretation. One metaphor is taken from ancient Israel's agricultural setting, that of harvesting and binding sheaves (vv. 5–8) and the other from astral observations (vv. 9–11). Upon sharing the dreams with his family, they adopted an interpretation that Joseph would rule over them, resulting in more hatred and incredulity (vv. 8 and 10). In fact, they may not have gotten the interpretation strictly correct, and the notion that Jacob "kept the matter in mind" hints at future fulfillment nonetheless (v. 11).[552]

Hatred, jealousy, and favoritism in the form of alloyed love, fuel the flames of betrayal and violence in the rest of the chapter (vv. 12–36). Reuben is unable to thwart his brothers' collusion against Joseph. Eventually their hatred is surpassed only by greed, so that Joseph's life is spared, although he is sold into Egypt as a slave.

Israel's ancestors are consistently portrayed as small-cattle pastoralists, tending flocks on the fringes of settled society.[553] Relocation of their flocks from a home base near Hebron to Shechem and further northward to the Valley of Dothan (vv. 12–17) reflects a custom practiced to this day by shepherds residing north of Hebron, who transfer flocks for summer grazing.[554] And placing the action in the rest of this text near Dothan also puts Joseph and his brothers along a major

---

[552] Unlike Pharaoh's two dreams, which Joseph says are "one and the same" (41:25), these two may have different interpretations, and on the possibility that Jacob and the brothers failed to get the interpretation correct, see Ron Pirson, *The Lord of the Dreams: A Semantic and Literary Analysis of Genesis 37–50* (JSOTSup 355; London: Sheffield Academic Press, 2002), 42–59. And for the idea that the second dream denoted the span of thirteen years between Joseph's dreams, when he is seventeen years old, and when he enters the service of the Pharaoh, at age thirty (41:46), see Ron Pirson, "The Sun, The Moon, and Eleven Stars: An Interpretation of Joseph's Second Dream," in *Studies in the Book of Genesis: Literature, Redaction and History*, ed. André Wénin (BETL 155; Leuven/Sterling, Va.: Leuven University Press/Uitgeverij Peeters, 2001), 561–68.

[553] See commentary on 26:12–14 (Isaac), and 29:1–31:55; 32:1–32; 34:8–10 (Jacob). Such mobile pastoralism, or transhumant pastoralism, involved seasonal migrations, typically from warm lowlands, where shepherds spent winters, to relatively cool highlands during the summers. For survey on the history of this phenomenon, see Daniel E. Fleming, *Democracy's Ancient Ancestors: Mari and Early Collective Governance* (Cambridge: Cambridge University Press, 2004), 34–39.

[554] Anson F. Rainey and R. S. Notley, *The Sacred Bridge: Carta's Atlas of the Biblical World* (Jerusalem: Carta, 2006), 115.

international trade route known from the time of the Bronze Age connecting Syria–
Palestine with Egypt, and preparing the reader for the introduction of the caravan
on its way from the transjordanian highlands to Egypt (v. 25). Jacob's concern
over the welfare of his sons and the flocks is justified in light of the history of
conflict with the Shechemites (Gen 34). If we understand the route from Hebron to
Shechem and finally to Dothan as a customary route for seasonal migrations, the
redirection provided by the anonymous stranger makes sense (vv. 15–17). Joseph's
meeting with the stranger is also transitional, from his association with his loving
and doting father, Jacob, to his association with this jealousy and conspiratorial
brothers.[555]

Verse 18 is the narrator's summary of the brothers' collusion, and vv. 19–20 give
the details in their own words. They plan to feign accidental death by animal attack.
The brothers do not mention in their reasoning Joseph's special robe or their father's
favoritism. They are fixated on the dreams. NRSV's "this dreamer" obscures their
contemptuous nickname for Joseph: "Here comes this Lord of Dreams." Their final
statement, "we shall see what will become of his dreams," implies they hoped to
thwart the fulfillment of an unwanted prophecy, implying further they believed
Joseph had actually increased the likelihood of the dreams' fulfillment by telling
their contents to his family.[556]

Reuben, in a futile attempt to save Joseph for his father's sake, argued that the
brothers should not make themselves guilty of bloodletting (vv. 21–22). Instead, he
argues, they should leave Joseph to die alone in a dry pit, from which he hoped to
rescue him at a later time. As firstborn son, Reuben was responsible for assuming
the role of his father in Jacob's absence, and he would need to answer for the loss
of Joseph.[557] In the description of the villainous deed, the narrator highlights the
removal of the robe, that loathsome robe of Joseph's, no doubt highlighting the
brothers' perception and their state of mind as they performed the act. They were
motivated by his dreams, but that garment is the tangible object of their father's
favoritism. The circumstantial clause of v. 24b lets the reader know the pit is empty,
since such pits were routinely used as cisterns holding water. Joseph is not yet
dead.

The seizure and sale of Joseph may be said to be a pivotal juncture in this text
(vv. 23–28).[558] Judah's proposal to turn a profit in exchange for Joseph has two
desired effects: it prevents the guilt of bloodshed and gets rid of Joseph for good,
with his dreams and robe. The designation of the caravaneers as both "Ishmaelite"

---

[555] W. L. Humphreys, *Joseph and His Family: A Literary Study* (Columbia: University of
South Carolina, 1988), 103.

[556] Thus the telling of a dream was tantamount to declaring a prophecy; R. E. Longacre,
Joseph, a Story of Divine Providence (2003[1989]), 41–42.

[557] C. Westermann, *Genesis 37–50* (1986), 41.

[558] Longacre's "peak" is a shifting of the dynamic flow of the discourse, and is marked
by specific grammatical-lexical characteristics; R. E. Longacre, *Joseph, a Story of Divine
Providence* (2003[1989]), 18 and 28–30.

and "Midianite" has long been one of the few indicators of source distinction in this text.[559] Many attempts have been made to harmonize these references, most assuming the terms are simply overlapping referents, typically the Midianites as a subset of Ishmaelites, or the like.[560] It is also possible, however, the narrator has intentionally preserved two variant threads because both were widely known to the readers and were both deemed authoritative.[561] It has even been recently proposed that v. 28 is intentionally ambiguous in order to connect the two alternative accounts of the episode.[562]

The consequences of their actions are narrated in quick succession. Reuben, for reasons not disclosed, was not present when his brothers decided to sell Joseph. When he discovers that Joseph is gone, he is full of remorse and anguish because he will bear responsibility for Joseph's loss (vv. 30–31). Jacob's sons then execute the original plan to feign death by animal attack (vv. 32–33).[563] The bloody garment is incontrovertible proof that Joseph has come to a tragic end, and Jacob's grief is palpable (vv. 34–35). The closing scene in Canaan is that of tragic mourning for the deceased Joseph. But the chapter's last verse is a circumstantial clause resuming the story of Joseph, who is very much alive, having been taken to Egypt (v. 36, cf. v. 28).[564] He has been sold to Potiphar, a prominent official of the royal court, who is "captain of the guard."[565] Joseph's father and brothers think they have seen the last of him, but the narrator knows otherwise. The rest of the narrative sets out "to show how all the sins of human beings were nevertheless incapable of impeding God's decision."[566]

---

[559] The older tendency to find priestly and Yahwistic sources behind the Joseph Novel has rightly been abandoned, yet it seems likely there were other precursors to the Novel itself, which are largely unreconstructable; D. M. Carr, *Reading the Fractures of Genesis* (1996), 283–89.

[560] John H. Walton, Victor H. Matthews, and Mark W. Chavalas, *The IVP Background Bible Commentary: Old Testament* (Downers Grove, Ill.: InterVarsity Press, 2000), 69. Or with a great deal of literary subtlety, Longacre argues that Joseph's brothers saw from a distance what appeared to be Ishmaelites, who proved upon closer examination to be Midianites; R. E. Longacre, *Joseph, a Story of Divine Providence* (2003[1989]), 29–30 and 305.

[561] C. Westermann, *Genesis 37–50* (1986), 35.

[562] That is, who is the "they" in "they drew Joseph up"? See Jan-Wim Wesselius, "Language Play in the Old Testament and in Ancient North-West Semitic Inscriptions," in *The Old Testament in Its World*, eds. Robert P. Gordon and Johannes C. de Moor (OtSt 52; Leiden: Brill, 2005), 253–65, esp. 263–64.

[563] Wenham observes the irony in the use of their brother's clothes and a goat to deceive their father, since it was with his own brother's clothes and a goat that Jacob had deceived his father Isaac (27:9–17); see G. J. Wenham, *Genesis 16–50* (1994), 356.

[564] The Hebrew word order marks pluperfect action, "*had sold* him in Egypt," and is the narrator's way of providing additional background information central to the rest of the story; Ziony Zevit, *The Anterior Construction in Classical Hebrew* (SBLMS 50; Atlanta, Ga.: Scholars Press, 1998), 15–32, esp. 27.

[565] The name Potiphar is the Hebrew spelling for the Egyptian name "He-whom-(the sun god)-Re-has-given"; J. K. Hoffmeier, *Israel in Egypt* (1997), 84–85. On the prestige of this official, based on his titles, see Kenneth A. Mathews, *Genesis 11:27–50:26* (NAC 1B; Nashville: Broadman & Holman Publishers, 2005), 702.

[566] H. Gunkel, *Genesis: Translated and Interpreted* (1997), 381.

A CLOSER LOOK — DREAMS IN THE HEBREW SCRIPTURES

In the ancient world, dreams were perceived as encoded revelations of a higher order, often needing specialists, oneiromancers, to decode their meaning. Message dreams usually require no interpretation, for in them a god or other figure appears in order to communicate by spoken word. In symbolic dreams, on the other hand, the dreamer observes enigmatic visual images that require interpretation.[567] For the Egyptians particularly, dreams were a portal to the divine realm, requiring great technical skill to interpret them. The Egyptians produced dream manuals as early as the thirteenth century BCE, listing various dream possibilities and their corresponding good or bad meanings. For example, one such manual begins "If a man see himself in a dream, . . . " followed by the various possibilities. Thus it is a good omen to see a large cat in one's dream because it means a large harvest is imminent. But seeing oneself peering into a deep well in one's dream is bad, because it means one can be expected to be put in prison.[568]

Dream interpretation is highly valued as an acceptable means of prophecy in the Joseph Novel (37:5–8; 37:9; 40:5–19; 41:1–36).[569] While dreams have occurred elsewhere in Genesis, they have served in those contexts as a kind of *deus ex machina*, in which God makes decrees or proclamations (20:3–7; 28:12–17; 31:10–13). Such message dreams did not require interpretation and they seldom functioned as prophecies of future events (28:15 may be an exception), or as acceptable means of

---

[567] On the limitations of this typology and the need for more nuanced approaches, see Scott B. Noegel, *Nocturnal Ciphers: The Allusive Language of Dreams in the Ancient Near East* (AOS 89; New Haven, Conn.: American Oriental Society, 2007), 6–9. While Noegel's volume is most interested in the use of punning in literary reports of enigmatic dreams, his work nevertheless provides a useful overview and recent bibliography on dreams and their interpretation in the ancient world, including Mesopotamian literature (where the earliest examples occurred in Sumer), Egyptian literature, where it developed later under Mesopotamian influence, Canaanite, Israelite, and early Greek and talmudic literature. See also Magnus Ottosson, Jan Bergman, and G. Johannes Botterweck, "*ḥālam*," *TDOT* 4:421–32.

[568] Robert K. Ritner, "Dream Oracles," *COS* 1.33:52–54. These are similar to the Mesopotamian compendium of dream omens; A. L. Oppenheim, *The Interpretation of Dreams in the Ancient Near East: With a Translation of an Assyrian Dream-Book* (Transactions of the American Philosophical Society; Philadelphia: American Philosophical Society, 1956), 256–344; and Ann K. Guinan, "Mesopotamian Omens," *COS* 1.120:421–26, esp. 426.

[569] Since the nineteenth century, scholars have often noted the role of dreams in the Elohist source of the classical version of the Documentary Hypothesis. See, e.g., Speiser's periodic comments on dreams in the Joseph narrative; E. A. Speiser, *Genesis: Introduction, Translation, and Notes* (AB 1; Garden City, N.Y.: Doubleday, 1964). The validity of dreams in a narrative, however, should be reconsidered as a criterion for source distinction; Murray Lichtenstein, "Dream-Theophany and the E Document," *JANESCU* 1 (1969): 45–54; contra Robert K. Gnuse, "Dreams in the Night – Scholarly Mirage or Theophanic Formula? The Dream Report as a Motif of the So-called Elohist Tradition," *BZ* 39 (1995): 28–53.

Israelite prophetic divination. In Joseph's case, the dreams are symbolic rather than the message-type, and they clearly need interpretation. Significant for his Egyptian context, Joseph credits God with the giving of useful interpretations of dreams that are otherwise unintelligible (40:8; 41:16).

The Bible's witness to ancient Israel's perception and approval of various types of divination is inconsistent. The Torah proscribes several forms of divination and other mantic disciplines (Lev 19:26, 31; 20:6, 27; Deut 18:10–11), but dream interpretation and certain other types of divination remained alternative means of seeking Yahweh's will.[570] Some scholars have attempted to explain the inconsistency by means of evolutionary processes, in which a gradual decline of such practices may be traced historically in ancient Israel. More likely, however, portions of the Hebrew Bible are polemical in nature, denigrating the use and effectiveness of foreign divinatory practices, while accepting the validity and usefulness of other practices in the hands of Israelite protagonists.[571]

The techniques and practices of other ancient Near Eastern prophetic communication are often indistinguishable from Israelite practices. As can be said of Moses and Aaron and their use of techniques quite similar to those used by the Egyptian magicians, so in Genesis the use of dream interpretation is not entirely different from the rest of the ancient world. Rather the biblical heroes hold to a different conception of divinity. So while the techniques may be similar or even the same, the difference is in Joseph's (or Moses' or Daniel's) understanding of God. The genius of the narrator's use of dream interpretation in the Joseph Novel is the way the text stresses the superiority of the Yahweh-inspired court diviner from *within* the tradition of such diviners.[572]

GENESIS 38:1–30 JUDAH AND TAMAR

(38:1) It happened at that time that Judah went down from his brothers and settled near a certain Adullamite whose name was Hirah.

(38:2) There Judah saw the daughter of a certain Canaanite whose name was Shua; he married her and went in to her.

(38:3) She conceived and bore a son; and he named him Er.

(38:4) Again she conceived and bore a son whom she named Onan.

(38:5) Yet again she bore a son, and she named him Shelah. She was in Chezib when she bore him.

(38:6) Judah took a wife for Er his firstborn; her name was Tamar.

---

[570] Such as divination by means of casting lots, otherwise known as cleromancy, as in Israel's use of Urim and Thummim; Bill T. Arnold, "Necromancy and Cleromancy in 1 and 2 Samuel," *CBQ* 66/2 (2004): 199–213.

[571] S. B. Noegel, *Nocturnal Ciphers* (2007), 113–21.

[572] Frederick H. Cryer, *Divination in Ancient Israel and Its Near Eastern Environment: A Socio-Historical Investigation* (JSOTSup 142; Sheffield, England: JSOT Press, 1994), 183.

(38:7) But Er, Judah's firstborn, was wicked in the sight of the LORD, and the LORD put him to death.

(38:8) Then Judah said to Onan, "Go in to your brother's wife and perform the duty of a brother-in-law to her; raise up offspring for your brother."

(38:9) But since Onan knew that the offspring would not be his, he spilled his semen on the ground whenever he went in to his brother's wife, so that he would not give offspring to his brother.

(38:10) What he did was displeasing in the sight of the LORD, and he put him to death also.

(38:11) Then Judah said to his daughter-in-law Tamar, "Remain a widow in your father's house until my son Shelah grows up" – for he feared that he too would die, like his brothers. So Tamar went to live in her father's house.

(38:12) In course of time the wife of Judah, Shua's daughter, died; when Judah's time of mourning was over, he went up to Timnah to his sheepshearers, he and his friend Hirah the Adullamite.

(38:13) When Tamar was told, "Your father-in-law is going up to Timnah to shear his sheep,"

(38:14) she put off her widow's garments, put on a veil, wrapped herself up, and sat down at the entrance to Enaim, which is on the road to Timnah. She saw that Shelah was grown up, yet she had not been given to him in marriage.

(38:15) When Judah saw her, he thought her to be a prostitute, for she had covered her face.

(38:16) He went over to her at the road side, and said, "Come, let me come in to you," for he did not know that she was his daughter-in-law. She said, "What will you give me, that you may come in to me?"

(38:17) He answered, "I will send you a kid from the flock." And she said, "Only if you give me a pledge, until you send it."

(38:18) He said, "What pledge shall I give you?" She replied, "Your signet and your cord, and the staff that is in your hand." So he gave them to her, and went in to her, and she conceived by him.

(38:19) Then she got up and went away, and taking off her veil she put on the garments of her widowhood.

(38:20) When Judah sent the kid by his friend the Adullamite, to recover the pledge from the woman, he could not find her.

(38:21) He asked the townspeople, "Where is the temple prostitute who was at Enaim by the wayside?" But they said, "No prostitute has been here."

(38:22) So he returned to Judah, and said, "I have not found her; moreover the townspeople said, 'No prostitute has been here.' "

(38:23) Judah replied, "Let her keep the things as her own, otherwise we will be laughed at; you see, I sent this kid, and you could not find her."

(38:24) About three months later Judah was told, "Your daughter-in-law Tamar has played the whore; moreover she is pregnant as a result of whoredom." And Judah said, "Bring her out, and let her be burned."

(38:25) As she was being brought out, she sent word to her father-in-law, "It was the owner of these who made me pregnant." And she said, "Take note, please, whose these are, the signet and the cord and the staff."

(38:26) Then Judah acknowledged them and said, "She is more in the right than I, since I did not give her to my son Shelah." And he did not lie with her again.

(38:27) When the time of her delivery came, there were twins in her womb.

(38:28) While she was in labor, one put out a hand; and the midwife took and bound on his hand a crimson thread, saying, "This one came out first."

(38:29) But just then he drew back his hand, and out came his brother; and she said, "What a breach you have made for yourself!" Therefore he was named Perez.

(38:30) Afterward his brother came out with the crimson thread on his hand; and he was named Zerah.

"*J*udah and Tamar" is a dramatic human interest story, with themes of injustice, vindication, and righteousness. Perhaps more importantly, it held the interest of Israelite readers because of the identity of the sons born to this illicit liaison, and so it was preserved in the Bible. Its surprise ending has an etiology of great significance for Israelite history in the births of the twins. I have used "Judah and Tamar" as a title, but the story is also about Perez and Zerah.

In the literary flow of Genesis, this chapter is an interlude, building suspense about what will happen to Joseph in Egypt. As the text now stands, the editor has purposefully suspended Joseph in Egypt (37:36, "Meanwhile the Midianites had sold him in Egypt . . . "), only to pick him up again afterwards (39:1, "Now Joseph was taken down to Egypt . . . "), intentionally framing the Judah–Tamar chapter. While interpreters have long speculated that Gen 38 may have been inserted by the final redactors of Genesis, making it something of an interruption to the Joseph story, it is more likely this text was originally incorporated by the author of the Joseph Novel as a means not only of creating suspense, but as a foil for Joseph.[573] Judah's indiscretion and callousness, which he himself acknowledges make him less than righteous, are contrasted with Joseph's unsurpassed morality in the very next chapter (39:8–12). In this way, the location of Gen 38, with its sordid and seedy details, invites comparison with Joseph's refusal to sleep with Potiphar's wife, throwing into bold relief the qualities that set Joseph apart from his brothers.

[573] The resumption of the narrative backbone at 39:1 is most likely original to the Joseph Novel, and this Judah text was probably always considered an important part of "the story of the family of Jacob" (37:2), especially since Gen 38 has several similar themes in common with the surrounding chapters. See Brevard S. Childs, *Introduction to the Old Testament as Scripture* (Philadelphia: Fortress Press, 1979), 156–57; and for literary arguments for inclusion of Gen 38 in the original Novel, see Robert Alter, *The Art of Biblical Narrative* (New York: Basic Books, 1981), 3–10.

The characters of this episode are introduced in vv. 1–6 in breakneck pace. Judah aligned himself with Hirah, attained a wife, the daughter of a man named Shua, and had three sons, Er, Onan, and Shelah. He also acquired Tamar as a wife for Er, his firstborn son. Judah's departure "from his brothers" is surprising, but his taking up residence with a man of Adullam more surprising still. The geography is clear from the various locations mentioned (Adullam, Timnah, Chezib, and Enaim), placing these events in the northern lowlands (the Shephelah) just west of the hill country of Judah.[574] Judah's actions become even more alarming when we consider two additional details. First, he appears to enter into a business arrangement with Hirah that approximates a departure from mobile pastoralism to assimilation with local inhabitants, such as Isaac and Jacob both resisted (see commentary at 26:12–14 and 34:10). The danger Jacob and his family resisted at Shechem appears to be one Judah is embracing at Adullam. Second, the ancestral practice of endogamy, marriage within one's kinship group, appears to have been cast aside by Judah (see Closer Look, "Endogamy in Ancient Israel" at p. 219). The identification of Judah's new wife as the daughter of Shua, "a certain Canaanite," is an unmistakable indictment of his actions. Whereas his grandmother came from Haran to Canaan to marry his grandfather (Gen 24), and his own father sojourned twenty years in Mesopotamia in order to marry suitably within the extended family, Judah has turned aside "from his brothers" in order to marry a Canaanite. He has chosen the way of Ishmael and Esau rather than that of Isaac and Jacob.

The next paragraph explains how Tamar became a childless widow, an exceedingly vulnerable position in ancient society (vv. 7–11). Her husband, Er, dies. Israelite narrators seldom give attention to secondary causes such as illness or accidental death, but simply record that Er displeased Yahweh, who put him to death (v. 7). Judah's instruction to Onan to fulfill "the duty of a brother-in-law" (v. 8) assumes the Israelite practice of Levirate Marriage, an institution intended to protect the childless widow and safeguard the continuance of ancestral lands in the family (Deut 25:5–10).[575] The practice, which is known in other ancient Near Eastern cultures and may have had Canaanite origins, has a purpose clearly articulated in this text as that of raising up seed or offspring for the deceased brother.[576] Onan's refusal reflects the sense of discomfort on the part of those who are asked to fulfill the duty of the *levir*, because concerns for one's self often override fraternal loyalties.

---

[574] For details, see A. F. Rainey and R. S. Notley, *The Sacred Bridge: Carta's Atlas of the Biblical World* (2006), 115–16.

[575] Raymond Westbrook, *Property and the Family in Biblical Law* (JSOTSup 113; Sheffield: Sheffield Academic Press, 1991), 69–89.

[576] For definition of the practice, summary of the biblical data, and bibliography, see Richard M. Davidson, *Flame of Yahweh: Sexuality in the Old Testament* (Peabody, Mass.: Hendrickson Publishers, 2007), 461–83; and Ernst Kutsch, *"ybm," TDOT* 5:367–73. The term "levirate" derives from Latin *levir*, "brother-in-law," and thereby designates the one qualified to perform the duty of levirate marriage in Israelite society.

Building up the seed of his deceased brother would forfeit an opportunity to build his own inheritance, because Er's "double portion" as firstborn would have passed to Onan's children otherwise.[577] When Onan also dies, Judah sends Tamar away, a childless widow, to her own "father's house" (*bêt 'āb*, see commentary at 12:1), leaving her vulnerable and without means to provide for herself in the future.[578] He does so with the promise that Shelah, the last of his three sons, will be given to her as husband once he is of marriageable age.

When Judah sent Tamar away, he had been uncertain what to do about giving Shelah to her.[579] However, the circumstantial clause in v. 14 clearly states that Shelah had reached marriageable age and that Judah had not fulfilled the duty of Levirate marriage. Thus Tamar has been wronged and is desperate. She has been abandoned and perhaps branded as a dangerous woman – an unmarriageable, childless widow – perhaps the most vulnerable state of ancient Semitic society. When she learns of Judah's trip to Timnah during the shearing season, she seizes an opportunity to vindicate herself by posing as a prostitute and conceiving by Judah himself (vv. 12–19). The fact that Judah's wife had died also makes the case for Tamar (v. 12), because in some cultures, the father-in-law was obligated to fulfill the levirate duty as well.[580]

Although prostitution was already viewed negatively as early as the mid-third millennium BCE,[581] this text in no way condemns Tamar for her actions. Instead, she is presented as resourceful and proactive in attempting to make right the wrongs done against her. Her use of garments to disguise herself as a prostitute and deceive Judah may be compared to Jacob's use of garments in his own ruse (27:15, 27), or the brothers' use of Joseph's garment to deceive their father (37:31–33). But the fact that Shelah had not been given to her as husband seems to justify these desperate actions. She also outwits Judah by asking for a pledge, specifically his signet, cord, and staff, to

---

[577] R. Westbrook, *Property and the Family in Biblical Law* (1991), 76. On the general reluctance to serve as *levir*, see Dvora E. Weisberg, "The Widow of Our Discontent: Levirate Marriage in the Bible and Ancient Israel," *JSOT* 28 (2004): 403–29.

[578] Judah could have set Tamar free to remarry, but suspecting she is a "lethal woman," whose sexual partners are doomed to die, he sends her to live as "a widow" in her family household, leaving her without marriage prospects and in limbo. See Tikva Frymer-Kensky, "Tamar 1," in *Women in Scripture: A Dictionary of Named and Unnamed Women in the Hebrew Bible, the Apocryphal/Deuterocanonical Books, and the New Testament*, eds. Carol L. Meyers, Toni Craven, and Ross S. Kraemer (Boston: Houghton Mifflin, 2000), 161–63.

[579] The narrator's statement that Judah was afraid "[Shelah] too would die, like his brothers" (v. 11) does not necessarily mean he planned to withhold him permanently, only that he needed to buy time to decide whether or not to give Shelah to Tamar as husband.

[580] Whether or not Judah saw this as his obligation is irrelevant. But Tamar may have been working from a different set of societal rules, and since Judah was now single, he had no reason to avoid marrying Tamar while preventing her from marrying someone else; R. M. Davidson, *Flame of Yahweh* (2007), 463. Note particularly the Hittite laws in this regard; Harry A. Hoffner, "Hittite Laws," *COS* 2.19:106–119, esp. 118.

[581] Jerrold S. Cooper, "Prostitution," *RlA* 11:12–22, esp. 13.

be held until he returns payment later. These are objects known throughout much of the ancient Near East as insignia of a prominent man, which would make it possible for her later to identify the father of her child unequivocally. The "signet" (*ḥōtām,* or in v. 25, *ḥōtemet*) was likely a cylinder seal rather than a ring, carried around one's neck on a cord threaded through its center, and used for signing contracts.[582] The staff (*maṭṭeh*) was the common rod or shaft most likely carved with distinctive markings to identify its owner. Judah turns these over to Tamar, whom he does not recognize because of her prostitute clothing and veil. The narrator then uses succinct but crude terminology to describe the liaison, denoting simply the sexual penetration: "[he] went in to her."[583] Tamar returns to her widowhood, but the narrator informs us she has conceived. She departs the wayside station at Enaim carrying the evidence of her own righteous vindication in her womb.

Judah sends his Adullamite friend, presumably Hirah, back with the payment, only to discover she is missing, and none of the local residents are able to identify her or confirm that a prostitute regularly works that corner (vv. 20–22). Judah had thought Tamar was a "prostitute" (*zônâ,* v. 15), but when Hirah investigates among the townspeople, he uses "temple prostitute" (*qĕdēšâ,* v. 21) to describe her. Most likely Hirah is using a euphemism in polite speech with the townspeople, while the narrator describes what Judah thought he saw in plain speech.[584] The outcome for Judah was the same – whether she was an escort, call-girl, or whore – he stands to become a laughingstock, a real joke (v. 23). He is more concerned about saving face than providing the goat such a woman would have needed for her next meal.

In the denouement, Tamar is quickly vindicated (vv. 24–26). Judah is hasty in passing judgment on her, and excessive in the nature of the punishment.[585] Her execution would have seemed like fitting retribution, assuming Judah continued to blame her unfairly for the death of his two sons. But the evidence she produces – his own signet, cord, and staff – is undeniable, and turns the tables on his accusations and judgments about Tamar. Judah immediately acknowledges that she is in the right and he is culpable. The circumstantial clause of v. 26 makes it clear that Judah and Tamar conceived no further children. But we are left wondering what kind of resolution this is. Did Judah provide Shelah as a husband? Was Tamar otherwise provided for in the family? Instead of answering these questions, the text moves immediately to a surprise ending.

---

[582] Benedikt Otzen, "*ḥātam,*" *TDOT* 5:263–69, esp. 265; *HALOT* 1:300 and 365; *DCH* 3:180 and 336.

[583] R. Alter, *The Art of Biblical Narrative* (1981), 8–9.

[584] Victor P. Hamilton, *The Book of Genesis, Chapters 18–50* (NICOT; Grand Rapids, Mich.: Eerdmans, 1995), 446–47.

[585] Stoning was the penalty for adultery in later Israelite law (Deut 22:23–24), which would have applied in this case since Tamar was technically betrothed to Shelah, while burning was a more severe punishment; C. Westermann, *Genesis 37–50* (1986), 54.

At the birth of twins, we see once again the pattern of reversal in Hebrew Scriptures, in which the younger son displaces the firstborn (vv. 27–30).[586] The midwife carefully flagged Zerah as the firstborn, and yet it was Perez who prevailed, even in birth. At the naming of Perez, the unsuspecting reader discovers a surprise. This apparent digression in the narrative is really a story about Israel's royal family. Perez would have been a name known widely as the ancestor of King David through the genealogical line of Boaz, Obed, and Jesse (Ruth 4:18–22). The naming of the twins thus makes the entire episode an etiological account of Perez and Zerah, the former being a direct grandfather of David. The hero of the story is Tamar, who earns a place of honor alongside Rachel and Leah among all who build the house of Israel, according to the blessing pronounced over the Moabitess Ruth at the time she entered the household of Boaz (Ruth 4:11–12).

Future kings of Israel will come from the tribe of Judah (49:8–12), through Perez. Yet this is no attempt to whitewash that history. Judah behaved badly and it was only through the proactive, even courageous steps of Tamar that the injustice was exposed and corrected. On one level this story is a defense of David and his sons as the legitimate dynasty in Jerusalem. But this is almost secondary to the overarching message of the text. On a different level, the text demonstrates that God can and will use the misguided decisions and behavior of his people to accomplish his purposes, working good out of evil. In a vastly different way, the Judah and Tamar episode buttresses the central theme of the Joseph Novel: God turns good from evil in order to preserve life (45:5–8; 50:20).

GENESIS 39:1–23 JOSEPH IN POTIPHAR'S HOUSE

(39:1) Now Joseph was taken down to Egypt, and Potiphar, an officer of Pharaoh, the captain of the guard, an Egyptian, bought him from the Ishmaelites who had brought him down there.

(39:2) The LORD was with Joseph, and he became a successful man; he was in the house of his Egyptian master.

(39:3) His master saw that the LORD was with him, and that the LORD caused all that he did to prosper in his hands.

(39:4) So Joseph found favor in his sight and attended him; he made him overseer of his house and put him in charge of all that he had.

(39:5) From the time that he made him overseer in his house and over all that he had, the LORD blessed the Egyptian's house for Joseph's sake; the blessing of the LORD was on all that he had, in house and field.

(39:6) So he left all that he had in Joseph's charge; and, with him there, he had no concern for anything but the food that he ate. Now Joseph was handsome and good-looking.

---

[586] Bill T. Arnold, "*bkr*," *NIDOTTE* 1:658–59.

(39:7) And after a time his master's wife cast her eyes on Joseph and said, "Lie with me."

(39:8) But he refused and said to his master's wife, "Look, with me here, my master has no concern about anything in the house, and he has put everything that he has in my hand.

(39:9) He is not greater in this house than I am, nor has he kept back anything from me except yourself, because you are his wife. How then could I do this great wickedness, and sin against God?"

(39:10) And although she spoke to Joseph day after day, he would not consent to lie beside her or to be with her.

(39:11) One day, however, when he went into the house to do his work, and while no one else was in the house,

(39:12) she caught hold of his garment, saying, "Lie with me!" But he left his garment in her hand, and fled and ran outside.

(39:13) When she saw that he had left his garment in her hand and had fled outside,

(39:14) she called out to the members of her household and said to them, "See, my husband has brought among us a Hebrew to insult us! He came in to me to lie with me, and I cried out with a loud voice;

(39:15) and when he heard me raise my voice and cry out, he left his garment beside me, and fled outside."

(39:16) Then she kept his garment by her until his master came home,

(39:17) and she told him the same story, saying, "The Hebrew servant, whom you have brought among us, came in to me to insult me;

(39:18) but as soon as I raised my voice and cried out, he left his garment beside me, and fled outside."

(39:19) When his master heard the words that his wife spoke to him, saying, "This is the way your servant treated me," he became enraged.

(39:20) And Joseph's master took him and put him into the prison, the place where the king's prisoners were confined; he remained there in prison.

(39:21) But the LORD was with Joseph and showed him steadfast love; he gave him favor in the sight of the chief jailer.

(39:22) The chief jailer committed to Joseph's care all the prisoners who were in the prison, and whatever was done there, he was the one who did it.

(39:23) The chief jailer paid no heed to anything that was in Joseph's care, because the LORD was with him; and whatever he did, the LORD made it prosper.

*T*his text resumes the story of Joseph, which had been placed aside in order to present the Judah and Tamar episode (Gen 38). The opening paragraph uses recurrence to emphasize the blessing of Yahweh on Joseph.[587] Because Yahweh is

---

[587] The several occurrences of "Yahweh" led early source critics to assume J, or the Yahwist, was responsible for the Joseph Novel; E. A. Speiser, *Genesis* (1964), 304. But for a variety of reasons, the search for original sources behind the Novel has rightly been abandoned (see Introduction). The sources behind the Joseph Novel are largely unreconstructable;

"with Joseph," he prospers greatly. He is promoted over Potiphar's house, and all the household's enterprises prosper because of Joseph. But when Potiphar's wife falsely accuses Joseph, he is thrown in jail. There too, Yahweh is "with Joseph" and God gives him favor with the jailer. In this recurring theme, the narrator carefully characterizes Joseph. He is once again attacked and unjustly treated because of his attacker's jealousy or anger (cf. 37:4, 18). Yet he is faithful to Yahweh regardless of the unfair treatment, and the presence of Yahweh blesses him and causes him to prosper in all circumstances.

The opening clauses of v. 1 pick up again the narrative from 37:36, which had been suspended in order to narrate the Judah and Tamar episode. This resumption served to remind the reader of the details, to refocus the attention where desired, and possibly also to shift from the general (brothers and Midianites) to the particular (Joseph and Potiphar).[588] The narrator has used a large number of off-line comments in this chapter that do not advance the narrative *per se* but inform and nuance it considerably in order to characterize Joseph and to prepare for events of the Novel to be narrated later.[589] Most of these narratival comments emphasize Joseph's upstanding character, the presence of Yahweh with him to bless him, and to make him and those around him prosper. So v. 2 contains three important background clauses in the narrator's voice to provide theological underpinning for the rest of the text, and indeed for the rest of the Joseph Novel. The first two are linked by causation: because Yahweh was with Joseph, he became a successful man. The observation that Yahweh is with Joseph is at least an echo of the ancestral promise of divine presence (see commentary at 26:3, 24; 28:15), although stated differently and used in a different context. Joseph illustrates the truth of the promise stated directly to his ancestors in the context of the ancestral covenant.

Further background is provided in the assertion that Potiphar became aware of Joseph's abilities and promoted him over the entire household (vv. 3–4). Even this Egyptian official could see that Yahweh was with Joseph. In another allusion to the ancestral promises, Joseph becomes a mediator of God's blessing (v. 5). Yahweh blessed Potiphar's household because of Joseph, who has no personal abilities to bless others on his own. Rather Joseph becomes the conduit for Yahweh's blessing to Potiphar, who is blessed by association with Joseph.[590] The "blessing of the LORD" is a subjective genitive, in which Yahweh is the subject of the act of blessing others.[591]

D. M. Carr, *Reading the Fractures of Genesis* (1996), 283–89. Interestingly, after eight occurrences of "Yahweh" in Gen 39, the name is not used again in the Joseph Novel, and only once more in the book of Genesis, at 49:18.

588 So the repetition of 37:36 and 39:1 serves both mnemonic-resumptive and particularizing functions; M. Sternberg, *The Poetics of Biblical Narrative* (1985), 414–15.

589 R. L. Heller, *Narrative Structure and Discourse Constellations* (2004), 78–81.

590 Christopher W. Mitchell, *The Meaning of* brk *"to bless" in the Old Testament* (SBLDS 95; Atlanta: Scholars Press, 1987), 70–71.

591 Bill T. Arnold and John H. Choi, *A Guide to Biblical Hebrew Syntax* (Cambridge: Cambridge University Press, 2003), 9.

Potiphar's trust and confidence in Joseph is so complete, he has no concern about anything in the household (v. 6).

Potiphar's problem is not Joseph, but his own wife. The text is nearly ready to proceed to her proposition except for one more background piece. "Now Joseph was handsome and good-looking" (v. 6b). This formulaic expression for attractiveness relates both to bodily physique and general appearance. NRSV's "and after a time" is literally "after these things" (v. 7), referring to Joseph's prosperity and promotion. Although everything had gone well for the hero of the story since being sold to Egypt, things were about to get complicated. Joseph rebuffs the advances of his master's wife quickly and decisively (vv. 7–9). And his reasons are clearly stated. His master has placed complete trust in Joseph, withholding nothing except, obviously, his own wife.[592] Yet his reason for refusal is more than because this liaison would break the trust with his master, Potiphar. He further names her proposal as a "great wickedness" and a "sin against God." He uses the generic word "God" because his master's wife is not Israelite, and yet she must surely understand, Joseph maintains, the religious ramifications of her proposal. They both have theological reasons for restraint.[593]

Joseph's answer was quick, well reasoned, and decisive, but it also needed to be persistent. This was not a one-and-done event, or some impetuous suggestion she may have regretted later (v. 10).[594] This was a daily temptation, not easily dismissed, and yet Joseph faithfully fulfilled his obligation to his master and to his God, rebuffing her advances all the while. Then one day, while they are completely alone, Joseph needed more than well-reasoned arguments. He needed to run (vv. 11–12). When his quick exit left his "garment" in her hands (*beged*, probably a long cloak worn over trousers), she was left with a decision. How would she explain his garment in her possession? Might she turn this to her advantage, giving up on Joseph entirely and attempting to save face? She decides to gather others of the household and alleges

---

[592] On the possibility of word play between Potiphar's "food" (v. 6) and his "wife" (v. 9), see Gary A. Rendsburg, "Word Play in Biblical Hebrew: An Eclectic Collection," in *Puns and Pundits: Word Play in the Hebrew Bible and Ancient Near Eastern Literature*, ed. Scott B. Noegel (Bethesda, Md.: CDL Press, 2000), 137–62, esp. 150–51. This interpretation was already proposed in Midrashic literature; Jacob Neusner, *Genesis Rabbah, the Judaic Commentary to the Book of Genesis: A New American Translation* (BJS 104–106; Atlanta, Ga.: Scholars Press, 1985), 3:225, ¶86:6.

[593] Although we have few actual Egyptian laws related to homicide, theft, and sexual offenses (adultery, rape, and seduction), it appears from what meager evidence we have that the penalty of death might be expected, or the wronged husband could hope for material compensation through the local courts. In most cases, the real issue was not the sexual misconduct but official malfeasance or the misappropriation of property, in which case Joseph's abuse of his position as overseer was the focus of the allegation. See C. J. Eyre, "Crime and Adultery in Ancient Egypt," *JEA* 70 (1984): 92–105, esp. 101–2 and 104–5.

[594] The narrative structure portrays an elapse of time, during which the narrative does not actually progress, but in which her proposal is repeated again and again, and Joseph's virtue is thereby highlighted even further; R. L. Heller, *Narrative Structure and Discourse Constellations* (2004), 78.

that Joseph attempted to rape her (vv. 13–15). Her allegation appeals to any natural jealousy or resentment they may have had of this foreigner who has been promoted over them, using what must have been a racial slur in referring to Joseph as "a Hebrew" brought to make them a laughingstock.[595] When her account of the story is compared to the report of the narrator, her words actually highlight Joseph's innocence and the injustice of his imprisonment.[596]

Her prevarication works. She keeps the garment as evidence, which is not the first time garments have been used to deceive in the Joseph Novel (37:31–33). When Potiphar returns home, she executes her plan, repeating her allegation in nearly the same words (vv. 17–18). Yet the subtle differences in this report compared to her first speech of the attempted rape dare to cast some of the blame on Potiphar himself, all while intensifying the allegation, presumably now with the full support of the rest of the household ready to confirm her statement, and defending her own innocence.[597] Enraged, Potiphar springs into action, incarcerating Joseph in the royal prison (vv. 19–20).[598] Execution for this offense would have been considered reasonable in Egyptian society, although the wronged husband may also have hoped for material compensation. Since Joseph was only a servant in Potiphar's household, he could not have hoped for gain and so imprisonment seemed fair.[599] Perhaps we are to assume a hint of uncertainty in Potiphar's mind about the truthfulness of the allegation. But the important detail is that Joseph was now in the royal prison, "where the king's prisoners were confined," an item important to the next episode.

The recurrence of "Yahweh was with Joseph" signals that all is not lost (v. 23, cf. v. 2). Indeed, the reader is hereby invited to compare Joseph's circumstances now with those of his arrival in Potiphar's house (vv. 23–24; cf. 1–6a). In both cases, God is *with Joseph* to make him prosperous. Joseph finds favor with his superior, who gives over to Joseph all in his charge. The superior (Potiphar/chief jailer) now has no cares, because all is well cared for in Joseph's keeping. The Lord makes the work of the household/prison prosperous because of Joseph. As Joseph prospered in Potiphar's house, so he will prosper in the prison.[600] The recurrence builds confidence in Joseph (and in Yahweh). Joseph was unfairly sold into Egypt, and yet the prospering presence of Yahweh turned his fortunes into a good-out-of-evil drama, striking the theme of the Joseph Novel (45:5–8; 50:20). Now he has

---

[595] The precise connotation of NRSV's "to insult us" (*ṣāḥaq*, v. 14) is impossible to determine, but options range from laughing, mocking, fooling with, toying with, making fun of, and dallying with another party. For references, see V. P. Hamilton, *The Book of Genesis, Chapters 18–50* (1995), 466.

[596] R. L. Heller, *Narrative Structure and Discourse Constellations* (2004), 82–83.

[597] M. Sternberg, *The Poetics of Biblical Narrative* (1985), 425–27.

[598] As "captain of the guard," Potiphar was overseer of the royal prison (40:7; 41:12), so that the chief jailer was under his purview. Joseph was providentially imprisoned in the same facility Pharaoh would use to incarcerate his highest ranking officials (40:1–3).

[599] C. J. Eyre, "Crime and Adultery in Ancient Egypt," 102.

[600] The last word of the chapter in Hebrew, as in English, is "prosper."

been unfairly thrown in prison, and the recurrences raise the possibility, even the expectation, of another good-out-of-evil outcome. The reader gets the sense that no matter the circumstances, all will be well because Joseph will do the right thing and Yahweh will make him prosper.

GENESIS 40:1–41:57 MASTER OF DREAMS, MASTER OF EGYPT

(40:1) Some time after this, the cupbearer of the king of Egypt and his baker offended their lord the king of Egypt.

(40:2) Pharaoh was angry with his two officers, the chief cupbearer and the chief baker,

(40:3) and he put them in custody in the house of the captain of the guard, in the prison where Joseph was confined.

(40:4) The captain of the guard charged Joseph with them, and he waited on them; and they continued for some time in custody.

(40:5) One night they both dreamed – the cupbearer and the baker of the king of Egypt, who were confined in the prison – each his own dream, and each dream with its own meaning.

(40:6) When Joseph came to them in the morning, he saw that they were troubled.

(40:7) So he asked Pharaoh's officers, who were with him in custody in his master's house, "Why are your faces downcast today?"

(40:8) They said to him, "We have had dreams, and there is no one to interpret them." And Joseph said to them, "Do not interpretations belong to God? Please tell them to me."

(40:9) So the chief cupbearer told his dream to Joseph, and said to him, "In my dream there was a vine before me,

(40:10) and on the vine there were three branches. As soon as it budded, its blossoms came out and the clusters ripened into grapes.

(40:11) Pharaoh's cup was in my hand; and I took the grapes and pressed them into Pharaoh's cup, and placed the cup in Pharaoh's hand."

(40:12) Then Joseph said to him, "This is its interpretation: the three branches are three days;

(40:13) within three days Pharaoh will lift up your head and restore you to your office; and you shall place Pharaoh's cup in his hand, just as you used to do when you were his cupbearer.

(40:14) But remember me when it is well with you; please do me the kindness to make mention of me to Pharaoh, and so get me out of this place.

(40:15) For in fact I was stolen out of the land of the Hebrews; and here also I have done nothing that they should have put me into the dungeon."

(40:16) When the chief baker saw that the interpretation was favorable, he said to Joseph, "I also had a dream: there were three cake baskets on my head,

(40:17) and in the uppermost basket there were all sorts of baked food for Pharaoh, but the birds were eating it out of the basket on my head."

(40:18) And Joseph answered, "This is its interpretation: the three baskets are three days;

(40:19) within three days Pharaoh will lift up your head – from you! – and hang you on a pole; and the birds will eat the flesh from you."

(40:20) On the third day, which was Pharaoh's birthday, he made a feast for all his servants, and lifted up the head of the chief cupbearer and the head of the chief baker among his servants.

(40:21) He restored the chief cupbearer to his cupbearing, and he placed the cup in Pharaoh's hand;

(40:22) but the chief baker he hanged, just as Joseph had interpreted to them.

(40:23) Yet the chief cupbearer did not remember Joseph, but forgot him.

(41:1) After two whole years, Pharaoh dreamed that he was standing by the Nile,

(41:2) and there came up out of the Nile seven sleek and fat cows, and they grazed in the reed grass.

(41:3) Then seven other cows, ugly and thin, came up out of the Nile after them, and stood by the other cows on the bank of the Nile.

(41:4) The ugly and thin cows ate up the seven sleek and fat cows. And Pharaoh awoke.

(41:5) Then he fell asleep and dreamed a second time; seven ears of grain, plump and good, were growing on one stalk.

(41:6) Then seven ears, thin and blighted by the east wind, sprouted after them.

(41:7) The thin ears swallowed up the seven plump and full ears. Pharaoh awoke, and it was a dream.

(41:8) In the morning his spirit was troubled; so he sent and called for all the magicians of Egypt and all its wise men. Pharaoh told them his dreams, but there was no one who could interpret them to Pharaoh.

(41:9) Then the chief cupbearer said to Pharaoh, "I remember my faults today.

(41:10) Once Pharaoh was angry with his servants, and put me and the chief baker in custody in the house of the captain of the guard.

(41:11) We dreamed on the same night, he and I, each having a dream with its own meaning.

(41:12) A young Hebrew was there with us, a servant of the captain of the guard. When we told him, he interpreted our dreams to us, giving an interpretation to each according to his dream.

(41:13) As he interpreted to us, so it turned out; I was restored to my office, and the baker was hanged."

(41:14) Then Pharaoh sent for Joseph, and he was hurriedly brought out of the dungeon. When he had shaved himself and changed his clothes, he came in before Pharaoh.

(41:15) And Pharaoh said to Joseph, "I have had a dream, and there is no one who can interpret it. I have heard it said of you that when you hear a dream you can interpret it."

(41:16) Joseph answered Pharaoh, "It is not I; God will give Pharaoh a favorable answer."

(41:17) Then Pharaoh said to Joseph, "In my dream I was standing on the banks of the Nile;

(41:18) and seven cows, fat and sleek, came up out of the Nile and fed in the reed grass.

(41:19) Then seven other cows came up after them, poor, very ugly, and thin. Never had I seen such ugly ones in all the land of Egypt.

(41:20) The thin and ugly cows ate up the first seven fat cows,

(41:21) but when they had eaten them no one would have known that they had done so, for they were still as ugly as before. Then I awoke.

(41:22) I fell asleep a second time and I saw in my dream seven ears of grain, full and good, growing on one stalk,

(41:23) and seven ears, withered, thin, and blighted by the east wind, sprouting after them;

(41:24) and the thin ears swallowed up the seven good ears. But when I told it to the magicians, there was no one who could explain it to me."

(41:25) Then Joseph said to Pharaoh, "Pharaoh's dreams are one and the same; God has revealed to Pharaoh what he is about to do.

(41:26) The seven good cows are seven years, and the seven good ears are seven years; the dreams are one.

(41:27) The seven lean and ugly cows that came up after them are seven years, as are the seven empty ears blighted by the east wind. They are seven years of famine.

(41:28) It is as I told Pharaoh; God has shown to Pharaoh what he is about to do.

(41:29) There will come seven years of great plenty throughout all the land of Egypt.

(41:30) After them there will arise seven years of famine, and all the plenty will be forgotten in the land of Egypt; the famine will consume the land.

(41:31) The plenty will no longer be known in the land because of the famine that will follow, for it will be very grievous.

(41:32) And the doubling of Pharaoh's dream means that the thing is fixed by God, and God will shortly bring it about.

(41:33) Now therefore let Pharaoh select a man who is discerning and wise, and set him over the land of Egypt.

(41:34) Let Pharaoh proceed to appoint overseers over the land, and take one-fifth of the produce of the land of Egypt during the seven plenteous years.

(41:35) Let them gather all the food of these good years that are coming, and lay up grain under the authority of Pharaoh for food in the cities, and let them keep it.

(41:36) That food shall be a reserve for the land against the seven years of famine that are to befall the land of Egypt, so that the land may not perish through the famine."

(41:37) The proposal pleased Pharaoh and all his servants.

(41:38) Pharaoh said to his servants, "Can we find anyone else like this – one in whom is the spirit of God?"

(41:39) So Pharaoh said to Joseph, "Since God has shown you all this, there is no one so discerning and wise as you.

(41:40) You shall be over my house, and all my people shall order themselves as you command; only with regard to the throne will I be greater than you."

(41:41) And Pharaoh said to Joseph, "See, I have set you over all the land of Egypt."

(41:42) Removing his signet ring from his hand, Pharaoh put it on Joseph's hand; he arrayed him in garments of fine linen, and put a gold chain around his neck.

(41:43) He had him ride in the chariot of his second-in-command; and they cried out in front of him, "Bow the knee!"[qq] Thus he set him over all the land of Egypt.

(41:44) Moreover Pharaoh said to Joseph, "I am Pharaoh, and without your consent no one shall lift up hand or foot in all the land of Egypt."

(41:45) Pharaoh gave Joseph the name Zaphenath-paneah; and he gave him Asenath daughter of Potiphera, priest of On, as his wife. Thus Joseph gained authority over the land of Egypt.

(41:46) Joseph was thirty years old when he entered the service of Pharaoh king of Egypt. And Joseph went out from the presence of Pharaoh, and went through all the land of Egypt.

(41:47) During the seven plenteous years the earth produced abundantly.

(41:48) He gathered up all the food of the seven years when there was plenty in the land of Egypt, and stored up food in the cities; he stored up in every city the food from the fields around it.

(41:49) So Joseph stored up grain in such abundance – like the sand of the sea – that he stopped measuring it; it was beyond measure.

(41:50) Before the years of famine came, Joseph had two sons, whom Asenath daughter of Potiphera, priest of On, bore to him.

(41:51) Joseph named the firstborn Manasseh,[rr] "For," he said, "God has made me forget all my hardship and all my father's house."

(41:52) The second he named Ephraim,[ss] "For God has made me fruitful in the land of my misfortunes."

(41:53) The seven years of plenty that prevailed in the land of Egypt came to an end;

(41:54) and the seven years of famine began to come, just as Joseph had said. There was famine in every country, but throughout the land of Egypt there was bread.

[qq] *Abrek*, apparently an Egyptian word similar in sound to the Hebrew word meaning *to kneel.*

[rr] That is *Making to forget.*

[ss] From a Hebrew word meaning *to be fruitful.*

(41:55) When all the land of Egypt was famished, the people cried to Pharaoh for bread. Pharaoh said to all the Egyptians, "Go to Joseph; what he says to you, do."

(41:56) And since the famine had spread over all the land, Joseph opened all the storehouses, and sold to the Egyptians, for the famine was severe in the land of Egypt.

(41:57) Moreover, all the world came to Joseph in Egypt to buy grain, because the famine became severe throughout the world.

*D*reams have played an important role in moving this narrative forward from the beginning. The dreams of Joseph's youth were simple and their interpretations appeared obvious (cf. 37:5–11).[601] Many years later and now in prison, Joseph displays the gift of dream interpretation. The dreams of Pharaoh's officers, who are with Joseph in the prison, are mysterious and need interpretation. Joseph's ability to discern the meanings of the dreams becomes his key to freedom, and after a delay of two more years, he is brought from the prison to interpret Pharaoh's dreams. His gift of dream-interpretation then becomes the means of elevation over Egypt and salvation of the masses. The theme of the Joseph Novel recurs, as the abuse and neglect of others fail to prevent providence from directing Joseph's steps and preserving life for others (45:5–8; 50:20).

The opening paragraph explains that two of Pharaoh's top officers, the chief cupbearer and chief baker, offended their master and were thrown into the same prison with Joseph (40:1–4).[602] NRSV's "some time after this" leaves vague the amount of time Joseph languishes in prison. Even after he is given charge of the two Egyptian officials, he spends "some time in custody" before the narrative resumes. By noting the passage of time, the text highlights the injustice of Joseph's situation.

"Chief cupbearer" and "chief baker" reflect the use of titles among high ranking officers, where lowly service titles are often exalted to positions of highest rank (as in English "Secretary" of State). They would have been central to any royal court as the two responsible for the king's food and drink. Potiphar continues to be an important character, although somewhat less so signaled by the absence of his name. He is "the captain of the guard" as we know from 37:36 and 39:1. Joseph is identified

---

[601] Although his family appears to have jumped to several incorrect assumptions about them. Simply stated, they took the dreams personally, as indications that they would become subservient to Joseph, whereas the first one related to Joseph's rulership of Egypt, and the second dream may have referred to the passage of time before fulfillment of the first; R. Pirson, *The Lord of the Dreams* (2002), 47–58.

[602] The use of "Pharaoh" has occurred in the Abraham narrative already as a title for the king of Egypt (Gen 12), and is used throughout the Joseph narrative in the same way. Derived from Egyptian for "Great House," the term pharaoh was used as an epithet for the monarch alone, without the specific pharaoh's personal name juxtaposed, from the fifteenth through the tenth centuries BCE. Subsequently the personal name was included, as is done in biblical practice as well (e.g., Pharaoh Shishak, Pharaoh Neco); Donald B. Redford, "Pharaoh," *ABD* 5:288–89; J. K. Hoffmeier, *Israel in Egypt* (1997), 87–88.

as a "young Hebrew . . . a servant of the captain of the guard" (41:12), and the prison itself is the house of Joseph's master (40:7). All of this leaves the impression that Potiphar's responsibilities as "captain of the guard" included overseer of the royal prison, explaining providentially why Joseph was imprisoned in the same facility as Pharaoh's highest ranking officers. Again the theme of the Joseph Novel is subtly sounded. The crimes of those around Joseph cannot thwart the purposes of God.

Both of Pharaoh's officers have dreams, each dream is interpreted by Joseph, and each is fulfilled immediately (40:5–19). Unlike Pharaoh's two dreams with one meaning (41:25), the cupbearer and baker have separate dreams in the same night, "each dream with its own meaning" (40:5). Their dreams were obscure and needed interpretation, leaving them troubled because they had no access to professional dream-interpreters with them in the prison. For Egyptians, dreams were seen as encoded revelations of a higher order, puzzles, or sometimes "knots," that could only be untied, decoded, and understood by a specialist, experts trained in the science of dream-interpretation (see Closer Look "Dreams in the Hebrew Scriptures" at p. 322). Joseph himself had his own dreams at the age of seventeen, which probably needed more interpretation than they were given (37:5–11). He understood, more than most, the importance of finding the right meaning for a dream. So he comforts the two Egyptians with the assurance that dream-interpretation belongs to God (40:8), a very different view for them.[603] We are probably to assume the Hebrew word "God" (*'ĕlōhîm*) would mean simply "deity" in Egyptian ears, but on Joseph's lips it means something more specific (see commentary at 41:25–36). The God of Joseph is not limited to professional oneiromancers and is even available to the cupbearer and baker in their confinement, in the form of this Hebrew servant.

The cupbearer's dream contained symbolism appropriate to his role in Pharaoh's service – vine, grape-clusters, and drinking cup (40:9–11). Joseph's interpretation takes the dream as a good omen. In three days corresponding to the three branches of the vine, Pharaoh will lift up the cupbearer's head in honor and restore him to his former service (40:12–13). The cupbearer's imminent freedom presents Joseph with an opportunity to plead his innocence and ask for a pardon (40:14–15). Joseph's use of "dungeon" to describe the prison echoes his experiences in life, since this is the same word used for the pit to which his brothers discarded him and from which he was sold into Egypt (*bôr*, 37:24, 28). From the pit in Canaan, to Potiphar's house, to this prison, Joseph is innocent and has been treated unjustly.

Encouraged by the favorable interpretation, the baker proceeds with his own dream (40:16–17). His too used symbolism appropriate to his service but in his

---

[603] Joseph assumes a role that will define his identity for the remainder of the narrative by claiming access to divine knowledge, while also effacing himself before the divine so that God, rather than himself, appears to be the source of the interpretation; Hugh C. White, *Narration and Discourse in the Book of Genesis* (Cambridge: Cambridge University Press, 1991), 257.

case, birds were consuming the Pharaoh's food from baskets on his head. The recurring mention of the baker's "head" strikes an ominous tone, and indeed, the interpretation is not good (40:18–19). In three days corresponding to the three baskets of food, Pharaoh will lift up the baker's head too, but not in restorative honor as with the cupbearer. Joseph uses a play on the idiom "lift up the head" in the two interpretations, in each case clarifying the meaning with the next clause: " . . . and restore you to your office" versus " . . . from upon you and hang you on a pole" (40:13 and 19).[604] The same clause means "exonerate" in the first case but "behead" in the second.

The dreams were fulfilled precisely as Joseph said, three days later on Pharaoh's birthday (40:20–22). Repetition of the idiom "lift up the head" to relate the fulfillment emphasizes the accuracy of Joseph's reading. The reader may well expect the exonerated cupbearer to free Joseph, and vindicate his innocence. But the text's redundancy reflects yet another disappointment for Joseph: "the chief cupbearer did not remember . . . but forgot him." In this way, dramatic suspense is sustained, and the denouement reserved for a great moment, in which Joseph stands before the Pharaoh himself.

The narrative moves quickly now from the prison to the royal court, although for Joseph it was a wait of another "two whole years" (41:1). Pharaoh dreams of both fat and thin cows, as well as good and blighted ears of grain (41:1–7). The reader begins to grow confident now that Joseph could solve this riddle, especially when Pharaoh is unable to find an interpreter among the experts and specialists available to him as king (41:8).[605] Pharaoh's dilemma, the inability to find a legitimate dream-interpreter, reminded the cupbearer that he once had the same problem. His confession bears testimony to Joseph's skill at giving truthful interpretations, because all had turned out precisely as Joseph predicted for the cupbearer, based on his dream and that of the ill-fated baker (41:9–13). The cupbearer's speech repeats details of Gen 40, which will become characteristic of this text in a way that allows the speaker to nuance the message.

Another two years had passed since the cupbearer's freedom. Now Joseph is hurriedly brought from the "dungeon" (again *bôr*, "pit," cf. 40:15). He shaves and throws off his prison garb, primarily to be presentable before the king of Egypt, but also as a symbol of his freedom from prison life (41:14). His transformation from Hebrew slave and prisoner to clean-shaven Egyptian courtier is also important background for the rest of the Joseph Novel, during which Joseph is not recognizable to his own brothers.

---

[604] For the possibility of several more word plays in the passage, see S. B. Noegel, *Nocturnal Ciphers* (2007), 128–32.

[605] On the many parallels between the Joseph Novel and the book of Daniel generally, and Gen 41 in particular, see Susan Niditch and Robert Doran, "The Success Story of the Wise Courtier: A Formal Approach," *JBL* 96/2 (1977): 179–93.

With no fanfare, Pharaoh launches into this problem – he needs to find a true dream-interpreter. But Joseph counters that his reputation is unjustified because it is God who gives the answers (41:15–16). As he had done with the cupbearer and baker, Joseph diminishes any special powers or magical authority he may appear to have, and instead, he identifies God as the source of dream interpretation (cf. 40:8).[606] Pharaoh may be impressed, but Joseph must point his interlocutor in another direction.

Pharaoh summarizes the two dreams for Joseph (41:17–24). There are a few changes in the dream report compared to the narration, such as Pharaoh's observation that the thin cows were the ugliest ever in Egypt or that they were so emaciated, one could not have detected they had eaten at all after consuming the fat cows. But beyond these, the dream report has included many changes much more subtle in nature that hint that Pharaoh was at odds with the Egyptian magicians and wise men who had not been able to give the interpretation. Together with his earlier comment to Joseph, "I have had *a dream*" (note the singular), it is likely he was convinced himself that they were really only variants of one dream and that his professional dream-interpreters were unable or unwilling to grasp it.[607] He concludes in exasperation that none of his experts have been able to explain it (41:24).

Joseph responds with the longest speech of this text, giving the dream interpretation and offering a proposal for action (41:25–36). A recurring theme of the speech is the role of God in revealing to Pharaoh God's plans for the future. True to his earlier claim that accurate dream interpretation comes only from God (41:16), Joseph now asserts that God has "announced" (*higgîd*, NRSV's "revealed") and "shown" to Pharaoh what God is doing (41:25, 28). The reason the single dream is doubled, using symbols of cows and ears of grain, is because the matter is "fixed by God" (or "established with God") and God is moving quickly to execute the plan (41:32). As dreams go, duplication means certitude. The four uses of "God" (*'ĕlōhîm*) in Joseph's speech have the definite article, which may imply his attempt to mark the distinctiveness or uniqueness of the deity he serves.[608] In the Joseph Novel, in conversation with Egyptian polytheists, "god" will mean simply "deity," as in Pharaoh's speech (41:38–39) whereas Joseph is making a subtle claim about the uniqueness of the God he serves, who is giving the dreams and inspiring their interpretation.

Joseph's interpretation rests on two simple observations. The two dreams are really only one (41:25) and the number "seven" has a temporal application, meaning seven years (41:26–27). As we have seen, Pharaoh most likely already saw the wisdom in assuming the dreams were only variants of a single message, while his magicians

---

[606] The text of Joseph's first statement to Pharaoh is in doubt. Wenham accepts an emendation proposed by Murray Lichtenstein, which I think is likely: "Except for God, who can announce Pharaoh's welfare?" See G. J. Wenham, *Genesis 16–50* (1994), 386 and 388.

[607] M. Sternberg, *The Poetics of Biblical Narrative* (1985), 395–400.

[608] The so-called "solitary" use of the definite article; B. T. Arnold and J. H. Choi, *A Guide to Biblical Hebrew Syntax* (2003), 31.

and wise men were unable to make that assumption. Here, finally, is an interpreter who agrees that they are single in meaning, and does so immediately. Joseph's opening words, "Pharaoh's dreams are one and the same" (literally singular, "the dream of Pharaoh is one") were immediate confirmation that he was on the right track, as far as Pharaoh was concerned.[609] Once Joseph made the additional observation that the one-dream-in-two was about seven-year intervals of feast and famine, the rest was simple. Seven years of plentiful harvests will be followed by seven years of severe famine, in which the previous abundance will be completely consumed and forgotten (41:29–32).[610] By means of the dream interpretation, Joseph assumes the role of prophet and reveals, with God's help, the future events.

The pivot of Joseph's speech is at "now therefore" (41:33), at which point he turns from predictive prophecy to a proposed food conservation program, advising Pharaoh to take full advantage of the divine knowledge revealed in the dreams (41:33–36).[611] The greatest need, of course, is finding the right person to supervise such a hunger relief program. Where in all Egypt will Pharaoh find the right man, just discerning and wise enough to do what is needed?

Pharaoh has just gone through all his magicians and wise man, and found none wiser than this young Hebrew servant standing before him now. In a rush of narrative peppered with four brief speeches, Joseph is promoted as grand vizier of all Egypt, second only to Pharaoh, and given nearly unrestrained power to supervise the famine relief efforts (41:37–45). Pharaoh acknowledges that he has no one like Joseph available in Egypt. The "spirit of God" is in Joseph and it is God who has shown Joseph the meaning of the dreams.[612] The use of "God" (*'ĕlōhîm*), this time without the definite article, on the lips of Pharaoh is more likely "deity," which is itself remarkable in light of the Egyptian belief that the Pharaoh was himself a divine being.[613] Joseph's meteoric rise is complete, when the Pharaoh places Joseph over

---

609 The dreams in the Joseph Novel follow a pattern in which one individual has two dreams that are different in their meaning but are interwoven (37:5–11), then two individuals have one dream each with a common element (40:5–19), and finally one person dreams two dreams that are one; R. Pirson, *The Lord of the Dreams* (2002), 59.

610 The description of such a seven-year famine in the so-called "Famine Stela" was once thought to be confirmation of this biblical account. Yet we now have other examples of a widespread tradition of seven years of famine in the literature of the ancient Near East; Miriam Lichtheim, "The Famine Stela," *COS* 1.53:130–34; John A. Wilson, "The Tradition of Seven Lean Years in Egypt," *ANET* 31–32.

611 The "logical" use of *wĕʿattâ*, "and now," signals a shift in the flow of the discourse without a break in the theme, and is common in prophetic speech when moving from imminent future events to present action; B. T. Arnold and J. H. Choi, *A Guide to Biblical Hebrew Syntax* (2003), 140.

612 Much as Babylonian polytheists testified to the spirit of the holy gods in Daniel (cf. Dan 4:8,9, 18 [Aram 4:5, 6, 15]; 5:11, 14).

613 From earliest times, Pharaoh was identified with Horus, and the deification of the Pharaoh was depicted iconographically in diverse ways throughout Egyptian history; Erik Hornung, "Ancient Egyptian Religious Iconography," *CANE* 3:1711–30, esp. 1727–29; and M. Heerma van Voss, "Horus," *DDD*² 426–27.

his "house" (like Potiphar and the chief jailer before him, 41:40, cf. 39:4, 22), and over all the land of Egypt.[614] At his installation, Joseph is given symbols of power signifying his remarkable rise: the Pharaoh's signet ring, royal garments, a necklace, the chariot of the second-in-command, and the honorific introduction "Bow the knee!"[615] In all of world literature, this is one of the greatest rags-to-riches stories ever told; the Hebrew lad sold unjustly into servanthood has become the Grand Vizier of all Egypt.

As one final indicator of Joseph's new authority, he is given an Egyptian name and wife (41:45). The meaning of his new name is often assumed to be "the God speaks and he [the bearer of the name] lives," but another suggestion is "[Joseph] who is called 'Ip-'Ankh [he who recognizes life]." The name Asenath may mean "she who belongs to [the goddess] Neith," although "she who belongs to you" is also a possibility.[616] The author of the Joseph Novel had no objection to exogamous marriage, at least in this setting, unlike the traditions behind other ancestral narratives (see Closer Look "Endogamy in Ancient Israel" at p. 219). Joseph's transformation is complete. He has shaved and laid aside his prison garb, been dressed and adorned as an Egyptian official, and now has an Egyptian name and family. Little wonder his own brothers failed to recognize him in the next episode (42:8).

The text establishes a general chronology by stating that Joseph was thirty years of age when he was elevated over all Egypt, thirteen years from the time he is introduced in the narrative (41:46a, cf. 37:2). The fulfillment of the food conservation program is described next, just as Joseph proposed it, without speeches or further digression (41:46b-49). Each city stored up food from its surrounding fields and over the course of seven years, so much surplus was stored it could not be counted.

The parenthetical birth narratives for Manasseh and Ephraim interrupt this narration (41:50–52).[617] The Joseph Novel has made no mention of Jacob's family since the favored son and despised brother was sold into Egypt. The last image we have is Jacob mourning the perceived loss of Joseph (37:35). But Joseph's names for his sons, "Manasseh" and "Ephraim," and their popular etymologies, remind us of a larger narrative (see NRSV's footnotes). Manasseh's name resonates with "God has made me forget all my hardship and all my father's house," and Ephraim's name

---

[614] That Pharaoh "set him over all the land of Egypt" employs an unusual infinitive absolute as a governing verb to tie off the end of the paragraph, summarize all and mark a preliminary conclusion (41:43); R. L. Heller, *Narrative Structure and Discourse Constellations* (2004), 112–13.

[615] On "Abrek," see NRSV's note. For options and bibliography, see V. P. Hamilton, *The Book of Genesis, Chapters 18–50* (1995), 506–7.

[616] For both names, see Kenneth A. Kitchen, "Genesis 12–50 in the Near Eastern World," in *He Swore an Oath: Biblical Themes from Genesis 12–50*, eds. Richard S. Hess, P. E. Satterthwaite, and Gordon J. Wenham (Carlisle, UK/Grand Rapids, Mich.: Paternoster Press/Baker Book House, 1994), 67–92, esp. 80–84 (Zaphenath-paneah) and 84–85 (Asenath).

[617] The syntax of these verses signals them clearly as an interruption, perhaps a later insertion, and the text flows more naturally from v. 49 to v. 53.

signals Joseph's pleasure at having a new family. All of this may expose a disposition in Joseph to settle down in Egypt and forget all about his family with its painful past.[618] It seems unlikely Joseph expects to see his father and brothers ever again, and perhaps without a sense of loss. But the final paragraph of this text prepares the reader for the next surprising and providential step. Just as the crimes and evil intent of those around Joseph could not thwart the will of God, neither will the good fortunate of Joseph's new life in Egypt impede the next step of divine providence.

The seven years of feast were followed by seven years of famine, just as Joseph had predicted (41:53–54). When the years of famine begin, Pharaoh instructs all the people to do as Joseph tells them, making it possible for Joseph to save the masses from starvation (41:55–57). This concluding paragraph contains distinct notations preparing the reader for the rest of the narrative in Gen 42–45. The first hint of that preparation is the observation that the famine hit "every country," while there was food in Egypt. This is developed further by the idea that the famine overpowered the entire land of Egypt, which however was well cared for because of Joseph. Finally, the last verse states more clearly still that "all the world" was coming to Egypt to buy grain. Joseph may have put his family behind him, but the reader is now aware that Jacob and his family in Canaan will need to come to Egypt for food. As Yahweh was "with Joseph" in the service of Potiphar's house and in the prison (39:2, 21), so the reader has a growing confidence in the hand of providence, moving in these events at the Egyptian royal court as well as in the tragic events of nature.

GENESIS 42:1–45:28 THE SONS OF JACOB ARE REUNITED

(42:1)   When Jacob learned that there was grain in Egypt, he said to his sons, "Why do you keep looking at one another?

(42:2)   I have heard," he said, "that there is grain in Egypt; go down and buy grain for us there, that we may live and not die."

(42:3)   So ten of Joseph's brothers went down to buy grain in Egypt.

(42:4)   But Jacob did not send Joseph's brother Benjamin with his brothers, for he feared that harm might come to him.

(42:5)   Thus the sons of Israel were among the other people who came to buy grain, for the famine had reached the land of Canaan.

(42:6)   Now Joseph was governor over the land; it was he who sold to all the people of the land. And Joseph's brothers came and bowed themselves before him with their faces to the ground.

(42:7)   When Joseph saw his brothers, he recognized them, but he treated them like strangers and spoke harshly to them. "Where do you come from?" he said. They said, "From the land of Canaan, to buy food."

(42:8)   Although Joseph had recognized his brothers, they did not recognize him.

---

[618] R. E. Longacre, *Joseph: A Story of Divine Providence* (2003[1989]), 45–47.

(42:9) Joseph also remembered the dreams that he had dreamed about them. He said to them, "You are spies; you have come to see the nakedness of the land!"

(42:10) They said to him, "No, my lord; your servants have come to buy food.

(42:11) We are all sons of one man; we are honest men; your servants have never been spies."

(42:12) But he said to them, "No, you have come to see the nakedness of the land!"

(42:13) They said, "We, your servants, are twelve brothers, the sons of a certain man in the land of Canaan; the youngest, however, is now with our father, and one is no more."

(42:14) But Joseph said to them, "It is just as I have said to you; you are spies!

(42:15) Here is how you shall be tested: as Pharaoh lives, you shall not leave this place unless your youngest brother comes here!

(42:16) Let one of you go and bring your brother, while the rest of you remain in prison, in order that your words may be tested, whether there is truth in you; or else, as Pharaoh lives, surely you are spies."

(42:17) And he put them all together in prison for three days.

(42:18) On the third day Joseph said to them, "Do this and you will live, for I fear God:

(42:19) if you are honest men, let one of your brothers stay here where you are imprisoned. The rest of you shall go and carry grain for the famine of your households,

(42:20) and bring your youngest brother to me. Thus your words will be verified, and you shall not die." And they agreed to do so.

(42:21) They said to one another, "Alas, we are paying the penalty for what we did to our brother; we saw his anguish when he pleaded with us, but we would not listen. That is why this anguish has come upon us."

(42:22) Then Reuben answered them, "Did I not tell you not to wrong the boy? But you would not listen. So now there comes a reckoning for his blood."

(42:23) They did not know that Joseph understood them, since he spoke with them through an interpreter.

(42:24) He turned away from them and wept; then he returned and spoke to them. And he picked out Simeon and had him bound before their eyes.

(42:25) Joseph then gave orders to fill their bags with grain, to return every man's money to his sack, and to give them provisions for their journey. This was done for them.

(42:26) They loaded their donkeys with their grain, and departed.

(42:27) When one of them opened his sack to give his donkey fodder at the lodging place, he saw his money at the top of the sack.

(42:28) He said to his brothers, "My money has been put back; here it is in my sack!" At this they lost heart and turned trembling to one another, saying, "What is this that God has done to us?"

(42:29) When they came to their father Jacob in the land of Canaan, they told him all that had happened to them, saying,

(42:30) "The man, the lord of the land, spoke harshly to us, and charged us with spying on the land.

(42:31) But we said to him, 'We are honest men, we are not spies.

(42:32) We are twelve brothers, sons of our father; one is no more, and the youngest is now with our father in the land of Canaan.'

(42:33) Then the man, the lord of the land, said to us, 'By this I shall know that you are honest men: leave one of your brothers with me, take grain for the famine of your households, and go your way.

(42:34) Bring your youngest brother to me, and I shall know that you are not spies but honest men. Then I will release your brother to you, and you may trade in the land.'"

(42:35) As they were emptying their sacks, there in each one's sack was his bag of money. When they and their father saw their bundles of money, they were dismayed.

(42:36) And their father Jacob said to them, "I am the one you have bereaved of children: Joseph is no more, and Simeon is no more, and now you would take Benjamin. All this has happened to me!"

(42:37) Then Reuben said to his father, "You may kill my two sons if I do not bring him back to you. Put him in my hands, and I will bring him back to you."

(42:38) But he said, "My son shall not go down with you, for his brother is dead, and he alone is left. If harm should come to him on the journey that you are to make, you would bring down my gray hairs with sorrow to Sheol."

(43:1) Now the famine was severe in the land.

(43:2) And when they had eaten up the grain that they had brought from Egypt, their father said to them, "Go again, buy us a little more food."

(43:3) But Judah said to him, "The man solemnly warned us, saying, 'You shall not see my face unless your brother is with you.'

(43:4) If you will send our brother with us, we will go down and buy you food;

(43:5) but if you will not send him, we will not go down, for the man said to us, 'You shall not see my face, unless your brother is with you.'"

(43:6) Israel said, "Why did you treat me so badly as to tell the man that you had another brother?"

(43:7) They replied, "The man questioned us carefully about ourselves and our kindred, saying, 'Is your father still alive? Have you another brother?' What we told him was in answer to these questions. Could we in any way know that he would say, 'Bring your brother down'?"

(43:8) Then Judah said to his father Israel, "Send the boy with me, and let us be on our way, so that we may live and not die – you and we and also our little ones.

(43:9) I myself will be surety for him; you can hold me accountable for him. If I do not bring him back to you and set him before you, then let me bear the blame forever.

(43:10) If we had not delayed, we would now have returned twice."

(43:11) Then their father Israel said to them, "If it must be so, then do this: take some of the choice fruits of the land in your bags, and carry them down as a present to the man – a little balm and a little honey, gum, resin, pistachio nuts, and almonds.

(43:12) Take double the money with you. Carry back with you the money that was returned in the top of your sacks; perhaps it was an oversight.

(43:13) Take your brother also, and be on your way again to the man;

(43:14) may God Almighty grant you mercy before the man, so that he may send back your other brother and Benjamin. As for me, if I am bereaved of my children, I am bereaved."

(43:15) So the men took the present, and they took double the money with them, as well as Benjamin. Then they went on their way down to Egypt, and stood before Joseph.

(43:16) When Joseph saw Benjamin with them, he said to the steward of his house, "Bring the men into the house, and slaughter an animal and make ready, for the men are to dine with me at noon."

(43:17) The man did as Joseph said, and brought the men to Joseph's house.

(43:18) Now the men were afraid because they were brought to Joseph's house, and they said, "It is because of the money, replaced in our sacks the first time, that we have been brought in, so that he may have an opportunity to fall upon us, to make slaves of us and take our donkeys."

(43:19) So they went up to the steward of Joseph's house and spoke with him at the entrance to the house.

(43:20) They said, "Oh, my lord, we came down the first time to buy food;

(43:21) and when we came to the lodging place we opened our sacks, and there was each one's money in the top of his sack, our money in full weight. So we have brought it back with us.

(43:22) Moreover we have brought down with us additional money to buy food. We do not know who put our money in our sacks."

(43:23) He replied, "Rest assured, do not be afraid; your God and the God of your father must have put treasure in your sacks for you; I received your money." Then he brought Simeon out to them.

(43:24) When the steward had brought the men into Joseph's house, and given them water, and they had washed their feet, and when he had given their donkeys fodder,

(43:25) they made the present ready for Joseph's coming at noon, for they had heard that they would dine there.

(43:26) When Joseph came home, they brought him the present that they had carried into the house, and bowed to the ground before him.

(43:27) He inquired about their welfare, and said, "Is your father well, the old man of whom you spoke? Is he still alive?"

(43:28) They said, "Your servant our father is well; he is still alive." And they bowed their heads and did obeisance.

(43:29) Then he looked up and saw his brother Benjamin, his mother's son, and said, "Is this your youngest brother, of whom you spoke to me? God be gracious to you, my son!"

(43:30) With that, Joseph hurried out, because he was overcome with affection for his brother, and he was about to weep. So he went into a private room and wept there.

(43:31) Then he washed his face and came out; and controlling himself he said, "Serve the meal."

(43:32) They served him by himself, and them by themselves, and the Egyptians who ate with him by themselves, because the Egyptians could not eat with the Hebrews, for that is an abomination to the Egyptians.

(43:33) When they were seated before him, the firstborn according to his birthright and the youngest according to his youth, the men looked at one another in amazement.

(43:34) Portions were taken to them from Joseph's table, but Benjamin's portion was five times as much as any of theirs. So they drank and were merry with him.

(44:1) Then he commanded the steward of his house, "Fill the men's sacks with food, as much as they can carry, and put each man's money in the top of his sack.

(44:2) Put my cup, the silver cup, in the top of the sack of the youngest, with his money for the grain." And he did as Joseph told him.

(44:3) As soon as the morning was light, the men were sent away with their donkeys.

(44:4) When they had gone only a short distance from the city, Joseph said to his steward, "Go, follow after the men; and when you overtake them, say to them, 'Why have you returned evil for good? Why have you stolen my silver cup?

(44:5) Is it not from this that my lord drinks? Does he not indeed use it for divination? You have done wrong in doing this.'"

(44:6) When he overtook them, he repeated these words to them.

(44:7) They said to him, "Why does my lord speak such words as these? Far be it from your servants that they should do such a thing!

(44:8) Look, the money that we found at the top of our sacks, we brought back to you from the land of Canaan; why then would we steal silver or gold from your lord's house?

(44:9) Should it be found with any one of your servants, let him die; moreover the rest of us will become my lord's slaves."

(44:10) He said, "Even so; in accordance with your words, let it be: he with whom it is found shall become my slave, but the rest of you shall go free."

(44:11) Then each one quickly lowered his sack to the ground, and each opened his sack.

(44:12) He searched, beginning with the eldest and ending with the youngest; and the cup was found in Benjamin's sack.

(44:13) At this they tore their clothes. Then each one loaded his donkey, and they returned to the city.

(44:14) Judah and his brothers came to Joseph's house while he was still there; and they fell to the ground before him.

(44:15) Joseph said to them, "What deed is this that you have done? Do you not know that one such as I can practice divination?"

(44:16) And Judah said, "What can we say to my lord? What can we speak? How can we clear ourselves? God has found out the guilt of your servants; here we are then, my lord's slaves, both we and also the one in whose possession the cup has been found."

(44:17) But he said, "Far be it from me that I should do so! Only the one in whose possession the cup was found shall be my slave; but as for you, go up in peace to your father."

(44:18) Then Judah stepped up to him and said, "O my lord, let your servant please speak a word in my lord's ears, and do not be angry with your servant; for you are like Pharaoh himself.

(44:19) My lord asked his servants, saying, 'Have you a father or a brother?'

(44:20) And we said to my lord, 'We have a father, an old man, and a young brother, the child of his old age. His brother is dead; he alone is left of his mother's children, and his father loves him.'

(44:21) Then you said to your servants, 'Bring him down to me, so that I may set my eyes on him.'

(44:22) We said to my lord, 'The boy cannot leave his father, for if he should leave his father, his father would die.'

(44:23) Then you said to your servants, 'Unless your youngest brother comes down with you, you shall see my face no more.'

(44:24) When we went back to your servant my father we told him the words of my lord.

(44:25) And when our father said, 'Go again, buy us a little food,'

(44:26) we said, 'We cannot go down. Only if our youngest brother goes with us, will we go down; for we cannot see the man's face unless our youngest brother is with us.'

(44:27) Then your servant my father said to us, 'You know that my wife bore me two sons;

(44:28) one left me, and I said, Surely he has been torn to pieces; and I have never seen him since.

(44:29) If you take this one also from me, and harm comes to him, you will bring down my gray hairs in sorrow to Sheol.'

(44:30) Now therefore, when I come to your servant my father and the boy is not with us, then, as his life is bound up in the boy's life,

(44:31) when he sees that the boy is not with us, he will die; and your servants will bring down the gray hairs of your servant our father with sorrow to Sheol.

(44:32) For your servant became surety for the boy to my father, saying, 'If I do not bring him back to you, then I will bear the blame in the sight of my father all my life.'

(44:33) Now therefore, please let your servant remain as a slave to my lord in place of the boy; and let the boy go back with his brothers.

(44:34) For how can I go back to my father if the boy is not with me? I fear to see the suffering that would come upon my father."

(45:1) Then Joseph could no longer control himself before all those who stood by him, and he cried out, "Send everyone away from me." So no one stayed with him when Joseph made himself known to his brothers.

(45:2) And he wept so loudly that the Egyptians heard it, and the household of Pharaoh heard it.

(45:3) Joseph said to his brothers, "I am Joseph. Is my father still alive?" But his brothers could not answer him, so dismayed were they at his presence.

(45:4) Then Joseph said to his brothers, "Come closer to me." And they came closer. He said, "I am your brother, Joseph, whom you sold into Egypt.

(45:5) And now do not be distressed, or angry with yourselves, because you sold me here; for God sent me before you to preserve life.

(45:6) For the famine has been in the land these two years; and there are five more years in which there will be neither plowing nor harvest.

(45:7) God sent me before you to preserve for you a remnant on earth, and to keep alive for you many survivors.

(45:8) So it was not you who sent me here, but God; he has made me a father to Pharaoh, and lord of all his house and ruler over all the land of Egypt.

(45:9) Hurry and go up to my father and say to him, 'Thus says your son Joseph, God has made me lord of all Egypt; come down to me, do not delay.

(45:10) You shall settle in the land of Goshen, and you shall be near me, you and your children and your children's children, as well as your flocks, your herds, and all that you have.

(45:11) I will provide for you there – since there are five more years of famine to come – so that you and your household, and all that you have, will not come to poverty.'

(45:12) And now your eyes and the eyes of my brother Benjamin see that it is my own mouth that speaks to you.

(45:13) You must tell my father how greatly I am honored in Egypt, and all that you have seen. Hurry and bring my father down here."

(45:14) Then he fell upon his brother Benjamin's neck and wept, while Benjamin wept upon his neck.

(45:15) And he kissed all his brothers and wept upon them; and after that his brothers talked with him.

(45:16) When the report was heard in Pharaoh's house, "Joseph's brothers have come," Pharaoh and his servants were pleased.

(45:17) Pharaoh said to Joseph, "Say to your brothers, 'Do this: load your animals and go back to the land of Canaan.

(45:18) Take your father and your households and come to me, so that I may give you the best of the land of Egypt, and you may enjoy the fat of the land.'

(45:19) You are further charged to say, 'Do this: take wagons from the land of Egypt for your little ones and for your wives, and bring your father, and come.

(45:20) Give no thought to your possessions, for the best of all the land of Egypt is yours.'"

(45:21) The sons of Israel did so. Joseph gave them wagons according to the instruction of Pharaoh, and he gave them provisions for the journey.

(45:22) To each one of them he gave a set of garments; but to Benjamin he gave three hundred pieces of silver and five sets of garments.

(45:23) To his father he sent the following: ten donkeys loaded with the good things of Egypt, and ten female donkeys loaded with grain, bread, and provision for his father on the journey.

(45:24) Then he sent his brothers on their way, and as they were leaving he said to them, "Do not quarrel along the way."

(45:25) So they went up out of Egypt and came to their father Jacob in the land of Canaan.

(45:26) And they told him, "Joseph is still alive! He is even ruler over all the land of Egypt." He was stunned; he could not believe them.

(45:27) But when they told him all the words of Joseph that he had said to them, and when he saw the wagons that Joseph had sent to carry him, the spirit of their father Jacob revived.

(45:28) Israel said, "Enough! My son Joseph is still alive. I must go and see him before I die."

The Joseph Novel continues in this text, which is arguably the finest narrative preserved in the Bible, and considered among the greatest literature ever written. Rhetorically, the use of speeches is masterful for building the characters and dramatic suspense, while the emotive language of the family relationships flows with a minimum of narrative insertions for background information. The sons of Jacob make two trips to Egypt during the famine to acquire food, the first narrated in Gen 42 and the second in Gen 43–45. Suspense is created when Joseph recognizes his brothers but does not reveal his identity to them. They are kept in the dark, while the narrative delays the revelation of Joseph's identity, building tension and heightening the suspense until the denouement in Gen 45, when the brothers are reunited in full disclosure of Joseph's identity. Reconciliation between brothers once alienated is itself a powerful theme. But in this case, the offended brother is innocent and his brothers seem wracked with guilt nurtured over many years. The narrator suspends this tension until the dramatic moment in which Joseph reveals his identity and calls for his father to be brought to Egypt to be near him. With the help and full blessing of the Pharaoh himself, Jacob's family is relocated to the best region of Egypt.

1. *First Trip to Egypt* (Gen 42). The narrative returns to Jacob in the land of Canaan after several chapters focused instead on his sons, Judah and Joseph (Gen 38–41). The paragraph immediately prior to this text noted the famine had spread over all lands, was severe in every country, and that all the world was coming to Joseph in Egypt to buy grain (41:54–57). In the opening verses of this text, we are therefore not surprised to learn that Jacob and his children in Canaan are suffering from the same famine (42:1–5). Having heard Egypt had grain to sell, Jacob sends his sons there to purchase food. While these ten are Jacob's "sons" (42:1), they are also "Joseph's brothers," who ironically are sent to Egypt to buy grain from Joseph (42:4). There are only ten of them, because Jacob is fearful the same fate might befall Benjamin as Joseph, and these two are the only sons of his favorite wife, Rachel. Thus Joseph's ten half-brothers set out unsuspectingly for Egypt – the six sons of Leah, two of Bilhah, and two of Zilpah – along with people from throughout the ancient world to buy grain.

The circumstantial clauses of 42:6a serve not only to remind the reader of Joseph's role in Egypt but also that he personally sold grain to those coming from elsewhere. Israel's sons are about to meet the Grand Vizier of Egypt. The centrality of Joseph to the story emphasizes his dominance over them, achieved through recurrence of his name combined with descriptions of the sons of Israel as his brothers, or simply by pronoun.[619] When Joseph's brothers meet him again thirteen years after their treachery, they bow before him with their faces to the ground (42:6b).

Joseph recognizes his brothers immediately and has the advantage over them because they do not recognize him (42:7–8, stated twice for dramatic effect). Word play is used to emphasize their lack of knowledge about Joseph's identity, " . . . he recognized them (*wayyakkirēm*), but he treated them like strangers (*wayyitnakkēr*)," establishing the tension suspended throughout the text until its great denouement in Gen 45 when Joseph finally reveals himself to them.[620] Joseph is not yet ready to reveal himself to them. He needs more time, and so he alleges that they are spies

[619] R. E. Longacre, *Joseph, a Story of Divine Providence* (2003[1989]), 144–45.

[620] The word play is metaphonic, since it depends on the use of the same verbal root in different derived stems: *nkr* in Hiphil and Hithpael. The word play itself may also be an intertextual echo of 37:18, "they saw him from a distance, and . . . they conspired to kill him," raising the possibility that Joseph's first instinct was to exact terrible retribution against his brothers; M. Sternberg, *The Poetics of Biblical Narrative* (1985), 288–89.

rather than honest men seeking relief from the famine (42:9). Their denial uses deferential lord–servant language and identifies them as "sons of one man" (42:10–11). Their claim to be "honest men" (*kēn*, upright, sound) is ironic, raising the possibility that Joseph might expose them immediately as dishonest and deceitful. Instead, he rejects their answer, restating his allegation a second time, which leads to another denial (42:12–13). Their denial this time adds more detail. They are ten of twelve sons of this certain man in Canaan; their youngest brother remains at home with their father and the twelfth one "is no more." The irony, of course, is that the expression implies the twelfth one is dead while they are, in fact, speaking to the twelfth son. Each speech in the dialogue has added a bit more detail and contributed to the text's mounting suspense.

Joseph responds for the third time with the allegation that they are spies (42:14). This time, however, rather than hear more protestation, he establishes a plan for a test (42:15–16). They shall send one brother back to Canaan to fetch their youngest brother Benjamin, while the rest stay in Egypt in prison. This will confirm whether they are telling Joseph the truth, and will allow them to vindicate themselves as honest men. Without explaining further, Joseph throws all ten of them into prison for three days, which might seem an ultimate irony in light of the years he spent in prison because of them (42:17).

The text to this point poses an interesting dilemma. Why is Joseph treating his brothers in this manner? Initially, he "spoke harshly" to them, and after he had opportunity to reflect on the dreams of his youth, he alleged that they were spies. Such an allegation was not unrealistic, since Egypt for many centuries had conflict with Semites from Syria–Palestine, and periods of famine tended only to renew those hostilities. Yet these hungry sons of Jacob are no political threat to Joseph and the Egyptians, as the narrator, the reader, and Joseph well understand. Why then does Joseph choose not to reveal himself now, rather than treat them in this manner? Most interpreters assume Joseph is punishing, testing, or teaching his brothers a lesson, while others think Joseph needs to ensure they bring Benjamin to Egypt so that all eleven of them will bow before him fulfilling his dream.[621] Literarily, of course, the idea is to suspend the revelation of Joseph's identity as long as possible. But I believe also we are to conclude that Joseph simply does not trust his brothers. And why should he? Perhaps Benjamin is not standing with them now because they have also sold him into slavery or worse. Perhaps Jacob too is dead. Joseph at first seems merely to stall for more time while he sorts out what he should do. Then he seems intent to ensure that Benjamin and Jacob are not also mistreated by this lot, and wants only to discern whether these ten can be trusted. So the idea of testing, as Joseph himself states in 42:15, seems to be his only motivation.

---

[621] Sternberg argues that each of these possibilities is correct in its own way, yet he seems to settle on testing as the primary motive for Joseph's behavior; M. Sternberg, *The Poetics of Biblical Narrative* (1985), 286–90.

On the third day of their imprisonment, however, Joseph proposes an alternate plan (42:18–20). The new plan would give opportunity to prove they were trustworthy "honest men," verifying their words. Moreover, detaining only one of them and allowing nine to return to Canaan was merciful because more grain could be carried back for the rest of the family. The rather awkwardly worded insertion revealing Joseph's motives for having mercy in this alternate plan, "for I fear God," uses the definite article on "God," reflecting Joseph's Egyptian persona and also inviting his brothers to consider their own sin.[622] This they do immediately and openly (42:21–23). Since Joseph has been using an interpreter to communicate with them, they assume he cannot understand their speech, and so they speak openly of their guilt in betraying Joseph those many years before. But Joseph was listening, and he heard first-hand their regret and acknowledgment of guilt. The "anguish" (*ṣārâ*, "distress") of this situation is the result of their refusal to respond to the "anguish" in Joseph's plea when he entreated them not to harm him (details not included in Gen 37). They assume they are reaping the harvest of that crime by suffering the same crime returned upon them now in the form of this powerful Egyptian ruler; punishment mirrors the crime.[623] They recall that moment in great pain and regret, and appear to have born the guilt of that particular moment for these many years, a moment in which they refused to hear the pleading of their brother Joseph but rejected him once and for all.

Their painful confession is more than Joseph can bear. In the first of three occasions in this text, Joseph is overcome with emotion and weeps (42:24a, see below at 43:30 and 45:2).[624] Yet he is not yet ready to reveal his identity, without knowing whether they can truly be trusted. He hides his tears, and almost mechanically selects Simeon as the one to be detained while the others return to Canaan (42:24b). Although we cannot be certain why Joseph chose Simeon, we know that he was aware of their birth order (43:33) and he presumably wanted the firstborn, Reuben, to return as a spokesman to their father (42:37).

Prior to the departure of the nine brothers for Canaan, Joseph gave orders not only to load their grain and provisions for the journey, but also to return to each one the money they had paid for the grain (42:25). While on the journey, one of them discovered his refunded silver in his pouch, causing great confusion and fear (42:26–28). As they assumed they are being punished for their sin against Joseph

---

[622] The statement also resonates with God's observation of Abraham, "now I know that you fear God" (22:12), and one wonders if intertextuality is intended here.

[623] The use of the word play – that sinful "anguish" caused this punitive "anguish" – expresses the Israelite belief in a sort of poetic justice. The penalty inflicted matches repayment in kind for the harm done, or a sort of commensurate form of justice, so that divine punishment mirrors the crime. The Joseph Novel announces a new kind of grace in which good is brought from evil, rather than the expected punishing-evil resulting from sinful-evil. See Patrick D. Miller, Jr., *Sin and Judgment in the Prophets: A Stylistic and Theological Analysis* (SBLMS 27; Chico, Calif.: Scholars Press, 1982), esp. 121–39.

[624] A fourth occasion in the extended narrative is anticlimactic, 46:29, and cf. 50:1, 17.

(42:21–22), so now they assume God is behind this turn of events, jeopardizing their relationship with the Egyptian ruler.

Upon their return to Canaan, Joseph's nine brothers report to Jacob all that has happened in a summative speech (42:29–34). The narrative delay adds suspense to the story, leaving Joseph and Simeon in Egypt. But their speech also adds features that attempt to soften the impact of the news that – yet again – one of Jacob's sons is missing.[625] To make matters worse, each of the remaining eight brothers discovers his money in his pouch, just as one had done along the way (42:35). All nine have arrived in Canaan with what can only appear to be stolen silver, causing more confusion and fear, and throwing Jacob into utter despair (42:36).[626] First it was Joseph, now Simeon, and they want Benjamin as well! His words make it clear that this is personally more than Jacob can tolerate.[627] Reuben's offer to become personally responsible for Benjamin, even offering to substitute his own two sons if things go badly, is not an acceptable solution for Jacob (42:37–38). The reason for Jacob's refusal is that Benjamin "alone is left" of the two sons of Rachel. To lose Benjamin would be tantamount to losing Jacob's chances for a timely and rewarding death. One's sons were the most dependable family members to assist the elderly in traversing the path to death, and since Jacob favors Rachel even in death, Benjamin is his last hope of a good passing.[628]

2. *Second Trip to Egypt* (Gen 43–45). Jacob refused to allow Benjamin to go to Egypt, but the fact remains, "the famine was severe in the land" (43:1). Perhaps if the famine had ended, Jacob would have accepted the loss of Simeon. But once the supply of food is consumed, Jacob proposes another trip to Egypt in order to purchase more (43:2). Judah, however, is clear in two conditional clauses: another trip is impossible unless Benjamin goes with them (43:3–5).[629] The prohibition against seeing Joseph's face and the questions attributed to Joseph in another of Judah's speeches (43:7) are not present in the narrative of Gen 42. This does not,

---

[625] Sternberg observes that they tell the truth this time, although not the whole truth. Specifically, they omit the bit about the returned money in one pouch, hoping to give Jacob time to decide to allow Benjamin to go with them back to Egypt, when suddenly they turn up the rest of the money, culminating in Jacob's vow not to allow it; M. Sternberg, *The Poetics of Biblical Narrative* (1985), 297. Heller observes that their speech closely parallels the earlier narrative prose, establishing the trustworthiness of the brothers, which will however deteriorate in subsequent speeches in Gen 43; R. L. Heller, *Narrative Structure and Discourse Constellations* (2004), 136.

[626] Note the specific and redundant mention of "their father" seeing the bundles of money as they empty their sacks (42:35).

[627] Jacob's words may imply he suspects they have sold Simeon into slavery in Egypt and are now trying to convince their father otherwise, raising suspicions about what really happened to Joseph as well; M. Sternberg, *The Poetics of Biblical Narrative* (1985), 298.

[628] Heinz-Josef Fabry, "*śêbâ,*" *TDOT* 14:79–85, esp. 82.

[629] Judah becomes the spokesman at this point in the narrative. Reuben's best has been rejected (42:37–38), Simeon is imprisoned in Egypt, and Levi is a man of violence like Simeon (49:5–7). Judah is next in line, and after his humbling experience in Gen 38, he becomes the leader of his generation.

however, mean they lied or falsely paraphrased their conversations with Joseph. Rather, they added further details that were not included in the narrative prose, and the narrator has deliberately included those details here.[630]

After Jacob's protestations that "the man" in Egypt should not have been given so much knowledge about the family (43:6–7), Judah makes another proposal (43:8–10). His offer to stand as "surety" for Benjamin is a metaphor from economics, in which one person pledges to cover another's losses, and in this figurative sense, Judah offers himself as a guarantor of Benjamin's safety.[631] Although we cannot know what this means in practice, the meaning is clear from the following clauses: Judah will be personally responsible and forever liable for any tragic outcome.

Finally, Jacob relents, without really accepting Judah's proposal to stand as surety for Benjamin (43:11–13). He gives instructions for taking gifts to the Egyptian ruler, including enough money to cover the first portion returned accidentally (perhaps). Jacob includes Benjamin last in the list of items to take, elevating the drama, as the brothers and readers await to see if Benjamin is released to go along to Egypt. Jacob concludes by placing himself at the mercy of God Almighty, praying that both Benjamin and Simeon will be returned to him (43:14).[632] Ultimately, however, Jacob is resigned to the reality that he may lose his sons, even though he has placed them in God's hands.

Armed with the gifts and Benjamin in tow, Joseph's brothers depart for Egypt (43:15). The narrator packs verbs together in a telescoping sentence, in which the brothers take the gifts, depart, go down to Egypt, and stand before Joseph. When they arrive, Joseph gives order to prepare an extravagant midday banquet with his brothers (43:16–17). In light of Joseph's harsh treatment of them the first time they came to Egypt, they could hardly have expected to be invited to the Grand Vizier's home for dinner. They assume instead they are being led into a trap (43:18). That Joseph may also be planning to "take our donkeys" may in fact be a humorous glance at their naiveté, as if Egypt's second-in-command had need of their donkeys from Canaan. In order to stave off what they fear may be catastrophe, they decide to approach the steward of Joseph's house in an effort at diplomacy (43:19–22). They come clean about the money and inform the steward they are returning it, along with enough money to purchase more food on this second journey. The Egyptian steward, who appears more theologically astute in this text than Jacob's sons, assures them he received their money the first time, and that their God – the God of their fathers – has provided the extra money as a treasure (43:23).[633] As further assurance

---

[630] C. Westermann, *Genesis 37–50* (1986), 121; contra R. L. Heller, *Narrative Structure and Discourse Constellations* (2004), 152–53.

[631] Edward Lipiński, "ʿārab," *TDOT* 11:326–30, esp. 328.

[632] On "God Almighty" (ʾēl šadday), see commentary at 17:1.

[633] The Septuagint is plural, "God of your fathers," which reminds the reader not only of Jacob, but of Isaac and Abraham too. The word "and" in "your God *and* the God of your fathers" is most likely *waw* epexegetical, identifying "your God" specifically as "the God

that all is well, the steward brings Simeon out to them before escorting all of them together into the house. Final preparations are made for their meeting with Joseph, including washing, feeding the donkeys, and setting out the various gifts for Joseph (43:24–25).

When Joseph arrives, they present the gifts and make obeisance (43:26). This second meeting of Joseph and his brothers has many similarities with the first (42:6–25) but Joseph's kindness toward his brothers here is a significant contrast, and no doubt a great relief.[634] Once Joseph confirms that father Jacob is still alive, he turns quickly to observe his younger brother, Benjamin (43:27–29). Fittingly, the narrator identifies Benjamin as "his mother's son," emphasizing the consanguinity between the full-brothers, Joseph and Benjamin. Without yet revealing his identity, and thereby continuing the narrative suspense, Joseph nonetheless blesses Benjamin as a stranger: "God be gracious to you, my son!" Not a common greeting among strangers, this expression must have been surprising to the brothers.[635] The articulation of the blessing itself is more than Joseph can bear. He is overcome with emotion (43:30). He leaves them for a private place to weep and regain his composure, and then returns ordering the food and commencing the meal (43:31).

We may wonder why Joseph continues his ruse at this point, but without question the narrative suspense is heightened by the depth of human pathos and brotherly affection. This is the second of three occasions in this text in which Joseph weeps, and the three contribute to the growing suspense and passion of the narrative. First Joseph weeps silently in their presence but conceals his tears (42:24). Second, he excuses himself to a private room to weep, continuing to hide his identity from them and his affection for them (43:30). Finally, he weeps loudly and openly before them, revealing his identity, and expressing his love for them (45:2, 14–15). The progression of Joseph's tears mirrors the emotive impact of the narrative upon the reader.

A narrative insert explains that they ate together but seated separately because of an Egyptian aversion to eating with Hebrews (43:32).[636] As a cultural aside, this detail contributes to Joseph's continued subterfuge that he is thoroughly Egyptian.[637] The

---

of your fathers"; B. T. Arnold and J. H. Choi, *A Guide to Biblical Hebrew Syntax* (2003), 147; GKC ¶154a, note 1b; Westermann's *waw* explicative, C. Westermann, *Genesis 37–50* (1986), 124.

[634] G. J. Wenham, *Genesis 16–50* (1994), 423.

[635] C. Westermann, *Genesis 37–50* (1986), 126; V. P. Hamilton, *The Book of Genesis, Chapters 18–50* (1995), 554–55.

[636] Egyptian society was characterized by a willingness to absorb diverse ethnic groups without prejudice, as long as the group was willing to be assimilated into the culture. Ethnic or cultural distinctiveness was discouraged; Anthony Leahy, "Ethnic Diversity in Ancient Egypt," *CANE* 1:225–34, esp. 232–34.

[637] The background detail in v. 32b is a narrative explanatory insert, or inner-paragraph comment, even though it is not marked as such in the syntax; R. E. Longacre, *Joseph, a Story of Divine Providence* (2003[1989]), 90–93; R. L. Heller, *Narrative Structure and Discourse Constellations* (2004), 57–58 and 151–55.

brothers are left in the dark. And yet, hints during the meal indicate that something extraordinary is happening. Joseph has them seated according to birth order, leaving them stunned, and leaving the reader to assume the brothers have not revealed so much to Joseph about the family (43:33). Only an insider could know so much. Then Joseph gives Benjamin quintuple the portion of the others (43:34). Having no idea why they were receiving such favored treatment by the Egyptian ruler, they nevertheless drank with him, which has cultural significance as a sign of acceptance and camaraderie. NRSV's "and were merry with him" (*škr*, become drunk) denotes an intoxicating time of companionship.[638] The tenderness of this scene is set against a backdrop in which Egyptians not only refuse to dine with Hebrews, but they ordinarily abhor shepherds altogether (46:34).

In preparation for their return trip to Canaan the next day, Joseph instructs his steward to return their money in their sacks again, as before, and this time to plant his own silver cup in Benjamin's sack (44:1–2). While they were still only a short distance away, Joseph sends his steward after them under the pretense of finding the lost cup (44:3–5). The use of vessel inquiry, or lecanomancy, as a divinatory technique is so far unattested in Egypt during pharaonic times although it is known from later periods.[639] Joseph the great dream-interpreter, is also portrayed in this text as capable of gazing hypnotically at the surface of oil on water to acquire answers to questions from the deities (such practices were expressly prohibited in later Israel, Lev 19:26; Deut 18:10–11, but not perceived as inappropriate in the ancestral period; cf. v. 15, and Gen 30:27).

When the steward tracks down the brothers and charges them with the crime, they declare that they will stand or fall together (44:6–9). If the cup is found among them, they declare the thief shall die and the rest of them become slaves. The steward, speaking on behalf of Joseph, declines such severe punishment (44:10). Instead the guilty party will become a slave, fittingly like Joseph himself long ago, and the rest will go free. The search is conducted, eldest to youngest, and at last the cup is found in Benjamin's sack (44:11–12). Thus Joseph has created another moment of crisis and decision for his brothers.

Joseph's motivation for this additional ruse becomes clear only when read in the context of the larger narrative complex. The warmth of the shared meal the day before established a perfect moment for Joseph to reveal his identity to his brothers. Indeed, the reader might fully have expected him to reveal himself in that moment of affable congeniality. Instead, Joseph devises yet another test for them. This trial of their character turns time back to the original crime against Joseph himself, in which his half-brothers, working in solidarity, acted in hatred, vengeance, and greed

---

[638] Manfred Oeming, "*šākar*," *TDOT* 15:1–5, esp. 1–2.
[639] László Kákosy, "Divination and Prophecy: Egypt," in *Religions of the Ancient World: A Guide*, ed. Sarah I. Johnston (Harvard University Press Reference Library; Cambridge, Mass.: Belknap Press of Harvard University Press, 2004), 371–73.

to inflict pain upon a son of Rachel.[640] Has anything really changed? Have they come to terms with their father's favoritism? Or now with Simeon released, will they take the food and the extra money, and run, abandoning Benjamin forever? Perhaps they would simply tell their father that a wild animal attacked Benjamin on the journey home. Joseph has devised this test to determine their character, to know the truth. The answer comes quickly when the cup is discovered in Benjamin's sack: they rend their garments in horror, and turn back to face Joseph – all of them together (44:13). Though free to go, all ten half-brothers return in solidarity to the Egyptian ruler to accept their punishment.

When they arrive back at Joseph's house, he presses his case (44:14–15). The narrator calls them "Judah and his brothers," which draws attention to the pledge Judah made to his father (43:8–10) and signals the new role Judah is to play. The presence of all the brothers together is as much in support of Judah as it is of Benjamin. Judah's offer to accept the guilt and punishment corporately is rejected by Joseph as it was by his steward (44:16–17). Only Benjamin will be detained, the rest are free to go. Joseph is not yet satisfied that he knows the whole truth about his brothers.

As elsewhere in the Joseph Novel in a series of speeches, each successive speech reveals more and more detail (see especially Gen 42). Judah's impassioned speech now goes back to the beginning and rehearses for Joseph what has led to this point of crisis, including certain features of the family's history that come to bear on the outcome (44:18–34). This is the longest speech in the Joseph Novel. It begins with the deferential lord–servant references, which gradually diminish as the speech progresses and Judah forgets himself eventually in his emotional fervor.[641] The essentials of Judah's discourse are as follows. (1) Jacob has lost the firstborn of his beloved Rachel, and he "loves" Benjamin, her only remaining child (44:18–20). The irony of Judah's words, "his father loves him," which is the only use of the term "love" in the Joseph Novel besides Jacob's love for Joseph at the beginning (37:3–4), elevates the passion and suspense of the narrative. How ironic that Judah would observe and accept the fact that Jacob loves Benjamin! (2) Jacob surely cannot survive the loss of another son of Rachel (44:21–29). Judah is not concerned only for Benjamin or for his own role as the one who stands for surety for Benjamin. More than anything else, Judah stresses what the loss of Benjamin will mean for Jacob, their elderly father. This second feature of the speech is driven home with the first of two "now therefore" conclusions, in which Judah states unequivocally that Jacob will die if they return to Canaan without Benjamin (44:30–31).[642] And since Judah

---

[640] For this assessment of Joseph's motives, see M. Sternberg, *The Poetics of Biblical Narrative* (1985), 301–5.

[641] R. E. Longacre, *Joseph, a Story of Divine Providence* (2003[1989]), 193.

[642] The "logical" use of *wĕʿattâ*, "and now" or "now therefore" in vv. 30 and 33; B. T. Arnold and J. H. Choi, *A Guide to Biblical Hebrew Syntax* (2003), 140.

himself has pledged surety for Benjamin, he is now ready to make an alternative proposal to the Egyptian lord (44:32).

Judah's speech comes to a close with the final "now therefore," in which he makes his proposal (44:33–34). He offers himself in place of his brother, to stand as a servant to the Egyptian master for the rest of his life. This offer is the main point of the discourse, as illustrated by several stylistic features, especially the central volitives "let your servant remain . . . " and "let the boy go back. . . . "[643] Judah has become a representative for the family. His willingness to sacrifice his freedom for the sake of his father and his brother Benjamin sets him justifiably in a place of honor among the sons of Jacob.[644] Judah has changed; he is not the same individual we encountered in Gen 38. And the presence of all the brothers signals a new day. They are resolved to treat Rachel's younger son differently than they did his brother, Joseph.

Genesis 45 has two parts. First, Joseph finally reveals his identity to his brothers and they are reunited in the denouement of the narrative (45:1–15). Second, in an anticlimactic post-denouement, plans are made to relocate Jacob's family, and the brothers return to Canaan to fetch him (45:16–28).

The Joseph Novel has had this moment in view from the beginning. The importance of the text is clear not simply because of its high drama and passion, but because here the theological thrust of the narrative is stated expressly by its main character. The transparency of Judah's speech (44:18–34) brings Joseph's emotions to the surface. He is unable to restrain himself (45:1). His "send everyone away from me" does not include his brothers, as is clear from the next verses, but only the Egyptian steward and attendants with him in the house. The suspense of the narrative, maintained from the moment Joseph decided not to reveal his identity to his brothers (42:7), will now be broken. In fact, the narrator informs us Joseph was alone with his brothers when he "made himself known" to them. Now that we know what is about to happen, suspense yields to anticipation, a narrative technique that intensifies the moment.

Joseph now releases his pent-up emotions (45:2). His weeping is loud enough to be heard by the Egyptian attendants in his house, as well as those of Pharaoh's house nearby. As we have seen, the text has a progression in Joseph's weeping, which mirrors the climax of the narrative generally (see commentary at 43:30). This is the third of three occasions in which Joseph weeps, culminating in this moment of self-disclosure. His silent weeping is at first concealed, although still in their presence (42:24), and a second time he excuses himself from their presence to weep (43:30), and finally here, he weeps loudly and openly.[645] The narrative suspense is

---

[643] R. E. Longacre, *Joseph, a Story of Divine Providence* (2003[1989]), 36.

[644] I am unconvinced that the subtle changes in Judah's account of the specifics narrated in Gen 42–43 reflect the "slightly deceptive nature" of his speech; R. L. Heller, *Narrative Structure and Discourse Constellations* (2004), 168.

[645] Beyond the Joseph Novel proper, there are other examples: 46:29; 50:1, 17.

heightened by such brotherly affection and pathos, and the gradual progression of Joseph's weeping mirrors the emotive impact of the narrative upon the reader.

Joseph's words are too much for his brothers; they needed a moment (45:3). He repeats "I am Joseph" twice (vv. 3–4), because they simply cannot grasp it the first time. The narrator intends us to assume Joseph sent the interpreter out of the room with the rest of the Egyptians, and transitioned to Hebrew for this revelation (see 42:23 on the interpreter).[646] The switch from speaking Egyptian with interpretation to using their native Canaanite dialect makes his assertion immediately comprehensible and irrefutable, all at one blow. The words themselves, perhaps with distinctive accent, were self-confirming. This was Joseph standing before them; there could be no disputing that fact! Before they catch their breath, Joseph hastens to ask again about their father's welfare. But they are left speechless.

Realizing the trauma he has caused, Joseph tries again (45:4). Drawing them closer, for they no doubt fell back in shock at his first attempt, he repeats the words "I am Joseph." This simple identifying nominal clause is modified this time with "your brother,"[647] followed by a relative clause, "whom you sold into Egypt." As they begin to absorb the reality that Joseph is alive, and indeed, stands before them as the Grand Vizier of Egypt, they must also come to grips with their own guile and corporate guilt. His very presence condemns them as culpable, and now he has added the detail that only the real Joseph could know – they sold him into Egypt.

To their great relief, Joseph's next words are reassuring (45:5). "And now..." signals a turn from past events.[648] It is time instead to think of the present, and especially for the brothers not to be distraught or too hard on themselves for their past actions. The reason Joseph can offer such comforting words is stated next in a causal clause, in which the Hebrew word order stresses the purpose for all these events: "because, *in order to preserve life*, God sent me ahead of you." There is a grand and noble purpose for all this! They must not beat themselves up over their actions because, through it all, God used their crime for his purposes, purposes they could not have anticipated. Here Joseph sounds forth the overarching theological conviction of the Joseph Novel: God's purposes are not thwarted by human sin, but rather advanced by it through his good graces. The hand of God is seen, not only in clearly miraculous interventions and revelations, but also in the working out of divine purposes through human agency, frail and broken as it is.[649] Joseph knows it to be true: "you sold me..." but "God sent me...." He quickly explains there remain five more years of famine, and then repeats the refrain "God sent me" ahead

---

[646] Hamilton is one of the few commentators to explore this possibility; V. P. Hamilton, *The Book of Genesis, Chapters 18–50* (1995), 575.

[647] NRSV's colloquial word order masks the precision of the Hebrew repetition, "I am Joseph," (v. 3) "I am Joseph, your brother,..." (v. 4).

[648] On the "logical" use of *wĕʿattâ*, "and now" for a temporal shift from past to present, see B. T. Arnold and J. H. Choi, *A Guide to Biblical Hebrew Syntax* (2003), 140.

[649] John Skinner, *A Critical and Exegetical Commentary on Genesis* (ICC 1; New York: Scribner, 1910), 487.

in order to preserve life during the crisis (45:6–7). And once more to conclude this portion of Joseph's speech, "it was not you who sent me here, but God" (45:8).[650]

Having established this theme of providential care, Joseph turns immediately to a plan to rescue Jacob and the entire family (45:9–11). He proposes that the whole household – women, children, and animals – settle in the land of Goshen, in order to be near him. This will need later to be confirmed by Pharaoh (46:31 – 47:6), but Goshen is Joseph's choice from the beginning. The region of Goshen in the eastern Delta was later equated by the narrator with "the land of Rameses" (47:11). Its precise dimensions are impossible to trace, but it was said to provide better pasturage for Jacob's livestock than elsewhere in Egypt (47:4–6).[651] Joseph approaches a conclusion by noting that they have actually seen (and had time to digest) that it is indeed the mouth of Joseph speaking to them, suggesting they cannot deny the distinctive dialect they share with him (45:12). After a closing summary, Joseph commands once more to bring his father down to Egypt quickly (45:13).

The express mention of "the eyes of my brother Benjamin" (v. 12) signals that Joseph's attention is once more drawn to the presence of his full brother, and he is again overcome with emotion (45:14–15). They weep together, and Joseph turns to be reunited with all his brothers. This wonderful scene hardly needs interpretation or commentary.[652] Afterward Joseph's brothers were able to speak again.

In the post-denouement, Pharaoh is informed of the reunion and is pleased (45:16–20). He instructs Joseph to send the brothers to Canaan to escort Jacob and the household back to "the best of the land of Egypt." Pharaoh provides wagons for transporting the women and children. Joseph implements Pharaoh's plans for relocation without delay (45:21). Before their departure, Joseph gives them plenty of provisions and gifts for Jacob, and new garments for each of them, including extravagant gifts of money and clothing for Benjamin (45:22–23). The gift of garments is ironic in light of the use of clothing in the Joseph narrative thus far, especially as a sign of Jacob's love for Joseph (37:3, 23, 31–34).[653] As they set out for Canaan, Joseph gives one final word, "do not quarrel along the way," as a hint that he knows their habits well (45:24).

---

650 Verses 7–8 serve as Joseph's own exposition of v. 5, because the words "you sold me . . . God sent me" needed elaboration.

651 A. F. Rainey and R. S. Notley, *The Sacred Bridge: Carta's Atlas of the Biblical World* (2006), 118–19; J. K. Hoffmeier, *Israel in Egypt* (1997), 121–22. On the evidence from the Septuagint and other versions for the identity and location of Goshen, see Mark W. Chavalas and Murray R. Adamthwaite, "Archaeological Light on the Old Testament," in *The Face of Old Testament Studies: A Survey of Contemporary Approaches*, eds. David W. Baker and Bill T. Arnold (Grand Rapids, Mich.: Baker Books, 1999), 59–96 esp. 73–75.

652 As observed modestly by one of the greatest interpreters of Genesis; G. von Rad, *Genesis* (1961), 397.

653 Cf. also 38:14, 19; 39:12–18; 41:14, 42; 44:13.

Upon their return to Canaan, the brothers relate the news to Jacob, whose heart nearly gives way (45:25–26).[654] His shock and disbelief is matched only by their own when they first heard the truth. But when he heard the whole story and saw the goods from Egypt, he recovered and was resolved to travel to Egypt to see Joseph before he dies (45:27–28).

GENESIS 46:1–47:31 JACOB SETTLES IN GOSHEN

(46:1) When Israel set out on his journey with all that he had and came to Beer-sheba, he offered sacrifices to the God of his father Isaac.

(46:2) God spoke to Israel in visions of the night, and said, "Jacob, Jacob." And he said, "Here I am."

(46:3) Then he said, "I am God, the God of your father; do not be afraid to go down to Egypt, for I will make of you a great nation there.

(46:4) I myself will go down with you to Egypt, and I will also bring you up again; and Joseph's own hand shall close your eyes."

(46:5) Then Jacob set out from Beer-sheba; and the sons of Israel carried their father Jacob, their little ones, and their wives, in the wagons that Pharaoh had sent to carry him.

(46:6) They also took their livestock and the goods that they had acquired in the land of Canaan, and they came into Egypt, Jacob and all his offspring with him,

(46:7) his sons, and his sons' sons with him, his daughters, and his sons' daughters; all his offspring he brought with him into Egypt.

(46:8) Now these are the names of the Israelites, Jacob and his offspring, who came to Egypt. Reuben, Jacob's firstborn,

(46:9) and the children of Reuben: Hanoch, Pallu, Hezron, and Carmi.

(46:10) The children of Simeon: Jemuel, Jamin, Ohad, Jachin, Zohar, and Shaul, the son of a Canaanite woman.

(46:11) The children of Levi: Gershon, Kohath, and Merari.

(46:12) The children of Judah: Er, Onan, Shelah, Perez, and Zerah (but Er and Onan died in the land of Canaan); and the children of Perez were Hezron and Hamul.

(46:13) The children of Issachar: Tola, Puvah, Jashub, and Shimron.

(46:14) The children of Zebulun: Sered, Elon, and Jahleel

(46:15) (these are the sons of Leah, whom she bore to Jacob in Paddan-aram, together with his daughter Dinah; in all his sons and his daughters numbered thirty-three).

(46:16) The children of Gad: Ziphion, Haggi, Shuni, Ezbon, Eri, Arodi, and Areli.

(46:17) The children of Asher: Imnah, Ishvah, Ishvi, Beriah, and their sister Serah. The children of Beriah: Heber and Malchiel

---

[654] NRSV's "he was stunned" is literally "his heart went numb/feeble."

(46:18) (these are the children of Zilpah, whom Laban gave to his daughter Leah; and these she bore to Jacob – sixteen persons).

(46:19) The children of Jacob's wife Rachel: Joseph and Benjamin.

(46:20) To Joseph in the land of Egypt were born Manasseh and Ephraim, whom Asenath daughter of Potiphera, priest of On, bore to him.

(46:21) The children of Benjamin: Bela, Becher, Ashbel, Gera, Naaman, Ehi, Rosh, Muppim, Huppim, and Ard

(46:22) (these are the children of Rachel, who were born to Jacob – fourteen persons in all).

(46:23) The children of Dan: Hashum.

(46:24) The children of Naphtali: Jahzeel, Guni, Jezer, and Shillem

(46:25) (these are the children of Bilhah, whom Laban gave to his daughter Rachel, and these she bore to Jacob – seven persons in all).

(46:26) All the persons belonging to Jacob who came into Egypt, who were his own offspring, not including the wives of his sons, were sixty-six persons in all.

(46:27) The children of Joseph, who were born to him in Egypt, were two; all the persons of the house of Jacob who came into Egypt were seventy.

(46:28) Israel sent Judah ahead to Joseph to lead the way before him into Goshen. When they came to the land of Goshen,

(46:29) Joseph made ready his chariot and went up to meet his father Israel in Goshen. He presented himself to him, fell on his neck, and wept on his neck a good while.

(46:30) Israel said to Joseph, "I can die now, having seen for myself that you are still alive."

(46:31) Joseph said to his brothers and to his father's household, "I will go up and tell Pharaoh, and will say to him, 'My brothers and my father's household, who were in the land of Canaan, have come to me.

(46:32) The men are shepherds, for they have been keepers of livestock; and they have brought their flocks, and their herds, and all that they have.'

(46:33) When Pharaoh calls you, and says, 'What is your occupation?'

(46:34) you shall say, 'Your servants have been keepers of livestock from our youth even until now, both we and our ancestors' – in order that you may settle in the land of Goshen, because all shepherds are abhorrent to the Egyptians."

(47:1) So Joseph went and told Pharaoh, "My father and my brothers, with their flocks and herds and all that they possess, have come from the land of Canaan; they are now in the land of Goshen."

(47:2) From among his brothers he took five men and presented them to Pharaoh.

(47:3) Pharaoh said to his brothers, "What is your occupation?" And they said to Pharaoh, "Your servants are shepherds, as our ancestors were."

(47:4) They said to Pharaoh, "We have come to reside as aliens in the land; for there is no pasture for your servants' flocks because the famine is severe in the land of Canaan. Now, we ask you, let your servants settle in the land of Goshen."

(47:5) Then Pharaoh said to Joseph, "Your father and your brothers have come to you.

(47:6) The land of Egypt is before you; settle your father and your brothers in the best part of the land; let them live in the land of Goshen; and if you know that there are capable men among them, put them in charge of my livestock."

(47:7) Then Joseph brought in his father Jacob, and presented him before Pharaoh, and Jacob blessed Pharaoh.

(47:8) Pharaoh said to Jacob, "How many are the years of your life?"

(47:9) Jacob said to Pharaoh, "The years of my earthly sojourn are one hundred thirty; few and hard have been the years of my life. They do not compare with the years of the life of my ancestors during their long sojourn."

(47:10) Then Jacob blessed Pharaoh, and went out from the presence of Pharaoh.

(47:11) Joseph settled his father and his brothers, and granted them a holding in the land of Egypt, in the best part of the land, in the land of Rameses, as Pharaoh had instructed.

(47:12) And Joseph provided his father, his brothers, and all his father's household with food, according to the number of their dependents.

(47:13) Now there was no food in all the land, for the famine was very severe. The land of Egypt and the land of Canaan languished because of the famine.

(47:14) Joseph collected all the money to be found in the land of Egypt and in the land of Canaan, in exchange for the grain that they bought; and Joseph brought the money into Pharaoh's house.

(47:15) When the money from the land of Egypt and from the land of Canaan was spent, all the Egyptians came to Joseph, and said, "Give us food! Why should we die before your eyes? For our money is gone."

(47:16) And Joseph answered, "Give me your livestock, and I will give you food in exchange for your livestock, if your money is gone."

(47:17) So they brought their livestock to Joseph; and Joseph gave them food in exchange for the horses, the flocks, the herds, and the donkeys. That year he supplied them with food in exchange for all their livestock.

(47:18) When that year was ended, they came to him the following year, and said to him, "We can not hide from my lord that our money is all spent; and the herds of cattle are my lord's. There is nothing left in the sight of my lord but our bodies and our lands.

(47:19) Shall we die before your eyes, both we and our land? Buy us and our land in exchange for food. We with our land will become slaves to Pharaoh; just give us seed, so that we may live and not die, and that the land may not become desolate."

(47:20) So Joseph bought all the land of Egypt for Pharaoh. All the Egyptians sold their fields, because the famine was severe upon them; and the land became Pharaoh's.

(47:21) As for the people, he made slaves of them[tt] from one end of Egypt to the other.

(47:22) Only the land of the priests he did not buy; for the priests had a fixed allowance from Pharaoh, and lived on the allowance that Pharaoh gave them; therefore they did not sell their land.

(47:23) Then Joseph said to the people, "Now that I have this day bought you and your land for Pharaoh, here is seed for you; sow the land.

(47:24) And at the harvests you shall give one-fifth to Pharaoh, and four-fifths shall be your own, as seed for the field and as food for yourselves and your households, and as food for your little ones."

(47:25) They said, "You have saved our lives; may it please my lord, we will be slaves to Pharaoh."

(47:26) So Joseph made it a statute concerning the land of Egypt, and it stands to this day, that Pharaoh should have the fifth. The land of the priests alone did not become Pharaoh's.

(47:27) Thus Israel settled in the land of Egypt, in the region of Goshen; and they gained possessions in it, and were fruitful and multiplied exceedingly.

(47:28) Jacob lived in the land of Egypt seventeen years; so the days of Jacob, the years of his life, were one hundred forty-seven years.

(47:29) When the time of Israel's death drew near, he called his son Joseph and said to him, "If I have found favor with you, put your hand under my thigh and promise to deal loyally and truly with me. Do not bury me in Egypt.

(47:30) When I lie down with my ancestors, carry me out of Egypt and bury me in their burial place." He answered, "I will do as you have said."

(47:31) And he said, "Swear to me"; and he swore to him. Then Israel bowed himself on the head of his bed.

*I*srael's ancestors leave Canaan, the land of promise, and settle in Egypt, the land of slavery, from which they would later need to be delivered.[655] With the support of Joseph and the Pharaoh in Egypt, Jacob relocates his family to the land of Goshen in the Delta of northern Egypt in order to survive the famine. The text opens with one last theophany at Beer-sheba before the departure for Egypt, at which time God restates the covenant promises for Jacob. The account of the actual departure is interrupted in order to enumerate the children of Jacob who made the journey. After arriving in Egypt, Jacob is reunited with Joseph, and he and some of his sons have audiences with the Pharaoh himself. They settle in Goshen, are well cared for by Joseph, and thrive and prosper for the remainder of the famine. The text includes also an account of Joseph's administration of Egypt during the famine.

[tt] Sam Gk Compare Vg: MT *He removed them to the cities*

[655] Wenham observes that the narrator here explains this relocation to Egypt not as a mistake but as divine providence working for Israel's good; G. J. Wenham, *Genesis 16–50* (1994), 450–51.

This text contains what is probably the conclusion of the original Joseph Novel, and raises a difficult historical problem. The Novel itself concludes with the settlement of Jacob and his family in the land of Goshen, either at 47:11–12 or 47:27.[656] The historical problem is raised by a lack of verifying evidence that Israel's ancestors ever entered Egypt under such circumstances, and the resulting intractable problem of dating these events.

It is possible these traditions contain little of historical value, and our attempts in this direction are simply futile.[657] On the other hand, Egyptian sources tell of a period near the end of what is generally known as the Second Intermediate Period, during which time the country was ruled by foreign Semitic rulers referred to as "Hyksos" or "rulers of foreign lands" (ca. 1720–1550 BCE).[658] Jacob's family might have migrated to Egypt during the reigns of one of these Semitic kings, at a time when migrations from western Asia into Egypt by Semitic tribesmen would have been accepted more naturally, with immediate bonhomie established with the ruling parties of Egypt. If so, the rise of a new king over Egypt "who did not know Joseph" (Exod 1:8) would have been the native Egyptians taking back their country under Ahmose after the Hyksos were thrown out.[659] Moreover, we know there was a constant presence of western Asiatics established in the eastern Delta much earlier, more than 150 years *before* the Hyksos rulers, and we have evidence of strong Semitic presence in the Egyptian navy and army as far back as the Old Kingdom period, and signaling the use of northeastern Delta around Goshen as the gateway of Egypt.[660]

We have an interesting Egyptian source, a model letter or scribal exercise, from the time of Merneptah (ca. 1213–1203 BCE), indicating that pastoralists were allowed to enter the eastern Delta peacefully, and in the case of this model letter, from

---

[656] I take 47:11–12 as the original ending of the Novel, for a variety of reasons, including the final resolution of the Novel's overarching problem; that is, food. For another view, see R. L. Heller, *Narrative Structure and Discourse Constellations* (2004), 38–39.

[657] Thomas L. Thompson, *The Mythic Past: Biblical Archaeology and the Myth of Israel* (New York: Basic Books, 1999), 130–43; Israel Finkelstein and Amihai Mazar, *The Quest for the Historical Israel: Debating Archaeology and the History of Early Israel*, ed. Brian B. Schmidt (Atlanta: Society of Biblical Literature, 2007), 41–51; Israel Finkelstein and Neil A. Silberman, *The Bible Unearthed: Archaeology's New Vision of Ancient Israel and the Origin of its Sacred Texts* (New York: Free Press, 2001), 27–47.

[658] Thompson, rather, denies the Hyksos rulers were foreign at all, and argues instead that our understanding of them has been misguided by political propaganda stemming from a civil war between Egypt of the Nile valley and Egypt of the Delta. In this interpretation, the Hyksos rulers were indigenous to the Delta; T. L. Thompson, *The Mythic Past* (1999), 138–43. Yet their Canaanite origin has been established by archaeological connections; Carol A. Redmount, "Bitter Lives: Israel in and out of Egypt," in *The Oxford History of the Biblical World*, ed. Michael D. Coogan (New York: Oxford University Press, 1998), 58–89, esp. 74.

[659] For this view, see R. de Vaux, *The Early History of Israel* (1978), 318–20.

[660] Manfred Bietak, "The Predecessors of the Hyksos," in *Confronting the Past: Archaeological and Historical Essays on Ancient Israel in Honor of William G. Dever*, eds. Seymour Gitin, J. E. Wright, and J. P. Dessel (Winona Lake, Ind.: Eisenbrauns, 2006), 285–93.

the region of Edom in order to preserve their lives and those of their livestock (cf. 45:5, 7; 47:4).[661] It is premature to assume these pastoralists, known as Shasu, were related to the early Israelites. But their journey and experiences are at least reminiscent of that described here for Jacob's family. So although we are not able to propose a date at which time Israel's ancestors may have made such a move to Egypt, the presence of Semitic tribal groups from Syria–Palestine moving to Egypt, even rising to positions of influence and power, was a political reality in ancient Egypt. The artistic and theological sophistication of this account should not lead us to conclude these events have no rootage in historical reality. Nor should the lack of archaeological confirmation leave us too skeptical, for there are explanations for its absence.

On his way down to Egypt, Jacob (here called Israel) comes to Beer-sheba, presumably setting out from Hebron at the start (46:1; cf. 35:27; 37:14).[662] Upon offering sacrifices there to the God of his father Isaac, God appears to him in one last patriarchal theophany (46:2–4, cf. Closer Look "Ancestral Religion" at p. 142). God's appearance in "visions of the night" reminds the reader of another important dream-revelation to Jacob (28:10–22). In this case, God repeats his name in a sense of urgency, "Jacob, Jacob." His response to God's call, "Here I am," denotes focused attention, and when spoken to one's superior, as here, is more like "At your service, sir" (cf. 22:1). God formally calls upon Jacob as he had his grandfather Abraham, and Jacob declares his readiness. In both examples, something momentous is about to happen.

As in most divine revelations in Genesis, God's speech begins with the revelatory predicate nominative, "I *am God*," which in this case is modified further by "the God of your father."[663] Such divine self-disclosures signify God's nature and identity, and introduce covenant promises, often also assuring the patriarch of guidance for the tasks ahead (cf. Closer Look "Divine Revelation in the Hebrew Scriptures" at p. 135). So here God's self-disclosure is followed immediately by assurances that Jacob has no reason to fear the trip to Egypt. This is substantiated by the promise that God will make Jacob a "great nation" while in Egypt, establishing lexical and ideological echoes with the original ancestral promise to Abram in 12:2. God further offers his protecting presence to go with Jacob and bring him up again, a promise important earlier in Jacob's journey (28:15; 31:3; cf. 26:3). Finally, God assures Jacob that Joseph will be present to comfort him at his death, reflecting Jacob's deepest concern to attain a good death, avoiding descent to the grave in pain (37:35; 42:38; 44:29). God's promises meet Jacob at his greatest need.

---

[661] James P. Allen, "A Report of Bedouin," *COS* 3.5:16–17.

[662] On the Jacob–Israel name interchange, see the commentary at 37:2–3. I assume 46:1–4 is an insertion into the original Joseph Novel, picking up again the traditional, oral materials of the ancestral narratives, Gen 12–36. The Novel itself is therefore suspended until vv. 5–7 and again until v. 28.

[663] See 15:1; 15:7; 17:1; 26:24; 28:13; 31:13. On the predicate nominative of identification, see B. T. Arnold and J. H. Choi, *A Guide to Biblical Hebrew Syntax* (2003), 6.

The report of the actual departure from Canaan and arrival in Egypt is given next in 46:5–7. Jacob brought his entire family, and all their belongings including the livestock, using the carts provided by the Pharaoh according to his instructions (45:19). The text refers twice to all Jacob's "seed" (*zera'*, NRSV's "offspring"), highlighting especially his many children and grandchildren. Implicitly, this presents a problem because Israel's ancestral "seed" is being carried away from the "land," i.e., the Promised Land. But in this way, a suspenseful digression is introduced to the overarching pentateuchal drama, and the text prepares for and anticipates the exodus.

The references to "seed" prompt an editorial insertion, listing the numbers of Jacob's children taken to Egypt (46:8–27). The phrase "Now these are the names of the Israelites, . . . who came to Egypt" is repeated verbatim in Exod 1:1a, intentionally creating intertextuality between Genesis and Exodus, and establishing a certain unity in the Pentateuch. Relying presumably on an ancient segmented genealogy for the ancestral family, this text enumerates the children and grandchildren according to birth order for each wife: Leah, Zilpah, Rachel, and Bilhah. The total is seventy, and the details of this list provide the reference point for the introduction to the book of Exodus (Exod 1:1–5).

The editor's summary in 46:27–28 is somewhat confusing because of two separate totals: sixty-six and seventy.[664] The sixty-six of v. 26 counts Dinah but not the deceased sons of Judah, Er and Onan, leaving Leah with a total of thirty-two. Furthermore, Joseph and his two sons were not included in this total, as the editor clearly states in v. 27, leaving Rachel with a total of eleven. Thus the totals are now Leah thirty-two, Zilpah sixteen, Rachel eleven, and Bilhah seven, for a total of sixty-six children who actually traveled with Jacob to Egypt. The alternative total of seventy, a number connoting the ideal growth of a family into a tribe (Judg 8:30; 12:14), is derived when Joseph and his sons, as well as Er and Onan are counted, but not Dinah, as the list in vv. 8–25 has it. This yields Leah thirty-three, Zilpah sixteen, Rachel fourteen, and Bilhah seven, for a total of seventy.[665] Years ago, Jacob set out for Haran frightened and alone (27:43–45; 28:10), and now he leaves for Egypt with God (46:4) and a growing tribe.[666] Jacob is, indeed, in the process of becoming the great nation promised to Abram.

---

[664] On the complexity of the list and reconstruction of its tradition history, see C. Westermann, *Genesis 37–50* (1986), 158–61. The absence of Yahwistic names among the theophoric types attests to the great antiquity of this list (p. 161).

[665] Sasson observes the use of seven and its multiples in the list, including the placement of Gad in the seventh position, whose gematria is 7 and who bears seven sons; Jack M. Sasson, "A Genealogical 'Convention' in Biblical Chronology?" *ZAW* 90 (1978): 171–85, esp. 181.

[666] Hamilton observes that the real number with Jacob is seventy-one, for he has God to guide him and his family to support him; V. P. Hamilton, *The Book of Genesis, Chapters 18–50* (1995), 599.

Jacob's relocation and settlement in Goshen is narrated in 46:28–47:12.[667] We have another occasion when Jacob sent messengers ahead to meet someone (32:3[Heb 32:4]), which seems an appropriate thing to do when a long absence is ending. Judah has assumed a new position of leadership among the brothers since his role in standing for surety for Benjamin and speaking persuasively on behalf of the family (43:3–10; 44:14–34). So now he leads the way to Goshen.[668] Joseph honors his father by going to meet him and presenting himself before him (46:29). The reunion is emotional, marked by weeping in the narrative for the fourth time (cf. the three weeping scenes in Gen 42–45, and commentary at 43:30 and 45:2). Jacob avows that he can die in peace now that he is reunited with Joseph, which has been a central concern repeated often in the narrative (46:30).[669] Death without Joseph attending to his needs would send Jacob to the grave in sorrow and pain.

Joseph immediately turns his attention to preparing his family for audiences with the Pharaoh himself (46:31–34). His instructions presuppose two facts. First, Goshen is an ideal region for pastoralists tending flocks and herds. This assumption lies at the heart of Pharaoh's query about their occupation. Joseph wants to establish their credentials as experts in tending livestock, so they may reasonably request the land of Goshen. Second, Egyptians have a natural disdain for shepherds, which is in fact stated by the narrator (46:34).[670] The implication is that Egyptians themselves have no interest in living in Goshen, which suits the shepherding lifestyle better. By emphasizing their natural talents and long history as pastoralists, Joseph establishes the logic of giving Goshen to his family as their new home. The plan works beautifully when five of Joseph's brothers are presented before Pharaoh (47:1–6). They speak just as Joseph prompted them, and Pharaoh grants their request to settle in Goshen. Pharaoh may have seen Goshen as a temporary location for them, assuming they would request domiciles in the cities. When they requested Goshen for pasturage, he was happy to let them have it. Moreover, he requested the best of Joseph's family, the most capable shepherds among them, to be in charge of his own livestock.

Joseph then presents his father before the Pharaoh (47:7–10). Jacob greets the Pharaoh and bids him farewell with the customary "blessing" of such formal social settings.[671] Yet this twice repeated blessing may also have in view the promise that Israel's ancestors would become a blessing to all families of the earth (beginning at 12:3). In any case, it is unusual for someone of inferior social status to bless the superior, and this may signal Jacob's advanced age compared to the Pharaoh. The latter's question about Jacob's age and life experiences implies great respect and

---

667 The syntax of 46:28 flows most naturally from 46:5–7, illustrating the intrusive nature of the list of names in vv. 8–27.

668 On Goshen, see commentary at 45:9–11.

669 Cf. 37:35; 42:38; 44:29.

670 Egyptians also refrain from eating with Hebrews, which appears to be purely a racial taboo (43:32). Scorn for shepherding as an occupation may just as easily be racially founded.

671 C. W. Mitchell, *The Meaning of* brk *"to bless" in the Old Testament* (1987), 106–8.

appreciation for one of advanced age, a deference extended cross-culturally in the ancient world. After Jacob's audience with Pharaoh, the family settles in Goshen and is cared for throughout the remainder of the famine (47:11–12). The provision of food resolves the narrative thread related to the famine, and together with the emphasis on Goshen as "the best part of the land," these statements illustrate once again the providential care of the ancestral family worked out through the messiness of human interaction.

According to Joseph in 45:6, only two years of famine have occurred; there remain five more years of hard famine. The syntax and content of 47:13 signal a new literary unit that extends through 47:26, describing Joseph's administration of Egypt and Canaan during the remainder of the famine. The unit ends with Joseph's Egyptian statute that one-fifth of all agricultural produce shall support Pharaoh's royal coffers, with the exception of the holdings belonging to the priests (47:26). That Joseph's statute continues "to this day" reflects an etiological focus familiar from the ancestral narratives of Gen 12–36 but absent in the Joseph Novel proper. And since 47:13–26 says nothing about Joseph's brothers or their relationship, we may assume this portion of the text had an independent tradition history.[672] Whether "to this day" is part of a later Deuteronomistic edition remains in doubt, but it at least reflects an eyewitness perspective some considerable amount of time after the events.[673]

Joseph supervises significant social and economic changes in Egypt as a result of the famine, and eventually acquires all Egypt for the Pharaoh. After the people deplete their financial resources (47:13–14), Joseph acquires their livestock as well (47:15–17), and then the land (47:18–20). This is more than land reform because they eventually agree to enter something akin to indentured servitude in order to survive, returning one-fifth of their produce to the Pharaoh, all except the priests, who are given special provisions (47:21–25).[674] Although we lack references to such practices in Egypt so far, we have several interesting texts from Mesopotamia relating to these legal practices, dating from early in the second millennium to the mid-first millennium BCE. Most impressively, we have texts from northern Mesopotamia during the thirteenth century that speak of enslavement during famine and of being "kept alive" in a way reminiscent of "you have saved our lives" in 47:25.[675]

---

[672] I do not believe it is possible to discern whether 47:13–26 was added to the Joseph Novel prior to its inclusion in the book of Genesis, or whether it was added by the final redactors of the book.

[673] Jeffrey C. Geoghegan, "Additional Evidence for a Deuteronomistic Redaction of the 'Tetrateuch,'" *CBQ* 67/3 (2005): 405–21, esp. 410–11 and for an interesting proposal that this text underscores the role of kings in providing for the interests of priests in later Israel, see pages 413–16.

[674] The Hebrew of v. 21 (see NRSV's note) implies urbanization, so that Joseph also relocated many from the now unproductive rural areas into the cities as part of the land seizure.

[675] Victor A. Hurowitz, "Joseph's Enslavement of the Egyptians (Genesis 47:13–26) in the Light of Famine Texts from Mesopotamia," *RB* 101/3 (1994): 355–62, esp. 358.

The text concludes with two summary notations. The first (47:27) returns to Jacob/Israel who settles in Goshen and acquires land possessions there. Jacob's family was "fruitful and multiplied exceedingly," which contributes to an overarching literary frame for Genesis as a whole (1:22, 28, etc.).[676] The seed of the ancestral family is growing dramatically in fulfillment of the divine promise, even if they are living far from the land of promise itself. By this statement, the editor affirms the theological themes of the Joseph Novel by emphasizing the providential fulfillment of the covenant promises; it was not the brothers who sold Joseph to Egypt, but God, in order to preserve a remnant and keep them alive (45:5–8). Now we learn they not only survive in Egypt, but thrive.

The second summary notation (47:28–31) prepares for the deathbed blessings of Jacob (Gen 48–49) and the account of his death and burial (50:1–14). It contains the sum total of Jacob's years, one hundred forty-seven, in formulaic language (cf. 25:7; 35:28). It then reports Joseph's promise to bury Jacob in Canaan in the ancestral tomb at Machpelah (cf. 23:19; 25:9; and 50:13). The custom of placing one's hand under another's thigh while making an oath occurred also in 24:2, 9, and seems to enact or ritualize the oath by the organ of precreation.[677] The closing statement, Israel "bowed himself on the head of his bed," is obscure but most likely means the old man is relieved to hear Joseph's promise and he relaxes in its comfort.[678] He wants to be buried in Canaan, in the Promised Land, no matter how long his children remain in Egypt. Jacob knows that Canaan is his home. After his long and torturous life-journey, he has come fully to embrace the covenant promises.

GENESIS 48:1–22 JACOB BLESSES EPHRAIM AND MANASSEH

(48:1) After this Joseph was told, "Your father is ill." So he took with him his two sons, Manasseh and Ephraim.

(48:2) When Jacob was told, "Your son Joseph has come to you," he summoned his strength and sat up in bed.

(48:3) And Jacob said to Joseph, "God Almighty appeared to me at Luz in the land of Canaan, and he blessed me,

---

[676] The parallels observed by Heller between this verse and 37:1 may mark this verse as the formal ending of the Joseph Novel, but can just as easily be explained as a final redactor creating an intertextual connection with 37:1 and at the same time, casting a look back to Gen 1; R. L. Heller, *Narrative Structure and Discourse Constellations* (2004), 38–39. I take 47:11–12 as the end of the original Joseph Novel, and 47:27 as the summary notation of a final editor of Genesis. The next summary in 47:28–31 then returns to the older epic materials to prepare for Gen 48–49.

[677] Gottfried Vanoni, "*śîm*," *TDOT* 14:89–112, esp. 104. The gesture may entail a threat of sterility if Joseph failed to keep his commitment, especially since children issued from their father's thigh (46:26; Exod 1:5); E. A. Speiser, *Genesis* (1964), 178. For a Sumerian parallel, see Yitschak Sefati, "The Women's Oath," *COS* 1.169A:540–41.

[678] C. Westermann, *Genesis 37–50* (1986), 183–84.

(48:4)   and said to me, 'I am going to make you fruitful and increase your numbers; I will make of you a company of peoples, and will give this land to your offspring after you for a perpetual holding.'

(48:5)   Therefore your two sons, who were born to you in the land of Egypt before I came to you in Egypt, are now mine; Ephraim and Manasseh shall be mine, just as Reuben and Simeon are.

(48:6)   As for the offspring born to you after them, they shall be yours. They shall be recorded under the names of their brothers with regard to their inheritance.

(48:7)   For when I came from Paddan, Rachel, alas, died in the land of Canaan on the way, while there was still some distance to go to Ephrath; and I buried her there on the way to Ephrath" (that is, Bethlehem).

(48:8)   When Israel saw Joseph's sons, he said, "Who are these?"

(48:9)   Joseph said to his father, "They are my sons, whom God has given me here." And he said, "Bring them to me, please, that I may bless them."

(48:10)   Now the eyes of Israel were dim with age, and he could not see well. So Joseph brought them near him; and he kissed them and embraced them.

(48:11)   Israel said to Joseph, "I did not expect to see your face; and here God has let me see your children also."

(48:12)   Then Joseph removed them from his father's knees, and he bowed himself with his face to the earth.

(48:13)   Joseph took them both, Ephraim in his right hand toward Israel's left, and Manasseh in his left hand toward Israel's right, and brought them near him.

(48:14)   But Israel stretched out his right hand and laid it on the head of Ephraim, who was the younger, and his left hand on the head of Manasseh, crossing his hands, for Manasseh was the firstborn.

(48:15)   He blessed Joseph, and said, "The God before whom my ancestors Abraham and Isaac walked, the God who has been my shepherd all my life to this day,

(48:16)   the angel who has redeemed me from all harm, bless the boys; and in them let my name be perpetuated, and the name of my ancestors Abraham and Isaac; and let them grow into a multitude on the earth."

(48:17)   When Joseph saw that his father laid his right hand on the head of Ephraim, it displeased him; so he took his father's hand, to remove it from Ephraim's head to Manasseh's head.

(48:18)   Joseph said to his father, "Not so, my father! Since this one is the firstborn, put your right hand on his head."

(48:19)   But his father refused, and said, "I know, my son, I know; he also shall become a people, and he also shall be great. Nevertheless his younger brother shall be greater than he, and his offspring shall become a multitude of nations."

(48:20) So he blessed them that day, saying, "By you Israel will invoke bless-ings, saying, 'God make you like Ephraim and like Manasseh.'" So he put Ephraim ahead of Manasseh.

(48:21) Then Israel said to Joseph, "I am about to die, but God will be with you and will bring you again to the land of your ancestors.

(48:22) I now give to you one portion[uu] more than to your brothers, the portion[vv] that I took from the hand of the Amorites with my sword and with my bow."

*T*he deathbed blessing, or testamental blessing, is of vital importance in Israelite culture. Such blessings, pronounced when death was imminent, were more than simple wishes or prayers but were legally binding wills, and the privileged status of being the firstborn was not necessarily determined by birth order.[679] This text ties such a blessing for Joseph together with the elevation of Joseph's sons Ephraim and Manasseh to positions of honor among Jacob's children.

The text begins with background information regarding Jacob's declining health, which prompts Joseph to take his two sons to him for blessing (vv. 1–2). The sequence "Manasseh and Ephraim" anticipates the etiological conclusion to the chapter, in which we learn the origins of the blessing "God make you like Ephraim and like Manasseh," and the narrator's conclusion that Jacob "put Ephraim ahead of Manasseh" (v. 20). The natural order of things should be Manasseh first and then Ephraim, but this text explains why the sequence is the other way round.

The role of Joseph's two sons in the family is in doubt. They were born to an Egyptian wife, the daughter of a priest, before the years of famine and before Joseph was reunited with the rest of the family (41:50–52). Such exogamous marriages were undesirable in the ancestral family. Marriage within one's kinship group was considered necessary to ensure continuity of cultural and religious values (see Closer Look "Endogamy in Ancient Israel" at p. 219). Moreover, their names, "Manasseh" and "Ephraim," signal a disposition in Joseph to settle down in Egypt *as an Egyptian* and forget all about his family with its painful past (see commentary at 41:50–52). Given the long history of dysfunction in Jacob's family, the relationship of Manasseh and Ephraim to Jacob's children and other grandchildren is of natural concern in a tribal society based on such close-knit kinship connections.

Before the blessing, therefore, Jacob establishes his reasons for elevating Manasseh and Ephraim in the family to the role of son rather than grandson, on an equal level with Reuben and Simeon (vv. 3–7). He begins by recalling the divine revelation

---

[uu] Or *mountain slope* (Heb *shekem*, a play on the name of the town and district of Shechem).

[vv] Or *mountain slope* (Heb *shekem*, a play on the name of the town and district of Shechem).

[679] Such testamental blessings were illocutionary or performative utterances, in that the pronouncement of the words in itself accomplished the act of blessing; C. W. Mitchell, *The Meaning of brk "to bless" in the Old Testament* (1987), 79–83. In Gen 49 especially, the deathbed blessing can also serve as a type of prophecy (Ibid., 85–88).

at Bethel (formerly Luz), where God Almighty appeared to him and blessed him (35:9–15). "God Almighty," *'ēl šadday*, as the archaic, revelatory name of God for the ancestors (see commentary at 17:1), and "appeared" is the common verb "to see" in its causative-reflexive form used for self-disclosure in revelatory theophanies (see Closer Look "Divine Revelation in the Hebrew Scriptures" at p. 135). The summary of God's blessing ties together the ancestral promises of "seed" (*zera'*, NRSV's "offspring") and "land" (*'ereṣ*) in a way familiar by now in the book of Genesis, beginning at 12:7 and frequently thereafter in the ancestral narratives (cf. 35:12). So Jacob begins his speech by reminding Joseph, and presumably Manasseh and Ephraim, that they are heirs of the ancestral trust, inheritors of the promise that God would establish their descendants in the land of Canaan.

It is at this point in the speech that Jacob turns his attention to Ephraim and Manasseh (note the sequence is already reversed), and declares they are his, on an equal level with Reuben and Simeon (v. 5). This is not simple adoption, since they are already his grandsons, but it stresses their inclusive and equal status in spite of their Egyptian mother. Jacob, as one of only three legitimate patriarchs, is the recipient of divine revelation in a way Joseph is not, and therefore only Jacob can legitimize Ephraim and Manasseh as fathers of tribes in Israel by declaring them to be his own sons.[680] Other children born to Joseph in addition to Ephraim and Manasseh will count as Joseph's sons with their own inheritance (v. 6). Jacob supports his declaration by referring to Rachel's untimely death (v. 7, cf. 35:16–20). The implication is that his favored wife gave birth to only two sons before her death, and so her grandsons, Ephraim and Manasseh, will count as hers.[681]

The physical presence of the lads is highlighted by Jacob's query, "Who are these?" Together with Joseph's presentation and Jacob's call to "bring them to me," this exchange is most likely a formulaic preface to blessing, signaled by Jacob's "that I may bless them" (vv. 8–9). Jacob kisses and embraces the boys, which continues the blessing ritual (v. 10).[682] Jacob's joy is reflected in his exceeded expectations; he never thought he would see Joseph's face again but now sees even his children (v. 11). Textual problems in v. 12 make it difficult to know precisely who is doing what to whom, but NRSV is probably correct in assuming Joseph removed the lads from Jacob's lap and himself bowed before his father.[683] The presentation is described in careful detail, making it clear that Joseph presents Manasseh as firstborn on Jacob's right and Ephraim on his left (vv. 13–14). Thus Jacob would lay his right hand on the

---

[680] C. Westermann, *Genesis 37–50* (1986), 185.

[681] Perhaps similar to the way a son born to Naomi's daughter-in-law became hers (Ruth 4:16–17).

[682] C. Westermann, *Genesis 37–50* (1986), 187. These ritual gestures have nothing to do with magical beliefs related to such customs; C. W. Mitchell, *The Meaning of* brk *"to bless" in the Old Testament* (1987), 84.

[683] The versions have the boys bowing before their grandfather.

firstborn at the time of blessing. But Jacob knows well that the "right of firstborn" (běkōrâ) is transferable (25:31–34),[684] and he crosses hands to indicate Ephraim's dominance over his brother.

The blessing of Ephraim and Manasseh is really a blessing of Joseph (v. 15a).[685] The pronouncement itself makes the boys heirs of the ancestral promises by first identifying the God in whose name Jacob blesses them (vv. 15–16). He is the God of Abraham and Isaac, the Shepherd of Jacob, and the angel who has protected Jacob from calamity.[686] The blessing furthermore establishes Ephraim and Manasseh as the bearers of the names of the three patriarchs, by means of their growth into multitudes. Despite their Egyptian mother, these two are full descendants of the patriarchs and recipients of the ancestral covenant promises.

Joseph attempted to correct Jacob's criss-crossed blessing, assuming perhaps his elderly father could not see well enough to get them straight (vv. 17–18, cf. v. 10). But Jacob knew well what he was doing, and so the younger son supplanted the older as Jacob supplanted Esau (v. 19). Nevertheless each will become a great people, signaling the important roles of these tribes in later Israel. There follows a second blessing, which is etiological in nature, and which may be taken as a summary statement of the whole instead of a completely different blessing (v. 20). This benediction explains two realities of ancient Israel. First, a blessing well-known in the narrator's day, "God make you like Ephraim and like Manasseh," finds its origins in Jacob's blessing of the boys those many years ago. Second, the priority of Ephraim over Manasseh is established by the old patriarch Jacob himself, as the narrator observes, "so he put Ephraim ahead of Manasseh."

Jacob concludes by affirming that God will some day bring Joseph to "the land of your ancestors," stressing once again his faith in the promises of God (v. 21). He is about to die, but he has confidence that God will be with Joseph. The final reference to a single portion given to Joseph more than to his brothers is obscure (v. 22). It is unlikely that we have here an overturning of the right of *primogeniture*, in which the firstborn is given a double-portion of the inheritance (the implied interpretation of NRSV). The gift of a "double portion" of the inheritance to the firstborn son is an entirely different expression (pî šěnayim, as in Deut 21:17, cf. 2 Kgs 2:9; Zech 13:8).[687] Instead, the word translated by NRSV as "portion" (šěkem) may also be "shoulder"

---

684 Matitiahu Tsevat, "běkôr," TDOT 2:121–127, esp. 126; Bill T. Arnold, "bkr," NIDOTTE 1:658–59.

685 And therefore supplements the formal blessing of 49:22–26.

686 In Genesis, the "angel, messenger" (mal'āk) of Yahweh/God typically represents the appearance of an unspecified supernatural envoy sent from God, which however is often identified with God himself, and is the personification of God sent to someone in need (cf. 16:7–12). Note the parallelism with "God" in v. 15, which avoids ambiguity about the identity of the angel.

687 HALOT 3:915 and 4:1605–6; BDB 805 ¶5,b; and cf. AHw 1242.

and may here mean "mountain ridge."[688] While this may be a word play on the city name "Shechem," it may also denote simply a mountain range in Canaan that Jacob is now bequeathing exclusively to Joseph. Perhaps the mention of a return to the ancestral homeland in v. 21 prompted this mention of a specific portion of land allotted to Joseph.

GENESIS 49:1–33 THE TWELVE TRIBES OF ISRAEL

(49:1) Then Jacob called his sons, and said: "Gather around, that I may tell you what will happen to you in days to come.

(49:2) Assemble and hear, O sons of Jacob; listen to Israel your father.

(49:3) Reuben, you are my firstborn, my might and the first fruits of my vigor, excelling in rank and excelling in power.

(49:4) Unstable as water, you shall no longer excel because you went up onto your father's bed; then you defiled it – you went up onto my couch!

(49:5) Simeon and Levi are brothers; weapons of violence are their swords.

(49:6) May I never come into their council; may I not be joined to their company – for in their anger they killed men, and at their whim they hamstrung oxen.

(49:7) Cursed be their anger, for it is fierce, and their wrath, for it is cruel! I will divide them in Jacob, and scatter them in Israel.

(49:8) Judah, your brothers shall praise you; your hand shall be on the neck of your enemies; your father's sons shall bow down before you.

(49:9) Judah is a lion's whelp; from the prey, my son, you have gone up. He crouches down, he stretches out like a lion, like a lioness – who dares rouse him up?

(49:10) The scepter shall not depart from Judah, nor the ruler's staff from between his feet, until tribute comes to him;[ww] and the obedience of the peoples is his.

(49:11) Binding his foal to the vine and his donkey's colt to the choice vine, he washes his garments in wine and his robe in the blood of grapes;

(49:12) his eyes are darker than wine, and his teeth whiter than milk.

(49:13) Zebulun shall settle at the shore of the sea; he shall be a haven for ships, and his border shall be at Sidon.

(49:14) Issachar is a strong donkey, lying down between the sheepfolds;

(49:15) he saw that a resting place was good, and that the land was pleasant; so he bowed his shoulder to the burden, and became a slave at forced labor.

(49:16) Dan shall judge his people as one of the tribes of Israel.

---

[688] See NRSV's notes; *HALOT* 4:1495 ¶2,b; taken as a word play by BDB 1014 ¶1,b.

[ww] Or *until Shiloh comes* or *until he comes to Shiloh* or (with Syr) *until he comes to whom it belongs.*

(49:17) Dan shall be a snake by the roadside, a viper along the path, that bites the horse's heels so that its rider falls backward.

(49:18) I wait for your salvation, O LORD.

(49:19) Gad shall be raided by raiders, but he shall raid at their heels.

(49:20) Asher's food shall be rich, and he shall provide royal delicacies.

(49:21) Naphtali is a doe let loose that bears lovely fawns.[xx]

(49:22) Joseph is a fruitful bough, a fruitful bough by a spring; his branches run over the wall.[yy]

(49:23) The archers fiercely attacked him; they shot at him and pressed him hard.

(49:24) Yet his bow remained taut, and his arms were made agile by the hands of the Mighty One of Jacob, by the name of the Shepherd, the Rock of Israel,

(49:25) by the God of your father, who will help you, by the Almighty who will bless you with blessings of heaven above, blessings of the deep that lies beneath, blessings of the breasts and of the womb.

(49:26) The blessings of your father are stronger than the blessings of the eternal mountains, the bounties of the everlasting hills; may they be on the head of Joseph, on the brow of him who was set apart from his brothers.

(49:27) Benjamin is a ravenous wolf, in the morning devouring the prey, and at evening dividing the spoil."

(49:28) All these are the twelve tribes of Israel, and this is what their father said to them when he blessed them, blessing each one of them with a suitable blessing.

(49:29) Then he charged them, saying to them, "I am about to be gathered to my people. Bury me with my ancestors – in the cave in the field of Ephron the Hittite,

(49:30) in the cave in the field at Machpelah, near Mamre, in the land of Canaan, in the field that Abraham bought from Ephron the Hittite as a burial site.

(49:31) There Abraham and his wife Sarah were buried; there Isaac and his wife Rebekah were buried; and there I buried Leah –

(49:32) the field and the cave that is in it were purchased from the Hittites."

(49:33) When Jacob ended his charge to his sons, he drew up his feet into the bed, breathed his last, and was gathered to his people.

*R*ealizing he is near death, Jacob summons his twelve sons, pronounces a deathbed blessing over each one, and concludes with another request to carry his remains back to Canaan to be buried in the ancestral burial plot. The final testament and death of Jacob come near the end of the Joseph narrative, but they relate more to the Jacob narrative begun in Gen 25. For this reason, this chapter is part of the composite narrative that concludes the Jacob narrative as well as the Joseph narrative. The tribal blessings themselves appear to be older than the surrounding epic narratives, based primarily on the antiquity of the poetry, which

---

[xx] Or *that gives beautiful words.*
[yy] Meaning of Heb uncertain.

is often obscure, and the text of which has suffered considerably more than the rest of Genesis.[689] The framing elements of vv. 1a and 28–33 are relatively obvious, and come from the hand of our narrator or final redactor of the book, making the poetry of the blessings identifiable as perhaps the oldest portions of the book of Genesis.[690]

The tribal blessings may be compared to Deut 33, and Judg 5:14–18, which have similar roots in an Israelite tribal federation of the premonarchic period.[691] The twelve-tribe system for ancient Israel is assumed as the foundation for these blessing–pronouncements, which is also related to three similar lists in Genesis: the birth narratives of the twelve children of Jacob, comprised of the birth of eleven sons and one daughter (29:31–30:24); a list of twelve sons (35:22b–26); and a list of seventy children and grandchildren of Jacob who went with him down to Egypt (46:8–27). The first four pronouncements (i.e., Reuben, Simeon and Levi, Judah, vv. 3–12) are of a different nature than the last eight (vv. 13–27). The focus in the first four is the misdeeds that disqualify Judah's older brothers from serving as the legitimate firstborn for the ancestral family, and the suitability of Judah instead. These first four also have intertextual links with other episodes in the Jacob and Joseph narratives whereas the last eight pronouncements do not.[692] The last eight blessings offer reflections on the future of each tribe, and make no mention of the virtues or vices of the ancestor for each.

The introduction contains three parts (vv. 1–2). First is a narrator's prelude, tying the original poetry of the blessings to the surrounding narrative (v. 1a). Second is a general introduction to Jacob's speech, which was most likely formulaic for such testamental blessings (v. 1b). The expression "in days to come" in this context denotes a limited future time, and takes on eschatological meaning only later in

---

[689] Some say the blessings are archaizing rather than genuinely archaic, but this begs several questions. The third masculine singular suffix for *"his* foal" and *"his* robe" in v. 11 (*–ōh*, rather than *–ô*) has the *hê*-ending occurring routinely in early Hebrew inscriptions rather than the expected *wāw*-ending of Biblical Hebrew; Sandra L. Gogel, *A Grammar of Epigraphic Hebrew* (SBLRBS 23; Atlanta, Ga.: Scholars Press, 1998), 159, n. 186. For more on the nature of the Hebrew here, see Frank M. Cross and David N. Freedman, *Studies in Ancient Yahwistic Poetry* (Biblical Resource Series; Grand Rapids, Mich.: Eerdmans, 1997), 46–63.

[690] John Van Seters, *Prologue to History: The Yahwist as Historian in Genesis* (Louisville, Ky.: Westminster/John Knox Press, 1992), 322–23; D. M. Carr, *Reading the Fractures of Genesis* (1996), 249–53.

[691] Bruce Vawter, *On Genesis: A New Reading* (Garden City, N.Y.: Doubleday, 1977), 457–58. For survey and critique of recent work on the tribal-list traditions in ancient Israel, see Kenton L. Sparks, "Genesis 49 and the Tribal List Tradition in Ancient Israel," *ZAW* 115/3 (2003): 327–47. The blessings of Issachar, Naphtali, and Joseph contain features of a northern dialect of ancient Hebrew; Gary A. Rendsburg, "Israelian Hebrew Features in Genesis 49," *Maarav* 8 (1992): 161–70.

[692] Suggesting the possibility that the first four have been modified in light of the overarching narrative and the last eight have not; C. Westermann, *Genesis 37–50* (1986), 223.

Hebrew Scriptures.[693] Third, is the specific call for the sons of Jacob to come and hear the words of their father (v. 2). We have seen the importance of the deathbed blessing, or testamental blessing, in Israelite culture (Gen 27 and 48). Pronounced when death is imminent, these blessings are more than simple wishes or prayers but are legally binding wills. In several cases, they also contain predictions and take on the nature of prophecies, making them more like final testaments rather than simple blessings as we might think of them, although they are clearly understood as blessings here (v. 28).[694] In his final moments, Jacob assumes the role of prophet to let his sons know what they can expect in the future.

First, of course, is Reuben, who is technically firstborn by birth order, but who lost that preeminent status because of sexual perversion (vv. 3–4, cf. 35:22). We have seen several times in Genesis the pattern of reversal, in which the younger son displaces the firstborn (25:31–34; 38:27–30; 48:19).[695] The Hebrew concept of "right of firstborn" (*bĕkōrâ*) is transferable; no guarantees of privilege come as an accident of birth order. Personal responsibility for one's actions is more important than ascribed privilege due to cultural norms. Similarly, Simeon and Levi are violent, conspiratorial, and cruel to humans and animals alike (vv. 5–7, cf. 34:25–30). Consequently, they will be divided and spread about in Israel, anticipating their lack of independent tribal allotment in the period of Israelite settlement (Num 18:24; Josh 19:1–9; 21:1–42). Thus the actions and character of Reuben, Simeon, and Levi make any one of them unsuitable as the firstborn for the family, and as figurative firstborn among the tribes of Israel.

The blessing of Judah is second only to Joseph's in length (vv. 8–12). Judah emerged gradually in the Joseph narrative as a leader, progressing from his bad behavior in the treatment of Tamar, his daughter-in-law (Gen 38), to his decision to stand surety for Benjamin (43:3–9), resulting in his courageous and passionate speech offering to sacrifice himself for the sake of his father and his brother (44:18–34, and see commentary there). At that time, Judah assumed a new position of leadership among the brothers (cf. also 46:28), and set himself justifiably in a place

---

[693] For discussion and other references, see Edward Lipiński, "*bᵉḥryt hymym* dans les textes préexiliques," *VT* 20 (1970): 445–50. Lipiński compares this text to David's deathbed prayer (1 Kgs 1:47–48), takes the clause in v. 1, "that I may tell you what will happen to you in days to come," as the center of a chiastic structure uniting 47:31b to 49:1b-2, and attributes this reconstructed introduction to a ninth century BCE Yahwist (pp. 446–47). On the development of eschatology in the Hebrew Scriptures generally, see Bill T. Arnold, "Old Testament Eschatology and the Rise of Apocalypticism," in *The Oxford Handbook of Eschatology*, ed. Jerry L. Walls (New York: Oxford University Press, 2008), 23–39.

[694] They were perceived as illocutionary or performative utterances, in that the pronouncement of the words in itself accomplished the act of blessing; C. W. Mitchell, *The Meaning of* brk *"to bless" in the Old Testament* (1987), 79–88. In this sense, the closest parallels to Gen 49 are Deut 33 and Judg 5:14–18.

[695] Matitiahu Tsevat, "*bĕkôr*," *TDOT* 2:121–127, esp. 126; Bill T. Arnold, "*bkr*," *NIDOTTE* 1:658–59.

of honor among the sons of Jacob. With his blessing, we appear to have arrived at an acceptable firstborn.

The pronouncement concerning Judah sets his preeminence over his brothers, who not only defer to him but praise him (v. 8). This is substantiated by leonine imagery stressing Judah's success and respect among others (v. 9), and royal imagery naming the tribe of Judah as the suitable source for Israel's kings (vv. 10–12).[696] The opening line of the blessing uses striking word play, *yěhûdâ . . . yôdûkā*, "Judah . . . they praise you," showing how appropriate it is for the other sons of Jacob to praise Judah. The syntax of this line is highly stylized and open to interpretation. I take the name Judah as a vocative (so too Reuben in v. 3), and the rest of the line centralizes Judah using the pronoun "you" as the object of his brothers' praise.[697] Alternatively, one can change the Masoretic accentuation slightly to derive a nominal clause (without needing the vocative): "You are Judah." This makes the next clause, "your brothers shall praise you," epexegetical, in which the word play highlights the suitability of the name Judah: "You are Judah; you are what your name means – because your brothers praise you."[698] In any case, the contrast with Reuben, Simeon, and Levi is obvious. The list of tribal blessings has finally arrived at a praiseworthy scion of Jacob. Further word plays in v. 8 underscore the traits that make Judah great, and result in adoration of him.[699]

The leonine and royal imagery of Judah's blessing takes on important significance elsewhere in the Bible. In Balaam's oracles, the imagery has messianic overtones (Num 24:9, 17), and with the appearance of David from the tribe of Judah (1 Sam 17:12), Judah's preeminence as a tribe increases. A Davidic interpretation of

[696] On leonine imagery as it relates to Judah's blessing, see Brent A. Strawn, *What is Stronger than a Lion? Leonine Image and Metaphor in the Hebrew Bible and the Ancient Near East* (OBO 212; Fribourg/Göttingen: Academic Press/Vandenhoeck & Ruprecht, 2005), 47–48 and 243. On kings from the ancestral line, see 17:6, 16, and 35:11. I assume the somewhat obscure descriptions of vv. 11–12 flow from the royal imagery of v. 10, and therefore take them also to be symbols of Judah's royal descendants. The meaning of "until tribute comes" (v. 10) is famously difficult textually and lexically (see NRSV footnote), and a theory that it contains a reference to the extension of Judah's royal authority as far as the ancient city of Shiloh should not be discounted; J. A. Emerton, "Some Difficult Words in Genesis 49," in *Words and Meanings: Essays Presented to David Winton Thomas on His Retirement from the Regius Professorship of Hebrew in the University of Cambridge, 1968*, eds. Peter R. Ackroyd and Barnabas Lindars (London: Cambridge University Press, 1968), 81–93, esp. 83–88.

[697] A most unusual *casus pendens*, in which the independent pronoun, "(as for) *you*," is the antecedent for both the genitive *and* the object in the sentence, "*your* brothers praise *you*." Contra GKC ¶135e. On the uses of the *casus pendens* in general, see Paul Joüon and Takamitsu Muraoka, *A Grammar of Biblical Hebrew* (SubBi 14; Roma: Editrice Pontificio Istituto Biblico, 1993), 586–87; and Takamitsu Muraoka, *Emphatic Words and Structures in Biblical Hebrew* (Jerusalem/Leiden: Magnes Press/Hebrew University. E.J. Brill, 1985), 93–99.

[698] C. Westermann, *Genesis 37–50* (1986), 227.

[699] G. J. Wenham, *Genesis 16–50* (1994), 476.

Gen 49:8–12 seemed inevitable, and the monarchy itself may have been the source of an elaboration of the first four tribal blessings in this text, reflecting Judah's royal significance. The connection of this text with a Davidic interpretation led to further messianic overtones in psalm and prophecy alike (Ps 2; Isa 11:1–9; Ezek 19), so that the role of "the Lion of the tribe of Judah" in biblical thought was secured forever (Rev 5:5).

In contrast to Judah's blessing, the next few are notable for their brevity. Zebulun's pronouncement is strictly geographical (v. 13). Issachar's animal imagery reveals great strength and symbolizes the tribe's role as a labor force (v. 14). Word play is used once again to highlight Dan's role as judge: *dān yādîn*, "Dan shall judge..." (vv. 15–18). The significance of the serpentine imagery is unclear, although it probably refers to the small size of the tribe, which however is surprisingly dangerous to its enemies.[700] The psalm-like insertion of v. 18 is likely a gloss that somehow buttresses Dan's favored position as seventh in the list of tribes.[701]

The word play continues with Gad, who will be raided by raiders (*gād gĕdûd yĕgûdennû*) but will raid (*yāgūd*) at their heels (v. 19). This pronouncement anticipates Gad's military prowess, whereas another word play used at his birth stressed the good fortune his birth signaled (see NRSV note at 30:11). Asher's agricultural productivity is its claim to fame (v. 20), and the animal imagery of Naphtali's blessing is clear, although a textual problem limits our ability to understand it precisely (v. 21, see NRSV's note).

This brings us to Joseph's blessing, which is the longest of the lot (vv. 22–26). Translating and interpreting the opening verse is treacherous, lexically and syntactically, and the text itself also appears to have suffered damage (see NRSV's note). "Fruitful bough" as in NRSV is possible, relying on viticultural imagery. But bovine imagery is also possible: "Joseph is a heifer by a spring."[702] The decision to assume faunal over floral imagery seems confirmed by the numerous other animal metaphors in the list of tribal blessings, perhaps most especially the description of Benjamin as a "ravenous wolf" in v. 27. Regardless of the specifics of v. 22, the central thesis of the pronouncement seems clear. Joseph will have a violent future, but he will prevail

---

[700] C. Westermann, *Genesis 37–50* (1986), 234–35. Yet we may have here an entirely new verbal root, yielding the meaning, "Dan – his people will be strong," which highlights that Dan will be comparable to the other tribes despite its small size; J. A. Emerton, "Some Difficult Words in Genesis 49," in *Words and Meanings* (1968), esp. 88–91.

[701] J. M. Sasson, "A Genealogical 'Convention' in Biblical Chronology?" esp. 183–84.

[702] Or even equine imagery is possible; E. A. Speiser, *Genesis* (1964), 363; G. J. Wenham, *Genesis 16–50* (1994), 484–85; V. P. Hamilton, *The Book of Genesis, Chapters 18–50* (1995), 683–84. Gunkel's word play association of *pōrāt* with Ephraimite is still reasonable, it seems to me, and therefore the bovine imagery seems preferable; H. Gunkel, *Genesis: Translated and Interpreted* (1997), 459. For the possibility that we have a reference here to the Euphrates River, and to a particular type of tree found near the Euphrates, yielding the meaning, "Joseph is a tamarisk of the Euphrates," see J. A. Emerton, "Some Difficult Words in Genesis 49," in *Words and Meanings* (1968), esp. 91–93.

through the help of God, who is described in a series of epithets: Mighty One of Jacob, Shepherd, Rock of Israel, God of your father, and the Almighty, i.e., Shadday (vv. 23–25). These are undoubtedly among the most ancient Israelite titles for God, and in the case of Mighty-One-of-Jacob (or "Bull-of-Jacob") we have a template of a larger religious tradition, which was later suppressed when the Canaanite bull mythology became unacceptable in Israelite thought.[703] The translation "Mighty One" captures only one aspect of a rich theological tradition. Similarly, Shadday, "Almighty" is a revelatory name for God with particular meaning for the ancestral period (see commentary at 17:1, and cf. Exod 6:3).

In addition to military ascendancy – though enemy archers press him bitterly, his bow is firm, his arms agile – Joseph will be the recipient of the Almighty's blessings (vv. 25–26). Such blessings extend beyond the natural gifts of heaven above and the sea below, and include reproductive fertility. But more than the gifts of nature, these are the blessings "of your father," which therefore flow from the ancestral covenant itself. They are stronger than the blessings of the eternal mountains and the everlasting hills, because they relate to things greater than material products, but include national and political greatness for Joseph.[704]

The table of tribal blessings concludes with Benjamin, the ravenous wolf (v. 27). The animal imagery continues here, as a means of highlighting Benjamin's perpetually dangerous character, since he is busy devouring his prey morning and evening. The youngest son and smallest tribe, he nevertheless enjoys military prowess during Israel's settlement and early monarchic periods (Judg 20:21; 2 Sam 2:25; cf. 1 Sam 9:21; Ps 68:27[Heb 68:28]).

Turning back to prose, v. 28 is a narrative summary of the blessings from the perspective of a twelve-tribe system: "these are the twelve tribes of Israel." Before closing the chapter with the formulaic announcement of Jacob's death (v. 33), the text relates the dying patriarch's final wish (vv. 29–32). He charges his sons to bury him at Machpelah with Abraham, Sarah, Isaac, Rebekah, and Leah (cf. 23:17–20). The precision with which the locale is described is more than providing information for finding the right spot, but the geographic features reflect the joy of holding a portion of the Promised Land. Jacob's dying wish therefore expresses faith in the ancestral promises, and anticipates a better day when his family will inherit the Promised Land permanently, fulfilling the promises of the covenant (cf. 47:29–31). By means of Jacob's dying wish, the text summarizes the overarching themes of Genesis, pointing to the fulfillment of the ancestral promises: Canaan is their homeland, Egypt is but a sojourn.

---

[703] For discussion and references to this epithet elsewhere in the Bible, see Susan Niditch, *Oral World and Written Word: Ancient Israelite Literature* (Library of Ancient Israel; Louisville, Ky.: Westminster John Knox Press, 1996), 15–16.

[704] S. R. Driver, *The Book of Genesis, with Introduction and Notes* (Westminster Commentaries 1; London: Methuen, 1943), 393.

GENESIS 50:1–26 BURIAL OF JACOB AND DEATH OF JOSEPH

(50:1) Then Joseph threw himself on his father's face and wept over him and kissed him.

(50:2) Joseph commanded the physicians in his service to embalm his father. So the physicians embalmed Israel;

(50:3) they spent forty days in doing this, for that is the time required for embalming. And the Egyptians wept for him seventy days.

(50:4) When the days of weeping for him were past, Joseph addressed the household of Pharaoh, "If now I have found favor with you, please speak to Pharaoh as follows:

(50:5) My father made me swear an oath; he said, 'I am about to die. In the tomb that I hewed out for myself in the land of Canaan, there you shall bury me.' Now therefore let me go up, so that I may bury my father; then I will return."

(50:6) Pharaoh answered, "Go up, and bury your father, as he made you swear to do."

(50:7) So Joseph went up to bury his father. With him went up all the servants of Pharaoh, the elders of his household, and all the elders of the land of Egypt,

(50:8) as well as all the household of Joseph, his brothers, and his father's household. Only their children, their flocks, and their herds were left in the land of Goshen.

(50:9) Both chariots and charioteers went up with him. It was a very great company.

(50:10) When they came to the threshing floor of Atad, which is beyond the Jordan, they held there a very great and sorrowful lamentation; and he observed a time of mourning for his father seven days.

(50:11) When the Canaanite inhabitants of the land saw the mourning on the threshing floor of Atad, they said, "This is a grievous mourning on the part of the Egyptians." Therefore the place was named Abel-mizraim;[zz] it is beyond the Jordan.

(50:12) Thus his sons did for him as he had instructed them.

(50:13) They carried him to the land of Canaan and buried him in the cave of the field at Machpelah, the field near Mamre, which Abraham bought as a burial site from Ephron the Hittite.

(50:14) After he had buried his father, Joseph returned to Egypt with his brothers and all who had gone up with him to bury his father.

(50:15) Realizing that their father was dead, Joseph's brothers said, "What if Joseph still bears a grudge against us and pays us back in full for all the wrong that we did to him?"

[zz] That is *mourning* (or *meadow*) *of Egypt.*

(50:16) So they approached Joseph, saying, "Your father gave this instruction before he died,

(50:17) 'Say to Joseph: I beg you, forgive the crime of your brothers and the wrong they did in harming you.' Now therefore please forgive the crime of the servants of the God of your father." Joseph wept when they spoke to him.

(50:18) Then his brothers also wept, fell down before him, and said, "We are here as your slaves."

(50:19) But Joseph said to them, "Do not be afraid! Am I in the place of God?

(50:20) Even though you intended to do harm to me, God intended it for good, in order to preserve a numerous people, as he is doing today.

(50:21) So have no fear; I myself will provide for you and your little ones." In this way he reassured them, speaking kindly to them.

(50:22) So Joseph remained in Egypt, he and his father's household; and Joseph lived one hundred ten years.

(50:23) Joseph saw Ephraim's children of the third generation; the children of Machir son of Manasseh were also born on Joseph's knees.

(50:24) Then Joseph said to his brothers, "I am about to die; but God will surely come to you, and bring you up out of this land to the land that he swore to Abraham, to Isaac, and to Jacob."

(50:25) So Joseph made the Israelites swear, saying, "When God comes to you, you shall carry up my bones from here."

(50:26) And Joseph died, being one hundred ten years old; he was embalmed and placed in a coffin in Egypt.

*H*ebrew narrative often concludes with the death of the leading protagonist. So here the narrator reports the deaths of Jacob (including 49:33) and Joseph, drawing to a close both the Jacob narrative and the Joseph narrative. The text includes the trek back to Canaan to bury Jacob in the ancestral burial plot, as agreed before his death, and the final reconciliation between Joseph and his fearful brothers. The poignant scene, in which Joseph forgives their sins, sounds the theological theme, "you-intended-harm . . . God-intended-good," and fittingly closes both the Joseph Novel and the book as a whole. The editor of the whole has thoughtfully wrapped together themes from both the Jacob narrative and the Joseph Novel in these last chapters of Genesis (chapters 46–50) in order to conclude the book as a whole.[705]

The first portion of the text narrates the burial of Jacob in Canaan (vv. 1–14). Joseph's immediate response is emotional (v. 1), not surprising for a man as passionate as Joseph, who has been through his experiences (42:24; 43:30; 45:2). In the

---

[705] C. Westermann, *Genesis 37–50* (1986), 211–14. Gen 50 itself is a composite of national epic materials (probably vv. 1–14), priestly materials (vv. 22–26), and free composition by the editor (vv. 15–21), although these are not entirely reconstructable. For somewhat different assessment, see B. Vawter, *On Genesis* (1977), 469–76.

ancient Near East generally, burial occurred within twenty-four hours of death. But in ancient Egypt, embalming and mummification were routine, in which the viscera and brain were extracted, preserved in jars and usually buried with the corpse, and the body wrapped in linen bandages.[706] The Hebrew word for this practice (*ḥānaṭ*, vv. 2, 26) occurs only here in the Bible, reflecting how foreign the concept was in ancient Israel, while in Egypt it was first and foremost a religious practice. In this case, it served the purposes of preserving Jacob's body long enough to return him to Canaan, in keeping with his dying wish.[707] The forty days of embalming and seventy days of mourning were concurrent (v. 3), since we have Egyptian texts describing a seventy-day postmortem period, in which embalming was included with other burial preparations and mourning ceremonies.[708]

Joseph speaks to "the household of Pharaoh," sending his request to return to Canaan to bury his father (vv. 4–6). The reason for sending his message through other high officials is most likely related to the rites of mourning just ended, presumably related to Joseph's appearance (cf. 41:14).[709] Having dutifully gained the Pharaoh's approval, Joseph returns to Canaan with a large company escorting him, including the elders of his own household, those of the Pharaoh's household, the elders of Egypt, and his brothers (vv. 7–9). Children and flocks were left behind in Goshen, perhaps as a sign of good faith that they would indeed return, and a chariotry battalion went along as military escort. The security force protects Joseph and the family against potential trouble in Sinai and Canaan on the journey. This is the most elaborate funeral recorded in the Bible, parading the pomp and ceremony of Egypt itself, suitable for the patriarch whose life-story covers nearly half of Genesis.[710]

When the funeral cortège arrives in the Transjordan, Joseph observes another elaborate seven-day mourning period, which makes quite an impression on the resident Canaanites (vv. 10–11). The location of "the threshing floor of Atad," renamed here in standard etiological form "Abel-mizraim" (see NRSV's note), is located only vaguely "beyond the Jordan," and is of uncertain identity. For reasons not

---

[706] Richard N. Jones, "Embalming," *ABD* 2:490–96.

[707] Embalmment honors Jacob's heritage by preserving him for the trip to the Promised Land but it also honors his Egyptian host by presenting an overture to Egyptian culture; Joshua Berman, "Identity Politics and the Burial of Jacob (Genesis 50:1–14)," *CBQ* 68/1 (2006): 11–31.

[708] A. J. Spencer, *Death in Ancient Egypt* (Pelican Books; New York, N.Y.: Penguin Books, 1982), 126–30.

[709] C. Westermann, *Genesis 37–50* (1986), 199.

[710] G. J. Wenham, *Genesis 16–50* (1994), 488. Moreover, the sheer amount of material devoted to the death of Jacob signals the end of an era – the end of the ancestral period formally; Patrick D. Miller, Jr., "The End of the Beginning: Genesis 50," in *The Ending of Mark and The Ends of God: Essays in Memory of Donald Harrisville Juel*, eds. Beverly R. Gaventa and Patrick D. Miller (Louisville, Ky.: Westminster John Knox, 2005), 115–26, esp. 116.

explained, the entourage travels around the southern tip of the Dead Sea and north-ward through the Transjordan, taking the long way around to Hebron for the burial itself. Perhaps we are to assume by this circuitous route that Jacob, even in death, was prefiguring the route of the later Israelites, showing the way for his descendants into the Promised Land. The narrator's summary highlights the faithfulness of Jacob's sons to fulfill his dying wish, and once again details the geographic features of the ancestral burial ground so important to the ancient Israelites (vv. 12–14, cf. 49:30).[711]

Returning to Egypt after the funeral, Joseph's brothers sense their vulnerabil-ity now that Jacob is dead (v. 15). Assuming their father had prevented Joseph from seeking revenge against them, they now suspect Joseph will retaliate for their mistreatment of him those many years ago. They ask "what if . . . ?" in tones that acknowledge their guilt. Their reference to "the wrong" they did to Joseph announces the catch term for this paragraph, *ra*, "evil, harm." In a way that consistently eludes abstract definition by philosophers and theologians, evil itself is everything that is "bad," including physical harm, moral harm due to human volition, and social harm caused by corporate injustice.[712] The brothers are painfully aware of the physical and ethical harm they have caused Joseph.

The brothers report to Joseph words spoken by their father before his death (v. 16). As they fulfilled Jacob's dying wish to be buried in Canaan, the brothers also hope Joseph will fulfill Jacob's wishes in forgiving them. Of course, we have no account of such words spoken by Jacob, and the narrator likely invites us to assume prevarication and collusion on their part in order to save themselves. The alleged speech of Jacob highlights the severity of their deeds (v. 17). Their "crime" (*pešaʿ*) is transgression or rebellion, their "sin" (*ḥaṭṭāʾt*, NRSV's "wrong") is a misdeed that results resolutely in guilt, and together these were acts of harm (*ra*, "evil") done to Joseph.[713] The brothers understand their guilt, expressed through these fabricated words of their father. They need forgiveness, which is here the "lifting or bearing away" of one's guilt (*nāśāʾ*).[714] Joseph weeps at their words, overcome again by the way God has superintended the affairs of his life, despite the deeds of these brothers of his, whom he seems to love nevertheless (v. 17b). Perhaps stunned by his emotional response, the brothers simply fall before Joseph and declare "we are here as your slaves" (v. 19). They resolve to accept their fate, which is clearly in Joseph's

---

[711] Vv. 12–13 may be a priestly insertion, which many scholars believe originally followed 49:29–33, revealing a priestly version of the non-priestly commission of Joseph to bury his father in Canaan in 47:29–31; D. M. Carr, *Reading the Fractures of Genesis* (1996), 95.

[712] Christoph Dohmen and D. Rick, "*rʿ*," *TDOT* 13:560–588, esp. 567.

[713] For *pešaʿ*, see *HALOT* 3:981–82; and for *ḥaṭṭāʾt*, *HALOT* 1:306 and *DCH* 3:198–200. Most English translations necessarily obscure the rhetorical effects of such an onrush of words: "Please, I beg you, forgive the transgression of your brothers, their sin, for they dealt out evil/harm against you. Now therefore please forgive the transgression of the servants of the God of your father!"

[714] *HALOT* 2:726; *DCH* 5:766.

hands, and their words resonate with those of the Egyptians who sell themselves into servitude to the Pharaoh because of the famine (47:25).

Joseph's response is a classic of biblical literature (vv. 19–21). Sensing their anxiety, he immediately assures them they have nothing to fear. He then puts his own role in their lives in perspective: "Am I in the place of God?" Only God can properly match punishment with crime, and Joseph refuses to act as judge on God's behalf. Joseph has seen evidence of their tortuous suffering over the years, and perhaps concludes they have endured enough punishment (cf. 42:21).

Next he puts their evil actions in perspective: "Even though you intended to do harm to me, God intended it for good." Using emphatic syntax, "You *certainly* intended, . . . " Joseph does not deny their evil intent. But the word play, using the same verb with different idioms, highlights the way God has turned the evil intent of humans into an opportunity to accomplish his good purposes. They planned harm (*ḥāšab* plus preposition *ʿal*), but God reconfigured their evil and produced good from it (*ḥāšab* plus preposition *lĕ*).[715] By revisiting the theme of reconciliation between estranged brothers (45:5–8), the narrator has provided a profound theological summary of the Joseph Novel. The brothers sold Joseph to Egypt with evil intent, but it was really God who brought him to Egypt in order to preserve life. Using the antithetic dyad "good and evil" as a paradigm, the text lifts even the wrongful and unethical behavior of humans as something God is capable of comprehending as an opportunity for good. Joseph's theological insight of v. 20 not only summarizes the themes of Joseph Novel, but also of the book of Genesis overall, since the "good-and-evil" dyad is so central to the Eden narrative as well (2:9). The persistent drumbeat of the Primeval History is that humans choose evil, but throughout the book we learn that God can turn it to good. Joseph closes with more words of consolation and comfort; they will benefit from God's life-saving plan (v. 21).

The narrator concludes the book with the death of Joseph (vv. 22–26). At the age of one hundred ten years, Joseph lived long enough to enjoy his great-grandchildren, a sign of abundant blessing (Ps 128:6).[716] Like his father, Joseph's dying words express triumphant faith that God will fulfill his promises to the ancestors (vv. 24–25, cf. 48:21; 49:29–33). His mention of the great triad – Abraham, Isaac, and Jacob (occurring here for the first time in the Bible, v. 24) – becomes an important reference point for the future and for the rest of biblical literature.[717] As the end of the beginning, Joseph's words in Gen 50 point the way to the future. When God fulfills his promise to the patriarchs, Joseph's descendants will carry him from Egypt to the Promised

---

[715] Klaus Seybold, "*ḥāšab*," *TDOT* 5:228–45, esp. 238–39; *HALOT* 1:360; *DCH* 3:327.

[716] NRSV's "children of the third generation" is great-grandchildren, and those "born on Joseph's knees" were likely adopted; C. Westermann, *Genesis 37–50* (1986), 208.

[717] P. D. Miller, Jr., "The End of the Beginning: Genesis 50," in *The Ending of Mark and The Ends of God* (2005), esp. 116.

Land. To this end, Joseph is embalmed and placed in a coffin, in order to wait for the day of journey (Exod 13:19).[718] In death as in life, Joseph represents the conviction that good can come from evil, so that even his burial plans are transformed by faith into plans for a journey to a better land.

---

[718] Such coffins (*'ārôn*, "box") were ubiquitous in ancient Egypt, and even occasionally in Syria–Palestine under Egyptian influence, such as the famous sarcophagus of King Aḥiram of Byblos; for photograph, see A. F. Rainey and R. S. Notley, *The Sacred Bridge: Carta's Atlas of the Biblical World* (2006), 158.

Scripture Index

Extrabiblical Index

Author Index

Subject Index